COMPUTERS

TOOLS FOR
KNOWLEDGE
WORKERS

JACK B. ROCHESTER

Lecturer, Plymouth State College

IRWIN

Homewood, IL 60430
Boston, MA 02116

This book is dedicated to the memory of

Charles Philip Lecht
(August 5, 1933– July 3, 1992)

Computer technology visionary and futurist
My mentor and my friend.

Senior sponsoring editor: Rick Williamson
Developmental editor: Lena Buonanno
Marketing manager: Scott J. Timian
Project editor: Susan Trentacosti
Production manager: Diane Palmer
Cover designer: Mercedes Santos
Interior designer: Maureen McCutcheon
Cover illustrator: Jeff Bryce
Art manager: Kim Meriwether
Photo research coordinator: Patricia A. Seefelt
Compositor: Progressive Typographers, Inc.
Typeface: 10/12 Galliard
Printer: Von Hoffmann Press

Library of Congress Cataloging-in-Publication Data

Rochester, Jack B.
    Computers: tools for knowledge workers/Jack B. Rochester.
        p.   cm.
    Includes index.
    ISBN 0-256-11015-8
    1. Computers.   2. Electronic data processing.   I. Title.
QA76.R6116   1993
650′.0285 — dc20   92 – 16801

Printed in the United States of America

1 2 3 4 5 6 7 8 9 0 VH 9 8 7 6 5 4 3 2

INTRODUCTION: THE KNOWLEDGE WORKER

Students taking an introductory computer course in the 1990s will almost inevitably become computer users in their chosen occupation. More and more jobs require a computer today; moreover, a U.S. government study states that by the year 2000, three out of five jobs people will need to be trained and educated for do not exist today because they involve the use of emerging computer technologies.

What used to be referred to as white-collar work has changed. This is not merely clerical tasks, but work that requires the use of computers to perform. The computer *adds value;* therefore, this is called knowledge work. The people who perform it are **knowledge workers** who use a computer to complete work tasks more quickly and easily. The computer enhances their *personal productivity.*

Knowledge workers are white collar professionals from many walks of life who need to understand how to use a personal computer, how to work with computer-based information, and how computer systems benefit business. They may be self-employed in a home office or cottage industry; they may use a computer for their work in the office, while traveling, and at home; or they may operate their own small business.

TODAY'S BUSINESS COMPUTING ENVIRONMENT

Computers: Tools for Knowledge Workers takes the approach that students need to understand computers within the broad computing environment. Business today uses individual personal computers, workstations, departmental minis, and database-bound mainframes, often linked together in a network, al-

most always working within a framework called enterprisewide computing. The knowledge worker of today and tomorrow needs to understand how computing works in all these contexts. Moreover, this understanding must have a managerial emphasis or orientation; knowledge workers in the 1990s are more likely to become *information technology managers* in the particular department or division they work in, rather than programmers in the information systems department. They will not only use computer technology in their own work, but may often be involved in developing new departmental applications, using a fourth-generation language or object-oriented programming tools. They may be PC managers or be responsible for training other knowledge workers in their department. They may be work group computing team leaders or LAN managers.

Therefore, students need to clearly understand the foundations — the basics of the business computing environment that matured in the 1980s — as well as the new and emerging technologies that make the 1990s an exciting time for knowledge workers. That is the intent and the goal of this textbook. All the latest hardware and software technologies, as well as managerial and organizational advances, are presented *from a knowledge worker's perspective rather than a technical one.* They are discussed in terms of their value to the business and how they can be used to achieve goals better, faster, or with less cost.

A unifying theme in *Computers: Tools for Knowledge Workers* for presenting this information is that of **the computer system, which is comprised of people, data, procedures, software, and hardware.** Computers today are not a machine science; rather, as presented here, they are part of the business-oriented human enterprise. You, the student, are either a knowledge worker now or will be performing knowledge work in your career. Thus, computer concepts are explained in the context of their everyday, actual business, and personal use with many case studies (both short and long) that demonstrate how those concepts apply in business situations using true examples and illustrations.

A Textbook Designed for You

Computers: Tools for Knowledge Workers has four key differentiating features: a sharper focus, a stronger organization, greater currency, and more enriching applications.

A Sharper Focus. This text is written for the student majoring in such subjects as accounting, communications, finance, marketing, management, and public relations. The topics, presentation level, and overall focus of the book are tailored to knowledge work, where technical depth serves the purpose of showing students how computer technology makes work more efficient and satisfying. Topics and concepts build one upon another so that students see the *relationship* between people, data, procedures, software, and hardware. Concepts and terms appropriate only for hardware or software engineers will not be found here. This method allows students to grasp the concept, understand its importance, and visualize its application in the real world.

A Stronger Organization. This text begins with an overview of hardware, with emphasis on the personal computer. Understanding the PC's components make it easier to grasp how larger computer systems work. In Module II the focus shifts to software, so students can see that systems software and application software make computers useful. Module III builds upon the usefulness applications provide by exploring hardware concepts — the CPU, input, and output — in more detail. Now that students clearly understand the relationship between hardware and software, Module IV explains how systems are created with programming, software engineering, and database, yet always from a knowledge worker's perspective. Module V puts it all together and shows the computer at work on tasks in business: management information systems, communications, and office automation.

Greater Currency. Students should understand how today's computer environment was shaped, but most important, they must be prepared for the computer systems they will encounter in tomorrow's workplace. *Computers: Tools for Knowledge Workers* describes all the latest technologies *as they are being utilized in today's business environment.* There is no coverage of technology simply for technology's sake. For example, the most powerful microprocessor is not necessarily the one most widely used; a promising software technology may be popular in the computer press but rarely implemented. These subjects are covered, but presented in a realistic business context, so students can appreciate the difference between "gee-whiz" technology and rock-solid implementation.

More Enriching Applications. This text's approach is to *show,* not simply to tell. This is done through hundreds of examples and case studies, all drawn from real-life business situations. The approach is people-oriented and explains how the technology is used to solve a business problem. In most cases, people and companies are portrayed by name, and the benefits drawn from computer technology are explained in terms of increased productivity and cost savings.

The Way Things Work: Personal Computer Anatomy. Chapter 2 has a feature that appears for the first time in a computer text: a set of six acetate overlays that show the various internal and external components of a personal computer and the way they work together. This Computer Anatomy feature is called The Way Things Work, and it begins with the basic electronic components, each overlay adding components and connections so that their relationships to one another are made clear. After studying this Computer Anatomy, the student should be able to identify the major electronic and electromechanical components, and perhaps even install a component in their own personal computer.

Text Organization

Computers: Tools for Knowledge Workers is organized into five self-contained modules that build one upon another, but can be reorganized if so desired.

Each chapter is clearly structured and is composed of the following elements:

- A *chapter outline,* clearly explaining chapter content and organization.
- *Learning objectives,* keyed to chapter sections and topics, with an accompanying summary at the end of each chapter.
- *Knowledge Checks,* intrachapter self-quizzes that allow the student to confirm understanding before proceeding to the next section or topic.
- *Practical, useful art* — photographs, drawings, and illustrations — that communicate how the technology is used, with captions that explain what the student is seeing in the photograph.
- *Three boxed features,* Yesterday, Today and Tomorrow, illuminate each chapter's topic. Yesterday is a history vignette that provides necessary perspective. Today is a story of how knowledge workers are using interesting or innovative computer technology today. Tomorrow describes where the computer technology is heading in the 1990s and toward the year 2000.
- An *Ethics essay* keyed to each chapter topic, concerning the personal, office, and social implications of computing. Students learn how the common understanding all people share for ethical and moral behavior in the workplace applies in knowledge work, how appropriate behavior is often misplaced when working with technology, and in some cases about overt criminal behavior.
- *Summary,* tied to the learning objectives.
- *Careers for Knowledge Workers,* true-life stories with an accompanying photo of individuals performing the kind of work the text describes. These knowledge workers are people working in business who, by and large, do not have a computer science degree. Rather, they are using computers to perform tasks such as newspaper publishing, marketing, public relations, or product development.
- *Issues* that accompany the Ethics essay present the student with a moral or ethical decision to make, based on a short, descriptive, realistic business scenario. These issues are meant to stimulate class or group discussion on the impact of technology in modern life and how it affects personal and group human behavior. There are no right or wrong answers, but students are encouraged to support their opinions with facts and examples from their own experience or outside reading.
- *Review and discussion questions* designed for either individual or class use. These questions, grouped by type (review, discussion, multiple-choice, fill-in-the-blank, true/false), may be used for class discussion, as a self-test, or to provide questions for in-class quizzes. The answers to the odd-numbered questions are included in the text.
- *Essential key terms,* those a knowledge worker needs to understand the technology and accomplish their work, referenced to the text page where they first appear. The Glossary contains all key terms and definitions.

Computers: Tools for Knowledge Workers is a textbook that is practical, rigorous, and complete. It is sharply focused on the student, tomorrow's knowledge worker. It is carefully organized and thoughtfully written. It has practical, pedagogically sound features. It blends traditional and current topics and exemplifies them through interesting, real-life examples, illustrations, and cases. Careers, ethics, social implications, and the history and future of computers are integrated with chapter topics for greater relevance.

ACKNOWLEDGMENTS

Benjamin Franklin, the great American statesman, writer, editor, publisher, and printer, once said "Either write things worthy of reading, or do things worth the writing." This text is, in the truest sense of the word, a collaboration among many knowledge workers. The author hopes he has written a textbook worthy of reading.

Many thanks to those knowledge workers who gave of their time and energy to develop the Careers for Knowledge Workers profiles. Sincere thanks to the reviewers listed below for their thoughtful comments and suggestions; their work has been more than worthy of the writing and they have substantially shaped the book. Now it is in the students' hands, where it is hopefully worth reading and will lead to knowledge work worth writing about in future editions.

Elvin H. Campbell, Jr.
Golden West College

Thomas B. Cannon
Danville Community College

Karen A. Forcht
James Madison University

Connie Morris Fox
West Virginia Institute of Technology

Thomas F. Jackson
Wingate College

Constance A. Knapp
Pace University

John N. Landon
University of LaVerne

Chang-Yang Lin
East Kentucky University

George Mundrake
Ball State University

Brenda C. Parker
Middle Tennessee State University

John Rezac
Johnson County Community College

Ronald D. Robison
Arkansas Tech University

Ali Salehnia
South Dakota State University

Susan Traynor
Clarion University of Pennsylvania

Janet R. Truscott
San Joaquin Delta College

Terry F. Urbine
Eastern New Mexico University

Special thanks to George Borhegyi of Cambridge Technology Partners for his review of the software engineering chapter.

I would also like to thank Dr. William J. Taffe, Chairman of the Department of Computer Science at Plymouth State College, Plymouth, New Hampshire, for the opportunity to teach the Introduction to Computers course. Thanks also to the faculty for their warm welcome, encouragement, and counsel.

The author would like to thank Lena Buonanno, the book's developmental editor, for her firm guiding hand, empathetic support, and intelligent counsel. Special thanks to Maureen McCutcheon for the handsome book design and to Mercedes Santos for the elegant and evocative cover art. Sarah Evertson of Photosynthesis was thoughtful and imaginative in her choice of photographs, and brought an extraordinary degree of visualization to the words and text. And deep appreciation to Larry E. Alexander, for his vision, diligent management, patience, and enthusiasm for this ambitious project. His knowledge of textbooks and understanding of the course have helped hone this book into an innovative, yet substantial, learning tool for tomorrow's knowledge workers.

Special thanks are due to Susan Trentacosti, my project editor. Sue and I worked together previously on *Computers for People,* and I was glad to have her in charge of this book project as well. I admire Sue's ability to keep the many complicated facets of the bookbuilding process in order and on schedule, and to coordinate the work of many other knowledge workers in editing, design, illustration, typesetting, and more. Together, as this text exemplifies, we are a collaborative work group using computer technology in a variety of ways to perform knowledge work.

The author also wishes to express his gratefulness and deep appreciation to Charles Philip Lecht, a computer industry pioneer, software entrepreneur, industry observer, columnist, and one of the few people who can rightly claim the title of futurist. After a long and successful career in New York, Charley moved to Tokyo where he launched a successful and innovative think tank and software development firm, Lecht Sciences. He was a constant friend and an extraordinary counsel to me for over a decade, and sadly did not live to see this book published. It is dedicated to his memory.

SUPPLEMENTS

Three excellent educators have been part of the team helping to develop the learning and teaching program for *Computers: Tools for Knowledge Workers.* Cathi Chambley-Miller of Aiken Technical College is author of the Study Guide. Ernest F. Hensley of St. Petersburg Junior College compiled and wrote the Instructor's Resource Manual. Eugene Stafford of Iona College prepared the Test Bank. The author appreciates the hard work that went into preparing these supplements and thanks each author.

COMPUTERS USED IN THE PREPARATION OF THIS TEXT

As a working author and computer industry journalist, I enjoy the opportunity to not only see how computer technology is utilized in business, but to use it myself. I used or reviewed all the personal computer hardware and software technology you read about in this text. I use both a PC and a Macintosh; my primary computer is a Zeos 80386 with 4MB of RAM and two Conner IDE hard disk drives: a 120 MB hard disk for word processing software and work files and an 80MB hard disk for all other application software. I use a Nanao Flexscan 9080i 16-inch color monitor with an ATI Graphics Ultra video card, a Hewlett-Packard LaserJet III printer with a Bitstream Type City font cartridge, a Fujitsu keyboard, a Supra modem, and the DAK Industries CD-ROM drive and disc reference library.

I cannot possibly thank all the publicists and marketing people from the many hardware, software, and research companies that provided assistance during this project. I would like to acknowledge the following:

Better Software Technology
Borland International
CompuServe
Dialog / Knowledge Index
InfoWorld Newsmagazine
Lotus Development Corporation
MCI Mail
Microsoft Corporation
The Open Systems Foundation
Quarterdeck Office Systems
Stairway Software
Supra Corporation
Symantec / Peter Norton
WordPerfect Corp.
Xerox Imaging Systems
XTREE Company
Zeos International

Jack B. Rochester

■

MODULE I
AN INTRODUCTION TO COMPUTERS

■

CHAPTER 1
THE COMPUTER, THE KNOWLEDGE WORKER, AND YOU
4

■

CHAPTER 2
THE PERSONAL COMPUTER
32

CHAPTER 3
A WORLD OF COMPUTERS: FROM THE LAPTOP TO THE SUPERCOMPUTER
66

■

MODULE II
PERSONAL PRODUCTIVITY APPLICATIONS

■

CHAPTER 4
WORD PROCESSING AND ELECTRONIC PUBLISHING
100

■

CHAPTER 5
THE SPREADSHEET AND PRESENTATION GRAPHICS
142

■

CHAPTER 6
FILE MANAGERS AND DATABASE MANAGEMENT SYSTEMS
178

CHAPTER 7
SYSTEM SOFTWARE AND APPLICATION SOFTWARE
204

MODULE III
HARDWARE CONCEPTS

CHAPTER 8
THE CENTRAL PROCESSING UNIT AND MAIN MEMORY
248

■

CHAPTER 9
INPUT, OUTPUT, AND SECONDARY STORAGE CONCEPTS AND DEVICES
276

■

MODULE IV
SOFTWARE CONCEPTS

■

CHAPTER 10
PROGRAMMING LANGUAGES AND CONCEPTS
316

■

CHAPTER 11
SOFTWARE ENGINEERING
344

CHAPTER 12
CORPORATE DATABASE CONCEPTS
366

■

MODULE V
COMPUTERS AND THE KNOWLEDGE WORKER

■

CHAPTER 13
MANAGEMENT INFORMATION SYSTEMS
396

■
Chapter 14
Voice and Data Communications Systems
430

■

CHAPTER 15
OFFICE AUTOMATION AND DEPARTMENTAL COMPUTING
470

COMPUTERS

TOOLS FOR
KNOWLEDGE
WORKERS

2

An Introduction to Computers

Each person approaches the study of computers with their own unique viewpoint, background, and skills. You may already know enough about computers that you are eager to learn more. You may know how to use one or two software programs, but be unaware of what makes them tick. You may be a complete novice or a skilled knowledge worker, but in any case you're a student who has enrolled in this course to gain a more thorough understanding of computers.

Welcome.

The three chapters comprising Module I introduce you to the wide-ranging uses of computers in modern society. As you read them and, indeed, all that follow, you will discover that the text is interspersed with features designed to expand your understanding and awareness of the computing field. The Yesterday feature provides background; the Today feature demonstrates a contemporary function or application; and the Tomorrow feature portrays how we will use computer technology in the future. Careers for Knowledge Workers feature portrays people, very like yourself, who are using computers in their work. And Ethics and Issues present current legal, ethical, and moral aspects of using computers.

Chapter 1 is a general introduction to how knowledge workers use computers in business and society. Are you a knowledge worker? You'll find out. "How Computers Do Their Work" explains how computer professionals program a computer so that it can perform data processing.

Chapter 2 introduces the personal computer system. Once you understand the fundamentals of the PC, you can understand a computer of any size or power. The distinction between processing hardware and peripheral hardware is explained. DOS is the operating system. It carries instructions from the knowledge worker and the application software to the computer hardware.

Chapter 3 builds on your understanding of the personal computer to explain the many other different types of computer hardware. You'll learn the distinctions between portable personal computers and how the workstation differs from PCs. Minicomputers, mainframe computers, and supercomputers are explored.

Once you finish these chapters, you should feel comfortable in your knowledge of computer hardware and ready to explore the personal productivity applications in Module II.

The Computer, the Knowledge Worker, and You

LEARNING OBJECTIVES

After reading and studying this chapter, you should be able to:

1. Explain the many uses for computers in modern life.
2. Describe the characteristics of knowledge workers.
3. Describe the components that make up all computers.
4. Name and identify the different types of computers.
5. Understand the difference between data and instructions.
6. Describe the five data processing steps.
7. Name the two types of software.

COMPUTERS ARE EVERYWHERE

Sarah Rolph is a marketing consultant who specializes in computers and high technology. She has combined her knowledge and skills in business practices, interpersonal communication, writing, editing, and print-media advertising to create a lively, interesting business for herself, with offices in a restored Victorian mansion. She has a Macintosh personal computer which she finds herself using more and more in her work, which includes writing, graphic design, and creative planning and strategies for her clients.

While reading her mail recently, Sarah came upon an envelope with a small cartoon beside the address. A man was sitting behind a desk with a big smile on his face, speaking to another man in his office. The caption read, "Hiring Sarah Rolph was one of the smartest things we've ever done." Sarah was, of course, a little startled until she looked more closely. The envelope contained direct mail advertising for an executive search firm, and the letter inside had been personalized with her name and address. By now, most people realize their names get on mailing lists and that it's possible to personalize letters using computerized *mail merge* capabilities. Yet what was truly amazing was that this company had used the laser printer to not only print the name and address, but to personalize the cartoon caption as well.

This illustration shows one of different and interesting ways computers are used in our world today. Refer to Figure 1.1 as you read the following. Most of us have grown comfortable with the bank's automated teller machine (ATM) and routinely make deposits and withdrawals or check account balances. The ATM makes the unseen computer behind it pretty simple to use. The same is true of the point of sale (POS) cash register and scanner at the supermarket. We trust it to correctly ring up the prices of the goods we buy. There are probably many more examples of computers you come into contact with in your everyday life. Perhaps you have a computer where you work or have one of your own that you use for your college coursework.

Computers are everywhere, seen and unseen. There are computers in cars that perform many tasks, such as monitoring engine performance and controlling the braking system. Computers fly airplanes, help find oil and natural gas deposits, analyze data from space probes, assemble electronic components in stereo systems, and shuttle billions of dollars between banks and across continents 24 hours a day. Computers are even used to design new computers. In short, there are very few aspects of modern life that have not been touched by the computer.

FIGURE 1.1

This is a hypothetical example of how an ATM network operates. Don Lewis is a manufacturer's representative for New England Pine Furniture Company of Portland, Maine. He travels the Eastern Seaboard from Canada to Florida. Running low on funds in Atlanta, Georgia, Don inserts his First Bank of Maine bank card into an Atlanta National Bank ATM. The ATM reader mechanism scans the magnetic strip on the back of Don's card for his name and account number. The reader determines that Don's card was not issued by Atlanta National Bank, so it sends an electronic signal across the telephone lines to the NationWide ATM Network computer in Minneapolis, Minnesota. The NationWide computer reads identifiers in Don's account number and sends a query to the First Bank of Maine computer, where his active account status is verified and sent back to Minneapolis. NationWide then sends an "OK" to the Atlanta computer and the ATM now prompts Don for his password. All this takes place in a matter of seconds. A second electronic transaction will occur, verifying that he has sufficient cash or reserves to make his withdrawal and debiting his account—as well as a fee for using the ATM and network services.

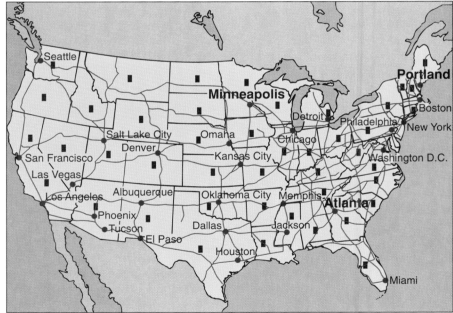

COMPUTERS IN BANKING

While the automated teller and checkout scanner seem like simple computer devices, they are just the tip of the iceberg. Each is a terminal in a large, complex web of computers and communications. Figure 1.1 shows how this computer system works. Say you want to withdraw $100 from your checking account. You insert your bank card into the ATM, then type in your password and withdrawal request. Each keystroke creates an electronic blip — just like a touch-tone telephone — that is sent over special telephone lines especially for computers. The blips arrive at the bank's data processing center and are routed to a large computer system that maintains thousands, perhaps millions, of bank customer accounts. The computer looks through your account data, verifying your password and checking your account balances. If everything checks out, it sends an electronic signal back across the miles to the ATM to count out $100 and to print a receipt of the transaction. As you know, all this happens in a matter of seconds, yet we take such transactions for granted as just another everyday part of our lives.

But the bank's computer may have hundreds of ATMs in use — many 24 hours a day — processing thousands of transactions *per second*. In addition, the bank's computer is linked to a nationwide ATM network, so that you can make your withdrawal from nearly any ATM in the country. The bank's computer is also linked to a government banking network that provides many services, such as clearing checks from foreign banks and making electronic funds transfers between banks. Literally billions of dollars are transferred every day in the form of electronic computer blips, traveling across networks that encircle the earth. In the near future, we may have ATMs that are able to recognize the human voice or provide a live video connection with a human teller when needed.

COMPUTERS BENEFIT SOCIETY

In addition to the many ways computers have made the wheels of commerce move more efficiently and conveniently, they also play a larger role in many more everyday activities than we might at first imagine. Computers make 24-hour, around-the-world stock market trading between New York, London, and Tokyo possible. Local law enforcement agencies can connect their computers to those of national and international law enforcement agencies to more quickly identify and apprehend dangerous criminals. Computers are weaving a complex web of information between newspapers, magazines, and libraries, so that people anywhere and everywhere can be better informed. And computers have shortened the time it takes to connect telephone calls. In the 1980s, a long-distance connection could take 30 seconds or more; in the 1990s, it's only a few seconds, even if it's an international call. Over the past decade, people have found a vast array of new uses for computers and the information they produce. For example:

- The computers at the National Center for Atmospheric Research in Boulder, Colorado, are being used to build a large, complex model of the earth's ecosystem, as shown in Figure 1.2, to better understand the trend in global warming, called the "greenhouse effect." The information is collected from a wide variety of sources, including meteorological observations from merchant ships dating back to 1854. In fact, they have collected the equivalent of over 12 million books full of information.

- Tiger is the U.S. Census Bureau's information mapping program. Tiger, which stands for Topologically Integrated Geographic Encoding and Reference, produces minutely detailed computerized maps of the entire United States and combines them with data collected in the

FIGURE 1.2   Supercomputers at the National Center for Atmospheric Research in Boulder, Colorado, create models of the earth's ecosystem to better understand the effects of global warming. These graphs indicate climate simulations: the globe on the left indicates temperatures at current CO_2 levels while the globe on the right shows a simulation of global warming due to doubled levels of CO_2.

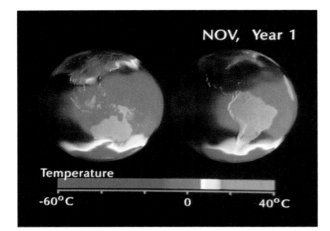
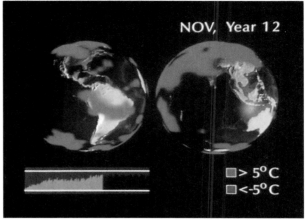

Census to provide vast amounts of information about the country and its citizens. These maps include streets, roads, waterways, railroads, census tracts, cities, and postal zone codes. Governmental agencies use Tiger to help determine demographics and to define political redistricting. People who market and sell products can use it to target customers, but package delivery companies can also use it to find the most efficient routes. The maps and data are shown in Figure 1.3.

We, as a society, increasingly take computers and their awesome ability to store and produce information for granted. Yet there are a number of reasons why we should not. Here are a few examples:

- Many people labor under the belief that whatever comes out of the computer must be accurate, yet often it is not. It only takes one misplaced character or one incorrectly typed number to create an error. There are numerous examples of errors in phone bills and credit card statements. For example, the European Airbus 300 airliner has been subject to a number of low-altitude crashes, thought to be the result of minute, and so far unidentified, programming errors in its automatic pilot computer system.

- With every passing day, computers collect more and more information about you. Some of this information is benign, such as your name and address for direct mail advertising as noted earlier, but credit bureaus know intimate financial details about you. It is extremely easy for others to obtain this information, while it is often troublesome for you to do the same. For example, Lizabeth Stephens, a.k.a. Elizabeth Ann Borruso, used eight Social Security numbers and six names to open accounts throughout Northern California at Citibank, Security Pacific, and Great Western Savings. She obtained an Army civilian

FIGURE 1.3
The U.S. Census Bureau was one of the first organizations to realize that computers could assist in the management of information. They presently use the Tiger Database system to provide vast amounts of information about the country and its citizens.

identification card under a false number and name. She faces a maximum sentence of five years in prison and a $250,000 fine. For this reason, the U.S. government has legislation pending that would rectify many of these abuses of our personal financial privacy.

- Unauthorized computer use is a growing problem. Untold billions of dollars are embezzled via computer every year by white-collar workers. Intruders gain unauthorized access to corporate and government computers. These are individuals with poor ethical and moral values, but in some cases they are spies and agents who steal secret information and sell it to others. In recent years, computer intruders in Germany and the Netherlands have been caught and in some cases convicted of stealing classified data from U.S. computers and selling it to KGB agents of the former Soviet Union.

These are just a few of the many risks associated with our high technology world, and they point up the need for an informed citizenry. Attempting to address the myriad issues of individual rights of privacy in the Information Age, Laurence Tribe, professor of constitutional law at Harvard University, has proposed the 27th Amendment to the U.S. Bill of Rights. In brief, Professor Tribe's amendment would read, "This Constitution's protections . . . shall be construed as fully applicable without regard to the technological method or medium through which information content is generated, stored, altered, transmitted or controlled."[1] Tribe believes that recent judges' decisions seem as if the Constitution were being reinvented according to new technologies. This amendment would create a uniform means of dealing with this new electronic frontier.

---

[1] *Computerworld,* April 1, 1991, p. 99.

COMPUTER LITERACY

Each of us must be responsible computer users, but it is also our duty as members of a free and democratic society to ensure that *all* computers are used responsibly, ethically, and morally. This is called **computer literacy** — being knowledgeable or educated about the computer and how it works in our daily lives. It also means being able to operate and use a computer properly and ethically.

It is very likely that you will use computers in your work, if you are not already doing so. Computer literacy is an essential skill for people in the 1990s. As the Information Age reaches maturity, being a computer-literate member of society is a responsibility we all share. Here is how the Information Age came to pass.

THE INFORMATION AGE.   In 1956, Harvard sociologist Daniel Bell identified most of Western civilization as entering the "postindustrial society," or what we now commonly refer to as the Information Age. Simply put, the **Information Age** describes a society in which information takes on the following three characteristics:

1. It has become a *commodity,* just as steel, plastic, cars, stereos, and other manufactured products are commodities.
2. It has *value;* companies carefully guard the formulas for their products and all kinds of market data.
3. It is *bought and sold,* whether in the form of a magazine or a computerized list of customer names.

Information has not replaced manufacturing, nor is it yet considered an aspect of the Gross National Product, but it is an essential component in many operations. It is not uncommon to see a machinist working on the factory floor with a computer monitor close by, referring to it for specifications and part numbers as he works.

We are indeed entering into a time when computers are everywhere. It is an exciting time, for we are using computers and computer technology for a variety of new and useful tasks. Who would have ever thought a computer could be shrunk to the size of a pinpoint and injected into the human bloodstream, where it can monitor a patient's health? Charles P. Lecht, a computer visionary, has said, "What the lever was to the arm, the computer is to the brain." [2] Like a lever, a hammer, a wrench, or a screwdriver, the computer is a tool. It enables us to perform tasks that would be difficult, time-consuming, or in some cases impossible without it. In the next section, we'll study the role people in the business world play in using computers. Then we'll learn more about this fascinating machine.

KNOWLEDGE CHECK

1. Describe two computers: one you can see and one you can't.   p. 5
2. Explain some ways computers benefit society.   pp. 7–8
3. What is a concern we should have about the ways computers are used?   pp. 8–9

---

[2] Jack B. Rochester, "Artificial Intelligence," *OMNI,* December 1986, p. 30.

THE KNOWLEDGE WORKER

What is a knowledge worker? **Knowledge workers** are people who routinely use a computer in their work to enhance their productivity. She or he is the critical component in a computer system. A **computer system** is made up of people, using data and procedures to work with software and hardware components. It takes all five working together to produce results. Knowledge workers are white-collar professionals from many walks of life who have the following characteristics:

- They understand how to use a personal computer.
- They know how to work with computer-based information.
- They understand how the computer benefits their work and the business.
- They regard the computer as a productivity tool.

Knowledge workers may be employed in a company of any size, large or small, at a wide range of tasks. They may be self-employed, working in their own office or at home. They may be sales representatives or managers who travel with a portable computer. Students are knowledge workers as well. Many of you may be preparing for a career in knowledge work in office automation, public relations, account supervision, social work, management, or a number of other occupations.

Knowledge workers use computers and information in many, many ways; often it is a highly personal process. But here is an example of how a typical white-collar division manager in a large marketing and distribution firm might spend part of her day. There is a meeting at 3:00 to discuss the quarterly sales for the company's six regions. Each manager must present a report to the director of marketing. Our manager, Kathleen, sits down at her personal computer and starts her spreadsheet application. From the corporate computer she then obtains the quarter's sales figures, which are loaded into her spreadsheet. She uses certain procedures known as spreadsheet formulas for processing the data, and comes up with total sales, year-to-date sales, and sales compared to the same quarter last year. The numbers show her division is doing extremely well. Using the graphics program with her spreadsheet, she turns those numbers into bar charts, highlighting the current quarter's outstanding performance. Then she switches to word processing to write a short report. Once she's finished, she transfers the three bar charts to the appropriate locations in the text. Now she prints the report and puts it in a handsome binder for her boss. Kathleen smiles. It's going to be a good meeting, she thinks to herself.

It's interesting to note that a recent U.S. government study concluded that by the year 2000, three out of five jobs that people will need to be trained and educated for *do not exist today.* Moreover, these jobs will almost certainly involve the use of a computer. Clearly, it is in your best interests to become a highly competent knowledge worker. Here are several snapshots of knowledge workers and how they use their computers.

- Tedd Martin is a management consultant who specializes in working with information systems in the newspaper publishing business. He works from his home in Oceanside, California, and has three computers. "The first one was just to see if it was a toy or not," says Tedd, "but every one after that was to fill a specific need. It's just that I got more knowledgeable and kept wanting to do more, and that meant getting better, faster computers that could handle the software!" Tedd writes and designs a newsletter that he sends to his friends and family every Christmas, filled with stories about his adventures (a week in the Mohave Desert), his hobbies (music, especially electronic keyboards), and computer-generated art — his photographs (he's also a photographer) and computer graphics he has created.

- R. Tucker Reynolds is, in his own words, "a country lawyer" in Medway, Massachusetts. After practicing law for several large firms in Boston, Tucker opted to open an office in the town where he lives so he could spend more time with his family and "for that thing they call 'quality of life.'" He uses his personal computer every day, mostly for word processing; he has all his legal documents stored so they can be revised and reused for different clients. He also uses a simple software program in place of an electronic address book. "At first I thought I'd hire a secretary, because I thought my clients would expect an attorney to have one. But between the computer and the FAX machine, I can do everything myself. And my clients are impressed by the fact that I do my own computing!" When he's not preparing legal briefs, Tucker is writing a book about his experiences coaching his eight-year-old son's soccer team.

- Jeffrey VanSkyhawk is a manager of end-user services. Bose Corporation manufactures high-quality stereo speaker systems for homes and automobiles. Bose designs custom, multiple-speaker systems for such cars as Cadillac and Infiniti. That same creative thinking applied when Bose decided to upgrade from several older computer systems and to put a Macintosh on the desks of over 600 knowledge workers in customer service, sales support, production planning — in short, throughout the company. Jeff was responsible for helping set up the customer service department. Over 200,000 customer records had to be transferred to the Macintosh. Jeff says they are able to gather data from various departments much more efficiently now, and that everyone seems happy and productive. The system helped Bose save over $1 million in inventory control in one year, and production planning has been extended from 1 month to 12. Office workers and executives alike utilize the Macintoshes, which are used for training and boardroom presentations as well.

Today, there are over 70 million knowledge workers in the United States, who generate nearly 2 *trillion* pieces of paper each year. These knowledge workers work 10 hours per week more than they did 10 years ago, and create over 15 billion new pieces of paper a year. According to a survey conducted by *Industry Week* magazine in 1991, 39 percent of U.S. management-level knowledge workers say paperwork is a problem. Further, *USA Today* reported in 1991 that the average knowledge worker has 36 hours of work stacked up on the desk. Clearly, the computer as a productivity tool must play an ever more important role in knowledge work. And knowledge work itself is steadily assuming larger proportions. According to several worldwide studies, urban centers in Canada, the United States, Europe, and other developed areas are increasingly using computer technology and thus evolving *knowledge-based cities.* These knowledge-based cities are characterized by: (1) a concentration of scientists and engineers, (2) business, university, and governmental research activities, (3) a high degree of interaction between individuals and the various institutions, and (4) a positive image that attracts college graduates to knowledge work. Clearly, the decade of the 1990s and the new millennium that follows are an exciting time for knowledge work.

KNOWLEDGE WORKERS AND INFORMATION

For many years, it has been said that computers work with and produce data, and that it is the human being who turns that data into information. In many cases, this is still true; the vast majority of computers at work today provide data, most often in the form of reports such as the one in Figure 1.4, that must be interpreted by a qualified knowledge worker.

Yet computer systems are becoming more sophisticated—better brain levers, if you will—and in some cases it is fair to say that they produce information. This is coming about due to an emerging concept known as the document. A **document** is a self-contained work, created by a knowledge worker using a computer and an application program, which can be saved and later retrieved as a file. A document contains data in the form of text and graphic characters, but it is also something more. It is the record of a transaction between two parties, such as a memo, letter, or report. A significant aspect of the document is that it has a life cycle that extends in time and in space. Over *time,* its content has immediate and possibly long-range value. In *space,* the document also has form; it may be paper and as such must conform to business

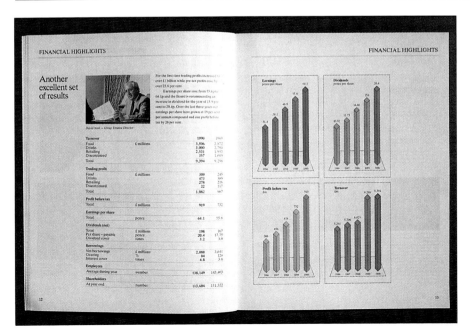

FIGURE 1.4

The report is the most common means of communicating information in business.

1. *Creation:* The author proposes the changes.
2. *Management:* The memo is reviewed and specifications are checked prior to approval.
3. *Manufacturing:* The memo is printed, copied, or reproduced.
4. *Delivery:* The memo is distributed via paper, mail, messenger, etc.

or company requirements for quality and presentation as, say, a report or an advertising brochure. The document may also be electronic, meaning it originates on a computer and is viewed on the computer screen. Figure 1.5 gives the four distinct activities involved in working with a common written document, in this case a memo suggesting changes in a manufacturing process.

Document-based information is the next great frontier for the knowledge worker. Data created by a number of applications (including word processing, the spreadsheet, and drawing and drafting programs) most frequently appear in a document of some kind. New systems have emerged, and continue to emerge, to work with the document: desktop publishing, electronic publishing, multimedia, text retrieval systems, the Xerox DocuTech machine, and others. You'll learn about all of them as you continue reading *Computers: Tools for Knowledge Workers*. But next, we will learn more about the computer itself.

KNOWLEDGE CHECK

1. What does a knowledge worker use the computer for?   p. 11
2. What are the five components of a computer system?   p. 11
3. What are some specific productivity problems confronting today's knowledge worker?   p. 12
4. What is the difference between data and information?   p. 13
5. Why is document-based information of greater value than data? pp. 13–14

WHAT IS A COMPUTER?

A **computer** is a device that accepts data, then performs arithmetic or logical operations that manipulate or change the data, and finally produces new results from that data. Given that definition, you might think there are many machines or devices that qualify as a computer—and you'd be right. Computers come in many shapes and sizes. Commonly, they are grouped into four types: the personal computer, the minicomputer, the mainframe computer, and the supercomputer. Let's briefly take a look at each, and the types of tasks it is commonly used for.

THE PERSONAL COMPUTER

For many people, the path to computer literacy begins with the personal computer, so that is our primary focus in this book. The **personal computer,** or microcomputer as it is sometimes called, is (1) one designed for use by a single individual, (2) usually small enough to fit on a desktop, and (3) affordable enough for the average person. The personal computer is sometimes called a *microcomputer,* reflecting the fact that it is smaller than a mainframe or a minicomputer. Today, we commonly use the term *personal computer* (or *PC*) generically to refer to many different kinds of microcomputers. This includes the IBM PC, the Apple Macintosh, the Commodore Amiga, and many others.

Personal computers come in many sizes. Besides the common desktop machine, there are portables, laptops, notebooks, and palmtops. The most powerful models are called *workstations,* which have the power and capabilities of a minicomputer. We'll learn all about the various types of personal computers in Chapter 3.

The first personal computers were like the old Volkswagen beetle: they came with only the bare essentials. Their owners had to know a lot more about electronics than today's personal computer users. In 1977, Apple and Tandy/Radio Shack became the first companies to introduce personal computers to the mass consumer market. Radio Shack's management wasn't sure there would be much interest in personal computers when the TRS-80 Model I came off the assembly line, so they only made enough so each retail store would have one. If it didn't sell, the store could use it for inventory or something, they reasoned. Needless to say, it sold very well and today Tandy is one of the leading personal computer suppliers.

Figure 1.6 shows a state-of-the-art personal computer. The **system unit** is where the computer's electronic and mechanical are housed. The **keyboard** is used to enter data and instructions. The **monitor** or video display screen is where you see your work. A separate **printer** provides a finished copy of the results. These hardware components are common to all computers, large and small. Large computers often fill many cabinets and can have hundreds of keyboards and monitors, so more than one person can use them at once.

FIGURE 1.6

This Macintosh IISI personal computer is shown with its system unit, color monitor, keyboard, and mouse and a separate laser printer.

THE MINICOMPUTER

The **minicomputer** is a versatile, medium-sized computer designed so that more than one person can use it at the same time. It was introduced as a smaller, less expensive alternative to the mainframe. Early minis were designed for use in a variety of *special-purpose* tasks (manufacturing, engineering, science, and process control, for example):

- Providing instructions for manufacturing equipment such as presses or robots.
- Use in guidance systems for aircraft.
- Measuring seismographic fluctuations in dangerous mines.
- Use in control processes such as keeping a constant temperature for cooking vats of soup, spaghetti sauce, or chocolate.

Yet over time, the mini became a viable computer for business purposes, serving the needs of a small to medium-size company or a department or division of a larger company.

Minis are often connected to other minis, and are commonly used to provide connections between mainframe computers and personal computers. It is a good idea to remember that many of the sharp distinctions between mainframes and minis and between minis and powerful personal computers have been blurred by technological advances, as you shall see in later chapters.

The mini was designed by Kenneth W. Olsen, an MIT graduate who went on to found Digital Equipment Corporation (DEC), the world's second-largest computer company. In 1959, Digital introduced the PDP-1 (for Programmed Data Processor). At a time when typical computer systems sold for over $1 million, the PDP-1's price tag of $120,000 shocked the industry. Of course, it was not able to perform all the tasks of a mainframe but it was a true

FIGURE 1.7

This engineer is using a mini-computer for the development of special software.

computer nonetheless. It was followed by several other PDPs, the last of which, the PDP-11, led to the VAX, introduced in 1975, which is now the most widely used family of minicomputers in the world. Today, there are minis of all sorts; some are as large or as powerful as mainframes, while others fit on a desktop. Figure 1.7 shows a minicomputer at work in an engineering department.

THE MAINFRAME COMPUTER

The computer most commonly used in business is the mainframe computer. A **mainframe** is a large, general-purpose computer capable of performing many tasks simultaneously, while permitting hundreds, even thousands, of people to use it at the same time. It is made up of many cabinets filled with electronic gear and connected to the main computer cabinet, which led to its being called a mainframe. One is shown in Figure 1.8.

In 1964, after spending four years and $5 billion on research and development, International Business Machines (IBM) introduced the System/360 mainframe computer. Bob Evans, the project manager, called it the "you-bet-your-company computer." Thomas J. Watson, Jr., IBM's chief executive, introduced it himself on April 7, 1964; he called it the most important product in the company's history. It became the most popular mainframe in computer history and set an early standard for the industry.

Mainframes dominated the corporate and government computing market for many years. However, in the 1980s people found many uses for the personal computer in business, and it became obvious that the mainframe needn't be used for all computing tasks. In fact, many tasks have been shifted off the mainframe and onto minis and personal computers. The mainframe is still an essential component; however, it is commonly a storehouse for vast amounts of data that organizations need to operate properly.

FIGURE 1.8

Chase Manhattan Bank installed mainframes in its new Metrotech facility in order to reduce its back-office expenses.

FIGURE 1.9   Discrete computer facilities used to be called islands of automation. Today, knowledge workers commonly don't need to know where the machine is physically located, as long as the information they need is on the screen.

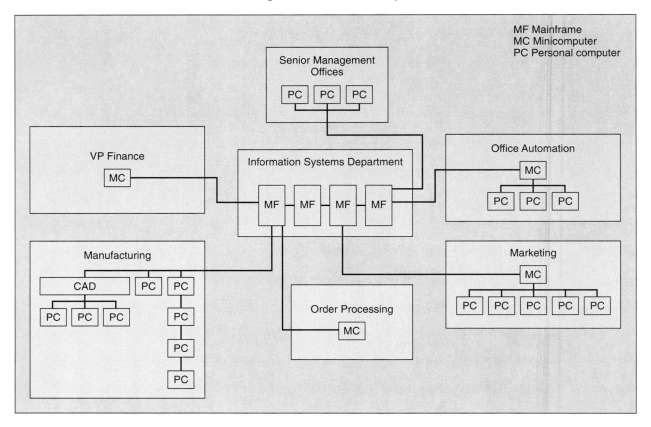

Yet this change has led to a dramatic shift in how computers are viewed and used, as shown in Figure 1.9. In the past, computers of all sizes were viewed as discrete machines, each separate and unable to connect with others. Today, it is more common to think of the computer *system* as an electronic infrastructure for the business, not unlike the human nervous system. As the diagram shows, today we think far less about the type of computer we're using, and far more about the resources and the information we need to do our work.

THE SUPERCOMPUTER

The **supercomputer** is a special type of computer that is commonly used to perform a single, very complex task that requires massive processing power. For example, a supercomputer may be given the task of analyzing how a chemical carcinogen attaches itself to a DNA molecule, a task that might take hours, days, or even weeks to compute. Supercomputers are the most powerful computers on earth. They are most often used in experimental government and scientific research facilities such as the Lawrence Livermore Labs in Cali-

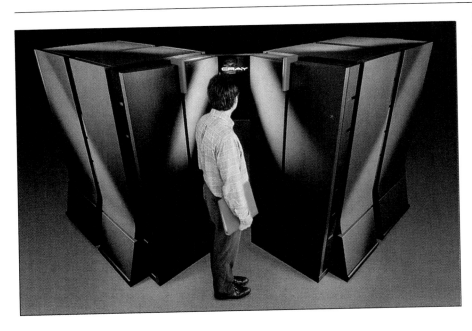

FIGURE 1.10

The Cray Y-MP/90 is one of the most powerful computers in the world. Supercomputers can quickly process enormous amounts of information. In a fraction of a second, they can perform calculations or programs that calculators or personal computers would take days to perform.

fornia and Los Alamos National Laboratory in New Mexico. They are also used in military weapons research, atmospheric and earth science research, and natural resource exploration.

A supercomputer must have its own installation platform, plus thousands of dollars worth of air-conditioning plumbing. It must be tested for months before it can be used. Once ready, the entire setup is put in a semitrailer truck and moved to the site. Figure 1.10 shows one of the most popular supercomputers, the Cray.

In 1957, William Norris and some other engineers formed a new company, Control Data Corporation in Minneapolis, to build supercomputers. In 1963, CDC introduced what was then the most powerful computer on earth, the CDC 6600. It was designed by a man named Seymour Cray.

Seymour Cray is probably the most brilliant supercomputer architect of our times. He left CDC in 1972 to start Cray Research, Inc., and built his own supercomputer, the Cray-1. Today, Cray Research, Inc., is the leading supercomputer maker and CDC is no longer in the supercomputer business. IBM has entered the market, and Japan's Fujitsu is a major competitor. Seymour Cray has gone on to form Cray Computer Corporation, where he and a team of engineers are building the next-generation supercomputer, the Cray-3. The market for supercomputers has grown beyond the research laboratory, as many businesses have found uses for supercomputers as well.

To get an idea how fast a supercomputer is, compare how long it took each of the following computers to perform a particular calculation:

- IBM PC: 35 hours.
- VAX mini: 7 seconds.
- Cray supercomputer: less than 2 seconds.

THE MODERN COMPUTER

All the types of computers we have been studying are machines that are both electronic and digital. By **electronic** we mean a machine that uses components such as vacuum tubes, transistors, or silicon chips. All these electronic devices require electricity. By **digital** we mean a computer that uses the binary arithmetic system as the basis for its operation. Binary arithmetic uses only two digits: the 0 and the 1. Thus the electronic digital computer is generally considered the *modern computer,* which dates from the early 1940s. This chapter's Yesterday feature describes ENIAC, the first electronic digital computer.

THE ANALOG COMPUTER

In contrast to the digital computer, there is also an analog computer. **Analog** means the computer does not count in two digits, but rather continuously measures and compares changing values. One example is a computerized thermostat, which regulates the heat or air conditioning in a building. An analog radio tuner has a needle or arm that moves from station to station when you turn the knob; a digital radio tuner displays the precise frequency when you touch a button. Analog computers are in wide use, but rarely for the same purposes as digital computers. However, there are important differences between the two in the types of work they perform.

KNOWLEDGE CHECK

1. What is the other term used to describe a personal computer?   p. 15
2. Name several different types of personal computers.   p. 15
3. What are the three components of every computer?   p. 15
4. How is the minicomputer different from the mainframe computer?   p. 16
5. How is the role of the mainframe changing?   p. 17
6. What are the primary uses for the supercomputer?   pp. 18–19
7. What are the two characteristics of the modern computer?   p. 20
8. What is a common example of an analog computer?   p. 20

HOW COMPUTERS DO THEIR WORK

In the definition of a computer, we learned that the computer accepts data. The term **data** is defined as facts and numbers suitable for communication or interpretation. Strictly speaking, a single unit of data is termed a datum; *data* is the plural term. When people or a computer act on that data, we call it processing. **Data processing** is the computer system using specific procedures that turn data into useful information for people. Data is the raw material of information. People turn the data computers produce into useful information through understanding, integrating, and applying them to our world.

YESTERDAY

ENIAC: THE FIRST ELECTRONIC DIGITAL COMPUTER

In 1937, the League of Nations commissioned the world's best minds to forecast future technologies. When these experts submitted their report, there was no mention of a computer. Yet even as they convened, John Atanasoff, a physics professor at Iowa State University, was at work on the first computer.

Many of his ideas would find their way into ENIAC, the Electronic Numerical Integrator and Calculator. ENIAC was a project commissioned by the U.S. Army's Ordnance Department, which was seeking a better way to plot ballistics trajectories. John Mauchly and J. Presper Eckert headed up the project, which got underway in 1943 at the University of Pennsylvania. Some of the best academics in the country worked on ENIAC. When it was completed in

1946, at a cost of $3 million, it stood two stories high, weighed 30 tons, and covered an area the size of two football fields. Its electronic circuitry was comprised of 18,000 vacuum tubes, 70,000 resistors, 10,000 capacitors, and 6,000 switches that made up 100,000 circuits. When ENIAC was turned on, it was said, the lights of Philadelphia dimmed. Yet ENIAC was not much more complicated than a modern hand-held calculator, and was only able to perform a mathematical computation about as fast.

Unfortunately for ENIAC, World War II ended in 1945; thus it was unable to fulfill its original purpose. However, ENIAC was put to work on calculations for atomic bomb research at the Los Alamos, New Mexico, government research

laboratories. Today, some portions of ENIAC are on display in the Smithsonian Institution in Washington, D.C.

ENIAC was a research computer, but its descendant, UNIVAC (both shown below), was designed for commercial purposes by Mauchly and Eckert. They formed their own computer company to build UNIVAC, the Universal Automatic Computer, but they were not good businessmen and eventually had to sell their interests to Remington Rand. The UNIVAC I was introduced in 1951, and the U.S. Bureau of the Census received the first one to tabulate census statistics. The government also bought two more. Shortly thereafter, a computer made its first television appearance. UNIVAC was used to predict the 1952 presidential election—and it did a good job, forecasting that Dwight Eisenhower would win 438 electoral votes to Adlai Stevenson's 93. The actual count was 442 to 89.

The next year, General Electric became the first private business to buy a computer. Then other businesses began clamoring for UNIVACs, which were sold in rapid succession to Metropolitan Life Insurance, U.S. Steel, Du Pont, and Franklin Life.

ENIAC.

UNIVAC.

PROGRAMMING COMPUTERS

We commonly turn to computers to help us solve a problem or perform a task that would take too long or that is too difficult for people to do themselves.

The problem or task must be presented in a very specific and precise manner. If it is not, the computer won't be able to help.

People can make the computer do many sophisticated and complicated tasks by issuing it instructions. We give the computer instructions, usually in the form of programs, so it will perform the data processing. An **instruction** is typically a group of characters the computer understands. A single instruction might be to total 2 + 2. A **program** is a series, or set, of instructions that gives us a more complex result, such as producing a report listing all the company's customers living in the postal ZIP code 95123.

COMPUTER OPERATIONS

The computer performs two types of operations on data: arithmetic and logical. **Arithmetic operations** are simply addition, subtraction, multiplication, and division, as in adding the numbers 2 and 2. **Logical operations** compare values to perform logical tests and make decisions. For example, is the number 2 *greater than* (expressed with the > sign) or *less than* (expressed with the < sign) the number 6? As you can see, the fundamental way computers operate is very simple.

THE FIVE DATA PROCESSING STEPS

We can now put everything we've just learned into a practical context and more clearly understand how the computer performs its tasks. There are five specific steps involved in processing data with a computer: input, processing, output, storage, and results. Refer to Figure 1.11 as we examine each.

When we give the computer either instructions or data, it is called **input.** An instruction is either an arithmetic or logical operation, such as addition. The data are the numbers, such as 2 and 2. The computer performing the addition of 2 and 2 is **processing,** as you have already learned. The product of the processing, or the answer we seek, is termed **output;** in our case, the number 4.

Once the data is processed and output from the computer, there are two additional steps. One is **storage,** or holding the data in computer memory. This may be for a short, indefinite period, or permanently, depending on the type of storage we choose. The final step is called **results,** or presenting the data in a form that a person can use. Most commonly, the results are displayed on the monitor or printed on the printer.

FIGURE 1.11

The five data processing steps.

1. *Input:* Either instructions or data.
2. *Processing:* The computer performing its instructions—either an arithmetic or logical operation—on the data.
3. *Output:* The data produced after processing.
4. *Storage:* The option of retaining the data indefinitely or permanently.
5. *Results:* Presenting the data in a useful form.

Needless to say, we don't often use the computer to perform the tasks a calculator can do. However, this example of adding 2 + 2 demonstrates the simplicity of the computing process. The computer is no more complicated than this; its primary virtue is its speed. It is able to count and compare its binary digits very, very fast. We'll study the computer's components and these five tasks in more detail in Module III on hardware.

SOFTWARE

Software is the programs and instructions that tell the computer what to do. The **programmer** is a person who understands the problem or task the computer is supposed to work on and can translate it into the language the computer understands. This process is called **programming.** Programmers, in the programming process, create software.

Computer software takes two forms. One is **system software,** which controls the computer's primary operations. The system software we most commonly come in contact with is called the *operating system* which, among other jobs, controls the programs we use to accomplish our tasks. You'll learn more about this form of software in Chapter 7.

The other form computer software takes is **application software,** the programs we use to produce useful work. This might be a bicycle parts inventory management application program or a zoological classification application program. There are applications for many thousands of interests and needs. The three most commonly used for personal productivity, schoolwork, and business are:

- **Word processing,** which lets you create and revise your writing.
- The **spreadsheet,** which lets you perform a variety of accounting and mathematical calculations.
- The **database management system** (DBMS), which lets you organize and obtain data stored in one or more databases.

We'll learn how to use each of these applications, along with several others, in Module II.

Therefore, programmers create the application software that we use to issue instructions to the computer in order to perform various tasks. The tasks we perform are often referred to as *procedures,* a set of clearly defined steps. When those procedures are applied to working with data, the result is information that we and others find useful in a variety of ways.

WHERE ARE WE GOING?

Dr. Robert Lucky, executive director of research at Bell Labs, a premier technology think tank, has written a book entitled *Silicon Dreams.* In it he says

> Perhaps information itself is best described in terms of organization, implying that organization per se is the intellectual effort that manufactures information out of such raw material as observation. The more the organization, the higher the level of information. In contrast, where there is total disorder there is no information. The level of organization can be described in terms of a hierarchy,

TODAY
CORNELL'S DIGITAL BOOKS

Over one-third of the books in the world's libraries are deteriorating, due to what is called the "brittle book" problem which arose due to manufacturing process changes around 1850. As a result, where book life had been measured in centuries, it is now measured in decades.

Cornell University has two libraries that contain over 5 million books, including world-renowned collections of the poets William Wordsworth and Petrarch. There is a large collection of older books on mathematics that are also valuable — and turning brittle. One such volume is the *Traite d'Analyse*

Traite d'Analyse.

by H. Laurent, a French work on calculus published in 1885. It was chosen as a work to be preserved in digital form using the Xerox DocuTech Production Publisher. Xerox is working with Cornell, supplying technology and expertise for its Commission on Preservation and Access project development team. Over the project's life span, about a thousand books will be scanned into a digital format.

The DocuTech machine is designed to accept both text and images from either paper or electronic sources, to digitize them, and then to organize, design, format, and print them in an-

How to Draw a Straight Line.

other new form. Large pages can be reduced and vice-versa. Photographs can be scanned in and then prepared for printing as halftones. Text and images can be moved, resized, or reformatted in a variety of ways.

Cornell has identified a number of benefits to digital preservation. There is no loss of information; the book appears in its original format. For example, the *Traite d'Analyse* is reproduced with its complex and varied mathematical symbols, its boldfaced and italicized type faces, and even an unintentional blob of printing ink that stuck to the type. However, a work can be easily reformatted as desired, as when someone only needs a few pages or chapters, not the entire book. Image capture is another benefit; drawings need not be redrawn, images can be enhanced and halftones created. An excellent example of this can be seen at left from a small, 50-page chapbook entitled *How to Draw a Straight Line: A Lecture on Linkages,* written by A. B. Kempe (a member of the council of the London Mathematical Society) and published in 1877. It contains many rare drawings of these "linkages" or mechanical drafting devices used in the drawing of lines. These drawings of the Victorian era preserve all their original charm and interest.

THÉORIE DES FONCTIONS ELLIPTIQUES.   191

Ses propriétés découlent de la théorie développée aux paragraphes précédents. Si l'on pose avec Jacobi

$$(2) \qquad K = \int_0^1 \frac{dz}{\sqrt{(1-z^2)(1-k^2z^2)}},$$

$$(3) \qquad K'\sqrt{-1} = \int_1^{\frac{1}{k}} \frac{dz}{\sqrt{(1-z^2)(1-k^2z^2)}}$$

ou encore, en faisant dans cette dernière formule $k'^2 = 1 - k^2$ et $1 - k^2 z^2 = k^2 t^2$,

$$(4) \qquad K' = \int_0^1 \frac{dt}{\sqrt{(1-t^2)(1-k'^2t^2)}}.$$

Les intégrales prises le long des lacets relatifs aux points critiques seront données par le Tableau suivant :

Le point $+ 1$ fournira la valeur ...... $2\,K,$

» $+ \frac{1}{k}$ »   ...... $2\,K + 2\,K'\sqrt{-1},$

» $- \frac{1}{k}$ »   ...... $2\,K - 2\,K'\sqrt{-1};$

en ce qui concerne les points critiques $+ 1$ et $- 1$, cela est

Fig. 7.

évident. Pour calculer la valeur de l'intégrale relative au lacet du point $\frac{1}{k}$ (*fig.* 7), on remarquera que le contour fermé qui se compose des lacets successifs du point $\frac{1}{k}$ et du

---

A LECTURE ON LINKAGES.   31

motion distributed in all directions. This species of motion is called by Professor Sylvester "tram-motion." It is worth noticing that the motion of the circular disc is the same as it would have been if the dotted circle on it rolled inside the large dotted circle; we have, in fact, White's parallel motion reproduced by linkwork. Of course, if we

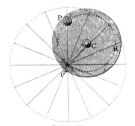

Fig. 20.

only require motion in one direction, we may cut away all the disc except a portion forming a bent arm containing C, P, and the point which moves in the required direction.

The double kite of Fig. 18 may be employed to form some other useful linkworks. It is often necessary to have, not a single point, but a whole piece moving so that all points on it move in straight lines. I may instance

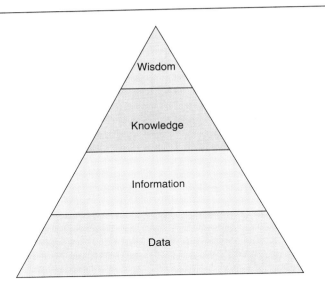

FIGURE 1.12
Dr. Lucky sees the computer
as a tool for organizing data
into information so that
knowledge workers can organize it into knowledge and,
in turn, integrate it into wisdom.

where we have borrowed the words sometimes used as synonymous with information to indicate the levels of organization—data, information, knowledge
and wisdom.[3]

Figure 1.12 shows Lucky's organizational-level pyramid. Lucky goes on to
say that *data* is the raw material from which information is extracted. *Information* is the raw data after it has been organized, such as a newspaper. "When
we take in information ourselves, for example by reading, and consciously or
not store it in our minds with the rest of our remembered information, we
create something personal, and at a higher level of organization. Now we call it
knowledge." Lucky concludes by saying that *wisdom* is organized, distilled, and
integrated knowledge. An integrated base of knowledge makes it possible to
create new knowledge. Wisdom is what we aspire to.

This, then, is the brave new world of the knowledge worker. We are indeed
fortunate to have a powerful tool to use as we turn data into information,
information into knowledge, and knowledge into wisdom. Let us begin.

KNOWLEDGE CHECK

1. What is data processing?   p. 20
2. What are the two types of computer operations?   p. 22
3. What are the five data processing steps?   p. 22
4. What are the two kinds of software?   p. 23
5. What are the four levels of information organization?   p. 25

---

[3] Robert Lucky, *Silicon Dreams* (New York: St. Martin's Press, 1989).

Tomorrow
The Challenges of Unmet Promises

What follows is the text of a thoughtful speech, "The Challenges of Unmet Promises," by Jim P. Manzi, president and chief executive officer of Lotus Development Corp. in Cambridge, Massachusetts, from 1990.

It seems an act of divine intervention that the decade just concluded will be remembered not by its first nine years but rather by its last nine weeks. When historians reflect on the 1980s, they will be drawn to this decade's punctuation mark—the unraveling of totalitarianism and the liberation of the people of Eastern Europe.

From one vantage point, these events can be viewed as the triumph of free information. It is now a time when information no longer respects national boundaries.

As we further reflect on the past decade and look beyond mere images, the 1980s will be defined as the dawning of the information age, an era when computers moved from the laboratory to the lap and satellite dishes made their way from radar stations to rooftops, providing Americans and others around the world almost instantaneous access to information.

Today, tens of millions of computers populate a world that a decade ago could count these machines in the thousands. It is this explosion of information power that is helping change the world's economic and political landscape.

In 1983, when Mitchell Kapor and Jonathan Sachs first brought Lotus' 1-2-3 to market, no one imagined that this software would ignite the personal computer revolution.

Seven years later, Lotus can count almost 10 million customers in more than 70 nations, each having access to a new, common language of global business.

In many instances, this access has enhanced productivity—the promise of the revolution. In many others, it has left people overwhelmed by a surfeit of facts and figures that they neither have the time nor the inclination to comprehend.

As one writer stated recently, "One of the great ironies of the information age is that as the technology of delivering information becomes more sophisticated, the possibility that we can process it becomes more remote."

So we now have more information, but not necessarily any greater understanding of the world around us. This is one of the unmet promises of information technology, and it is one that we—and other companies like us—plan to meet in the 1990s.

Another challenge for PC hardware and software suppliers in the 1990s will be meet-

Information Age Ethics: Privacy and the Law

The Information Age has brought with it a whole new set of concerns. People work harder and longer than ever before, seemingly trying to keep pace with computers. We often face "information overload" because there is so much information to assimilate. Computers also test our ethics and our values on both personal and societal levels. Computers make it all the more important for each of us to act ethically and responsibly.

If you believe that information will improve the quality of life, then you must accept the fact that computers will be full of data about you. The government wants statistical data about your occupation, your race, your age, your income tax status, and so forth. Business wants data on your buying habits, how you like its products, and your address for its mailing lists. The bank wants data on your credit. The insurance company wants data on your

ing the service requirements of our customers who are attempting to take maximum advantage of the advances in hardware and software that have occurred in the past 10 years.

Service, rather than raw technology, will drive the next cycle of growth in the PC industry. We have given our customers tremendous raw processing power and hundreds of new applications that attempt to harness that power. We now must recognize that there is a great need to provide the support offerings that will help our customers achieve the highest payback from the technology we've provided them.

Another challenge of the 1990s will be meeting the advances of foreign competitors, particularly the Japanese.

Unlike the automobile industry, software companies did not face stiff competition from the Japanese in the 1980s. But we cannot afford to be complacent and convince ourselves that software technology is the only computing technology that will elude the grasp of the Japanese.

Some say the Japanese lack the individual creativity for developing good software. This is nonsense. In the 1970s, some said the Japanese could not build cars that would sell in the U.S.

The Japanese are no longer confined to capital- or manufacturing-intensive industries. Recent data suggests that the Japanese in 1988 began spending more on research and development than on capital investment for the first time in history. Creativity — called *soozoo* — is now Japan's corporate battle cry. Matsushita executives sport badges saying "Create!" In many firms "innovation groups" have replaced "quality circles."

A significant portion of the U.S. economy is based on information industry compa-nies such as Lotus. The members of this sector must act cohesively but, at the same time, remember that global competitive battles are not fought industry versus industry but rather company versus company. We must compete aggressively and not retreat into an era of techno-nationalism, nor should we abandon our commitment to free markets.

As the decade's end approached, I was often asked if the PC revolution is over or whether it has just begun. My answer is similar to the close of Philip Roth's novel, *Portnoy's Complaint*.

After Portnoy recounts the story of his life for nearly 300 pages, in the very last line of the book his psychiatrist finally speaks up and says, "So, now vee may perhaps to begin. Yes?"

Begin, indeed. Welcome to the 1990s.

health. It's conceivable that these computers know more about you, in terms of the amount of data amassed, than you realize. How do you feel about that?

Back in the 1960s and 1970s, some people thought of computers as intrusive; they were tools of Big Brother, who was always Watching You. Over the years, many of these attitudes have diminished; with the exception of instances involving criminals and political dissidents, there are few cases of personal data being misused by the government. But privacy is becoming a social issue again. In 1991, an editor for a business magazine was able to become a client of a credit reporting agency with remarkable ease. Using his personal computer at home, he was able to read the credit files of colleagues at the magazine and even Vice President Dan Quayle! He learned that Quayle has a big mortgage and shops often with his charge card at Sears; the reporter even got a list of the vice president's credit card numbers. For many such firms, information — public or private — has become a commodity for sale. Yet who is the legitimate owner of personal information about you?

CAREERS FOR KNOWLEDGE WORKERS
GARRY FAIRBAIRN, EDITOR, *WESTERN PRODUCER*

Alberta, Saskatchewan, and Manitoba are known as the three prairie provinces of Canada. They border the United States north of Montana, North Dakota, and Minnesota, and are known for their rich agricultural bounty—especially wheat. The Prairies, as they are known, produce over a billion bushels of wheat per year.

Garry Fairbairn is editor of *Western Producer,* a weekly newspaper for farm families in the prairie provinces and eastern British Columbia. Journalism and writing runs in the family; Garry's father was a journalist who formerly worked for the paper, and his mother is a freelance writer. The *Western Producer* is published in Saskatoon, Saskatchewan (the largest city in the province), and is read by 400,000 Canadians.

Garry spent 11 years with the Canadian Press, a news wire service, prior to joining the paper. He had assignments in many Canadian cities as well as Washington, D.C., before settling down in Saskatoon. "It's a modern city, a very nice city for a family, and the University of Saskatchewan is here as well," says Garry. He knows this land well, having written the book *From Prairie Roots: A History of the Saskatchewan Wheat Pool.*

When he came to the paper, a mainframe computer and typesetting system were in use. Garry realized they had to modernize not only typesetting but writing, editing, and graphics. So Garry brought in a Macintosh to show the company its graphical capabilities; its first task was producing weather maps. It was well received, and soon a few more Macs were added for writing and typesetting the editorial page.

Today, *Western Producer* has over two dozen Macintoshes in use at every stage of the publishing process. The computers are connected in a network and the entire editorial staff uses them. Reporters write their stories and then send them electronically to the editors, who edit the copy and lay out the full pages on screen, complete with stories and graphics.

Garry is proud of their latest addition, an imaging system that takes the final electronic layout and produces the actual film that goes to the printer. Completed pages are printed to film on the editorial department's imagesetter, and the film goes straight to the printer's plate-making machines, eliminating the need for traditional composition and typesetting. "There are only a few dozen newspapers in North America that have a setup like ours," he says.

Garry Fairbairn manages a staff of 20 knowledge workers. He knows they could be more productive and creative with computers. "We've seen impressive benefits in flexibility, productivity, and design innovation with desktop computers," says Garry. "But the real revolution in office operations will come when the current high school generation hits the work force after having grown up with user-friendly computers."

Within the government computers, there are levels of security that restrict access to computer data, to protect your privacy and prevent misuse of information. In the United States, there is the Freedom of Information Act that allows us to see the files the government maintains on us. In fact, there are a number of laws in the United States designed to protect your rights and your privacy, but they often have loopholes. Consider these laws:

- Fair Credit Reporting Act (1970): Forbids giving credit information to anyone other than "authorized customers," but that means anyone can gain access who has a "legitimate business need."
- Privacy Act (1974): Bars federal agencies from using information for a purpose other than for which it was obtained — but exceptions in the law let them do it anyway.
- Right to Financial Privacy Act (1978): Restricts the government's access to citizens' bank records, but does not cover state and local governments, the FBI, or U.S. attorneys.
- Video Privacy Protection Act (1988): Retailers cannot disclose (or sell) video-rental records. Privacy advocates want the same rules to apply to medical and insurance files.
- Computer Matching and Privacy Protection Act (1988): Regulations cover cross-referencing federal data when verifying eligibility for federal benefits or programs, or for delinquent debts, but there are many holes and gaps.

Clearly, vigilance is the price of freedom. That is why we, as knowledge workers and members of the Information Age, must accept the personal responsibility for being computer literate in this complex, high technology world we live in.

SUMMARY

1. *Explain the many uses for computers in modern life.* Computers are used in business and government around the world. There are the computers we see and those we don't — both large and small, from banking to auto brakes.

2. *Describe the characteristics of knowledge workers.* Knowledge workers are people who routinely use a computer in their work to enhance their productivity. They are white-collar professionals from many walks of life who understand how to use a personal computer, know how to work with computer-based information, understand how the computer benefits their work and the business, and regard the computer as a productivity tool. The knowledge worker is the critical component in a computer system, which is made up of people, working together with software and hardware components.

3. *Describe the components that make up all computers.* The system unit is where the computer electronics are stored. The keyboard is used to enter data and instructions. The monitor or video display screen is where you see your work. A separate printer provides a finished copy of the results.

4. *Name and identify the different types of computers.* The personal computer, or microcomputer as it is sometimes called, is designed for use by a single individual. It's usually small enough to fit on a desktop and is affordable for the average person. The minicomputer is a versatile computer designed so that more than one person can use it at the same time. It is a smaller, less expensive alternative to the mainframe. A mainframe is a large, general-purpose computer capable of performing many tasks simultaneously, while permitting hundreds, even thousands, of people to use it at the same time. The supercomputer is a special type of computer that is commonly used to perform a single, very complex task that requires massive processing power.

5. *Understand the difference between data and instructions.* Data is defined as facts and numbers suitable for communication or interpretation. An instruction is typically a group of characters the computer understands.

6. *Describe the five data processing steps.* When we give the computer either instructions or data, it is called input. The computer executes the instructions, which is processing. The product of the processing, or the answer we seek, is termed output. One additional step is storage, or holding the data in computer memory. This may be for a short, indefinite period or permanently, depending on the type of storage we choose. The final step is called results, or presenting the data in a form that a person can use. Most commonly, the results are displayed on the monitor or printed on the printer.

7. *Name the two types of software.* One is system software, which controls the computer's primary operations. The other form computer software takes is application software, the programs we use to produce useful work.

INFORMATION AGE ISSUES

1. What is the proper response when you are told that the mistake on your bill or invoice was a "computer error"?

2. Each of us must grapple with ethical and moral issues every day of our lives. What, if anything, makes computer ethics different? Do you think we need a separate set of ethical guidelines to follow when working with a computer? What makes it any different than the ethics we use on the job or in our lives? Do you think computer ethics, or any other kind of ethics, can be taught?

3. What does the term Information Age mean to you? Do you feel you are living in the Information Age? Are you a knowledge worker? Do you enjoy working with information, or has it caused more stress in your life? What do you think the Information Age will be like in the year 2000?

CHAPTER REVIEW QUESTIONS

REVIEW QUESTIONS

1. What is computer literacy? Who is responsible for it?

2. What are the three characteristics that define a personal computer?

3. What are the three components in a personal computer? What is a fourth commonly used with a personal computer?

4. What other type of computer lacks these characteristics? Describe some its uses.

5. Describe the five data processing steps and what process or processes characterize each.

6. Why are there two different types of software?

7. What is the difference between data and a document?

8. When do we need to use a supercomputer?

DISCUSSION QUESTIONS

1. Why is it important to understand what occurs behind the ATM when we make a transaction?

2. Discuss some benefits of computers in society, beyond the ones described in this chapter.

3. Discuss some reasons why we should not take computers in society for granted, beyond the ones described in this chapter.

4. Do we need an amendment to the U.S. Constitution to protect our privacy rights?

5. Are you a knowledge worker? Explain why you are or aren't.

6. Discuss the data-to-wisdom hierarchy. Is it reasonable to assume that computers will help people attain more or better wisdom?

MULTIPLE-CHOICE

1. The characteristics of information in the Information Age are:
   a. It is a commodity.
   b. It can be bought and sold.
   c. It has its own value.
   d. All of the above.

2. The following are names of personal computers (check all that apply).
   a. Apple Macintosh.
   b. Commodore Amiga.
   c. IBM.
   d. Tandy/Radio Shack.
   e. Digital VAX.
   f. CDC 6600.

3. How have the uses for a mainframe computer changed over the years? (Check all that apply.)
   a. It is being used mostly in foreign countries.
   b. It is mostly used as a storehouse for corporate data.
   c. It is used in conjunction with minis and personal computers.
   d. It is not used for all computing tasks.

e. It is the computer of choice when price is no object.

4. A knowledge worker is:
   a. Someone who uses a computer in his or her work.
   b. A white-collar worker.
   c. The owner of a small business.
   d. Someone who wants more work productivity using computers.

e. All of the above.

5. Data processing is (check all that apply):
   a. Programming information into computers.
   b. Storing one datum.
   c. People turning computer data into information.
   d. Input, processing, output, storage, and results.

FILL-IN-THE-BLANK

1. The two central characteristics of a modern computer are _____ and _____.

2. The name of the first modern computer was _____.

3. A computer system is made up of _____, _____, _____, and _____.

4. The Information Age states that information has the following three characteristics: _____, _____, and _____.

5. The personal computer has as its standard components a _____, _____, and _____.

6. The modern computer is _____ and _____.

TRUE/FALSE

1. The minicomputer was invented because mainframes became too large to fit in buildings.

2. The software most commonly used by a knowledge worker is systems software.

3. Knowledge workers, using computers, are creating less paper every year.

4. A document is always paper.

5. The three components that make up a personal computer are not the same ones that make up larger computers.

KEY TERMS

analog, 20
application software, 23
arithmetic operation, 22
computer, 14
computer literacy, 10
computer system, 11
data, 20
database management system, 23
data processing, 20
digital, 20
document, 13
electronic, 20

Information Age, 10
input, 22
instruction, 22
keyboard, 15
knowledge worker, 11
logical operation, 22
mainframe, 17
minicomputer, 16
monitor, 15
output, 22
personal computer, 14
printer, 15

processing, 22
program, 22
programmer, 23
programming, 23
results, 22
software, 23
spreadsheet, 23
storage, 22
supercomputer, 18
system software, 23
system unit, 15
word processing, 23

The Personal Computer

LEARNING OBJECTIVES

After reading and studying this chapter, you should be able to:

1. Identify the processing and peripheral hardware components in a personal computer.

2. Describe the steps involved in working with DOS.

3. List some commonly used DOS commands.

4. Explain the way DOS organizes files and directories.

5. Describe different types of personal computer configurations.

6. Identify the more commonly used types of personal computers.

MASTERING YOUR PERSONAL COMPUTER

One of the most satisfying experiences in life is the ability to master a task, a subject, or the operation of a machine. Whether it's knowing how to cook chicken cacciatore, learning ancient Celtic mythology, or driving a car, we all enjoy that sense of accomplishment and self-confidence that comes from doing something well.

This is certainly true when it comes to mastering the computer. In this chapter, you'll learn how to use a personal computer. Today, the term *personal computer* (PC) is most often used to refer to specific computers made by IBM, Apple, or a number of other computer makers; they are all personal computers. The personal computer is intended to help you become more personally productive in your work and your life.

Chapter 1 introduced you to the fundamental computer concepts. This chapter presents the personal computer from a "hands-on" perspective, actually taking you inside the machine to see its physical components. You'll learn about their components, how to begin and end a work session, and how to master some basic operating system commands that perform everyday tasks. The most popular personal computers are described.

A firm grasp of personal computer concepts provides a foundation for understanding Chapter 3's description of larger computer systems and for understanding many other chapters in this book. The personal computer has all the same components, both in hardware and software, as its larger predecessors. It differs primarily in power, size, and scale, but the components and operating principles are the same.

GETTING ACQUAINTED WITH PERSONAL COMPUTER HARDWARE

Learning to use a personal computer is really no more difficult than learning to drive a car or use a VCR. Contrary to popular opinion, it's difficult to damage a personal computer in normal usage; at the very worst, you might lose something you typed. The two most important things to remember are: (1) take your time and (2) do things carefully. If you follow these two simple guidelines, you'll have very few problems with your personal computer.

In Chapter 1 we discussed the five data processing steps: input, processing, output, storage, and results. We also learned that a computer system is made up of people, data, procedures, hardware, and software. The computer system utilizes the following four hardware components to perform data processing operations:

- A *system unit,* a cabinet that houses the electronic and mechanical components that comprise what we call the computer. This is where the data is input and processed according to the program instructions.

- *Input/output devices* or *peripherals,* such as the keyboard and printer. The keyboard is an **input device** people use to enter data into the computer for processing. The printer is an **output device** that gives people a way to see and use the results of the processing.
- *Storage devices,* such as disk drives or tape drives to store data for later use. These devices often have removable disks and tapes that actually contain the stored data.
- *Routing and control components,* which direct the instructions and/or data from one component to the next, making sure each does its task properly. Some of these components are electronic in nature, and may reside within the system unit; others take the form of cables and other connecting devices.

All computer systems are made up of these four components, whether a personal computer, minicomputer, mainframe, or supercomputer system. The personal computer's system unit usually houses the processing, storage, and routing and control components. In larger computers, each component may be housed in its own refrigerator-sized cabinet; often there are multiple processing and storage cabinets.

In many ways, a computer system is similar to a stereo system. Figure 2.1 compares the two. Most component stereo systems have an amplifier (or a receiver). Like the computer's system unit, the amplifier is the central component of the system. The amplifier receives input from a tuner, cassette deck, compact disc player, or turntable. Likewise, the computer's processor receives input from the keyboard. The amplifier processes the input, amplifies it, and then sends it to output devices, such as speakers or headphones. Similarly, the computer's processor sends output to the monitor or printer.

FIGURE 2.1

The similarity between computer technology and entertainment technology—whether sound or video—underscores the way people use information, whether for business or pleasure. It also demonstrates how technology crossover will eventually integrate these various forms of information.

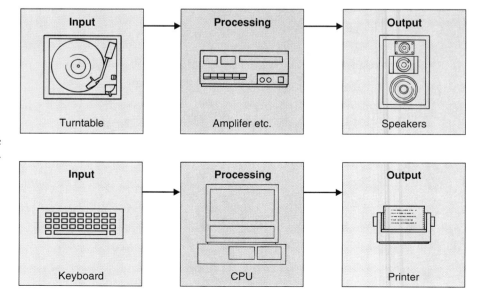

Yesterday

What Was the First Personal Computer?

Many computer historians say the first PC was born in 1975, when the electronic hobby kit Altair 8800 was offered for sale. Others date the first PC to 1977, when the first Apple II computer was built. That was the same year Radio Shack introduced its TRS-80 Model I, and Commodore introduced the PET. In truth, both the Apple II and the TRS-80 can be considered the first *popular* PCs, but neither was the very first. Let's take a look at a few selected "firsts."

The kitchen computer. One contender dates back to 1969, when Nieman-Marcus, an elegant Texas department store, offered the Honeywell H316 "Kitchen Computer" in its mail order catalog. It cost $10,600 and could be programmed for menu planning, tracking golf scores, monitoring stock market investments—even managing a charity ball membership list.

The kit computer. Another PC kit similar to the now-famous Altair 8800 was introduced in 1973, two years before the Altair 8800. Called the Mark-8, it was the creation of Jonathan Titus of Blacksburg, Virginia. It had no keyboard, but could be programmed by flipping eight toggle switches. One magazine called it a minicomputer; perhaps the term microcomputer hadn't yet been invented.

The first IBM PC? IBM created what might be termed a PC in 1973. It was called the SCAMP, for Special Computer APL Machine Portable. It had a keyboard, a cassette tape drive for storage, and a tiny screen. While amusing, it was never sold to the public.

The Sol-1. Les Solomon, an editor at *Popular Electronics* magazine, suggested the design for an early PC and ended up having it named after him. The Processor Technology Sol-1 was designed by Lee Felsenstein, who went on to design the Osborne-1. The Sol-1 debuted in 1976 in a typewriter-style enclosure with wooden sides. Only one program worked on it, Electric Pencil, a word processor.

The Commercial PC. By 1976, several California companies had decided there was a market for a personal computer. Among them were Altos, Vector Graphic, North Star, and Alpha Micro. Small businesses that couldn't afford a minicomputer were their target market. These "high-end" micros, as they were called, were expensive—some in the $10,000-plus range.

Altair 8800.

First Apple logo.

Radio Shack's TRS-80.

We can also compare the media used with a stereo to computer media. **Media** refers to the physical material used to store data and instructions. It might be a record, a cassette tape, a floppy disk, or a CD. In both systems, we have some devices that can only play, or *read,* media. Compact disc players only play CDs but do not record them. But both stereos and computers have other forms of media that can be recorded, or *written* on, such as tapes and disks. Reading and writing to media are discussed again shortly.

Although there are these similarities between stereo systems and computer systems, there is one big difference. Stereos play music, period. They don't have programs that allow them to perform a variety of tasks, as computers do. They produce sound but they can't switch between doing the payroll, word processing, spreadsheet analysis, inventory control, and organizing the quarterly sales figures.

It's helpful to think of the personal computer as a stereo boom box. All the components — usually excepting the printer, which is similar to the speakers — are contained within the system unit. Next, we take a look inside a personal computer to find out what hardware components look like and how they perform the five data processing operations.

FIGURE 2.2

This chip was designed for applications that require complex timing, such as plotters, digital cellular, engine control, antilock braking, robotics, stepper motors, and servo control.

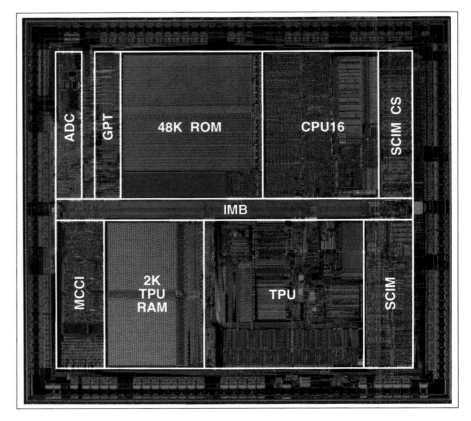

1. What is the reason for using a personal computer in your work or your private life?   p. 33

2. What are the two most important things you can do when learning to use a personal computer?   p. 33

3. Name the four components found in all computer systems.   pp. 33–34

4. What term do we use to refer to the components that people use and that are connected to the system unit?   p. 34

5. What is stored on media?   p. 36

PROCESSING HARDWARE

Hardware is the term we use to describe the computer's physical components —the machine itself. **Hardware** is any and all the components or physical devices —those things we can touch and feel —that make up a computer system. We're going to take a personal computer apart, figuratively speaking, so you can see what these hardware components actually look like and where they are physically located. As you already know, most of the PC components are located within the system unit.

As we discuss personal computer hardware, use the Computer Anatomy transparencies in The Way Things Work. The Computer Anatomy is designed to illustrate how a computer is assembled and how its various hardware components interact with one another. We'll start with the basic electronic circuitry inside the system unit and work our way out to the peripheral devices. Begin by lifting all the overlays away from the text page, so that only portion A is displayed. As you see subsequent pages referred to in the text, overlay the corresponding transparency.

THE MOTHERBOARD

The **motherboard** is where the computer's primary electronic circuitry resides. As you can see in The Way Things Work part A, this is a *printed circuit board* that contains a number of electronic components which perform the processing, storage, and some routing and control steps. Note the row of connections on the motherboard; these are called **expansion slots,** into which other printed circuit cards are plugged. They provide electrical connections from the processor to other hardware components, as we shall see. Note also the connectors at the rear of the motherboard. These are called **ports,** or interfaces, to which cables are connected for peripherals such as the keyboard, monitor, and printer.

Among the electronic components on the motherboard are a number of integrated circuits. An **integrated circuit** (IC) has hundreds, often thousands, of electronic circuits in a single piece of silicon, which is housed in a casing with a number of tiny electrical connections or "feet" as shown in Figure 2.2. The large black square on the motherboard is one type of integrated circuit; it is the processor chip, or what we call the CPU.

A. The computer's basic circuitry resides on, or is
connected to, the motherboard. It is a printed
circuit board upon which the expansion slots,
ports, and sockets for integrated circuits are
mounted.

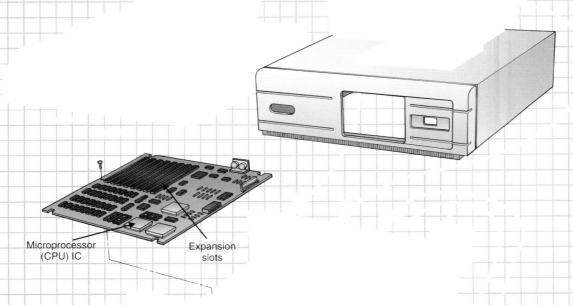

Microprocessor
(CPU) IC

Expansion
slots

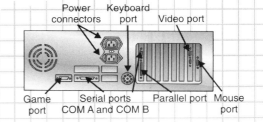

Power
connectors

Keyboard
port

Video port

Game
port

Serial ports
COM A and COM B

Parallel port

Mouse
port

The CPU

Look at The Way Things Work transparency overlay B. The **central processing unit** (CPU) is the computer's brain. As its name implies, it is where the *processing* step takes place. Instructions are executed and data is processed. The CPU consists of three components: the control unit, the arithmetic/logic unit, and main memory. The personal computer's CPU is commonly a single chip; in larger computers, it may be many chips.

The **control unit** directs the *step-by-step operation* of the computer. Like a traffic policeman at a busy intersection, the control unit directs electrical impulses between itself, the ALU (described next), and storage. It also controls operations between the CPU and the peripheral devices. These electrical impulses consist of instructions and the data being processed.

The **arithmetic/logic unit** (ALU) performs the *arithmetic and logical operations* you learned about in Chapter 1. You'll recall that the arithmetic operations are addition, subtraction, multiplication, and division. The logic operations compare two pieces of data to determine if one is greater than, less than, or equal to the other.

Random access memory (RAM), also called *main memory,* is the third component of the computer's CPU. RAM carries out the *storage* step for the CPU, providing temporary storage for the programs being executed and for data as it passes through processing. RAM is short-term, **volatile memory;** that means everything stored there is lost when the computer's power is shut off. RAM is not a physical part of the CPU chip. Rather, it is made up of a number of additional chips electrically connected — what is termed *logically connected* — and in close proximity to the CPU chip. This can be seen in the rows of RAM memory chips installed beside the CPU, and the arrows indicating the flow of data within the CPU and between the CPU and main memory.

There is another type of memory associated with the CPU called **read only memory** (ROM). It is memory chips that are used to store permanent instructions that perform many routine tasks for the CPU; these instructions cannot be changed.

The motherboard, as you can see, is the most important single hardware component. It contains all the circuitry for the CPU, control and routing components, and short-term storage. However, it is not the only component in the system unit. Next look at The Way Things Work transparency overlay C. The power supply provides the proper electricity to each component. The cooling fans do just what the name implies, moving cooling air across the electronic components. Proper cooling can extend their life by a factor of 10. Now that you have a good idea what's inside the system unit, let's see how the peripheral devices are connected to it and what they do.

---

1. What do we call the portion of the computer that we can touch? p. 37
2. Where does the computer's primary electronic circuitry reside? p. 37
3. What does CPU stand for? p. 39
4. What two units make up the CPU? p. 39
5. What is volatile memory? p. 39
6. How does ROM differ from RAM? p. 39

KNOWLEDGE CHECK

Peripheral Hardware

Peripheral hardware completes the remaining three data processing steps of input, output, and results. These **peripheral devices,** or just peripherals for short, are the CPU's senses; without them, we could not communicate with the computer. Peripherals are connected to the CPU, or motherboard, either by an expansion slot or through a cable to a port. Peripheral devices fall into three categories: input, output, and storage devices.

Input Devices

Look at The Way Things Work transparency overlay D. Input devices allow us to enter instructions and data into the computer. A common input device is the keyboard, which allows us to use our fingers to type data or instructions into the computer. Another is the mouse, which is used solely for issuing commands or instructions.

Output Devices

Look at The Way Things Work transparency overlay E. Output devices allow us to see the results of the computer's processing. A common output device is the monitor or video display, which provides what is known as *soft copy,* or one that we can only view but cannot keep. Whenever we type a character on the keyboard, we see it output to the monitor. Another output device is the printer, which gives us *hard copy,* a permanent paper record. Printing begins when we issue the proper software instruction.

Storage Devices

Storage devices, also known as **auxiliary storage,** are used to keep instructions (in the form of programs) and data permanently. A common auxiliary storage device is the disk drive. It can copy data that is being held in RAM onto a magnetic disk; this is called **writing** to the disk. The disk drive can also copy instructions or data from the disk into RAM so that the computer can perform its processing; this is called **reading** from the disk.

MEDIA.   See The Way Things Work transparency overlay F. The two most common types of auxiliary storage media for personal computers are magnetic disks. There is the **floppy disk;** the two most common types are the 5¼-inch disk and the 3½-inch disk, shown in Figure 2.3. People can insert and replace floppy disks in an auxiliary storage device, which of course is called a **floppy disk drive.** Refer back to overlay F. Just beneath the two floppy disk drives is the **hard disk drive,** which has a rigid magnetic disk enclosed in a permanently sealed housing. Hard disk drives have greater capacity than floppy disk drives. Both types of drives are connected to a *controller circuit board,* or card, which is plugged into an expansion slot in the motherboard.

Auxiliary storage, also called auxiliary memory or secondary storage, is memory that supplements RAM. This type of memory is long-term, nonvolatile memory. **Nonvolatile** means it stores and retains programs and data, regardless of whether the computer is turned on or off. We'll learn more about auxiliary storage in Chapter 9.

RAM is auxiliary storage's working partner. In fact, RAM is sometimes called the "working memory" of the computer because it holds the data and instructions during data processing. RAM is read-write memory: it can read or write data and instructions to auxiliary storage. Refer to Figure 2.4 as we use this example to see how the two different kinds of memory work together:

- *Input.* You type a short memo that reads, "Department meeting at 3:00 P.M. today."
- *Processing.* The CPU executes the instructions to turn the keystrokes into characters.
- *Output.* The characters are displayed on the monitor.
- *Storage.* The memo is stored temporarily in RAM.
- *Results.* You want to post the memo on the bulletin board, so you send it to the printer for a paper copy.
- *Storage.* At this point, you could also send the memo from RAM's working memory to a storage device, where you could save it permanently.

Computers differentiate between main storage and auxiliary storage in terms of speed and efficiency. RAM storage is very fast, because it's usually on a chip or circuit board physically close to the CPU. The shorter the distance

FIGURE 2.3

To accomodate changing technology, many personal computers have disk drives for both 3½-inch and 5¼-inch floppy disks.

FIGURE 2.4

RAM is the computer's working memory, working with the CPU to facilitate the five data processing steps and directing data to permanent storage when necessary.

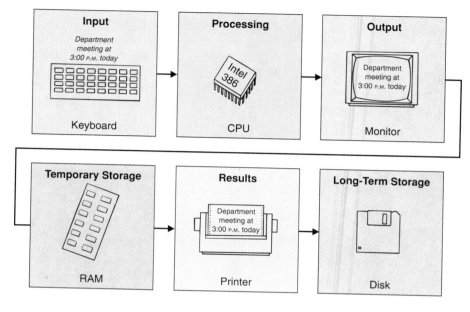

electrical signals have to travel, the faster the processing. Auxiliary storage is usually slower, not only because of the electrical distance, but because it involves some type of mechanical operation. For instance, disk drives must spin the disk to store data.

Let's review what we've just learned about the personal computer's hardware components, both processing and peripherals. Part A of The Way Things Work showed the motherboard and the expansion slots and ports; overlay B showed the RAM and ROM memory; overlay C showed the power supply and cooling fans; overlay D showed the connections of the input devices; overlay E showed the output devices; and overlay F showed the disk drives installed, completing the view of the system unit hardware components. Now that you understand the different personal computer hardware components, we shall learn how the operating system software makes it possible for them to function together.

KNOWLEDGE CHECK

1. What do we use peripherals for?   p. 40
2. What is the mouse used for?   p. 40
3. What type of output device provides soft copy?   p. 40
4. Why is RAM needed when reading or writing data to auxiliary storage?   p. 40
5. Name the two types of disk drives.   p. 40
6. What type of drive does not permit removing the media?   p. 40
7. What type of memory is nonvolatile?   p. 41

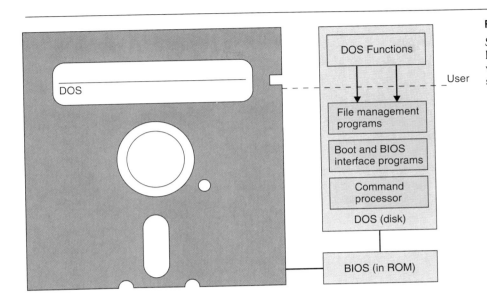

FIGURE 2.5

Software (such as DOS) and hardware (such as BIOS) work together to issue instructions to the computer.

DOS, THE DISK OPERATING SYSTEM

Turning the personal computer on is not enough; it must have instructions for the tasks it is to perform. These instructions come in the form of software. The primary tasks and functions the personal computer performs come from the instructions in systems programs.

You have already learned that there are specific systems software instructions embedded in chips that make up ROM (read only memory). These instructions help the computer give itself a checkup when you switch the power on, to make sure everything is in working order. Most of these instructions occur without our being aware of them. However, one that you often can see when you first turn the power on is the computer checking its RAM.

The other aspect of systems software, the one we can actually interact with, is called the operating system. The operating system for the personal computer is called **DOS,** for **disk operating system.** DOS must be loaded into the personal computer's main memory before it can be used. There are also a number of instructions given to the computer by the operating system, as shown in Figure 2.5. As you can see, many are unavailable to you, the knowledge worker. One that is very important that you can't see is the Basic Input/Output System (BIOS). It contains instructions specific to the computer you are using; for example, there is a BIOS that only works on an IBM PC.

When you load the operating system into the computer's memory, it is called a **boot** or booting the computer. The term comes from the old saying, "Pulling himself up by his own bootstraps," meaning someone who is able to do something on his own. Starting a program in the early days of computers was called bootstrapping, shortened to boot. Once booting is completed, you can issue DOS instructions and use application programs such as word processing.

FIGURE 2.6

Filenames, and their extensions, help knowledge workers identify the types of files and their uses. Word processing files often end with a .DOC extension, while spreadsheet files often end with a .WKS (for worksheet) extension.

ANSI.SYS	A DOS file that issues system commands
SORT. EXE	A DOS file that performs a DOS task
WP.EXE	A file that starts word processing application
THREE.100	A user-created data or text file (word processing)

DOS awakens the hardware and allows you to control the personal computer. It is responsible for managing all the input and output tasks, such as assuring that when you type a character on the keyboard, that same exact character appears on the screen and is stored in memory. Think of yourself as the personal computer's manager; DOS makes sure all your instructions are carried out accurately and promptly.

DOS FILES

DOS is actually a collection of programs, each of which performs specific tasks. Programs and data are stored in files. The **file** is a group of related records and the primary unit of data storage in DOS-based computers (as well as most others). It is very similar to the file folder in a common filing cabinet. Just as a file folder might contain memos with instructions or informational letters and reports, so a DOS file can contain either program instructions or data. There are files that are unique to DOS; files that both DOS and an application uses; and files created by the user while working with an application. Figure 2.6 shows these types of files. DOS uses files itself, performs operations on applications files, and allows you to create your own files.

DOS FILENAMES

Each file in DOS has a unique **filename,** which can be up to eight characters long, followed by an optional period or dot and three-character filename extension. DOS requires an .EXE or .COM extension for a program file, but you can give your files any extension (or no extension) you want. For example, the filename for this chapter is TWO, which may be typed without the dot or extension. But in order to keep track of each revision, the filename TWO.100 was used the first time, then TWO.101, TWO.102, and so forth, each time the chapter was subsequently worked on.

There are five different types of files used in DOS itself, and they are distinguished from one another by their filename extensions. All five types of filename extensions are shown in Figure 2.7. Of the five different types, .COM, .EXE, and .SYS are the most commonly used. Batch (.BAT) files contain instructions that perform a special grouping of commands and are often created by the user. .CPI files are used by skilled programmers.

The two types of files you'll work with most commonly in DOS are .COM and .EXE files because they perform the widest variety of tasks. For example, PRINT.COM will print a file, and DOS executable (.EXE) files are used to start almost all application programs. The most common DOS commands appear in the Today feature. A complete Glossary of terms with definitions follows Appendix C.

.COM	A command file that issues a specific command
.EXE	An executable program file, more complex than a .COM file
.SYS	An operating system file
.BAT	A batch file, which starts other programs
.CPI	A Code Page Information file

FIGURE 2.7

These are files that DOS uses. The one knowledge workers will create and use most often is the AUTOEXEC.BAT file, used to group commands and launch applications.

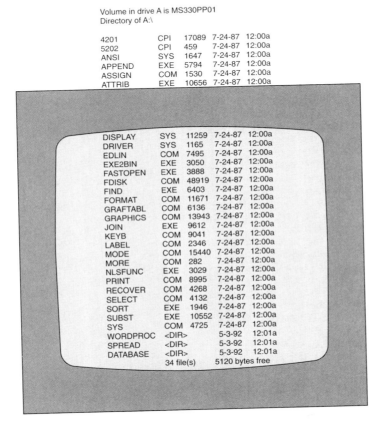

Volume in drive A is MS330PP01
Directory of A:\

4201	CPI	17089	7-24-87	12:00a
5202	CPI	459	7-24-87	12:00a
ANSI	SYS	1647	7-24-87	12:00a
APPEND	EXE	5794	7-24-87	12:00a
ASSIGN	COM	1530	7-24-87	12:00a
ATTRIB	EXE	10656	7-24-87	12:00a

DISPLAY	SYS	11259	7-24-87	12:00a
DRIVER	SYS	1165	7-24-87	12:00a
EDLIN	COM	7495	7-24-87	12:00a
EXE2BIN	EXE	3050	7-24-87	12:00a
FASTOPEN	EXE	3888	7-24-87	12:00a
FDISK	COM	48919	7-24-87	12:00a
FIND	EXE	6403	7-24-87	12:00a
FORMAT	COM	11671	7-24-87	12:00a
GRAFTABL	COM	6136	7-24-87	12:00a
GRAPHICS	COM	13943	7-24-87	12:00a
JOIN	EXE	9612	7-24-87	12:00a
KEYB	COM	9041	7-24-87	12:00a
LABEL	COM	2346	7-24-87	12:00a
MODE	COM	15440	7-24-87	12:00a
MORE	COM	282	7-24-87	12:00a
NLSFUNC	EXE	3029	7-24-87	12:00a
PRINT	COM	8995	7-24-87	12:00a
RECOVER	COM	4268	7-24-87	12:00a
SELECT	COM	4132	7-24-87	12:00a
SORT	EXE	1946	7-24-87	12:00a
SUBST	EXE	10552	7-24-87	12:00a
SYS	COM	4725	7-24-87	12:00a
WORDPROC	<DIR>		5-3-92	12:01a
SPREAD	<DIR>		5-3-92	12:01a
DATABASE	<DIR>		5-3-92	12:01a
34 file(s)		5120 bytes free		

FIGURE 2.8

Both floppy disks and hard disks have root directories, and may have subdirectories as well. This floppy disk has three subdirectories named for the most commonly used applications.

THE DOS DIRECTORY

DOS stores files on a disk in a **directory,** a list of the files stored on a disk or a portion of a disk. The primary directory is called the **root directory.** DOS also allows you to create subdirectories under the root directory. Thus, you can keep your programs and data well organized and easy to find. For example, you could keep your DOS program in the root directory, your word processing program in a subdirectory, and the files you create in word processing in a subdirectory off the word processing subdirectory. Both floppy disks and hard disks can be organized into directories; Figure 2.8 shows the DOS program listing in the root directory of a floppy disk (A:\) and three subdirectories (e.g., WORDPROC) at the bottom.

TODAY

COMMONLY USED DOS COMMANDS

These DOS commands will help you understand DOS better and perform some important tasks at the same time. It's extremely important that you type DOS commands precisely, using the correct DOS syntax, or else you will get the "Bad command or file name" error message. DOS requires that you insert blank spaces (using the keyboard's space bar) or certain punctuation marks in many commands; watch for them.

DIR (directory). One of the most important things we need to know about a disk, whether floppy or hard, is what files it contains. We learn this by using the DIR command, which lists a directory of the disk's contents.

FORMAT. All disk drives do not work in exactly the same way; therefore, the blank disks you buy must be formatted for the type of personal computer you use. FORMAT is a command that formats or creates an electronic pattern on the floppy disk. This pattern divides the disk into *tracks* and *sectors,* where specific parts of application programs and data will later be stored. Tracks are concentric rings, like growth rings in a tree, while sectors are like slices of a pie. Once a disk is formatted, it

can be read from and written to by your computer.

DISKCOPY. The DISKCOPY command copies the entire contents of one disk to another. The correct DOS syntax is that the first drive designation (A) is the drive you are copying from, and the second is the drive you are copying to.

Certain hidden files make a disk bootable or able to awaken the personal computer. A **hidden file** contains software information that is the copyrighted property of the computer company; we have no need to gain access to these hidden files. If the disk we were copying from contained the hidden files, they will be copied along with all the others, thus making the new disk bootable as well. The DISK-COPY command has another useful feature. If the target disk has not been previously formatted, DISKCOPY will format it as well. When DISKCOPY is finished, a message asks, "Copy another diskette? (Y/N)." You can make another copy of the same disk in drive A, or you can insert another disk to copy. If you are finished, type

N

then press ENTER, and you will be returned to the DOS prompt, ready to issue a new command.

Changing drives. The command to change a drive is simple: just type the drive designation and a colon together. If you are on the A drive and wish to change to the C drive, type

C:

then press Enter.

COPY. The COPY command is a much more flexible command than DISKCOPY. It allows you to copy a single file, a group of files, or all the files on a disk.

DELETE. The DELETE command eliminates an unwanted file from a disk, thereby making room for new file storage. When typing, DELETE can be abbreviated DEL. The DEL command syntax performs identically to COPY; we can delete a single file or, using the asterisk (*) wildcard, a group of files, or all files.

RENAME. Since a DOS filename can only be eight characters long, we often must abbreviate a name or make it unintentionally difficult to understand. Later, however, we might think of a filename that is easier to remember or that better identifies the file contents. The RENAME command allows us to change the file's filename, its filename extension, or both. The RENAME command can be abbreviated REN.

BEGINNING A WORK SESSION

A common term for a period of time during which a knowledge worker is computing is **work session.** The first step is loading DOS, the operating system. Personal computer software, whether it's the operating system or an application, usually comes on a floppy disk. It's from that disk that the per-

```
Phoenix 80386 ROM BIOS PLUS Version 1.10.10
Copyright (C) 1985-1989 Phoenix Technologies Ltd.
All Rights Reserved

MYLEX Corporation
386

640K Base Memory, 01408K Extended
Current date is Sun  8-19-1990
Enter new date (mm-dd-yy):
```

FIGURE 2.9

DOS provides useful information about the computer system on the opening screen. It's a good idea to get into the habit of using the clock and date functions in DOS so you can maintain a record of when files were created and last revised.

sonal computer's DOS got its name. The acronym DOS (disk operating system) dates back to the early 1970s when it was used to refer to an IBM mainframe operating system. **Loading** is the process of reading software, whether the operating system or application software, into the computer's memory. When we load DOS, we do so by copying the DOS disk's magnetic contents into the personal computer's RAM. Once this process is complete, DOS displays a screen as in Figure 2.9. DOS lets you check the computer's internal clock to date and time stamp your files. If the date you see is correct, press the Enter key; if the time is correct, press Enter again. If the date and time are not correct, DOS lets you type in the correct date and time by displaying on the screen "Enter new (date:)." Now you are at the DOS prompt.

DOS VERSIONS.   All good software is revised and improved over time, and DOS is no exception. Microsoft, now the world's largest software company, has made a number of improvements to DOS, each of which is called a *version;* they are described in Figure 2.10. Which version does your computer use? When you boot up, the copyright notice and version are usually displayed on the screen prior to seeing the date and time. If you are already at the DOS prompt, simply type

VER

and the version is displayed. The most common version in use is 3.3. Version 4.0 was developed by IBM and is most commonly used on portables. Microsoft introduced 5.0 in 1991 and 6.0 in 1993, and plans subsequent versions every 18 to 24 months.

Version	Date	Features
1.0	1981	Original disk operating system
1.25	1982	Support for double-sided disks
2.0	1983	Support for subdirectories (especially hard disk)
2.01	1983	Support for international symbols
2.11	1983	Bug corrections
2.25	1983	Extended character set support
3.0	1984	Support for 1.2MB floppy disk, up to 32MB hard disk
3.1	1984	Support for PC networks
3.2	1986	Support for 3.5-inch micro-floppy disk
3.3	1987	Support forIBM PS/2 computers
4.0	1989	Menu-driven user interface; support for 1.44MB floppy disk, hard disks over 32MB
5.0	1991	Windows interface; better memory use
6.0	1993	Highly integrated support for Windows 3.1; more built-in utilities, such as antivirus program

THE PROMPT

The **prompt** is a character or message that tells you the computer system is
ready to accept a command or input. A **command** is an instruction you give to
the computer. A prompt may be textual, such as "ENTER COMMAND," or a
character such as a question mark (?) or a period (.). In DOS, the prompt is a
right-pointing arrow or *caret* that looks like this: >.

THE COMMAND LINE

The prompt appears on the command line. The **command line,** as its name
implies, is the portion of the screen where you issue DOS commands or
instructions. Once you have typed the command and reread it to make sure it
is accurate, you must press the Enter key to issue the command.

THE CURSOR

Commands are issued at the prompt on the command line by typing them on
the keyboard. But first, we need to know if the command line is ready to accept
a command. The **cursor** is usually a blinking rectangle or a blinking underline
that tells us where the next keyboard character we type will appear on the
screen. It appears just to the right of the prompt. Other types of personal
computers that use a mouse, such as the Macintosh, often display an arrow for
pointing at the menu and issuing commands. Figure 2.11 shows screens with
rectangle and arrow cursors. Regardless of the type of task we're working at,
the cursor is our constant point of reference.

USING APPLICATION PROGRAMS

Once the operating system is loaded into the computer's main memory, we
can remove the DOS disk and load the application program. In most dual
floppy disk systems the application is loaded from the **program disk** that is

FIGURE 2.11

Operating systems: The top screen shows a DOS screen; the bottom screen is a Macintosh. The cursor, whether a blinking dash or a solid block, shows us our place on the screen — it is where data will next be entered. The pointer is used in the same way as certain key combinations — to issue commands.

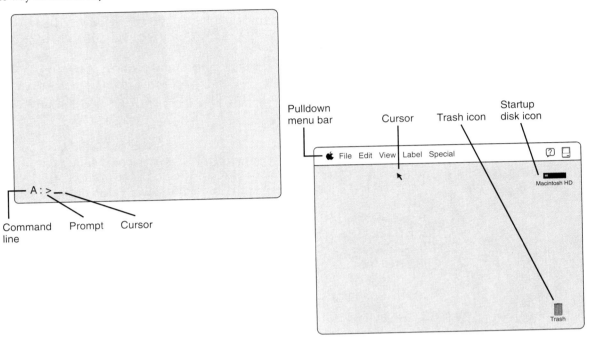

inserted into the A drive, and the **data disk** (where our files are stored) is inserted into the B drive. On a hard disk drive system, both the program and data files may be stored on the hard disk or C drive. Alternately, programs may be stored on the C drive and data files on a disk in the A drive. Many application programs allow you to create separate directories, one for the program and one for the data files, which often makes it more convenient to find your files. Chapters 4 through 7 explain the most popular personal computer applications in more detail.

ENDING A WORK SESSION

Learning how to properly end a work session with your personal computer is as important as knowing how to begin one. If you are working with an application, you must properly save your files before exiting the program. To save a file means to store the data you have created on a disk so that you can work with it again at another time. These procedures are explained in more detail in the applications chapters.

The first and most important step in ending a work session is to make protective copies of your work. The process of making extra, or duplicate, copies of your programs and files for safekeeping is called **backup.** The backup disk becomes your working copy that you use every day; put the original away for safekeeping.

Whether you are working in DOS or an application, your floppy disks should be removed from the drives before turning off the power. Make sure the disk drive indicator light is off, assuring that the disk is not in use. If the light is on, you run the risk of harming the disk or corrupting the data stored there. If your personal computer has a hard disk drive, there is a special DOS program you can use to safely shut down the system. Just as we powered up when we began our work session, shutting the power off is often called powering down.

TROUBLESHOOTING.   At the beginning of this chapter, you learned that the two most important things about working with a computer are to (1) take your time and (2) do things carefully. But as someone named Murphy once said, things can go wrong. What most commonly goes wrong when working with a personal computer?

According to computer service and repair technicians, the most common hardware problem people encounter with their personal computers is an unplugged power cord. Often, the plug has wiggled loose from the wall socket or from the socket on the back of the computer. Next most common is circuits that have been burned up by a power surge or electricity brownout. Service and repair technicians advise everyone to buy a high-quality surge protector and line filter power strip that the personal computer, monitor, and printer can all be plugged into. The most common software problems are (1) the disk is inserted into the drive upside down and (2) the disk is inserted but the drive door latch is not locked in place. As you can see, the two rules of computing clearly overcome the most common problems.

KNOWLEDGE CHECK

1. What does the term DOS stand for?   p. 43
2. What is the term used for loading the operating instructions into the personal computer to awaken it?   p. 43
3. What is the primary unit of data storage in DOS computers?   p. 44
4. Describe how a filename is organized and how many characters it contains.   p. 44
5. How are the primary units of data storage orgainzed in DOS?   p. 45
6. Name the device that tells you where you can type the next character. Name the area where they both appear on the screen.   p. 48
7. What are the names commonly used for the two types of floppy disks used with an application program?   pp. 48–49
8. What steps should you always take before powering down?   p. 50

THE DESKTOP PERSONAL COMPUTER

A **desktop personal computer** is the most commonly used personal computer today. It is a computer that fits on a desktop, is designed for a single user, and is affordable for an individual to buy for personal use. Personal computers come in what we call configurations.

PERSONAL COMPUTER CONFIGURATIONS

Knowledge workers often use the word configuration to describe a computer's attributes. **Configuration** refers to the various hardware components that together make up a computer system. This includes the type of monitor or video display (color or monochrome, which may be green, amber, or black/white), the quality of the video display, the amount of RAM (random access memory), and the number and type of floppy or hard disk drives. It also includes other devices that may be connected either internally or externally. Adding a printer makes sense.

A personal computer can be configured as a desktop personal computer like the Macintosh, or as a lightweight, portable laptop computer, or even as a more powerful workstation. If we were describing the configuration of a stereo or an auto, we'd probably refer to its features or accessories. A full-featured auto is often termed *fully loaded*. A full-featured personal computer is called *fully configured*.

BITS AND BYTES

Before we go any further in explaining configurations, you need to understand the bits and bytes of computers. At their most basic level, computers only understand the language of electricity: positive and negative, or on and off. Since computer hardware is electronic, to communicate with it we must speak its simple language. For this reason, we use the **binary number system,** a system based on just two numbers or digits: 1 (for on) and 0 (for off). Each of these numbers is called a **bi**nary digit, or bit for short. A **bit** is the basic unit of data recognized by a computer. See Appendix A for more on number systems.

Computer designers realized that they could make computers work faster by grouping bits together for presentation to the CPU. This is like our language — it's easier for us to speak in words, rather than spelling out each letter as we talk to one another. The term we use for a grouping of bits is a byte. A **byte** is a group of bits that can be operated on as a unit by the computer. Most modern computers have eight bits to a byte. The relationship between bits and bytes is shown in Figure 2.12.

The binary number system is called a **base 2** number system, since it has only two numbers. By contrast, we use the base 10 number system in our everyday lives. In that system, we count by powers of 10; in the binary system, we count by powers of 2. For example:

$2^1 = 2$
$2^2 = 4$
$2^3 = 8$
$2^4 = 16$

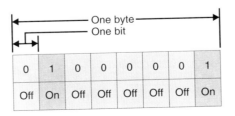

FIGURE 2.12

Like the DNA of a living organism, bits and bytes are the building blocks for computer data.

A very important measure of the computer's power is the number of bytes of memory and storage it has. We commonly count bytes in the thousands, called **kilobytes** (KB), but using the base 2 number system. Therefore, 1KB is 2^{10} bytes, or 1,024 bytes. When memory and storage goes into the millions, it is called **megabytes;** 1MB is 2^{20} (1,048,576) bytes. A **gigabyte** (GB) is 1 billion bytes, and a **terabyte** (TB) is 1 trillion bytes. With that understanding, let's explore configurations in more detail.

A SIMPLE CONFIGURATION

The basic, or least expensive, configuration for a personal computer is a monochrome monitor, a minimal amount of RAM, and one disk drive. RAM is measured in KB or MB; a simple configuration has 640K (655,536 bytes). Most PC-compatibles have either 1MB or 2MB of RAM as standard equipment. The Macintosh Classic II comes standard with 4MB. Figure 2.13 shows common personal computer RAM configurations.

A FULL CONFIGURATION

While you may not need a fully loaded car, it is often sensible to have a fully configured personal computer. A full configuration for a state-of-the-art personal computer system includes a color monitor with high-quality screen display, at least 2MB (and up to 8MB) of RAM, two floppy disk drives (one for 5¼-inch and one for 3½-inch disks), and one hard disk with at least 30MB of storage capacity. A color display is useful if you plan to use graphics software. In addition, many nongraphic programs, even word processing, are primarily

---

FIGURE 2.13

The amount of RAM available has a dramatic impact on how efficiently the CPU can process data and thus how productive a knowledge worker can be with an application. Thus, RAM size has grown exponentially over the years.

Type	CPU	RAM	Disk Drive	Notes
Early IBM PC	8088*	64K	1 or 2 5¼" floppy	
IBM PC/XT	8088	512K	1 Fl, 10MB hard drive	Added hard drive
IBM PC/AT	80286	640K	1–2† FL, 20MB hard drive	CPU speed increase
Compaq Deskpro	80386	4MB+	1–2† Fl, 30-650MB hard drive	Also IBM PS/2s
Zeos 386SX	80386SX	2MB+	Same as Compaq	Replaced by 486SX
Macintosh Plus	68000‡	1MB	1 Fl, 40MB hard drive	B/W; replaces SE
Macintosh LC	68020	4MB+	1 Fl, 40–80MB hard drive	Color
Macintosh IIsi/fx	68030	4MB+	1 Fl, 80–160MB hard drive	Expandable
Macintosh Quadra	68040	8MB+	1 Fl, 80–400MB hard drive	Designer workstation

* All 8080 series microprocessors manufactured by Intel.

† All 386 computers and most 286 computers can use either or both 5¼-inch and 3½-inch disk drives.

‡ All 68000 series microprocessors manufactured by Motorola.

intended for a color monitor, and can be awkward to use on a monochrome display. Figure 2.14 shows how the same program appears on color and monochrome monitors.

Many applications have grown more complex and have added more features, requiring more RAM. For example, word processing programs often include a spelling or grammar checker. Complex spreadsheets, filled with numbers and calculations, require large amounts of memory too. Generally speaking, the more RAM, the better. It is not uncommon to use applications that require most of the 640K of main memory. Likewise, hard disk drives become more useful when working with large programs that come on multiple disks. Without a hard disk, you have to swap the floppies in and out of the floppy disk drive when you need to perform different operations. A hard disk allows you to store the entire program, with no disk swapping. Programs often run more smoothly from a hard disk.

TYPES OF PERSONAL COMPUTERS

Desktop personal computers are commonly used for education, running a small business, or, in large corporations, to help knowledge workers be more productive. Some of the more common types of desktop personal computers are:

- The IBM PC and PC-compatible.
- The IBM PS/2®.
- The Apple® Macintosh™.

While there are many other desktop personal computers, such as the Amiga, Apple II, Apricot, and Atari, their use is not as widespread. People tend to choose a personal computer based on the software they wish to use. Software developers, hoping to sell as many copies of their programs as possible, write applications for the personal computers they believe will be widely used for a

Many programs are more difficult to use without the advantage of color monitors. Text commands are easier to discern when they are highlighted in color.   FIGURE 2.14

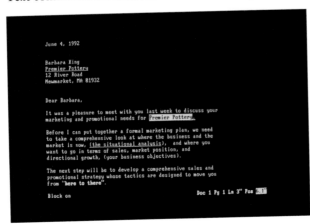
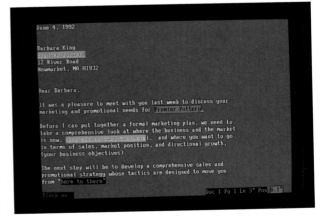

long time — in other words, they try to bet on the winner. In this way, the software industry actually can make a new personal computer either a success or a failure.

IBM PCs and PC-Compatibles

The IBM Personal Computer, or IBM PC, was the most widely used — and widely copied — personal computer. Originally, IBM considered its PC a home computer. However, corporate America was quick to recognize the PC's usefulness in boosting knowledge worker productivity. Up until this time, when knowledge workers needed to use a computer, it was usually a mainframe or a minicomputer. But sometimes it wasn't possible to accommodate everyone who needed to work on the computer. In addition, applications suited to an individual worker were limited.

The IBM PC was designed as an open architecture machine. **Open architecture** means the specifications are available to outside organizations so they may develop compatible software and hardware products. The open architecture philosophy also made it possible for other computer companies to design personal computers that worked almost identically to the IBM PC. Thus, the PC-compatible market was launched, and eventually eclipsed IBM's sales of its own PCs. Companies such as Compaq, Tandy/Radio Shack, Zenith, Epson, and NEC built PC-compatibles with the same types of microprocessor. They used the MS-DOS® operating system, developed by Microsoft Corporation, which was nearly identical to IBM's PC-DOS. This made it possible to use almost any software for the IBM PC on a PC-compatible. Figure 2.15 shows the genealogy of personal computers.

These companies followed in IBM's footsteps, introducing an XT-compatible and then an AT-compatible shortly after IBM's machines debuted. But in 1986, Compaq decided to take a chance and beat IBM to market with a personal computer that used the newest and fastest microprocessor, the Intel 80386. It was called the Deskpro 386/20 and was followed shortly by the Portable 386. Figure 2.16 shows the 386 computers that made Compaq the leader in PC-compatibles. Compaq went on to set the record for reaching the Fortune 500 faster than any other company in history.

FIGURE 2.15

Genealogy of personal computers.

1977	Apple II
	Radio Shack TRS-80
1981	IBM PC
1982	Epson QX-10
1983	Leading Edge PC/XT
1984	Macintosh
1986	Compaq Deskpro 386
1987	Toshiba Laptop
	IBM PS/2
1988	NeXT Workstation
1989	Zeos 386SX
1990	AST Premium 486/25

Today, the 386 microprocessor is the standard for most personal computers in the office. However, many personal computers already use its successor, the 80486, and Intel plans to introduce the 80586 in 1993; the 80686 will follow sometime thereafter. These microprocessors bring even greater speed and efficiency and represent the promise of the desktop supercomputer.

USING PCs AND PC-COMPATIBLES.   PCs and PC-compatibles are used in organizations of all sizes. A case in point is H&R Block, the largest income tax

---

Although the IBM PC was developed as a home computer, it was the business world that propelled its popularity.

FIGURE 2.16

Compaq was the first to use the Intel 386 microprocessor in its desktop and portable PC-compatibles. This new microprocessor brought greater speed and efficiency to operations and forever changed the rules of computer marketing and composition.

The popularity of the desktop led to development of an even smaller, lighter computer. This Zeos Notebook 386SX has the speed and memory of a desktop combined with the extreme portability of a computer which weighs under seven pounds.

preparation firm in the United States. Block has headquarters in Kansas City, Missouri, with 7,000 offices nationwide. Using over 4,000 personal computers, Block offered its Rapid Refund program to all its customers for the 1990 filing year. Block uses personal computers in the Kansas City office to connect directly to the Internal Revenue Service computers, thus electronically filing income tax returns. The regional offices use portable and desktop computers to prepare returns and electronically send them to the PCs in Kansas City. This speeds up the entire process and results in far less paperwork for everyone involved. Refunds for electronic filing usually arrive in three weeks. If they so desire, Block customers can take a Rapid Refund loan in anticipation of their refund check. The participating bank makes the loan, and the IRS pays the bank. In 1990, using personal computers, H&R Block filed 2,892,000 electronic tax returns.

THE IBM PERSONAL SYSTEM/2

In 1987, IBM launched a new line of personal computers that were technologically more sophisticated. They are called the Personal System/2 (PS/2) computers. PS/2s are smaller, sleeker machines that use the 3½-inch microfloppy and are capable of utilizing some advanced internal components that enhance speed and make the machine more versatile. There are many different models of PS/2s, including one that works just like the original PC, a PC/AT, and several 386 and 486 models. Figure 2.17 shows PS/2s in an office publishing environment.

IBM chose to make the PS/2 a **closed architecture,** meaning a competitor would need permission to obtain the specifications and duplicate it. More in

FIGURE 2.17

The PS/2's additional power and versatility allows this office to develop advertising promotion and publish such materials as catalogs and magazines for its clients.

keeping with its corporate philosophy, IBM hoped to keep the market to itself. Most computers have a closed architecture; the Apple Macintosh is another example. Two aspects of the PS/2's closed architecture are the Micro Channel Architecture (which permits connections to other larger IBM computers) and the operating system, called OS/2®. It provided advantages over DOS such as utilizing more random access memory (RAM) and multitasking, the ability to use two or more applications at the same time (discussed in more detail in Chapter 7). Although slow to catch on in the early years, PS/2 use is growing; and IBM has made OS/2 available for sale to anyone who wants to use it. There are many factors in the computer industry that are leading away from any type of closed architecture.

USING PS/2s.   Banks have traditionally used the latest computer technology to automate their own operations. First New York Bank for Business found a way to use personal computers to improve customer service. In the past, when a customer wanted to cash a check, the signature card had to be compared to verify identity. That meant looking through a card file or contacting central bookkeeping, which could take as long as 30 minutes.

New York Bank for Business installed PS/2s with special graphics capabilities and software called Signet to perform this task. Now, when tellers retrieve customer account information from the computer, they see the authorized signatures appear right on the screen. The system also tells them what other signatories are permitted on the account or if two signatures are required to cash a check. Using the powerful PS/2s and Signet, they can cash a customer's check in a minute or less, while offering the customer superior protection against forgery at the same time.

THE APPLE MACINTOSH

The Apple II, introduced in 1977, is still in wide use in homes and schools. It was also the first personal computer to gain widespread use in business because VisiCalc®, the first spreadsheet program, was written for it. Apple Computer is also the company that created the Macintosh. Steven Jobs conceived the idea for the Mac while visiting the Xerox Palo Alto Research Center, a think tank and laboratory for extending the frontiers of technology. There he saw the Xerox Star, a computer with color graphics and a mouse that moved the cursor around the screen, touching graphic symbols to issue commands. It was Jobs' inspiration for the Lisa® (1982) and then the successful Macintosh (1984). The Macintosh was designed with a closed architecture, like the IBM PS/2 computers, allowing Apple to maintain a strict degree of quality control over software and accessories developed by other companies. Figure 2.18 shows several Macintosh models in an office.

USING THE MACINTOSH.   The Macintosh is one of the popular personal computers with Westinghouse employees at the Savannah River nuclear power plant in Aiken, South Carolina. Engineers use them for engineering design and drafting; knowledge workers use them for traditional word processing and spreadsheet analysis. These knowledge workers found two other interesting uses for the Macintosh. Since it lends itself to high-quality graph-

FIGURE 2.18

This international design firm uses Macintosh computers with oversize monitors for their creative work.

ics, they began designing their own slides and overhead drawings for speeches and presentations. And since it has a variety of type fonts (styles), they began designing new office forms and redesigning old ones that needed updating. Not only did they end up with better forms, they saved a great deal in graphic design charges and printing costs.

Although there are three different types of personal computers commonly in use, there is a strong drive in business for connectivity, the ability to share data between machines of different types. Computer makers prefer to have customers buy all one brand—theirs—but certain types of machines are better suited to different tasks. In addition, different people prefer different types of computers. When many types are used throughout an office, connectivity becomes essential. This topic is discussed in more detail in Chapter 15.

Now you know how DOS works with the personal computer to carry out your commands, as well as the basic operations of your personal computer. You can see how the software and hardware, working under your direction, comprise a computer system. Regardless of their size, all computers use the basic principles you've learned here. Therefore, let's apply the concepts we've learned as we begin studying other types of computers in Chapter 3.

INFORMATION AGE ETHICS: PERSONAL COMPUTING MANNERS AND MORES

Human beings tend to be competitive and to want to get ahead in life. For many years, people have used war terminology and metaphors to describe business practices. It's no secret that certain people will do unethical—even illegal—things to make money or boost their careers. But can we say, "All's fair in love and war—and business"? This is an issue of particular concern in the office, where so many people can easily gain access to your computer and the data stored in it.

TOMORROW

TIPS FOR BUYING A PERSONAL COMPUTER

1. *Conventional wisdom suggests you choose the application(s) you like and then buy the appropriate computer system.* In many cases, there are compromises you must make between software and hardware; just try to make as few as possible. If you're like most people, you'll probably have to live with your system for quite a while. Make sure the applications you want to use will run on the personal computer you intend to buy. One way to do this is to obtain demonstration disks, when available. They can be ordered from the software company, but software stores often have a large stock of demo disks you can obtain for free or for just a few dollars.

2. *Fill in the gaps in your knowledge about computers.* Read magazines, periodicals, and specialty books on computers. The newsstands are filled with good magazines on PC-compatibles and Macintoshes. In addition, many larger bookstores have an entire section devoted to computer books. Look for magazines like *Computer Shopper,* which features articles on purchasing as well as a huge assortment of advertisements.

3. *Talk to friends who own computers and solicit their opinions.* A word of caution: Most personal computer owners are proud of their decision and their computer system, so you probably won't get unbiased information. For that reason, you might want to prepare a list of questions in advance that help you get the answers you seek.

4. *Shop around.* Personal computers are sold in retail computer stores, specialty stores, and electronics and appliance stores as well as by direct mail. Unless you are proficient with electronics, it's a good idea to avoid the "clones" with names you've never heard of. They often contain the least expensive parts and components, or require some assembly, and may not prove as reliable or easy to use as name brand machines. Several magazines now evaluate computers and make recommendations; check these brands first. Several mail order companies, such as Dell and Zeos, make very high quality computers and stand behind their products; look for their advertisements in most major computer magazines. In addition, mail order generally means more computer for less money than you'd pay retail.

5. *Select your configuration with the future in mind.* It's highly likely that you'll want to upgrade the RAM or the hard disk, or add certain peripherals; all these things can be accomplished without problems or penalties. However, it makes sense to buy a computer with a CPU, or microprocessor, that will serve you today and tomorrow as well. For that reason, buy as much CPU as you can afford. There are few things more chafing than having to use an underperforming computer.

6. *Spend some time working with the computer.* Make sure that you like the monitor and the keyboard, and that the CPU is fast enough to suit you.

7. *Take notes; make a comparison chart.* Be sure to record your impressions along with the price, features, and performance.

8. *Think about service.* What is the manufacturer's warranty? Where can you take the machine for service? Some retail stores don't service what they sell. Overall, remember that if a computer breaks down, it is most likely to do so in the first 30 days or less. During this period, in most cases, you can return it for a full exchange. Therefore, don't allow service to be a dominant factor in choosing a particular retailer or computer.

9. *Don't let a salesperson snow you with jargon.* Every time you hear a term you don't understand, ask for an explanation. If it isn't forthcoming, shop elsewhere.

10. *Ask about setup, training, and support.* If you buy from a computer store or mail order, your computer should arrive with the software installed, ready to use. Some may try to charge for this service, but they should not; they make it back in their software profit margins. Make sure you get what you pay for; be a good negotiator.

CAREERS FOR KNOWLEDGE WORKERS
SUSAN WELLS, DIRECTOR OF PUBLIC RELATIONS, IRWIN INK

Susan Wells doesn't just use a personal computer in her work. She uses a personal computer to work with companies in the personal computer industry. That's because Susan is the director of public relations for Irwin Ink, a company specializing in microcomputer and marketing communications. For someone who majored in business and journalism in college, it's nearly a dream job. When she was offered the position at Irwin Ink, she thought to herself, "There must be an interesting side to computers. I just have to find out what it is." She did.

Susan took an Introduction to Information Systems course, where she was introduced to a programming language and the spreadsheet. She got some hands-on experience with a Macintosh in her journalism courses. "As a result, I felt it was OK to be interested in computers." After graduation, she used an IBM Personal Computer on her first job in marketing communications; now she was familiar with both types of PCs.

Susan's clients are mostly software companies, but she also represents a computer book author. Irwin Ink provides additional marketing and advertising services to its clients. Its offices are very high-tech. Ten personal computers connected in a network allow knowledge workers to use various applications such as word processing and to exchange "electronic mail" messages. Susan uses computer telecommunications to send various documents to her clients on a regular basis.

She also uses several special application programs for her public relations work. One is an electronic directory of the national business and computer press, television and radio media, and other parties interested in the computer industry. It provides her with detailed information on publications such as what specific items editors are interested in, reader demographics, and trade show information. The directory is published quarterly and supplied on computer disk. Susan uses it in conjunction with a special database program designed specifically for public relations work. It lets her track her activities for clients and with editors — the date she last spoke with an individual, any notes she took, and correspondence or documents she sent. The program automatically reminds her on the date scheduled for the next follow-up contact.

Susan Wells has successfully combined her interests in business, public relations, and computers into a challenging career. Her enthusiasm is evident in nearly everything she does: "I think it's so important to establish and maintain good relationships with everyone — industry gurus, product reviewers, freelance writers, and editors. I know that I may not always get the product review or feature story that I want, but I continue to learn from these people so that I can do my own job better. And along the way, I've made some good friends. I believe in giving back to others because I know that I'm going to learn something about myself and my work along the way."

One way Susan "gives back" while also combining her talents and interest in journalism is by writing a monthly column, "Public Relations and You," for *Reseller World* magazine. Readers, mostly software and hardware producers, learn from Susan's tips, techniques, and strategies for presenting themselves to the public and the press. One of her columns told how to prepare a press kit, explaining that "a polished, professional-looking Press Kit is a vital part of any good PR campaign." Using the example of Dorothy traveling the yellow brick road to the land of Oz, Susan skillfully led her reader to the conclusion that "no matter what the size of your budget, you can create a Press Kit that has courage, brains, and a heart." Just like its author!

Knowledge workers must work together to achieve common goals. There should be respect for others' rights, privacy, and data in such an environment. However, it is likely that in the real world, unethical people will read other peoples' private files; in fact, some might even sabotage a colleague's work to make him or her look bad. To some extent, security systems should take care of this, but as the old saying goes, locks only keep honest people honest.

What can you do? Don't create temptations. Keep your computer secure, conceal your password, and follow the company's security precautions. Keep your personal data on a floppy disk; lock it in your desk or take it home with you at night. Be sure that all your important work is backed up and stored in more than one physical location—on more than one computer system or on a disk you keep with you.

Finally—and this is the hardest part—realize that you are part of the problem as well as part of the solution. Encourage your fellow employees,

through polite conversation and example, to behave ethically. Find mutually shared values and beliefs and discuss them; people who are basically moral and honest find it difficult to wrong those they know personally. And when you see illegal or unethical things occurring, discuss them with your superior. To do otherwise makes you an accomplice to wrongdoing, and it also makes it easier to look the other way the next time it happens.

Kenneth R. Andrews, a former professor of management and editor of the *Harvard Business Review* for many years, writes in the Introduction to his book *Ethics in Practice: Managing the Moral Corporation* (Boston: Harvard Business School Press, 1989), "Commitment to quality objectives—among them compliance with law and high ethical standards—is an organizational achievement. It is inspired by pride more than by the profit that rightful pride produces." Everyone must work together for an ethical workplace.

SUMMARY

1. *Identify the processing and peripheral hardware components in a personal computer.* All computers have four hardware components: a system unit, input/output devices or peripherals, storage devices, and routing and control components. Processing components include the motherboard, CPU, and main memory. Peripheral hardware includes the keyboard, mouse, monitor, printer, and floppy and hard disk drives.

2. *Describe the steps involved in working with DOS.* There are several ways to boot DOS and thus begin a work session: the cold boot and the warm boot. Booting works somewhat differently, depending on whether you are using a floppy disk or a hard disk. Commands are the way we issue instructions or perform tasks with the computer system. It is important to enter these commands in the proper syntax, or language, that DOS will understand. The key to working successfully with a personal computer is to take your time and do everything carefully.

3. *List some of the commonly used DOS commands.* DOS commands allow us to perform work and solve problems with the personal computer.

Some commands list files; some start application programs; others prepare disks for use. Some commonly used DOS commands include DIR, FORMAT, DISKCOPY, COPY, DELETE, and RENAME.

4. *Explain the way DOS organizes files and directories.* The operating system provides the instructions that make personal computers perform tasks. DOS is an integrated set of programs that provide access to the CPU and the peripherals that allow us to perform a number of important tasks when working with applications. Files are the primary unit of data storage in personal computers. Files have filenames and are grouped into directories, such as the root directory or various subdirectories. DOS must be loaded into the computer; once it is, we can issue instructions at the prompt, which is found on the command line. The cursor shows us where the prompt is located.

5. *Describe different types of personal computer configurations.* Personal computers come in different configurations, which determine the complexity and sophistication of the tasks they are able to

perform. The hardware elements that change a configuration include the monitor, the quality of the video display, the amount of RAM, the number and type of floppy and hard disk drives, and other devices such as the printer.

6. *Identify the more commonly used types of personal computers.* The most common personal computers are the IBM PC, the PC-compatible, the IBM PS/2, and the Apple Macintosh.

PERSONAL COMPUTER ISSUES

1. Ethics is a subject of concern on all levels of society. Is it true when it comes to violating the ethical uses of computers, "Everybody's doing it"? Read some current articles on software piracy and unauthorized computer usage; then compile a list of questions concerning ethical computer use. Take a random survey or, if your professor permits it, survey your class on their computer ethics. Is everybody doing it? What is it that they're doing? What is your assessment of today's attitude toward the ethical use of computers?

2. Computers are a significant financial investment. There's the computer, the printer, and the software to buy, plus accessories and other items. But the computer also requires a significant in-

vestment of your time to learn the hardware, the operating system, and the applications. This could be literally hundreds, perhaps thousands, of hours. Yet the personal computer industry is still growing and changing rapidly. Given this investment in time, how would you feel if your hardware suddenly became obsolete? What if the maker suddenly introduced, for example, a new operating system with a significantly changed human-computer interface that you had to learn all over again? What if the software company came out with a new, improved version of your favorite application but you found it was riddled with programming errors that were destroying your files?

CHAPTER REVIEW QUESTIONS

REVIEW QUESTIONS

1. What steps and components are dependent on human control and interaction? What steps and components are not?

2. Describe the manner in which DOS works with files and filenames. Why are there five types of files?

3. How is a command like an instruction?

4. What are the major differences between a simple configuration and a full configuration? Why is the configuration important?

DISCUSSION QUESTIONS

1. Why is it so important to take your time and do things carefully when working with a personal computer?

2. Discuss the relationship between the five data processing steps and the four hardware components.

3. In what ways are the computer system and the stereo system similar? What is the main difference between the two?

4. Discuss the various ways we most effectively utilize input, output, and storage devices.

5. Describe an ideal computer configuration for your own personal computer from the three types described and why you chose each characteristic or component.

6. Discuss why there seem to be so many more aspects of the PC-compatible configuration to choose from than there are with a Macintosh.

7. Discuss the manner in which DOS stores files in directories. Why do we need a root directory and subdirectories? Why not just store everything in one directory?

8. Discuss the relationship between commands, instructions, and programs.

9. Describe how we keep application programs and data separate on a personal computer with two floppy disk drives versus how we would do so with a single hard disk drive.

MULTIPLE-CHOICE

1. The CPU consists of (check all that apply):
   a. The control unit.
   b. The arithmetic-logic unit.
   c. Random access memory.
   d. The power supply.

2. The advantages in using the binary number system for computers are (check all that apply):
   a. It is easy to keep track of only two digits.
   b. The two digits represent the two electrical states.
   c. Binary digits are easy to group into bits and bytes.
   d. The 1 stands for on and the 0 stands for off.

3. The main differentiating characteristics between IBM's Personal Computer and its PS/2 are (check all that apply):
   a. The PS/2 uses Micro Channel Architecture.
   b. The IBM PC has more models.
   c. The PS/2 has a newer operating system.
   d. The PS/2 uses microfloppy disks.
   e. The IBM PC is a closed architecture.

4. Which of the following is not a consideration when purchasing a personal computer?
   a. Buying the best hardware and not worrying about the application.
   b. Service and support.
   c. The opinions and experience of others.
   d. Studying up on the advantages and disadvantages of different types of personal computers.
   e. None of the above.

FILL-IN-THE-BLANK

1. Media that can only be read is called _____.

2. Media that can be written to and read from is called _____ / _____.

3. Create your own scenario, as illustrated in Figure 2.4, for how you would use the five data processing steps to create and store your work.
   Input: _____
   Processing: _____
   Output: _____
   Storage: _____
   Results: _____

4. The binary number system uses the _____ and _____ numbers or digits.

5. 1,024 bytes, or 2^{10} bytes, is commonly called _____.

6. Which of the following are not DOS commands?
   a. DELETE.
   b. RENAME.
   c. REBOOT.
   d. COPY.
   e. HIDEFILE.

TRUE/FALSE

1. The motherboard is one of the components of the CPU.

2. An integrated circuit can only be a CPU chip, not a RAM memory chip.

3. The prompt indicates the disk drive in use.

4. The cursor is always found on the command line.

5. When using a mouse, the cursor may be an arrow instead of a blinking line.

6. When ending a work session and powering down, it doesn't matter whether or not the disk is in the drive.

7. The Macintosh is the only closed-architecture personal computer.

KEY TERMS

arithmetic/logic unit (ALU), 39
auxiliary storage, 40
backup, 49
base 2, 51
binary number system, 51
bit, 51
boot, 43
byte, 51
central processing unit (CPU), 39
closed architecture, 56
command, 48
command line, 48
configuration, 51
control unit, 39
cursor, 48
data disk, 49
desktop personal computer, 50

directory, 45
disk operating system (DOS), 43
expansion slot, 37
file, 44
filename, 44
floppy disk, 40
floppy disk drive, 40
gigabyte, 52
hard disk drive, 40
hardware, 37
hidden file, 46
input device, 34
integrated circuit, 37
kilobyte, 52
load, 47
media, 36
megabyte, 52
motherboard, 37

nonvolatile, 41
open architecture, 54
output device, 34
peripheral device, 40
port, 37
program disk, 48
prompt, 48
random access memory (RAM), 39
read, 40
read only memory (ROM), 39
root directory, 45
terabyte, 52
volatile memory, 39
work session, 46
write, 40

A World of Computers From the Laptop to the Supercomputer

LEARNING OBJECTIVES

After reading and studying this
chapter, you should be able to:

1. Describe the difference between
   general-purpose computers and
   special-purpose computers.

2. Explain the difference between
   the various types of portable
   computers.

3. Describe the different types of
   workstations and how each is
   used.

4. Describe the characteristics of
   the minicomputer and its three
   different uses.

5. Describe the characteristics and
   uses of the mainframe computer.

6. Describe the characteristics and
   uses of the supercomputer.

A World of Computers

"The world will only need five computers," Thomas J. Watson, founder of IBM, is reported to have said. The year was 1953, and it was the elder Watson's opinion that this was an enterprise in which IBM had no business. Yet three years later, with his son Tom, Jr., at the helm, IBM was competing furiously in the nascent computer field.

How could Watson, Sr., a man of great vision, have been so wrong about computers? Indeed, he can probably be forgiven, for at the time the few such machines in existence filled entire rooms. Computers were thought of as people thought of electrical generating plants or waterworks: one was surely enough for an entire community. Far more popular in business was the electronic calculator, a "computing" machine about the size of a radiator that could be rolled from desk to desk, room to room. At that time, it was probably hard to conceive of computers that fit on a desktop — much less computers in autos, cash registers, watches, stereos, and telephones.

Big computers haven't gone away, but today we have computers of all sizes and descriptions — there is a computer for every need, every lifestyle, and almost every pocketbook. If the computer industry had but one motto, it would be "Better, faster, cheaper." There has been a constant drive to produce more reliable computers, computers that perform their tasks ever more speedily and at a lower cost. *Computerworld,* the leading weekly newspaper of the computer industry, once used the advertisement in Figure 3.1 to point out how the computer industry's technological advances have outpaced those of the auto industry. The analogy is not far-fetched.

General-Purpose and Special-Purpose Computers

Computers are generally classified as general-purpose or special-purpose machines. A **general-purpose computer** is one used for a variety of tasks without the need to modify or change it as the tasks change. A common example is a mini or mainframe computer used in business that runs many different applications — payroll, order entry, inventory control, and computer-integrated manufacturing.

A **special-purpose computer,** on the other hand, is designed and used solely for one application. The machine may need to be redesigned, and certainly must be reprogrammed, if it is to perform another task. Special-purpose computers might be used to read the gas or electric meter; in a factory to monitor a manufacturing process; in research to monitor seismological and other natural occurrences; in the office for dedicated work processing; or in

YESTERDAY

THE FATHER OF THE MODERN COMPUTER

John Vincent Atanasoff had a problem. The year was 1937 and Atanasoff, a professor of mathematics and physics at Iowa State University, needed to find a better way to help his college students solve long, complex math problems called simultaneous differential equations. "We needed practical solutions for practical purposes," he recalls. For Atanasoff and his students, that meant getting more accurate answers and getting them more quickly.

Wrestling with the problem kept him working in his lab, many times until three or four in the morning. "Tormented" is the way he described himself. Driving helped him work out problems. One night he drove 200 miles before stopping at a roadhouse to rest. "I realized that I was no longer so nervous and my thoughts turned again to computing machines. Now I don't know why my mind worked then when it had not worked previously, but things seemed to be good and cool and quiet. During this evening . . . I generated within my mind the possibility of regenerative memory . . . and I gained an initial concept of what is called today the 'logic circuits.'" The concept for the computer was emerging.

Working with a modest grant of $650 from the college, Atanasoff began designing his computer. With help from his graduate assistant, Clifford Berry, the first prototype of the Atanasoff-Berry Computer, or ABC, was completed in 1939. Atanasoff was quick to realize that vacuum tubes, although subject to failure, were more reliable than mechanical relays. He also developed some of the essential concepts that would be incorporated into future computers, including using binary mathematics over the decimal system. The combination of vacuum tubes and binary mathematics made the ABC an electronic, digital computer.

Atanasoff never permitted a commercial version of the ABC to be built, mainly because the two companies to whom he showed it—IBM and Remington Rand (which went on to develop the UNIVAC)—asked him to sign away all his inventor's rights. In a letter to Remington Rand, Atanasoff wrote, "This procedure would furnish your company with all of my information without any corresponding obligation on your part. . . ."

In 1942, Dr. Atanasoff was requested to accept employment with the Naval Ordnance Labo-

ratory in Washington, D.C. He left the details of the patenting process in the hands of Iowa State officials and a patent lawyer. To his chagrin, and despite periodic inquiries, the patent applications were never filed. Even so, the ABC became the prototype of the first large-scale programmable electronic computer, ENIAC. Patents granted to ENIAC, constructed at the University of Pennsylvania under a U.S. Army contract between 1943 and 1946, were invalidated by an unchallenged U.S. District Court decision in 1973. The court found that basic electronic digital computer concepts in ENIAC were "derived from one Dr. John Vincent Atanasoff."

Yet true and formal recognition of Atanasoff's contribution was not made until 1990, when President George Bush presented him with a National Medal of Technology at a White House ceremony. Atanasoff, the program for the ceremony read, was being honored "for his invention of the electronic digital computer." At 87 years of age, John Atanasoff was finally recognized as the father of the modern computer.

FIGURE 3.1

This *Computerworld* ad from the 1970s underscores the tremendous success achieved by the computer industry in their drive to produce more efficient, affordable computers.

science to forecast severe weather events. Figure 3.2 shows several special-purpose computers. We'll identify general-purpose and special-purpose computers elsewhere this chapter.

Computers today range in size from those you can hold in the palm of your hand to those so large you can stand inside of them. Let's learn about each and how they are used. We shall begin small with the portable personal computer, working our way up to the supercomputer.

THE PORTABLE PERSONAL COMPUTER

While desktop personal computers are designed for a desktop, the portable computer is one you can take with you. Like a desktop computer, a **portable computer** is used by a single individual; the difference is that it can be used in many different places. It is not confined, by its size or weight, to a desktop. It has the same components as a desktop machine, but in most cases the monitor and keyboard are integrated. The printer is usually separate. What sets the portable apart is that all its components, including its special monitor, are self-contained in a very small package. These factors contribute to making it somewhat more expensive than a desktop. However, cost has done little to dim its popularity.

FIGURE 3.2

Underscoring the fact that the computer is capable of performing many varied tasks, these special-purpose computers (clockwise from top left) are being used for advanced medical research, video editing, television production purposes, and in manufacturing.

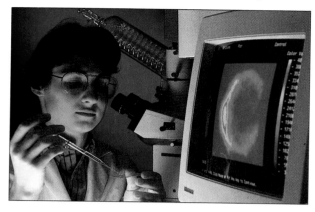

TYPES OF PORTABLES

Today, the three most popular portables are laptops, notebooks, and palmtops. Let's look briefly at each.

- **Laptops** weigh between 8 and 15 pounds, have a desktop-quality keyboard, and often offer special features such as a color monitor. Most are Macintoshes and PC-compatibles.
- **Notebooks** weigh between 4 and 7 pounds, have a somewhat limited keyboard, and offer many of the features of a common desktop PC-compatible or a Macintosh built in.
- **Palmtops** are hand-held personal computers that weigh less than a pound, often have a restricted or low-quality keyboard and a small monitor, and usually come with their own built-in software.

Let's take a closer look at the many different types of portable computers.

FIGURE 3.3

The Osborne-1 was the first traveling computer. Its convenience quickly changed the way many people used computers.

PORTABLES AND LAPTOPS

The first traveling computer was the Osborne-1, introduced in 1981 (Figure 3.3). The Osborne-1 was termed a portable or "luggable" computer because it was a self-contained system unit, monitor, and keyboard—with a handle. It even came complete with application software programs, and there was a special slot beside the monitor to hold the disks! The Osborne-1 changed the way people used computers because now they could be taken to any place of work. People didn't particularly enjoy toting a 20- or 25-pound computer through airport terminals, but most felt it was worth the effort to have the portability. The portable computer market took off when Compaq Computer Corporation introduced the luggable PC-compatible.

PC-COMPATIBLE LAPTOPS AND NOTEBOOKS. PC-compatible laptops and notebooks are the downsized equivalent of PC-compatible desktop computers. They commonly use 3½-inch floppy disk drives and 2½-inch hard disk drives to reduce size and weight. They usually do not have all the keys that a desktop computer keyboard has, such as the numeric keypad. Most have a rechargeable battery pack which is good for several hours of use. The notebook is the most popular portable computer these days, given its light weight, powerful microprocessor, powerful memory and storage, and crisp, clear monitor—and low price, often under $2,000.

PS/2-Compatible Laptops.   In 1991, IBM introduced the first of a family of PS/2 laptop computers that will eventually include between 6 and 10 models. The first release of the new lineup is the 7.7-pound L40 SX, which can use either DOS or OS/2. Since the PS/2 uses IBM's advanced Micro Channel architecture, it is possible to add more functions such as a cellular telephone that will transmit both voice conversations and computer data. Figure 3.4 shows such a PS/2 compatible.

Macintosh Portables.   Apple's first Macintosh portable was heavy and expensive. Its new Powerbook series of three notebook computers is comparable with PC-compatible laptops and notebooks. They are somewhat slower than a desktop Mac, due to the type of screen used, but the display is crisp and clear. All come with a built-in trackball, innovatively centered below the keyboard for ease of use. The most popular model is the 14S, with 4MB RAM and a 40MB hard disk drive standard. Figure 3.5 shows a current Macintosh notebook.

Using Laptops

People use laptops for many of the same tasks that they use desktops — and more. Sales and marketing representatives in business use laptops to gather inventory and ordering information, to transmit orders and reports to headquarters, and to show customers new products and services. Executives use them for a variety of tasks while traveling.

Tom Temple, a resident of Seattle, Washington, uses his laptop to aid him

---

Figure 3.4

Look how far we've come: The Darius ProPortables incorporate integrated tape backup, a hard disk drive, a plain-paper high-resolution printer/plotter, and a modem in a computer which weighs no more than 20 pounds.

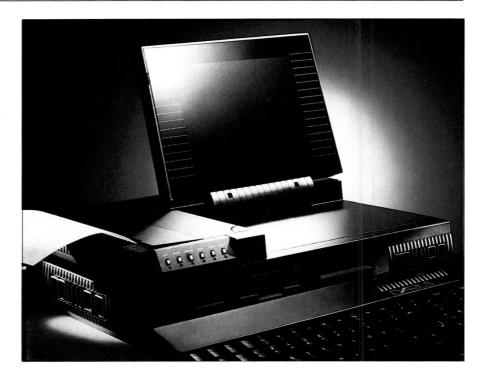

in competition sailing with his boat, the *Argonaut.* On a race from Victoria, British Columbia, to Maui, Hawaii, he used his Toshiba laptop to navigate and track the other boats he was competing with. "I wouldn't go off shore without the computer," says Tom. "I can't imagine not using it. To be competitive, you have to use methods other than the old pencil and paper."

The laptop is just one more step forward in the computer industry's drive to create better, smaller computers. Laptops have made working with computers much easier for businesspeople. Before departing on a business trip, it is possible to transfer the data stored in your desktop to a laptop. And when you return, all the data you created on the laptop can be transferred back to the desktop machine. It may not be long before we see the desktop computer replaced altogether by the desktop "dock" that connects the laptop to a standard monitor and keyboard.

THE PALMTOP COMPUTER

The palmtop computer is a computer with the functionality of a desktop PC, yet is small enough to fit in your pocket or hand. It is the smallest and lightest of portable computers, and often runs on two AA batteries. The palmtop is often the most difficult to describe as well, for no two are quite alike, and they should not be confused with calculators or organizers with business functions (such as a memo pad, address book, or scheduler). A palmtop computer has its own operating system plus separate, often selectable, application software programs; calculators and organizers do not. Here are two palmtops.

The Poqet PC (Figure 3.6) is a PC-compatible with no moving parts; its software comes in integrated circuit chips that plug in. It comes with a scheduler, word processing, a calculator, an address book, and a communications

FIGURE 3.5

Industry analysts estimate that the demand for note-book computers such as this Macintosh Powerbook is growing at a annual rate of 25 percent, making it the fastest-growing segment of the personal computer in-dustry. Their advanced com-munications capabilities make "anytime, anywhere" computing a reality.

program. Additional programs, such as Lotus 1-2-3, are available on *RAM cards,* integrated circuits on credit card – like cards that slip into the machine. A nice feature is the Poqet's ability to "remember" where you stopped your work when you turn the power off, and return you to the same place.

FIGURE 3.6

The Poqet PC, a 1.2-pound IBM-compatible PC, can take additional software on RAM cards that slip into the machine.

FIGURE 3.7

The Hewlett-Packard HP 95LX is an 11-ounce computer with many built-in programs, including the Lotus 1-2-3 spreadsheet, which makes it very popular with financial professionals.

The Hewlett-Packard HP 95LX (Figure 3.7) is an 11-ounce PC-compatible computer with a phone book, appointment scheduler, memo writer, and other features. Most notably, however, it comes with the Lotus 1-2-3 spreadsheet built in, making it an ideal computer for the accountant or auditor on the go. It performs all the 1-2-3 functions (including graphics, database, and macros) and can be connected to standard personal computer printers. It can communicate over phone lines with other computers. But more interestingly, it can also exchange data with another HP 95LX, while they are sitting side by side, via infrared beam. The palmtop spreadsheet was so impressive that it was featured on the "NBC Nightly News."

KNOWLEDGE CHECK

1. What is the difference between a special-purpose computer and a general-purpose computer?   p. 67
2. What is the main difference between a desktop and a portable?   p. 69
3. What were the first traveling computers called?   p. 71
4. What was the most important factor in making portables popular?   p. 71
5. What are the three most popular types of portable computer?   pp. 71–72
6. In what way might a laptop and a notebook be similar?   p. 73
7. What makes the palmtop different from other portables?   p. 73

THE WORKSTATION

A **workstation,** like its personal computer counterpart, is a computer that fits on a desktop and is most commonly used by a single individual, but it may also be shared among users. The workstation combines the ease of use and convenience of a personal computer with some of the power and functions of larger computers. Workstations differ in often costing more than most individuals can afford for personal use.

WORKSTATION CHARACTERISTICS

Workstations have three main characteristics:

- They use powerful microprocessors, often with special operating system software and commonly with special application software.
- They have an easy-to-use interface.
- They are capable of multitasking.

While these three characteristics used to be unique to workstations, they are being adapted to the more powerful personal computers over time. Let's take a closer look at each characteristic.

THE MICROPROCESSOR.   Today, we have personal computers that are based on many different microprocessors and operating systems. **A microprocessor** is a single integrated circuit chip that contains all the control unit and arithmetic/logic unit electronic circuitry that comprise the CPU. Early microprocessors condensed the CPU circuitry down to five chips; then, in the early 1970s, it was shrunk onto a single chip. The two most popular microprocessors are made by Intel, notably for the PC-compatibles and PS/2s, and Motorola, for Macintoshes.

Yet one thing almost all microprocessors have in common is the manner in which they process instructions. **Complex-instruction-set computing** (CISC) is a microprocessor or CPU architecture and operating system design that allows it to recognize 100 or more instructions, enough to carry out most computations. CISC is the most prevalent architecture today; virtually all popular personal computers use CISC. Most people feel CISC computers are adequate for our computing needs; besides, all our application software is based on the CISC instruction set and operating system.

Reduced-instruction-set computing (RISC) is a microprocessor or CPU architecture that uses a condensed set of instructions for its operating system. RISC microprocessors have the advantage of simplicity and elegance over CISC microprocessors. They are also extremely fast. The increased performance and lower price of RISC microprocessors have had a profound effect on the computer industry, prompting companies such as IBM (which created RISC technology) to introduce an entire line of RISC workstations. For that reason, more and more workstations are based on RISC microprocessors.

In the 1980s, four companies became well known for their workstations: Sun Microsystems, Hewlett-Packard (H-P), Apollo Computer (now part of H-P), and Digital Equipment Corporation. These companies manufacture their own proprietary microprocessors. Proprietary means the chip is made exclusively by or for a certain manufacturer. A RISC microprocessor that shows great promise for the 1990s is Digital's Alpha.

THE INTERFACE.   Workstations were the first computers to make the friendly human-computer interface of prime importance. The **human-computer interface** is the point of meeting between the person using the computer and the computer itself. The interface was intended to make it as easy as possible for users to get their work done, rather than having to spend time manipulating the computer system. A research report published in 1981 said, "the [interface of the] integrated workstation is meant to represent a natural technological extension of a person's mind. [It] comes the closest to setting the pace for future information systems."[1]

MULTITASKING.   **Multitasking** is the ability of the computer to run two or more applications at the same time. Using a conventional computer, the operating system must first be loaded, then the application software is loaded. When the knowledge worker wants to change work — say from word processing to the spreadsheet — the first application must be exited, down to the operating system, then the second application is loaded.

Multitasking permits loading and running multiple applications. Each appears in its own area of the screen, often called a *window,* which can be opened, closed, made larger or smaller, and moved around the screen. In addition, multitasking permits taking portions of one application's file and copying

---

[1]"All about Executive and Professional Workstations," Datapro Research Corp., 1981, p. 101.

them into another — for example, the spreadsheet data can be inserted in a word processing report. Figure 3.8 shows a video display on a workstation computer multitasking; each window is a different software program. The workstation also makes it possible to have a small multiuser computer that can be shared by others. These were significant benefits that, over time, have led to new and innovative ways for people to utilize computers.

TYPES OF WORKSTATIONS

Workstations were first used by engineers to design everything from airplanes to computers. But in the late 1970s, Allen Michels saw an emerging need among office workers and business executives for a computer more powerful than a personal computer, with many different software functions. He founded Convergent Technologies, based in Silicon Valley, and introduced the Integrated Work Station in 1979. Today, workstations are designed for three markets: scientific and engineering, office automation, and education.

SCIENTIFIC AND ENGINEERING WORKSTATIONS. Workstations are used to design everything from gears and pulleys to microchips and telephone networks. Workstations permit not only drawing and designing in two and three dimensions, but testing and simulation as well: an aircraft designer can create a computer simulation to test wind shear, or an electrical engineer can test a new chip design in a simulated circuit. Models of microscopic molecules can be viewed in three dimensions, rotated, and even animated using graphics superworkstations.

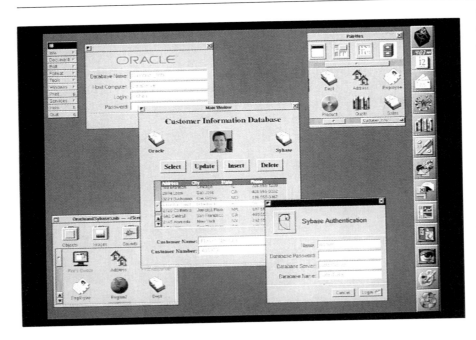

FIGURE 3.8

The NeXT workstation video display is showing multi-tasking; the computer is able to run several applications simultaneously.

OFFICE AUTOMATION WORKSTATIONS. Workstations are used for a variety of tasks throughout the office. People who perform similar jobs or who perform tasks in cooperative work groups often use personal computers and workstations that are connected to one another. Senior management and executives use workstations with special executive information systems software to keep their fingers on the company's pulse. Doctors often have a workstation in their office that is connected to the hospital where they practice. When a patient needs to be admitted, the file and proper forms can be transmitted to the hospital admissions office in a matter of seconds, shortening the paperwork process and helping the patient obtain speedy and proper care.

EDUCATIONAL WORKSTATIONS. Many colleges and universities make workstations available for engineering students or for general use with a variety of personal computers in computing labs. Steve Jobs, who co-founded Apple and created the Macintosh, introduced the first personal workstation for students, the NeXT Computer System. Although it is more expensive than a personal computer, it offers many more features. The NeXT has highly detailed graphics, sound, and even music. It has many built-in applications and special tools such as a library containing a dictionary, a thesaurus, a book of famous quotations, and the works of William Shakespeare. The newest NeXT computer uses a RISC microprocessor, which makes it three times faster than it was when it used a CISC microprocessor.

From the beginning, Allen Michels envisioned a workstation that would integrate many tasks and functions in an easy-to-use computer. This would come about through the marriage of a variety of hardware and software technologies, combined with new insights into **ergonomics,** the study of how to create safety, comfort, and ease of use for people who use machines such as computers. As computer engineers learn more about how we think and work, workstations will just keep getting more useful.

USING WORKSTATIONS

Astrophysicists at the Harvard-Smithsonian Center for Astrophysics use Sun Microsystems workstations for their engineering work. They routinely sketch graphs and diagrams on the screen using computer-aided drafting software, as well as sophisticated calculation software to test mathematical equations. (See Figure 3.9.) They also exchange ideas and information with each other in electronic messages. One project they have worked on in cooperation with NASA is the Advanced X-Ray Astrophysics Facility. It is an observatory in space that will measure cosmic X-rays, which are invisible on earth. The astrophysicists hope that the information provided will help them understand better how the universe was formed and what its eventual fate will be.

The Sun workstation performed an additionally important task: helping gather visual and textual information into a comprehensive report for NASA to explain how an X-ray telescope would function aboard the observatory. Using electronic publishing software, they combined graphics screens, mathematical equations, and textual explanations into a document that took just six hours to prepare. Previously, it would have taken two days. Equally important, the report's professional preparation made it much easier for the NASA people to understand.

FIGURE 3.9

A draftsman uses CAD programming to design and test new products.

While most workstation applications are oriented to science and engineering, here is one that is designed for creative people. The William Morris Agency has installed an "interpersonal network" of NeXT workstations at its offices in Beverly Hills, New York, London, and Nashville. William Morris's clients are people in the entertainment business, including motion picture and television actors, directors, writers, producers, news anchors, and musicians. It's important that the agents — creative but very busy people — share ideas and information throughout the organization. The NeXT workstation was chosen because its graphical interface and advanced design make using the database and exchanging electronic messages from one workstation to another extremely easy. The agents can send each other client information and look at talent profiles on the screen. In addition, using a special application called "Who's Calling?", they can schedule meetings with other agents and clients and track previous phone calls. They can also work with multimedia project material that includes text, visual images (including full-motion video), and high-fidelity stereo sound recordings. When completed, the system will have 250 NeXT workstations in five countries.

KNOWLEDGE CHECK

1. What is the primary difference between a personal computer and a workstation?   p. 75
2. How were the first workstations used?   p. 77
3. What are the three markets or uses for workstations?   pp. 77–78
4. Name two ways workstations can be used in the office.   pp. 78–79
5. What is the study of human factors in the use of computers called?   p. 78

TODAY

THE FAST-CHANGING WORLD OF COMPUTER RETAILING

It used to be that you bought a personal computer at a small mom-and-pop computer store or at a store owned and operated by a computer maker such as IBM. But all that has changed now. The mom-and-pop stores took a beating from the franchise and chain store retailers, such as ComputerLand and Businessland. Yet they have not thrived either, due to poor management and/or sales help. During their heyday, it was not uncommon to see a diversity of former used-car salesmen, electronics technicians, and Ph.D.s in computer science selling computers. One thing they often shared was an inability to fulfill the uneducated customer's needs. "Customer service is one of the hottest things in retail today," says Stewart Neill, vice president of information systems

at Saks Fifth Avenue. Computer retailing is still changing, and today the primary ways to buy a personal computer are via a wholesale club, through mail order, or at a computer "superstore."

- *Wholesale clubs.* Wholesale clubs such as Sam's, Price Club, Wholesale Club, and BJ's sell personal computers. Many carry models made by Positive Corp. exclusively; the prices are rock-bottom. Other brands seen in wholesale clubs include Packard Bell, Emerson, Cordata, and KLH.

- *Mail order.* Some companies, such as Zenith, Toshiba, and BSR, liquidate their older models to mail order companies like C.O.M.B., Damark International, and DAK Industries. Other companies, such as Dell, Gateway, Everex,

and Zeos, sell direct to the consumer, eliminating the distributor and retailer and thus saving you money. CompuAdd sells both in its own retail stores and via direct mail.

- *Computer superstores.* Computer superstores sell nothing but personal computers, often at deeply discounted prices. The Big Five are Businessland, ComputerLand, ValCom, NYNEX, and MicroAge. There are many regional superstores, such as The Laptop Store which sells only portables.

What conclusions may we draw from the changing retail market? That the personal computer is becoming a *commodity,* not unlike the stereo, VCR, or toaster oven—although it's got a long way to go before it's as easy to use.

THE MINICOMPUTER

A notable event in computer history occurred on a sunny fall day in 1957: the founding of Digital Equipment Corporation by Kenneth H. Olsen in an abandoned woolen mill in Maynard, Massachusetts. He created the minicomputer and developed a company that is the second largest computer company in the world, with annual revenues in excess of $12 billion. Olsen has helped make computer history; in 1986, *Fortune* magazine featured him on the cover as "the most successful entrepreneur in history." [2] After leading Digital for 35 years, Olsen retired in 1992.

The minicomputer, or mini, is a versatile special- or general-purpose computer designed so that many people can use it at the same time. Minis operate in ordinary indoor environments; some require air conditioning while others

---

[2] *Fortune* 114, no. 9 (October 27, 1986), p. 24.

do not. Minis also can operate in less hospitable places such as on ships and planes and in manufacturing shops. Minis cost more than personal computers, typically $20,000 to $500,000, but they are also more powerful. Up to 200 people can use the minicomputer at the same time.

Like all computers, the minicomputer is designed as a system. There is a system unit containing the CPU and main memory. There are multiple keyboards and monitors which in combination are called a **terminal,** which we'll study in more detail in Chapter 9. All system components, including storage devices and printers, can be purchased separately to design a specific system or to upgrade an existing one.

Mini systems are more mobile, easier to set up and install, and more versatile than mainframes. It is common to see a minicomputer system combined with specialized equipment and peripherals and designed to perform a specific task. These are called *original equipment manufacturer* (OEM) systems, which means a company buys various hardware from original manufacturers, customizes it with hardware add-ons and software tailored to a specific business or task, and markets it all together as a system. OEM systems are used in publishing, brokerage houses, hospitals, manufacturing, and hundreds of other ways.

TYPES OF MINICOMPUTERS

Digital's VAX minicomputer is the most widely used mini. Digital ensured the VAX's success by making it possible to connect all computers in the VAX family, some from the PDP family, and those of other manufacturers as well. Figure 3.10 shows a Digital minicomputer system. Today, there are many

FIGURE 3.10

The minicomputer shows its versatility here in scientific research.

minicomputer makers such as Data General, which was started by ex-Digital employees. Some, such as Prime Computer, specialize in scientific and engineering systems. Banks use special Tandem Computer "nonstop" systems with two complete CPUs, so that if one fails, the other immediately takes over. Wang has created entire office automation minicomputer systems. In 1988, IBM, best known for its mainframes, introduced a mini called the AS/400, which is widely used in business.

USING MINIS

Here are three examples of how minicomputers are used. The first is a special-purpose application, the second is for general business, and the third is an OEM.

SPECIAL-PURPOSE MINIS. Special-purpose minis can be used in places mainframes would find inhospitable. One such use is atop Mount Kilauea in Hawaii. The Hawaiian Volcano Observatory uses two minis to collect and analyze volcanic and seismic data. In this location, 4,000 feet above sea level, hundreds of tiny earthquakes occur daily as a result of volcanic activity. The minis collect data from dozens of sensors throughout the active areas of the island at the rate of 100 samples per second. The minis then analyze the data showing the effects of ground movement, temperature changes, electromagnetic variations, gravitational fields, and the chemistry of volcanic gases and lava. Telecommunication links allow the resident geologists to share the data they collect with other geological research stations all over the world. Networking with other minis allows this research site to play a vital part in understanding and predicting geologic events in the Pacific.

MINIS IN BUSINESS. Minis are often used as small-business computers. They are widely used by companies whose data storage and processing needs are smaller, and in large banks or government agencies where specific tasks can be handled by one or perhaps a few minis. In these situations, the minicomputer works much like a mainframe, although the volume of usage is lower. Company sales, inventory, and financial records are stored on disks. Terminals give people access to the data, and specially designed software allows executives to translate data into reports, charts, and graphs.

AN OEM MINI. *People with Great Lifestyles,* a fictitious national newspaper, uses a minicomputer. It is kept in a temperature-controlled room, like a mainframe, but you don't see the large cabinets. Instead, the entire mini is in a single cabinet. Against the wall are several disk drives, but much of the other equipment is associated with the newspaper's publishing system.

This is an OEM mini. The company that developed the publishing system software installs the minicomputer, along with any of their own special hardware for publishing. There are about 70 terminals, used mostly by reporters for writing their stories. They send the finished story electronically to the editor, who works at a page makeup terminal. It shows columns of text just as they will appear on the newspaper page.

The mini also keeps other business data. For example, the entire subscriber list, including the dates their subscriptions expire, is stored in a database. The mini automatically sends them a renewal notice and stops their subscription when it is up. *People with Great Lifestyles* often sells portions of its subscriber database, in the form of lists of names and addresses, to companies that want to send advertising literature to potential customers. In addition, the sales representatives can learn how often their clients buy ads and which ones get the most replies on reader response cards.

The mini has become a valuable, versatile computing resource over the years. It has also taken on several other guises: as a supermicro or workstation, as a mini-mainframe for larger business applications, and as an extremely powerful superminicomputer used in science research. Even though the trend is toward smaller computers, minis in various forms will be around for a long time. So will mainframes, which we shall learn about next.

KNOWLEDGE CHECK

1. Name two ways the minicomputer is different from the mainframe. pp. 80–81
2. What do we call a minicomputer that is fitted with special devices to perform a specific task?   p. 81
3. Who is considered the creator of the minicomputer?   p. 80
4. What acronym is used to describe the most successful minicomputer family?   p. 81
5. Describe several ways in which the minicomputer is versatile.   p. 82

THE MAINFRAME COMPUTER

The mainframe is the largest general-purpose computer. It was also the first computer to be used in business, dating back to the early 1950s. It is designed to be used by hundreds — even thousands — of people. Mainframes generally cost at least $700,000 and must be housed in special rooms where temperature and humidity are carefully maintained within certain limits. Most mainframes are employed in situations with continual, heavy processing and many users.

Mainframes consist of the basic building blocks of a computer system: the CPU, various I/O devices, and external memory. The main difference is that these building blocks are considerably larger than, say, a personal computer's. In some cases, mainframes are so large that there is more than one CPU. There might be a cluster of CPU cabinets forming a very powerful mainframe that requires so much main memory that it, too, takes several cabinets to house. In almost all mainframe systems, the controller is in a separate cabinet as well. Figure 3.11 shows a mainframe system.

An extensive array of peripheral equipment is connected to the mainframe: terminals, a variety of printers, many different kinds of storage devices, and communications equipment. A mainframe uses the same peripherals you will find with a minicomputer or a personal computer. What sets the mainframe apart from other types of computers is its powerful CPU, its vast memory and storage capabilities, and the number of terminals that can be connected. For

FIGURE 3.11

The mainframe is the largest general-purpose computer. Hundreds of knowledge workers can use a multitude of applications simultaneously, attesting to its power and versatility.

example, Pillsbury, the food products company with headquarters in Minneapolis, has built an entire underground building the size of a football field to house its mainframe computer equipment.

TYPES OF MAINFRAMES

In the Yesterday feature, you learned that John Atanasoff built the Atanasoff-Berry Computer (ABC), the first electronic, digital computer. It was a special-purpose computer designed for a single task: solving simultaneous differential equations. But the ABC was also the basis for ENIAC, the world's first electronic, digital general-purpose computer.

Most mainframe computers are general-purpose machines. One of the earliest and most effective uses of general-purpose computers in business was the insurance industry's application of ENIAC's descendant, the UNIVAC computer system. The enormous amount of accounting required, together with the need to calculate complex actuarial tables for risks and premiums, gave the UNIVAC just the test it needed to prove its usefulness. It wasn't long before other large U.S. corporations were clamoring for their own computers.

Today, general-purpose mainframe computers play a major role in virtually every aspect of business and organizational life. IBM is largely responsible for this. IBM devised many accounting, calculating, and automatic tabulating machines and the first successful electric typewriter. But it was Tom Watson, Jr., who was mostly responsible for IBM's aggressive pursuit of the computer market. "By 1958, 1959," he said, "I realized that I had water in relatively large quantities and I had a dry sponge for a market. And if I could just learn to introduce that water into the sponge in acceptable form, there was no limit to where this business could go."[3] In 1964, after investing four years and $5

---

[3] Jack B. Rochester, "An Interview: Thomas J. Watson, Jr.," *Computerworld,* June 13, 1983.

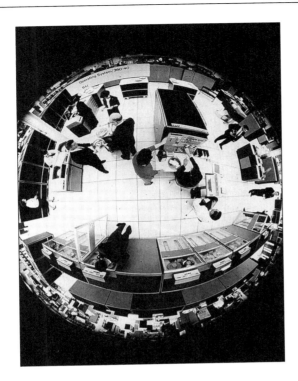

FIGURE 3.12

Computer in the round: The IBM 360, named after the circle it forms, set a standard of the industry.

billion, IBM introduced the System/360 mainframe computer, shown in Figure 3.12, so named because a perfect circle has 360 degrees. It became the most popular mainframe in computer history and the standard for the industry.

USING MAINFRAMES

In the past, mainframes were used in large companies to perform nearly all computing tasks. As the company grew or as new applications were needed, more CPU power or terminals were added to the system. In the 1970s, many companies learned that it was less expensive and often more efficient to install a minicomputer in a department or division than to add on to the mainframe. In the 1980s, companies learned this same lesson again with personal computers and workstations.

As a result of these changes, computers are assuming different roles in the 1990s. Now, the mainframe is commonly used for applications that affect the entire company, such as accounting or maintaining the corporate database. Minicomputers are used as departmental systems in marketing or manufacturing. Workstations and personal computers are used by individuals or small work groups within departments. The notion that a single computer can satisfy an entire company's needs has been overturned. In the same way that a carpenter or a mechanic chooses the right tool for the job, there are a variety of computers to choose from.

Whitbread & Company PLC is a large English food-and-drink company. It brews Whitbread beer, distills Beefeater's gin, operates 6,000 pubs, and owns Pizza Hut, TGI Fridays restaurants, and a number of hotels and inns. In 1983, Whitbread reorganized 10 divisions into four: breweries, trading, inns, and retail. Ten large mainframe data processing centers were reduced to two, and Whitbread began installing new computer systems.

Whitbread's five breweries each has its own computer system for manufacturing. The pubs have a special terminal that is used to place orders with the mainframe computer and to file weekly sales reports to the bank. At London headquarters, a manager in the inns division can use a personal computer connected to the centralized mainframe database to learn which inn had the highest sales on, say, Fridays and Saturdays. Whitbread has diversified its computer facilities and in the process has gained what it calls flexible systems that help the company solve problems — not create new ones.

KNOWLEDGE CHECK

1. What special conditions do large mainframe installations require?   p. 83
2. In terms of its components, what makes a mainframe different from the mini?   p. 83
3. What was the first general-purpose computer called?   p. 84
4. What company developed the System/360, the most successful mainframe computer?   p. 84
5. How are mainframes being used differently in the 1990s?   p. 85

THE SUPERCOMPUTER

A supercomputer is a very, very fast special-purpose computer designed to perform highly sophisticated or complex scientific calculations. Supercomputers are large and quite expensive. They start at around $5 million and can cost as much as $20 million. They often contain state-of-the-art circuitry and require special installation because of their complexity and power requirements plus the need for their own specially designed cooling systems. Figure 3.13 shows a supercomputer installation.

TYPES OF SUPERCOMPUTERS

Supercomputers are known best for their sheer power and massive storage capabilities. Their task is to process large, complex problems at high speed. Early supercomputers had a single, enormous CPU; today, it is possible to have up to eight CPUs, which may be used for different purposes or all applied to a single computing task. All the other computers we've discussed in this chapter operate at speeds measured in *millions of instruction per second;* a supercomputer performs *billions of operations per second*. An **operation** is a set of instructions or a programming statement. With supercomputers, an operation is often a complex mathematical equation called a *floating point operation*.

FIGURE 3.13
The Thinking Machine supercomputers serve the highly
complex needs of the business and scientific communities. Specific applications
include the search for oil, design of helicopters and jet engines, vision studies, on-line
retrieval of information, and
research in areas ranging
from astronomy to new
sources of energy.

Therefore, we often refer to supercomputer performance in FLOPS, for floating point operations per second. A supercomputer that can perform at 2
billion floating point operations per second is referred to as having 2-gigaflops
performance.

As you learned in Chapter 1, supercomputers are made by Cray, IBM,
Fujitsu, and several others. The market for supercomputers has grown beyond
the research laboratory as many businesses have found uses for supercomputers as well, as we shall see in the sections that follow.

USING SUPERCOMPUTERS

Supercomputers are often used to solve complex mathematical problems —
for example, calculating a prime number (one that is divisible only by 1 and
itself) or the distance between planets. But computers permit turning many
other problems into numbers, such as molecular modeling, geographic modeling, and image processing.

A Cray X-MP supercomputer was used to help make a movie called *The Last
Starfighter*. Computer animation isn't new, but using the X-MP added a whole
new dimension of sophistication. Its most remarkable accomplishment was
creating the entire bridge of the alien starship, complete with animated aliens
walking around next to real actors. Because the Cray could process the image
in incredibly fine detail, the average viewer would think it looked absolutely
real. The X-MP allowed animators to make illusion as convincing as reality
itself.

TOMORROW

A CHILLY SUPERCOMPUTER

In 1962, an English computer scientist named Brian Josephson came up with an idea for a way to make electronic circuits work faster. The circuit, called the *Josephson Junction,* takes advantage of a weird property electrons have when they get very cold: They move through circuits much faster than they ordinarily would. The Josephson Junction is similar to an integrated circuit but with a difference: It is cooled to 4 degrees above absolute zero. At this superconducting temperature, the circuit uses one ten-thousandth the energy of a regular circuit and operates at speeds 10 to 100 times faster than the fastest computer in existence. Fujitsu has built logic circuits using Josephson Junctions. Research is underway at IBM to create a Josephson supercomputer the size of a baseball that will consume no more electricity than a 60-watt light bulb.

Less dramatic but of far greater importance was the role a Cray supercomputer played in the San Francisco earthquake on October 17, 1989. Frieder Seible, associate director of the Powell Structural Systems Laboratory, used the Cray at the San Diego Supercomputing Center to build a model of the I-880 freeway that had collapsed. By subjecting the model to earthquakelike vibrations, he was able to determine within two days what joint had failed, causing the upper deck to collapse. This information was used by the transportation department officials to decide on closing several other highway structures.

PARALLEL PROCESSING

Over the past few years, a new kind of supercomputer has emerged. Instead of having a single powerful CPU, this machine has many microprocessors working together so that many programs, operations, or transactions can be processed simultaneously. This is called **parallel processing.** One of the first commercial successes is the Connection Machine, created by MIT graduate Danny Hillis. It has 65,096 microprocessors all working together. The Connection Machine was used to simulate the airflow around helicopter blades, which is critical to the aircraft's stability, at United Technologies. It was able to perform the computations five to six times faster than the most powerful Cray supercomputer. Figure 3.14 shows the Connection Machine. Even more powerful parallel processor computers are being developed, using dozens to hundreds and even thousands of microprocessors. This is termed **massively parallel processing.**

USING PARALLEL PROCESSING

Prudential Securities in New York has installed an Intel IPSC high-performance supercomputer for its bond traders. The "Hypercube," as it is called, can be configured with between 8 and 128 CPUs (processors); when

FIGURE 3.14

Parallel processing allows for high-speed computational diagnosis, five to six times faster than the most powerful Cray Supercomputer.

configured with 64 or more processors, it becomes a massively parallel processor. Each processor is responsible for executing its own program, in concert with all other processors. Termed *multiple instruction, multiple data* (MIMD) organization, it is the most sophisticated type of high-speed parallel processing.

When faced with a buy/sell situation, a broker wants to quickly run an analysis and make an offer. Say the broker is working on the trading floor at Prudential Securities (along with dozens of other brokers) and receives a call asking if he or she would like to bid on a bond. The trader turns to the terminal and enters the bond's unique identification number into a screen form. It is followed by menus that provide options — for example, market conditions, various factors or variables, comparisons with other bonds — for the type of analysis. The trader chooses the options and each analysis begins. Some of these analyses are computationally intense, and they are routed to the Hypercube for processing. Once finished, the results are routed back to the Hypercube and then to the trader's screen.

The Hypercube has given the trader a powerful analysis tool, on call, whenever there is a time-critical buy or sell situation. It's similar to an auto with a turbocharger; the car runs on the regular engine most of the time, but when the driver needs additional power the turbo kicks in. The Hypercube is a turbocharger on Prudential Securities' computing engine, and it can provide the analysis in anywhere between 30 and 40 seconds and several minutes, depending on its complexity. The traders find they can hedge a security better now, because they are better able to quantify it. They are able to control their risk and exposure better because they don't have to use crude computational analysis tools or their own intuition. In addition to the Hypercube, the trader can use one of Prudential Securities' RISC workstations, such as an IBM

RS/6000 or Sun Microsystems Sparcstation, to design custom bonds — you might call them financial engineering workstations.

Supercomputer research has been on the forefront of new computer technology for some time. Even so, Neil Lincoln, who worked with Seymour Cray designing supercomputers at CDC, once defined a supercomputer as "a machine that is one generation behind the problems it is asked to solve." That problem, at least in processing hardware, is to create ever smaller, faster, cheaper computers.

KNOWLEDGE CHECK

1. How does the supercomputer differ from the general-purpose mainframe computer?   p. 86
2. How does a supercomputer's speed compare to that of other computers?   p. 86
3. What type of problems do supercomputers excel at?   p. 87
4. What are the two main types of the supercomputer?   pp. 87–88
5. What types of processing does a supercomputer like the Connection Machine perform?   p. 88

THE EVER-EVOLVING COMPUTER

The human race doubled its technological knowledge — which is another way of saying the creation of new technology tools — from the year 1 A.D. to the year 1750. But then, in just 150 years — by 1900 — that technological knowledge doubled again, and once again between 1900 and 1950. Since then, we have made more progress than in the preceding 10,000 years.

The computer is part of our expanding technological knowledge, but it is also a tool used to advance that knowledge. One reason is that the computer, unlike a plow or an airplane, can be used for many different things. Back in the 1940s and 1950s, no one imagined we would have computers in wristwatches or cash registers. No other technology has grown so fast, nor provided us with so many benefits, as the computer.

It's easy to look at a computer and perceive only its external cabinetry, the keyboard, and the monitor screen without comprehending all the ingenuity that went into creating a successful, functional computer system. Sometimes it's easy to slip into thinking about computers, or even cars or toaster ovens, as machines that somehow simply exist. Yet each was devised or developed by people. Someone saw a problem, then sat down and figured out a way to solve it.

The computer industry has produced some of America's greatest thinkers, entrepreneurs, corporate leaders, and, yes, mavericks. They share a vision centered on three goals: better, faster, cheaper computers. In the social context, the purpose is to provide more computers for people to use, and in the process, improve the quality of life for all.

Computers have the power to be great tools of democracy. Sir Francis Bacon said, "Knowledge is power," and St. John said, "The truth shall make

FIGURE 3.15
No more typing—the pen-based computer uses an electronic stylus that writes, rather than relying on a keyboard.

you free." Therefore, gaining access to information and knowledge is essential to learning the truth. In this quest, the Japanese government has launched a high technology program to make computers as common as pay telephones, so that its citizenry can be better informed.

The introduction of personal computers in the former Soviet Union has played a significant role in that area's moving toward democracy. Indeed, one of the world's most popular computer games, Tetris, was created by a Russian. According to the *Fort Worth Star – Telegram,* computers and communications technology played an important role in the attempted coup attempt in the Soviet Union. The paper stated:

> While messages from Russian President Boris Yeltsin and other coup opponents were being sent throughout Asia, Europe and North American this week, the committee that tried to seize power either didn't know about or couldn't keep up with the instantaneous network transmissions. . . . The unprecedented connection, made possible by the introduction of thousands of personal computers into the Soviet Union under President Mikhail Gorbachev, put a kink into plans to control the flow of information.[4]

What is the next great challenge for computer hardware? Today, it appears to be portable computers that have no keyboards, known as **pen-based computers.** They use an electronic stylus to draw simple characters when issuing instructions, as shown in Figure 3.15. Pen-based computers are currently being used to fill out forms or complete reports that only require writing in

[4] *Fort Worth Star – Telegram,* August 22, 1991.

CAREERS FOR KNOWLEDGE WORKERS
MICHAEL DELL: PRESIDENT AND CEO, DELL COMPUTER CORP.

It is very popular in the computer industry to create a story about the company birthplace — especially if it's in a garage, which is where companies like Hewlett-Packard and Apple got their start. But Michael Dell, 19 years old, started his computer company with $1,000 in his dorm room at the University of Texas in Austin. Michael sensed a need for low-cost personal computers that retail stores weren't addressing, and it paid off.

That was in 1984; today, Michael Dell's office at Dell Computer Corporation is on the top floor of his own building, atop a hill that allows him a view of his old campus. Dell Computer is one of the 10 top personal computer companies in the world, and Michael is one of the 100 wealthiest Texans.

Michael's success was no fluke. He was avidly interested in personal computers and studied the market. He saw that retailers reaped a great profit on each computer but provided few services after the sale — something he believed new users needed. His strategy was simple: buy the parts, assemble the computers, and sell them directly to individuals and businesses.

In person, Michael is a quiet but hard-working man, often putting in 16 long business hours a day. He keeps his private life very private, and acknowledges the contributions of others in making Dell Computer a success. "This company is 3,200 people; this company is 16 vice presidents; this company is 5 directors; this company is a $890-million company that has a lot of people behind it. It is not a one-person company," he says.

Michael talked about the importance of service and support in a keynote speech to the computer industry. He pointed out how personal computers have grown more complex from the 1980s to the 1990s, where often it is simply "technology for technology's sake."

"We, as an industry, need to work on things that make people more productive, which means we need to understand our customers' businesses. That is really hard to do if you're focused on the latest technology and buzzwords. I believe our company has succeeded primarily because we have listened and responded to customer needs."

"It's important for companies to be able to configure service and support, just as easily as they configure hardware and software to specific customer needs. And these needs are evolving. The PC five years from now will be very different from the PC of today. The one constant will be that users will have their own ideas of what they want, where they'll buy, and what they want the computer to do for them. Customers want computers that make them genuinely more productive. They want computers that interface like humans do, not like computers do. They want computers that are a tool to leverage their abilities." If Michael Dell practices what he preaches, he will clearly be a successful entrepreneur and businessman for a long, long time.

block letters. This includes salespeople who must collect data in the field or at the job site—for example, sales representatives taking orders in grocery stores; construction site supervisors, who must evaluate drawings and reports; equipment maintenance, public utility, or safety workers; and a variety of data collectors, such as census takers. But in time these computers will be able to "learn" our handwriting, opening up the use of computers to a large population that cannot or will not type on a keyboard.

COMPUTING MACHINE ETHICS: IS THE MACHINE WRONG?

How can we determine when computers are being used ethically? Is it ethical to create nuclear missiles or nuclear power plants? Is it ethical to use computers in business to outmaneuver or outperform a competitor? Is it ethical to break into or disable a computer system that belongs to someone else, regardless of the reason?

In the 17th century, Dutch factory workers kicked their wooden clog shoes, called *sabots,* into factory machines, causing them to break down. This act became known as *sabotage.* In 1987, a young woman named Katya Komisaruk broke into the NAVSTAR satellite control computer complex at Vandenberg Air Force Base, California, and sabotaged a $1.2 million mainframe computer. "I used my crowbar to haul out all the chips," she said. "I piled them on the floor, jumped up and down, and did a dance over them." A peace activist, Komisaruk claimed the act was an expression of her commitment to help the United States avoid nuclear war.

The NAVSTAR computer serves several purposes. In addition to pinpointing the locations of Soviet missile silos, it is used by aviators and sailors as a navigation system to plot their courses. At her trial, Komisaruk's defense was that she destroyed the computer to prevent a greater crime. "It's better to destroy a few machines than to let those machines destroy millions of people," she claimed. The prosecuting attorney responded by saying, "That's like calling a typewriter a weapon of destruction because it can be used to write the attack order." The judge sentenced Komisaruk to five years in prison and ordered her to pay $500,000 in restitution for the computer. She considered her actions ethical and moral as they were intended to save lives. Yet, what if she had cost the lives of people on board an airplane or a ship?

SUMMARY

1. *Describe the difference between general-purpose computers and special-purpose computers.* A general-purpose computer is one used for a variety of tasks without the need to modify or change it as the tasks change. A common example is a mini or mainframe computer used in business that runs many different applications. A special-purpose computer is designed and used solely for one application. It may need to be redesigned, and certainly must be reprogrammed, if it is to perform another task. Special-purpose computers range from the smallest hand-held device to the largest supercomputer.

2. *Explain the difference between the various types of portable computers.* A portable computer is used by a single individual; the difference is that it can be used in many different places. It is not confined, by its size or weight, to a desktop. It has the same components as a desktop machine, but in most cases the monitor and keyboard are integrated. The three most popular portables are laptops, notebooks, and palmtops.

3. *Describe the different types of workstations and how each is used.* A workstation, like its personal computer counterpart, is a computer that fits on a desktop. It is most commonly used by a single

individual, but it may also be shared among users. The workstation combines the ease of use and convenience of a personal computer with some of the power and functions of larger computers, and thus often costs more. Workstations are characterized by their microprocessor, their easy-to-use interface, and their multitasking capabilities. They are used in science and engineering, office automation, and education.

4. *Describe the characteristics of the minicomputer and its three different uses.* The minicomputer, or mini, is a versatile special- or general-purpose computer designed so that many people can use it at the same time. Special-purpose minis can be used in places that would be inhospitable to mainframes. Companies whose data storage and processing needs are smaller than those of large banks or government agencies find they can do the job with one or perhaps a few minis. In these situations, the minicomputer works much like a mainframe, although the volume of usage is lower. An OEM mini is a system offered by a company that develops special software that runs on the minicomputer, along with any of their own special hardware for publishing.

5. *Describe the characteristics and uses of the mainframe computer.* The mainframe is the largest general-purpose computer. It is designed to be used by hundreds or even thousands of people. Most mainframes are used when there is continual, heavy processing and many users. Most mainframe computers are general-purpose machines. General-purpose mainframe computers play a major role in virtually every aspect of business and organizational life.

6. *Describe the characteristics and uses of the supercomputer.* Supercomputers are known best for their sheer power and massive storage capabilities. Their task is to process large, complex problems at high speed—for example, calculating a prime number (one that is divisible only by 1 and itself) or the distance between planets. We often refer to supercomputer performance in FLOPS, for floating point operations per second. But computers permit turning many other problems into numbers, such as molecular modeling, geographic modeling, and image processing.

COMPUTING MACHINE ISSUES

1. How do you feel about the fact that there are so many different standards for personal computers? If you buy a PC-compatible, you can't use software created for the Macintosh. There is CISC, now RISC. Why do computer makers create differing standards? From your perspective, what are the advantages and disadvantages of each? Which standard would you choose? Should all computer makers be required to adopt the same standard?

2. The business press is prone to sensationalize downturns in the computer industry. Over the years, companies such as IBM and Digital Equipment Corporation occasionally have a poor quarter or perform less well than expected. The press tends to exaggerate this news, suggesting the demise of the mainframe or mini, or that the company may be about to go out of business. For instance, in 1989, a front-page story in a leading business newspaper said, "Today, Digi-

tal is nearly dead in the water." And in 1991, an internal IBM memo was leaked to the press revealing how upset the president of IBM was with people's performance. What do you think of this kind of reporting? What are its effects on stockholders? Ask your economics professor what it means when a multibillion dollar company has a flat quarter, and try to assess the real impact.

3. You walk into a friend's room or a colleague's office. The personal computer is on but no one is around. On the screen is the text of something that appears to be extremely personal. You're curious; should you read it or not? You glance at it, not sure. The last sentence on the screen makes you want to read what follows. That means touching the keyboard to scroll the screen up. What if you touch the computer? What if you don't? Is reading the screen ethical? Is touching the keyboard to read the text more unethical? Is there any difference between the two?

CHAPTER REVIEW QUESTIONS

REVIEW QUESTIONS

1. What is the difference between general-purpose and special-purpose computers?
2. What are the advantages and disadvantages between CISC and RISC microprocessors?
3. In which of the three markets do you think workstations are most useful?
4. What will be the future role of the mainframe computer?
5. Compare the difference in processing speeds between a mainframe and a supercomputer. Why do you think a supercomputer is so much faster?
6. Discuss the notion that computers — especially personal computers — are tools of democracy.
7. How would a pen-based computer make you more productive?

DISCUSSION QUESTIONS

1. Why do we need to constantly improve computer performance?
2. History tells us that it's fairly common to overlook the true inventor or creator. For example, Edison did not invent the first light bulb, nor did Bell invent the first telephone. Does this tell us that it's not the very first, but the first *successful* invention or creation that counts?
3. When might you prefer a notebook to a laptop? A palmtop to a notebook?
4. Discuss some ways you would use a portable computer in your life. Do you think you would use it as your sole and only computer, or would you want both a desktop and a portable?
5. Discuss the advantages and disadvantages of multitasking. When would you use it? How would it help you be more productive?
6. Discuss the future of the mini, in light of the fact that workstations and personal computers can perform many of its tasks.
7. Why has the mainframe remained a general-purpose computer? Why has it never become an OEM computer?

MULTIPLE-CHOICE

1. The portable computer (check all that apply):
   a. Is usually more expensive than a desktop PC.
   b. Does not always have a floppy disk drive.
   c. Performs all the same tasks as a desktop PC.
   d. Can transfer data to other computers.
   e. Sometimes comes with built-in software.
2. What do the terms *human-computer interface* and *ergonomics* mean to you? (Check all that apply.):
   a. Making the computer amenable to the way knowledge workers work.
   b. A colorful, graphic screen display.
   c. Keyboards and monitors that are easy to use.
   d. A marketing concept to get more people to buy computers.
   e. A government regulation that manufacturers have to comply with.
3. Why are mainframes losing their "do-everything" role in business? (Check all that apply.):
   a. They are too expensive.
   b. They have grown too old.
   c. Knowledge workers want processing power on their desktops.
   d. The mainframes were too busy for all the tasks required of them.
   e. Many shoulders make a light burden.
4. A mainframe computer:
   a. Can run hundreds of applications simultaneously.
   b. May have more than one CPU.
   c. Is the same as a PC, only bigger.
   d. Is primarily used in business.
   e. All of the above.

FILL-IN-THE-BLANK

1. The computer continues to become
   _____, _____, and
   _____.

2. CISC stands for _____
   _____ _____
   _____.

3. RISC stands for _____
   _____ _____
   _____.

4. Packaging a computer, special hardware, and custom software are called _____
   _____ _____.

5. A palmtop computer often has its software built into an _____ _____.

6. The most advanced supercomputer technology is called _____ _____.

TRUE/FALSE

1. The development of portable computers was propelled by a need to perform business computing tasks when away from the office desktop.
2. Parallel processing is changing the nature of the supercomputer as a special-purpose computer by making it possible to perform business tasks with ease.
3. The people who design and create computers are often thought of as mavericks.
4. The first portable computer was called a *luggable* and was invented by Compaq Computer.
5. Workstations were the first computers to emphasize ergonomics.
6. Some minicomputers can be confused with workstations, and some other minis can be confused with mainframes.

KEY TERMS

complex-instruction-set computing (CISC),   76
ergonomics,   78
general-purpose computer,   67
human-computer interface,   76
laptop,   70
massively parallel processing,   88

microprocessor,   75
multitasking,   76
notebook,   70
operation,   86
palmtop,   70
parallel processing,   88
pen-based computers,   91

portable computer,   69
reduced-instruction-set computing (RISC),   76
special-purpose computer,   67
terminal,   81
workstation,   75

Personal Productivity Applications

Knowledge workers work with information; that's our job. We work with many different kinds of information, primarily in the form of words, numbers, sets of facts, and graphic images. To do so more productively, we use the computer and application software. The chapters in Module II show you how to use the most popular personal productivity applications: word processing, the spreadsheet, the database management system, graphics, and desktop publishing software.

Chapter 4 discusses word processing, a program that lets you work with ideas and text to create a variety of documents: memos, letters, reports, poetry, short stories, magazine articles, books, and more. It also covers electronic and desktop publishing, the more sophisticated counterpart to word processing. Publishing software brings words, numbers, and images together in an application used by many types of knowledge workers, from an individual with a home office business to a large corporation's marketing department.

Chapter 5 discusses the spreadsheet, a program designed to analyze mathematical or financial situations and produce possible solutions in a matrix or table. It combines the accountant's paper ledger sheet, the pencil, and the electronic calculator. Although the spreadsheet can display text, its principal task is performing calculations. An additional advantage is its ability to present numerical data graphically or in pictures. And speaking of graphics, the chapter concludes by covering the various types of graphics software, the visual application that turns information into images.

Chapter 6 discusses the database management system, a program that allows you to store, organize, and retrieve information stored in a database. The database can be something as simple as an address book or as complex as the personnel records for a huge corporation.

Chapter 7 presents the fundamental concepts of software. System software, which guides the CPU operations, is explained. Operating systems for all sizes and types of computers are covered, followed by operating environments designed to make it easier to work with operating systems. The different categories of business application software are also described.

Let's begin exploring these applications, their uses, and their advantages in more detail.

CHAPTER 4

Word Processing and Electronic Publishing

LEARNING OBJECTIVES

After reading and studying this chapter, you should be able to:

1. Explain why it is important for knowledge workers to know how to use word processing.

2. Describe how word processing is used to create various types of documents.

3. Explain the five steps involved in using word processing.

4. Explain the four phases of the writing/word processing process.

5. Describe the word processing keyboard and screen.

6. Understand how to use the commands and steps involved in creating, formatting, revising, saving, retrieving, and printing a document.

7. Describe some advanced word processing tools and how they are used.

8. Understand the difference between corporate electronic publishing and desktop publishing.

9. Explain the steps in creating a desktop publishing document.

The Knowledge Worker and Word Processing

Mark Twain was traveling in Europe when he read in a newspaper that he had died. He fired off a letter to the paper saying, "Reports of my death are greatly exaggerated." Reports of the death of the printed word are similarly exaggerated. The same can be said for knowledge workers with writing skills. Amy Wohl, the leading office automation consultant in the United States, says that throughout this decade, the highest requirement in hiring knowledge workers will be their ability to use a personal computer and word processing.

Indeed, word processing is the leading software application. According to Merisel (the largest worldwide software distributor), almost 40 percent of all personal computer software sold is word processing software. And over half of all knowledge workers — whether they are senior managers, supervisors, administrative assistants, or secretarial staff — spend at least one hour a day using it. They use word processing to write memos, correspondence, and reports in the office, on airplanes, in hotel rooms, and at home. These knowledge workers are convinced that they can get more work done — in other words, be more productive — using a personal computer and word processing, says Wohl.

Clearly, your ability to work with words is critical to your job success. It is the primary way that information is formally shared in business, whether it is a memo directed to a work group, a report to senior management, or an annual report to stockholders. In fact, sharing information has been shown to improve employee motivation. The more workers understand about their work and the nature of the business, the better they perform.

The book *Workplace 2000* reports that by the millennium we will rarely see the old company bulletin board with its typed memos, informal notes, and such. It will be replaced by professional-looking publications designed to help workers increase their knowledge and thus improve their productivity. These newsletters and magazines will be filled with articles about business trends, charts and tables analyzing company performance, various internal reports, information about new products, and educational articles that help knowledge workers improve their skills. Many of these publications will be written, designed, typeset, and even published on personal computers, using a combination of word processing and desktop publishing software. The power of the computer-written word continues to assume ever greater importance.[1]

Whenever knowledge workers work with information, it must be structured in such a way that it is meaningful to its intended audience — whether that is a single colleague, a work group, a management committee, the presi-

---

[1] Joseph P. Boyett and Henry P. Conn, *Workplace 2000: The Revolution Reshaping American Business* (New York: E. P. Dutton, 1991), pp. 55–56.

YESTERDAY
THE AUTOMATION OF THE WRITTEN WORD

For thousands of years, people could only scratch words on paper with a sharp-pointed device — often a pointed feather called a *quill.* The first mechanically printed book was the Bible, produced in Europe about 1455 on a press invented by Johann Gutenberg. Originally a goldsmith, Gutenberg developed his process of printing by using movable type made from punch-stamped matrices, a press similar to a wine press, and oil-based printing ink. Each page of the Bible held about 2,500 individual pieces of lead type in the German Gothic type style of the period. Six presses worked on the Bible simultaneously, printing 20 to 40 pages a day. Fewer than 50 copies are still in existence.

Printing remained in the shops of the printers for another 400 years, until W. A. Burt, an American, built the first working typewriter. Then in 1857, Christopher Latham Sholes developed the first commercial typewriter, WHICH COULD ONLY TYPE IN UPPERCASE LETTERS. Remington bought the rights to

it, and Mark Twain was the first author to buy and use one.

Thomas Edison invented the electric typewriter in 1872, but it was so crude it could only be used as a stock market ticker tape printer. A commercial electric typewriter wasn't available until IBM introduced one in 1935. IBM proceeded to lead the field in typing innovation, introducing the "golfball" typewriter in 1961.

The term *word processing* was coined by IBM (and derived from data processing) to signify using computers that could manipulate written words. The first word processing system was created by IBM in 1964. Called the MT/ST (for Magnetic Tape/Selectric Typewriter), it used magnetic tapes to store work. In 1969, IBM updated it so that it stored information on magnetic cards — and logically named it the MC/ST.

There followed a number of computer systems that were designed solely to perform word processing tasks. Word processing became a buzzword in busi-

ness, and companies such as A.B. Dick, Xerox, and even Exxon introduced *dedicated* word processing systems — meaning that's all the systems did. In 1976, the Wang WP 55 was introduced, and it became the most highly successful office word processing system. Digital Equipment Corporation followed suit with a very popular word processing system called the WPS-8.

When personal computers became popular, word processing turned from a hardware orientation into a software application. MicroPro International Corporation introduced WordStar® in 1979, a program that relied on pressing a combination of keys, such as CONTROL-K-S, to issue commands. Since then, we have seen several word processing programs ascend the best-seller lists, with WordPerfect topping that list since the mid-1980s. More importantly, today we have a wide variety of word processing programs tailored to unique needs and individual preferences.

---

dent, or the board of directors. Such structured information is called a *document,* the subject we shall take up next.

WORKING WITH DOCUMENTS

Knowledge workers use word processing so that they may work efficiently with a document, which was introduced in Chapter 1. As you know, a document contains data, but it is also the record of a transaction between two parties. A document has both content and form. Its *content* — the information itself — has immediate and possibly long-range value. The document also has

FIGURE 4.1

Your credibility rests upon the quality presentation of your documents; letters must be error-free and printed for easy reading.

form, whether it is a poem, short story, memo, letter, report, proposal, company policy, quote, contract, design, warranty, newsletter, or invoice. A document's form may also be a formally printed and published brochure, pamphlet, manual, or even a book. Its form must conform to business or company requirements for quality and presentation. For example, a letter must be error-free, typed or printed so that it can be easily read, and laid out according to corporate conventions, as seen in Figure 4.1.

Xerox Corporation has studied the document for many years. It defines the document as "a package of information having organizational impact, which is transmitted, filed and maintained for the purpose of informing or influencing others." Using the document effectively leads to mastering the use of information. By the year 2000, Xerox claims, the companies that have thrived, not merely survived, will be those that have mastered their information and the document processes that originate, produce, and use that information.

Proper document management is crucial. In one example, Xerox was able to demonstrate to a shipping company that a simple Request for Proposal (RFP) was re-keyed on at least 10 word processors, passed through 50 engineering workstations, and still had to be re-keyed once again to integrate the graphics. Eliminating repetitive work reduces errors, improves productivity, and saves money.

To summarize, knowledge workers use word processing to create documents. A document takes on a specific form, depending on its purpose. It contains data that takes the final form of valuable information, depending on the recipient. Now let us see how we use word processing and then electronic (desktop) publishing to create these various documents.

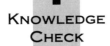

KNOWLEDGE CHECK

1. Why must information be structured when shared with fellow knowledge workers?   p. 101
2. What is the structure we use when working with word processing software?   p. 102
3. What do we mean by the *content* of a document?   p. 102
4. What do we mean by the *form* of a document?   p. 103
5. Name at least three different types of business document.   p. 103
6. What benefits can a company derive from using documents successfully?   p. 103

WHAT IS WORD PROCESSING?

Word processing is a software application designed to write, revise, format, save, and print documents. As mentioned, the document can take many forms. Word processing is a tool for working with two primary forms of human communication: ideas and text. Whether writing term papers or letters, composing the lyrics to a tune, or creating a business memo, word processing helps us write more easily. This is because it has distinct advantages over noncomputerized writing tools and methods. There are five advantages found in using word processing: writing, revising, formatting, saving, and printing.

WRITING

Word processing makes **writing,** the process of conveying information with words, easier for us in two ways. First, word processing automates many actions we perform manually on typewriters. For example, we can type continuously without executing a carriage return at the end of each line of text, because word processing does it for us automatically, pushing the text to the next line. Also, we don't have to insert a new piece of paper at the end of each page as we do with typewriters because of a feature called **scrolling,** which continuously feeds us an electronic sheet of paper. If you are using one of the newer word processing packages, scrolling and a number of other functions can be accomplished using the mouse.

Author Alice Kahn tells an interesting story about writing using word processing. "When Delacorte Press was working on *My Life as a Gal,* they sent me a mock-up of the cover, a photograph of my face rolling out of a typewriter. I was embarrassed enough at being on the cover, but seeing the typewriter made me sick because I didn't associate it with my career as a writer. I had them replace it with a picture of my face on a computer screen."

Many word processors give us a second advantage by incorporating additional writing tools such as a spelling or grammar checker, a thesaurus for finding the appropriate word, an outliner, and footnoting. We'll discuss these and other ease-of-use features later in this chapter.

REVISING

Revising (or *revision*) is the process of re-reading, changing, and replacing text that you have written. Each time you revise, you create a new **draft,** a term used to describe successive versions of your document. Most knowledge workers realize the need to edit a document once or twice, making changes and corrections. Word processing has made this procedure as painless as possible, since changes can be made on the computer monitor instead of paper. Using a typewriter, you may spend many hours typing and retyping to produce a good final draft. With word processing, changes can be made over and over until you are satisfied with the document; then the final draft can be printed. Revising includes:

- Moving or rearranging portions of the document.
- Replacing specific characters, words, or phrases.
- Deleting and undeleting portions of the document.
- Adding new text.

We'll study each of these features in detail in the section that follows.

FORMATTING

Formatting is the process of emphasizing and arranging text on the screen or the printed page (not to be confused with formatting disks). Word processing allows us to format and stylize our written documents. We format *words* by underlining, boldfacing, or italicizing. We format *lines* by centering text and by setting margins and tab spaces. We format *pages* by setting line spacing, justification, and page breaks. We format *documents* by choosing a specific typeface, setting page numbering, and creating headers or footers. Figure 4.2 defines these common formatting terms.

Boldface:	Accentuating type characters by making them darker, for example with key terms.
Center:	Placing text equidistant from each side of the page.
Footer:	Information about the document that appears at the bottom of the page, in most cases repetitively throughout a document, such as the page number.
Header:	Information about the document that appears at the top of the page, in most cases repetitively throughout a document, such as the document title.
Italics:	Tilting characters for *emphasis;* often used for publication titles.
Justification:	Aligning text against the left, right, or both margins.
Line spacing:	The space between lines of text, as in single space, double space, and so on.
Margin:	The blank space on each side of the text, usually one inch.
Page break:	Determining the last line of text at the bottom of a particular page.
Tab:	An automatic indentation from the margin, usually to begin paragraphs.
Typeface:	Also called the **font;** the type character design. This is Times Roman; this is Helvetica.
Underline:	Drawing a line under words, as in book titles.

FIGURE 4.2

Formatting terms.

We can do many of these things with a typewriter; however, the word processing advantage is that many can be done automatically. For example, you can issue the instruction to begin page numbering on page 2, leaving page 1 unnumbered. Another advantage is that you can change a format setting whenever you want. If you want to remove a boldfaced word, change the line spacing or the type font, or insert new headings, you may do so easily. It's all done on the screen rather than on paper; you create a printed document when you are ready to do so.

SAVING

Saving is the process of storing the document in a file, which you learned about in Chapter 2 on DOS. It is the means by which we frequently protect our work while writing, as well as the step we take to preserve our work for posterity. We can use the DOS filenames as a way to store and identify successive drafts, so that we have a complete record of our revisions. The most important thing to remember is to save your work frequently, regardless of the application software you are using. A good rule of thumb is to save at the end of every page or every 10 minutes, whichever comes first. Some word processing programs have a built-in automatic save feature set on a timer so you don't have to worry about it.

PRINTING

What you see on the monitor is referred to as **soft copy,** since it is visual only and intangible. But at any point in the writing process, you can print what you have written. **Printing** lets you read and review a draft of your document in a paper form, what is often termed **hard copy.** Hard copy provides a permanent record of a document that can be conveniently shared with other knowledge workers. It is also another form of backup for a disk file in case of loss.

Printing combines software and hardware technology. The word processing software must be able to take advantage of the printer's capabilities, but the hard copy is only as good as the printer itself. Yet using the two together, it is possible to create simple documents that look typewritten, or to create complex documents as elegant as the typeset page you are reading, as the examples in Figure 4.3 demonstrate. Some word processing programs have a feature that allows you to see what the document will look like when printed, including the headers, footers, pagination, and type fonts.

KNOWLEDGE CHECK

1. Word processing is a tool for working with what two aspects of human communication?   p. 104
2. Describe several advantages in writing with word processing instead of a typewriter.   p. 104
3. What do we create each time we revise a document?   p. 105
4. Describe at least two ways in which to revise text.   p. 105
5. What are the four levels at which we can format a document?   p. 105
6. Into what DOS structure do we save a document?   p. 106
7. What is another name for a printed document?   p. 106

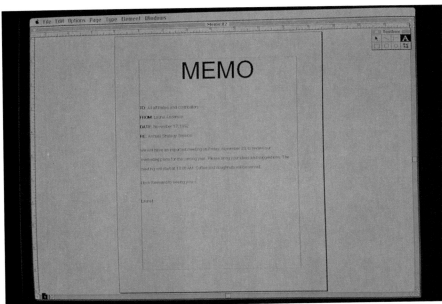

FIGURE 4.3
This document began as an on-screen draft and was printed so corrections could be made on hard copy. The presentation copy produced included formatting changes such as the font decision.

THE WRITING/WORD PROCESSING PROCESS

In Chapter 1 you learned that the computer system uses specific *procedures* that turn *data* into useful *information* for people. Application software predetermines our procedures for accomplishing specific tasks such as word processing. This is true of the other applications you'll learn about in the chapters that follow. We'll see that these procedures are easy to understand. If we carefully follow the procedures, it makes learning to use the application easier and, actually, a lot more enjoyable. Don't forget the two computer caveats: (1) take your time and (2) do things carefully.

There are four different activities of the writing/word processing process, as described in Figure 4.4. The first activity is *prewriting,* the preparation before you actually begin using the computer and application software. Prewriting, usually done with pencil and paper, helps you *brainstorm,* pull your ideas together; *plan* how you will present your information to the audience; perform any necessary *research* before you start writing; and *prewrite,* which might be hand writing a rough draft or outline that forms a structure and sketches in some content.

The second activity is *word processing,* actually writing using the application software. The primary task throughout the process is *keying in text,* or writing. However, we perform some simple *formatting* as we go along, such as using the Tab key to indent paragraphs, boldfacing, underlining, or italicizing words. We might *block edit,* for example, to move a sentence or a paragraph. Surely we will perform some simple *deletions* of a word or a phrase if we mistype or if better words come to mind. If we make a mistake or change our minds, we might *undelete,* to correct a text deletion. We might want to change a word or correct its spelling if we've been using it repeatedly and use the

---

FIGURE 4.4   The word processing process.

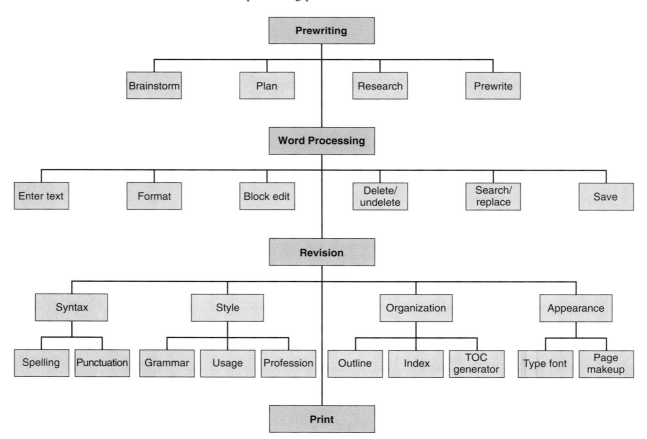

search/replace function to do so. And most important, at intervals throughout our writing and as we finish the first draft, we'll *save* our document in a file.

The third activity is *revision,* the work we do on a document after we've completed the first draft. There is a good reason why we separate the word processing, or creation, phase from the revision phase. Most people, upon completing a document, feel it's reasonably good and that it doesn't need much revision. That's just human nature, and it's true of the occasional writer as well as the professional who writes every day. Yet by stepping back from it for a period of time, whether a few hours or a day or two, we will see many ways in which the document can be improved. Those improvements fall into four categories:

- *Syntax,* concerning spelling and punctuation. Often we can use built-in software tools to check these mechanics.
- *Style,* primarily grammar and word usage, meaning choosing the most precise words to convey meaning. Using terminology specific to your profession or your company—those words that are quickly understood by your audience—are another aspect of style.
- *Organization,* the way your document is structured. For example, you might compare the draft to your original outline to see if any important topics have been left out. You may need to create an index or a table of contents, which reports often require.
- *Appearance,* the final polished and professional way the document is printed. As mentioned earlier, this involves the typeface (font), headers, footers, pagination, titles, and page design.

Once the document looks just as you want it, the final activity is *printing.* This is simply issuing the command through the word processing software to print the file, producing the hard copy. With this basic understanding of the process, it's time to familiarize ourselves with the word processing keyboard and screen.

KNOWLEDGE CHECK

1. What do we call the preparation done before using the computer and application?   p. 108
2. Identify and describe the activities of the writing/word processing process.   pp. 108–109
3. What is the single most important thing we do during the word processing activity?   p. 108
4. Why is the revision activity separate from the word processing activity?   p. 109
5. Name several improvements we make during the revision activity.   p. 109

THE WORD PROCESSING KEYBOARD AND SCREEN

In this and each of the following chapters, we'll examine the manner in which knowledge workers use the application software program. We use our senses to interact with the computer—specifically touch and sight, or our fingers and our eyes. Thus, it is important to understand how the application takes advantage of the keyboard and screen.

THE KEYBOARD

When Christopher Sholes invented the typewriter, he significantly advanced written communications. However, he had to do so with available technology. In this case, that meant the keys were attached to long bars with the type characters on the end; they traveled forward and struck the ribbon and paper to make an impression. Typing too fast caused the bars to get tangled up, so Sholes designed the typewriter keyboard to slow down the typing process. We call this the QWERTY keyboard, and it is the one most people use for typewriters and computers alike.

There is, however, another keyboard that was designed by a man named August Dvorak in 1936, which permits higher typing speeds, more comfort, and fewer typing errors. It places the most frequently used keys under the strongest fingers, reducing wasted finger motions and awkward strokes by 90 percent.

If this is so, then why don't more people use the clearly superior Dvorak keyboard? The simple answer is they learned on the QWERTY, and it is hard for most people to change and relearn another. Both keyboards are shown in Figure 4.5.

THE COMPUTER KEYBOARD.   The typewriter keyboard is only a portion of a computer's keyboard. The first computer keyboards were nearly identical to a typewriter's, with one or two additional keys for issuing computer-related commands. Today, both Macintosh and PC-compatible computers have an *enhanced keyboard,* as shown in Figure 4.6, with a number of differences. There is a full array of function keys, a separate set of cursor movement keys, as well as specific keys for use within applications. These are often referred to as a "101-key enhanced keyboard," and some allow the knowledge worker to program specific keys.

FIGURE 4.5   A better idea? The QWERTY is more familiar, but the Dvorak keyboard is laid out to be considerably more efficient.

Refer to Figure 4.6 and follow the color coding as we discuss the personal computer keyboard features. Starting at the bottom, note the addition of the pink **Control** (Ctrl) and gold **Alternate** (Alt) keys; they are used in conjunction with standard keyboard keys to issue commands or instructions to the application software. The typewriter's purple **Return** key has been replaced by the **Enter** key, which is often pressed to complete and issue a command or instruction to the computer.

Moving to the top, note the white **Escape** (Esc) key at the far left; this is a nearly universal key that removes control of the computer system from the program in use, either stopping a task in progress or exiting from the program altogether. Directly below or to the right of the Esc key (depending on the type of computer) are the white **Function** keys, which programmers assign to commands or instructions that you use while working with the application program. If you guessed that Function keys perform the same tasks as the Ctrl and Alt key combinations, you're right. The function keys are often employed by the application software in conjunction with the Shift, Alt, and Ctrl keys to multiply the number of available functions. Two common commands are SAVE and PRINT.

Just to the right of the keyboard are green keys specifically for the computer keyboard. The **cursor control** arrow keys move the cursor you learned about in Chapter 2 around on the computer monitor (for example, in word processing, through the lines of written text). Above these keys are six other keys. Four of them, **Home, End, Page Up,** and **Page Down,** may be used in conjunction with the cursor keys, depending on the way the programmers designed the

---

In addition to its standard typewriter keyboard, the computer keyboard is able to issue commands to application programs using additional keys or several keys in combination.

FIGURE 4.6

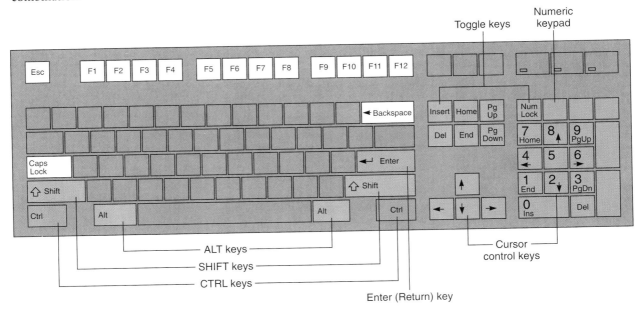

application software. For example, the Home and "up" arrow key may move you to the beginning of a file. The Page keys move the text up or down, one screen or page at a time.

Most people are familiar with the white **Backspace** key from the typewriter, which in word processing removes the next-to-the-last typed character. But there is also a green **Delete** key. It is used to remove the character upon which the cursor rests, and will continue to remove every character to the right as long as you press it. So, Backspace deletes to the left, while Delete deletes to the right.

The green **Insert** key is called a **toggle** key, which means it is used to alternate between two related tasks. In **Insert mode,** every character you type is placed at the position of the cursor, pushing all the text in front of the cursor ahead. Nothing you wrote before is deleted; every new character you type is inserted into the existing text. If you press the Insert key, it toggles to the **Typeover mode,** where every character you type replaces any character that was there previously. Typeover mode, sometimes called **Overstrike mode,** deletes each old character as you type a new character.

There are several other toggle keys on your computer keyboard. The ones you'll use most frequently are the white **Caps Lock,** to the left of the **A** key, FOR WHEN YOU WANT ALL CAPITALS. The other is the green **Number Lock** (Num Lock) key, which we shall take up next.

To the right of the cursor keys is the green **numeric keypad,** so called because it is laid out like the keys on an electronic calculator. When the Num Lock is toggled on, the keypad is used by people working with numbers—most frequently with the spreadsheet application discussed in the next chapter. The Ins key (identical to the other Insert) becomes the numeral 0 (zero), and the Del key (identical to the other Delete) becomes the decimal point. When Num Lock is toggled off, the 2, 4, 6, and 8 keys become cursor control keys and function identically to the arrow keys.

Now that we know what the keyboard is used for in word processing, let's examine what we see on the computer monitor.

THE WORD PROCESSING SCREEN

Refer to the word processing screen shown in Figure 4.7. As you can see, most word processing screens are designed to look like a sheet of paper—with a few electronic improvements, of course! Even though each word processing application may take a slightly different approach to screen design, they have certain similar screen characteristics that provide you with essential information for working with the program. Let's take a look at them.

THE STATUS LINE. The **status line** provides information about your word processing session at the top or bottom of the screen. The status line usually includes the name of the file in use, the page number, and the line, column, and space the cursor presently occupies.

THE TITLE LINE. The **title line** presents the name of the program and often the document name. In programs capable of opening simultaneous multiple documents, it presents the document number. It may also have the date, the time, and the available space on disk information displayed.

Word processing screens help you feel more comfortable by resembling a piece of paper and by adding such features as status lines and menus.

FIGURE 4.7

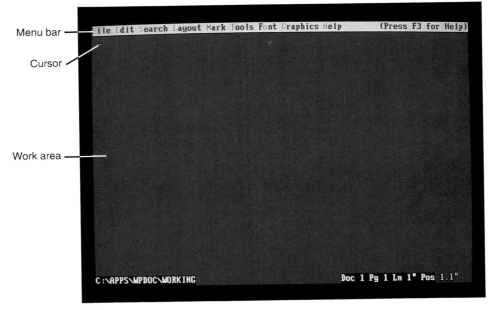

Menu bar

Cursor

Work area

File Edit Search Layout Mark Tools Font Graphics Help   (Press F3 for Help)

C:\APPS\WPDOC\WORKING   Doc 1 Pg 1 Ln 1" Pos 1.1"

THE MENU LINE. The **menu line** displays the various options you have for working with the document. Generally speaking, these options are the same as those available using the Function keys, but are grouped into logical organizations. For example, the File option provides commands for opening, saving, listing, and printing files. These additional commands are found in pulldown menus that are displayed when you activate the option on the menu line. A **pulldown menu** is a menu hidden behind the individual menu options that provides more options. Think of it as a window shade that is rolled up and hidden until you pull the cord. The pulldown menu for the File option is shown in Figure 4.8.

Menu options and pulldown menus are activated in one of two ways. The first way is by pressing a specific key such as Alt, which displays the menu line. The cursor keys move across the menu, and the option is selected and activated by pressing the Enter key. The second way is by using a mouse to move the cursor to the menu line, and then pressing the mouse button — in computer jargon called *clicking* on the selection.

THE ICON BAR. Many of the newest word processing applications use an **icon bar** (see the Tomorrow feature). An **icon** is a pictorial figure or representation that is designed to be easily recognized by most people. Each icon represents a word processing command or task that is more quickly or easily accomplished by clicking on it. For example, the icons often represent open-

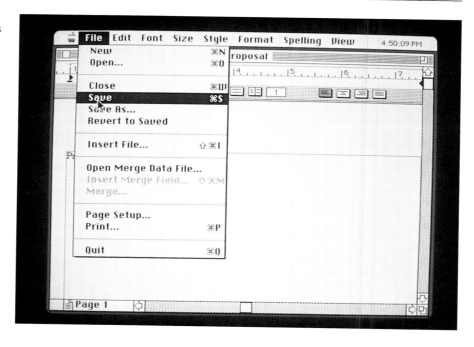

ing, closing, or printing a file, boldfacing or italicizing text, performing a
spelling check, or other revision tools.

THE SCROLLING BARS.   You will also see **scrolling bars** on the newer word
processing screens. The vertical scrolling bar is on the right side of the screen,
and the horizontal scrolling bar is at the bottom. Within each bar you can see a
square block that indicates where the text is positioned. Using the mouse, the
cursor is positioned in the box while holding the mouse button down, then
moving — called *dragging* — the box up and down or left and right. The
alternative is holding the cursor key down or using the Page Up/Down
buttons. Scrolling bars make it quick and easy to move through long documents.

THE WORK AREA.   So far, we've discussed the periphery of the screen. However, most of the screen is blank. This is the **work area,** and it is waiting for you
to fill it with text! To do so, the first and most important thing is to locate the
cursor, for it tells you where you can begin keying in text.

CURSOR MOVEMENT.   Word processing uses the cursor for the same purpose
as DOS. The cursor is a dashed line or square in the work area on your screen. It
may be blinking or solid, but regardless it indicates where the next character
you type will appear. When you begin working with a new file, it is usually
found at the top left-hand corner of the screen. If you're using word processing
that employs a mouse, then the cursor becomes an arrow when you use it to
issue commands.

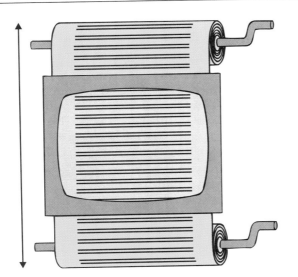

FIGURE 4.9

Although the computer screen only displays a fixed number of lines at a time, the scrolling feature makes the entire document available for viewing.

WORD WRAP. When using an electric typewriter, you must press the carriage return key at the end of each line you type. **Word wrap** is a feature that automatically moves a word from the end of one line to the beginning of the next. This feature lets you type without stopping to look at the screen to decide if the typed line is too long. It saves keystrokes and makes keying in text a more natural process. However, when you wish to end a line manually — for example, to end a paragraph and begin a new one — pressing the Enter key inserts what is called a **hard return.** Then whatever you type next will appear on the following line.

SCROLLING. The vertical movement of text on the screen is called *scrolling,* a continuous flow of lines and paragraphs from bottom to top. The term was borrowed from ancient days when people wrote on scrolls — long rolls of paper attached to round cylinders at each end. To read scrolls, people unrolled the paper from one cylinder as they rolled it up with the other, leaving text between the rolls exposed for viewing.

Word processing works similarly, as illustrated in Figure 4.9. Twenty-five single-spaced lines are commonly displayed. The remainder of the document either precedes what is shown or follows it. We can scroll through the text using the up and down arrow keys to move a line at a time, or the Page Up and Page Down keys to move a screen or a page at a time. Scrolling occurs automatically when we enter text. When you are keying in and reach the bottom of the screen, the text scrolls up, displaying the newly entered text one line at a time.

EDITING MODES. Most word processing programs allow you to toggle between the two editing modes mentioned earlier. In addition, most use Insert as the **Default mode;** that means the program automatically begins in Insert. You can often tell which mode you're in by referring to the status line. Figure 4.10 gives examples of Insert and Typeover modes.

FIGURE 4.10

Word processing has two text entry modes: insert and type-over. In typeover, see how the word **noted** has been typed over the word **pushed.**

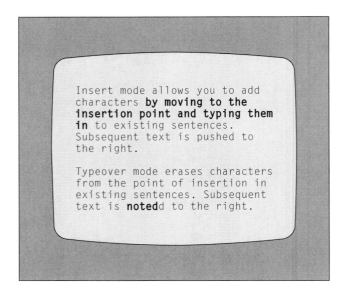

Insert mode allows you to add characters **by moving to the insertion point and typing them in** to existing sentences. Subsequent text is pushed to the right.

Typeover mode erases characters from the point of insertion in existing sentences. Subsequent text is **noted**d to the right.

HELP. Sometimes we need more information on how to use an application. Knowing this, programmers created a **Help** function, built into the application, that contains instructions, tips, pointers, explanations, and guidance. It is always available while you are using the program, usually by pressing a key such as F1 or by clicking on the word "Help" in the menu line. Help often provides information on current format settings, tells which keys perform specific tasks, says how to use advanced features, and more. Figure 4.11 shows a word processing Help screen. Familiarize yourself with how Help works; it's a good idea to get in the habit of using it. It's especially important to learn how to exit Help.

KNOWLEDGE CHECK

1. How do we move the cursor?   p. 111
2. What is a toggle key?   p. 112
3. What does the status line tell us?   p. 112
4. What do we call the area where text is typed?   p. 114
5. Define insert and typeover editing modes.   p. 115
6. Explain how word wrap works.   p. 115
7. What is scrolling?   p. 115
8. When and how do we use the Help feature?   p. 116

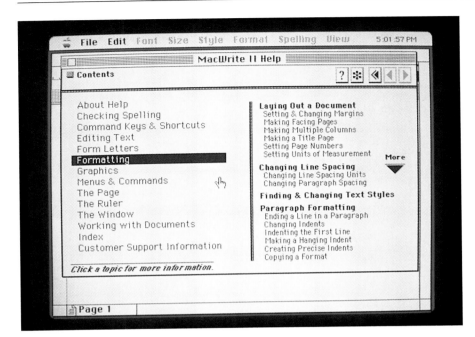

FIGURE 4.11

Help screens show you the steps of using various word processing features.

USING ADVANCED WORD PROCESSING FEATURES

Learning to get the most from the basic word processing features takes some time, but the sense of accomplishment makes it all worthwhile. Advanced word processing features build on that knowledge, making it possible to create sophisticated, elegant, and more useful documents. Here are some of those features.

THE MACRO

A **macro** is a sequence of keystrokes or instructions, recorded and saved in a file, that you use while working in word processing and other applications. These keystrokes may activate a command or series of commands (for example, combining saving and printing the file). The keystrokes may be a character string that you have to type repetitively, such as "Consolidated Electrical and Plumbing Supply Corporation." In either case, the macro stores all these keystrokes in a file, thus making it possible to type them automatically by hitting a few keys. Macros are commonly activated by holding down the Alt key while pressing a letter or number, or by selecting the macro from a menu with the appropriate function key.

TODAY

WORD PROCESSING AND DESKTOP PUBLISHING TIPS

Word Processing

1. Use word processing to brainstorm and for prewriting exercises. Because you can move, add, delete, and edit so easily, your work will take shape much more quickly. It's tedious and rather pointless to write ideas or drafts on paper and then type them into a word processing file.

2. If your word processing software has a multiple document feature that allows you to open and work with more than one file at a time, use it. Multiple documents make it easy to view and edit more than one manuscript or several portions of the same manuscript at the same time.

3. Strive to edit on the screen as much as possible. The idea behind word processing is that we don't need to retype drafts over and over; if you always edit drafts on paper, you're defeating one of word processing's major advantages.

4. Don't overuse print fatures. Underlining, **boldface,** and *italics,* not to mention TYPEFACE SIZES, should be used sparingly, otherwise the text becomes difficult to read.

5. If you're using software that only allows you to use the standard DOS eight-character filenames, name your documents carefully. Choose words that convey the content rather than the type of file. For example, it's much easier to remember what's in a file called TOYSTORY than one called FICTION.

6. Most people use about 10 commands on a regular basis. Learn and memorize the commands you use most frequently, so that you don't have to look them up each time. Use mnemonics, or associative words, to help you master the commands and functions (for example, "Press F10, save it again.").

7. Use a keyboard template that identifies the Function keys until you are thoroughly familiar with the commands. If your software doesn't come with a template, get one at your local retail software store or order one from the publisher.

8. Learn keyboard shortcuts that save you keystrokes. For example, if you are

MAIL MERGE

An advanced feature often used by knowledge workers is **mail merge,** which permits combining information from separate files to create special documents. Mail merge is most commonly used in letters to add the recipient's name and address, along with the salutation, to make the letter more personalized. This was one of the first uses for dedicated word processors. It can also be used to create address lists for printing labels or envelopes. A complementary function is *sort,* which permits alphabetizing words or ordering numbers. For example, all the key terms created during the writing of this text were saved into a single file and then sorted to create the glossary that appears at the end of the book.

using the * asterisk to "bullet" a group of headlines, use the multiplication key above the numeral 9; that saves you pressing Shift-8. Another shortcut is using search and replace when you have to type in a long phrase, such as "Consolidated Electrical and Plumbing Supply Corporation." Type a unique character set, such as ZX, each time the phrase occurs; then search and replace it when you're through. Use macros, described elsewhere in this chapter, for phrases you use repeatedly in a variety of documents.

9. Strive to learn a new command or technique once a week or once a month—whatever works best for you. Extend your knowledge and your software's capabilities to make your work more productive, interesting, and fun.

10. Save your work frequently. Although this applies to any application you use, most people find it incredibly frustrating to lose their work. If your word processing software has an automatic Save feature, set it to save frequently. If it doesn't, get in the habit of performing a quick save at the end of every page.

Desktop Publishing

1. Create a style sheet and save it, without text or graphics, so that you have a fresh template each additional time you need it.

2. Keep pages simple. Avoid embellishing margins and overusing different type fonts or styles. Study book or electronic publishing design to see how the experts do it.

3. If you use a dot-matrix printer, keep a separate, "fresh" ribbon that you use just for final, camera-ready printouts.

4. Use the COPY and PASTE sequence of commands to replicate a page or portion of a page design. For example, a business card can be replicated eight times on an $8\frac{1}{2}'' \times 11''$ sheet of paper, thus reducing printing costs.

5. Learn to use the extensive graphics capabilities of DTP to enhance your typewritten documents. Even simple line images or enhanced alphabetic characters add value to a printed work.

THE OUTLINER

Many word processing software packages include an **outliner** feature that helps you create an outline with paragraph numbering, as you use it. Here is an example of how the outline feature works:

```
                         Levels
                 1     2     3     4     5
Paragraph        1.    a.    i.    (1)   (a)
Outline          I.    A.    1.    a.    (1)
Legal (1.1.1)    1     .1    .1    .1    .1
Bullets          .     o     -     .     *
User-defined
```

THE SPELLING CHECKER

When you want to be sure you spell a word correctly, you probably turn to a dictionary. But that can be a frustrating experience. How do you look up a word you don't know how to spell? A word processing spelling checker can solve this problem for you. This tool requires only that you type the word as closely as possible to how you think it should be spelled and select the spell checking option. If you spelled it incorrectly, most word processing programs stop at the word and then show you a list of alternatives from a built-in dictionary. You can select a word to replace what you typed, edit it, or ignore it. Figure 4.12 shows one program's spelling checker display. You can also add to the built-in dictionary and add words it does not include, such as special terminology associated with your study, work, or discipline.

Various word processing programs check spelling in different ways, but all perform the same function. Most will read through every word in your document, comparing against the words in their dictionaries and flagging words that don't match. Most allow you to replace your words with those from a list, and to add words you have written in your document that aren't already in the dictionary. Some even allow you to do a global replace—replacing every occurrence of your misspelled word with the correct word in the spelling checker. In addition, some spelling checkers locate duplicate words. For example, if you accidentally type a word twice, like "the the," your spelling checker will ask you if you want to eliminate the second occurrence.

A spelling checker helps even the best writers and typists, catching mistakes that might otherwise require a good copy editor. It allows us to write continuously, without pausing to look up words in a dictionary. We can leave the final spelling check and corrections until we are finished keying in text. Most

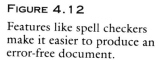

FIGURE 4.12

Features like spell checkers make it easier to produce an error-free document.

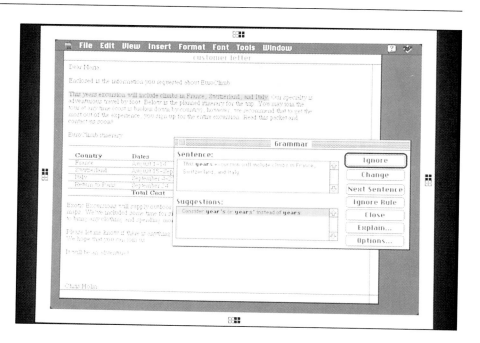

spelling checkers work within the word processing software, so select the appropriate function key, and then follow the screen instructions to correct misspellings and add unknown words. However, spelling checkers do not catch the mistaken use of properly spelled works — that is, words — so don't forget to proofread your documents before they leave your desk!

THE THESAURUS

The dictionary was the first lexicon, a collection of words and their definitions. The thesaurus was the second, designed to help people look up *synonyms,* words with similar meanings. To make this easier and bring all the tools of writing together, some word processing programs have a built-in thesaurus. Figure 4.13 shows the difference between a spelling checker and a thesaurus.

While the spelling checker verifies spelling, the thesaurus helps you determine if you're using the word that's correct or most precise. You position the cursor on the word in question, then press the function key to activate the thesaurus. A list of noun synonyms is displayed in the first column, while verb synonyms are in the second column. The first menu choice at the bottom of the screen allows you to select a synonym for replacement.

Using a thesaurus in book form to find the perfect word, or *mot juste* as the French say, can be time-consuming. Much of the value of using a word processing thesaurus lies in its speed; the searching is done quickly by the computer. Your writing flow and momentum aren't interrupted as much when you use this tool.

PAGE DESIGN

Page design changes a sheet of plain word processing text into a unique and attractive page like a newspaper, magazine, annual report, or other document. Once the text is written and corrected, page design makes it more presentable

---

FIGURE 4.13

The thesaurus assists in the selection of the perfect word.

Your on-screen dictionary gives you word definitions and corrects spelling.

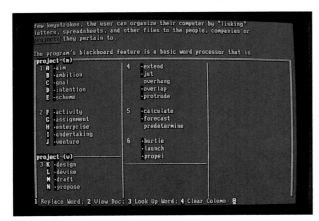

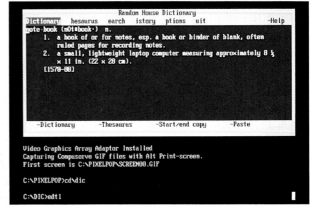

FIGURE 4.14

A. A wide range of fonts are available through various software packages.

B. Advanced word processing tools allow you to combine text and graphics to create professional-looking documents.

to its audience. Using page design, it is possible to select different typefaces or fonts (shown in Figure 4.14A), organize the text into multiple columns, and even insert graphic images. Once you have designed the page, you can preview on the monitor what it will look like once it is printed, using the word processing *page view* feature. An example of such a page is shown in Figure 4.14B.

While word processing does a creditable job with page design, it may not always be sufficient for more complex documents that demand the skills and attention to detail of typesetting. For those jobs, it is better to use electronic publishing, our next topic.

KNOWLEDGE CHECK

1. What two types of keystroke sequences is a macro used for?　p. 117
2. What are some additional features a spelling checker offers, besides flagging misspelled words?　pp. 120–21
3. What types of words does a thesaurus help you find?　p. 121
4. What three design elements might be found in page design?　p. 122
5. How is page view useful?　p. 122

ELECTRONIC PUBLISHING

Electronic publishing is the process of converting text materials, commonly produced with word processing software, into a professionally published format. Electronic publishing makes it possible to compose, design, typeset, and

FIGURE 4.15

Electronic publishing has simplified and streamlined the publishing process, making it possible for businesses to internally design and create many more professional-looking documents.

1. **Begin with a General Layout**

   The built-in layout tools will help you develop a format for your document. Place text and graphic elements exactly where you want them on each page.

2. **Enter Text**

   Enter the text for your document by either typing it in with the built-in word processor, or import your text directly from any other program with an ASCII text format.

3. **Create Graphics**

   Use the built-in drawing tools to create your own graphics or import them from your favorite drawing program.

4. **Add Finishing Touches**

   The layout and typesetting features allow you to explore different creative options directly on your screen. You can reposition graphics, change a type size, or use other special effects.

5. **Print**

   Once your page looks just the way you want it to, press a key and your document is delivered to you via your dot matrix or laser printer.

incorporate artwork into a professional-looking document or a form ready for a printing press. Typically, documents include anything from books and instruction manuals to magazines, brochures, leaflets, flyers, advertisements, newsletters, and pamphlets.

Electronic publishing creates *typeset* as opposed to *typewritten* documents. You can change or combine type fonts, type sizes, and styles, and display boldface, underlining, and italics. Electronic publishing justifies individual text characters to create perfectly aligned margins — left and right and top and bottom — as well as multiple columns on a page.

Electronic publishing also allows you to insert graphics to visually enhance the publication. These graphics range from simple line drawings to photographs, computer-generated art, and what is known as **clip art,** universally recognized images available in books or stored on computer disks. Finally, electronic publishing creates finished (camera-ready) pages that can be printed on a high-quality laser printer or a magazine-quality Linotronic typesetter. At this point, the conventional printing process takes over. Figure 4.15 shows the steps in electronic publishing.

TYPES OF ELECTRONIC PUBLISHING

Today there are two types of electronic publishing. One is **corporate electronic publishing** (CEP), which companies use for both external documents such as user manuals and advertising brochures, as well as internal use (for example, to publish a company newsletter). CEP usually employs either stand-alone personal computers or larger workstation- or minicomputer-based electronic publishing systems.

The second type of electronic publishing is **desktop publishing** (DTP), which is word processing and graphics applications combined with advanced formatting capabilities, used with a personal computer or workstation. DTP is used in many schools for flyers and announcements, in small businesses for advertising, and by entrepreneurs to publish their own newsletters or to offer

Tomorrow

Character-Based versus WYSIWYG Word Processing

The earliest word processing software was called an *editor,* which was used by programmers to write notes. The editor could only reproduce the characters the keyboard was capable of typing, and such was the case with early word processing. This was so because, to some extent, the hardware components dictated what the software was capable of producing. If the monitor could not display anything but keyboard characters, then that was all you could see. The same was true of the printer.

Thus word processing of this era was called **character-based,** meaning it could only reproduce the symbols in the ASCII character set. ASCII characters are the letters, numbers, and punctuation marks that appear on your keyboard. For a more complete discussion of ASCII and other character sets, see Appendix A.

But it didn't take long for people to begin asking for the ability to reproduce type styles —*italics,* **boldface,** and underline— and later, different type fonts and sizes. Most early word processing programs obliged on the type styles, but you still couldn't see them on the screen. Instead, they were coded into the document. For example, Ctrl-B would toggle on boldfacing; after typing the word or words, you pressed Ctrl-B again to toggle it off. And, as you might expect, people often forgot to toggle off, with predictable results! A notable advance was the introduction of color, which meant you could see the styles in color or in reverse. This made it easier to remember toggling off.

But in the mid-1980s, word processing grew more sophisticated, adding the ability to re-

produce a variety of type fonts and sizes, so the demand grew to be able to see the real thing on the screen. The first computer to offer this capability, which became known as What You See Is What You Get **(WYSIWYG),** was the Apple-Macintosh, using MacWrite or Microsoft Word software. Even though its display was only black and white, the Macintosh displayed crisp-looking type styles and fonts.

IBM PCs and PC-compatibles were slow to catch up with the WYSIWYG trend, but the high-quality, color displays made the wait worthwhile for most knowledge workers. In addition to providing true text characters and a color display, many modern word processing programs display many of the features discussed earlier in this chapter. There are tools such as a tool

professional DTP services to businesses in their communities. Figure 4.16 shows examples of some corporate and desktop publishing systems.

The Evolution of Publishing

Printing changed very little from the 11th century to the 20th century. Type was first made of wood, then lead; printing presses were in the hands of the few: newspapers, book printers, and the like. The computer industry was among the first to perceive a need for internal publishing operations: a typical computer system comes with a shelf of instruction manuals between 6 and 20 feet long! Xerox and IBM were early participants in CEP in the mid-1970s. Today, to quote industry expert David H. Goodstein, "Publishing is every company's second business."

The first desktop publishing program was the brainchild of Rob Doyle, son of astrophysicists, inventors, and Cambridge, Massachusetts, residents Robert

"palette" of icons from which you can select the ones you'll use most frequently. Once chosen, they are displayed in an icon at the top or side of the screen. Graphic images, of course, appear on the screen in color. Some let you place a color note, like a Post-It note, in documents, which is very handy when several people are working together.

Today, we speak of the *graphical user interface environment* (GUI), which means we can use the operating system, word processing, and many other applications in a WYSIWYG mode. This is only natural, for we enjoy our work more when it's easier to visualize what we're doing. One drawback, however, is that WYSIWYG often causes the

CPU to run more slowly, and thus many tasks such as retrieving and saving files, or printing, take longer to accomplish. This is a trade-off each knowledge worker must assess. In time, however, almost all computers will employ some form of GUI. Their displays will grow more alike, and even easier for knowledge workers to use.

MacWrite.

Ami Pro.

WordPerfect.

and Holly Doyle. While he was editor of his high school newspaper, the Macintosh was introduced, causing Rob to speculate that it might be useful to have a program to combine text and graphics and then format pages. With his father's support, Macpublisher was introduced in the summer of 1984. A small announcement in *MacWorld* magazine brought 3,000 inquiries. Although other desktop publishing programs are now more popular, Macpublisher was the first.

Benjamin Franklin, America's first truly successful publisher and printer, would be astounded at the progress we've made.

Using Electronic Publishing

In CEP, workstations and software create everything from marketing materials to reference manuals to user documentation. For example, Lotus Development Corporation uses a workstation system to produce its documentation

FIGURE 4.16

Every company's second business: Electronic publishing has made it possible for many businesses to design and publish a wide range of documents—from newsletters to reference manuals—saving untold dollars every year.

Publishing companies now turn to desktop publishing systems for the timely production of newspapers, magazines, and even books.

for 1-2-3 and other software products. Others that use CEP systems include General Electric, Boeing, and the National Center for Health Statistics. Networking now permits sending typeset documents from a personal computer to a satellite system that links a business to its printer, so that the entire photocomposition and pagination process is electronically transmitted. No paper need be exchanged. The daily contents of both *USA Today* and *The Wall Street Journal* are electronically transmitted to remote printing sites across the country where the newspapers are printed and then distributed so that readers have today's news first thing every morning.

DTP is used in many different industries and walks of life. Newsletters that used to be typewritten and then typeset are now written using word processing, then typeset, designed, and illustrated using DTP. The owner of a hobby store uses DTP to create his own newspaper advertisements, saving $1,300 per ad—money he formerly paid a graphic artist. DTP is not just for small business either. *USA Today* uses Macintoshes to create many of the simple charts and graphics used in the newspaper—as well as using a more expensive system for photograph preparation.

DTP shows more and more signs of replacing expensive workstation- or mini-based corporate electronic publishing systems. At the same time, stand-alone word processing software has more and more DTP capabilities such as page layout, multiple typefaces or fonts, and inserting graphics. Perhaps most amazing of all is the fact that there have been more changes in the publishing process in the past 20 years than there were in the preceding 1,000.

1. What is the difference between corporate electronic publishing and desktop publishing?   p. 123
2. What is clip art?   p. 123
3. What does the term *camera-ready pages* mean?   p. 123
4. When electronic publishing and networking are combined, what is eliminated?   p. 126
5. Which shows more growth potential, DTP or CEP systems?   p. 126

■ KNOWLEDGE CHECK

THE DESKTOP PUBLISHING PROCESS

Figure 4.17 shows the desktop publishing process. There are five activities: designing the layout, keying in and copy-fitting text, creating and sizing graphics, formatting, and printing. Let's take a closer look at each.

Layout involves determining what type of publication you wish to create. It might be a one-page flyer, newsletter, report, brochure, advertisement, business form, catalog pages, stationery, invitations, menu, program, directory, manual, or book. From a single page to a bound and printed 500-page book, it can all be done with DTP.

Knowing the scope of the project helps plan the work. Some documents have more than one page design; for example, your textbook uses a one-column design for text, but a three-column page design for the boxed features. DTP pages use a **frame,** or box containing text or graphics. The frame may be a column, as when it is text, or it may stand alone as a graphic element. It may also be a header (as in a newsletter masthead) or a footer (such as newsletter subscription information). A frame is not restricted by the column layout or format. The **ruler** is a tool for measuring the size of frames and columns.

The use of a template or **style sheet** makes document design progress more quickly and smoothly. If your layout indicates there are four different page designs; then a style sheet can be created for each and used when necessary.

Text is the written content of the document. It may be **imported** from word processing; most DTP programs permit importing text in its **native format,** meaning the way the word processing program saves its files, from a menu including WordPerfect, Microsoft Word, WordStar, and so forth. In addition, most DTP programs have a built-in word processing editor so that text can be entered directly into a column or template. The only real drawback to doing so is that the DTP software often formats the text as you write, making the program work somewhat slowly.

DTP permits designing text just as a typesetter would. Different fonts or type styles may be selected, in a variety of sizes and in boldface, italics, bold-faced italics, and so forth. Like sophisticated word processing software, DTP also permits deciding if words are to be **hyphenated** at the end of a line; the program knows where to properly separate a hyphenated word, and it makes it easier to justify margins. In addition, the process called **kerning** proportion-

FIGURE 4.17 The desktop publishing process.

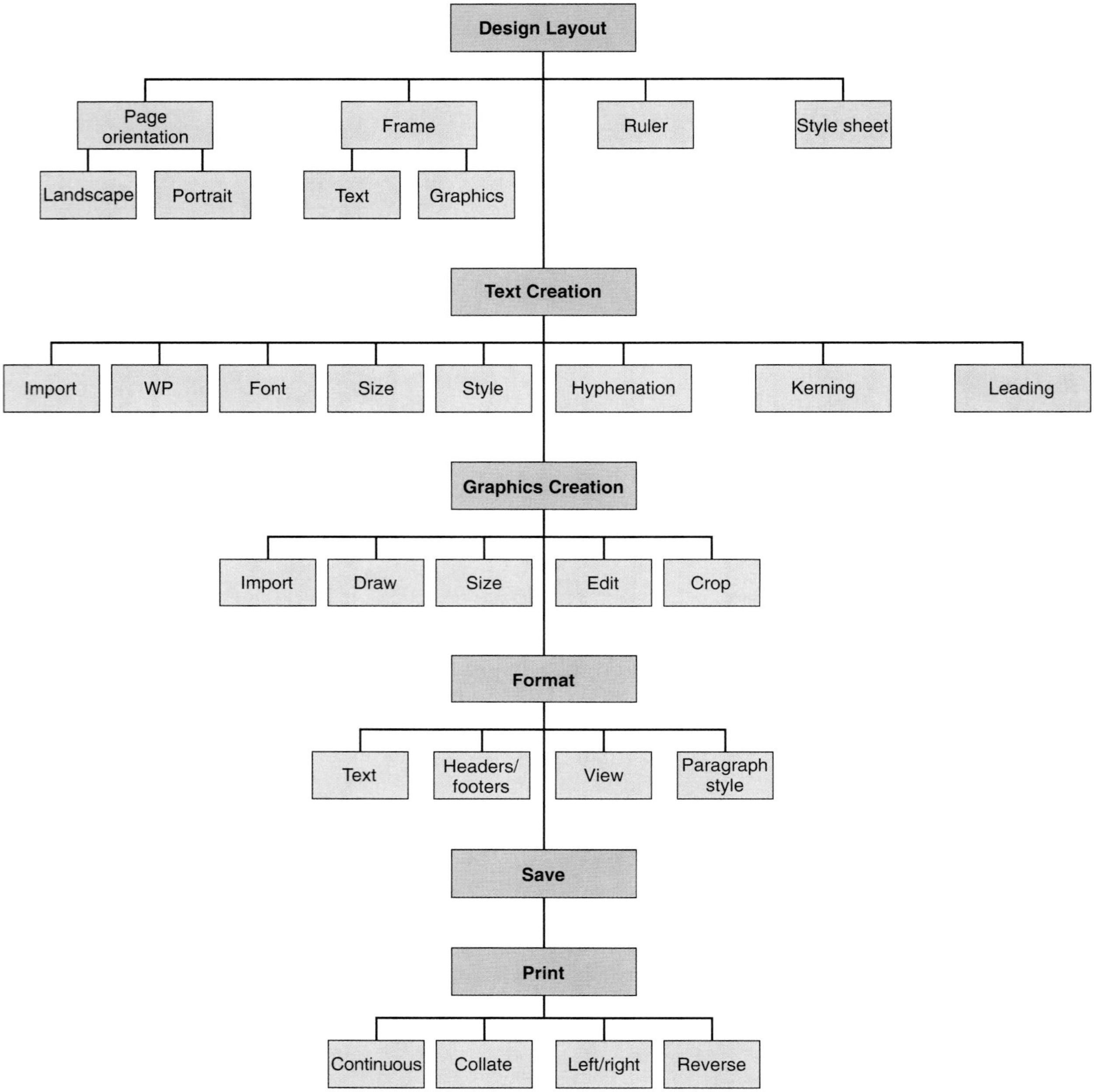

ally separates individual characters within a word to make text easier to read. The space between lines is altered by a process called **leading** in order to make each column exactly the same length.

Graphics are the images used in desktop publishing. Either a graphic can be created or a ready-made graphics file can be imported into the DTP style sheet.

Electronic publishing requires close attention to details. Neither paragraphs nor pages should end with a dangling word, called a widow. Page breaks should facilitate the reader's eye moving smoothly from one page to the next.

FIGURE 4.18

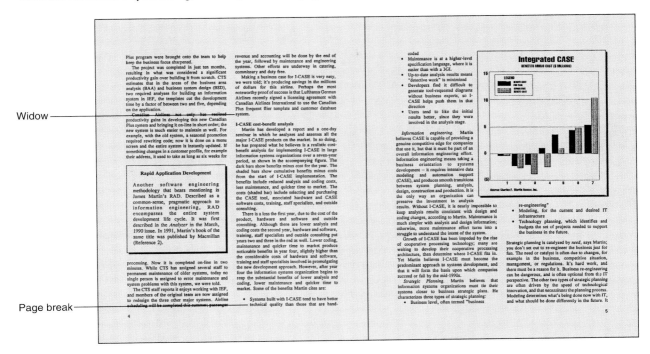

In addition, most DTP programs have a drawing program built in to create simple line drawings. Like text, graphic images are stored as files; often the DTP program comes with a selection of graphic images and clip art.

The graphic image can be edited and manipulated, the same as with text. It can be **sized** to fit in a predefined frame. It can be **cropped,** meaning leaving out portions such as superfluous background. And the image can be edited too, meaning it is possible to change the nature of the image — for example, drawing a mustache on the Mona Lisa!

Format is the step after all the text and graphics have been manipulated and set in place. Now we begin to use the DTP program in earnest, to design and create a professional document. Text must be checked to make sure margins are neat and that there are no **widows,** a single word on a line left dangling at the end of a paragraph. Similarly, a page break (or column break) must be checked. For example, you wouldn't want a paragraph to end at the top of a new page or column, nor would you want a chapter or topic heading to begin at the bottom of a page or column. Figure 4.18 shows examples of widows, page breaks, and column breaks to be avoided.

In addition, formatting often involves altering paragraph styles between type fonts or between plain, boldface, and italics. It also includes page styles. The most common page style is called **portrait** which is taller than it is wide. We commonly use 8½″ × 11″ paper in portrait style. The other is **landscape,** which simply means laying the sheet on its side; thus it is measured 11″ × 8½″. Using style sheets, we can combine the two in a single document.

Most DTP programs have a view feature that lets you see what the document will look like before you begin printing. In some cases there are multiple views: a single page, side-by-side pages, partial pages, and so forth. The most important step before printing is, of course, to save the file.

Printing is the final step, but one that takes on added dimensions in desktop publishing. Most people look forward with great anticipation to seeing what the finished product looks like, and with good reason. The text, with its various fonts or styles, combined with the graphic images, looks as if it just rolled off a printer's press. The print function lets you select if you want a single page or the whole document printed, continuously. It lets you print specific pages, such as just left or just right, or have the pages collated. In some cases you can print pages in reverse order. Some DTP programs will print cropping or printer's alignment marks as well.

KNOWLEDGE CHECK

1. What is the purpose of the frame in DTP layout?   p. 127
2. What is another name for the style sheet?   p. 127
3. What is the difference between kerning and leading text?   p. 127–28
4. When would you size and when would you crop a graphic image?   p. 129
5. Name two problems you should look for in editing.   p. 129
6. What is the difference between portrait and landscape?   p. 129
7. Name several ways DTP software make printing more versatile.   p. 130

THE DESKTOP PUBLISHING KEYBOARD, MOUSE, AND SCREEN

As with the graphic program you just studied, the desktop publishing keyboard and mouse permit more versatility, and the screen is highly visual. Unlike the other applications you've studied, a distinguishing characteristic of DTP is the fact that you work with several different types of data and manipulate it in many different ways.

THE KEYBOARD AND MOUSE

The keyboard is used to enter text and numbers, but the mouse plays an essential role when it comes to issuing commands and manipulating the program and data. A major reason for this is because DTP is a highly graphical application; another is that the amount of text changing, moving, and manipulation is made easier using mouse techniques. Therefore, the keyboard commands are often used in a secondary capacity or as a shortcut by experienced knowledge workers. For example, a command that requires pointing the mouse at a menu item and clicking its button is replicated on the keyboard by, say, the Ctrl-Alt-F key combination. Therefore, we'll concentrate on using the mouse and understanding its relationship to the screen. There are two ways the mouse is used: (1) to issue commands or initiate functions and (2) to manipulate the style sheet and data.

COMMANDS AND FUNCTIONS.   The mouse is used to issue commands or initiate functions by moving the pointer to the item on the menu bar and clicking. This usually invokes the pulldown menu with its additional commands and functions. An example is moving the mouse pointer to the File menu bar selection, then pulling down to OPEN (a file), and then moving the pointer to the next menu listing the data files.

MANIPULATING STYLE SHEETS AND DATA.   The mouse is used to control or change characteristics of the style sheet. When activated, it can draw frames, resize columns, and move text or graphic elements on the screen. It is also used to shift various portions of the style sheet into or out of view. The mouse is also used in much the same way as the cursor in word processing to enter, move, and delete textual and graphic data.

To help the knowledge worker understand its various manipulative "modes," in most DTP programs the mouse pointer changes from task to task. Figure 4.19 shows a few examples.

THE SCREEN

DTP brings out many of the computer's text and graphics capabilities, as you can see in Figure 4.20. Across the top of the screen is the menu bar. Just below is the Toolbox. These tools let you select from four work modes:

- *Frame mode* for creating frames.
- *Text mode* for working with text.

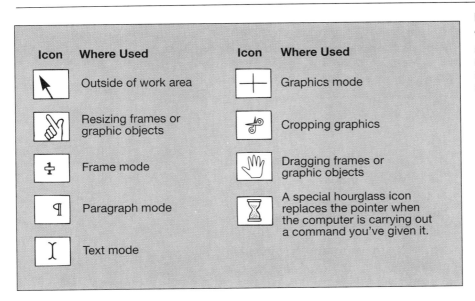

FIGURE 4.19

The program pointers. The shape of the pointer will change when it is in diffrent areas of the screen or is being used for different functions.

FIGURE 4.20

DTP publishing programs like PageMaker give you the tools to become writer, editor, typesetter, and printer.

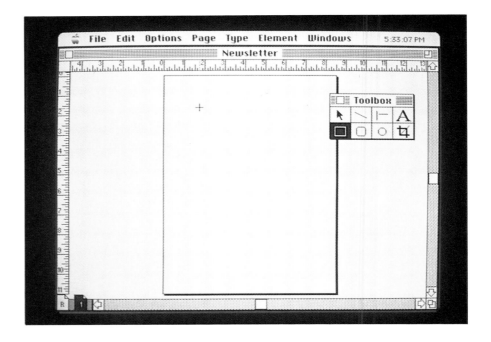

- *Paragraph mode* to create style sheets, select type fonts and sizes, design paragraphs, and so on.
- *Graphics mode* for using the drawing tools in the DTP program.

At the side and bottom of the screen you'll see the scrolling bars, which are used to position portions of the document in the viewing screen. By moving the pointer to any arrow and holding down the mouse button, it is possible to move the document up, down, left, or right. Note also the solid portion of the scroll bar; you can place the pointer on it and hold the mouse button down to click and drag the scroll bar, and thus the document, in the same way you used the arrows. **Click and drag** is a technique used with pointing devices, such as the mouse, to issue commands and accomplish tasks. Click and drag on the scroll bar is a simpler one; as we shall see, it has many uses.

KNOWLEDGE CHECK

1. Why is the mouse so useful in DTP?   p. 130
2. How is the mouse commonly used to invoke commands and functions?   p. 130
3. How is the mouse commonly used to manipulate data?   p. 131
4. What are the four most common DTP working modes?   pp. 131–32
5. What purpose do the scrolling bars serve?   p. 132

ADVANCED DESKTOP PUBLISHING

Desktop publishing provides many satisfactory returns for a significant investment of your time and attention. DTP programs are complex yet versatile tools that are capable of importing not only word processing files, but those of spreadsheets and DBMSs as well. The latest DTP programs are now compatible with Windows, making it possible to work consistently in a graphic computing environment.

MULTIMEDIA AND HYPERTEXT

Multimedia is the next step toward becoming totally conversant with the computer, as if it were a friend joining you for a stimulating conversation. **Multimedia** is sometimes referred to as *interactive,* which means it lets you and the computer engage in an ongoing exchange or presentation of information.

Multimedia is often thought of as a tool either for training and education or for personal entertainment. But Business Research, Inc., a business and technology research and information resource firm in Stowe, Vermont, has developed a multimedia information delivery system. BRI used to deliver its research and reports to clients in traditional, paper-based bound documents. However, upon querying people about their usefulness, BRI learned that most did not read the reports; that, since a specific report may contain up to 1,500 separate items, they were often impossible to update; and that the report was often difficult to locate when it was needed. Therefore, BRI concluded, a different way of *presenting and delivering information* was called for. The firm felt that the goal of presenting information was to make people more productive, and that data should be delivered in a way that provided greater efficiency than did paper.

BRI decided against using icons, menus, and windows — in other words, nothing should come between the user and the information. And further, that meant the technology itself should be utterly and completely transparent, whether it was hardware or software. This, BRI reasoned, was the true meaning of "multimedia." Figure 4.21 shows a BEST multimedia screen.

The BEST system uses a hypertext program to link and present information. **Hypertext** is software that dynamically associates words and concepts, so that searching for a specific word also produces other related words or text. For example, searching for "desert" may also produce "oil" and "Middle East." The BEST hypertext program combines information from a number of applications: text, graphics, imaging, still and full-motion video, audio (voice or music), and computer-aided design (CAD). The base machine is a PC-compatible, an IBM PS/2, or a Macintosh. Among the outboard accessories are an indexable VHS videocassette recorder/playback deck, a digital still-photo camera, and high-quality stereophonic speakers. The DOS machines use Windows as the operating environment, yet the user does not see it or manipulate it. And the system uses a wide variety of software: DBMS, graphics, hypertext, spreadsheet, CAD, communications, and utility programs.

To use the system there is a table of contents, which shows four choices: Alerts, Reports, BRI Anatomy, and News. Alerts are short items on new technology developments. By clicking on Reports, the user can read any or all

FIGURE 4.21

The BEST multimedia system represents the state of the art in combining text, graphics, sound, and video. Thus, knowledge workers can format and present information in the ways they find most useful.

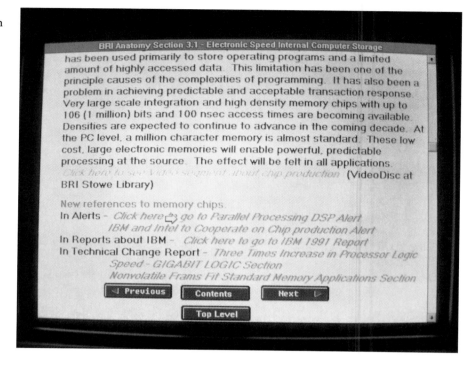

portions using a hypertext function, moving intuitively from topic to topic, either more deeply or tangentially into related topics.

Some information is presented as technical drawings and schematics, and provides an interesting feature of the system. Some reports have drawings embedded; they are not only easy to view but are often dynamic in nature, allowing the user to "click" deeper for more detail.

Samuel Harvey, who conceived the system, says it is based in part on comments made by Vannevar Bush, an early figure in computing at MIT, who wrote in his book *As We May Think:* "Publication has been extended far beyond our present ability to make real use of the record. A record, if it is to be useful to science, must be continuously extended, it must be stored, and above all it must be consulted." [2]

KNOWLEDGE CHECK

1. DTP programs can import files from what applications?   p. 133
2. What is another term for multimedia?   p. 133
3. What is hypertext used for?   p. 133
4. Name several applications that will run under multimedia.   p. 133
5. What is the output from multimedia?   pp. 133–34

---

[2] Vannevar Bush, "As We May Think," *The Atlantic Monthly,* 1945.

What Lies Ahead?

Word processing has grown more sophisticated, as we have moved from text- or character-based programs to the newest WYSIWYG entries on the market. Yet word processing has become more specialized too; there are hundreds of programs designed for all kinds of special purposes and uses. There are very simple programs, such as PFS-WRITE and Volkswriter, for occasional users. Q&A Write is an "executive word processor" for managers. Journalists and newspaper reporters have a program designed just for them, Xywrite. Scholars use Nota Bene, which is capable of preparing documents in several foreign languages. Thoughtline asks questions that help stimulate your thinking and then links ideas together into an outline that helps you get the writing ball rolling. At the top of the spectrum are the professional word processing programs (such as Ami Pro, WordPerfect, and Word for Windows) used mostly by knowledge workers; they have nearly every conceivable feature and capability.

We are on the threshold of computing with a pen, where instead of typing on a keyboard we use a special stylus to write directly on the computer's screen. In the not-so-distant future, we may use word processing programs that allow us to dictate our thoughts, ideas, and sentences into a microphone, almost magically transforming the spoken word into the written word. Yet for many, the mental and physical process that links brain and fingers, thoughts and words, eyes and monitor, are irreplaceable. It is as if they are still using a typewriter — albeit one far more powerful, efficient, ~~creative~~ ingenious, and ~~uuseful~~ useful!

Color desktop publishing is just ahead as well. Some DTP programs now have full color capability; it is the expense of color printing hardware that is still prohibitive. Xerox has introduced color laser printers for corporate users, but the complexity of working in color may inhibit the home desktop publisher for a few more years.

Word Processing Ethics: Plagiarism

Plagiarism is the theft and use of another person's original writing. You may have heard discussions at your college about plagiarism, for it has been around a long time. In the past, people would often plagiarize by copying another's writing from a book or a term paper. The Information Age and word processing make it even easier to plagiarize. For example, a college student loaned a fellow student the disk containing her bibliography for a term paper. He used it for his term paper and then passed it along to 10 other students. The professor saw identical bibliographies in their papers, and all received a reprimand for their actions. This means each student must take more stringent measures to avoid plagiarizing, even unintentionally.

It is common to see all kinds of information distributed on floppy disks and optical disks these days. This includes magazine articles, the works of William Shakespeare, and book excerpts — the list goes on and on. In addition, it is not uncommon to obtain information from electronic sources over the telephone lines.

All this information can easily be plagiarized, simply by copying portions of text into a word processor and creating a file. The plagiarist changes a few words, modifies some sentences, adds or deletes a paragraph here and there, and calls it an original work. But the plagiarist knows that he or she has committed an unethical act. And while a short-term goal has been met — getting a term paper in on time

CAREERS FOR KNOWLEDGE WORKERS
MARIA HOATH, WORD PROCESSING AUTHOR

Maria Hoath is a writer who uses word processing to write about word processing! As a student of journalism at the University of Georgia, Maria enrolled in an Introduction to Microcomputers course. Her interest was so great that she helped teach other students how to use personal computers and software applications. She used what she learned in this course to obtain a summer job as an office temporary, where she continued to improve her skills. "I felt that if I had computer skills I could make more than the minimum wage, and for someone going to college that was important," Maria says. "These skills opened up a world of opportunities for me."

Indeed they did, for Maria landed a job with a computer services company the following summer, followed by a part-time job during her junior year with a computer training and consulting firm. This company trained other companies' employees in how to use personal computers and software applications, and had a need for clear, well-written training materials. Maria was hired to write the training documentation. "Most people had a lot of difficulty with the manuals, so I wrote 'quick guides,' reference cards, and manuals for the applications they most often used. I liked this kind of writing

—the long-term goal of acquiring knowledge through the learning process and disseminating it through the effective use of language has not. Plagiarism, like other unethical acts, really hurts the plagiarist most of all.

A recent college graduate was hired as associate editor of a well-known investment advice newsletter. Key to the newsletter's success was its original insights into the market and its unique perspective on how to invest. This young woman worked hard but often ran late on her deadlines. Afraid she would not have her article done in time, she plagiarized an article from a magazine published by an investment services company, typing it into her word processor as an original piece. The editor immediately sensed the lack of insight in the work and challenged its originality. The young woman confessed she had plagiarized the work. Although her editor understood the reason, it was grounds for dismissal. The writer couldn't be trusted to report and write ethically and responsibly again.

and found out that there were only a few people who did it."

Maria continued to hone her skills in her senior year as a co-op student, working as a consultant in the training services department for a large utility company. When she graduated, she was hired by a computer training firm as an instructor. Six months later the utility created an opening for a technical writer, and Maria was their first choice. Working with two others, Maria helped shape the new department and within a year was made director of technical writing, managing a staff of seven.

Maria developed some fundamental concepts about how manuals should be written. First, they should be task-oriented, showing how to use software rather than explaining how the software works. Second, there should be consistency in the way

tasks are explained, so that students see the relationship between the functions, keystrokes, and tasks. This consistency extended to all the corporate manuals, making it easier to learn new applications.

By 1990, Maria had a thorough knowledge and understanding of all the popular personal computer applications. She wanted to try her hand at writing a book, "to see what it was like." She studied *Writer's Market* and learned she needed to write a proposal explaining the book's purpose, along with several sample chapters, to show to publishers. After choosing WordPerfect 5.1 as her topic, she sent the proposal and chapters to 10 publishers. It was accepted and published by a small publisher in Texas "who gave me a lot of personal attention," says Maria.

Since then, Maria Hoath has written several more books and articles for computer magazines. Today she has a literary agent who takes care of the business details of her writing contracts, and is often approached by publishers asking her to write for them. Her most recent book, *Inside Ami Pro: Tips and Techniques,* concerns one of the new breed of graphical word processing programs. "Ami Pro is an amazing software product that makes its most powerful features easy to use," she says, "but that doesn't mean people don't need training. I know this from experience.

"Anyone who wants to work in business today must be computer-literate," Maria continues. "You must be confortable working with computers, for no matter what field you go into, you're going to be using one."

SUMMARY

1. *Explain why it is important for knowledge workers to know how to use word processing.* Working with words and information, ideas and text, is critical to job success. Word processing is the most popular computer-based application for this purpose.

2. *Describe how word processing is used to create various types of documents.* There are many kinds of documents, from personal (poetry, short stories) to business (memos, forms, reports). Documents must be error-free and must conform to standards; word processing is a way to ensure this. Word processing also makes document preparation and management more productive.

3. *Explain the five steps involved in using word processing.* Word processing is a software application designed to write, revise, format, save, and print documents. We can write continuously because

of word wrap and scrolling. Each revision is a new draft. Formatting lets us emphasize and arrange text. Saving the document to a file is most important. Printing gives us a paper (hard copy) document.

4. *Explain the four phases of the writing/word processing process.* Prewriting helps you brainstorm, plan, and research your work. Word processing is the act of writing, using the software. Revision is the work done once the first draft is completed. Printing gives us hard copy.

5. *Describe the word processing keyboard and screen.* The keyboard is organized into the typing keys; the function keys to perform commands and tasks; the cursor movement keys; and the numeric keypad. The screen may contain a status line, title line, menu line, icon bar, and scrolling bars, and it always contains a work area. The cursor tells us our position in the text, and is also used to issue commands.

6. *Understand how to use the commands and steps involved in creating, formatting, revising, saving, retrieving, and printing a document.* Creating a document means keying in text. Simple formatting means centering text or indenting paragraphs.

Revising involves block editing, changing text appearance, copying or moving text, saving text, deleting text, undeleting text, and search and replace. Saving the file should be done often, every five minutes or after every page. Once a file is saved, it can be safely retrieved and revised. Printing the finished document is the final step.

7. *Describe some advanced word processing tools and how they are used.* Advanced word processing tools give us additional capabilities. The most common one is the spelling checker, closely followed by the thesaurus. The macro helps us automate repetitive keystrokes for commands and text. Many page design tools, such as fonts, graphics, and multiple columns, help us make our documents more attractive.

8. *Understand the difference between corporate electronic publishing and desktop publishing.* Corporate electronic publishing often utilizes dedicated systems that permit working with more complex or longer documents.

9. *Explain the steps in creating a desktop publishing document.* The steps are: design the layout; create the text; create and position the graphics; format the document; and print.

ISSUES WITH WORDS AND TEXT

1. Science tells us that the average human is able to memorize 10 basic commands or key combinations associated with using an application. There are also certain conventions that are common to the way we use computers, such as pressing the Enter key after issuing a command. How do these apply to the concept of "ease of use"? Should a word processing program have the most important commands on the first 10 function keys? When should a command be on a toggle key, and when should it use the Enter key? What is ease of use?

2. Computers are supposed to help us do things better, faster, and cheaper. However, some of the most popular word processing programs require extensive training. How can we evaluate the advantages in using computers and word processing against the human costs, in both time and money, of learning how to use them?

3. Plagiarism is unethical behavior. Is there ever a time when it is OK to use someone else's writing in your documents? How should that be properly done? How would you feel if you saw something you had written in a document another student or coworker submitted as his or her own original work? Is it plagiarism to reuse something that you previously wrote?

4. It often takes a great deal of time to learn a new software application; indeed, some require extensive, expensive training. Moving to graphics software, especially desktop publishing, is a considerable investment in time as well as system cost. Do you feel it's worth it? Should all knowledge workers learn these more complex programs, or should there be a special DTP staff?

CHAPTER REVIEW QUESTIONS

REVIEW QUESTIONS

1. How has word processing changed the way knowledge workers work with words, ideas, and information?
2. What are the five advantages of word processing over manual forms of writing?
3. Discuss the advantages in word wrap and scrolling.
4. Why is it necessary or important to work with separate drafts?
5. What makes the spelling checker a versatile tool?
6. How do macros make a knowledge worker more productive?
7. What are some uses for the style sheet?
8. When would you use word processing, as opposed to desktop publishing?

DISCUSSION QUESTIONS

1. Discuss the importance of working with words in business.
2. Discuss ways in which you would use the word processing advantages of formatting words, lines, pages, and documents.
3. Discuss why it is important to use and save successive drafts.
4. Discuss the relationship between procedures, data, and information as they pertain to word processing.
5. Why is prewriting so important? Discuss the advantages to prewriting with pen and paper over doing it on the word processing screen.
6. Discuss the advantages of the keyboard and its function keys versus using the mouse and pull-down menus.
7. Discuss what you feel are the most important word processing tips. Why did you choose those particular tips?
8. Discuss how corporate electronic publishing will differ from desktop publishing in the near future.

MULTIPLE-CHOICE

1. A document may take the form of:
   a. A poem.
   b. A letter.
   c. A memo.
   d. An invoice.
   e. All the above.
2. Hard copy is important because (check all that apply):
   a. It can be used as evidence.
   b. If you lose the disk file, you have paper.
   c. It can be shared conveniently with others.
   d. It justifies the cost of a printer.
   e. All the above.
3. WYSIWYG (check all that apply):
   a. Makes commands graphical.
   b. Only works on the Macintosh.
   c. Makes good use of a color monitor.
   d. Doesn't require the use of toggle on/off keys.
   e. Is more fun to use.
4. The advantages of a typeset versus typewritten document are:
   a. It looks more professional.
   b. It takes advantage of different type styles.
   c. It can include graphic images.
   d. It is ready for printing.
   e. All the above.
5. Multimedia (check all that apply):
   a. Is only for training and education.
   b. Is a very sophisticated form of electronic publishing.
   c. Allows mixing movies and sound with text and graphics.
   d. Only runs on PCs with Windows.
   e. Takes good advantage of hypertext.

FILL-IN-THE-BLANK

1. Structured information is often called a
   _____.

2. Some _____ have more immediate
   value than long-term value.

3. The most popular keyboard is the
   _____; its counterpart is the
   _____ keyboard.

4. WYSIWYG stands for _____.

5. Multimedia is the computer's way of presenting text, graphics, imaging, video, and audio
   _____ together.

TRUE/FALSE

1. A document's value is based on its content.

2. Word wrap and scrolling are most important
   when you have long sentences.

3. A file should be saved to disk at least once a day.

4. The main advantage in waiting for a period of
   time to revise a document is that it will be permanently stored on disk.

KEY TERMS

The Spreadsheet and Presentation Graphics

LEARNING OBJECTIVES

After reading and studying this chapter, you should be able to:

1. Explain what a spreadsheet is and how a spreadsheet program works.
2. Describe the different uses for a spreadsheet.
3. Identify the various characteristics of the spreadsheet screen.
4. Explain the steps in creating and editing a spreadsheet.
5. Name some of the advanced functions and features of the spreadsheet.
6. Describe the various types of graphics software.
7. Describe the computer graphics keyboard, mouse, and screen.
8. Explain the steps in creating presentation graphics.

The Knowledge Worker and the Spreadsheet

In the previous chapter, you learned how knowledge workers work with ideas and words. In this chapter, you'll learn how to work with numbers, the second most important "language" of the modern office. Working with numbers isn't new; the Babylonians were proficient in arithmetic more than 4,000 years ago. They developed a number system that used 60 as a base and included place values. (For a complete discussion of number systems, see Appendix A.) This base-60 system was used to measure time, assigning 60 seconds to each minute, 60 minutes to each hour and so forth.

The Hindu-Arabic base-10 number system (Figure 5.1) we use today was developed by the Hindus and brought to Europe by the Arabs before the year A.D. 1200. Ten was used as a base, or conversion point, probably because a person has 10 fingers. (Europe, however, used Roman numerals — I, II, III, IV, and so forth — until the 17th century.) The major advantage of the Hindu-Arabic system over other number systems is the inclusion of a zero; this permits using the decimal place, so we can also count below whole numbers while still using only 10 different symbols.

The base-10 system is obviously the one used most often for measuring the value of money, what business terms *keeping a record of accounts*. Accounting is the orderly, systematic compilation of financial information used in making economic decisions. Accountants record the monetary value of business events and transactions, then organize, summarize, and communicate the information in the form of financial statements. Accountants frequently interpret this financial information in reports that explain trends and suggest various future courses of action.

In the 1700s, businesses began recording financial transactions, such as credits and debits, in a large book called an *accountant's ledger*. Each page in the ledger book was called a *columnar page* or **ledger sheet** because there were a number of vertical **columns** running down the page. In addition, lines drawn across the page created **rows** running from left to right. A typical blank ledger sheet is shown in Figure 5.2.

As business grew more sophisticated and complex, columnar or ledger sheets were used for other purposes besides just calculating the company's profits and losses. They were used to keep track of manufacturing, advertising, and research and development costs. They were used to calculate interest, taxes, salaries, and sales figures. They were used for tracking a company's current financial picture, but also by management to project what would occur in the future.

Over the years, the green-tinted ledger sheet grew in size to accommodate these more complex financial situations. As ledger sheets grew in size, they also became more complex to work with. People created ledger sheets with

FIGURE 5.1

The Hindu-Arabic base-10 number system is the basis for our financial system.

Arabic	Roman	Arabic	Roman	Arabic	Roman
1	I	16	XVI	90	XC
2	II	17	XVII	100	C
3	III	18	XVIII	200	CC
4	IV	19	XIX	300	CCC
5	V	20	XX	400	CD
6	VI	21	XXI	500	D
7	VII	22	XXII	600	DC
8	VIII	23	XXIII	700	DCC
9	IX	24	XXIV	800	DCCC
10	X	30	XXX	900	CM
11	XI	40	XL	1,000	M
12	XII	50	L	2,000	MM
13	XIII	60	LX	3,000	MMM
14	XIV	70	LXX	4,000	M̄V̄
15	XV	80	LXXX	5,000	(V̄ (or ϑ)

FIGURE 5.2

Tabula rasa: the blank ledger sheet is the model for the spreadsheet screen.

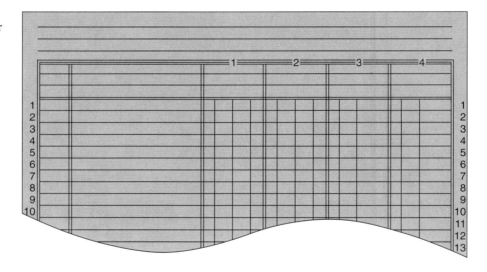

pencils and erasers for many years, working with columns and rows of figures they had to total either by hand or by using an electronic calculator. If an incorrect number was written into one of the boxes, or if projections changed, it meant a great deal of tedious erasing, refiguring, and recalculating — that is, until the electronic spreadsheet came along.

An electronic spreadsheet, or simply a **spreadsheet,** is an application that uses mathematical formulas to perform calculations on data arranged in a matrix or grid. It is the software version of the paper ledger sheet. A spreadsheet has the same columns and rows as a ledger sheet and serves the same purpose as its paper counterpart. The spreadsheet is a very popular application with more than just accountants and auditors. Now anyone, from marketing managers to automobile salespeople to corporate financial officers, can take advantage of a spreadsheet program.

YESTERDAY

BIRTH OF THE SPREADSHEET

The spreadsheet is an interesting example of creating a software application to solve a problem. In 1978, Dan Bricklin was a student in the Master's of Business Administration program at Harvard University. Like the other MBA students, Dan had to use paper, pencil, and calculator to solve problems posed in the case studies. There had to be a better way, he thought. Couldn't a computer help? Dan asked Bob Frankston, a programmer friend, if he could help solve the problem.

Frankston was fascinated with the idea of creating a new kind of software program. "Our goal was to provide a high-performance tool that would allow financial planners the same kind of flexibility enjoyed by people using word processors," Frankston said. He worked every night, pounding the keys of his Apple II in his attic apartment, and then slept all day. By January 1979, Frankston was done. Bricklin chose the name VisiCalc (for Visible

Calculator), and he and Frankston formed a company named Software Arts to market it.

VisiCalc was a success because it helped people do their work more efficiently. News of the spreadsheet traveled slowly at first; then in 1981, VisiCalc took off. Businesspeople flocked to computer stores to buy Apple IIs just so they could use it. Software Arts' 1981 sales projections (prepared using VisiCalc) had to be revised from $1 million to $2 million, then to $2.5 million, then to $3 million!

But it wasn't long until along came another spreadsheet — 1-2-3® from Lotus Development Corp. As its name implies, it was three separate programs that all worked together. This was called *integrated software*. Integrated software makes it relatively easy to switch from one program to another and to share data between programs; we'll learn more about integrated software in Chapter 7.

The primary application in 1-2-3 is the spreadsheet. There is

a graphics program that transforms spreadsheet data into pictorial representations commonly used by businesspeople. There is also a database management program for keeping track of simple information such as addresses or telephone numbers. Even though it is integrated software, users worked with the spreadsheet more than the other programs. Lotus 1-2-3 debuted in 1983 and, by this time, corporate America had made the IBM Personal Computer its machine of choice. This caused Lotus 1-2-3 to shoot to the top of the software best-seller list, where it has remained ever since.

Between VisiCalc and Lotus 1-2-3, the spreadsheet program is generally considered the reason for the personal computer's enthusiastic acceptance in the business world. Even though word processing is still the most widely used application in businesses large and small, the spreadsheet is a very close second.

WORKING WITH A SPREADSHEET

The spreadsheet's principal task is performing calculations, which it does very efficiently. The spreadsheet combines the paper ledger sheet, the pencil, and an electronic calculator to provide several advantages over its paper counterpart. For example, the electronic ledger sheet is much larger. Where the largest paper ledger sheets have about 30 columns and 51 rows, a modern spreadsheet usually has at least 255 columns and 255 rows.

The spreadsheet is designed to work with numbers and mathematical formulas. A **formula** is a mathematical statement that sets up a calculation with values. A **value** is a quantity assigned to a variable, or simply a number. The simplest formula is $A + B$, where the letters A and B represent values (variables) that can change. A formula is different from a mathematical *problem,* such as $1 + 2$, where the values are numbers. Although a spreadsheet can solve a math problem with ease, its real advantage lies in storing the formula while allowing you to change the variable values at will.

Other advantages include speed and convenience. The spreadsheet's calculator is built in, so it can total a column of figures in less than a second; if you want to correct or insert another value, it will give you the new total just as quickly. All adding, subtracting, multiplying, dividing, and many other mathematical functions are performed automatically. A **function** is a formula or set of formulas already created and programmed into the spreadsheet for you to use. These formulas perform mathematical, financial, statistical, and other functions to quickly produce a mathematical result or value. We'll learn more about functions and values later in this chapter.

The spreadsheet makes it possible to speculate about the financial future. In the same way that we can quickly retotal a column of numbers when a mistake has been made, we can test a variety of financial models. A **financial model** is a mathematical representation of a real-world financial or economic situation used to test different hypotheses in order to find a solution.

One of the stranger events involving a computer model occurred in Boston in 1970. The "World Dynamics Model" was intended to help the mayor solve some of the problems confronting a large city, but its conclusions proved somewhat puzzling. For example, aiding the unemployed, the program concluded, would draw more unemployed people to the city. This in turn would cause the planned social reforms to backfire. For example, free public transportation would result in overcrowded subways, creating more traffic from commuting workers. And building city-funded housing would take up space that businesses would have occupied, resulting in fewer jobs. Ultimately, the model was useful because it raised issues that city planners had not considered.

Using the spreadsheet for financial modeling is called performing a what-if analysis. A **what-if analysis** involves substituting one number for another to see what difference it will make. For example, *what if* the company has a 20 percent increase in sales next year? *What if* we build a new manufacturing facility with twice our current capacity? *What if* we decide to raise or lower the price of our product by 6 percent? Numerical data can be replaced easily in the spreadsheet to see what would happen in such scenarios. The ability to perform what-if analyses and test different speculative financial models is one of the spreadsheet's most useful features. It has provided business with a powerful planning tool that is used extensively. What-if analysis has become a common business term.

Knowledge Check

1. The spreadsheet is the software version of what kind of paper form? p. 144
2. What three tools does the spreadsheet combine?   p. 145
3. What is a formula?   pp. 145–46
4. What is the difference between a value and a number?   p. 146

5. What type of model can the spreadsheet create?   p. 146
6. In what way does the spreadsheet's handling of functions and values differ from the calculator's?   p. 146
7. What type of analysis feature does the spreadsheet employ for speculating about the financial future?   p. 146

WHAT IS AN ELECTRONIC SPREADSHEET?

The spreadsheet makes it possible to create a visual, mathematical model of a specific financial situation on the personal computer's screen. A model is a replica or copy that can be tested or charged without disturbing the original, in the same way an engineer creates a model of an auto or an airplane. The spreadsheet model is financial; thus it involves the use of mathematical numbers and equations.

Consider a model used to compute a company's sales figures. The spreadsheet stores sales by month. At the end of the year, sales are totaled, costs are subtracted, and the resulting figure is profits. Now management can use the spreadsheet to plan next year's sales. If the sales force sells 20 percent more this year than last, what will the company earn in profits? The spreadsheet will quickly calculate the new figures. This is a simple mathematical model, and it is possible to get all this information and more using a spreadsheet.

The spreadsheet was the first software program originally developed for the personal computer; later it was adapted for use on larger computers (see the Yesterday feature). Before this, most software was first created for mainframes, and later adapted to run on minicomputers and then on personal computers. There were other kinds of specialized financial software programs available for mainframes and minis, but there was nothing quite like the spreadsheet.

Like word processing, the spreadsheet has distinct advantages over other, noncomputerized calculating methods. There are five steps in using the spreadsheet: creating the worksheet, organizing it, revising it, saving it, and printing the results.

CREATING

The spreadsheet makes working with numbers much more efficient than working with a paper ledger. *Creating* a spreadsheet means putting all the information we need to work with—both words and numbers—into the proper form. Automating the process of entering letters and numbers means no more pencils; the computer's penmanship is always readable. Further, mistakes are much easier to correct than on paper, so no more erasers. The spreadsheet can be made almost infinitely large, so the size of the paper is no longer a constraint.

ORGANIZING

Organizing the spreadsheet involves entering the formulas in the appropriate places, so they may perform the proper calculations on the values and numbers. Using a calculator, the numbers and formulas must be rekeyed every time a new calculation is made. Again, the spreadsheet shows its superior ease and convenience of use by automating this process, so that formulas need only be entered once to be used again and again.

REVISING

Revising a spreadsheet is almost as easy as creating and organizing one. Like word processing, *revising* means changing something, whether it is words, numbers, or formulas. Since all these changes can be simply made by typing them in, where they appear on the computer screen, we can have new results in moments. Making changes on a paper ledger sheet is arduous, to say the least. What's more, we are likely to make fewer errors using the spreadsheet, since values that don't change needn't be rewritten.

SAVING

The computer's ability to *save* our work in files makes using the spreadsheet a distinct advantage over using paper. Instead of having to erase and rewrite, or copy information from one ledger sheet to another, the spreadsheet lets us quickly and easily save each version in a separate file. This is particularly handy when a large quantity of data, or many formulas, are in use. Saving at intervals makes it much easier to save different versions of a what-if analysis, or to find where a mistake was made. Again, the need to save your work frequently cannot be overemphasized.

PRINTING

Printing lets us see the results of our work in hard copy. It gives us a permanent paper record in case the computer file is lost or destroyed. It provides another important advantage when working with spreadsheets as well. Often, many knowledge workers are involved in the financial planning process, and each needs to study the results. It is quick and easy to print (or copy) legible, easy-to-read spreadsheets that display important formulas, so that fellow knowledge workers understand how you arrived at your results. This not only saves time explaining your work in meetings, but it also gives others the opportunity to suggest improvements in the spreadsheet construction or formulas.

KNOWLEDGE CHECK

1. What language do we use when working with the spreadsheet?   p. 147
2. Describe several advantages to working with a spreadsheet instead of a paper ledger sheet.   p. 147
3. What do we work with when we create a spreadsheet?   p. 147
4. What do we work with when we organize a spreadsheet?   p. 147
5. Describe some advantages of the spreadsheet revision process.   p. 148
6. Describe an additional benefit in the process of saving a spreadsheet.   p. 149

THE SPREADSHEET PROCESS

The first modern digital computer was used to perform tedious logarithmic calculations. Today's fastest supercomputers are also used to perform complex calculations and sophisticated modeling. Therefore, as we use the spreadsheet we will see the computer doing what, in a sense, it knows how to do best: perform calculations very quickly. The procedures we must follow are to enter the formulas and values very carefully, so that we get the most accurate results. For that reason, it's useful to understand the spreadsheet process shown in Figure 5.3.

There are four steps in the spreadsheet process. It begins with *worksheet design,* which most knowledge workers do with paper and pencil. The **worksheet** is the document we work on using the spreadsheet program. This is the planning phase, where such things as the spreadsheet's objective, size, and complexity are determined. How many columns will it have? How many rows? Will the column or row contents be described or labeled? What formulas will be needed for totaling columns or other more complex mathematical functions? Finally, what is the objective — what precisely do we wish to obtain from the spreadsheet once it's built? It is much easier to work out and finalize these details on paper before setting up the spreadsheet on the computer monitor.

The next step is creating the worksheet, which is the actual work of building it as described in the design phase. As we enter the words, values, formulas, and so forth, we begin to see the worksheet take form and shape. After finish-

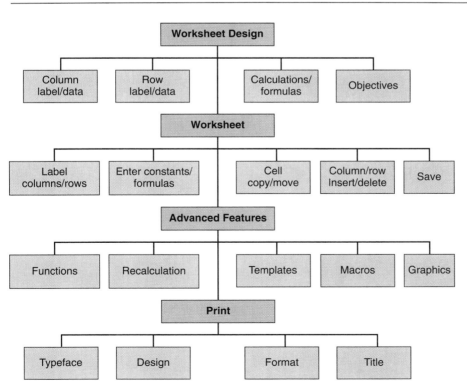

FIGURE 5.3
The spreadsheet process.

ing certain stages, it makes sense to save our work. The last step is saving the finished version.

Commands issue instructions to the spreadsheet program to perform tasks or manipulate the design of the spreadsheet itself. Most commands are issued by you, the knowledge worker. Here are some of the most commonly used commands.

COPY, sometimes called REPLICATE, copies the contents of a cell or group of cells into another cell or group of cells.

DELETE removes a column or a row.

INSERT adds a row or column; it is the opposite of DELETE.

MOVE takes the contents of a cell or group of cells and moves it into another cell or group of cells.

RETRIEVE gets a spreadsheet file you have previously created and saved, and displays it on the screen.

SAVE safely stores on disk the spreadsheet file you are currently working on.

PRINT prints your spreadsheet.

There is an additional spreadsheet command that is frequently in use, but is not normally executed by the knowledge worker. It is **CALCULATE,** a command built into the spreadsheet's operation. Say you have entered the proper constants and formula to add the contents of five cells. By pressing the Enter key in most spreadsheet programs, calculation occurs automatically.

The third step is using *advanced features,* which make our work go more smoothly or efficiently, or make the information we produce more useful. There are special spreadsheet functions that combine several different mathematical tasks into just a few keystrokes. As we shall see, recalculation is a powerful tool when performing what-if analyses. Templates are the recyclable building blocks of the spreadsheet. Spreadsheet macros perform tasks similar to word processing macros, and the graphic feature turns rows of numbers into businesslike charts and graphs.

The fourth step is *printing,* which involves the way we present information to others. Therefore, it is possible to make the spreadsheet look very professional and attractive in this step. There are different typefaces to choose from, not only for the spreadsheet but for its title. It is possible to format the information (for example, use it within a report written in word processing) or to combine a spreadsheet with a graphical depiction of its numerical data, such as a pie chart. As you can see, the spreadsheet is a useful and versatile tool for knowledge workers. To use it properly, we must become familiar with the keyboard and screen.

KNOWLEDGE CHECK

1. Why should the spreadsheet design process be done on paper?   p. 149
2. Describe some examples of the objective for a spreadsheet.   p. 149
3. Why does it make sense to build the spreadsheet in versions? pp. 149–50
4. What do functions do?   p. 150
5. Why are there different print options?   p. 150

THE SPREADSHEET KEYBOARD AND SCREEN

The spreadsheet replaces three manual tools for working with numbers: the ledger sheet, the pencil, and the calculator, shown in Figure 5.4. The ledger sheet is what you see on the computer screen. The keyboard or mouse takes the place of the pencil. The calculator is actually your personal computer's microprocessor — to be more precise, its arithmetic-logic unit or ALU. It's activated by the spreadsheet software when you issue certain commands to the spreadsheet called formulas.

While you're already familiar with the keyboard layout from Chapter 4, using the spreadsheet application shifts the emphasis to different keys. And, while the basic areas of the screen are similar, we use the screen and cursor differently than in word processing. In addition, many modern spreadsheets now have graphic, or WYSIWYG, capabilities, which permit using various type fonts and graphics on the screen while you work.

THE SPREADSHEET KEYBOARD

We use the numeric keypad extensively with the spreadsheet, so to make our work easier we can simply toggle the Num Lock key on. Now the numbers, instead of the cursor movements, are activated. The Enter key serves the same purpose as the other key of the same name, but it is more convenient to use. Most spreadsheet programs utilize the Function keys, and permit using Esc to stop or reverse the last activity. In addition, many spreadsheet programs identify a key that can be used to activate the menu on the screen. A common key used for this purpose is the diagonal or / key. Once the menu appears, commands may be selected by pressing the key corresponding to the first letter, such as "W" for "Worksheet."

FIGURE 5.4

Before the advent of the spreadsheet, these were the tools for working with numbers.

Some of the more modern spreadsheet programs take advantage of the mouse, which is often used in place of the / key to activate the menu. Many people find it easier and quicker to move the mouse pointer to the desired command and click the mouse button to activate it. The mouse also permits moving around the work area.

THE SPREADSHEET SCREEN

While sharing some things in common with its paper counterpart, such as columns and rows, the spreadsheet has a slightly different look and feel. A paper ledger sheet is static; the lines are drawn and you can't change them. It's quite another case with the spreadsheet. Let's see why. Refer to Figure 5.5 as we explain the spreadsheet screen's features.

COLUMNS AND ROWS.   The spreadsheet has a border that runs horizontally across the top of the screen, and vertically down the left-hand margin. The horizontal border displays the columns, which are designated with the letters of the alphabet: A, B, C, and so on. Once the columns reach Z, they begin again with AA, AB, AC, and so on. The vertical border displays the rows, which are numbered 1, 2, 3, and so on.

Columns are commonly used to create time categories such as months or years. For example, in a spreadsheet for managing a personal budget, the first column might start with September and end with June. Columns are designed in a uniform width, but you can widen them when necessary. People often

---

FIGURE 5.5   The spreadsheet screen displays a great deal of information. Labels, constants, and formulas are essential for understanding and working with the data in spreadsheet cells.

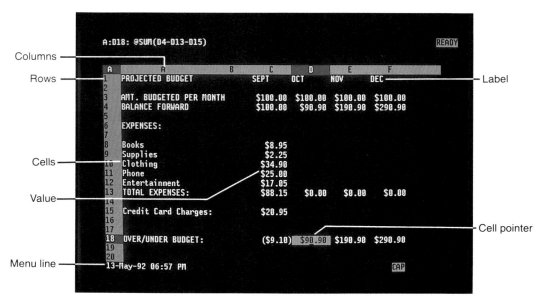

widen the first column so they can type in words or phrases to identify the columns that follow.

Rows are commonly used for listing entities such as sales regions, companies the firm does business with, or areas of expenditures such as manufacturing, marketing, and shipping. In a personal budget, the rows might list such things as clothing, entertainment, books, and supplies. There is no need to change the size of a row, since the cell content is always typed on a line by itself to the width of the column.

CELLS.   On the ledger sheet, the vertical columns and horizontal rows form squares on the paper. In the spreadsheet, this square is called a **cell,** indicating a place where we can type in data. Usually, there are no visible lines separating them. Cells are identified by their column-and-row position. For example, when you begin working with a new spreadsheet, the command line shows the pointer is located in column A, row 1, so the cell designation is "A1."

CELL POINTER.   The **cell pointer** takes the place of the cursor found in other programs. The cell pointer illuminates the particular cell it is located in, to indicate where data may be entered. If your computer has a green monochrome monitor, the cell pointer glows green, as if reminding us of the accountant's green ledger sheet paper and green eyeshade. The arrow keys or the mouse can be used to move the pointer from cell to cell. Other keys move the pointer to specific locations such as the home cell, A1, or to a particular cell such as B155.

When the cell pointer is positioned in a cell, its contents appear on the status line. If there is a formula in a particular cell, the number is highlighted by the pointer, while the formula appears on the status line. Therefore, if the answer is incorrect the formula can be checked for accuracy.

LABELS AND VALUES.   Cells may contain labels or values. **Label** is the term used to refer to text in a spreadsheet. As you already know, values are numbers and they take two forms. One is the **constant,** the raw number or data we enter for processing. The other is the mathematical formula used for performing calculations on the constants. For example, say the constant 12 is in cell A1 and the constant 24 is in cell A2. Using the formula $+A1+A2$, we can arrive at the answer, 36. Any time the cell contains a constant, that is what we see.

MENU LINE AND COMMAND LINE.   Most spreadsheet programs display some type of **menu line,** which lists a description of commands and other valuable information about the spreadsheet. Sometimes it is at the top of the screen; other spreadsheet programs display it below the spreadsheet itself. Some programs show the menu line on the screen at all times; others require that you press a key, commonly the diagonal or / mark, to display it.

The **command line,** as its name implies, displays the commands we use to work with the spreadsheet. It too may be either above or below the spreadsheet. The command line is usually easy to recognize because the first item indicates which cell the pointer is in, as determined by the column and row identifiers—A1, C3, and so on.

The command line commonly shows the contents of the cell the pointer is positioned in, a label (text) or a value (either a constant or a formula). This is sometimes referred to as the **status line,** whether it is combined with or separate from the command line. The formula is not displayed in the cell itself; it is usually seen only in the command line. You can enter either a label or a value at the command line. If you enter a label or a constant, such as "February," that is what you will see in the cell. If you enter a formula, the cell will display only the constant that results from calculating that formula. The formula itself may contain constants and/or another formula but not a label. The formula can act only on numbers, not text. Figure 5.5 shows how the spreadsheet displays labels, constants, and formulas.

The command line also displays the commands used in creating a spreadsheet for such tasks as entering data, editing, copying, printing, and saving the completed work. The command line may display other information too, such as the data and time or the status of certain special keys on your keyboard, for example, Num Lock. We'll learn more about commands when we begin creating our own spreadsheet.

SCROLLING WINDOW. You may remember we said there are hundreds of cells in the average paper ledger sheet (30 columns and 51 rows). The average spreadsheet program contains as many as half a million cells; one claims to have a billion! That's great, but how can you possibly see all of them? With a scrolling window, as shown in Figure 5.6, you see only a portion of the spreadsheet on the screen. The pointer and page movement keys allow you to scroll from left to right and up and down, moving to the different areas of the spreadsheet as you enter labels or values into the cells. In most cases, you fill the cells in the portion of the spreadsheet visible on the screen, then scroll to the right or downward to continue filling more cells. As your spreadsheet grows larger than a single screen, you can use other commands that shift the spreadsheet an entire screen or permit jumping to a particular cell such as L22 or BB655.

FIGURE 5.6

The spreadsheet's scrolling window functions similarly to the word processing scrolling window; however, its dimensions are often much greater.

Monitor

Spreadsheet/ ledger sheet

■
KNOWLEDGE
CHECK

1. What keys do we use more frequently with a spreadsheet, and how do we activate them?   pp. 151–52
2. What key commonly activates the menu?   p. 151
3. In the spreadsheet grid, what do the vertical lines form?   p. 152
4. In the spreadsheet grid, what do the horizontal lines form?   p. 152
5. What is the box formed by a column and a row called?   p. 153
6. What is the cursor called in a spreadsheet program?   p. 153
7. What is the term used to refer to text? To numbers?   p. 153
8. Where do we see commands and instructions on the screen?   p. 153
9. What is the purpose of the scrolling window?   p. 154

USING ADVANCED SPREADSHEET FEATURES

When someone becomes proficient with a particular application and a computer, they are often referred to as a *power user*. As you learned in the previous chapter on word processing, there are special advanced features that help you work more efficiently with an application program and its data. This is also true with spreadsheet software. Let's look at some of the most commonly used power-user spreadsheet features.

FUNCTIONS

A function combines built-in formulas that perform special mathematical tasks for us with a minimum of keystrokes. Functions, like formulas, work with the data in the spreadsheet, as opposed to commands, which work with the spreadsheet itself. In some spreadsheet programs, the function is typed in at the command line; in others, a special key such as the @ sign is used to activate a function. The following are the five most common functions:

1. AVERAGE (@AVG) takes the average of a set of constants.
2. COUNT (@COUNT) literally counts or tallies the contents of cells, for example, the number of cells with a dollar amount of $5 or more.
3. MAXIMUM (@MAX) gets the greatest number within a range of cells.
4. MINIMUM (@MIN) gets the lowest number within a range of cells.
5. SUM (@SUM) totals the contents of a range of cells.

@AVG is one of the most useful functions, since knowledge workers are often interested in averages—the average cost of a procured item over time, the average sales figures for all 12 territories, etc.

RECALCULATION

Recalculate, or recalc, refigures your spreadsheet whenever you make a change. It is one of the spreadsheet's most powerful features, working in place of an eraser and pencil to make corrections and updates. If you have to change

TODAY

SPREADSHEET AND PRESENTATION GRAPHICS TIPS

Spreadsheet

1. Plan your spreadsheet on paper before you begin working with the program on the computer. Think through the problem you want to solve, drawing a rough sketch of the data on a sheet of blank paper or a ledger sheet. Jot down the mathematical equations you'll need to come up with answers. This saves you a great deal of time, and you'll make fewer mistakes.

2. Learn to use macros to record, save, and reuse formulas, equations, labels, and such. A macro lets you fill a cell with data by tapping a key or two, rather than dozens or hundreds of keystrokes. In addition, macros are a way to customize your keyboard.

3. Use COPY or REPLICATE when you need to copy data from one place in the spreadsheet to another.

4. When you build a model, even a simple one, you have created a template. Save it blank, without any data, so you can reuse it over and over again.

5. If your completed spreadsheet doesn't work, you'll have to edit it. Make a copy of the spreadsheet and save it under a different filename. Then make corrections to the copy and test it. If it works, fine; if not, you can start over again with the original.

6. Spreadsheets can take up a great deal of disk space. Make sure you have plenty before you start working.

7. Recalculate your spreadsheet before you print it. Otherwise, it may print out the previous version.

8. Use headers to identify your spreadsheet, as well as to describe various formulas or procedures you have used so that others will understand your work.

9. Take advantage of the auditing function, if your spreadsheet has one, to check your spreadsheet formulas for errors.

10. Save your work often. If you're building a complex spreadsheet, saving each iteration makes it much easier to correct.

Presentation Graphics

1. Analyze the audience before determining the type of graphic presentation you need to make. Make sure the medium — and the message — suit the occasion.

2. Select the best visual medium, based on the audience, room size, type of information, and cost to produce.

3. Remember that not all information needs to be shown on a screen. Use handouts to augment your visuals.

4. Use more graphic images than text. The text should help make the image more understandable, but should not replace image information.

5. Use the storyboard technique to plan the presentation and to determine the content and sequence of the graphic images.

a number for any reason, you don't have to reenter the entire column of constants all over again, one at a time, as you would with a calculator. Instead, simply enter the change, and recalc totals the column for you. This makes creating what-if analyses easy. As spreadsheet users say, you "plug in" some numbers or constants, and calculate them; then you "plug in" some new numbers that change the scenario and recalculate to get another outcome. An interesting use for recalc is to figure a down payment, the interest rate, or the length of a large purchase, such as company equipment, a new car, or a home.

In most spreadsheet programs, recalculation occurs automatically. Every time you make a change, recalculate runs through all the constants and formulas, making all subsequent changes for you. That's fine if you are only making one change. However, if the spreadsheet is very large and there are a number of changes in different areas, manual recalculation is more convenient. The spreadsheet doesn't have to perform unnecessary and time-consuming recalcs after every change; instead, it is done after all the changes are completed. Recalculation significantly sets the spreadsheet apart from the ledger sheet.

Three other useful advanced spreadsheet features are templates, macros, and graphics. Let's look at each.

TEMPLATES

It's often possible to use a spreadsheet design over and over. A **template** is a worksheet with labels, commands, and formulas already created and saved in a file so that you can begin entering data without doing all the other tedious, repetitive work. It is like a blank form, waiting to have data entered into its cells. For example, you can create templates for a monthly or annual budget, for loan or credit card calculations, and for cumulative departmental expenditures on personal computer software.

There are templates for everything from accounting to tax preparation to home budgets. Many people create their own templates, but you can also buy ready-made templates. Some are in books and magazines, so you must key in the one you want and save it as a file. Often you can buy ready-made templates on disk, so you don't have to do the keying. Once you are in the spreadsheet program you simply load the template, as you would any other file, and then fill in the cells. All the calculations are performed automatically.

MACROS

A **macro** contains commands or formulas that you create and then store in the spreadsheet so that you can use them again and again. Macros help you program your spreadsheet in many different ways, so you can use it more productively. They are also time-saving devices that save you keystrokes on tasks you frequently perform in your spreadsheet work. For example, you could create a macro that keeps a running total of the interest you have paid, or the point at which you begin paying down the principal, or many other calculations that change over time. Every time you wish to use the macro, you simply type its filename. Macros are typed directly into a cell as a label.

SPREADSHEET GRAPHICS

Spreadsheet **graphics** are pictorial representations of the numerical data produced by the spreadsheet. A number of spreadsheet programs are able to turn numerical data into business presentation graphics. These pictorial representations are most commonly in the form of a pie chart, a line graph, or a bar chart, as shown in Figure 5.7. Although graphics software is discussed in greater detail later in this chapter, it's important to recognize the graphics aspect of spreadsheet programs.

Spreadsheet data often must be presented to other people, for example, in business meetings. Sometimes it's hard to see the importance of a row of numbers or to properly grasp their relationship to other numbers. This is where spreadsheet graphics comes in. The graphics program may be a com-

FIGURE 5.7

Spreadsheet graphics make complex financial information easier to comprehend.

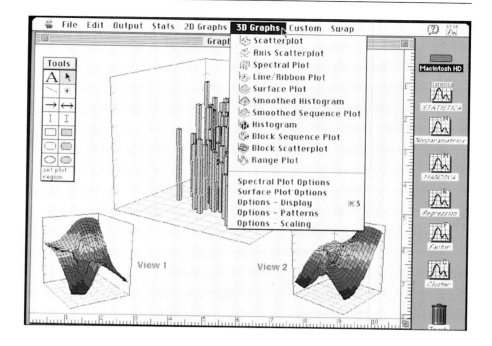

panion program to the spreadsheet or a separate program capable of accepting and converting spreadsheet data. In either case, the finished graphics can be printed out and displayed on paper, as overhead transparencies, or even as color slides.

KNOWLEDGE CHECK

1. What feature uses built-in keystrokes to perform mathematical tasks?   p. 155
2. What feature makes it possible to change figures and perform what-if analyses?   p. 155
3. What feature makes it easy to store and reuse commands and formulas?   p. 157
4. Name the special files that store commands and keystrokes for reuse.   p. 157
5. What do we call pictorial representations of spreadsheet data?   p. 157

SPREADSHEET APPLICATIONS

The spreadsheet can be used in hundreds of different ways, not only for business applications but for many personal ones as well. The spreadsheet can be used to collect, organize, and calculate many kinds of data into orderly,

TOMORROW

THE CHARACTER-BASED VERSUS WYSIWYG SPREADSHEET

The first graphical spreadsheet was Microsoft Excel, introduced for the Macintosh in 1985. In fact, it was the Macintosh that made the personal computer industry aware of the greater potential of graphical applications. Over the next few years, today's character-based (often termed *text-based*) standard will give way to the graphic, or WYSIWYG, application.

WYSIWYG is particularly useful when working with a spreadsheet. Yesterday's character-based spreadsheet made it necessary to go through a complex set of plotting procedures, keystroke by keystroke, to transform the numerical data into a chart or graph. Today's most advanced spreadsheet programs make it possible to do so with a click or two of the mouse button. These include horizontal bar charts, column charts (pie charts scrunched into vertical bars),

area charts, and combination line/bar charts. In most cases, the charts appear on the screen in color and can be transferred to color transparencies. Or you can string the graphics together so they can be displayed consecutively for a presentation. Graphic information can often be displayed in three dimensions, for example, showing three years' sales information stacked one on top of another. Bars have a three-dimensional perspective, pies appear as three-dimensional disks, text is large and legible (and you can select different typestyles and sizes), and different types of data are distinguished by pattern as well as by color—which means you don't need a color printer to get decent-looking printouts.

The newest graphic spreadsheets provide the knowledge worker with a drawing or charting option for creating bullet

lists and freehand drawings. You can add arrows, boxes, and clip-art images (for example, money symbols). In addition, different type fonts, sizes, and styles can be selected, just as with word processing, for emphasis and attractiveness. And now graphic representations can be displayed side by side with the spreadsheet itself, so the data can be viewed from both perspectives. You can even reference data in external worksheets, just as any worksheet formula can. Thus, it is possible to graph consolidated figures without creating a separate consolidation worksheet.

In many respects, the spreadsheet of tomorrow is here today. However, as software engineers expand and improve their WYSIWYG design skills, we can look forward to many of today's features becoming easier to use.

informative reports. Reports are commonly used in business to share information with management. The spreadsheet is ideal for creating reports because it not only permits organizing and calculating numerical data but also because it lets you use text that identifies the numbers. Here are a few examples of business spreadsheet applications.

BALANCE SHEET, INCOME STATEMENT, AND FINANCIAL ANALYSIS RATIOS

These three financial tools—the balance sheet, the income statement, and financial analysis ratios—form a common business report that is prepared at least annually and can often be found in a company's annual report. The simple spreadsheet in Figure 5.8 shows each of the three categories. The balance sheet gives the difference between assets and liabilities. The income statement shows how much profit the company made after expenses. The

FIGURE 5.8   The balance sheet, income statement, and financial analysis ratios form a common business report.

```
            A       B       C       D       E       F       G      H
                              BALANCE SHEET
 1    - - - - - - - - - - - - - - - - - - - - - - - - - - - - - - - - -
 2
 3    COMPANY NAME:    XYZ Company        AS OF : December 1982
 4
 5    ASSETS                              LIABILITIES
 6      Cash............   1300             Accounts Pble...   1600
 7      Accounts Rec....   2600             Notes Pble......   1900
 8      Notes Rec.......      0             Interest Pble...      0
 9      Inventory.......   7300             Taxes Pble......    300
10      Oth cur assets...   300             Oth Cur Liab....    800
11         Tot Cur Assets........  11500       Tot Cur Liab........        4600
12
13      Land...........   1200             Bonds Pble......   2000
14      Building........      0             Loan Pble.......      0
15      Equipment.......   5200             Mortgage Pble...    200
16      Less accum dep...  1300             Oth LT Liab.....      0
17      Other assets.....     0
18         Tot Non-cur assets.....  5100        Tot Non-cur Liab......  2200
19                                              Owners Equity.........  9800
20         Total Assets........  16600          Total Liabilities.....  16600
21               INCOME AND RETAINED EARNINGS STATEMENT
22    - - - - - - - - - - - - - - - - - - - - - - - - - - - - - - - - -
23    COMPANY NAME:    XYZ Company        FOR PERIOD ENDED: December 1982
24
25    Sales Revenue..............  25900        Tax Rate(.XX)=   40.00%
26    Other Revenue..............    200
27
28                TOTAL REVENUE.....   26100
29    Less Expenses:
30      Cost of Goods Sold........  20500
31      Selling..................   2120
32      Administrative...........   1300
33      Interest................     180
34      Income Taxes...........      800
35            Total Expenses...........   24900
36               NET INCOME.......   1200
37    Less:
38      Dividends........................   600
39            RETAINED EARNINGS.......    600
```

financial analysis takes the form of profitability and liquidity ratios that are created with data from the balance sheet and income statement.

PAYROLL INFORMATION

Collecting and calculating payroll information is simple with a spreadsheet. Figure 5.9 shows that once the basic salary and tax information is entered, an employee's number of hours worked is entered and the spreadsheet does the calculating. Changes in withholding tax or a raise are easily entered, with the spreadsheet automatically performing the recalculations.

Collecting and calculating payroll information is simple with a spreadsheet

FIGURE 5.9

```
       A         B         C         D         E         F         G         H         I         J         K         L         M         N
 1                      PAYROLL DATABASE
 2   ------------------------------------------------------------------------------
 3   ASSUMPTIONS: OVERTIME FACTOR(eg 1.5)     1.50      FICA RATE....      0.06
 4                DAILY REGULAR      7.00     8.00      FICA MAXIMUM.37000.00
 5
 6   DATABASE:                                                    TAX %-    TAX%-    TAX%-    PAY  $ THIS WEEK'S HOURS WORKED AND
 7   --------------------------- ----------------- -------- ------ -------  ------ ------ -------  ---------------------------
 8   NAME                        SS#                MAR-CODE   EXEMPT FEDERAL  STATE  LOCAL  HOURLY        SUN        MON        TUE
 9   SPARKS, BOB                 765782343                 1      3    0.47    0.05   0.02   15.12    ENTER #       7.00       7.00
10   REINDER, NANCY              234233454                 1      2    0.43    0.05   0.00   14.75    ENTER #       7.00       7.00
11   LEWIS, PAULETTE             786903984                 0      1    0.27    0.03   0.00    7.56       4.00       9.00       9.00
12   GERMAN, STANELY             447326987                 0      1    0.35    0.04   0.00   11.34    ENTER #       7.00       7.00
13   HOWARDS, PETER              132568567                 1      1    0.47    0.05   0.02   15.12    ENTER #       7.00       7.00
14   NORMAN, LESLIE              786465876                 0      1    0.25    0.04   0.02    7.34       4.00       8.00       9.00
15   PHILLIPS, PETER             396785634                 1      4    0.32    0.02   0.02   11.17    ENTER #       7.00       7.00
16   ENTER LAST, FIRST, MI       ENTER #           (1=R/0=S) ENTER # ENTER # ENTER # ENTER # ENTER #  ENTER #    ENTER #    ENTER #
17   ENTER LAST, FIRST, MI       ENTER #           (1=R/0=S) ENTER # ENTER # ENTER # ENTER # ENTER #  ENTER #    ENTER #    ENTER #
18   DUMMY END RECORD
19   --------------------------- ----------------- -------- ------ -------  ------ ------ -------  ---------------------------
20   TOTALS                                                                                           8.00      52.00      53.00
21
22
23   MACRO INSTRUCTIONS FOR UPDATING Y-T-D TOTALS AND DATABASE
24   ---------------------------------------------------------
25   THIS IS FOR THE INITIAL STORAGE OF Y-T-D TOTALS:
26             /FXVTEMPPR-A09.AW17-(Home)/FSPAYROLL-(HOME)
27
28   THIS IS FOR THE WEEKLY LOADING OF PREVIOUS Y-T-D TOTALS:
29             (GoTo)AF9-/FCCETEMPPR-(Home)
30
31
32   THIS IS FOR THE WEEKLY STORAGE OF Y-T-D TOTALS:
33             (Calc)
34             /FXVTEMPPR-A09.AW17-R
35             (GoTo)L9-''ENTER #-/C-L9.R17-(Calc)
36             (Home)/FSPAYROLL-R/WEY
```

FIGURE 5.10   Add-on programs.

A. Budget Express collects data from the spreadsheet and presents it for more effective financial planning.

B. Instant Analyst is an easy-to-use tool for highlighting trends and exceptions in spreadsheet data.

C. ForeCalc helps you use your spreadsheet data to profile future financial scenarios.

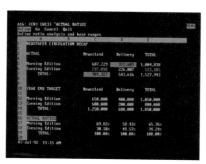
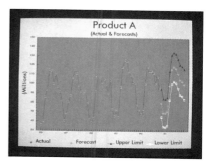

BUDGETING

Both people and businesses must budget if they are to live within their means. A budgeting program, such as the one in Figure 5.10A, lets you set up a budget and then analyze it according to your financial goals, such as achieving a 20 percent increase in sales or setting a specified amount aside each month for a down payment on a house. A range of cells may be modified by an amount and a percentage in order to reach the goals. In addition, you can perform a month-by-month analysis to find out why the goals aren't being achieved.

ANALYSIS

Although it's true that the computer provides the data and the person analyzes the data to make it useful information, sometimes a helper like Instant Analyst, shown in Figure 5.10B, makes the job easier. One of the most useful tools is ratio analysis, which allows identifying relationships between different trends or types of data. This "add-on" program helps spot trends and differences, termed *exceptions,* in a handy way: The data you specified is shown in one color and the exception data is displayed in another.

FORECASTING

Financial forecasting is the next logical step beyond budgeting; it's the spreadsheet equivalent of a crystal ball. An add-on program such as ForeCalc, shown in Figure 5.10C, can make this task much easier. ForeCalc lets you assess trends over time and display them graphically. It also presents a diagnostic screen that displays the values of the different parameters used in a forecast, along with the statistical methods used in calculating the forecast.

1. What two tasks is the spreadsheet good at performing?   p. 159
2. What are some of the most common spreadsheet applications in business?   p. 159
3. How does the spreadsheet add value to business reports?   pp. 158–59
4. What are three add-on tools that the spreadsheet makes use of?   p. 162

KNOWLEDGE CHECK

THE KNOWLEDGE WORKER AND PRESENTATION GRAPHICS

Human beings are visually oriented; therefore, if computers are going to be useful, they should be visually oriented too. It seems a shame to be constrained by a screen filled with text characters when the computer is capable of providing highly detailed, colorful graphic images.

Graphics are pictorial representations; **presentation graphics** are pictorial representations of data. Without graphics, we wouldn't have user-friendly interfaces. Presentation graphics used to be reserved for the few (mostly artists and engineers) but the Macintosh changed all that. It demonstrated that the computer was capable of producing high-quality graphics at an affordable price and brought many people flocking to computers who hadn't been interested before.

The first graphics software was created in 1962 by Ivan Sutherland, a graduate student at the Massachusetts Institute of Technology. Sketchpad allowed drawing on the face of a video display with a light pen. It was a visionary work, and it inspired Philippe Villers, another MIT graduate student, to create the first commercial computer-aided drafting system: The Designer Studio. This software combined computer graphics and drawing software for use on a special terminal with a drawing tablet, and set the course from computer graphics to computer-aided design (CAD).

In its simplest form, an image on the computer screen is simply a character: a letter, a number, or a symbol. This is called *text*. Many applications display text only. Text is contrasted with graphics, which displays shapes, lines, and images, often in color. Early, simple graphics programs allowed you to connect lines between points on the screen (say, to make a box or a star) and were called **vector graphics.**

But what we call computer graphics today is **high-resolution graphics,** a sharp, crisp video display that can display curving lines, shading, detail, color, and so forth. **Resolution** refers to the amount of detail in the graphics display. High-res graphics can be just about anything you can imagine, from a photograph of a butterfly to a video game to an engineering drawing to a transparency of a business graph or chart. When it comes to working with graphically oriented applications, the higher the better.

To produce high-resolution graphics you must have the right hardware, including an internal video display board and the right video monitor. Personal computer video monitor resolution is rated according to the number of **pixels** or dots of light it can display on the screen. Pixels form a grid on the screen to create graphics. A typical personal computer color monitor displays 640 by 220 pixels, or about 14 million dots. That means the picture can show a great deal of fine detail or resolution.

Another hardware device necessary to create computer graphics is known generically as a *pointing device,* meaning something that can be used to draw, design, and move efficiently across the screen. Most commonly we know this device as a **mouse,** a hand-held device moved across the desktop surface to electronically move the **pointer** correspondingly across the screen. Certain other graphics applications use different pointing devices, as we shall see.

■ KNOWLEDGE CHECK

1. What is the difference between graphics and computer graphics?   p. 163
2. Name an example of vector graphics.   p. 163
3. Describe an example of high-resolution graphics.   p. 163
4. What is a pixel?   p. 164
5. What is the most common pointing device?   p. 164

TYPES OF GRAPHICS SOFTWARE

Graphics software programs let you create, design, and manipulate graphic images, from simple line drawings to detailed, three-dimensional engineering drawings to business graphics to animated figures. In addition, some utility software programs use computer graphics to display recognizable images on the screen to help the knowledge worker better utilize the computer. The

FIGURE 5.11   Today's knowledge workers have the option of using a graphical user interface to make computers easier to use.

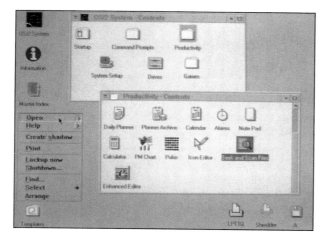
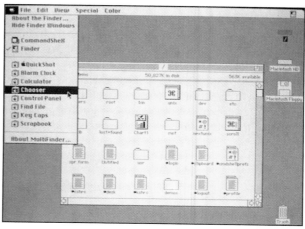

Macintosh was the first to do this, with its graphical user interface; however, it was a black and white screen display. Today, knowledge workers using both Macintoshes and PC-compatibles can take advantage of a similar color program called Windows®. Figure 5.11 shows some aspects of both these graphical interfaces. Let's take a closer look at some of the different computer graphics applications.

PRESENTATION GRAPHICS

Of the several types of graphics software, the one we see most commonly is called presentation graphics, computer graphics or visuals used for business. Presentation graphics present numerical, statistical, financial, or other quantitative data in a visual form, usually a pie chart, a bar chart, a line graph, or scatter graph, as shown in Figure 5.12. These graphics are intended to convey information about a situation quickly and clearly, either in a printed report or on a transparency master or slide.

Presentation graphics software comes in two forms. One is as a stand-alone program, meaning it produces graphics only. Two popular stand-alone graphics programs are Corel Draw!© and Lotus Freelance Graphics. Both are powerful, capable of creating everything from simple drawings and charts to color slides. They are full-featured, including clip art and a variety of typefaces. Both are designed for Windows; Corel Draw! is even available on a CD-ROM disc.

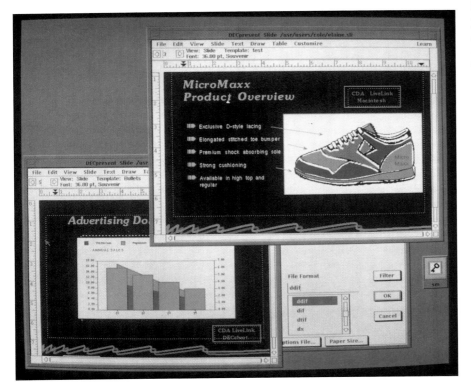

FIGURE 5.12

Presentation graphics offer many different sophisticated manners in which to organize data; the graphics chosen should suit the intended audience.

DRAW AND PAINT GRAPHICS PROGRAMS

The Macintosh made it possible to create artwork or designs from scratch, using a program called MacDraw as the palette and the mouse as a pencil or brush. Now there are many color draw and paint programs for personal computers. A draw program is designed to create line drawings, which is useful for illustrators, drafters, and designers. A paint program permits use of color and more creativity, including changing brush thickness and creating sprayed or spattered designs. Figure 5.13 shows an illustration created with a draw and paint program.

COMPUTER-AIDED DESIGN

CAD is engineering design software that replaces the drafting table, special drafting tools, pencils, and templates, permitting knowledge workers to create designs in three dimensions. Many CAD programs use a special input device called a **digitizer tablet** for creating drawings. A decade ago, CAD required an expensive terminal, but like many other mini and mainframe applications, there are programs now for the personal computer. Today, CAD is only one phase of the automated process known as *computer-integrated manufacturing (CIM)*.

CAD designs are now tested on the computer screen and then revised and refined. The designs are turned into working specifications, both graphics and text, in a process called **document and image processing.** For example, the

FIGURE 5.13

Draw and paint programs have resulted in a new medium — computer art.

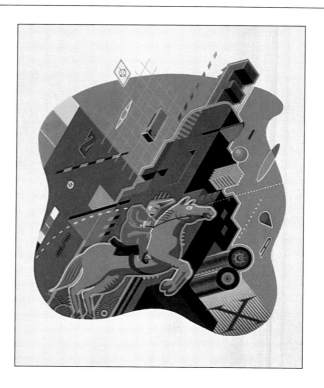

manufacturing specifications for an aircraft engine accompany the drawing itself. Once the specs are complete, they are sent, as computer instructions, to the manufacturing floor for computer-aided manufacturing (CAM).

COMPUTER ART

Back when graphics systems were expensive, they were used mostly by engineers designing automobiles, aerospace vehicles, computers, electronics circuits, and the like. Even so, many people were drawn to computer graphics terminals for artistic expression and amusement, and in 1973 the First Annual Conference on Computer Graphics and Interactive Techniques (now called SIGGRAPH) was held. In addition to its speakers, a SIGGRAPH conference is like an art opening of the finest, most interesting computer-generated art in the world.

COMPUTER ANIMATION

The next step beyond still drawings is moving figures, or computer animation. Animation makes objects (such as a bouncing ball) and characters (such as animals or people) move. There are many uses for computer animation, most notably in cartoons and movie sequences. One area where computer animation shows great growth is training and education, where instructions can be explained and demonstrated step by step.

USING COMPUTER GRAPHICS

Today, computer graphics touch many areas of life:

- Artists, designers, and special effects technicians use computer graphics for many creative projects, including fine art, television commercials, graphical novels, and illustrations (Figure 5.14A).

FIGURE 5.14

A. Joni Carter has used her computers to create fine art. Her sports art achieved national prominence when the U.S. Postal Service selected it for the 1992 Summer Olympics stamps.

B. Thomas Banchoff combines the possibilities of computer graphics and physics to visualize the fourth dimension.

C. Photographs recording loss or damage can be stored directly into the insurance claim record.

FIGURE 5.15

This is one of a series of CAT scans taken through the patient's chest. The red mass at the center is the heart.

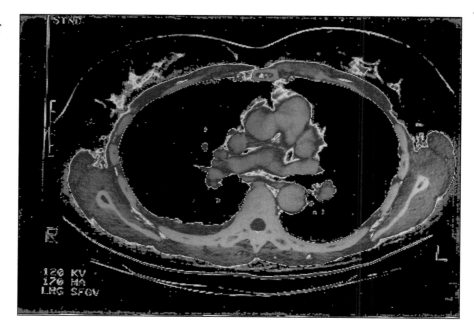

- Thomas Banchoff of Brown University experiments with computer graphics and theoretical physics to visualize the fourth dimension (Figure 5.14B).
- Wang and other computer companies now offer insurance information systems that capture a photograph of a damaged car or house in the claims database, accompanying a text explanation (Figure 5.14C).

Computer graphics is evolving into image processing, where information that was once represented in words can now be captured, stored, and manipulated pictorially in the computer. But as CAD applications evolve, so do others. Surgeons can manipulate an image of a diseased organ, captured from a computerized axial tomography (CAT) scan. They can simulate the surgery to see if it will correct the problem without ever touching the patient (Figure 5.15). Computer graphics have certainly come a long way since pie charts.

KNOWLEDGE CHECK

1. What are some of the most common business graphics?   p. 164
2. What is the most commonly used type of computer graphics?   p. 165
3. What has replaced traditional drafting methods and tools?   p. 166
4. What do we call a computer system that captures and stores visual images and text?   p. 166
5. What software turns engineering designs into working specifications?   p. 166

THE COMPUTER GRAPHICS KEYBOARD, MOUSE, AND SCREEN

As mentioned earlier, using a computer graphics program requires a pointing device, most commonly a mouse. (Pointing devices similar to the mouse are described in Chapter 9.) The mouse combines the arrow (cursor movement) keys with keys that would be used to issue commands. These commands are issued by "clicking" a mouse button. Most mouses have two or three buttons, but commonly the left button is used most frequently.

THE SCREEN

Graphics programs divide the screen into a workspace, occupying the center portion, and the graphics tools, which are gathered to one side or the other and sometimes across the top or bottom. These tools are generally a grouping of squares, each with a graphic symbol to indicate their purpose: a line, square or circle, a paintbrush, spray can, and so forth. The tool is activated by pressing the mouse button—clicking—and then remains active until another is selected. When the graphics program is representing numerical data, the values are usually identified for the various portions of the chart or graph. When done, the graphic aspect is activated, and the chart or graph is presented on the screen for viewing.

KNOWLEDGE CHECK

1. What is a commonly used pointing device?   p. 169
2. What two activities does the mouse combine?   p. 169
3. How is the computer graphics screen organized?   p. 169
4. How are graphics tools activated?   p. 169
5. How is numerical data identified for presentation?   p. 169

THE COMPUTER GRAPHICS PROCESS

Figure 5.16 explains the steps involved in the computer graphics process. The process is not complicated, and is very straightforward because the computer and software do most of the work for you. In step one, basic page design decisions are made, or you may choose to make a color slide. In step two, the frame(s) are created. You may draw, paint, or both; add text, clip art images, or create special effects such as airbrushing. Display permits viewing and zooming in for touch-ups. Step three permits saving, but also importing or exporting graphics to or from other applications. An additional advantage in creating computer graphics files is that they may be used in other programs' files, as with the graphic of a personal computer in our word processing or desktop publishing file in Chapter 4. The fourth step is printing. If you don't have a color printer, the chart will print out in different designs and shades of black and white.

FIGURE 5.16   The computer graphics process chart.

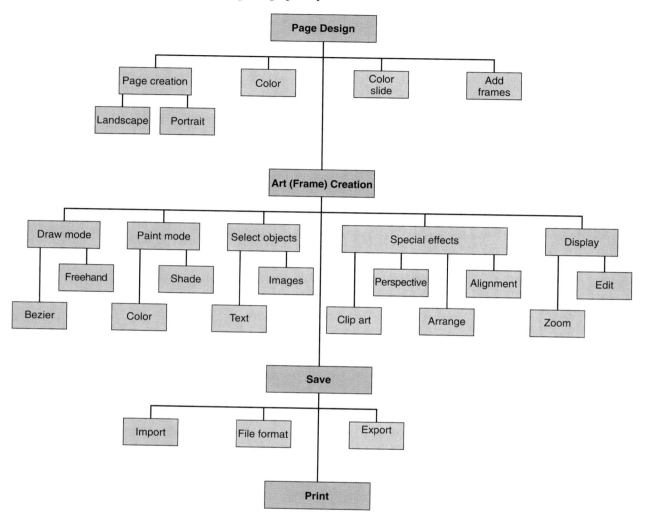

KNOWLEDGE CHECK

1. What do you primarily work with in the first step of the computer graphics process?   p. 169
2. Why are frames important?   p. 169
3. Name several ways to customize a computer graphic.   p. 169
4. How does it help to preview the graphic?   p. 169
5. What is an additional advantage in saving a computer graphic file?   p. 169

FIGURE 5.17

A. If you have imagination and 3-D animation software you can produce animated films such as this.

B. A visual cornucopia—new graphics applications are always emerging. This computerized car map tells you where you are.

C. PV-WAVE graphically presents large volumes of data. The unique feature is that the graphic renditions are in motion and respond to additional input as it is occuring.

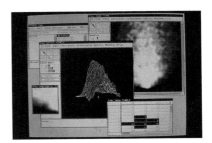

WHAT LIES AHEAD?

The spreadsheet—a unique product of the personal computer generation of software—is the most widely used productivity tool for managers in business. It is not uncommon to find people who use it as much as five hours a day. It continues to evolve with such features as the three-dimensional spreadsheet, which allows you to overlay several spreadsheets one on another. Nearly every major software company has a powerful spreadsheet for its customers, for both the Macintosh and DOS-based personal computers.

More uses for the spreadsheet are found every day. For example, during corporate research into DNA, Cetus Corporation engineers found they needed to analyze enormous amounts of real-time data generated by the experiments. Using a spreadsheet and personal computer, they wrote macros that were used to collect temperature data, which were then stored in specific ranges for analysis. This spreadsheet-based research alleviated the need to repeat experiments. Using spreadsheets in lab-wide experiments now cuts costs on an ongoing basis.

Most software originated on large computers and later was made available for personal computers. In an interesting reversal, Lotus 1-2-3 is now available in a mainframe version. Clearly, the spreadsheet is a useful tool, one that people are constantly using to find more ways to work with numbers. And making numbers make sense is the most important goal of all.

Presentation graphics is easily the most exciting application area in computing today. As computers become more powerful, as well as less expensive, more graphic applications are emerging. Here is a sampling:

- *3-D animation software* is available for a personal computer from Autodesk (the leading CAD software company), making it possible to produce animated films—if you have the cartooning and drawing experience, that is (Figure 5.17A).
- *Computerized maps* are currently available on disk and on CD-ROM and soon will be widely available in autos (Figure 5.17B).

CAREERS FOR KNOWLEDGE WORKERS
TIM TRAN, CFO, JOHNSTONE SUPPLY

Tim Tran is an all-American success story if there ever was one. He was raised in the village of Gia Dinh, near Saigon, South Vietnam, and believed that through diligence and hard work he could see his dreams come true. Aided by a U.S. Department of State scholarship, he graduated from the University of California at Berkeley (UCB) with honors and a degree in accounting.

Tran's interest in mathematics, which began in graduate school, blossomed at UCB and led to taking a number of computer courses. "I learned to program in both COBOL and BASIC," he says, "and I took a course in management information systems too." After graduation, Tim returned to Vietnam but was soon caught up in the war. He was viewed with suspicion by the Communists, who suspected the U.S.-educated citizen was a spy because he bore the title CIA — which actually stood for certified internal auditor.

Tim and his wife Cathy soon decided they must escape the country, which was only possible by hiring a boat on the black market. Four times Tim paid a captain for the trip, and four times it ended in disappointment. The fifth time they did escape, only to be repeatedly robbed by Thai pirates as they crossed the South China Sea. Tim arrived in Portland, Oregon, and "with a burning desire, really *burning,*" began his job search. He landed a position as an accountant at Johnstone Supply, a distributor of parts and equipment for heating, ventilation, air conditioning, and refrigeration equipment.

Through hard work, Tim has risen to the position of chief financial officer at Johnstone, where he also oversees the data processing center. He uses a personal computer that is linked to the company's ultramodern computer network. "I spend about half my time at the computer," Tim says, "and 90 percent of that time I use the spreadsheet. Every morning I look at our cash flow to determine what money to invest, borrow, or keep in the bank. I use a model to see what checks are in transit and which have cleared." This model, or template, is one Tim designed himself, which analyzes the checks by zip code, sorted into the 12 Federal Reserve bank regions, so that he'll know exactly how long it takes a particular check to clear.

Tim also uses his spreadsheet to analyze sales reports from Johnstone's 135 locations. He can track trends, see where sales are flat, compare sales from different periods or times — by month, year, or year-to-date — and then make predictions for the future. "The computer is a tool that can provide quantitative information," he says, "but a person must provide the qualitative, or 'why' aspect. What makes managers good at their work is knowing the numbers, but also investigating, asking intelligent questions, and doing some research to analyze. You have to use your common sense and understand the business." Clearly, Tim Tran has made it his job to do so — with a little help from his personal computer and spreadsheet program!

- *Animated data representation* is available in a product called PV-WAVE from Precision Visuals, which takes spreadsheet data and transforms it into 3-D, moving visuals (Figure 5.17C).

One day soon, almost all the work we do with personal computers will be accomplished in a graphic mode or with the aid of graphic-based programs. Graphics not only makes our computing experience more pleasant, it makes it easier as well.

SPREADSHEET ETHICS: MAKING NUMBERS LIE

There is an old saying in business: "Figures do not lie." But spreadsheet users must be careful about trusting the figures they see, for the figures are only as accurate as the person who entered them. It's possible to make errors in formulas, slip a decimal place, or forget to recalculate when you change something. People have made errors with pencil and paper, adding machines, and electronic calculators for years. Now they make errors with spreadsheet models too. A faulty model with incorrect formulas will produce errors in the spreadsheet.

It's possible to make a spreadsheet lie, in the same way any numbers can be made to lie. A product manager can simply pluck sales projections out of the air, plug them into the spreadsheet, and project success. Inaccurate data produces inaccurate results: garbage in, garbage out.

Using a spreadsheet program ethically means entering the correct data to arrive at a correct conclusion—and accepting the results. Since it's possible to create what-if scenarios with the spreadsheet, it's easy to keep feeding numbers in until the desired results are produced. This is not a good use of the computer, and it doesn't make sense morally, ethically, or practically—from a business perspective.

It's often hard for humans to own up to their mistakes. It's not uncommon to hear people blaming the computer for errors in many walks of life. In fact, some companies have brought lawsuits against software companies, alleging the program made a mistake that cost them money. Lacking merit, none have been brought to trial. The problem, as might be expected, is garbage in, garbage out. The spreadsheet needs to be used accurately and sensibly. If that's done, using it ethically should follow.

PRESENTATION GRAPHICS ETHICS: ALTERING REALITY

The greatest dangers in using graphics and desktop publishing programs are in misrepresenting reality and plagiarism. It is now possible to alter photographic images, which in turn opens up the possibilities for altering them to achieve an unethical, illegal, or immoral end. Using graphics software, people can be shown in places they haven't been; objects can be shown with or without things they should have.

When graphics software is combined with desktop publishing software, it becomes possible to deliberately misrepresent the truth by creating an entirely fraudulent publication. Similarly, documents from stock certificates to bills of sale, even currency, can be forged. There is no simple cure for these problems except education in why the deeds should not be done. Yet, like any safeguards, these will only work when the people involved wish to be ethical and honest.

SUMMARY

1. *Explain what a spreadsheet is and how a spreadsheet program works.* The spreadsheet is an application that allows us to create sophisticated mathematical models for financial and economic planning. It is the electronic counterpart of the paper ledger sheet, the pencil, and the hand-held calcu-

lator. The spreadsheet was invented by an MBA student who saw a real need for it in his schoolwork.

2. *Describe the different uses for a spreadsheet.* The spreadsheet can add, subtract, multiply, and divide. However, it can also let us create and test financial models, using its what-if analysis capabilities. The spreadsheet allows us to use formulas, some of them by using built-in spreadsheet functions to perform a series of mathematical operations.

3. *Identify the various characteristics of the spreadsheet screen.* The spreadsheet screen represents the paper ledger sheet. Vertical columns and horizontal rows create cells, which may contain labels (text) and values (numbers) in the form of constants or mathematical formulas. The cursor in a spreadsheet is called a *cell pointer,* and wherever it is placed is where labels or values will be placed. Spreadsheet programs commonly have a menu line and/or a command line, where commands and other important information are displayed, and a status line, where labels, constants, and formulas are typed and displayed.

4. *Explain the steps in creating and editing a spreadsheet.* First, a spreadsheet is designed on paper. Then the labels are created, followed by entering data, or constants. Next, the formulas necessary to perform calculations on the data are entered. The spreadsheet does the calculating. The COPY, MOVE, INSERT, or DELETE commands affect the contents of cells, whether in columns or rows. As with other applications, the file is saved when work is finished; RETRIEVE recalls it to work some more. PRINT provides a hard copy to look at and also serves as a backup.

5. *Name some of the advanced functions and features of the spreadsheet.* Advanced features help knowledge workers become power users. Functions, which are often identified by the @ symbol, perform special tasks with a minimum of keystrokes. Recalculate helps to quickly see the results of changing figures or performing a what-if analysis. The spreadsheet normally recalculates automatically, but can usually be set to manual as well. We can create templates for spreadsheet designs that are used over and over. Macros store labels, constants, and formulas used frequently, which can be recalled with just a few keystrokes. There are thousands of business and personal uses for the spreadsheet.

6. *Describe the various types of graphics software.* Graphics software is able to display lines, shapes, and colors. The older type was called *vector graphics;* today, we work with high-resolution graphics. Some of the types of graphics software are presentation graphics, draw and paint, computer-aided design, computer art, and computer animation.

7. *Describe the computer graphics keyboard, mouse, and screen.* Graphics programs usually require a pointing device to augment the keyboard. It is used to issue commands and initiate functions, but also to perform the drawing, painting, and manipulation tasks.

8. *Explain the steps in creating presentation graphics.* There are four steps: creating labels or text to define and describe the numerical data; customizing the color and design of the various elements of data; screen display and saving the chart; and printing.

ISSUES

1. A construction company used a spreadsheet to create a bid for building a multimillion-dollar office complex. One of the line items, overhead costs totaling $250,000, wasn't inserted in a cell that was part of the formula. As a result, it didn't get calculated into the final bid. The company won the bid but found it would lose money because overhead wasn't factored in.

   The construction company sued the software developer, claiming the problem was a bug or malfunction of the spreadsheet. Was it? Or was it carelessness? One spreadsheet expert says that formula errors are very common. Do you think the construction company had cause to sue? Should the instruction manual have made special mention of this kind of error? Who, if anyone, is at fault?

2. You have a personal computer that you share with a colleague — let's call her Jane. Jane is an avid sports fan and follows all the team's games.

She is using a spreadsheet to record team statistics. One day you walk in and there are two other people in the room, hovering over Jane and the computer. She is performing a what-if analysis on how certain players will perform in Saturday's game. The other two people take out money and begin placing bets. It seems to you that Jane is a bookie! Is this illegal? Is it an unethical use of the computer?

3. With more and more text and various graphics available on computer disks, it seems as though it is getting harder to know when or how it is permissible to use copyrighted materials. Do you think that computer technology is going to force a reconsideration of proprietary ownership of words and images and, thus, cause changes in the copyright laws? Is this a good or bad development?

CHAPTER REVIEW QUESTIONS

REVIEW QUESTIONS

1. What are the advantages of working with a mathematical model?
2. How do what-if analyses help a business make better decisions?
3. Explain the difference between a formula and a constant, and where they appear on the spreadsheet screen.
4. When is it most useful to turn worksheet data into a graphic representation?

5. What are the major differences between a character-based and a graphically based application?
6. Name several graphics programs that are not necessarily business-oriented.
7. What is a pixel? What role do pixels play in high-resolution graphics?

DISCUSSION QUESTIONS

1. Discuss the purpose of macros and what you would use them for.
2. What types of knowledge workers get the most benefit from using a spreadsheet?
3. What are some risks in using a spreadsheet?
4. Why is it important to be able to see the constant and the formula for a cell simultaneously?

5. Discuss the advantages and disadvantages of using a graphically based application.
6. Discuss the reasons why the spreadsheet and graphics programs were integrated first (along with the database).

MULTIPLE-CHOICE

1. What are the advantages offered by integrated software packages such as Lotus 1-2-3? (Check all that apply.)
   a. Several applications can work together.
   b. It's easy to exchange data between applications.
   c. All applications work similarly.
   d. Price is lower.
2. During the spreadsheet design step, the following things are determined (check all that apply):
   a. The purpose of the spreadsheet.

   b. Size.
   c. Labels and formulas.
   d. cell colors.
   e. Number of columns and rows.
3. Presentation graphics software creates (check all that apply):
   a. Bar charts.
   b. Pie charts.
   c. Area charts.
   d. Line charts.
   e. All of the above.

4. The most common business uses for a spreadsheet program are (check all that apply):
   a. Budgeting.
   b. Forecasting.
   c. Analysis.
   d. Tax planning.
   e. Balance sheet.

5. Some other uses for graphics software include (check all that apply):
   a. Illustrating documents.
   b. Animation.
   c. Graphic novels.
   d. Finger painting.
   e. Mapping.

FILL-IN-THE-BLANK

1. The three manual tools built into a spreadsheet are _____, _____, and _____.

2. We use the _____ number system for our currency.

3. A worksheet with all the labels and formulas in place, waiting to accept data for calculation, is called a _____.

4. Cells are designated with a _____ and a _____.

5. The spreadsheet has both a _____ line and a _____ line.

6. The most common pointing device is called a _____.

7. The name used for the graphics used in business is _____.

TRUE/FALSE

1. The spreadsheet's primary task is to keep track of very large worksheets.

2. One of the spreadsheet's most powerful features is recalculate.

3. The Scroll Lock key is used extensively when working with a spreadsheet.

4. The & symbol is used to indicate a spreadsheet function.

5. A pointing device is highly desirable for creating graphics.

KEY TERMS

CALCULATE, 150
cell, 153
cell pointer, 153
column, 143
command line, 153
constant, 153
digitizer tablet, 166
document and image processing, 166
financial model, 146
formula, 145
function, 146

graphics, 157
high-resolution graphics, 163
label, 153
ledger sheet, 143
macro, 157
menu line, 153
mouse, 164
pixel, 164
pointer, 164
presentation graphics, 163
recalculate, 155

resolution, 163
row, 143
spreadsheet, 144
status line, 154
template, 157
value, 146
vector graphics, 163
what-if analysis, 146
worksheet, 149

File Managers and Database Management Systems

LEARNING OBJECTIVES

After reading and studying this chapter, you should be able to:

1. Explain the difference between a database and a database management system (DBMS).

2. Describe the advantages of a DBMS.

3. Identify the four types of DBMS and the data elements they use.

4. Explain the steps in creating and editing a database.

5. Describe some advanced database management functions and features.

6. Describe some features of the modern database-like personal information manager.

The Knowledge Worker and the DBMS

Many knowledge workers collect information they must use on a regular basis. How about you? If you do, you probably are familiar with some of the problems of managing information. One way to keep track of information is to create a **database,** defined as a group of related records and files.

Libraries are in the business of collecting books. For most of this century, libraries used card catalogs as databases to manage their book collections. Card catalogs hold three kinds of cards to represent each book the library owns. First, there is a title index, which has one card for every book in the library, filed alphabetically by book title. Second, the card catalog has an author index, which has one card for every book, filed alphabetically by author name. Third is the subject index, which has a card for each book according to topic. When a book falls into several subject categories, it has several subject cards. Card catalogs file subject cards in alphabetical order too.

The card catalog is an excellent manual database — it allows library users to search the entire contents of a library book collection by flipping through cards, rather than walking through the library reading book spines. It also allows people to search for books in three ways: by title, author, and subject. But a card catalog has several limitations. It is slow; you often have to flip through many cards to find the one you're looking for. It is a single-user system; if someone else is using the drawer pertaining to the subject you're exploring, you have to wait to use it. And it is limited in its scope. For example, if you want to find all the books written by Isaac Asimov pertaining to Mars, you have to manually search either all the Mars subject cards or all the Asimov author cards, carefully reading each one. Some searches require looking through several dozen (even several hundred) cards.

When computer use became widespread, libraries found that turning their card catalogs into computerized databases, for use with a database management system, could make searches easier and simpler. Let's find out why.

Working with a Database Management System

Managing databases with computers has become very popular. A DBMS allows you to use a database in many ways that aren't possible with traditional paper records. One DBMS advantage is *flexibility*. A DBMS allows you to search for many kinds of data. While a card catalog can only be searched according to title, author, or subject, a computer database can be searched and manipulated by any type or category of data. For example, you could design a library database so that a DBMS searches it by book publication date, by the number of pages in its book, or even by the language in which books are written. Figure 6.1 shows the relationship between a library card catalog, an office filing system, and a DBMS.

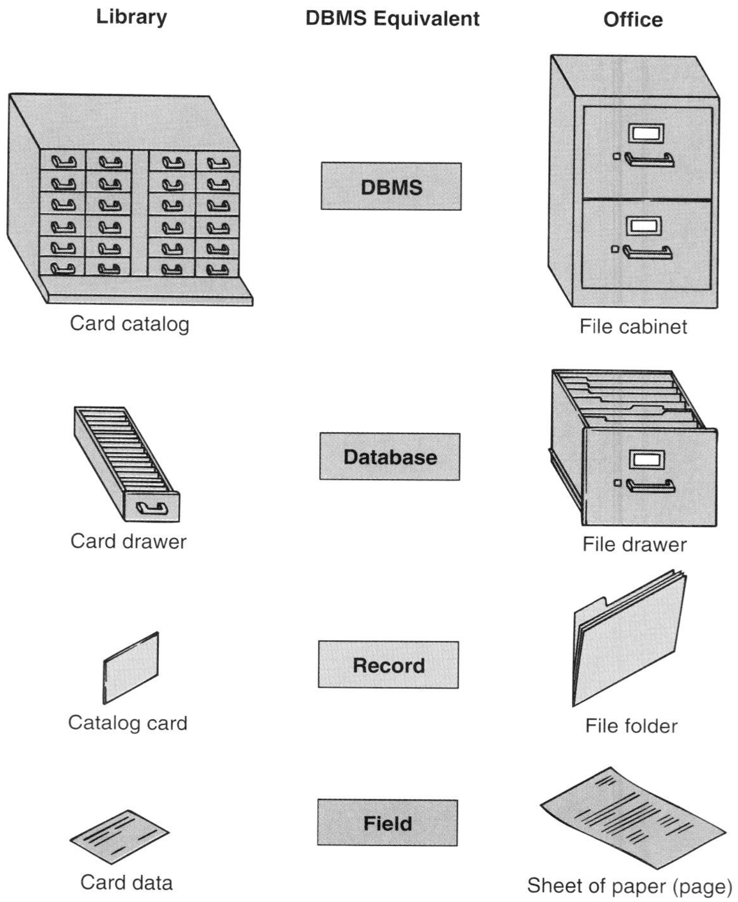

FIGURE 6.1

The structure of the library card catalog, an office filing system, and the DBMS are the same; however, it can be more efficient to locate information using a DBMS.

Library   **DBMS Equivalent**   **Office**

Card catalog   DBMS   File cabinet

Card drawer   Database   File drawer

Catalog card   Record   File folder

Card data   Field   Sheet of paper (page)

A second DBMS advantage is *discrimination*. A DBMS allows you to search selectively. For example, a DBMS can provide you with a list of all books by Isaac Asimov, written about Mars, before 1979; or a listing of all science fiction novels over 400 pages long.

A third DBMS advantage is *extensibility*. You can often use a DBMS to search many different kinds of databases. For example, you can search through databases in a dozen university libraries from one location, so long as the basic file structure is the same.

The features and advantages of word processing, the spreadsheet, and the database management system overlap to some extent. It is possible to search word processing files for a name and address or a specific phrase, but its strength is in its ability to manage text. A spreadsheet is capable of producing sales or manufacturing reports, but its strength is in its ability to perform mathematical calculations. A database management system is able to draw on the strengths of word processing by sorting through large quantities of text, or the strengths of a spreadsheet by tabulating numerical data and making them available in many different ways. Let's learn more about databases and the software — the DBMS — we use to manipulate them.

YESTERDAY

WAYNE RATLIFF: FATHER OF THE PERSONAL COMPUTER DBMS

The idea of a DBMS for a personal computer seemed far-fetched in 1980. Could the personal computer, with its tiny 64K of RAM and floppy disks that held only 241K bytes, ever produce a truly useful database? Wayne Ratliff thought so.

Wayne Ratliff was an aerospace engineer who developed the first DBMS for personal computers using the now-defunct CP/M operating system in the late 1970s. He called it DBMS Vulcan, and it had all the personality of that other Vulcan, Mr. Spock, until George Tate and Hal Lashlee came along.

They were business and marketing whizzes, and saw Vulcan's potential. Together, the three formed the software company Ashton-Tate.

But when it came time to market the software, they learned another company owned the Vulcan name. An advertising man suggested dBASE II, saying it sounded "high tech." The "II" was added to make it sound like a new and improved dBASE I — which, of course, had never existed.

dBASE II was a success, and when the IBM PC came out, there was a real, improved ver-

sion of dBASE II — dBASE III. With these products, Ashton-Tate reigned as the king of DBMS software for personal computers for many years. However, dBASE IV was put on the market with literally hundreds of bugs, or errors, which allowed competitors to erode its market. In 1991, Ashton-Tate was purchased by Borland International (see Careers for Knowledge Workers), its main rival, with its own DBMS program called Paradox.

For his part, Wayne Ratliff has continued as an innovator in personal computer software.

KNOWLEDGE CHECK

1. What is a database?   p. 179
2. Name an advantage and a disadvantage of a library card catalog database.   p. 179
3. What do we call a computerized database?   p. 179
4. What is the difference between flexibility and extensibility?   pp. 179–80
5. Why is discrimination so important in a database?   p. 180

WHAT IS A DATABASE MANAGEMENT SYSTEM?

A **database management system** (DBMS) is application software that lets you organize, store, and retrieve data from a single database or several databases. A DBMS helps you manage data better by:

- Providing a logical, orderly way to organize data.
- Allowing great versatility in ways to manipulate the data by modifying, searching, sorting, and organizing them in various ways.
- Providing many ways to format and print the data in reports.

The DBMS is able to work with both letter characters (usually words) and numbers, and is able to compare and organize them in ways unlike either word processing or spreadsheet software. In database technology, there is a specific language used for describing these characters, which are generally referred to as *data elements*.

DATA ELEMENTS

In a DBMS, data is arranged from the smallest to the largest. These are referred to as **data elements** or data items, individual pieces of data that are joined to produce information. Without data elements, we would not have consistent data organization or effective data management. There are two levels of data elements used in the DBMS: physical data representation and logical data representation.

PHYSICAL DATA REPRESENTATION

Physical data representation refers to how data is stored and retrieved on the computer system's auxiliary storage devices. Physical data elements include the bit, byte, and word that you learned about in Chapter 2. These elements are stored in files on some form of magnetic media, such as a disk.

LOGICAL DATA REPRESENTATION

Logical data representation is an organized method for storing data about an entity in a database. An **entity** is something about which we are interested in collecting data. In the library, it's a book; in business, it can be a customer. For example, a database of customer files may be organized by name, address, phone number, and most recent order; or it may be organized by credit card number, phone number, zip code, address, and name. All logical data may be in one file or it may be in a number of files, depending on the way it was designed and hence represented.

Most people organize things in logical ways. For example, a library card catalog has these data elements: data item, card, drawer, and index. Several data items pertaining to each book are written on a card. Cards are collected in drawers. Drawers are assembled into the title, author, and subject indexes.

Office filing systems use data elements similar to the library card catalog system. Sheets of paper, like data items, are stored in folders. Folders are collected in file drawers. Drawers are components of file cabinets. These are effective manual data management systems and they are used extensively all over the world.

Just as the card catalog and filing system use logical data elements, so does the DBMS. Its logical data elements are called *characters, fields, records, files,* and *databases.* Let's examine them one at a time to see how they work together. As you read, it may be helpful to refer to the comparisons shown in Figure 6.2.

CHARACTERS. A **character** is a single symbol, letter, number, or punctuation mark defined in the database. It is the smallest unit of data manipulated by a DBMS. Characters work together to form meaningful data such as words and social security numbers.

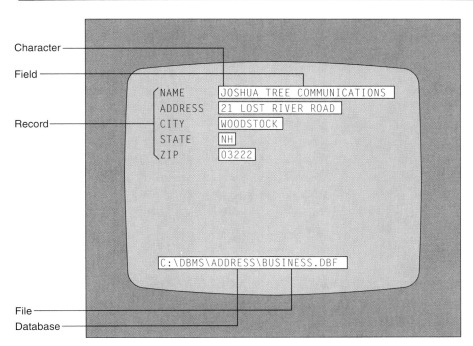

FIGURE 6.2

Working with logical data elements follows a natural progression. Typing single characters creates fields, several collected fields create a record, related records make a file, and one or more files form a database. Note that **BUSINESS** is one file in the **ADDRESS** database, or subdirectory; another file might be created for **PERSONAL** addresses.

FIELDS.   A **field** is a group of characters that represent an **attribute,** or characteristic of an entity. An example of a field is a customer (the entity) first or last name and their account number or hat size (the attribute). In other words, it is a data item that is part of a larger whole. A field is similar to a data item on a library card or a blank line to fill in on an employment application. In a card catalog database, the card is an entity, a book; each field on the card contains an attribute of the book, such as its title, author, subject, publication date, and page count.

RECORDS.   A DBMS **record** is a collection of related data items or fields that a DBMS treats as a unit. For example, a record contains all the information about a customer that is needed to process an order. A record holds all the attributes necessary to complete an entity, such as the address. A record is like a card in a card catalog database. Card catalogs have one card for each book. Office systems may have one folder for each employee or customer.

FILES.   Within the DBMS, a **file** is a collection of related records that serves as a unit of storage. The file holds all of the company's customer records. Of course, there are many types of files, and they may be organized however people want. Customers may be grouped into files by state, by alphabetical order, and so forth. As with any other computer file, there can be backup files as well. DBMSs hold related records in a file in the same way all the subject cards, say those for the letter R, are kept together in a card catalog.

DATABASES.   The simplest database is a single file. However, DBMSs really shine when they bring large quantities of data together. They do this by grouping many files into a database (for example, all the customers who have purchased items from a specific product line). A database is a common pool of data — a single, common storage entity used by the DBMS. A database may have dozens, even thousands, of files. In the library, it is the entire card file cabinet. A DBMS can manipulate multiple databases, too.

KNOWLEDGE CHECK

1. What are the two types of data elements in a DBMS?   p. 182
2. What are the three types of physical data elements?   p. 182
3. What is the smallest logical data element?   p. 182
4. What is the relationship of an entity to an attribute?   p. 183
5. What is the relationship of a field to a record?   p. 183
6. Is there a difference between a DBMS file and a DOS file?   p. 183

TYPES OF DATABASE MANAGEMENT SYSTEMS

The evolution of DBMS software over the years, from mainframes to personal computers, also sets it apart from the other software we've studied so far. As with other applications we have studied, people and hardware, combined with DBMS software, form a computer system that helps us effectively perform database management tasks. People design databases, but in the past they were constrained by the available hardware and software technology.

By the late 1950s and early 1960s, many businesses had recognized the value of a computerized database. Meanwhile, computer technology was improving. These events stimulated computer professionals to begin developing different database models to accomplish jobs more efficiently. Let's examine this evolution.

FLAT FILE

The first computerized databases were simple file management systems. In fact, one was named just that, referred to by its acronym, FMS. The file management system was useful for gathering and storing data, but in design it was nothing more than a library card catalog. For that reason, the file management system is often called a **flat file database,** because each file is stacked on top of the previous one. If you wanted to find something, you started at the beginning and looked through each file until you got the right one. There was no way to group similar files together, or to look for files that shared similar characteristics (for example, all the customers who live in Rockville, Maryland).

The earliest flat file database files were stored on reels of magnetic tape, which we will discuss in more detail in Chapter 9. That meant the data was stored sequentially, or one item following another. For example, letters might be stored in chronological order by date, or purchase orders might be stored in numerical order. Business quickly outgrew file management systems, and the following requirements emerged:

- The need to quickly retrieve specific data.

- The need to update data only once, in a file used by the entire corporation, rather than having to update multiple copies of the same file located in different databases.
- The goal of working with all the corporate databases as if they were a single, unified entity.

Large companies found it increasingly difficult to keep track of all the data in the computer: personnel files, equipment maintenance files, correspondence files, purchase order files, inventory files — the list goes on and on. Figure 6.3 shows a large bank's database management system. Note the complex interrelationships between the various databases. In business or government, a database of this size and complexity may be located on many computers. The customer file is only one database; others may include the company's payroll, inventory, assets, business correspondence and records, and a host of other stored data.

But the new DBMS requirements were also a response to diversity in the corporate environment. Each department often had its own way of managing files. There was no way to exchange data between departments that used different computer systems or DBMSs except the old way — paper. Managers seeking information on parts, prices, or inventory, for example, had to go from department to department, and from one DBMS to another, to gather all related data.

The advent of the disk drive in the late 1950s, with its ability to access data in random order instead of sequentially, made it easier to design databases according to relationships between different data. Now it was possible to quickly identify all citizens who didn't pay their income taxes in 1985 or every customer who bought a blue queen-size blanket.

Savings Deposits

account id
data
amount
identification
teller id
location
branch location
batch #
sequence id
work request?
supervisor verify IRA?

CD Withdrawals

account id
amount
date
closeout?
extension
branch location
teller id
location
domicile
check #

Quarterly Interest Payments to Account

account id
date paid
date credited
withholding
begin balance
calculated rate
calculated period

Activity

customer id
type
amount
date
process date
teller id

Deposits

account id
date
bank float amt
cust float amt
IRA year
mature date

Withdrawals

account id
date
check serv #
check issue id

Adjustments

account id
date
adj type
reason code

Interest Payment

account id
date
date paid
amount paid
amount withheld

FIGURE 6.3

Here are some of the databases in a typical large bank's DBMS. Note how certain file information recurs in various databases.

Flat file database management systems are still in use today. The most common ones are used for simple organizing chores on personal computers. Many are specially designed to perform specific tasks such as creating an address book, a personal belongings inventory, a recipe file, or just about anything that can be logically organized.

HIERARCHICAL

The **hierarchical database** model allows you to create relationships between logical data elements by establishing an inverted or upside-down tree structure from the central root to the branches, as shown in Figure 6.4A. Its main limitation is that you have to move from the root to a branch to access one file or record, then back to the root and out to a different branch to access another file or record. Therefore, we say the hierarchical database creates *one-to-many relationships* because you begin with the root and then move to the branches. An example of a hierarchical database is IBM's Information Management System (IMS).

Database designers knew the idea of using many branches was a good one, but they needed to solve the problem of having to return to the root every time they wanted to go out to another branch. In database terminology, they needed the ability to establish more relationships.

NETWORK

If the tree is a good model, database designers reasoned, the human cardiovascular system is even better. After all, its branches are interconnected and blood flows anywhere, as long as it passes through the heart. Therefore, the next step in DBMS evolution was the **network database** model. In DBMS terms, the network database system utilizes what are termed *many-to-many relationships,* just as veins intricately intertwine throughout the body. You don't have to enter the network database through the root, as in a hierarchical database; you can enter it anywhere. The most widely used example is IDMS, from Computer Associates. Figure 6.4B shows a network database. The network model is sometimes called the CODASYL model, and should not be confused with a communications network.

Flat file, hierarchical, and network DBMSs were created for large computer systems — mainframes first, then minicomputers. The network database was a big step forward in database design in the 1970s; but an even more efficient model, the relational database, emerged in the 1980s. It too was designed for mainframes, but was quickly adapted to the personal computer.

RELATIONAL

A **relational database,** often called an RDBMS, allows you to interchange and cross-reference data between different records. Most personal computer DBMSs use the relational model. In fact, the relational database has become the computer industry standard.

The relational database model is the most modern, easy to understand, and flexible of the three. In a relational database, all data is viewed as essentially alike; therefore, it creates *any-to-any relationships.* Data is stored in tables, as shown in Figure 6.4C.

Compare the relationship characteristics between the three DBMS schemas shown in this figure.   FIGURE 6.4

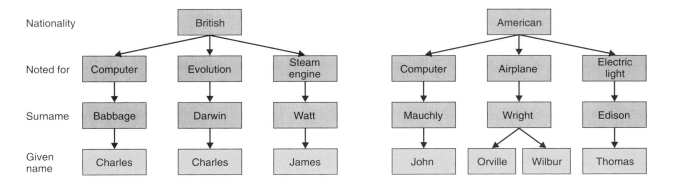

A. Hierarchical

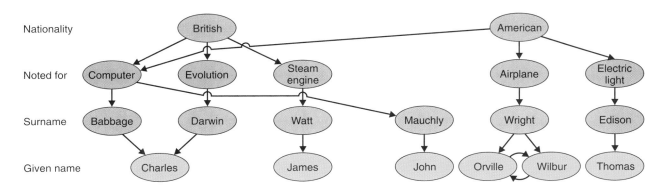

B. Network

C. Relational

Surname	Given name	Nationality	Noted for
Edison	Thomas	American	Electric light
Babbage	Charles	British	Computer
Wright	Orville	American	Airplane
Mauchly	John	American	Computer
Darwin	Charles	British	Evolution
Watt	James	British	Steam engine
Wright	Wilbur	American	Airplane

Source: Reprinted with permission, *High Technology* magazine (December 1984). Copyright © 1984 by High Technology Publishing Corporation, 38 Commercial Wharf, Boston, MA 02110.

Study all three types of databases so you can see how they organize the same data. The concept of the filing cabinet, which represented the hierarchical and network models, no longer applies. In fact, the RDBMS resembles nothing so closely as it does the human brain's ability to freely associate people, places, and things. For example, if you were trying to find the personnel file for Josh in the Oregon territory but couldn't recall his last name, the RDBMS would find all files with those two relations: Josh and Oregon. It is possible to classify, organize, analyze, cross-reference, and access data as if every item were indexed — or related. Note too that the relational database avoids creating duplicate data elements and is more flexible in organizing data. Because of this flexibility, you can focus on working with your data, rather than spending time maneuvering through the DBMS.

A simple example of the RDBMS in action is direct mail solicitations for bank credit cards. Have you ever received a solicitation for a credit card that you already hold? That means the bank either is not using a RDBMS or is using it inefficiently, since it sends all direct mailings to everyone in the database. However, the RDBMS permits narrowing the list to send to people by selecting relationships. For example, the RDBMS could select only customers who have a home mortgage, who earn in excess of $25,000, who do not have the bank's Visa card, but who have reserve checking.

■

KNOWLEDGE CHECK

1. What are the advantages in being able to access data in random order, versus sequentially, in a DBMS?   pp. 184–85
2. What is the flat file database used for today?   p. 186
3. Why is the tree a good analogy for a hierarchical database?   p. 186
4. What major advantage did the network database provide?   p. 186
5. What term is used to describe the fact that the relational database views all data as essentially alike?   p. 186

THE DBMS PROCESS

The clearest way to understand the process of creating a database with a DBMS is by studying the DBMS process chart in Figure 6.5. There are five steps in the process: design, in which the database is conceived; creation, in which it is built; the all-important step of saving your work to disk; manipulation, where you actually use the database; and printing, in which you gather specific data to analyze in a report. And, as you have already learned, the thinking and planning stage that precedes actual computer work is essential to creating a useful database.

DATABASE DESIGN

In **database design,** the nature and purpose of the database are determined and planned out, using paper and pencil. An example is shown in Figure 6.6. What is the scope of the database? It could be companywide, for a particular department or product line, or perhaps for individual use. What data will be collected, from the smallest to the largest? What are the relationships between the various types of data? For example, will people be grouped according to geographic area, sex, job description, or salary range? As each of these questions is considered, the design grows clearer, and the process or data refine-

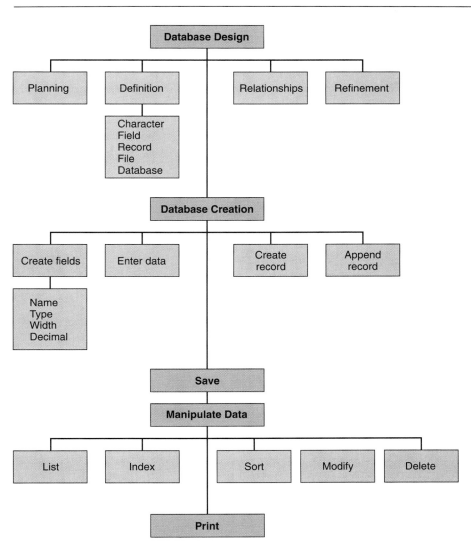

FIGURE 6.5
The DBMS process.

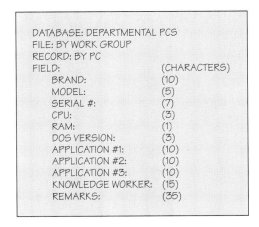

FIGURE 6.6

Database design is best done by hand. Sketching the database design helps you understand the relationships between the various logical data elements, and makes for a more efficient database once it is operational. This database is designed to keep track of a department's personal computers and their configurations.

ment takes place. Refinement means that some ideas change, while decisions about what stays in and what is left out are made. The mental picture of the database grows clearer as it is transferred to a diagram on paper.

There are two steps in database design. The first is data definition, and the second is data refinement. Once the database is built with the DBMS software, it's often difficult to go back and change it, so a little planning goes a long way.

DATA DEFINITION. **Data definition** involves creating a detailed description of the data you plan to use. Since you're learning about computers, suppose you were going to create an inventory database that catalogues the hardware and software components in a personal computer system. There are many kinds of characteristics we could collect about the system: the computer's brand name and type, name and type of monitor, name and type of printer, and names and types of software applications. We could also collect data such as year purchased, serial numbers, software version, and price paid — the list goes on and on. In database terms, each characteristic is an attribute, all of which make up an entity, the computer system. The entity is stored in the DBMS as a record, which might be the name of the knowledge worker who uses the system.

What do you *need* to know? What are the most important things you want to store about the office computer systems? It may be that if every fact is collected in the database, it would be too large or impractical to use. One way to determine what you need to know is by thinking about how you'll use the database. Is its purpose to manage ownership and security matters? Is it to ensure compatibility among knowledge workers? Is it for accounting, to amortize expenditures? It's very important to make these determinations during the planning process, for they affect how the data is defined and organized.

DATA REFINEMENT. **Data refinement** is the interaction of relationships between various data elements, and is the condensing and ordering phase in database design. You don't want your database cluttered with data you'll rarely use, so decide which attributes are least important and take them off the list. There is another important reason for data refinement. As you set up the DBMS software to enter each system's attributes and so forth, you must allocate a specific number of blank spaces to be filled in. Each is a character — the smallest unit of data manipulated by the database. If you allow for too many characters, it uses up memory space on your data disk. On the other hand, if not enough space is made, you won't be able to fit everything in.

DATABASE CREATION

Database creation is the computer work of transferring the design from ideas and diagrams to the software. Here we load the DBMS software, open the database file, and begin creating fields and their characteristics, according to the design.

CREATING FIELDS. Remember how attributes are chosen for entities in database design? Now each entity, or computer system, will become a record, and each attribute about that entity will become a field.

Fields must be of the correct type and size. There are four possible characteristics for each field: name, type, width (in characters), or number of decimal
places (for numeric data such as money). Here are some guidelines:

- *Name.* Any characters, including text, numbers, or symbols, may be used.
- *Type.* This defines what kind of data will be entered into this field —
  characters, numbers, or a date.
- *Width.* A field has a definite limit on the number of characters it can
  hold, usually 254. As mentioned earlier, do not allocate any more
  characters than absolutely necessary.
- *Decimal.* This tells the database how many decimal places to assign to
  numeric data such as dollars and cents.

With the fields created, the biggest job of all — the task of *entering data* —
begins. Once all the fields on the screen are filled in, a *record is created*. A
database may have a number of records. *Appending records* is the process of
creating new records to accompany those already created. For example, a new
customer would occasion appending a record.

SAVE

Saving the file that contains the records should be done frequently. With files
and records created and saved, the DBMS can now *manipulate data* and thus
make the database useful. The data can be organized in a variety of ways, to
create a list or index, or to sort it according to special criteria. The data can be
modified (changed) as business conditions change, and obsolete data can be
deleted. Finally, once the data is organized, it can be *printed* in the form of a
report. The next two sections explain these steps in the process in more detail.

MANIPULATING DATA

After safely saving the file, you have completed the data entry aspect of the job
and can actually *use* the database. This is called *manipulating the data,* because
the DBMS allows us to selectively retrieve and examine data. Here are a few
ways.

- **LIST** shows your data in many ways. For example, you can list all the
  records, or you can list the fields in different groupings such as all CPUs.
- **INDEX** puts data into either alphabetical or numerical order; it is useful for ordering information. It helps us find what we're looking for
  more quickly, whether it is customer records stored by invoice number
  or by customer name. Record numbers are sequential and can't be
  changed, but an index is organized the way we want it. It's much
  quicker to find data once they have been indexed, and if two databases
  have been combined, indexing becomes even more important.
- **SORT** is used to order and often to separate one or more records in a
  database. The fields it uses are termed **sort keys;** the first is the primary key, and there may be others. It indexes records in either ascending or descending order, while indexing only allows ascending. You
  can also sort across fields, whereas you can only index within a single
  field.

- **MODIFY** lets us change the width of a field, redefine it (as character, numeral, or date), or even add additional fields.
- **DELETE** is used to remove a record from the database.

PRINT

Like word processing and spreadsheet applications, database management systems provide a means of printing data, or producing hard copy output. Sometimes this function is termed a **report writer.** Basic features built into most DBMS report writers allow you to take data you have organized and then attractively format and print them.

Some personal computer DBMSs have a report writer with many useful features: the formatting capabilities of word processing, the number processing of spreadsheets, graphics output capabilities, and versatile database search and select features. With such a DBMS, we could design a report with a pie chart showing the percentage of knowledge workers with, say, a DBMS. With this basic understanding of the DBMS process, the next step is to learn about the keyboard and screen.

THE DBMS KEYBOARD AND SCREEN

In word processing, the screen resembles a blank sheet of paper. In the spreadsheet, the screen is a worksheet, ready for you to enter data into cells. Some DBMS programs use the command line interface, while others use a menu to guide you through the process. Several types of DBMS screens are shown in Figure 6.7.

Within the DBMS, we work with two basic types of screens. The first is where we issue commands or use a menu to create a database and subsequently work with it. The second is the database screen where we actually enter data, or fill in the blanks, so to speak.

THE DBMS KEYBOARD. The DBMS does not require any special uses of keys, as does the spreadsheet. Commands are commonly issued via the menu, by using the arrow keys or mouse to move to the appropriate selection. The alternate method is using the Ctrl, Alt, and Shift keys, in conjunction with the

---

FIGURE 6.7   The DBMS interface is usually a command line or a menu.

dBASE IV.   Paradox.   FoxPro.

Function keys, to guide the work. Otherwise, the keyboard is used to enter data in much the same way as it is used in word processing.

THE DBMS SCREEN. The DBMS cursor most often appears as a highlighted rectangle, in either color or reverse video, similar to the spreadsheet. The arrow keys are used to move from command to command in the menu, pressing Enter to issue the command. The same is true in entering data into database screens. As mentioned before, there is a certain degree of consistency across different applications. Like its counterparts, the DBMS uses the Backspace, Delete, Page Up, and Page Down keys, and may use the Function keys as well. Don't hesitate to use Help as you learn about the keys and the program.

Like the other applications, the DBMS usually has a status line to indicate where you are in the task. The status line may tell you things such as how to perform the task you are currently working on. Often you will see a helpful additional message that describes the purpose of the particular command or function you are contemplating using.

1. What are the five steps in the DBMS process?   p. 188
2. What tools are used in database design?   p. 188
3. What takes the most time in database creation?   p. 190
4. How many characteristics are there in a field?   p. 191
5. What do we call actually working with the database data?   p. 191
6. What do we call the data when it is printed?   p. 192
7. How are keyboard commands normally issued in a DBMS?   pp. 192–93
8. What is the main characteristic of the DBMS screen?   p. 193

KNOWLEDGE CHECK

ADVANCED DBMS FEATURES

At the beginning of this chapter, you learned that the DBMS has three capabilities: flexibility, discrimination, and extensibility. These capabilities are heightened when the more powerful, advanced DBMS features are used. In this chapter, several of the advanced features of personal computer DBMSs are discussed. The more extensive capabilities of large-system DBMSs are covered in Chapter 12.

RELATING DATABASE FILES

In most cases, it is impractical to store all the operational data needed in one database file. For example, it wouldn't make a great deal of sense to have the addresses, phone numbers, and contact names for each hardware and software vendor stored in the workgroup database file. Since each is used for different purposes—for example, the vendor information is used most often by the purchasing department—it makes sense to have a separate supplier database. However, it would be helpful if Jane could look up vendor information when

Today
DBMS Tips

1. DBMS programs range from easy-to-learn and intuitive to extremely difficult. The simplest is the flat file address book; the most difficult require the use of a programming language, creating the database nearly from scratch. Choose your DBMS carefully; study comparison reviews before you buy.

2. Design your database carefully and thoroughly on paper before you begin using your DBMS program. Study it frequently to determine if you've left anything out and to assure that the structure is logical.

3. Be judicious in defining data fields; don't make them larger than they need to be. Define data that you'll want to search for. If you want to search for an area code or zip code, be sure you distinguish them as such. Otherwise, the DBMS will stop every time it sees any numbers in sequence.

4. Use your word processor to enter large quantities of existing information into your database. This is accomplished by creating a file in the format the DBMS can read. The specifics for performing this task can be found in the DBMS user manual.

5. Create data entry forms, or templates, to enter repetitive data and automate its collection.

6. Use the DBMS programming language to create the command files that automate your work and simplify ways to commonly retrieve data.

7. Use the DBMS query language in lieu of the programming language to learn easier, quicker ways to retrieve data.

8. Explore the features of the report writer for there are many types of reports and numerous ways to use reports. Master the various ways to format reports, from the use of type fonts to formats.

9. Learn to use the DBMS's relational characteristics. There are many more ways to define relationships between files than are immediately apparent.

10. Find out if there are add-on utility programs that will assist in automating tasks that you commonly perform with the DBMS.

her workgroup needs a new piece of hardware or software, so relating the two database files makes a great deal of sense.

When relating two database files, they must share something in common. In this case, each hardware or software item in the departmental inventory database has a relationship to a vendor record in the purchasing department's supplier database. A **link,** or relationship between data, between the two must be established, commonly by finding a data item in common. For example, Zeos is the brand name of a computer and the vendor name, so it is a link.

Using a Query Language

Until the mid-1980s, programming was the most common way to access a database. One early personal computer DBMS program had no menus, only a blank screen with a period — not even a blinking cursor. To work with a database listing household items for your insurance agent, you typed in commands like

```
.DISP ALL DESCRIP VALUE
```

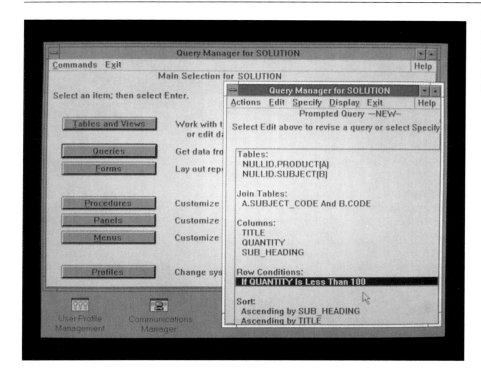

FIGURE 6.8

SQL provides a more English-like database query. Query language makes it easier for you to search your database for information.

Now we have much more English-like commands for searching a database, called *query languages*. A **query language** is a type of programming language that allows knowledge workers to make DBMS inquiries without using programming "codes" or keywords. Instead of using commands with formal syntax like just shown, we can simply type

LIST ITEMS AND PRICES

The query language combines several techniques that make it possible to collect disparate data in the database and view it on the screen in several different ways. There are many advantages in using a query language:

- Its main task is to manage data.
- Commands and statements are very similar to sentences in English.
- It creates a database, puts data into it, and then modifies and retrieves that data.
- It helps use the data more efficiently.
- It provides more ways of browsing through data.
- It can be used interactively, while working with the DBMS.
- It can merge data from different sources and databases.
- It can execute many DBMS commands with a single statement.
- It executes commands, such as SEARCH, up to four times faster.

Most query languages work by presenting a screen called a *work surface* that lets you make queries. An example is shown in Figure 6.8.

One of the most popular query languages was developed for mainframes and minicomputer relational DBMSs, and is now available for personal computer programs. It's called **SQL** and was developed by IBM. SQL stands for **structured query language,** which has many easy-to-use features that made it instantly popular. Now a number of software vendors have their own SQL products. Query languages are discussed in more detail in Chapter 12.

DATABASE PROGRAMMING

A unique feature of the DBMS is that it can be used to create applications. This is accomplished using the DBMS's built-in programming language. In this respect, it is often referred to as an **application development environment** because, with the computer hardware, a knowledge worker can develop and use a complete computer system. For example, the owner of a small mail order business could use the DBMS programming language to create an application that:

1. Presents an order entry screen.
2. Manages inventory.
3. Prepares replenishment orders.
4. Prepares customer orders.
5. Prints the invoice and shipping label.
6. Tracks payments and prints reports.

FIGURE 6.9

Working with a DBMS application generator. Application generators can take the drudgery out of customizing your database applications.

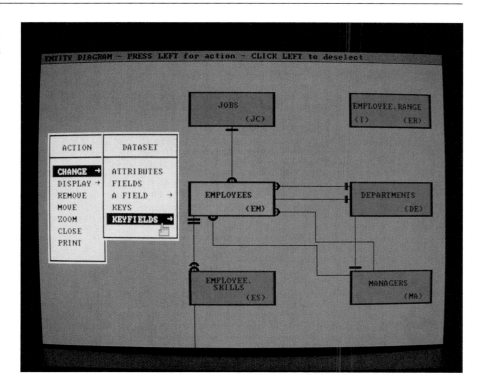

In the past, the owner would have needed to know a formal programming language or would have to hire a programmer to write such an application. Today, the DBMS programming language makes this a do-it-yourself project. What's more, the knowledge worker can do most of the programming work either using English-like commands or making selections from menus. These are often referred to as **application generators.** Figure 6.9 shows a typical application generator screen.

KNOWLEDGE CHECK

1. What is a link used for?   p. 194
2. What does a query language replace?   p. 195
3. When would you use an application generator?   p. 197

WHAT LIES AHEAD?

The trend in DBMS applications, as in other areas, is toward greater ease of use. New applications continually strive to bring the full power of the computer to the knowledge worker. As mentioned earlier, the advance from magnetic tape to disk technology made it possible to design entirely new types of databases. Greater processing speed has improved personal computer DBMS applications. Rapid advancements took RAM from 256K to 1MB and more, while disk storage grew from 140K to 1.2MB and more—not to mention hard disk auxiliary storage advances. With these changes, a personal computer could provide an effective platform for using a DBMS.

Most DBMSs for personal computers are considered relational and often have their own programming languages to help knowledge workers design the database more easily. Personal computer DBMSs also continue to grow in data capacity. dBASE II, for example, has been upgraded to dBASE IV. It is now capable of storing over 1 billion records, each with 128 fields containing 4,000 characters each—if you have enough auxiliary storage, of course.

The next generation of DBMSs allows us to connect personal computers and workstations in a network so they can work with other computers, including personal computers, minis, and mainframes. But the process of giving us easy access to the data we use most often is still under development. Now DBMS designers are striving to make the computer follow human work styles, rather than requiring people to work like the computer. In doing so, they are beginning to see the potential in *graphical databases* that store images instead of text. And thus storing text and graphics together—creating a complete view of information in images as well as words—cannot be far away.

DBMS ETHICS: PRIVACY

Clearly, we are in the midst of an information explosion. The computer's ability to store and maintain massive volumes of data has greatly expanded the information available to people. Since a lot of such data is private, relating to individuals and corporations, we have to be concerned with privacy.

TOMORROW

THE PERSONAL INFORMATION MANAGER

```
Highlight the date and press ENTER. Use arrow keys, PgUp, PgDn,
CTRL (with arrows) to move to other months and years.
High                                                        When
   !! Call John today at 2:00 on preparation for merger    -10/26/90 2:00pm
      meeting next Tues.
   · Call John next Monday about whether Q2 sales results   -10/29/90
     will be as strong         October 1990
   ⌐ Meet Chris about                                       -10/30/90
                          Sun Mon Tue Wed Thu Fri Sat
Medium                                                      When
   @ Staff meeting tod         1   2   3   4   5   6  ities -10/26/90 4:00pm
     for preparation f     7   8   9  10  11  12  13
   · Ask John on Monda     14  15  16  17  18  19  20   or  -10/29/90
     FY'91 will be rea     21  22  23  24  25 [26] 27
     Committee next Fr     28  29  30  31                   -11/09/90
   · Meet Lee in two w                                  on
     growth plans for

Low                                                        When
   · Call Fred to arrange lunch with new CFO after he       -11/09/90
     arrives on board in two weeks

No Priority Assigned                          Priority When
F1      F2      F3      F4      F5      F6      F7    F8    F9    F10
Help                                   SetTime
```

Lotus Agenda, a PIM.

One problem with the traditional DBMS is that data has to be structured—organized by fields, records, and files. But the data people use doesn't always fit neatly into this structure. Several people working with personal computers in the mid-1980s came up against this problem and resolved to do something about it. What has emerged is a new kind of relational DBMS called the **personal information manager (PIM).** It is actually a product of several different fields of research, combining some traditional desktop tools like the appointment calendar, calculator,

and "to-do" list, as well as word processing and a DBMS. The screen of a typical PIM is shown here.

PIMs go a step further in the way they organize data. For example, a PIM might associate information by items or topics, and sort through the topics using a specific category or a **keyword**—key term common to several topics. This is effective for keeping small bits of information: phone messages, reminders, names and addresses, or a to-do list.

Some PIMs also have special software that lets you make assumptions and create relation-

ships between information. For example, your things-to-do list says get the leaky faucet fixed; there is no listing in your phone book for a plumber, but a handyman named Jim did some repair work for you once. A PIM might use the keyword repair to help you find his phone number and address.

In some of the newer PIMs, the file structure is superseded by the information base. An information base, which resembles a cross between a text file and a free-form database, may contain many kinds of files. It can keep data in many formats. Instead of being organized by filenames, the information base structures data by logical relationships; for example, short text (notes), long text (letters, reports, and book chapters), databases, appointment books, business forms. One type of data can be easily linked to another, according to your needs, and changed often. Links can be created for any kind of searching and ordering. These links can be more effective for organizing data than keywords, which have to be in the text somewhere.

For many years, we have had to work with data in ways that conform to the computer's way of data processing. There is a trend toward designing software that guides the computer to do our work the way we do it. PIMs are a step in that direction.

CAREERS FOR KNOWLEDGE WORKERS
PHILIPPE KAHN, FOUNDER, BORLAND INTERNATIONAL

Paris-born Philippe Kahn used to tend goats in the Pyrenees mountains. Today, he is president and chief executive officer of Borland International, Inc., a software company located in Scotts Valley, California. Philippe was an undergraduate student at the University of Zurich, in Switzerland, where he studied under famed computer scientist Niklaus Wirth. It was Wirth who created the Pascal programming language, named after the French mathematician Blaise Pascal (1623–62), who created the Pascaline calculating machine. Philippe Kahn went on to earn the equivalent of an MS and a teaching degree, *Capes de Mathematiques,* from the University of Nice. As a mathematics professor, he was intrigued by computers from the beginning. Be-

fore long he realized he had to get to Silicon Valley and become part of the high tech industry. He could only afford a one-way plane ticket to California; there was no turning back.

Philippe formed Borland in 1983 as a software company, and it got its start with Turbo Pascal, an improved version of the Pascal programming language for personal computers. Soon after, Borland introduced the powerful utility program called Sidekick, which automates and organizes many business desktop tasks. Today, Borland is well known for Quattro Pro, a spreadsheet, and Paradox, a DBMS. In 1991, Philippe bought Ashton-Tate corporation and all rights to dBASE software, making him and his company the king of DBMS programs.

"Our corporate customers told us there is a place for both dBASE and Paradox in the organizations," he says, "and that they'd like the two products to become more integrated. Customers will benefit by continuing to choose the product that is right for them. Also, frankly, Ashton-Tate is not known for technical innovation, but Borland is. We're committed to boosting the functionality of dBASE. Our plans are to deliver Windows versions of both dBASE and Paradox."

Philippe Kahn is an outspo-

ken man who believes strongly in communication and frequently uses computers connected to phone lines for electronic mail exchanges. "I like the fact that it makes the organization flat, and anybody can have access to me at any time. It's the ultimate open-door policy and I take it very seriously. I read between 100 and 150 messages per day. Really, I believe that the best way to run a company and motivate employees is to communicate, and I want to have as many opportunities and channels to do that as possible." So Philippe has not only a cellular phone in his car, but a laptop computer for reading and writing electronic mail as well!

Philippe has a unique personal and business role model: the barbarian. "Lean and efficient, that's what a barbarian is," he says. "To me, the barbarian represents our dream of the free man. When he looks out, the sky is the limit. He lives by his friendship and trust in his people. He is direct, trustworthy and disdains luxury or useless possessions. The barbarian has to be his own warrior, priest, doctor, philosopher. Borland qualifies as a barbarian technology-driven culture. We focus on essentials, substance over form, the things that really make a difference to our customers and our shareholders."

Privacy involves boundaries. In earlier times, it was easier to establish those boundaries. Statements such as "one's home is one's castle" were the basis of law. No one had a right to invade the sanctuary of your personal four walls or disturb your home's contents, without a publicly demonstrated, authorized need.

But today, our personal concerns are extended beyond the home. Personal information is no longer simply recorded on paper and protected by walls. It has become much more elusive, in the form of bits and bytes that can travel over wires and even be beamed to and from satellites.

Now the boundaries of personal information are more abstract. The statement for our times might be "Who needs to know?" By this we mean, "For what purpose does the world at large seek information about me that I consider personal and private?" This is pertinent to us all. Here are some questions to demonstrate this fact:

- If you subscribe to a magazine, you have given its publisher your address. Should that publisher have the right to share or sell your address to other publishers without your consent?

- If you allow an insurance company to cover your medical, dental, or psychological services, this company has a legal right to view your records. If your employer is providing your insurance coverage, should it have the right to see your medical information?

- If you use a Visa or MasterCard credit card, your purchases are recorded in the bank's corporate database. Who should be allowed to view this personal information? Should data on your buying habits be used to help companies pursue you as a customer?

These are just a few examples of how our everyday activities can become data items in corporate databases. When the lines among these corporations or the boundaries between corporations and government and the public become blurred, our privacy becomes more than a philosophical matter. How data is interpreted can become misinformation that has a direct impact on our lives.

SUMMARY

1. *Explain the difference between a database and a database management system (DBMS).* A database is a group of related records or files used to keep track of information. A database may be manual, on paper, or on magnetic media for use with computers. A database management system is the application software that lets you organize, store, and retrieve data from one or more databases.

2. *Describe the advantages of a DBMS.* Database management systems provide an effective way to use computers to enter, manipulate, and print data that has been organized in specific ways. There are three primary advantages. A DBMS is flexible, allowing us to use or examine data in many different ways. It allows discrimination, the ability to search very selectively for data. The DBMS's third advantage is extensibility, the ability to use many databases so long as the structure is the same.

3. *Identify the four types of DBMS and the data elements they use.* There are four major types of DBMS: the flat file, like a stack of recipe cards; the hierarchical, like a tree, that uses one-to-many relationships; the network, like the body's circulatory system, that uses many-to-many relationships; and the relational, which cross-references between tables, that uses any-to-any relationships. In the DBMS, data is arranged into physical and logical data elements. The three types of common physical data are the bit, byte, and word. The five logical data elements are the character, field, record, file, and database.

4. *Explain the steps in creating and editing a database.* The first step in working with a DBMS is database design, which includes data definition and refinement. This helps plan for creating fields, the first step in creating a database. Once fields are designed, they may be filled with data to form records. Once the database is ready, the

data in it may be manipulated in several different ways, using commands such as LIST, INDEX, and SORT. The DBMS lets you print data in neat, attractive reports.

5. *Describe some advanced database management functions and features.* DBMS software has extensive capabilities for manipulating data. It is possible to relate different files, or databases, that have data elements in common. The query language makes it possible to explore relationships between data that would not be possible using conventional commands or in reports. The DBMS application programming environment lets knowledge workers create entire applications that would have required professional programming skills in the past.

6. *Describe some features of the modern database-like personal information manager.* The personal information manager (PIM) combines a relational DBMS with other desktop organizing tools. It is useful for keeping a variety of different kinds of information, from phone numbers to desktop reminders to an appointment calendar. Some PIMs utilize an information base, which permits organizing data in more useful formats than the conventional file. Then it is possible to find specific information through links.

ISSUES

1. An employee was fired after six weeks on a new job when a background check turned up a drug conviction. Equifax Services, Inc., had pulled the criminal record of a man with the same first and last names, but a different middle name, while collecting job applicant data from databases. Such companies mix information from various data bases and produce summaries that describe the applicant's financial condition, criminal and driving records, and business relationships. Sometimes this is raw, unchecked data from credit bureaus, motor vehicle departments, courthouses, and other sources. Often it is illegal for employers to have such information; for example, listings of arrests that ended in acquittal, discharge, and no disposition. In another case, an employee who collected workers' compensation was "blacklisted" from obtaining employment and turned down for over 200 jobs. What do you think of this practice? Should such database gathering be prohibited? Should it be screened by a government agency or subject to federal legislation guidelines?

2. Data security remains a big issue in business and government. A secretary created phony vendor records in her company's database and paid bills totaling $80,000 to them. Then she and her boyfriend cleaned out the bank accounts and left the country. Estimated losses due to such crimes by insiders total at least $100 million a year, per-haps as high as $3 billion. Nobody knows, because businesses are often reluctant to admit the crimes. They fear the stockholders and the public will think ill of them. Is that the right attitude? How would you feel if, instead of dismissing guilty employees and covering up their crimes, a company that was robbed by employees prosecuted them and made the event public knowledge? Which approach is more likely to prevent future crimes?

3. Credit card companies collect and analyze data about cardholders' shopping habits. Citibank is collecting extensive data about card-holding consumers in Chicago, Dallas, Denver, and Los Angeles through bar code scanning. American Express Gold Card customers receive an annual summary of what they've used their card to charge: hotels, meals, entertainment, consumer goods. The new generation of "smart" credit cards promise — or threaten — to hold not only transaction information, but the cardholder's personal health information, including insurance and prescription information. Perhaps all this is fine — except when the data is organized into patterns and sold to companies that wish to market their products to you. Do you feel that is ethical? Do credit card companies make it clear enough when they ask your permission to remarket this information? Do you recall any instances of being asked for permission?

CHAPTER REVIEW QUESTIONS

REVIEW QUESTIONS

1. Explain the difference between a database and a DBMS.
2. Why is it important to organize data in a DBMS carefully?
3. What are the database design steps?
4. What is the report writer used for?
5. Explain the differences between hierarchical, network, and relational DBMSs.
6. What are the advantages of a report writer over simply printing what is shown on the DBMS screen?
7. When would you use a database programming language?
8. How can a DBMS enhance a knowledge worker's productivity?
9. Why is it important to be able to access data on a variety of databases? Why not just keep it all in one centralized database?

DISCUSSION QUESTIONS

1. What are some advantages of using a DBMS?
2. What are some limitations of using manual databases?
3. Discuss the relationship between fields and records, and how that relationship affects the way we can organize and use data in the database.
4. Discuss several ways you would use the database manipulation commands—LIST, INDEX, SORT, MODIFY, DELETE—to extract specific information from a customer database.
5. Discuss the advantages of the RDBMS.
6. Design a database application based on your personal or work experience. Follow each step in the process, and define the logical data elements.

MULTIPLE-CHOICE

1. Identify the logical data elements common to all DBMSs:
   a. Record.
   b. Character.
   c. Relation.
   d. Index card.
   e. Field.
   f. Database.
   g. File.
   h. Folder.
2. A query language (select all that apply):
   a. Uses English-like commands.
   b. Manages the data in a variety of ways.
   c. Makes it easy to execute commands.
   d. Takes the place of database design.
   e. All of the above.
3. A personal information manager (PIM) (check all that apply):
   a. Is a spreadsheet and DBMS combined.
   b. Helps manage daily work activities.
   c. Can store data in more than one format.
   d. Works the way the knowledge worker works.
   e. Uses keywords to form associative links.
4. When creating fields, it is important to (check all that apply):
   a. Limit the width.
   b. Select and create the proper types of fields.
   c. Fertilize the soil prior to use.
   d. Indicate decimals for dollars and cents.
   e. Create fields of the correct type and size.

FILL-IN-THE-BLANK

1. The four types of databases are
   _____, _____,
   _____, and _____.
2. The simplest way of organizing data is with a
   _____ _____ program.
3. Database planning is most effectively done
   with _____ and _____.

4. The smallest data element is called a
   _____.
5. Entities must have _____.
6. SQL stands for _____
   _____.

TRUE/FALSE

1. The rational database is most common in a personal computer DBMS.
2. Entering data is the most time-consuming aspect
   of database creation.
3. Appending a record is the process of modifying
   existing records in a database.

4. The flat file database is no longer used.
5. Saving the database file is not as important as it is
   in other applications.

KEY TERMS

application development
environment, 196

application generator,   197

attribute, 183

character, 182

data definition, 190

data elements, 182

data refinement, 190

database, 179

database design, 188

database management system,
DELETE, 192

entity, 182

field, 183

file, 183

flat file database, 184

hierarchical database, 186

INDEX, 191

keyword, 198

link, 194

LIST, 191

logical data
representation, 182

MODIFY, 192

network database, 186

personal information manager
(PIM), 198

physical data representa-
tion, 182

query language, 195

record, 183

relational database
(RDBMS), 186

report writer, 192

SORT, 191

sort keys, 191

structured query language
(SQL), 196

System Software and Application Software

LEARNING OBJECTIVES

After reading and studying this chapter, you should be able to:

1. Explain the various tasks performed by operating systems software.

2. Identify leading personal computer, minicomputer, and mainframe operating systems.

3. Understand the purposes of operating environment software.

4. Understand the difference between stand-alone and integrated software.

5. Describe some other commonly used applications.

6. Describe the uses for utility software for applications and operating systems.

UNDERSTANDING SOFTWARE

Software. The word is so new that it didn't appear in the 1971 edition of the *Oxford English Dictionary*. Yet software has made dramatic changes in society and has created an entirely new industry. Indeed, software has made many people wealthy; Bill Gates, cofounder of Microsoft, the leading personal computer software company, was a billionaire at 32. Today he is the richest man in America.

In the previous chapters, you learned about the most popular application software packages. Now you're ready to learn more about software, the seemingly intangible component that makes computers able to do so many different, versatile things. Software helps us with tasks that control the machine. More importantly, it does many tasks that we as people think about or use our brains to perform. Indeed, without software, computers would be of little value.

This chapter builds on what you learned in Chapter 2 about operating systems. It presents a complete overview of system and application software. The operating system and its many functions are explained so that you'll come to appreciate all the things it can do for you. The second half of the chapter explores the many business software applications and utility programs that augment operating system software.

SYSTEM SOFTWARE

System software runs the computer system, performing a variety of fundamental tasks or operations that make the computer available for use. These tasks include:

- Booting the computer and making sure all aspects are operational.
- Performing operations such as retrieving, loading, executing, and storing application programs.
- Storing and retrieving files.
- Performing a variety of system utility functions.

System software includes the operating system software (OS for short) which controls the execution of computer programs. It also controls programming tools, which are used to translate and help improve computer programs. It acts as an intermediary between the user or application programs and the computer hardware to control and manage the operation of the computer. In a sense, the OS is the resident authority in your computer, as portrayed in Figure 7.1. Whatever you want to do has to be done with the help and cooperation of

FIGURE 7.1

The operating system orchestrates four essential operations in the computer: input and output control, CPU task scheduling, data management and storage, and command languages and utilities.

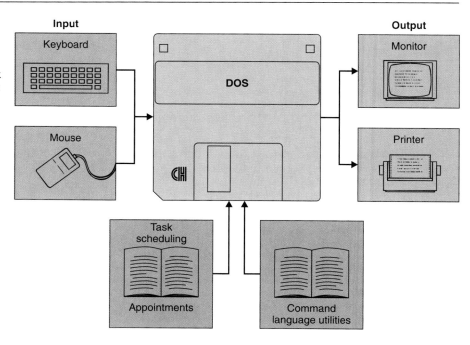

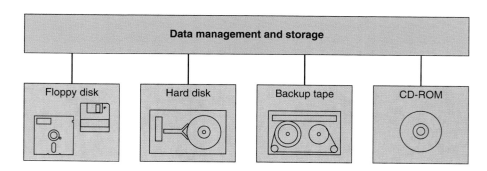

the operating system. The OS performs four important operations essential to the hardware resource allocation and usage:

1. Input and output control.
2. CPU task scheduling.
3. Data management and storage.
4. Command languages and utilities.

Some of these operations are directed and controlled by you, the knowledge worker, while others are usually performed without intervention. Yet all four are necessary for smooth computer functioning and are essential to support the use of individual software applications. Let's explore them in more detail.

INPUT AND OUTPUT CONTROL

Whether you are using a personal computer or a mainframe, your computer has many input and output (I/O) devices. A typical personal computer uses a keyboard, a monitor, and a printer. Like a skilled traffic officer, the operating system coordinates between these various I/O devices and other peripheral devices such as hard or floppy disk drives, making sure data flows properly between them and sorting out possible confusion.

For example, let's see how the operating system manages the printing process. When you want to print a file, you type the PRINT command. First, the operating system translates your command into the binary language of bits and bytes that makes sense to the CPU. Second, like a traffic officer seeing a car's turn signal, it realizes that you want to produce output on a specific device. Third, it stops whatever the CPU is doing and redirects its attention to the printing function. Fourth, the operating system searches the available peripheral devices, chooses the correct one, translates its name for the CPU, and commands the CPU to send your file to that device. Lastly, after the file is printed, the operating system tells the CPU the job is done so it is free for the next request.

CPU TASK SCHEDULING

With few exceptions, the computers we work with have but one CPU and can do only one thing at a time. However, in order to make knowledge workers more productive by helping them do their job better and faster, it must *seem* like the computer is performing many tasks or serving the needs of many knowledge workers simultaneously. Therefore, the OS must be a master appointment secretary.

How does the single CPU perform multiple tasks, such as permitting input (keyboarding) while producing output (printing)? How does it serve many knowledge workers while making it seem like we are the only user? With speed, scheduling, and memory management.

SPEED. The CPU works very fast. Processing time is measured in nanoseconds, or billionths of a second. Figure 7.2 illustrates some physical comparisons of the speed light — and thus electricity — travels.

SCHEDULING. The OS is very efficient at **scheduling** — making maximum use of the CPU by performing tasks in a precise sequence. By establishing rules and priorities among users and by making use of every nanosecond, the OS takes advantage of a brief pause in one task or user's activity to perform another request. Scheduling makes it appear as though the CPU is doing many things at once, when in fact it's only capable of doing one thing at a time — albeit very quickly. The CPU is always working at maximum efficiency.

Another aspect of scheduling involves **multitasking** — using more than one application at the same time. Most popular operating systems are designed for multitasking (sometimes called **multiprogramming**), permitting numerous applications to share the CPU so that many users can perform a variety of tasks consecutively. Mainframe and minicomputer operating sys-

FIGURE 7.2

Electricity travels at the speed of light — 186,282 miles per hour, or nearly one foot per second. The faster electricity travels between computer components, the faster instructions may be carried out. Shortening electrical distance is a major factor in circuitry and chip design.

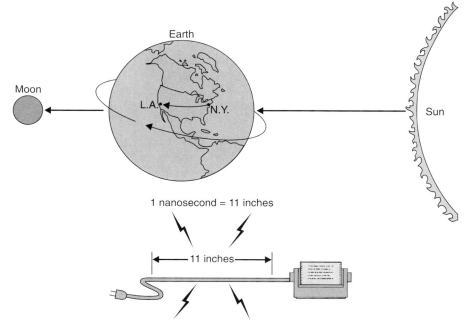

tems have had this capability for many years. In the 1990s, we can expect to see multitasking for personal computers become the *de facto* standard for knowledge workers.

MEMORY MANAGEMENT. The CPU and the operating system work together to perform **memory management,** or controlling the quantity of data and instructions that can be held in RAM at any one given time. A way to understand memory management is by envisioning a bucket brigade trying to put out a fire. At one end of a long line of people is the building on fire; at the other end is the water source. For our example, the blazing building is the CPU and the water source is the disk drive containing the application program's instructions. The people on the line are passing buckets of water as quickly as they can, but there is always a lag at one end or the other. Either the people can't fill the buckets quickly enough or there are too few people to toss buckets of water on the fire. For the computer, this means either that it is taking too long to access instructions from the disk, or that the instructions are piling up while waiting, one at a time, for processing.

To remedy this, two memory management schemes are commonly used. One is called *virtual memory,* and the other *cache memory.* **Virtual memory** means the CPU regards a portion of hard disk space in the same way it does RAM; therefore, RAM appears *in essence* to have more capacity than it does in *actual fact.* **Cache memory** is a small memory accumulation area, often part of the CPU integrated circuit chip; however, a cache can also be created using a special software program. In both cases, the idea is the same: create an *additional* memory staging area just before the CPU where instructions can be gathered and then promptly and efficiently passed on for processing. Cache memory is much faster than RAM, especially when it is part of the CPU chip. It's as if an additional group of people gathered together near the head of the line, just behind the people tossing water on the fire, to make sure they always have plenty of buckets.

DATA MANAGEMENT AND STORAGE

If you've ever visited or used a large library, you are aware of the tremendous quantity of information people have at their fingertips. A library collects and organizes information, primarily in the form of books and periodicals. One of its many virtues is making the information we seek easy to locate and use. The library is similar to a computer's auxiliary memory, where we organize and store data in files. Knowledge workers need to know the location, size, date, and composition of the files in the computer. They also need the assurance that the files are safely stored and available when needed. The operating system is essential in properly managing and storing vast amounts of data.

DATA MANAGEMENT.   The operating system's data management function is responsible for organizing and storing files and programs in auxiliary storage. It does so in a very orderly fashion by storing files alphabetically by filename in directories, which you learned about in Chapter 2. In addition to the filename, the operating system records other important facts about the file: the date and time it was stored, its size (usually in kilobytes, or Kbytes for short), and the directory in which it is located. It is often possible to know what application was used to create the file by its filename extension.

DATA STORAGE.   The data storage function, or saving a file on disk, is accomplished in a somewhat more haphazard way. When the operating system saves a file, it gathers several individual storage compartments into what are termed **clusters,** using as many as necessary to store the entire file contents. When you want to retrieve the file, the OS uses its file allocation table (FAT) function to link all the clusters together and restore the entire file. Fortunately, the operating system does all this work itself, without your having to concern yourself with it.

COMMAND LANGUAGES AND UTILITIES

Effective working relationships depend on effective communication, and this is certainly true with computers. Over the years, a fairly common vocabulary of codes, words, and phrases has evolved that allows us to communicate quickly and efficiently with the CPU. We call this a **command language.** For example, when you type DIR at the DOS prompt on your personal computer screen, the operating system issues a command to the CPU to list the files it finds on the disk or directory you are working in. Each operating system has a collection of these commands; Figure 7.3 shows some that are common in DOS.

Some commands activate OS programs called *utilities* that perform disk and file tasks; several, such as COPY, MOVE, and DELETE, were mentioned in Chapter 2. Operating system commands and utilities can be quite extensive, filling whole volumes. Some are difficult or awkward to use, and have given

FIGURE 7.3

This chart shows some commonly used DOS commands.

COPY	Makes copies of files
DATE	Sets the date
DIR	Lists the files on a disk
DISKCOPY	Copies an entire disk
ERASE	Removes files from a disk
FORMAT	Prepares a disk for use
PRINT	Prints a file on the printer
RENAME	Changes file names
TIME	Sets the time
TYPE	Displays the contents of a file on the monitor

birth to an entire segment of the software industry devoted to producing more effective and useful utility software programs. You'll learn more about them later in this chapter.

Now that you have a general idea of what operating systems do, let's take a look at some of the most common types. The next section describes some of the most popular types of personal computer, mini, and mainframe operating systems.

TYPES OF OPERATING SYSTEMS

The operating system is essential software in the computer system. It coordinates all activities between hardware and software components. Without it, nothing else happens. Yet at the same time it is software that we prefer to have as little to do with as possible; after all, our productivity depends on using application programs. This section is a brief introduction to the various operating systems. The following section explains the graphic user interface, a type of software intended to make it easier for knowledge workers to use the operating system.

PERSONAL COMPUTER OPERATING SYSTEMS

Most personal computers in use today are single-user computers, with one person using one application at a time. Instead of having to handle the requests of multiple users and sort out the inputs and outputs of many devices, the operating systems running these personal computers execute instructions in a very straightforward manner, serving one user and performing one function at a time.

Some personal computers have more advanced operating systems with multiuser, multitasking capabilities. **Multiuser** operating systems process the work of two or more users, working at different terminals or personal computers, at the same time. Multitasking operating systems perform two or more functions or tasks simultaneously for a single user. Multitasking is the personal computer equivalent of multiprogramming for minis and mainframes. A multitasking system allows you to write with a word processor while per-

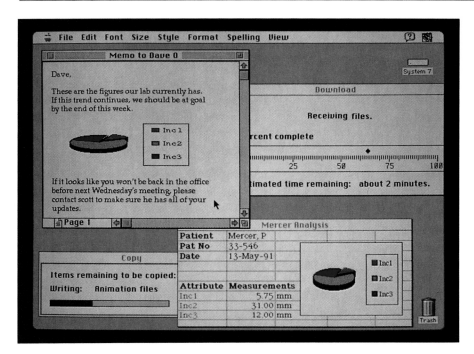

FIGURE 7.4

Multitasking on the Macintosh. From left to right: word processing, communications, spreadsheet, and operating system activities are in concurrent use.

forming spreadsheet calculations in the background, for example. Figure 7.4 shows multitasking at work. Chapter 14 covers the subject of personal computers linked in networks, and the special network operating systems they use. For now, let's compare several personal computer operating systems.

DOS. The most common personal computer operating system is MS-DOS, developed by Microsoft Corporation of Redmond, Washington. MS-DOS stands for Microsoft Disk Operating System. PC-DOS is a similar operating system developed for the IBM PC. Today we simply refer to these operating systems as DOS.

DOS is a simple operating system. It includes several basic utilities but its primary function is telling the personal computer to perform whatever task the application you're using tells it to. The first version of DOS was not very easy to use. For example, if you wanted to enter the date, you had to type it as 12-18-1944. It would not accept a date entered as 12/18/1944 or 12/18/44. A more serious drawback is that DOS makes no provision for an electrical outage or other system failure. Unless you frequently save your work, an unexpected system failure can destroy a lot of effort. In addition, its outdated memory management characteristics make it an awkward base from which to use the newer software.

Another problem has to do with memory management. DOS, as it was originally designed, could only access up to 640K of RAM. However, as software requirements grew, this became an extremely limiting factor. Thus, special memory management software was created. These utility programs, such as QEMM and 386MAX, find unused memory space above 640KB and

FIGURE 7.5

DOS versions. When problems are corrected or minor improvements made, the current version is modified and numbered with a suffix, as with 3.3. A major new version gets a new number, such as 6.0.

Version	Date	Features
1.0	1981	Original disk operating system
1.25	1982	Support for double-sided disks
2.0	1983	Support for subdirectories (especially hard disk)
2.01	1983	Support for international symbols
2.11	1983	Bug corrections
2.25	1983	Extended character set support
3.0	1984	Support for 1.2MB floppy disk, up to 32MB hard disk
3.1	1984	Support for PC networks
3.2	1986	Support for 3.5-inch micro-floppy disk
3.3	1987	Support for IBM PS/2 computers
4.0	1989	Menu-driven user interface; support for 1.44MB floppy disk, hard disks over 32MB
5.0	1990	Window interface; better memory use
6.0	1993	Better Windows integration, more utilities, networking

make it available to the operating system by making it appear to be extra RAM space. By quickly shuttling data and instructions around, this software can trick DOS into thinking it has access to as much as 32MB of RAM. This software, once installed, does its work without human intervention.

Despite its shortcomings, DOS has been a workhorse operating system for a long line of personal computers. As Figure 7.5 shows, it has been improved and revised extensively over the years and now provides user-friendly features such as a menu. MS-DOS 5.0 incorporated many features that make it easier for new or casual users. Its features include menus, the use of the mouse, an improved file editor, and many utility tasks that were previously unavailable. Figure 7.6 shows the menu-oriented version of MS-DOS 5.0. The latest version, 6.0, adds networking capabilities.

OS/2. The **OS/2** operating system was jointly developed by Microsoft and IBM for its PS/2 line of personal computers, so named because it was the second-generation DOS. OS/2 offers features not found in DOS. It has more RAM capacity (which allows it to run more complicated applications), multitasking capabilities, and a graphic interface. The OS/2 graphic interface, called Presentation Manager, allows you to run several applications in **windows,** or individual boxes displayed on the monitor screen. This makes it possible, for example, to perform word processing in one window while working with a spreadsheet in another. The current version, OS/2 2.0, is a single-user operating system, but works much faster than DOS.

MACINTOSH SYSTEM 7. System 7, the Macintosh operating system, uses icons and graphics instead of the command line common to DOS and OS/2. A file folder holds various documents, which are visually displayed on the screen. The mouse is used to move files and folders from one place to another; a trash can icon is used to erase them from the disk. A menu is displayed across the top of the screen, with "pull-down" menu commands connected to each.

Apple has improved its Macintosh operating system many times since its

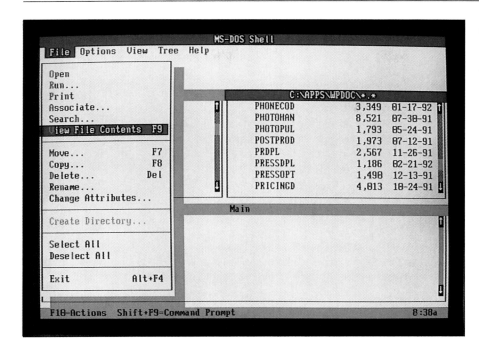

FIGURE 7.6

The DOS 5.0 menu provides a great deal of information in several different windows, a vast improvement over the plain command line interface.

introduction. While it has been known generically as the "system" in the past, with the release of System 7 it entered a new phase of maturity—much as MS-DOS 5.0 did. It permits multitasking and most recently has added a variety of desktop publishing capabilities as standard features. Additionally, other software companies have introduced programs that make System 7 even more useful, such as one that permits multiple users.

MINICOMPUTER OPERATING SYSTEMS

Minicomputer operating systems are more complex than those for personal computers. Most are multiuser, multiprogramming systems that control an extensive array of peripheral devices. Mini operating systems are fast, handle large volumes of data, and perform many I/O operations.

UNIX. UNIX is an operating system developed at AT&T Bell Laboratories in New Jersey. UNIX was initially designed to offer a powerful and convenient programming environment for experienced users. UNIX commands are abbreviated and extremely powerful. Steps required by many simpler operating systems are eliminated to make UNIX faster. Novice knowledge workers often find UNIX rather unfriendly and unforgiving.

But people who can do many things at once find UNIX especially valuable. UNIX allows you to, in effect, be many knowledge workers at once. This is accomplished by making it easy to run several subprocesses or work sessions at the same time. Each subprocess can perform several tasks at once.

UNIX use is widespread, especially in the college community. Its popularity is also due in part to its being a more portable operating system than most.

FIGURE 7.7

Digital minicomputer VMS
commands. Note that they
maintain an ease-of-use factor.

AUTHORIZE	Allocates system resources to users
COPY	Copies a file from one disk or directory to another
DELETE	Deletes a file
DIFFERENCE	Show the differences between two files
DIRECTORY	Lists contents of the default directory
EDIT	Edits a file
HELP	Displays help on commands
LOGIN/LOGOUT	Begins/ends a user session
MAIL	Sends/reads mail messages
PURGE	Deletes prior versions of files
RECOVER	Restores a file lost by system failure
RENAME	Changes file names
SET DEFAULT	Sets default disk and directory
SET PASSWORD	Sets a new user password
SHOW PROCESS	Shows use of system resources
SHOW PROTECT	Shows users allowed access to a file
SHOW QUEUE	Lists printer and batch jobs being executed or waiting to be executed
SHOW USERS	Lists current users of computer
SPAWN	Begins a user session within an active user session

Portable means it can be used on several different computers, regardless of their manufacturer. Because of its effective use of computer processing capabilities, many UNIX features have been added to some personal computer operating systems. UNIX is the preferred operating system for most workstations and is available for use with some personal computers as well.

VMS. **VMS** is the operating system Digital Equipment Corporation developed for its family of VAX (Virtual Address Extension) computers. VMS stands for Virtual Memory System, and it works as described earlier in this chapter.

VMS uses a technique called the Swapper to make the virtual memory seem larger than it actually is. It "swaps" users in and out of the CPU and its RAM very quickly, to make them each feel they have exclusive access to processing. VMS is by far the most popular operating system for minicomputers. Its widespread use and versatility have made it an ideal choice for the trend in business toward **open systems,** where all types and sizes of computers, regardless of their operating systems, can work together. VMS, as a proprietary operating system, is being upgraded, both in terms of compatibility with other open systems and in the features that made it so popular. Figure 7.7 lists some VMS commands.

MAINFRAME OPERATING SYSTEMS

One of the main advantages of using mainframes is that they permit the largest number of knowledge workers to simultaneously use the computer system. In addition, many different kinds of peripherals and auxiliary storage devices can be connected to the mainframe. In fact, a mainframe can send different types of output to a number of different printers or other output devices, all at the

IBM mainframe MVS commands, demonstrating this operating system's degree of   **FIGURE 7.8**
complexity.

```
    //*         -----------------------------------------------------  00000010
    //*         FORTCLG-FORTRAN COMPILE, LINK, AND EXECUTE.            00000020
    //*         -----------------------------------------------------  00000030
    //          PROC DECK=NODECK, SOURCE=,MAP=NOMAP,LOAD=LOAD,LIST=NOLIST  00000040
    //FORT      EXEC PGM=IEYFORT,REGION=100K,                          00000050
    //               PARM='&DECK,&SOURCE,&MAP,&LOAD,&LIST'             00000060
    //SYSPRINT  DD   SYSOUT=A                                          00000070
    //SYSPUNCH  DD   SYSOUT=B                                          00000080
    //SYSLIN    DD   UNIT=SYSDA,SPACE=(CYL,(1,1)),DISP=(,PASS)         00000090
    //LKED      EXEC PGM=IEWLF440,COND=(4,LT,FORT),REGION=96K,         00000100
    //               PARM=(XREF,LIST,LET)                              00000110
    //SYSLIB    DD   DSN=&&FORTLIB1,DISP=(SHR,PASS)                    00000120
    //          DD   DSN=&&FORTLIB2,DISP=(SHR,PASS)                    00000130
    //SYSLMOD   DD   DSN=&&GOSET(GO),DISP-(,PASS),UNIT=SYSDA,          00000140
    //               SPACE=(CYL,(1,1,1))                               00000150
    //SYSPRINT  DD   SYSOUT=A                                          00000160
    //SYSUT1    DD   DSN=&&SYSUT1,UNIT=SYSSQ,SPACE=(1024,(100,50),,,ROUND)  00000170
    //SYSLIN    DD   DSN=*.FORT.SYSLIN,DISP=(OLD,DELETE)               00000180
    //          DD   DDNAME=SYSIN                                      00000190
    //GO        EXEC PGM=*.LKED.SYSLMOD,COND=((4,LT,FORT),(4,LT,LKED))  00000200
    //FT05F001  DD   DDNAME=SYSIN                                      00000210
    //FT06F001  DD   SYSOUT=A                                          00000220
    //FT07F001  DD   SYSOUT=B                                          00000230
    //*         -----------------------------------------------------  00000240
```

same time. Yet another mainframe advantage is their extraordinary ability to work with large amounts of data. All these advantages, and many others, are possible because of the sophisticated operating systems mainframes employ. Thus, we refer to mainframe operating systems as being *multiuser* (many simultaneous workers), *multiprogramming* (many simultaneous tasks) systems that are capable of performing at greater processing speeds than either personal computer or mini operating systems.

MVS. MVS is a well-known operating system in the mainframe world. Developed by IBM, **MVS** specializes in batch processing, which involves collecting several user requests or programs into batches for processing at a later time. Batch processing is used primarily for large, periodic jobs such as corporate billing or payroll.

MVS also has extensive multiuser capabilities. That is because it was created using principles established during Project MAC at the Massachusetts Institute of Technology. Project MAC's goal was to create a time-sharing computer system (see the Yesterday box). **Time-sharing** means it could be used by many people simultaneously for different purposes or applications — thus its name, Multiple-Access Computer.

MVS is a big operating system, containing 520 million 8-bit characters, coded into 13 million instructions. Because it's big, it can do big things: one MIS department has 7 interconnected CPUs, with approximately 15,000 terminals in over 450 locations, running under the MVS operating system. Between 500 and 700 users can have access to the CPU at a time, using between 300 and 400 different applications. Figure 7.8 lists some MVS commands.

YESTERDAY
PROJECT MAC, THE FIRST OPERATING SYSTEM

Time-sharing was a significant breakthrough in computing. It permitted more than one user to simultaneously interact with the computer. Being able to share programs and data among users was a great boost to productivity and creativity. The first computer time-sharing system (CTSS) permitted a total of three users.

In 1962, MIT computer scientists J. C. R. Licklider and Robert Fano put together a research team to work on Project MAC, which was intended to extend the frontiers of time-sharing. The acronym had a double meaning: Multiple-Access Computer, for the time-sharing system, and Machine-Aided Cognition, the project's larger aim.

Project MAC began working toward the multiple-access computer with CTSS, refining it; within six months, it was serving 200 users in 10 MIT departments. It connected teletypewriter terminals via the MIT telephone system and could serve up to 24 users simultaneously. As a result, computers were becoming more practical and useful. Today multiuser systems are commonplace, thanks to the pioneering efforts at MIT.

Project MAC thrived for seven years, during which time it helped develop a more advanced type of time-sharing, an on-line computer system called Multics (Multiplexed Information and Computing Service). Multics, jointly developed with Bell Labs and General Electric, incorpo-

rated for the first time many sophisticated features such as sharing and managing files and systems security, now common in most computer operating systems software. Multics became the operating system for Honeywell computers (bought from General Electric in 1970). Bell Labs participated in the research and development of Multics and later implemented a similar operating system known as UNIX. And as you already know, IBM's MVS is yet another operating system influenced by Project MAC. Today all modern computers utilize the precepts set forth by the early time-sharing systems.

TRENDS IN OPERATING SYSTEMS

Personal computer operating systems such as System 7 are becoming increasingly sophisticated. Not only do they handle the traditional chores of managing memory and controlling peripherals but they now include such features as user-friendly interfaces, type fonts, and networking capabilities. Many features such as multiuser and multiprogramming/multitasking capabilities, previously found only in mainframe and minicomputer operating systems, are now available with personal computer operating systems.

In the past, computer manufacturers chose to keep the operating systems they developed for their computers **proprietary,** meaning the exact workings of these operating systems were private, protected information. This meant that if you wanted to use a particular manufacturer's hardware, you had to use the operating system designed for it and no other. System 7 is a proprietary operating system; it works only on Macintosh computers.

The opposite of a proprietary product is an open system. UNIX is an example of an open system, a product that can be altered for use with many manufacturers' hardware. Because the inner workings of UNIX are available to the public, anyone can develop applications to work on this operating system. The result is the first nonproprietary operating system that works with personal computers, workstations, minis, and mainframes.

The operating system is an undeniably essential link in the computer system. It links the CPU, peripherals, software, and knowledge worker together, much in the same way the human nervous system links the brain to the spinal cord, limbs, and sensory organs together for smooth functioning. And although the operating system performs many of its functions autonomously, there are still times when we need to direct its tasks. Unfortunately, the operating system is not always easy to use; therefore, a new type of software called an *operating environment* has emerged to help knowledge workers. In addition, many commonly used operating system commands and functions, such as COPY, MOVE, and SAVE, have been incorporated into application programs and other software designed to make the computer easier to use. We shall learn about both in the sections that follow.

KNOWLEDGE CHECK

1. What kind of software is the operating system?   p. 205
2. Identify the four functions of an operating system.   p. 205
3. What is a multiuser system?   p. 210
4. Define the term *multitasking*.   p. 210
5. What is the most common personal computer operating system?   p. 211
6. What is a portable operating system?   p. 214
7. What is the difference between a proprietary system and an open system?   p. 216

OPERATING ENVIRONMENTS

The operating system also determines how certain things look on the screen. In its unmodified form, the view may be as unadorned as the disk drive letter character, providing no hints or clues as to how to use the computer system. When this view is enhanced, it is called an operating environment. The **operating environment** is a form of software that works between the operating system and the application software that makes the computer system easier for knowledge workers to use. What we actually see on the screen is called the **human-computer interface,** the way the computer and its software are presented to the human being who is about to use them. The hardware interface is primarily the monitor and the keyboard, as well as a mouse if one is available. The software interface is composed of the operating system, the operating environment, the application program, and the way they appear to us on the screen. Figure 7.9 shows the relationship between the various levels of the human-computer interface.

When only skilled computer professionals used computers, the human-computer interface was very simple and straightforward. These people under-

FIGURE 7.9

In order to make computers easier to use, it becomes necessary to add more layers of software between the hardware and the knowledge worker.

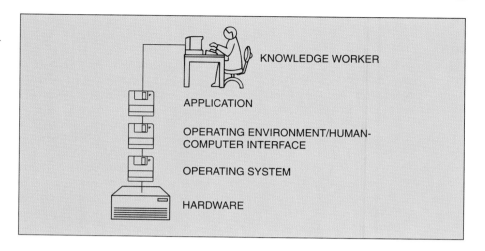

stood the computer quite well and wanted a no-frills interface so they could do their programming work quickly. But today's knowledge workers often have different needs, so different human-computer interfaces have been designed. Perhaps the most distinguishing characteristic of the human-computer interface is the way in which commands are issued to the computer system. There are three basic types of human-computer interfaces available for personal computers today: the command line interface, the menu-driven interface, and the graphic user interface.

THE COMMAND LINE INTERFACE

The original DOS interface is a good example of a command line interface. The **command line interface** requires typing a command to make something happen. However, you must already know what that command is. For example, to learn what programs or data are stored on the disk in the floppy disk drive, you must type DIR. When using DOS, you type a command and then press the Enter or Return key to actually issue that command. If you don't know the command and don't have a manual or guide, you're lost. In addition, DOS does not forgive errors, so all commands must be typed with scrupulous accuracy. On the other hand, using commands at the command line interface is the fastest way to issue commands and explore the computer system. Figure 7.10A shows a directory at the command line.

THE MENU-DRIVEN INTERFACE

As more knowledge workers with little prior experience began using computers, they wished for a human-computer interface to help them remember commands or see what to do next. One of the first friendly interfaces was called a *menu* because it presented a list of the commands, tasks, or projects the user most often worked with. The **menu-driven interface** was developed to make the command line interface easier to use. Figure 7.10B shows a menu-driven interface program.

FIGURE 7.10

A. The command line interface is the simplest to manipulate, if you know the proper commands and syntax.

B. Switch-It's menu makes it easy to toggle between the various programs you want to use.

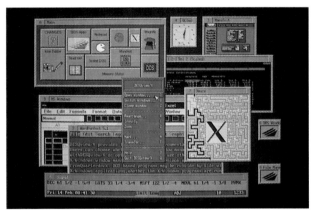

C. DESQView combines the best features of multitasking in a menu-oriented interface.

Some menu-driven interface programs provide additional features and tools, such as disk and file management functions. Such programs facilitate the use of operating system commands; for example, it is possible to see all the files on one disk, select those to be copied, and then confirm their presence on the second disk.

Another useful feature is called *task switching,* which is similar to multitasking. **Task switching** permits keeping several applications, or tasks, active at the same time, switching from one to another as you work. The CPU only works with the *foreground* application at a time, but *background* applications and their files need not be closed when switching between tasks. Some menu-driven interface programs have task switching. The one shown in Figure 7.10C not only offers both task switching and multitasking, but boasts a more graphic interface, the topic we shall take up next.

THE GRAPHIC USER INTERFACE

The most popular human-computer interface for new users is the **graphic user interface** (GUI) popularized by the Macintosh (see the Tomorrow box). The previous two interfaces use only text — numbers, letters, and standard keyboard characters. The graphic user interface uses images in the form of drawings, boxes, and characters in addition to text. It commonly employs *icons,* which are pictorial figures or representations designed so that most people easily recognize them. To see what work is stored on a disk, you must have a mouse or pointing device to position the character — usually an arrow — on the icon that resembles a disk. Press or click the mouse button twice and the disk contents appear. Knowledge workers using a PC-compatible and DOS can use a GUI operating environment such as Microsoft Windows or Geo Works.

THE GUI SCREEN.   The working screen on your monitor is quite different when using a GUI operating environment. If you were simply using MS-DOS, you would see the command line prompt. With a GUI, you see a colorful, graphic screen with text and icons. Whether you wish to work with the operating system commands or with an application, you do so from the GUI operating environment (although you can always "exit to DOS" if you want to!). Here is how it works.

Regardless of the type of computer, whether PC-compatible or Macintosh, there are several characteristics all GUIs share. Refer to Figure 7.11, which shows four popular GUIs, as you study their features. One is a menu bar across the top of the screen, with a number of basic commands used for both operating system software and application software. In the case of the latter, there are often many more commands. Commonly, though, you will see such commands as FILE, EDIT, SETUP, VIEW, TOOLS, and HELP when you are working in the operating environment. These are basic commands that are always in use. Each command represents a **pulldown menu,** which means there are additional commands that appear when you click on it.

The GUI screen below the menu bar displays icons that help you work with files and applications. The icon of a file folder is often used to depict an application, while a sheet of paper with one corner bent over is used to depict a file. These folders and pages are commonly named using everyday English. For example, the database folder is named Paradox and a file is named Last Month's Production. These icons replace the directory structure common to DOS; instead of having to issue commands to change from one directory to the next, you simply move the pointer (commonly using the mouse to do so) from one folder to another. Starting applications is much easier with a GUI. Double-clicking the mouse on the folder launches the application; in many cases, double-clicking the particular file you wish to work with will launch the application that was used to create it.

Today's GUIs have added color and *truly* graphical images to icons. It is possible now to choose the software publisher's *logo,* or image, to identify an application. If you prefer, you can choose more representational icons instead: a quill or typewriter for word processing or a calculator for a spreadsheet, for example. Just as there is clip art for graphics programs, there are literally thousands of choices in "icon art" for GUIs.

A GUI portrait gallery.   FIGURE 7.11

A. Macintosh interface.   B. Windows interface.

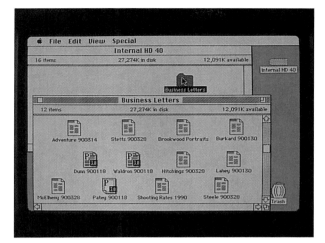

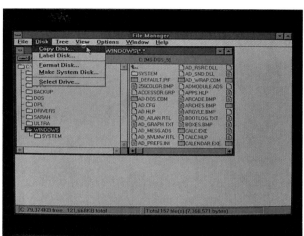

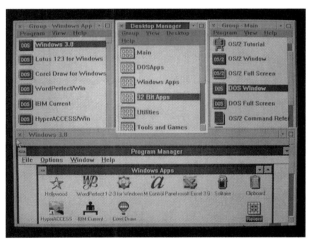

C. OS/2 interface.   D. Motif interface.

ADVANTAGES OF THE GUI

The main advantage a graphic user interface provides is ease of use. **Ease of use**
means that anyone, regardless of their computer knowledge, skills, or background, can quickly become productive. This is accomplished through using
commands (such as the menu bar) and graphic images (icons) that are readily
understood without prior training or experience. The Macintosh extends the
ease of use concept throughout all its application software; all applications
work nearly identically to one another. This is a prerequisite Apple established
within its closed architecture for independent software developers.

Unfortunately, no such standard exists for the open-architecture DOS machine. Although there are uniform characteristics within the operating envi-

ronment, each application performs somewhat differently, according to the way it was designed. In large part, the reason for this is that most applications were designed long before a GUI was available on DOS machines. Even so, many of the new GUI versions of DOS applications are conforming to many of the design principles that were established for the Macintosh; thus, uniformity in commands and characteristics are spreading throughout the DOS environment as well.

DESK ACCESSORIES. GUIs usually come with a number of **desk accessories,** helper programs that make it easier and more interesting to work with the computer. These desk accessories include a clock, a calendar, an appointment book, an address book (and telephone dialer), a scratch pad for notes, and even an alarm clock. These accessories are always readily available, even while using a personal productivity application. To understand desk accessories better, see the section on utility software later in this chapter. As you can see, these desk accessories literally replace the items found on a knowledge worker's desk and put them on the computer monitor screen.

MULTITASKING. Most GUIs have multitasking capabilities as well. In true multitasking, background applications continue processing even while you work with the foreground application. Thus, you could leave the spreadsheet application while it performs a lengthy recalculation and begin writing in word processing. And, unlike a menu with task switching, since the interface is graphic, the windows that applications appear in can be resized, moved, opened, and closed. Thus, it is possible to view a number of applications on the screen at the same time; for example, you could work in word processing while you watch the spreadsheet finish its recalculations.

FILE COMPATIBILITY. GUIs also provide a high degree of file compatibility. Applications designed to work under the GUI have almost 100 percent compatibility, which permits moving portions of files from one to the other. This is termed **cut and paste,** meaning you can cut a portion of your spreadsheet and paste it into the report you're writing in word processing.

Most GUI programs make it easy to use many operating system commands for working with files, without your having to return to the command line. For example, copying a file is as easy as placing the mouse pointer on it, holding the button down, and moving it to the icon of the disk you want it copied to. This is often referred to as *click and drag.*

The graphic user interface is becoming more widely accepted as the standard for personal computing. Many computer makers now offer their computer systems with a graphic interface. The GUI is also spreading to workstations and mini and mainframe systems as well, as exemplified in the Open Systems Foundation *Motif* (Figure 7.11), but it is Microsoft Windows that is most widely used.

MICROSOFT WINDOWS

Even though the Macintosh was the first personal computer to sport a GUI, Microsoft Windows deserves special mention due to the fact that at least four out of five personal computers in use today are DOS machines. In addition,

Windows has opened up the world of graphical computing applications for knowledge workers using DOS machines.

Windows was first introduced in the mid-1980s, but it was awkward and there were few applications available for it. (Although DOS applications will perform as normal under Windows, applications must be specifically created or rewritten to take advantage of Windows and the GUI). It wasn't until the third revision, Windows 3.0 in 1990, that it gained wide acceptance. Windows 3.1, released in 1992, is becoming a mature product; many bugs have been worked out and there are many more features that knowledge workers asked for. Refer again to Figure 7.11. Here is how it is designed.

PROGRAM MANAGER.   Program Manager does exactly what its name implies: it is in charge of all applications, large or small. Applications can be grouped together into functional categories, which then appear as a "window" on the screen. For example, desk accessories, personal productivity applications, utility software, and games could each be a separate category/window. Even Program Manager is a window itself. Individual applications are "installed" in the Program Manager and then "launched" from their category/window. Windows also permits creating a Start window, in which all the applications you normally use can be stored; then, when you boot the computer and start Windows, all these applications are automatically launched.

Once running, an application usually occupies the entire screen; however, each window can be sized to whatever dimensions you choose. You can split the screen and run two side by side, run one in a small window and another in a large one, or stack windows of any size one on top of the other like shuffling a deck of cards. The application window can be closed while the application is still active; when this is done, the icon for the application appears at the bottom of the main Windows screen.

FILE MANAGER.   Another major Windows component is the File Manager, which also does exactly what its name implies. File Manager allows knowledge workers to manipulate files either graphically, as icons, or in the conventional directory structure. Using the mouse, files are easily clicked on, dragged to the new directory, then dropped into place. This eliminates typing those long, tedious move and copy commands you learned in Chapter 2. File manager also graphically depicts each of the computer's disk drives, and even distinguishes between types of floppy drives and hard drives. Again, you change drives by pointing to the one you want and clicking the mouse.

CONTROL PANEL.   The other major feature of Windows is the Control Panel, a window in which all Windows' accessories and options are stored for use. Typically, the Control Panel lets the knowledge worker make changes such as:

- The colors Windows uses.
- Typefaces, or fonts.
- Selecting the printer(s).
- Adjusting the sound.
- Changing the date and time.

USING THE GUI.   How do knowledge workers take advantage of the GUI? Bonnie works at a travel agency that plans and promotes adventure tours, such as rock climbing in Yosemite National Park and kayaking the Colorado River. Experienced tour guides propose their own tour itineraries. Bonnie is responsible for preparing the cover letter and descriptive brochure, as well as coordinating airline flight schedules and reservations. She uses a PC-compatible personal computer running Windows and a number of unique applications. For example, in preparing the brochure Bonnie uses a map program, from which she cuts a graphic of Yosemite section of California for cover art, pasting it into the document she is creating with her graphical word processing program. She also cuts text from a U.S. Forestry Service publication on computer disk describing the physical characteristics of the climbs in the park (being certain to give copyright credit to the publication). She overlays the text on the map graphic.

Next, Bonnie writes her own marketing copy describing the tour, using various text fonts and clip art symbols to highlight the copy. Then she opens the word processing file from the disk provided by the tour guide, and cuts and pastes the itinerary. She has several different fee schedules that she's worked up using the spreadsheet application, so next she cuts and pastes them into the document. Finally, she opens the travel reservation system window, cuts the appropriate airline flight information schedules, and pastes them into her brochure. These tasks are made simpler—and more fun—because of the GUI.

TRADE-OFFS IN THE GRAPHICAL ENVIRONMENT

The GUI, and thus its compatible applications, *requires* the use of a mouse or pointing device. This is one of the trade-offs associated with working in a graphical environment. Using the mouse to the selected icon and double-clicking on it are often slower and require more hand-eye coordination than simply pressing a few keys to issue a command. On the other hand, the mouse often makes certain tasks easier to accomplish or combines a series of key commands; what's more, knowledge workers don't have to remember the command names. However, for those who find they tire of moving the mouse around, there is a software program that replaces pointing with the function keys—just like character-based applications.

Another common trade-off is speed. A GUI like Windows requires more CPU horsepower, more random access memory, and a great deal of hard disk space. Tasks are performed more slowly due to the size of the operating environment program itself, because the input and output functions take longer, and due to the time it takes to create graphic images on the monitor.

The development of the GUI is almost paradoxical in the respect that it was created for first-time or novice knowledge workers. Yet its development took so long (even with the Macintosh, which was not introduced until 1984), that many already learned to use the command line interface or had settled comfortably into using a menu. However, each day there are many new knowledge workers who can derive great benefit from GUIs like Windows. In addition, the operating environment familiarizes people with both the operating system and its commands, as well as the manner in which applications work. New knowledge workers often use the GUI while they're learning and then switch to the command line interface as they grow more proficient. For many, it is the best of both worlds.

KNOWLEDGE CHECK

1. What is the purpose of an operating environment?   p. 217
2. Name the five levels of the human-computer interface.   p. 218
3. What is the main advantage of the command line interface?   p. 218
4. Name a benefit from the menu-driven interface.   p. 218 – 19
5. What graphic images are commonly used with a GUI?   p. 220
6. What additional hardware device is needed for the GUI?   p. 224
7. What are some trade-offs between the three types of human-computer interfaces?   p. 224

APPLICATION SOFTWARE

Now let's turn our attention to the software you'll be interacting with most: application software. At first, there was only one application: a calculator that solved mathematical problems. Over the years, as Figure 7.12 shows, applications have shifted from the computer "back room" to knowledge workers.

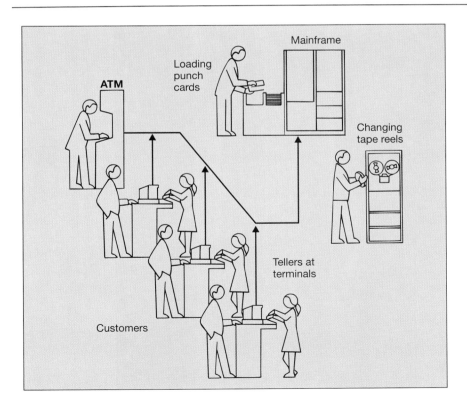

FIGURE 7.12

Upper right: In the past, transactions were processed in batches, often at the end of the workday. Lower left: Today, many transactions are processed once and only once, at the time they occur. This saves time, money, and human resources.

Today thousands of applications exist, ranging from powerful productivity tools to small utility programs that help manage small but important tasks. There are programs for astronomy, sports, geography, dieting, music, religious studies, genealogy, and more.

In this section, we'll learn specifically about business application software. First we'll study integrated software, a combination of individual applications. Then we'll learn about several individual business programs, followed by the world of helpful programs called *utilities*. Finally, we'll look at what lies ahead in software.

INTEGRATED SOFTWARE

The application programs for personal computers you studied in the preceding chapters — word processing, the spreadsheet, and the DBMS — are commonly known as **stand-alone programs.** That means they work alone, by themselves. There is nothing wrong with that if you spend a large proportion of your time using one application such as the spreadsheet. But what if you frequently need to write memos to accompany your spreadsheet analysis? What if you want to create a bar chart from the statistical information in your spreadsheet for a presentation? What if you keep your address book in a DBMS and need to look up phone numbers all the time?

It would be nice to switch between applications rather than store the file you're working on, quit the application, return to the operating system prompt, change disks or directories to the new application, and then run it. Only then can you begin working with a new file. To return to the previous application or change to another means going through all these steps once again. What's more, if you want to transfer data between two applications, it is either difficult, unlikely, or impossible.

ADVANTAGES AND DISADVANTAGES OF INTEGRATED SOFTWARE

Integrated software combines several stand-alone applications capable of freely exchanging data with each other into a single program. Figure 7.13 shows the versatility of integrated software. There are several advantages:

- You can switch from one application to another merely by pressing one or two keys, rather than using the complicated exit-enter process just described.
- The applications all work similarly to one another, so it is not as difficult as learning separate applications created by different software publishers.
- Because the applications work similarly, there is often a user-friendly interface such as a menu bar for selecting functions or switching between applications.
- Files, or data from files, can be transferred from one application to another. For example, a portion of a spreadsheet can be removed and then inserted into a word processing report.

There are disadvantages in using integrated software too. One is that a particular application may be very good, while others may have shortcomings.

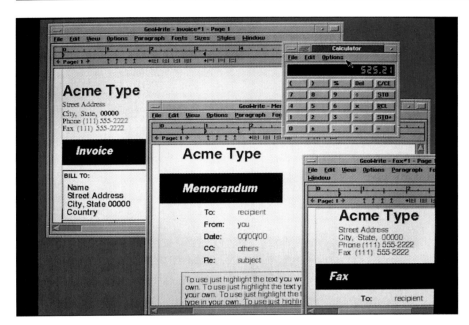

FIGURE 7.13

GeoWorks: the power of integration. Once the invoice has been prepared (using the calculator), data can be moved to a new document and even to a new application, such as transmitting by FAX.

For example, the word processing may be excellent but the DBMS may be poor. Another is that transferring data from one application to another may not work properly. For example, when transferring numbers from the spreadsheet to word processing, the columns may not line up properly. Over time, most integrated software programs have been revised and improved to overcome many of these disadvantages.

THE EVOLUTION OF INTEGRATED SOFTWARE

The first integrated software package, Context MBA, combined word processing, the spreadsheet, database management, and graphics. It was launched in 1982 but wasn't marketed effectively enough to really get off the ground. Lotus 1-2-3 was introduced at a gala party, high atop New York's World Trade Center, a year later. The brainchild of Mitchell Kapor, who had envisioned an integrated software package years before while writing programs for the Apple II, Lotus 1-2-3 combined the spreadsheet, graphics, and a database management system into one program. It is easy to switch between them, and it is possible to share data between them as well. Lotus 1-2-3 topped $1 million in sales its first week on the market, so Mitch Kapor is generally credited with introducing the first popular integrated software for the IBM PC. Figure 7.14 shows how Lotus 1-2-3 shares data between applications.

What happened to word processing? Mitch says it was part of the original plan but the programmer quit and he wasn't replaced. Today there is a Lotus 1-2-3 with word processing called Symphony®.

Commonly, integrated packages have four or five applications: word processing, a spreadsheet, graphics, database management, and telecommunications or networking. This is extremely useful. It means you can write a memo

FIGURE 7.14

Integrated programs such as Lotus 1-2-3 let you share data between spreadsheets, graphics, and database functions.

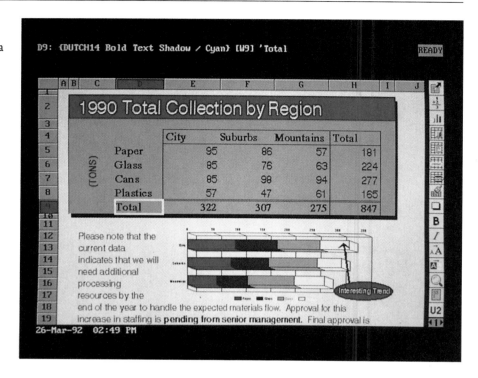

in word processing and, with just a few keystrokes, send it to another computer. Some integrated packages provide additional utility programs such as a spelling checker, calendar, calculator, or outliner.

How Integrated Software Works

Integrated software is loaded into your computer and runs like most other programs. However, since it consists of several different applications, it is usually much larger than a stand-alone program. If there is insufficient space in memory to hold the entire program, it is often necessary to switch disks to perform various tasks. A hard disk drive gets rid of this annoyance. Integrated software usually favors one application; for example, Lotus 1-2-3 favors the spreadsheet, while WordPerfect Executive favors—you guessed it—word processing. Although the other applications work just fine, you might think about which you'll use more often, for that one will have the most features.

The ability to share data or files between applications has been one of the most nagging problems besetting personal computer users. Integrated software addresses this problem head on but with varying degrees of success. In computer jargon, some programs are highly integrated, meaning they let you pass data back and forth very easily. Others are loosely integrated, meaning their main advantage is that they enable you to switch quickly between applications. Some software companies let you purchase loosely integrated applications separately.

TODAY

TIPS FOR BUYING PERSONAL COMPUTER SOFTWARE

People commonly buy their application software in a retail store such as Egghead Software or from a mail order software company. Both retail stores and mail order houses offer discounts and guarantee software, but how do you know what's best? There is a best-seller list, but that doesn't tell you if the software fits your expertise level or needs. Therefore, you may find this checklist useful in making your selection:

1. List the tasks you would like the software to perform.

2. Determine whether the features of a particular application match your task list.

3. Some software is designed exclusively for particular brands of personal computers and operating systems. Make sure the application runs on the hardware and operating system you use.

4. Check how much memory the software requires and make sure your personal computer has adequate memory space.

5. Try it out! Determine whether the application is easy to use. Many retail software stores permit you to return software.

6. See if the application includes good documentation. If it doesn't, there are software- and hardware-specific books, written by knowledgeable people, available in bookstores and computer retail stores.

7. Check for on-line help built into the application and try it out for ease of use.

8. Some applications offer technical support you can call when you have problems. Is this true of the application you are considering? Is there an additional charge for this support? Is there a toll-free 800 telephone number?

9. Is the software copy-protected? Most is not these days. If it is, does the copy-protection make it hard to install on your personal computer or awkward to use? Does the publisher provide backup disks? Is there a charge for them?

10. How long has the software been available? Look at reviews and advertisements in trade publications. Is it highly regarded? Are there user testimonials? Applications are updated, so be sure you get the latest version. Mail in your warranty card so you will be notified when a new version is available.

One last consideration: If you haven't yet purchased your personal computer, conventional wisdom suggests you choose the application(s) you like and then buy the appropriate computer system. In many cases, there are compromises you must make between software and hardware; just try to make as few as possible. If you're like most people, the investment means you'll probably have to live with your system for quite a while.

Even so, exchanging data between files or applications, commonly called *cut and paste,* is extremely useful. You can put monthly sales figures from the spreadsheet into a database of year-to-date corporate revenues. You can insert a name and address from the DBMS into a word processing letter's address heading. Some integrated software programs (and some stand-alone programs as well) also permit opening more than one file in a single application and then switching between them. For example, using the DBMS, you can switch between two different databases, one for your address book and another for company sales figures. Or let's say you wrote an analysis of industrial pollution for your earth sciences class last semester. Now you're taking a political science course and you're writing a paper on environmental politics.

FIGURE 7.15   Cut and paste.

First we highlight the text to be moved.   Next the text is moved to the clipboard.

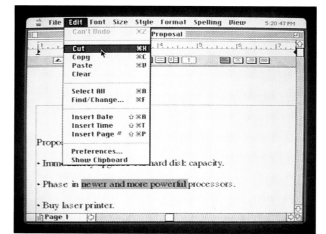

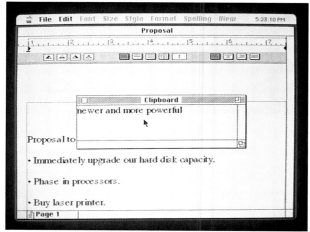

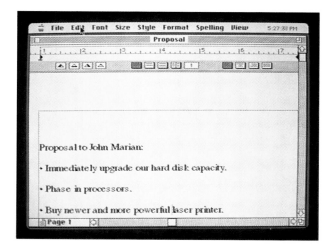

Then it is inserted at the new position.

In your previous paper, you quoted a Sierra Club spokesperson and want to reuse the quote. All you have to do is open the previous file, cut the quote from it, and paste it into the new file. Figure 7.15 shows the steps in cut and paste.

KNOWLEDGE CHECK

1. What is a program such as word processing or a DBMS called?   p. 226
2. What type of software combines several programs into one?   p. 226
3. Why do we need to switch between applications?   p. 226
4. Describe the difference between highly integrated and loosely integrated.   p. 228
5. Describe a use for the cut and paste function.   p. 229–30

BUSINESS APPLICATION SOFTWARE

Business software programs make it possible to automate many tasks that previously required many hours of human labor. For example, when an item is sold it must be taken off the inventory list and its replacement added to the order list. Business software is capable of recording the sale, subtracting the item from inventory, and placing the order, all automatically. Let's look at a few of the most popular business software applications.

ACCOUNTING SOFTWARE

Accounting, or bookkeeping, software is the financial bedrock of any business. You must know what you're taking in, what you're spending on, and how profitable you are. Accounting software replaces manual bookkeeping by providing specific modules. The most common modules are:

- General ledger, consisting of journal entries, trial balance, and financial statements.
- Accounts receivable, consisting of invoice entry, cash receipts, and customer statements.
- Accounts payable, consisting of disbursements entry and check preparation.

In addition, some accounting packages include time and billing, inventory control, invoicing, automatic monthly billing, automatic monthly payables, posting to accounts, and check printing.

Accounting software is generic enough that it can be used in many different industries, such as distribution, manufacturing, service, and retail. But many programs are oriented to the size of the business, from light-duty to heavy-duty. A heavy-duty accounting package generally runs on a mini or mainframe and is designed for 5 to 10 or more accounting knowledge workers. Modules for such a package can cost between $500 and $2,500. On the other hand, many packages are designed for a single accountant or for a small company with up to four or five knowledge workers. Modules can cost up to $250, but there are also integrated packages that cost under $100.

INTEGRATED ACCOUNTING SOFTWARE. An integrated accounting package includes all three modules, but each has a specific design orientation, for example, the general ledger or the check-writing capability may be its strongest asset. Integrated packages are easiest to learn and often have add-on modules that make them more useful as your needs grow and change. For example, Intuit, shown in Figure 7.16, allows you to send a check disbursement request over the phone lines to a company that electronically pays the bill.

PROJECT MANAGEMENT

Project management software is designed to help you plan, organize, track, and control a project. The project may be as simple as launching a new office procedure or as complex as building an office park or designing a new software application. The software provides a number of task points, typically 1,000,

FIGURE 7.16

Integrated accounting software provides many more services and benefits than a manual, paper-based system.

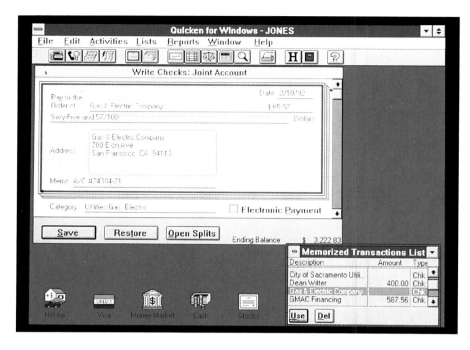

per project; it is possible to work on numerous projects. Activities and resources are logged, then managed. Project personnel data is organized, along with job assignments; subcontractor data can be managed as well. Reports are generated at specific times or project checkpoints, providing a wealth of information on progress. Figure 7.17 shows a project management software screen.

INVESTMENT MANAGEMENT SOFTWARE

Both companies and individuals have financial investments, most of which can be more efficiently managed with an application program. Investment management software, often called *portfolio management*, measures the performance of stocks, bonds, and real estate and calculates the long-term return on investment (ROI). Some packages are able to connect over phone lines to Wall Street services, thus updating the investment data on an hourly or daily basis. In addition, some calculate capital gains and help determine tax liability. A specialized type of investment management software is used for cash management, which is a short-term reinvesting of the liquidity of a check between the time it is mailed and when it is cashed.

MAILING LIST MANAGEMENT SOFTWARE

Information on customers is one of a business's most valuable assets. As you probably know, accurate, up-to-date mailing lists are an information commodity that are often sold to other businesses. Good mailing list management software keeps lists up to date by adding new names, deleting those of people

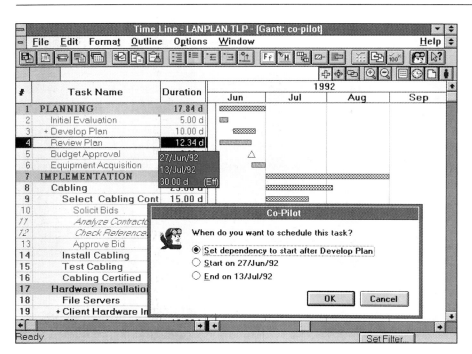

FIGURE 7.17

Project management software allows you to monitor, evaluate, and quantify the results of projects large and small.

who have moved, and eliminating duplications. Mailing list programs can also sort a list by name, region, zip code, product category, and other criteria. Most programs are able to print a variety of labels or envelopes, and also combine names to the salutation of a form letter, often termed *mail-merge*.

SPECIALIZED BUSINESS APPLICATION SOFTWARE

Large companies often develop their own applications to address specific needs. For example, Otis Elevator developed a business application called Contract Tracking, which is similar to a project management package. Its purpose is to assure that an elevator is designed, built, and delivered to the job site — the building in which it will be installed — at precisely the right moment, a process called *just-in-time* (JIT) manufacturing. Knowledge workers who use Contract Tracking include the sales representative who sells the elevator, schedulers, shop floor manufacturing personnel, corporate management, field operations managers, and on-site construction superintendents. It took Otis two years to develop Contract Tracking, but today it is used by 800 people in their daily work. It has become more than a project manager; it is a strategic management tool that provides valuable information on how the business operates on a day-to-day basis. Everyone understands better what it takes to get an elevator to the job site on time.

There are as many business application programs available as there are business needs. There are programs for managing rental properties, for calculating taxes and payroll, and for contractor estimating and job costing. There are also what are termed *vertical market* software packages for managing the business details of hundreds of specific industries such as real estate, dairy farming, and hotel and restaurant management. There is little doubt the number and diversity of business application programs will only continue to grow.

KNOWLEDGE CHECK

1. What are the three most common accounting software modules?   p. 231
2. What advantages does integrated accounting software offer?   p. 231
3. What are some uses for project management software?   pp. 231–32
4. What is another name for investment management software?   p. 232
5. What are the advantages in using mailing list management software?   pp. 232–33
6. What is a vertical market software program?   p. 233
7. Why do large businesses need to develop their own applications?   p. 233

UTILITY SOFTWARE

There are few computer users who couldn't use a little help now and then. That's why we have utility software. **Utility software** performs tasks that are difficult, awkward, or hard to remember with the ease and efficiency of an application program. Additionally, utility software improves performance and makes many tasks more useful or valuable.

TYPES OF UTILITY SOFTWARE

There are three basic types of utility software:

1. *Systems-level utility programs* that help us work with the operating system and its functions.
2. *Operating environment-level programs* that perform operating system functions and enhance the human-computer interface operations.
3. *Application utility programs* that augment and extend the usefulness of our application programs.

These utility software packages are usually purchased separately from, and in addition to, the operating system, operating environment, or application program.

THE EVOLUTION OF UTILITY PROGRAMS

Computers have always had utility programs. They accompany operating system software to perform tasks such as printing what's on the screen, formatting a disk, or setting the date and time. We often take these built-in utilities for granted because an operating system just wouldn't be complete without them. Yet sometimes a built-in DOS utility is less than satisfactory; perhaps it's hard to use or doesn't have all the functions we need. That's why there are separate systems-level utility programs.

USING SYSTEMS-LEVEL UTILITY PROGRAMS

EDLIN, the DOS text editor, is an example of a built-in utility. You can use it to create and edit an operating system program such as the AUTOEXEC.BAT file used to customize the way we start programs. However, EDLIN is a line editor, which means you can only work with a single line at a time. Moreover, it's like programming; you have to type a command such as

```
(n),(m),destM
```

A man named Philippe Kahn thought of a better way to create and edit files like these and created the Sidekick utility program to do it. But instead of providing just a text editor, Sidekick is a set of integrated utilities: a calculator, calendar, telephone dialer, and an ASCII table to help programmers recall the various keyboard characters.

Sidekick is a **terminate and stay resident (TSR)** type of program. That means it boots up and then waits in the background while you're using your application program until you need it. Say you're busily writing a paper in word processing and need to check your class schedule for tomorrow. You press the Control and Alt keys together and Sidekick pops up, displaying the main menu. You press the key for the calendar. After checking it, you realize you must cancel an appointment with Bob. Since Sidekick uses windows that present each utility in its own box on the screen, you simply press the key for the phone book and it appears on the screen with the calendar. You search for Bob's initials and then hit Return to dial the call. Once it rings, you can pick up the telephone receiver and talk to Bob. When you're through using Sidekick, hit the Escape key and Sidekick disappears until you're ready to use it again. Figure 7.18A shows Sidekick and several of the following types of systems-level utility programs.

- DOS shell (Figure 7.18B), a program that helps you manage and view the contents of a hard disk. It arranges directories and files in a graphic display on the screen, and provides many DOS functions such as copy, delete, rename, and create a new directory.

- Disk maintenance utilities (Figure 7.18C) that restore accidentally erased files, help you recover from an emergency such as a power outage, reconstruct the hard disk when it "crashes" or fails to operate properly, and offer other utilities for easier operating system maintenance.

- Peripheral management utilities that make it easier to use the keyboard, printer, or monitor. A keyboard utility creates keyboard macros that enable you to press two keys in combination that spell out an entire phrase—*peripheral management utilities,* for example. A printer utility called a *spooler* makes it possible to send a large file for printing, while freeing up the CPU to return to other tasks. A monitor utility called a *screen blanker* turns off the display when a key has not been pressed for a preset time, such as five minutes. This prevents characters from burning the screen phosphor.

- Security and virus protection utilities (Figure 7.18D) that protect a computer from unauthorized use. Security programs perform one of two tasks: encryption of text so it cannot be read; and system locking, usually by means of a password. Virus protection programs scan computer disks to locate and identify these destructive programs.

FIGURE 7.18   Systems-level utility programs.

A. Sidekick is a TSR program, whose desktop accessories pop up for use regardless of the application you are working in.

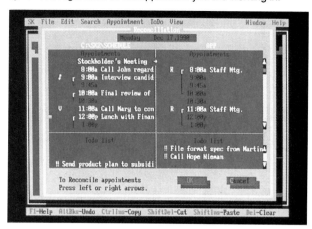

B. XTree Gold is a visual presentation of DOS directories and files, and includes many DOS management file functions.

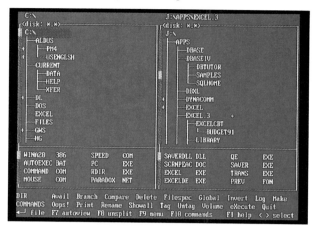

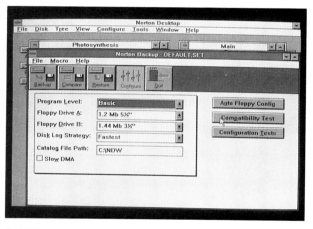

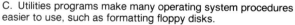

C. Utilities programs make many operating system procedures easier to use, such as formatting floppy disks.

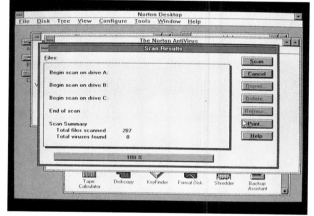

D. Virus scanning programs are often included with utility software programs such as Norton Desktop.

USING OPERATING ENVIRONMENT-LEVEL UTILITY PROGRAMS

Many of the types of system-level utility programs have been redesigned and have found new uses within operating environments. Some perform many of the same tasks: managing printing, virus-checking desk accessories, and replacing operating system tasks. The main difference is that most have been adapted to the GUI and are easier to work with—and often a delight to the eyes. Using these utilities can often seem more like playing a computer game than performing work tasks! A notable example is After Dark, a screen blanker program for both PC-compatibles running Windows and the Macintosh (Figure 7.19A).

Two other examples are programs that were designed to enhance Windows operations. One is New Wave, which uses special icons called *agents* to man-

Operating environment-level utility programs.

FIGURE 7.19

A. After Dark proves that screen savers don't need to be boring.

B. New Wave uses a more visual interface to install, present, and work with Windows-based applications.

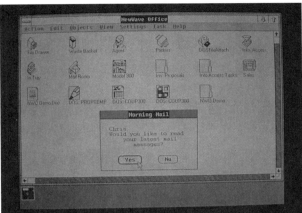

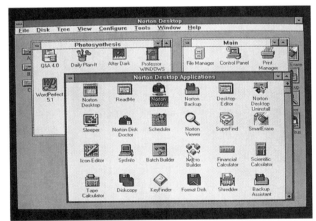

C. Norton Desktop for Windows makes Windows easier to manage, and adds powerful antivirus and backup utilities.

age applications (Figure 7.19B). These agents behave like macros to automate and speed up everyday tasks. For example, a New Wave icon could be built that would automatically back up your files or connect to the phone lines to check your electronic mail at preset times, such as every four hours.

Another is the Norton Desktop for Windows (Figure 7.19C), which enhances and improves upon many Windows characteristics. Screen icons show all disk drives and directories; a mere click of the mouse button changes from one to another. Clicking on a file icon opens it and the application that you used to create it. Norton Desktop also performs routine disk backup automatically, as a background application, while you work. It also includes the utility that made the Norton Utilities famous, *Unerase,* which permits recovering a previously deleted file.

Tomorrow

The Future of the Human-Computer Interface

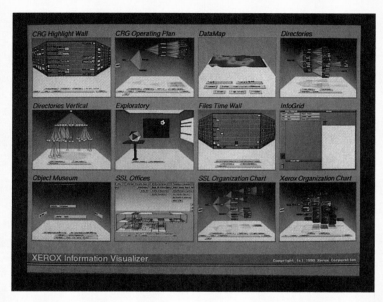

One of the greatest technology think tanks in the world is Xerox Corporation's Palo Alto Re-search Center (PARC), which celebrated its 20th anniversary in 1990. PARC pioneered many computer innovations that we take for granted today, including the human-computer interface. Steven Jobs, Apple Computer's cofounder, visited PARC in the early 1980s and saw the Xerox Star workstation, with its mouse, graphic screen, and icons. He vowed to develop a similar computer that anyone could learn to use—and afford (The Star cost $20,000!). His first attempt, called the Lisa®, later became the Macintosh.

The latest innovation from PARC is the *Information Visualizer* (IV). IVs are three-dimensional, animated tools that turn the computer screen into a passageway that leads to various types of information. Stuart Card is a cognitive psychologist and computer scientist who has been developing user interfaces at PARC since the be-

Using Application-Level Utility Programs

Application programmers don't always think of everything users would like to have in their programs. There are probably more utilities for word processing than any other application. These include the outliner, thesaurus, spelling checker, grammar checker, syntax and usage checker, and print spooler, which allow you to print a file while continuing to enter text into another.

Other utilities for any kind of application include:

- Keystroke managers that create macro keys for various applications or the operating system, like those you learned about in the spreadsheet chapter.

- Envelope or label printers that capture a name and address and then print them on the envelope.

ginning. He says the old ways of retrieving information are based on *content,* such as words or dates in time. The new way is to present information in the same manner in which the brain thinks about it: in structure and context as well as content.

The PARC workstation screen presents an *overview* room with 12 information visualizers, or screens. Eleven are 3-D rooms; the knowledge worker moves from one to another via connecting "doors." One IV room displays the Xerox organizational chart. Previously, it was an 80-page document, like one created in word processing. In the IV, it is a rotating drum with revolving names. When a person is chosen, his or her name is moved to the front of the screen, like a label, but that person's relationship to others in the orga-

nization is graphically presented.

By clicking the mouse, the knowledge worker can *navigate* closer to the individual. All screen objects, such as name labels, are *interactive* and can be moved into various relationships, such as a work group. The view can be narrowed on the person, displaying a color photograph, biography, papers he or she has written, and other public information. The view can also be widened to show people's offices, the floor plan for their work group, and biographies of their fellow knowledge workers. In fact, the interactive nature of the screen objects even permits showing parallels or differences between the various individuals' work.

Stuart Card believes that the ultimate goal of interface design is to make the interface vanish

so that there seems to be nothing between the knowledge user and the task at hand. Today there is too much manipulation of the computer system required. An ideal interface takes the focus off the machinery and puts it on the work.

Scientists and engineers at Xerox will be the first knowledge workers who get to take advantage of IVs. But Card and his team are working to develop IVs that help visualize information for business applications. It took Steven Jobs only four years to take the Star GUI from PARC to the marketplace. Perhaps it won't take even that long for IVs to reach the office.

- Text finders that search for any file, regardless of the application in which it was created, locating it by name or by key word search.
- Formatting programs that make spreadsheet and DBMS reports more attractive and informative.

KNOWLEDGE CHECK

1. What are the three types of utility software?   p. 234
2. Why would you need a utility program?   p. 234
3. What does TSR stand for?   p. 235
4. What is the difference between system-level and operating environment-level utility programs?   p. 236
5. Why would you use a keyboard macro program?   p. 238

CAREERS FOR KNOWLEDGE WORKERS
KENNY SHULTS, DIRECTOR OF MARKETING, WELLSOURCE

What do shreddin' and computers have to do with one another? Ask Kenny Shults. "Shreddin' is the slang word we use for playing footbag," he says. Not only is Kenny the World Footbag Association all-around men's champion, he's the director of marketing for

Wellsource, a company that publishes personal computer software for fitness and wellness. Not only can Kenny intercept a footbag serve flying parallel to the ground, returning the bag at speeds the eye can barely see; he can demonstrate, using the Personal Wellness Profile software,

how you can make changes in your lifestyle that will help you become a far more healthy knowledge worker.

Wellsource sells a wide variety of health and fitness software, mostly to healthcare organizations and companies that want to help employees become more healthy. Healthier employees require less in the way of health insurance benefits; thus, health insurance costs are lowered and employees are happier and more productive. Everybody wins.

The Personal Wellness Profile program is administered with a simple questionnaire, accompanied by health and fitness tests. It analyzes and identifies health risks and problems having to do with fitness, stress, and nutrition, and assesses the heart, lungs, and body composition. It also identifies the risks from cancer and those associated with the use of tobacco and alcohol. After assessing all these factors and analyzing them in light of the individual's family and per-

WHAT LIES AHEAD?

Where is software taking us? Clearly, operating systems are becoming more useful, and operating environments are helping make their commands and functions easier to use. Both are making it easier for us to work with applications, which are growing ever more powerful. Yet both the operating systems and operating environments in current use are growing dated, and it has become clear to many in the computer industry that new systems and environments are necessary to make tomorrow's knowledge worker more productive. Thus, Apple Computer and IBM have formed a new company, Taligent, and

sonal health history, the program provides recommendations with accompanying educational guidelines for how to improve health.

This information is commonly provided in a bound report that the software prepares and prints out on the computer's laser printer. It begins with a personal wellness summary, rating the individual in 16 areas and providing a bar chart showing how each measures up.

Kenny's journey to Wellsource took many interesting turns. He started college as a computer science major, but soon changed to advertising. "There are lots of careers that use computers that don't require a computer science degree," he says. "What I was really interested in was advertising." After graduation, Kenny was awarded a fellowship for a graduate degree in advertising. It was a one-year Master's program and he took it.

With his Master's, he applied for a job as a graphics design as-sistant at Wellsource, but Kenny still longed to be "an advertising person." In the interview, president Don Hall saw the reference to footbag on Kenny's resume. "Don makes a point of hiring people who are into fitness," he says. That started more conversation, and soon Don realized he wanted Kenny for his marketing and sales director.

On the job, Kenny uses both a PC-compatible and a Macintosh. "I've done a great deal of research on the high-risk employee," he says, "using the Personal Wellness Profile software and the PC to do cost-benefit analysis. What I learned is that 10 percent of a total employee population is responsible for 10 times the median health care claims for the entire company. These are the people who need to improve their wellness the most, and reduce the employer's healthcare premium.

"Using the software, I can take 5,000 employees who look healthy and separate out that 10 percent I'm looking for. The software identifies them and prints out their names. Now, helping them become more healthy, we can begin working on making the company's bottom line healthy too. I've turned this into a template so that our customers can do it themselves."

Kenny uses his Mac II to write and create marketing brochures. He used word processing to write, and desktop publishing to design and produce, a 12-page brochure, "Elements of Successful Wellness Programs." It includes text, bar charts, pages from the Profile, and some effective graphic layouts to convey its message.

And it's all about the things Kenny is personally interested in. "Landing this job was sheer luck," he says, "but it sure helped that I had my personal activities, such as playing footbag, on my resume. Often, the interests you have outside your work can affect your career."

are jointly developing a new operating system that will take advantage of all the latest hardware and software technologies.

In addition, Microsoft Corporation hopes to establish a new level of operating efficiency and functionality with its latest advanced operating system. It is called Windows NT, for New Technology, and combines the operating system and operating environment. Windows NT provides superior performance characteristics over today's MS-DOS and Windows, and is primarily designed for the more powerful, faster personal computers connected in networks. Microsoft has committed to continuing improvements and integration between DOS and Windows for all types of PCs. It may not be long before knowledge workers never have to issue commands from the command line interface.

SOFTWARE ETHICS: SOFTWARE PIRACY

Illegal or unauthorized software copying used to be called *software piracy,* perhaps in part to alert people to the seriousness of the act. It is a problem that plagues the software industry because it is so widespread. People who would never think of photocopying a book so they could read it will often make a copy of someone else's software program without giving it a second thought.

Software copying hurts both software publishers and computer users. It hurts publishers by taking revenues they would otherwise have earned that could have been used to develop new and better software. It hurts users because they do not usually copy the documentation manuals, so they often don't learn to take full advantage of the program. In addition, they can't take advantage of technical support or obtain new versions of the program.

In the past, many personal computer software publishers used copy-protection programs embedded in the disk that either did not permit copying or only allowed one or two copies, say to a hard disk and for an extra backup copy. But many people resented copy-protection, for it made it awkward to use the program. For example, even if the program would copy to the hard disk, you still had to insert the original program disk (sometimes called a *key disk*) in its drive before the program worked.

The software industry finally bowed to consumers—very few programs are copy-protected these days. Large corporations purchase a site licensing agreement to obtain multiple copies for office workers. But individuals still copy office software and then use it at home, and that is still software piracy.

The software publishers have said to us, in effect: "All right, we trust you to buy our program and not to make unauthorized copies of it." Each and every individual should strive to live up to that trust.

SUMMARY

1. *Explain the various tasks performed by operating systems software.* Software is the link between people and computer hardware. It provides two types of tools that bridge this gap: system software and applications. System software runs the computer and provides tools that assist application programmers. The operating system controls the computer's basic functions. It does so by providing command languages and utilities, controlling input and output, scheduling, managing data and instructions, and maintaining libraries.

2. *Identify leading personal computer, minicomputer, and mainframe operating systems.* There are many operating systems. The most common personal computer operating systems are DOS and the Macintosh System 7. The most common minicomputer operating systems are UNIX and VMS. The most common mainframe operating system is MVS. Some operating systems are proprietary, meaning they work on one brand of computer only; others are called portable, meaning they work on computers from different manufacturers. Portable operating systems make it possible to have open systems, which permit connecting different computers together.

3. *Understand the purposes of operating environment software.* Operating environment software works between the operating system and application software, making it easier to use the former. The human-computer interface is presented on the screen. It may be command-driven, menu-driven, or a graphic user interface.

4. *Understand the difference between stand-alone and integrated software.* A stand-alone application program works solely by itself; the applications in Module II are stand-alone. An integrated program combines four or five (or more) stand-alone applications that work similarly to each other. You can easily switch from one to another and exchange files or data between them. The main disadvantage is that one application tends to be very good, while the others have shortcomings.

5. *Describe some other commonly used applications.* Computer graphics programs that can draw, paint, or create three-dimensional drafting are in

wide use. Most common are presentation graphics and computer-aided design (CAD). Electronic publishing combines word processing with advanced formatting capabilities, including adding graphics, to produce high-quality documents.

6. *Describe the uses for utility software for applications and operating systems.* Utility software provides commonly used services and specific tasks that make our computing work easier. There are systems-level utility programs, such as DOS shells and windowing programs. Examples of application-level utility programs include text finders and formatting programs. HyperCard is an emerging new type of utility program.

SOFTWARE ISSUES

1. A major headache in selecting software is making sure it runs on your computer. There are many factors that must be considered: is your computer an IBM PC, PC-compatible, or a PS/2? What model of Apple II or Macintosh? Does it have the proper operating system and enough RAM? In the name of free enterprise, computer makers make their hardware distinct, while software publishers must adapt their products to specific hardware types. Should computer manufacturers conform to standards so that any software could be used with any hardware?

2. Many computer users "swap" copies of software, whether it is the latest operating system upgrade or an application. This is properly termed *software pirating* and when it happens, neither the programmer who wrote the program nor the software publisher that produced and promoted it are rewarded for their work. Do you feel software pirating is ethical? Is it stealing? What if the programmer or the software company only intended to cover their costs in the price of the update?

3. A growing concern for knowledge workers at home, in small business, and in large corporations is the computer virus. Like its biological counterpart, this software program is able to find its way into system software or applications and hide itself on a disk. Then, often at a preappointed time, it is activated, destroying files and the data contents of entire hard disks. The Michelangelo virus seems to be becoming an annual occurrence, "infecting" computers every March 6. Viruses are programs, written by individuals with prodigious computer skills. Why do they wish to inflict harm on others? What can be done to stop them, and what measures would you recommend for protecting computers against viruses?

CHAPTER REVIEW QUESTIONS

REVIEW QUESTIONS

1. What role does system software play in the computer system?
2. What is the difference between system software and the operating system?
3. Name the four tasks the operating system performs and state what each does.
4. What is a command language?
5. How are multitasking and multiprogramming commonly distinguished from one another?
6. What is the main difference between virtual memory and cache memory?
7. Name as many kinds of business software as you can.
8. When is it appropriate to use project management software?

DISCUSSION QUESTIONS

1. Discuss the advantages of multitasking. How often would you use it?
2. Discuss the advantages and disadvantages of the three different operating environments.
3. Discuss the advantages and disadvantages of integrated software.
4. When would it be preferable to use a stand-alone application over integrated software?
5. Describe some of your criteria for buying software.
6. Discuss the benefits to some of the application-level utility software packages described.
7. Discuss some reasons why software security is an important issue for knowledge workers.

MULTIPLE-CHOICE

1. MVS is (check all that apply):
   a. Only available on IBM mainframes.
   b. Capable of driving several CPUs.
   c. A single user system.
   d. Designed for all types of processing.
   e. Able to run hundreds of simultaneous applications.
   f. All of the above.
2. The graphic user interface (check all that apply):
   a. Is faster than the other types.
   b. Is designed for ease of use.
   c. Is for single users.
   d. Allows cutting and pasting data between applications.
   e. Requires the use of a mouse.
3. What type of utility software takes the place of integrated software?
   a. Terminate and stay resident.
   b. Screen blanker.
   c. Operating environment.
   d. Security.
4. Data storage is organized into (check all that apply):
   a. Sectors or triangular slices.
   b. Tracks that encircle the disk.
   c. Shells, which hold all command line data.
   d. Clusters, which store portions of a file.
   e. All of the above.

FILL-IN-THE-BLANK

1. The VM in VMS stands for _____ _____.
2. An operating environment where you select applications from a list is called a _____.
3. The first popular integrated software for the PC was _____.
4. The three types of utility software are _____, _____, and _____.
5. The five levels of the human-computer interface are _____, _____, _____, _____, and _____.
6. The PC-compatible operating system is called _____; the Macintosh operating system is called _____.

TRUE/FALSE

1. A multiuser system always has a mainframe computer.
2. UNIX is designed to work on many different hardware platforms.
3. The command line interface was the first operating environment.
4. Integrated accounting software is like regular integrated software—it's easy to learn, but may have one module stronger than the others.
5. The graphic user interface is slower than the other two.

KEY TERMS

cache memory,   208

clusters,   209

command language,   209

command line interface,   218

cut and paste,   222

desk accessories,   222

ease of use,   221

graphic user interface,   220

human-computer interface,   217

integrated software,   226

memory management,   208

menu-driven interface,   218

multiprogramming,   207

multitasking,   207

multiuser,   210

MVS,   215

OS/2,   212

open system,   214

operating environment,   217

portable,   214

proprietary,   214

pulldown menu,   220

scheduling,   207

stand-alone program,   226

System 7,   212

task switching,   219

terminate and stay resident (TSR),   235

time-sharing,   218

UNIX,   213

utility software,   234

virtual memory,   208

VMS,   214

windows,   212

To see the world in a grain of sand And heaven in a wild flower, Hold infinity in the palm of your hand And

Hardware Concepts

Knowledge workers don't *have* to know what's under their computer's hood. However, the concept underlying computer hardware advances can be summed up in these three goals: **better, faster, cheaper.** When you consider that the first computer was little more than a grossly overgrown hand-held calculator, the proposition becomes a little more interesting. The reason computers can perform so many tasks for us today is because computer engineers have pursued the better-faster-cheaper goals with such relentless zeal.

The two chapters in this module introduce the basic hardware concepts. Chapter 8 describes the central processing unit, which is truly the "computer" itself, and main memory, which manages the program instructions and data. Chapter 9 explains the concepts of input, or what we put into the computer, and output, or what the computer returns to us. It also describes the various devices we use for input and output tasks, as well as secondary storage — the how and where instructions and data are saved more permanently.

The Central Processing Unit and Main Memory

LEARNING OBJECTIVES

After reading and studying this chapter, you should be able to:

1. Describe the different types of integrated circuits used in computers.
2. Explain the tasks performed by the three components that make up the CPU.
3. Explain the differences between arithmetic and logical operations.
4. Describe the three different types of computer memory.
5. Describe the steps in CPU operation.
6. Explain the terminology used to measure computer speed.
7. Describe the three methods of data processing.

The Computing Engine

In a 1929 book entitled *Men and Machines,* author Stuart Chase wrote: "Technology is developing at an incredible pace. In a single week I have listed as many as fourteen important new inventions and discoveries."[1] Technology has continued its incredible pace throughout the 20th century, expanding its frontiers into ever new areas. At the time Chase wrote his book about the dangers of *mechanization,* there were no such things as electronic digital computers or genetic engineering. Today they are considered facts of life.

It would probably be conservative to estimate that there are 14 new inventions or discoveries each week in the field of personal computing alone. If you have any doubts, pick up a copy of *InfoWorld* or *PC Week,* two weekly PC newspapers. When we speak of invention and discovery in computing, we often use the term *technological innovation.* **Technological innovation** refers to the pace of new advances in technology and the propagation of those advances throughout the culture, toward the goal of performing work better, faster, and at less cost. The human race doubled its technological knowledge — which is another way of saying the creation of new technology tools — from the year A.D. 1 to the year 1750. In just 150 years — by 1900 — that technological knowledge doubled again, and then once again between 1900 and 1950. We have made more progress in just the past 50 years than in the preceding 10,000.

The computer is part of our expanding technological knowledge, but it is also a tool used to advance our technological knowledge. One major reason is that unlike a plow or an airplane, the computer can be used for many different tasks. Back in 1929, no one imagined we would have computers as we know them today. No other technology has grown so fast, nor provided us with so many benefits, as the computer.

The computer's versatility is due to its engine — the component that does the processing. Stuart Chase wrote with pleasure about how the automobile extends the possibilities for travel "together with the genuine thrill that comes from controlling its forty horses."[2] Today's auto engine has, on average, four to six times that amount of horsepower; some special cars have engines with eight to nine times the "horses."

But those comparisons dim — nay, are obliterated — when compared to the advances in the computer's engine. A simple hand-held calculator is 5,000 times faster than ENIAC. Today's microprocessor is millions of times faster. And so it is with a certain degree of interest, even fascination, that we approach the subject of the computing engine — that small sliver of silicon that empow-

---

[1]Stuart Chase, *Men and Machines* (New York: Doubleday, 1929), p. 292.
[2]Ibid., p. 5.

ers us knowledge workers, aids our personal productivity, and continues to make our work more interesting and enjoyable to perform.

THE COMPUTER SYSTEM

In Chapter 1 you learned that the computer is a system comprised of people, software, and hardware. Knowledge workers make up the people aspect; the personal productivity software aspect was presented in Module II. In Chapter 2 the concept of the central processing unit (CPU) was introduced, and you saw the physical layout of components inside the system unit.

All computer systems are made up of people, software, data, instructions, and hardware. Some computer systems have more hardware components than others and thus are more complex. The simplest computer system is a personal computer since it only has four basic components: the system unit, keyboard, monitor, and printer. The most complex computer hardware is the mainframe computer, which can have hundreds of components that can fill the entire floor of an office building.

In this chapter, we'll use the personal computer to study the CPU and main memory, and see how they work together to process data. That's why these components are referred to as *processing hardware*. Let's quickly review the five data processing steps as they were explained in Chapter 1:

1. *Input:* Either instructions or data.
2. *Processing:* The computer performing its instructions — an arithmetic or logical operation — on the data.
3. *Output:* The data produced after processing.
4. *Storage:* The option of retaining the data indefinitely or permanently.
5. *Results:* Presenting the data in a useful form.

In this chapter, we'll study the hardware devices that perform step 2: the processor unit and main memory. Let's begin by learning about the electronic components of which they are comprised.

THE INTEGRATED CIRCUIT

> To see the world in a grain of sand
> And heaven in a wild flower,
> Hold infinity in the palm of your hand
> And eternity in an hour.

These words were written by the poet William Blake over 200 years ago, but eloquently describe today's silicon chip, or integrated circuit. The integrated circuit (IC) is created from silicon refined from ordinary beach sand. The photo essay in Figure 8.1 shows the process of manufacturing integrated circuit chips.

Complex computer circuitry that once filled entire rooms now rests in a sliver of silicon you can hold on the tip of your finger. ENIAC, two stories high and covering 15,000 square feet, was composed of 18,000 glass vacuum tubes that made up 100,000 circuits. A ¼-inch square IC contains over a million circuits. Is it any wonder we call it a miracle?

Manufacturing integrated circuit chips.

FIGURE 8.1

Stages of integrated circuit creation
(photo inserts of each stage).

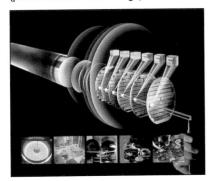

Crystal growing in furnace containing
molten silicon.

Photolithography patterning
process.

Silicon wafers baking in a diffusion furnace.   Etching operation.   Assembly bonding and packing phase.

Early computers were plagued by problems associated with the vacuum tube. These large, fragile devices generated excessive heat and were relatively unreliable. Many scientists and engineers seeking solutions paved the way to the silicon wizardry we call an IC. In the early 1950s, John Bardeen, William Shockley, and Walter Brattain earned a Nobel prize for developing the first transistor at AT&T's Bell Laboratories. Soon after, a British radar engineer proposed the idea of creating an entire electronic circuit on a block of semiconductor material. Then the breakthrough in integrated circuits arrived.

Jack St. Clair Kilby was an engineer at Texas Instruments in Dallas, an electronics firm working on what it termed "Micro Modules," or miniaturized circuits, for the military. While at work Kilby says he "realized that, since all of the components could be made of a single material, they could also be . . . interconnected to form a complete circuit." This discovery meant that the three main components in a circuit — the transistor, the resistor, and capacitor — could all be made simultaneously, or *integrated*, on a single slice of silicon. Kilby created the first integrated circuit in 1958. Because electricity didn't have to travel as far, the circuits were faster. Clearly, ICs were practical and had great potential.

FIGURE 8.2

Miniaturization shortens the distance electric signals must travel, making integrated circuits faster and more powerful. This blood pressure sensor microprocessor has been made so small that it can actually be inserted in a patient's blood stream.

Texas Instruments demonstrated it in a computer for the U.S. Air Force that used 587 ICs in a space of only 6.3 cubic inches. The circuitry it replaced required over 150 times as much space. Figure 8.2 illustrates the degree of miniaturization today by comparing an IC with 200 circuits to the diameter of a human hair.

TYPES OF INTEGRATED CIRCUITS

Integrated circuits perform many tasks today, depending on how they are designed and programmed. They are found in wristwatches, cameras, phones, cars, musical instruments — the list is endless. In computers, ICs may be used as:

- A central processing unit, or microprocessor.
- A ROM (read only memory) chip.
- A RAM (random access memory) chip.
- A controller for routing electrical signals from one place to another (for example, between input and output devices).

As you might expect, the most demanding task for an IC is that of the computer's engine. In large computer systems, there may be a number of ICs working together as the CPU. In a personal computer, there is but one engine — albeit a very powerful one.

THE MICROPROCESSOR

Ten years after the IC was created, a microelectronics firm named Intel was starting up near Palo Alto, California, an area that has come to be known as "Silicon Valley." Marcian E. (Ted) Hoff, a Stanford University graduate and

YESTERDAY

WHO REALLY INVENTED THE MICROPROCESSOR?

In 1991, a man named Gilbert Hyatt claimed he invented, and holds the patent to, the first microprocessor. He was awarded a patent in 1970, when he began working on a way to combine transistors on a single silicon chip. If he were to prove his patent, Hyatt could be the recipient of millions upon millions of dollars in royalties from Intel, Texas Instruments, AMD, Motorola, and every other microprocessor manufacturer. The U.S. Patent Office stood by Hyatt's claim at first, but then agreed to reexamine the patent it awarded to independent inventor Gilbert Hyatt in 1970.

Texas Instruments, Inc., claimed that Hyatt's original filing date goes back only as far as 1977, but a patent held by Gary Boone, who worked on microprocessor design at TI, dates back to 1971. Hyatt also claims he holds a patent on technology for improving the performance of integrated circuits for memory.

In late 1991, the Patent Office upheld Hyatt's claim; the 20-year struggle was over. The complete patent covers a wide range of technologies, including most microprocessor-driven devices ranging from dishwashers to computers. As proof of validation, North American Philips,

a consumer electronics company, agreed to license 23 of Hyatt's inventions for use in its many products. Although terms weren't disclosed, the deal was estimated to be worth around $35 million to Hyatt and could eventually amount to more than $100 million. North American Philips has agreed to help Hyatt obtain licensing agreements from other companies. Even though Hyatt holds this patent, we credit Intel for the commercial microprocessor and Texas Instruments for the commercial integrated circuit.

an engineer at Intel, was asked to design a set of 12 chips for electronic calculators; each chip would perform certain functions. Hoff thought that was rather inefficient, so he redesigned them into four chips sharing a single processor that could be programmed to perform many tasks. This was exactly what mainframe computers did, using far more circuits. Ted Hoff's creation was named the Intel 4004 and the company often referred to it as "a computer on a chip" or what we call a microprocessor today. It was the first in a family of Intel microprocessor chips that led to the IBM PC.

Today there are microprocessors in cash registers, videogames, toys, automobiles, stereos, and appliances, to name just a few uses. Jack Kilby and Ted Hoff dramatically changed the world we live in. Now that we know how ICs are created, we will next learn how they perform their tasks in the computer.

KNOWLEDGE CHECK

1. From what common material are integrated circuits made?   p. 250
2. What company developed the first transistor?   p. 251
3. What does the term *integrated* mean?   p. 251
4. What four tasks do ICs perform in computers?   p. 252
5. What company developed the first microprocessor?   p. 252–53

THE CENTRAL PROCESSING UNIT

The central processing unit (CPU) contains circuitry that controls the interpretation and execution of instructions. Figure 8.3 shows the CPU in its actual size, with corresponding views of its placement on the motherboard. The CPU integrated circuit chip contains the control unit and the arithmetic/logic unit. It is physically separate from the main memory, or RAM, integrated circuit chips. Yet all three — the control unit, the arithmetic/logic unit, and main memory — work together to perform the computing tasks. Collectively, they are often referred to as the *processor.*

THE CONTROL UNIT

The **control unit** directs the step-by-step operation of the computer. Like a traffic policeman directing cars, the control unit directs electrical impulses between itself, the ALU, and main memory. It also controls operations between the CPU and the peripheral devices. These electrical impulses consist of the data and instructions being processed.

THE ARITHMETIC/LOGIC UNIT

The **arithmetic/logic unit** (ALU) performs two types of operations: arithmetic and logical. The **arithmetic operations** are addition, subtraction, multiplication, and division. The **logical operations** compare two pieces of data to determine if one is greater than, less than, or equal to the other.

ARITHMETIC OPERATIONS.   Even though addition, subtraction, multiplication, and division are described, the ALU is actually only able to perform addition — albeit very fast. If it is asked to perform subtraction, it adds negative numbers.

LOGICAL OPERATIONS.   Logical operations play many important roles in computing by comparing data and values. There are three operations:

- *Greater than, or > condition:* The data or value is larger than the existing one. For example, the bank's computer checks to see if the amount you wish to withdraw from the ATM is greater than the prescribed $350 daily limit.
- *Less than, or < condition:* The data or value is smaller than the existing one. For example, an inventory management program alerts the purchasing manager that the stock of size 9 ski boots has fallen below the required stock level.
- *Equal to, or = condition:* The data or value is supposed to be the same. For example, the spelling checker in word processing compares a word you spelled against the one in its dictionary, looking for a 100 percent match.

There is a second type of processor chip often found in personal computers. Called a **math co-processor,** it is a completely separate microprocessor designed to improve the speed of ALU functions. Its mathematical processing

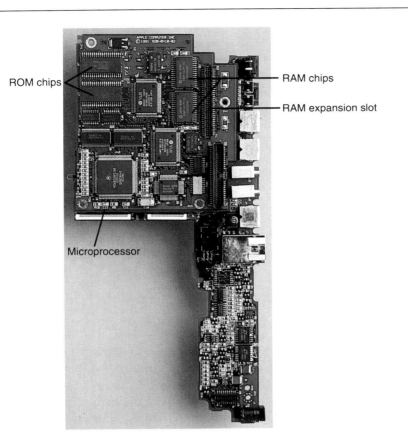

ROM chips

RAM chips

RAM expansion slot

Microprocessor

FIGURE 8.3

This is the motherboard of an Apple Powerbook notebook computer. Note the different types of integrated circuits, particularly the microprocessor CPU chip and the row of random access memory (RAM) chips. The CPU chip and RAM chips together make up the processor.

power makes it useful for knowledge workers who use the spreadsheet, computer-aided drawing (CAD), and project management, as well as graphically oriented applications. You can see the socket for the math co-processor in the Computer Anatomy transparency in Chapter 2.

The third part of the processor, main memory, is usually a number of ICs physically separate from the CPU. It is our next topic of discussion.

1. What tasks does the CPU perform?   p. 254
2. What three functions make up the processor?   p. 254
3. Between what four components does the control unit direct electrical impulses?   p. 254
4. What is an arithmetic operation?   p. 254
5. What are the three types of logical operations?   p. 254
6. Where is the CPU's main memory physically located?   p. 255

KNOWLEDGE CHECK

COMPUTER MEMORY

Memory is the general term used to describe how the computer holds data and instructions before and after processing. Memory's job is to store the instructions and data in the computer. In this section, we will discuss several types of computer memory. Memory can be divided into three major categories: main memory, read only memory, and auxiliary storage.

MAIN MEMORY

Main memory, also called RAM for random access memory, is the storage area directly controlled by the computer's CPU. Main memory assists the control unit and the ALU by temporarily holding the *programs* being executed, and for *data* as it passes through. Main memory is usually a number of additional ICs, electrically connected and in close proximity to the CPU, as you can see in Figure 8.3.

Main memory (also called *main storage, internal storage,* or *primary storage*) is associated with the CPU. It assists in processing tasks, but also directs its contents to output devices, such as the monitor or a printer, or to auxiliary storage. Main memory is short-term, **volatile** memory, meaning its contents are removed when replaced by new instructions and data, or when electrical power to the computer is turned off.

Throughout the remainder of this book we will refer to main memory as random access memory (RAM). Sometimes called the "working memory" of the computer, RAM holds the data and instructions during data processing. RAM is read-write memory: it can read or receive data and instructions from other sources; it can also write or transfer data to other sources such as auxiliary storage.

READ ONLY MEMORY

There is another kind of memory called *read only memory* (ROM). ROM is called read only memory because it holds instructions that can be read by the computer, but not written to. These are permanent instructions used to start the computer and direct many of its operations; they cannot be changed. ROM instructions are generally stored on a single integrated circuit chip.

ROM holds the startup program that begins when the computer power is turned on; this program is, in fact, what *boots* the computer. Each computer's startup program is a little different, but in general its tasks are to check the amount of RAM (you can often watch this counting process on the screen); check the video and monitor; identify the external connections, such as the keyboard or printer, to make sure they are operational; and check for a disk drive to load the operating system and execute any other instructions it finds on the disk.

HARDWARE MEMORY MANAGEMENT

You learned how the operating system works with memory in the previous chapter. But memory management is a critical *hardware* technology concern as well, and warrants discussion before we proceed to auxiliary storage. The first improvements in memory management began with IC design. Early RAM chips held approximately 16,384 kilobits (16K-bit), but soon grew to 64K-bit and 256K-bit. Today memory IC technology has boomed with the advent of chips that can hold 1M-bit, 4M-bit, 16M-bit, and so on.

In another advance, RAM is becoming less volatile through a technology called *dynamic memory*. The circuits are designed so that they not only hold the data or instructions in memory for as long as the electricity is applied, but they are periodically refreshed, or restored, while power is applied. This new technology is producing memory ICs called DRAM (dynamic random access memory). The latest 64M-bit DRAM chip is the highest-capacity chip developed to date; it is capable of storing more than 250 pages of newspaper text. DRAM chips are being manufactured by such Japanese firms as Matsushita, Fujitsu, and Mitsubishi. Interestingly, Japan dominates the market for memory IC technology, while the United States is the world leader in microprocessor technology.

Memory management has also been a factor in overall computer design. In the early days of personal computers, the standard RAM was 65,536 kilobytes; for convenience, it was rounded off and called 64KB. It was a small vessel to hold an entire application's program instructions as well as data; therefore, when the knowledge worker typed a command to perform a task that wasn't being held in RAM, the CPU had to fetch it from the auxiliary storage device (floppy or hard disk drive). But memory quickly grew; the first Macintosh had 128KB and rose to 1MB. IBM PCs and compatibles grew to the memory limit of 640KB, which quickly ushered in more sophisticated memory management techniques. Since it was theoretically possible to access many megabytes of memory, the 640K barrier had to be broken. Today, it is common to see personal computers with 2MB, 4MB, and even 16MB of RAM.

AUXILIARY STORAGE

Auxiliary storage, also called *auxiliary memory* or *secondary storage,* is memory that supplements main storage. This type of memory is long-term, **nonvolatile** memory. Nonvolatile means it stores and retains programs and data, regardless of whether the computer is turned on or off. The two most common types of auxiliary storage devices for personal computers are floppy and hard disks. Figure 8.4 summarizes computer memory and shows its relationship to hardware in the computer system.

Let's see how the different kinds of memory work together. Say you wrote a short memo to your fellow knowledge workers that read, "Department meeting at 3:00 P.M. today." It is stored temporarily in main memory or RAM, then you send it to the printer for a paper copy. You decide you don't need to store it

Type	Media	Retention	Location	Storage
RAM	IC	Volatile	Motherboard	Short-term
ROM	IC	Nonvolatile	Motherboard	Permanent instructions
AUX	Disk	Nonvolatile	Peripheral	Long-term

FIGURE 8.4

Computer memory.

TODAY
HIGH-PERFORMANCE COMPUTING

According to David Lowry, an executive consultant for the Research Consortium, Inc., of Minneapolis, "High-performance computing can be broadly defined as the most powerful machines in their class, whether they be a mainframe, a minicomputer, or a workstation." Thus, a supercomputer is a high-performance mainframe; a parallel or massively parallel computer is a high-performance mini; and a RISC-based machine is a high-performance workstation. Not many years ago, the only HPCs were supercomputers, but today HPC is entering into mainstream business computing. This trend is widely in evidence with IBM's RS/6000 RISC workstations. But it is also growing among the more powerful parallel processing computers made by Alliant, Convex, Intel, MIPS, and Sequent.

Parallel processing makes a quantum improvement over traditional computer architecture, which is called *von Neumann architecture* and was invented in 1945. In a von Neumann computer—which nearly all are today—each and every instruction must pass through the CPU one at a time. But with parallel processing, there are many processors, each performing its work simultaneously, side by side with the others. When the computer isn't busy, only a few are active; when the workload increases, one after another begins processing. Parallel processing makes sense for transaction-intensive applications, such as a bank's automated teller machines (ATMs). During the day, use may be light; but once people get out of work and begin withdrawing money, the demand surges.

Massively parallel processing computers (MPPC) do exactly the same thing as mainframes, according to Stephen Colley, president of nCUBE, a company that makes such machines. The major difference is they perform their tasks *10 to 20 times faster*. A MPPC has at least 64 CPUs and as many as 128.

Not quite as powerful—or expensive—is a parallel processing computer (PPC), which usually has between 2 and 30 CPUs. For example, Millipore Corporation, a company that makes analytical instruments and devices for analysis, synthesis, and purification in life science research, bought several Sequent Symmetry PPCs. One was installed with 28 processors, which may be either Intel 80386 or 80486 microprocessors. Millipore's rationale for PPC included the fact that it is an international company with offices in the United States and Europe that need to share data on a regular basis. The firm was looking for a computing environment that closely resembled personal computers, but with more power, flexibility, and a centralized database.

Millipore's previous system was a large minicomputer that used batch processing. It was slow; knowledge workers often had to wait days for the system to provide information. They wanted real time response, and parallel processing seemed to provide it.

The Sequent system provided "stunning performance," Millipore reports. Instead of knowledge workers waiting in a CPU queue for their request to be processed, each is routed to another microprocessor; now there is no waiting. The old system ran at 27 MIPS; the Sequent system runs at 350 MIPS. If the firm had installed an IBM mainframe, it would have cost about $200,000 per MIP; the Sequent system, which expanded to three machines, cost between $6,000 and $15,000 per MIP. If Millipore needs more power, it simply adds more microprocessors. Plus, it got on-line, real time transaction processing in the bargain.

for posterity, so it can be removed from memory. However, you do want to save the five-page report on new products you wrote for the marketing manager. This document passes from main memory into auxiliary storage for long-term safekeeping.

Computers differentiate between main storage and auxiliary storage for the sake of speed and efficiency. The CPU can work faster if the data and instructions it is processing are physically nearby. Main storage is usually on a chip or circuit board along with the CPU. However, auxiliary storage is usually slower because it involves some type of mechanical device. For instance, disk drives must spin the disk to store data. There is also a slowdown when the CPU must send signals back and forth between remote auxiliary storage devices. Auxiliary storage is explained in detail in Chapter 9.

KNOWLEDGE CHECK

1. What is the common name for main memory?   p. 256
2. What is the difference between RAM and ROM?   p. 256
3. What is the difference between volatile and nonvolatile memory?   p. 256–57
4. What is the term used to describe long-term supplemental memory?   p. 257
5. What is the primary disadvantage with long-term storage devices?   p. 259

CPU OPERATION

Now that you understand the way the CPU and RAM operate, let's see how they work together. The CPU, by itself, can do nothing; it is like an engine without fuel. Therefore, it must receive input, so that it has instructions and data to act upon, so that it can produce output. Knowledge workers provide the input and utilize the output.

In the early days of computing, having the computer able to solve a problem was often satisfaction enough. But the speed with which it could do so quickly became a key factor. Today computers utilize several techniques to increase and enhance the speed of operation. Memory plays a significant role in enhancing the computer's processing speed in more ways than one. This section explains, step by step, how this works.

THE REGISTERS

Since the CPU processes faster with instructions and data nearby, the control unit and ALU each have **registers,** temporary storage areas that are designed to hold both instructions and data during processing. Registers are built into the CPU integrated circuit, so they are electrically very close to the control unit and ALU; hence, they enhance processing speed. There are several types of registers; most common are:

- The **instruction register** holds an instruction; for example, add, multiply, or a logical comparison operation.

- The **address register** identifies memory locations for specific instructions or data.

- The **storage register** holds data retrieved from RAM temporarily, prior to processing.

- The **accumulator** temporarily stores the results of continuing arithmetic and logical operations.

Remember, registers are very short-term memory; they hold instructions or data only during a processing sequence and then pass it back to RAM. In summary, there are three types of storage used in processing:

- Registers for immediate storage.

- RAM, or main memory, storage for data or instructions that must be processed very soon.

- Secondary storage for data or instructions that may be processed at a later date or stored indefinitely.

DATA REPRESENTATION

What, you might be asking, do these instructions and data look like to the computer? Our everyday language symbols—those characters on the keyboard—must be translated into the binary language the computer understands. This is called **data representation.** As you know from Chapter 2, the computer only understands the binary language of 1s (for on) and 0s (for off). When a unique string of 1s and 0s are linked together, they create a representation the computer understands. Each 1 or 0 is a **bi**nary digit (**bit** for short), and the representation they form (a letter or number, for example) is called a *byte.* You can see how a byte represents a word in Figure 8.5. The computer can process data in byte sizes.

Bytes are sometimes organized into **words,** logical units of information. *Word length* is the term used to describe their size, counted in numbers of bits. However, a word to a computer is not the same as a word in our language. Most bytes represent just one letter, digit, or symbol. It takes several bytes to represent most human language words.

An early standard established a byte as a group of eight bits. So each byte contained exactly eight binary digits, a combination of eight 1s and 0s. We call a computer whose CPU is designed for bytes of eight bits an *8-bit machine.* In the early 1980s, most personal computers were 8-bit machines. But larger

---

FIGURE 8.5

The word "computer" in computerese.

C	O	M	P	U	T	E	R
0	0	0	0	0	0	0	0
1	1	1	1	1	1	1	1
0	0	0	0	0	0	0	0
0	0	0	1	1	1	0	1
0	1	1	0	0	0	0	0
0	1	1	0	1	1	1	0
1	1	0	0	0	0	0	1
1	1	1	0	1	0	1	0

computers were faster because their CPUs were designed to work with bigger bytes. As engineers were able to pack more components on a chip, it became possible to build 16-bit and 32-bit desktop computers. Supercomputers are at the leading edge of this drive for greater speed; some of their CPUs work with 64 or 128 bits. Once the instructions and data are in a language the computer understands, the CPU can perform its processing.

THE MACHINE CYCLE

The length of time it takes the CPU to process one machine instruction is called a **cycle.** The cycle is a useful term for measuring CPU performance, in the same way the term *horsepower* is used for internal combustion engines. Information systems professionals often use the term as a way to monitor computer resources consumption. For example, more cycles are needed late in the afternoon, after people have left work, for ATM transactions.

Machine cycle is the term used to describe the steps involved in processing a single instruction. Figure 8.6 shows the CPU machine cycle. Actually, it is comprised of two cycles: the instruction cycle and the execution cycle. Let's use the example of spell-checking a word to see how the machine cycle works. The word is "all" but let's say you have mistakenly typed a fourth character so that it reads "allk." The ALU has performed its equals condition operation on the first three letters and is beginning on the fourth. As we work it through, follow along in Figure 8.6.

THE INSTRUCTION CYCLE.   In the **instruction cycle,** sometimes called the *I-cycle,* the control unit of the CPU fetches, or retrieves, an instruction from RAM and gets ready to perform processing. There are four steps in the instruction cycle:

1. The control unit *fetches* from primary memory the next instruction for execution — in this case, the logical operator for *equals.*

2. The control unit decodes the instruction to issue the logical operation comparing the fourth letter of the word. (The word, previously considered "all," is now determined to be "allk.")

3. The control unit puts the part of the instruction for the equals condition into the *instruction* register; it's waiting for the ALU to compare the fourth letter.

4. The control unit puts the portion of the instruction that indicates the location of the needed data — the "k" — into the *address* register.

To summarize, the computer now has the instruction (the = logical operator) ready and waiting in the instruction register, and the data (the "k") ready and waiting in the address register.

THE EXECUTION CYCLE.   The next phase is the **execution cycle** (E-cycle) in which the data is located and the instruction is executed. Again, there are four steps:

1. Using the equals condition instruction, the control unit retrieves the "k" from RAM and places it in a storage register.

2. The command to compare is issued.

FIGURE 8.6   The machine cycle processes a single instruction. A typical personal computer CPU
                       processes millions of instructions per second.

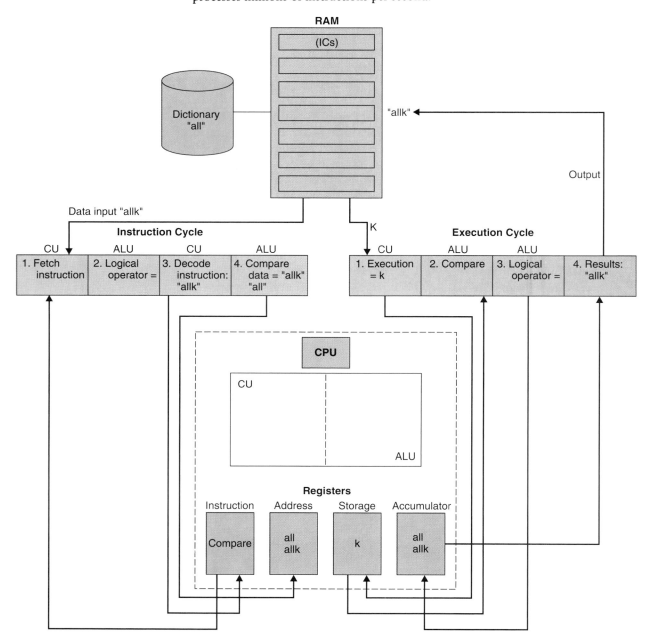

3. The ALU performs its equals (=) condition logical operation on the
    values it has found in the storage register and the accumulator
    (which is holding the results of performing the equals condition on
    the first three letters of the word).

Chip Manufacturer	Microprocessor	Word Size (bits)	Clock Speed (MHz)	Used in
Mostek	6502	8	1	Apple IIe Atari 800
Zilog	Z-80A	8	4	Radio Shack TRS-80 Model 1 Epson QX-10
Intel	8086	16	4.77	Leading Edge XT
Intel	8088	16	4.77–10	IBM PC and PC/XT Compaq Portable
Intel	80286	16	8–12	Toshiba T1600 Laptop IBM PS/1
Intel	386SL	32	16–25	Zeos Freestyle/SL Notebook
Intel	80386	32	16–33	Compaq Deskpro 386
Intel	486SX	32	20–25	ALR PowerFlex
Intel	80486	32	25–66	Dell Dimension 486DX2/50
Motorola	68000	32	8–12	Apple Macintosh
Motorola	68020	32	12–33	Macintosh LC
Motorola	68030	32	16–50	Commodore Amiga 3000
Motorola	68040	32	25–50	NeXT workstation Hewlett-Packard workstations Macintosh Quadra

FIGURE 8.7

The evolution of micro-processor chips.

4. The result of the operation is placed in the accumulator, replacing the values previously stored there. The word has now been completely — and incorrectly — spelled as "allk." The spelling checker, not having found such a word, will ask you to verify its spelling.

The computer machine cycle is very fast — a mere fraction of a second. It's an important measure of computer performance. Let's take a look at just how fast computers really operate.

SPEED

Personal computer microprocessors measure CPU speed in **Hertz,** a term used to describe machine cycle frequency. One Hertz equals one cycle. The basic unit of measurement is 1 million Hertz (HZ), abbreviated MHz. The early personal computer performed significantly more slowly than minis and mainframes, but over the past few years have shown a more than tenfold increase in microprocessor speed; in less than 10 years it has gone from 4.77 MHz to 66 MHz. Figure 8.7 depicts the evolution of microprocessors and their speed in MHz.

Minicomputers and mainframe computers measure CPU speed in **millions of instructions per second** (MIPS). The VAX line of Digital minis ranges from 1 to 12 MIPS. The IBM 3090 mainframe line ranges from 30 to 60 MIPS. Clearly, the machine cycle distinction between different classes of computers is blurring; however, that does not mean that PCs are equal in

TOMORROW
MORE POWERFUL, MORE VERSATILE CPUs

Today we have personal computers that are based on many different microprocessors and operating systems. Yet one thing almost all microprocessors have in common is the manner in which they process instructions. Complex-instruction-set computing (CISC) is a microprocessor or CPU architecture and operating system design that recognizes 100 or more instructions, enough to carry out most computations. Most people feel CISC computers are adequate for our computing needs; besides, all our application software is based on the CISC instruction set and operating system. Do we need yet another CPU architecture? Proponents of reduced-instruction-set computing (RISC) seem to think so.

Reduced-instruction-set computing is a microprocessor or CPU architecture that uses a condensed set of instructions for its operating system. RISC microprocessors have the advantage of simplicity and elegance over CISC microprocessors. They are also extremely fast. The increased performance and lower price of RISC microprocessors have had a profound effect on the computer industry, prompting companies such as IBM to introduce an entire line of RISC workstations.

However, older technologies are kept alive by the huge investments individuals and companies have already made in them. Users who have invested heavily in CISC, for example, are reluctant to purchase incompatible RISC machines. The abundance of existing software for CISC machines is also a factor in the continuing support of that technology. Many questions concerning the RISC versus CISC remain unanswered.

The debate over reduced-instruction-set computing versus complex-instruction-set computing typically focuses on which architecture is better, rather than which architecture best handles a specific set of problems. RISC is fast, but simple applications such as word processing do not require greater speed. CISC computers offer a wide diversity of applications, but these applications are often constrained by fundamental limitations in the CPU (or microprocessor) design. RISC is well suited for applications requiring great power, complexity, and diversity such as computer-aided design (CAD).

Converging forces may make it unnecessary to choose one over the other. The newest CISC microprocessors, such as the Intel 80486, are capable of RISC speeds. And RISC workstations are now able to utilize several different operating systems, like DOS, so they can run a wide variety of application software. With the introduction of the Intel 80586, the distinction between CISC and RISC begins to blur; microprocessors this powerful are capable of running two, three, or more operating systems and their applications as well. But no matter how powerful the CPU, as knowledge workers know, the first criterion for any decision regarding the "best" computer to purchase is the software application.

power to minis and mainframes. There are other considerations, such as the amount of RAM, multiple processors, and the number of knowledge workers and applications that are simultaneously on the system.

The fastest computers are supercomputers, where the measure is in **floating operations per second** (FLOPS), a distinctly mathematical term. Supercomputers perform FLOPS by the millions, called *megaflops,* and even by the billions, called *gigaflops.* The next generation of supercomputers will perform in the *teraflops* (trillions of floating point operations per second) range.

We've learned a great deal about CPU operation. Now let's put everything together and see how the data processing actually works.

■

KNOWLEDGE
CHECK

1. What is the purpose of the registers?   p. 259
2. What are the three types of registers?   pp. 259–60
3. Why does the CPU need data representation?   p. 260
4. What is processed during one machine cycle?   p. 261
5. What are the two types of machine cycle?   p. 261
6. What term describes the length of time it takes to process an instruction?   p. 261
7. What term is used to measure the speed of microprocessor CPUs?   p. 263

A DATA PROCESSING EXAMPLE

Each time we use a computer to perform data processing, a sequence of steps or operations occurs. The steps vary, depending on the software we use and the requirements of the problem we wish to solve. The four data processing operations (Figure 8.8) reflect this process in general. Let's look at a specific example to get a better understanding of how computers work.

In this example, the computer adds a list of 42 numbers. First, the CPU loads the software necessary for processing the data into RAM. Then the process begins at the keyboard, with the input operation. We enter the data to be processed—the 42 numbers we want added—and indicate that we want them totaled. As we type, the keyboard sends electrical signals representing

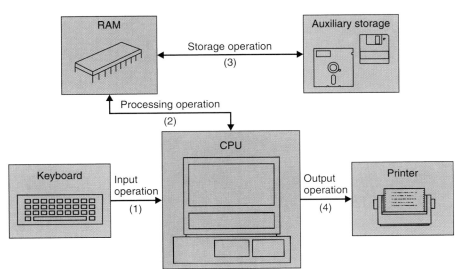

FIGURE 8.8

The four data processing operations: (1) the input operation sends keyboard input to the CPU; (2) interactions between the CPU and RAM execute processing operations; (3) data from RAM is stored on a floppy disk in the memory operation; and (4) the CPU sends data to the printer in the output operation.

each letter and number to the CPU, performing the data representation or translation into the binary language the computer understands. This is the input operation, shown in Figure 8.9. The CPU's control unit stores the input in RAM and sends signals to the monitor, causing it to display the input on the screen. This portion of the sequence is shown in Figure 8.10.

Next, the ALU performs the addition (or processing) operation. The control unit sends the addition instruction to the ALU 42 times — once for each number — adding the numbers together as it goes. For example, say the first three numbers are 2, 6, and 5: $2 + 6 = 8$ and $8 + 5 = 13$. In a simple calcula-

FIGURE 8.9

The input operation sends data from the keyboard to the CPU.

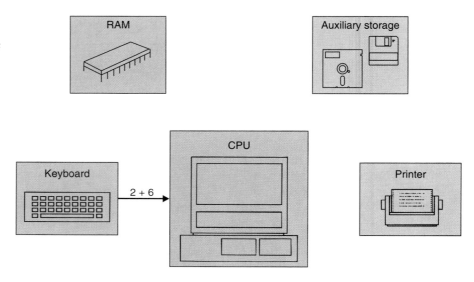

FIGURE 8.10

The CPU stores the data in RAM and sends data to the monitor for display.

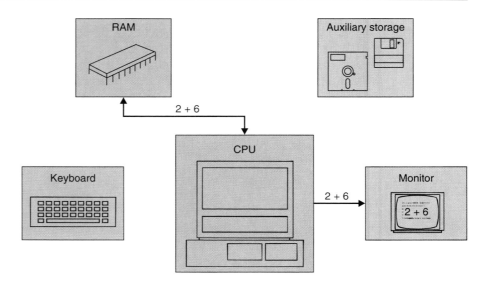

tion of this sort, the ALU adds the numbers in a tiny fraction of a second. Results of the calculation are sent to RAM for temporary storage. This portion of the sequence is shown in Figure 8.11.

In the output operation, the control unit obtains the results from RAM and routes the data wherever the software instructs it to. Typical output operations send the result to the monitor so we can see it, or to the printer so we can have a printed copy. Output can also be directed to auxiliary storage. This portion of the sequence is shown in Figure 8.12.

Depending on the software instructions, in the memory operation the

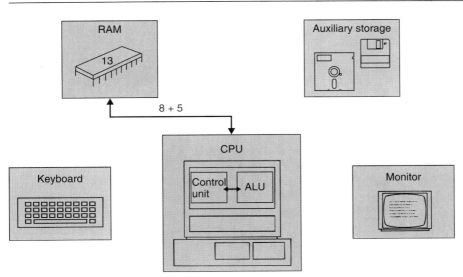

FIGURE 8.11

The ALU interacts with RAM to perform the next processing operation.

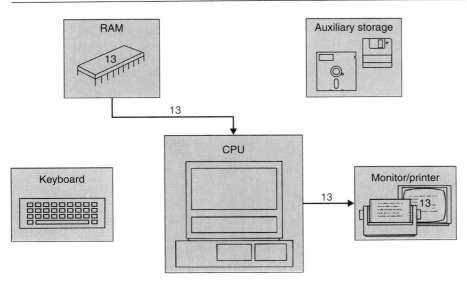

FIGURE 8.12

In the output operation, the result is sent to the monitor or printer.

FIGURE 8.13

In the memory operation, the result is sent to auxiliary storage.

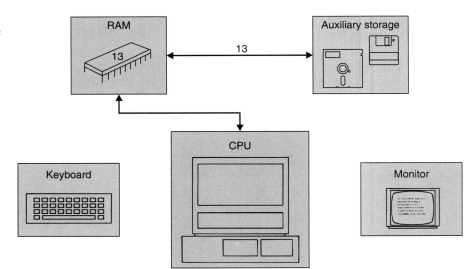

result is also sent to auxiliary storage, such as a disk drive, for permanent storage. It can also be retrieved into RAM at another time, as the arrow indicates. This portion of the sequence is shown in Figure 8.13.

This process has many variations, but this example is typical and shows the role of each device: the keyboard, the control unit, RAM, the monitor, the ALU, the printer, and auxiliary storage. It begins when a knowledge worker needs to solve a problem, whether it is processing an order or preparing sales projections for next quarter. The software issues the instructions to the hardware, which performs the processing. Once finished, the computer system presents its results and the knowledge worker has the information needed to solve the problem.

THREE METHODS OF DATA PROCESSING

Most computers commonly perform the four data processing operations using either the batch processing or the on-line processing method. **Batch processing** means the data is collected in a batch over a period of time, then usually input, processed, and output all at once. Batch processing helps people use the computer more efficiently; the computer can be used for important tasks during the day and can then perform the more repetitious and less important tasks overnight. It is best suited to tasks where there are many transactions to perform or tasks that are not particularly time-sensitive. For example, say a steel company only makes concrete reinforcement bars once a week, on Thursday. It accumulates hundreds of orders Monday through Wednesday; the computer batch processes them Wednesday night. The computer tallies the orders and determines how much steel to make on Thursday and then prepares the invoices and shipping forms so the orders can be shipped to customers on Friday.

On-line processing means that data is processed immediately, as soon as it is input. On-line processing is more frequently used as people and businesses require more speed and efficiency in handling transactions. For example, an on-line order entry system at a mail-order sporting goods company allows the operator to enter the transaction immediately, producing an invoice and sending the paperwork to the warehouse for packing and shipping.

There is a third method that is becoming more widely used. It is **on-line transaction processing** (OLTP), where the computer system completes the entire transaction as soon as it is entered. This is used in businesses where up-to-date information is critical, such as the airline industry. It is sometimes referred to as real time processing, since it is happening now, not later. With on-line transaction processing, for example, the computer reserves seat 11B for you the moment your travel agent selects it.

KNOWLEDGE CHECK

1. What components are involved in the input step?   p. 265
2. What components are involved in storing the numbers?   p. 266
3. What component does the addition, or processing?   p. 266
4. What component performs the routing during the output operation?   p. 266
5. What kind of processing takes place all at one time?   p. 268
6. When is it advantageous to process data immediately?   p. 269

WHAT LIES AHEAD?

When asking this question about processing hardware, the axiom "It's getting better, faster, and cheaper" comes to mind. Indeed, it is the correct answer.

Microprocessor technology is getting better. Engineers and architects are able to pack more features, such as cache memory, into each chip. The industry is becoming competitive as well, with companies like Advanced Micro Devices and Cyrix entering a market that has been dominated by Intel and Motorola. All are innovating and reaching out into noncomputer markets, where microprocessors are used to control everything from kitchen appliances to antilock automobile braking systems.

Faster microprocessors are being introduced faster. Until the 1980s, Intel's plan was to introduce a new generation of its 8000 series every five years. It didn't work; the 80386 and 80486 were only four years apart, and the 80586 was introduced three years after the 486. What's more, *upgradable* PC-compatibles are now available, so the old 386 microprocessor can be removed and replaced with a 486.

And personal computers are becoming less expensive. Both Apple and DOS machines have fallen dramatically in price over the past several years, making the personal computer an affordable consumer item. Today it is possible to purchase a powerful, flexible, useful computer system for under $1,000 that, just a few years ago, would have cost three or four times as much.

What lies ahead? More computers that are better, faster, and cheaper!

CAREERS FOR KNOWLEDGE WORKERS
AN INTERVIEW WITH LASZLO BELADY, MITSUBISHI ELECTRIC RESEARCH LABS

Laszlo A. Belady is chairman and director of Mitsubishi Electric Research Laboratories, Inc., a basic research institute established in Cambridge, Massachusetts, in July 1991. This appointment is just the most recent chapter in a varied and notable career that has included stints as manager of software engineering at Japan Science Institute (a branch of IBM's worldwide research organization, now called IBM's Tokyo Research Laboratory) and as vice president at Microelectronics and Computer Technology Corp. (MCC) in Austin, Texas.

Born in Hungary, Belady began his career at IBM and spent 23 years there before moving on to MCC. In the 1960s, his primary concentration was on virtual machines and virtual memory—notions that he pioneered. During the 1970s, he was a leader in the development of software engineering and, in his words, "made software maintenance respectable to scientists."

In a conversation* with *Computerworld* Senior Editor Michael Alexander, Belady discussed some of the new challenges for basic researchers and for people who aspire to a career in the computer industry.

Q. What do you think about the quality of Japan's computer science graduates compared with here?

A. They aren't as able to be immediately useful. On the other hand, with respect to the whole Japanese population, I think their mathematical and basic scientific backgrounds are very thorough and very good. There is another interesting aspect to this: The distribution of talent and capability is skewed differently. We have a small percentage of absolute superstars, then we have lesser stars and finally the plain-vanilla scientist or engineer. In Japan, there are perhaps no superstars, but on average, the scientists and engineers are slightly better than in the United States.

They miss these superstars and, therefore, many good ideas, but everybody on average is extremely solid and capable. In addition to that, they are avid readers and, therefore, much more aware of a broad selection of relevant topics than in the United States.

---

* *Computerworld,* October 31, 1991, p. 19.

ETHICS: COMPETITION IN THE COMPUTER BUSINESS

What does *proprietary* mean to you? In the computer industry, it means that computer vendors develop their own, independent, proprietary technologies and then make them available for lease or for sale to customers. The initial reasoning behind proprietary technology was to protect one's research and development investment, and to ensure customer loyalty to a product line. For example, the compatibility of applications and data could only be assured if one upgraded from model to model with the same vendor's computing machines. And even that was not always assured.

Q. If a young person, a college person, came to you for advice about what to study to prepare himself or herself for a career in computer science, what would you say?

A. I could tell him or her a few things. One of them is, don't take any branch you are studying seriously, but learn how to learn. That is, be flexible and be aware that whatever you learn now is just the basics upon which you will have to build by continuously learning new things as the world changes around you.

I'd say, learn the basics: mathematics, physics, logic. Once you have the basics, you can build any kind of knowledge and expertise by continuing your education, reading research papers and so forth.

Don't be narrow. You should not just learn things that are related to programming. Pick another discipline that appeals to you, because applications-oriented systems design will be the future. For example, be a

programmer plus a medical doctor to some degree, be a civil engineer plus a programmer, or be a lawyer who also knows a lot about software.

Q. Any insights about which areas of computer science might be the most promising?

A. Probably for the next five years, visualization will be a very fruitful area. So will computer graphics and man/machine interfaces— the whole field of improving communication with machines, whether it involves extension of traditional programming languages, more advanced two-dimensional languages or, in general, the ergonomics of working with computers, making them user-friendly and so forth.

Computer-aided design and very large-scale integration will also be growth areas. So will anything that has to do with efforts that help people work together through the computer.

If you look at the last 30 or 40 years, computers have been supporting the individ-

ual. But when it comes to cooperation, we do it outside of computers. The only thing we use the computer for is as a communications device; namely, to send electronic mail to one another.

Q. Do you see your center interacting to any great degree with the university environment?

A. Very much so. This center is meant to be an open center —not a secret, closed company.

We expect to sponsor graduate work and, in the long run, to have postdocs accommodated here who would work with us before they go somewhere else.

I have to build up this organization. We have a very small number of researchers so far, most of whom are senior. We have to have a balanced staff—some senior people but also a large number of young Ph.D.s who are coming out of the universities. That is something we have started doing already.

Think of what proprietary might mean to you in the music business. Say you bought a MellowTone stereo receiver; you would have to buy a Mellow-Tone compact disk player or tape deck. The CD player would only play MellowTone CDs, and the tape deck would only record on MellowTone tapes. Your selection, and the ability to share CDs or tapes with friends, would be severely limited. Now, factor in that there are seven competitors in the market.

When considering proprietary versus nonproprietary, consider this: When AT&T developed the transistor (mentioned earlier in this chapter), the company gave its use to the world without charge. The feeling was that it was a creation that many minds would find countless uses for, and that its propagation would benefit all. Contrast that with the fierce competition between various microprocessor manufacturers and the long battle to determine who held the first patent (see the Yesterday feature). Who was the ultimate victor, what was ultimately won, and how has it helped humankind?

There was a time when competition was viewed as healthy, indeed essential, for a free-market economy. It was possible for a computer vendor to dominate a market (for example, business data processing, scientific computing, or manufacturing process control). But the world and the nature of individual nation-states' economies has changed dramatically since World War II, and with it the way companies do business. Today most large companies need computers for all the preceding tasks as well as for office automation and many other things. It just isn't possible to have one computer system that does everything for everyone. Besides, the free-market economy has proven that the best solutions to computing problems don't necessarily come from the vendor with the largest share of the market.

Today, companies want "open systems," the ability to interconnect many different computers from a wide variety of vendors. They want their Macintoshes to work compatibly with their Sun workstations and want both to share data with their IBM mainframe and Digital VAX. Characteristically, many vendors are offering an open systems solution but one that is often proprietary. They still want to "lock the customer in," to use the marketing phrase.

The actor Charles Chaplin wrote in his autobiography that "Man is an animal with primary instincts for survival. Consequently, his ingenuity has developed first and his soul afterwards. Thus the progress of science is far ahead of man's ethical behavior." What are the ethics of proprietary versus open computer systems? Is it reasonable to say that what was ethical 50 years ago could be unethical or irresponsible today? Where is the line crossed between protecting the vendor's best interests and ensuring that the customer gets a useful computer system?

SUMMARY

1. *Describe the different types of integrated circuits used in computers.* ICs may be used as the central processing unit or microprocessor; the ROM (read only memory) chip; the RAM (random access memory) chip; or as a controller for routing electrical signals between input and output devices.

2. *Explain the tasks performed by the three components that make up the CPU.* The CPU consists of the control unit, the arithmetic/logic unit, and main memory. The control unit and the ALU are combined in one IC; memory is usually separate chips. The control unit directs the step-by-step operations of the computer. The ALU performs arithmetic and logical operations.

3. *Explain the differences between arithmetic and logical operations.* Arithmetic operations are add, subtract, multiply, and divide; the computer can only add. Logical operations are greater than (>), less than (<), and equal to (=).

4. *Describe the three different types of computer memory.* Main memory is also called RAM; it is the working memory of the computer. It is volatile,

meaning it holds data and instructions only temporarily. ROM holds permanent instructions for the computer. Auxiliary storage is memory that supplements main memory; it is nonvolatile and can hold data and instructions after the power is turned off.

5. *Describe the steps in CPU operation.* The CPU must process instructions as quickly as possible; registers make it possible to hold instructions nearby for speedy processing. There are four common types of registers: instruction, address, storage, and accumulator. Data representation is the important step in translating keyboard symbols into the binary 0s and 1s that the computer understands. The machine cycle is comprised of eight steps involved in processing a single instruction; four are the instruction cycle, four are the execution cycle.

6. *Explain the terminology used to measure computer speed.* Hertz is used to measure personal computer speed; MIPS is used for minis and mainframes; FLOPS is used for supercomputers.

7. *Describe the three methods of data processing.* Batch

processing means collecting the data over a period of time and then processing it all at once. On-line processing means data is processed at the time it is input. On-line transaction processing is continuous, as soon as the data is entered.

ISSUES

1. The competition in chips and computers between the United States and Japan is intense. In the 1980s, Japan was charged with "dumping" (selling below cost) their chips in the U.S. market. Sometimes there are chip shortages, which cause prices to skyrocket. Do you think dumping is unethical or just a clever business strategy? Do you think limiting competition by setting up trade barriers would help or hurt the development of computer technology?

2. Consider these scenarios from your everyday life. One, you buy something at the grocery store with a sticker stating the price is $1.98. However, when the clerk passes the item over the scanner, it rings up $2.49. Two, you believe you have paid your last VISA card bill on time, but this month's statement shows a late charge. Are these examples of a computer error? Why do they occur? Who should be responsible for correcting them — the originator of the error or you, the consumer? Do we need to be more alert to computer errors? Should there be more responsive mechanisms in place for correcting computer errors?

3. Here is a true account of an IBM mainframe computer installed at an American college campus. How would you feel about having a computer with this much information stored in it on your campus?

> The computer, which might be found at a Fortune 500 company with a spare $10 million, handles tuition bills, class enrollment records, freshman applications, administration records and correspondence, college payrolls and investments, student essays, classroom exams, polling data, student and faculty bulletin boards, and messages between professors and students. It handles campus crime records and patterns, investment and marketing plans for hypothetical student companies, all articles for the student newspaper, faculty lecture notes, campus parking permits, files on every Marist alumnus, all personnel records, every college bill and invoice, every grade for every student in every course, the records for every telephone on the 120-acre campus, and communications between Marist and campuses worldwide. Oh, and it holds the library's entire card catalogue and circulation files including when every book is due.

CHAPTER REVIEW QUESTIONS

REVIEW QUESTIONS

1. What major characteristic differentiates the computer from other types of machines?
2. What is the difference between the processor and the CPU?
3. Name the three components of the CPU.
4. Explain the two operations the ALU performs.
5. Which CPU component is physically separate?
6. What is the difference between volatile and nonvolatile memory?
7. What are the two individual cycles of the machine cycle?

DISCUSSION QUESTIONS

1. Discuss the impact of the concept "better, faster, cheaper" on the evolution of computers.
2. Discuss the different types of memory and their purposes.

3. Discuss the advances in memory IC storage capacity.
4. Discuss how main memory and auxiliary storage work together.
5. Discuss the difference between von Neumann architecture and parallel processing.

6. Discuss the four data processing operations.
7. Discuss when it makes sense to use batch processing and when it makes sense to use one of the on-line processing methods.

MULTIPLE-CHOICE

1. The integrated circuit (check all that apply):
   a. Was invented by Jack Kilby.
   b. Was invented at Texas Instruments.
   c. Integrates many electronic circuit components into a single chip.
   d. Was first used in the Air Force's ENIAC.
   e. All of the above.
2. The microprocessor (check all that apply):
   a. Was invented by Ted Hoff.
   b. Was invented at Intel.
   c. Is often called "the computer on a chip."
   d. Was not patented by Gilbert Hyatt.
   e. All of the above.

3. The length of time it takes the computer to process an instruction is called:
   a. A machine cycle.
   b. A cycle.
   c. A bit.
   d. A Hertz.
4. Supercomputer speed is measured in:
   a. Millions of instructions.
   b. Floating point operations.
   c. The number of processors.
   d. The size of main memory.

FILL-IN-THE-BLANK

1. Integrated circuits are made from common _____ _____.
2. ICs are typically used in computers for _____, _____, _____, _____, and _____.
3. *ROM* stands for _____ _____ _____.
4. *DRAM* stands for _____ _____ _____ _____.

5. In data representation, _____ are grouped into _____, which are often organized into _____.
6. The two competing types of microprocessor technology are _____ and _____.
7. The oldest method of data processing is _____ _____.

TRUE/FALSE

1. The ALU can only perform the addition function.
2. It is a program in ROM that actually boots the computer.
3. Memory does not help improve the computer's processing speed.

4. The fastest personal computers are not as powerful as some mainframes and minis.
5. Another name for on-line transaction processing is real time processing.

KEY TERMS

accumulator,   260

address register,   260

arithmetic-logic unit
(ALU),   254

arithmetic operations,   254

batch processing,   268

control unit,   254

cycle,   261

data representation,   260

execution cycle,   261

floating operations per second
(FLOPS),   264

Hertz (Hz),   263

instruction cycle,   261

instruction register,   259

logical operations,   254

machine cycle,   261

main memory,   256

math co-processor,   254

millions of instructions per
second (MIPS),   263

nonvolatile,   257

on-line processing,   268

on-line transaction processing
(OLTP),   269

register,   259

storage register,   260

technological innovation,   249

volatile,   256

word,   260

CHAPTER 9

Input, Output, and Secondary Storage Concepts and Devices

LEARNING OBJECTIVES

After reading and studying this chapter, you should be able to:

1. Define the peripheral device and explain the purposes of the different kinds of interfaces.

2. Identify the methods of data entry and the different types of input devices used.

3. Describe the different types of output devices and the uses for various output technologies.

4. Explain the uses and purposes for direct access and sequential access storage methods.

THE COMPUTER INTERFACE

In Chapter 3, you learned about the knowledge worker aspects of the human-computer interface. In this chapter, you'll learn about the computer side of that same interface. The term **interface** is used to describe the point where either a peripheral device or a human meets the computer. Let's look at each.

Whether we can use a particular peripheral device with a particular processor depends on the availability of the proper physical interface. The physical interface is a connection on the system unit that permits connecting the peripheral device. A cable or wire is often needed to plug the peripheral into the interface. The two most common physical interfaces are called *serial* and *parallel;* the keyboard has its own special interface. Generally speaking, a peripheral is designed to work with specific processing hardware — a Digital mini, a Macintosh personal computer, and so on. The most common physical interfaces are shown in Figure 9.1.

The serial interface is used to connect a variety of devices, such as a mouse or modem. (You'll learn about the modem and communications in Chapter 14.) **Serial interface** means the data passes through the interface sequentially. It is often referred to as COM1, for communications.

The parallel interface is commonly used to connect the printer. **Parallel interface** means the data passes through the interface simultaneously (all at once). It is often referred to as LPT1, for line printer. Both interfaces have been standardized and given names. Serial is usually referred to as RS-232, while the term *Centronics* is commonly used to describe parallel. When additional interfaces are added, they become COM2, LPT2, etc. In some cases, special software is required in order to use a peripheral; such software is called a *logical interface.*

As you know, the point at which people use input and output devices is referred to as the *human-computer interface.* One goal for many designers is to provide the most humanlike interface possible between human and machine. In other words, it should be possible to communicate with a computer as simply as we do another person. In the simplest terms, that means designing a keyboard (the most commonly used input device) that responds well to the touch of fingers, or a video monitor (the most common output device) that is easy on the eyes. When we refer to these complementary input and output devices, we often use the term **I/O.**

Therefore, we have three types of interface: the physical interface and the logical or software interface between the computer and the peripheral, plus the human-computer interface between the peripheral and you. In this chapter, we'll look at all the different kinds of peripheral devices: input, output, and storage. Then we'll see examples of how they are commonly used with particular processing hardware. It should also be mentioned that the human-

FIGURE 9.1

The rear view of a typical PC showing its various physical interfaces, or ports.

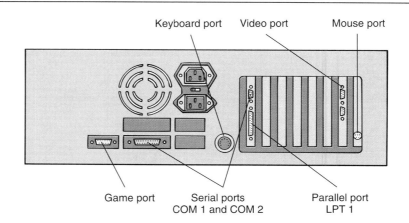

Keyboard port   Video port   Mouse port

Game port   Serial ports   Parallel port
               COM 1 and COM 2   LPT 1

computer interface extends to software design, such as the graphic user interface (GUI), as you saw in Chapter 7.

PERIPHERAL DEVICES

A peripheral is a device that performs input, output, or storage functions and is connected to the CPU. Without peripheral devices, the CPU is of no use to people. Figure 9.2 shows a variety of peripherals connected to a personal computer. As you can see, some are externally connected, while others are installed inside the cabinet.

You are familiar with the five data processing operations; this chapter explains the concepts and devices used in three of the five. Each of these operations is performed by specific hardware devices, often assisted by software. These devices make it possible to complete processing by the CPU. In this chapter, we take what we've learned about computer systems concepts, combine it with our understanding of processing hardware, and put it all together with peripheral devices. We explore the three types of hardware peripherals that permit us to utilize processing hardware in performing the primary transaction processing methods — batch processing and on-line processing.

HERMAN HOLLERITH AND THE FIRST I/O DEVICE

Herman Hollerith had a problem to solve: trying to count the 1890 census data in less than the seven years it took to do the 1880 census. Hollerith applied punched card technology, first employed by the Frenchman Joseph-Marie Jacquard in knitting machines, to mechanical tabulating machines. His card, called the Hollerith card, was the same size as a dollar bill. By 1884, Hollerith had developed an electromechanical tabulating machine. It used some of the same technology as an electric telegraph and had the same mechanical counters as an adding machine.

The **punched card** has a pattern of holes punched in it to signify program instructions. To read the cards, electrical contact was made by a pin passing through holes in the card, touching a bath of mercury below. The machine could read between 50 and 80 cards a minute. Counting the census involved

A PC showing the variety of peripheral devices that can be connected. The keyboard **FIGURE 9.2**
and video monitor are the most common input and output devices, respectively. A
number of storage and other devices may be installed internally.

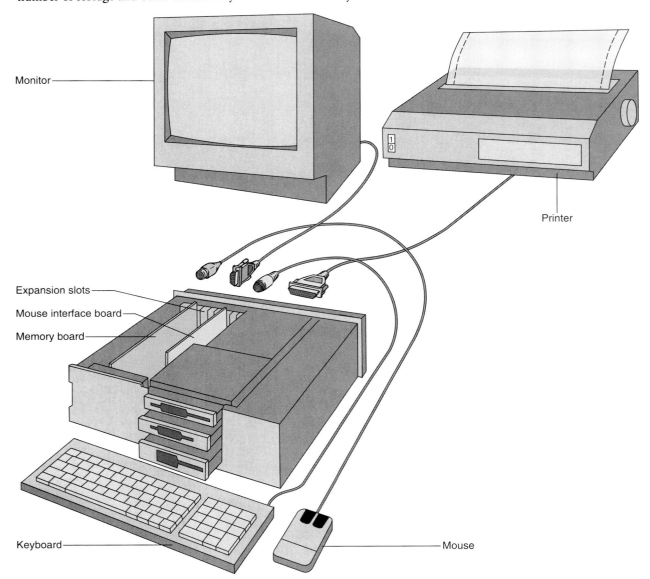

Monitor

Printer

Expansion slots

Mouse interface board

Memory board

Keyboard

Mouse

tabulating data on 62,622,250 citizens. That amounted to 2 billion holes in
punched cards. Hollerith's machine did it in just over two years. An article in a
magazine of the time said, "This apparatus works as unerringly as the mills of
the gods, and beats them hollow as to speed."

Hollerith leased his equipment to the U.S. government and to other countries as well. In 1896, he formed the Tabulating Machine Company. That
company became International Business Machines, and the punched card
became known as the IBM card. Billions and billions of punched cards have

been used for storing both programs and data over the years. But now, other forms of input and output have replaced the punched card. The last IBM punched card plant closed its doors in 1986. Today the Bureau of the Census uses the most modern VAX computers from Digital Equipment Corp. Yet it took as long to process the census in 1990 as it did in 1890, primarily because the population has grown so much.

■ KNOWLEDGE CHECK

1. What is a peripheral-to-computer connection called?   p. 277
2. What is a human-to-peripheral connection called?   p. 277
3. Name two common I/O devices.   p. 277
4. Name the two ways peripherals are connected with computers.   p. 277
5. What three functions do peripherals perform?   p. 278

INPUT

We use input devices to perform the two most basic computational tasks: **data entry,** the process of entering data into computer memory, and issuing commands. Nothing happens in the CPU until there is data for it to process. Once data is available, we must give the CPU instructions for what to do with it. For many years, knowledge workers have entered data manually into computers, usually by typing it on a keyboard. This method is slow and prone to typing errors. Therefore, developing faster, more accurate — better — data entry or input devices has been a high priority.

INPUT DEVICES

Most input devices depend on knowledge workers using their limbs, in conjunction with their senses, to perform data entry. In most cases, that means our fingers and our eyes — although, as we shall see, that too is changing.

THE KEYBOARD

The most widely used input device is the keyboard, which was adapted from the typewriter. Computer keyboards use the standard QWERTY alphanumeric keys. This convenient and familiar layout makes it possible for typists to learn word processing quickly. In addition, many keyboards have a numeric keypad to aid knowledge workers who work with numbers. Spreadsheet users find the numeric keypad especially useful. Most computer keyboards also have a set of function keys and keys to control cursor movement. Figure 9.3 shows the three most common personal computer keyboards.

The original PC keyboard places the Function keys to the left. The enhanced keyboard places them above the keyboard. The Macintosh extended keyboard replaces the less ergonomic original model.

FIGURE 9.3

IBM XT keyboard.

Enhanced PC keyboard.

Mac extended keyboard.

POINTING DEVICES

There are several types of pointing devices that are used to move the cursor, usually working in conjunction with a keyboard. A **pointing device** is used to move the cursor on the screen and to issue commands. The most common pointing device is the mouse, so named because it slides over your desktop and has a wire or "tail" attached to the computer. A mouse commonly has two or three buttons that are used to issue commands and provide input to the computer. Using the mouse to move the cursor to the menu and pressing a button, commonly called *clicking,* issues the command to open and close a file. The mouse can also be used to highlight a block of text you wish to move or delete. The cursor is placed at the beginning of the text, a button is pressed and held down, and then the cursor is dragged to the end of the block. Then the button is released and the block can be moved or deleted.

TYPES OF MICE. There are two common types of mice: electromechanical and optical. Usually the electromechanical mouse has a hard rubber ball in its base, which turns movement into electrical signals. The optical mouse projects a beam of light downward and must be used on a special metallic pad. Some tasks such as drawing lend themselves to efficient use of a mouse. However, tasks such as word processing would be awkward, extremely tedious, and time-consuming without a keyboard.

THE TRACKBALL. Another commonly used pointing device is the **trackball,** which performs like a stationary, upside-down mouse, as shown in Figure 9.4. Many people prefer the trackball over the mouse because it does not require as much hand-eye coordination, nor does it require the extra desk space necessary to move the mouse. The Macintosh portable has a built-in trackball.

THE JOYSTICK. The **joystick** is another pointing device, one that is usually associated with playing computer games. Joysticks used to produce jerky movement and were awkward to hold; however, newer models such as the one shown in Figure 9.5 use advanced technology for smooth movement; some are ergonomically designed to fit the hand.

FIGURE 9.4

The trackball is an alternative
to using a mouse.

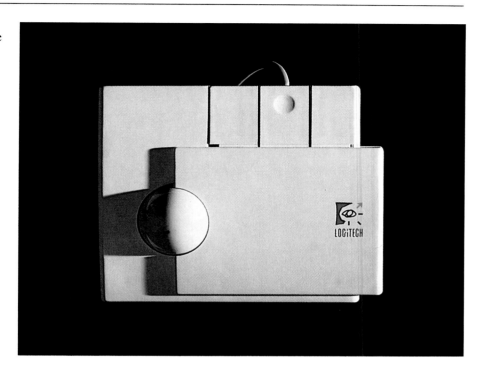

FIGURE 9.5

Joysticks are commonly used
with computer games.

YESTERDAY
GREAT MOMENTS IN I/O DEVICE HISTORY

Input Devices: Father of the Mouse

Douglas Englebart pioneered the mouse. His first model, built in 1963, was made of wood and used two wheels for movement. "We were experimenting with lots of types of devices at the time," Englebart recalls. Indeed, he and his colleagues at Xerox's highly respected Palo Alto Research Center were also exploring such futuristic concepts as

the workstation, graphic user interfaces, and networking, to name a few. "I felt until something better came along, the mouse would definitely remain the best pointing device for computer users."

Output Devices: Son of EP

The first dot-matrix printer for a personal computer was created by the Japanese company Epson, which in Japanese means

literally son of EP. The EP stands for electronic printer, which was part of an extremely accurate timing device that Seiko, Epson's parent company, built for the 1964 Summer Olympics in Tokyo. It was used to clock various events and print out the winning times. The timing device became the quartz watch, and the electronic printer became the dot-matrix printer.

WRITING AND DRAWING INPUT DEVICES

There are several ways to use a device similar to a pen for entering data. One is the **light pen,** used to draw, write, or issue commands when it touches the specially designed video monitor screen. For example, a circuit designer can draw the interconnecting wires in electronic circuits with a light pen. The light pen was originally developed for computer-aided drafting at MIT in 1964.

Even simpler than the light pen is your finger, which can be used as an input device on a video monitor with a **touch-sensitive screen.** You may have used a touch-sensitive screen to obtain information at an airport or the grocery store.

Do you remember the Etch-A-Sketch or Magic Slate? A drawing tablet or **digitizer** is similar and makes a good input device. Some have a form overlay that the data entry clerk fills out with a light pen or stylus. Others have more sophisticated stylus or pointing devices that are useful for designers, architects, artists, desktop publishers, or map makers, to name a few. Skip Morrow, the cartoonist shown in Figure 9.6, uses a digitizing tablet to produce his humorous work such as *The Official I Hate Cats Book.*

VIDEO INPUT

Images from video cameras, camcorders, VCRs, and optical disc players can be input into computers as static "snapshots" with a video digitizer peripheral, then used in many different ways. A series of snapshots can describe a process such as assembling a machine or an athlete's movements. The most recent video input device is the **digital camera,** which takes still photographs and transfers them directly into the computer through the serial port. A digital camera is shown in Figure 9.7.

FIGURE 9.6

Skip Morrow uses a digitizing tablet to create his cartoon art.

FIGURE 9.7

A recent innovation is the digital camera, which captures still images and converts them directly into digital files.

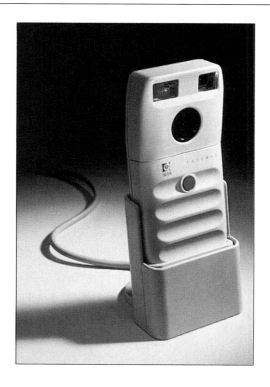

Scanners make it possible to input text and images from previously published sources.   **FIGURE 9.8**

Flatbed scanner.   Handheld scanner.

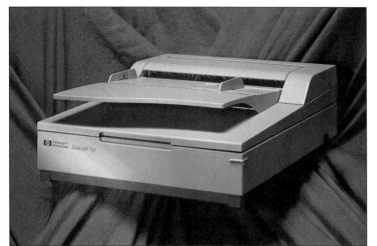

TEXT INPUT

One of the most tedious data entry tasks is to retype printed or previously word processed or typewritten text. A **scanner** uses a light-sensitive device to enter text (and, depending on the software, graphics) into the computer. Early scanners were only able to recognize text that was printed in a specific type font called OCR for **optical character recognition.** Early optical character reading equipment could read only one typeface, WHICH LOOKED LIKE THIS. Today scanners can read just about any type font. Their ability to do so, and the degree of accuracy in text input, depend in large part on the text, or character, recognition software used.

Figure 9.8 shows types of scanners in use today. The *flatbed* allows you to feed in sheets continuously. The *hand-held* scanner is able to capture images from source material such as a soup can label that can't be conveniently fed through a flatbed scanner.

VOICE INPUT

Perhaps the easiest way to enter data into a computer is by speaking; this is called *voice input* or **voice recognition.** However, since everyone pronounces words somewhat differently, and because of regional accents, the knowledge worker must teach the computer to understand his or her voice. Raymond Kurzweil has led voice recognition research with his Voicesystem, which can understand over 5,000 words. Doctors, notorious for bad handwriting, have successfully used the Voicesystem when evaluating patients and diagnosing illnesses. As Figure 9.9 shows, the spoken words appear on the screen and can then be printed out as patient records.

SOURCE DATA INPUT

Source data input refers to data fed directly into the computer without human intervention. Commonly, three types of media are used, which require special readers. One is **magnetic ink character recognition (MICR),** which allows the computer to recognize characters printed using magnetic ink. MICR is used by banks for processing checks. Another is the **magnetic strip,** used on the back of credit cards and bank debit cards; it allows readers such as an automated teller machine (ATM) to read account information.

A third source data input method is the **data collection device,** commonly used by sales and inventory people to check and replenish stock in retail stores or supermarkets. You'll often see these people standing in the shopping aisle, scanning *Universal Product Code* (UPC) symbols, often called *bar codes,* on bags of potato chips; they are counting what's in stock. They may use a light pen attached to a laptop or palmtop computer, or the hand-held computing device may have a bar code reading tip built right in. The number of bags sold will automatically be ordered when the hand-held data collection device is linked to its host computer. Figure 9.10 shows two methods of source data input.

Many retail businesses and grocery stores use yet another type of source data input: the **point-of-sale (POS) terminal,** part of the checkout register. It scans the bar codes of the UPC to register the price, which is programmed into the host computer, as well as to deduct the item from inventory. Figure 9.11 shows three different types of POS scanners.

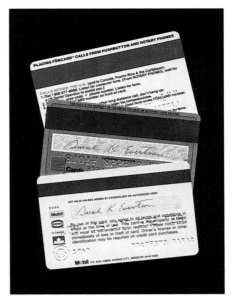

FIGURE 9.10
MICR on checks and magnetic strips on credit cards are used to enter account information.

FACSIMILE

Facsimile (FAX) machines have been in use for many years. Recently, however, we have seen a marriage of computers and FAX, so facsimile has become a type of source data input. A printed circuit board peripheral is installed inside the computer, which translates the computer's bits and bytes into the pattern of dots transmitted via FAX. However, the reverse is not true; a FAX machine cannot send a data file to a computer, it can only send the pattern of dots that can be viewed on the screen.

Computers and facsimile are now being used to deliver information via FAX. The Special Request system lets callers listen to a recording that lists such things as ski reports, sports information, product prices, investment tips, and interest rates; whatever callers select will then be FAXed to them.

INPUT DEVICES FOR THE DISABLED

Some interesting advances in input devices have come from small computer companies to aid the disabled. Voice recognition is one of these techniques. Stephen Hawking, a brilliant physicist who is almost completely immobilized from a rare type of sclerosis, is unable to use either his arms or his voice, so he wrote his best-selling book *A Brief History of Time* using a mouthstick to press the computer's keys. Special keyboards have been developed for people with cerebral palsy and muscular dystrophy. For the blind, there is a special braille keyboard that translates phrases into conventional letters and words.

People who can't move their limbs but have some head movement can use special pointing devices that attach to their heads. One such device is a small camera that projects a beam of light at a simulated keyboard. By holding the

FIGURE 9.11

POS scanners come in different types. The counter scanner and wand register the price and deduct the item from inventory. The hand-held scanner (below) is used to take inventory for replenishing stocks.

beam of light on the selected key for a moment, the character is sent as input to the computer. Research is under way at the IBM National Support Center for Persons with Disabilities to create a brain wave scanner. By reading electrical brain waves, the scanner would be able to sense when the person thought about an object such as a baseball, causing the word to appear on the screen. Figure 9.12 shows an input system for the disabled.

FIGURE 9.12

Special input systems compensate for a lack of mobility, as well as other disabilities.

1. What is the most common input device?   p. 280
2. What is a scanner commonly used for?   p. 285
3. What advantages does voice recognition offer?   p. 285
4. Name three different kinds of input.   pp. 285–86.
5. Describe two kinds of source data input.   p. 286.

KNOWLEDGE CHECK

OUTPUT

As the acronym I/O implies, you don't have much use for input without output. Output refers to the product of data processing, delivered in a form that knowledge workers can understand or that can be read by another machine. Today most output is visual in nature, produced by two devices: a video display screen or a printer.

TYPES OF COMPUTER OUTPUT

Most computer output comes in two forms: text and graphics. Text output is, simply, the characters that make up our language. Text output appearance ranges from typewritten to typeset quality. Graphic output includes line drawings, presentation business graphics, computer-aided design, computer painting, and photographic reproduction. As input or data entry methods improve, so do forms of output. As we shall see, sound output is growing more sophisticated and useful. Let's take a look at the devices that provide us with the output we need.

OUTPUT DEVICES

Text and graphic output devices fall into two categories: soft copy and hard copy devices. **Soft copy** refers to output we cannot touch, such as video or audio. The most common soft copy output device is the video display. **Hard copy** is output we can hold in our hand, such as a printed sheet of paper. The most common hard copy output device is the printer. We shall look at each in detail, as well as several other forms of output.

THE VIDEO MONITOR

The video monitor or display provides soft copy output. The most common video monitors, such as those used with personal computers, are very similar to a television screen; both use a cathode ray tube (CRT) to project an image. Video displays come either in monochrome or color. A monochrome display is a single color displayed against a background, such as green on black, amber on black, or white on black. A color display is able to show a variety of colors.

TYPES OF VIDEO DISPLAYS. *Resolution* is the term used to describe the degree of detail in a video display. The higher the resolution, the sharper and crisper the characters or images formed. For example, a conventional television display is low-resolution because you can see lines and graininess in the image. The newer, high-definition (HDTV) or high-resolution sets display a picture as sharp and crisp as a film image in a Hollywood movie. The same is true with computer displays. The Macintosh has a monochrome, **bit-mapped** display that is extremely high-resolution. This makes it good for graphics. Figure 9.13 shows both monochrome and color resolution.

Many other personal computers, whether monochrome or color, have **character-mapped** displays, which are not as high in resolution as a bit-

FIGURE 9.13   Monochrome and color resolution on a Macintosh.

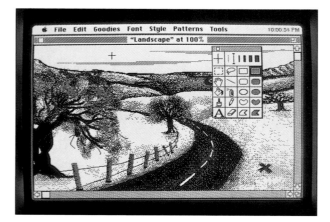

mapped display. To overcome their grainy display, successive generations of personal computers have employed improved video technologies. The first color display, called CGA (color graphics adapter), could display up to 16 colors. The EGA (enhanced graphics adapter) had better resolution and a palette of 64 colors. That was followed by the VGA (video graphics array), which is even sharper than HDTV and has a palette of 256 colors. Another popular color graphics adapter, the HGC (Hercules Graphics Card), became the standard for displaying graphics in Lotus 1-2-3. The 8514/A technology for IBM PS/2s with the Micro Channel has almost twice the resolution of VGA, a palette of 262,000 colors, and the ability to display 256 colors on the screen at a time. The latest advance, called Super VGA (S-VGA), was approved in 1992 by the Video Electronics Standards Association. It allows for easier installation and configuration of high-level video boards that work with the older video graphics array technology. The chart in Figure 9.14 lists the difference between EGA, VGA, Super VGA, and other video displays.

SPECIAL VIDEO DISPLAYS.   Some computers require special display technology because of either power requirements or the needs of special application software. Here are a few examples. The **gas plasma display** (Figure 9.15) is easy to recognize since it is a deep orange. It is a flat-panel display composed of three sheets of glass with plasma (an illuminant gas) between them. When electricity is applied, the screen glows. The gas plasma display has several distinct advantages. First, it is very thin, so it can be hung on a wall. Second, there is no limit to its size; one could be as large as a movie screen. Third, it is extremely easy to view. Some laptop computers use a gas plasma display, making it possible to view the screen from any angle and in any light.

The **liquid crystal display (LCD)** is also a flat-screen display commonly used with laptops. To make LCD screens easier to read in dim or bright light, they are backlit (lighted from behind the screen). Some use what is termed *supertwist technology* that also enhances visibility. Some laptops now have a color LCD display.

TERMINALS

Computer video displays are found on all types of computers, not just personal computers. Mainframes and minicomputers use terminals that commonly consist of a video display and a keyboard for input. These terminals can

Type	Resolution	Colors
Hercules	720 × 328	Monochrome
CGA	640 × 200	16
EGA	640 × 350	16
VGA	640 × 480	16
E-VGA	1024 × 768	16
S-VGA	1280 × 1024	256

FIGURE 9.14

IBM PC video displays.

FIGURE 9.15

A gas plasma display makes portable computers much easier to use.

be used for anything from data entry to computer-aided design (CAD). There are two basic types of terminals. One is the **dumb terminal,** which performs the simplest input and output operations but no processing. A bank ATM is a dumb terminal. The other is the **intelligent terminal,** which has its own CPU or processing capabilities built in. A point-of-sale (POS) cash register and a personal computer are examples of an intelligent terminal.

PRINTERS

A printer provides hard copy output on paper. The basic criteria for evaluating printers are the quality of the output and the speed, although the sound level is often a consideration. Printers fall into two primary categories: impact and nonimpact. **Impact printers** strike characters on the paper. The most common types of impact printers are the dot-matrix and letter-quality printers. **Nonimpact printers** form a character by other means, most commonly using laser technology or by spraying ink. Different types of printer output are shown in Figure 9.16. Let's look at the most common printing technologies today. Refer to the chart in Figure 9.17 as you compare the following printing technologies.

DOT-MATRIX PRINTING

Dot-matrix output is produced by printers that utilize wires in the print head. These wires extend out to create patterns, pressing against the ribbon to print the characters on the paper. For this reason, dot-matrix printers can produce

Dot-matrix output.

```
"I don't 'think them up,' to use your phrase.  They
come from some other place, really, it's hard to tell you
where it is, but I can feel it right there and it makes me
think of Montana, Big Sky Country.  When I'm a cowboy on
that range, nothing can stop me."
```

Near-letter-quality (NLQ) output.

```
"I don't 'think them up,' to use your phrase.  They
come from some other place, really, it's hard to tell you
where it is, but I can feel it right there and it makes me
think of Montana, Big Sky Country.  When l'm a cowboy on
that range, nothing can stop me."
```

Letter-quality output.

```
"I don't 'think them up,' to use your phrase.  They
come from some other place, really, it's hard to tell you
where it is, but I can feel it right there and it makes me
think of Montana, Big Sky Country.  When I'm a cowboy on
that range, nothing can stop me."
```

Laser output.

```
"I don't 'think them up,' to use your phrase.  They
come from some other place, really, it's hard to tell you
where it is, but I can feel it right there and it makes me
think of Montana, Big Sky Country.  When I'm a cowboy on
that range, nothing can stop me."
```

FIGURE 9.16

Different types of printer output.

both text and graphics. Early dot-matrix printers had nine wires in the print head and were very fast, but the print quality was often unacceptable for professional or business documents. To improve quality, printer makers created 24-pin print heads, which produce **near-letter-quality (NLQ)** output. The primary disadvantages with dot-matrix printers are that they are noisy and their print quality is often insufficient to meet business standards.

FIGURE 9.17   Comparison of popular personal computer printing technologies.

Type	Speed	Print Quality	Font Selection	Graphics/ Quality	Color/Quality	Noise	Cost
Dot-matrix, 9-pin	250 characters per second	Fair	Good	Yes/Low	Yes/Medium	High	Low
Dot-matrix, 24-pin	80 characters per second	Good	Good	Yes/High	Yes/Medium	High	Medium
Letter-quality	50–80 characters per second	Excellent	No	No	No	High	High
Laser	6+ pages per minute	Excellent	Excellent	Yes/High	Yes/High	Medium	High
Inkjet	12+ pages per minute	Excellent	Excellent	Yes/High	Yes/High	Very low	Medium

LETTER-QUALITY PRINTING

Letter-quality printers are most similar to typewriters and produce the same high-quality output. The two most common letter-quality technologies are the daisy wheel and the thimble. The **daisy wheel** resembles a daisy; a print hammer strikes each "petal" against a ribbon to form the impression. The **thimble** resembles the IBM Selectric "golfball," but like the daisy wheel, it utilizes a print hammer. Letter-quality printers offer a wide selection of interchangeable type fonts; however, you cannot change fonts in the middle of a print job, since it necessitates changing the daisy wheel or thimble. Nor can letter-quality printers print graphics. The impact printer's other major disadvantages are cost, noise, and slow speed.

LASER PRINTING

Laser printers provide high-quality nonimpact printing. Output is created by directing a laser beam onto a drum, creating an electrical charge that forms a pattern of letters or images. As the drum rotates, it picks up black toner on the images and transfers them to paper.

Laser printers have the advantages of speed and a wide selection of type fonts, as well as high-quality graphics. A variety of fonts permit using many type sizes, as well as italics and boldface text. Laser printers for personal computers can print up to eight pages per minute; commercial laser printers, such as those that produce bank statements, can print 400 to 500 pages per minute.

Laser printing offers the highest-quality text and graphics printing for the desktop. Color laser printers, like the one shown in Figure 9.18, promise to be the next great advance. Although laser printer prices have fallen dramatically over the past few years, the primary disadvantages are expensive maintenance and the high cost of toner cartridges. Another recent advance employs a liquid crystal display (LCD) shutter, like a camera, instead of a laser beam, offering greater reliability and longer life.

Laser printers often require special software, called *drivers,* that make them work compatibly with a particular type of computer or application software package. Various typefaces or fonts for a particular laser printer are provided as

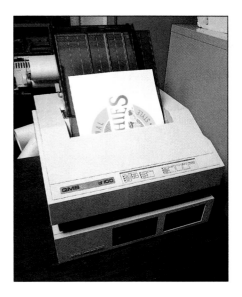

FIGURE 9.18

The color laser printer gives you WYSIWYG hard copy output. A portable printer lets you generate hard copy wherever you are.

software. This is also true of some dot-matrix printers. In addition, laser printers often have hardware peripherals of their own, such as add-on memory boards or *font cartridges,* a plug-in circuit board.

INKJET PRINTING

Inkjet printers were first used for high-volume printing, such as direct mail brochures. They transfer characters and images to paper by spraying a fine jet of ink. Like laser printers, they are able to print many different type fonts and graphics. In recent years, inkjet printing has come to the personal computer, offering the same high quality as a laser printer but at a more affordable price. Inkjet printers are slow, and their output may smear if it gets wet.

PLOTTERS

Plotters use inkjet technology to create scientific and engineering drawings, as well as other graphics, often in color. Color plotters use ink pens that switch on and off according to instructions from the computer and software. Plotters can create very large documents; for example, a chip designer created a schematic drawing of an integrated circuit 7 by 9 feet. Figure 9.19 shows plotter printing.

THERMAL PRINTING

As the name implies, **thermal printers** use heat to form a nonimpact image on chemically treated paper. Thermal printing combines high speed with a low-maintenance printing technology. However, the paper is expensive and not as desirable as plain bond paper. Thermal printing is mostly used for low-cost calculators or high-quality color printing.

FIGURE 9.19   Plotters use inkjet printing to produce high-quality color commercial documents. Color inkjet technology is now available in low-cost printers for personal computers.

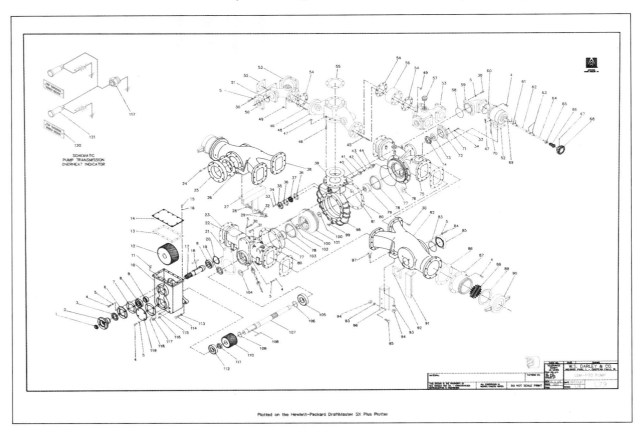

Plotted on the Hewlett-Packard DraftMaster SX Plus Plotter

COMPUTER-TO-MACHINE OUTPUT

Computer output can also be sent to another machine, including another computer. For example, computers are used for process control in factories, buildings, and even the home. With **computer-to-machine output,** the I/O process controls machine operations, maintains heating and cooling, and turns lights on and off at prescribed times. At a Panasonic factory in Japan, computer-controlled robots make vacuum cleaners without any human help (unless something breaks!).

It is possible to produce high-quality color slides directly using computer-to-machine output. Using a cameralike device connected to the computer interface, the image on the screen (whether text, graphics, or both) is output to 35mm film, which is exposed just as it would be in a camera. The film is then developed normally.

Another interesting computer-to-machine output task involves computer-output microfilm. **Computer-output microfilm (COM)** uses miniature photography to condense, store, and retrieve data on a film-like media called *microform.* The two most common types of microform are microfiche (which

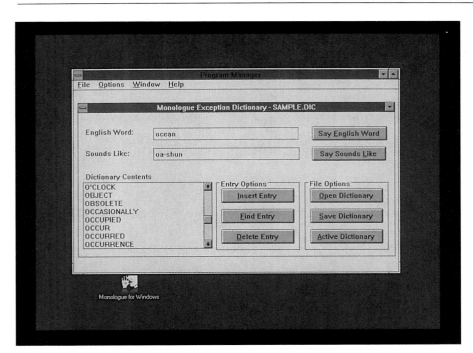

FIGURE 9.20
Monologue, a program that outputs text to a loudspeaker, is useful for the visually impaired.

are 4 × 6-inch sheets of film) and microfilm (which comes in rolls). Both are used with special readers that magnify the information and display it on a screen. Microform holds up well under sustained usage.

Computer output such as newspaper copy, canceled checks, or invoices is sent to a special COM machine that reduces it in size and then records it 10 to 20 times faster than printing. The film is developed and copied for distribution. For example, book distributors prepare weekly microfiches listing books by title, author, price, and number in stock. A single sheet of microfiche holds almost 1,000 sheets of standard paper.

VOICE OUTPUT

Voice output, or *speech synthesis,* is the machine's ability to "speak" like a human. Some computers already talk to us. The soft drink machine thanks us for our purchase. Autos tell us to buckle our seat belt. Monologue, the speech synthesis program shown in Figure 9.20, reads screen text; a voice pronounces the words through a speaker. But when will computers talk to us like the HAL 9000 in the movie *2001: A Space Odyssey?*

Raymond Kurzweil, creator of the Voicesystem mentioned earlier, thinks we will have quite natural-sounding speech synthesis by the first decade of the next century. He describes a very practical use for speech synthesis: a translating telephone system. It uses three technologies: automatic speech recognition for voice input; language translation performed as real time processing; and speech synthesis for voice output. Then two people, regardless of their native language, can speak to each other over the telephone or understand one another during meetings of the United Nations, as if they were both speaking the same language.

KNOWLEDGE CHECK

1. What are the two types of output copy called?   p. 289
2. Give examples of low-resolution and high-resolution monitors.   p. 290
3. What are the two types of terminals?   p. 292
4. What are the two common categories of printers?   p. 292
5. List the different types of printers, from the highest- to the lowest-quality output.   p. 294
6. What is the main advantage of computer-output microfilm?   p. 296

AUXILIARY STORAGE

Auxiliary storage is the critical link between input and output. In the previous chapter, you learned about main memory. Auxiliary storage or secondary storage is permanent storage. Once data is safe in auxiliary storage, it can be recalled again and again. Application programs can be stored and reused. A report can be revised and printed again; new figures can be inserted in a spreadsheet and recalculated; an address book database can be updated when someone moves. Auxiliary storage is our primary interest in this chapter.

There are two methods for storing and accessing instructions or data in auxiliary storage. One is direct access, and the other is sequential access. **Direct access,** sometimes called *random access,* means the data is stored in a particular memory location with a specific address so that any data can be found quickly. This is similar to selecting a song on a compact disc; it doesn't take the CD player any longer to find and play selection 8 than selection 3. Direct access is the most widely used auxiliary storage method; the most common direct access storage medium is the disk.

Sequential access storage means the data was stored in a particular order, perhaps alphabetically or by date and time. Just as you must search sequentially for a particular song on a cassette, so the computer must sequentially search for data. The most common sequential storage medium is magnetic tape on reels or cassettes. Today sequential access storage is mostly used to make protective backup copies of data stored on direct access devices.

As you recall, we use the term *backup* to describe the process of making copies of data and instructions for safekeeping. Backup is the best insurance against the computer or hard disk crashing. The simplest backup process on a personal computer is copying from one floppy disk to another. When you purchase an application software package, the publisher recommends you make backups or **working copies** of your original disks. It is essential that you back up all your data often.

Storage technology has improved dramatically over the years. In many cases, what was once a primary storage medium is today a backup medium. In this section, we'll examine the types of auxiliary storage peripherals most commonly used today.

TODAY

A WALKING TOUR OF A MAINFRAME INSTALLATION

Let's see what the many different computer peripherals look like when they're used together. The best way to do so is by visiting a large corporation's central data processing center, or information systems organization.

- *The control console.* Computer room personnel work here, monitoring and controlling the system. They view special monitor screens that display system performance. A special line printer prints out every system transaction and the time it occurs, so there is a permanent record and a way to trace problems.
- *The mainframe.* The tall cabinets, grouped closely together, are the mainframe (CPU). A very powerful system may have as many as 50 of these cabinets. Inside is the CPU circuitry and main memory; on the back are interfaces for connecting cables to the routing and control devices. The cables snake down beneath the false floor, connecting the various peripherals. The floor is made up of removable panels, which are lifted with a suction handle.
- *Controllers.* The cabinets to the left are the controllers that manage the entire system, routing instructions between the CPU and the I/O devices, as you learned in Chapter 2.
- *Terminals.* On the consoles are computer screens and keyboards, the terminals used to monitor various aspects of the system. They're just a fraction of the total number of termi-

nals in use, however; knowledge workers use most of them. Terminals may be directly connected to the computer by cabling, or tied in via phone lines through the data communications devices. A terminal in New Delhi, India, can be connected to a mainframe in Yonkers, New York.

- *Hard disk drives.* Over to the left are two hard disk drives. This company has a separate room in which most of their disk drives are kept in an area that is often called the *disk farm,* the principal storage area for data not currently being used. One way to assess a computer's power is by the amount of data it can store and manage. A mainframe computer can utilize literally hundreds of disk drives capable of storing billions, even trillions, of bytes.
- *Tape drives.* At the far left are the magnetic tape drives, which are used to make copies of important data for safe-keeping. This process, called *backup* or *backing up,* is valuable if data is lost due to a power failure, a system crash, or sabotage.
- *Mass storage systems.* Mass storage systems allow huge quantities of data to be stored for example, sales and production statistics or personnel or tax records. Such data may be infrequently used, but must be stored in a cost-effective manner. The trick is to rapidly retrieve that data when needed. Over a dozen types of mass storage systems were

developed over the years, but only two are in wide use today: magnetic tape on reels and mag tape cartridges in honeycombs.

- *Tape.* Data is stored on large reels of magnetic tape that hang in long racks, very much like books in a library. A mechanical unit rolls down the aisle, retrieves the tape, copies its contents to a hard disk, and returns it. Mass storage libraries can hold thousands of such rolls and are employed by large organizations (such as the Internal Revenue Service to store taxpayer records). Tape's main advantage is that it's fast, but it doesn't store vast quantities of data.
- *Cartridges.* Since the late 1960s, these mass storage systems have been called "chicken pluckers." Cartridges holding a strip of magnetic tape are stored in a large honeycomb, then a mechanical hand comes along and plucks one out. Cartridges are slower than tape, but hold far more data.
- *Communications.* Mainframes utilize a vast quantity of communications equipment, which connects the computer to other computer equipment over the telephone lines. This process is commonly termed *data communications* or *telecommunications,* which is discussed in more detail later in this text.

FIGURE 9.21

DASD is an acronym for mass storage device.

This hard disk is only 1.3 inches, yet provides 20MB of storage capacity. The primary advantage is reducing the size and weight of portable notebook computers.

DIRECT ACCESS STORAGE DEVICES

Direct access storage devices (DASD) are magnetic disk drives used for auxiliary storage. They may use floppy disks or hard disks. We have Alan Shugart of IBM to thank for inventing magnetic disk storage. He built the first hard disk drive for the RAMAC computer in 1957 and then invented the floppy disk in 1961. Figure 9.21 shows several different types of DASD drives.

DASD devices employ a moving **read/write head** that scans the magnetic surface of the disk. We say it is *reading the disk* when it searches for data or instructions, and that it is *writing to disk* when it is storing data or instructions. Figure 9.22 shows the two most popular floppy disks. Note the read/write window; this is where the head moves back and forth. The head floats above the spinning disk surface on a cushion of air. As you can see from the figure, this cushion is very thin; think of a Boeing 747 flying an inch above the ground at 3,000 miles per hour and you get an idea of the close tolerances. You can also see why it's so important to keep disks clean. When the head encounters a particle of foreign matter that causes it to fail in either reading or writing to the disk, it is termed a *head crash.*

Figure 9.22 also shows how a disk is magnetically laid out into tracks and sectors. **Tracks** are concentric circles upon which data is recorded. **Sectors** are pie-shaped wedges that compartmentalize the data into the addresses we mentioned for the head to locate. In addition, multiple hard disk drives organize tracks into **cylinders,** a vertical stack of tracks which, again, make it easier to locate data. Let's take a closer look at the various DASDs.

THE FLOPPY DISK. Floppy disks come in two popular sizes: 5¼-inch **minifloppy** and 3½-inch **microfloppy** for most computer systems. The first floppy disks were 8 inches in diameter. Over the years floppy disks have become smaller, yet they have increased in data capacity. One technique was developing **double-sided disks** that could be written to on both sides; the other was developing **high-density disks** that doubled and quadrupled the number of tracks. Today, a 5¼-inch disk can hold as much as 1.2MB, and a

FIGURE 9.22

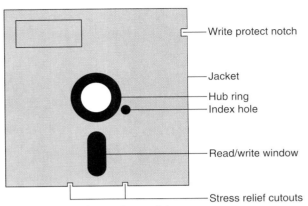

Write protect notch

Jacket

Hub ring
Index hole

Read/write window

Stress relief cutouts

Anatomy of a 5¼-inch floppy disk.

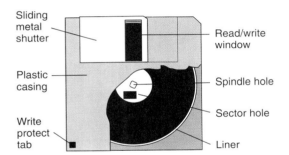

Sliding metal shutter

Plastic casing

Write protect tab

Read/write window

Spindle hole

Sector hole

Liner

Anatomy of a 3½-inch disk.

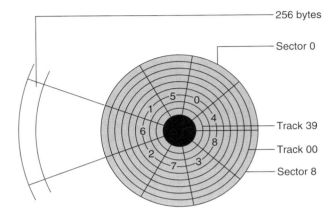

256 bytes

Sector 0

Track 39

Track 00

Sector 8

One floppy disk format, showing tracks and sectors. Format design and the number of tracks and sectors affect disk storage capacity.

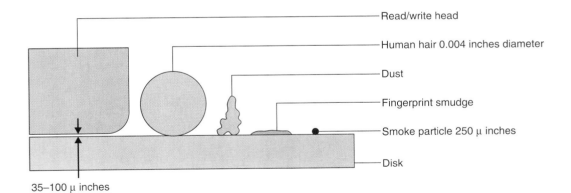

Read/write head

Human hair 0.004 inches diameter

Dust

Fingerprint smudge

Smoke particle 250 μ inches

Disk

35–100 μ inches height above disk

The head floats very closely above the spinning disk surface on a cushion of air. Note the relative size of disk pollutants.

FIGURE 9.23	A guide to floppy disks. IBM PCs/PC-compatibles may use either 5¼-inch or 3½-inch disks. Macintoshes use only 3½-inch disks. A 5¼-inch double-sided, double density disk is identified by a hub reinforcement ring. A 3½-inch high density disk is identified by a second square cutout hole at the top left corner. Both kinds of PCs use the same types of 3½-inch disks.

	5¼-Inch Minifloppy		3½-Inch Microfloppy	
IBM PC/PC-compatible	Double-sided, double density	360 KB	Double-sided, double density	720 KB
	High density	1.2 MB	High density	1.44 MB
			Extra-high density	2.8 MB
Macintosh	N/A		Double-sided, double density	800 KB
			High density	1.44 MB

3½-inch disk can hold as much as 1.44MB. Figure 9.23 shows various disks and their capacities.

The floppy disk drive begins to spin when it senses a disk is present, timing the speed of rotation very precisely. Some disk drives have a lever or button that locks the disk in and starts it spinning, while others are activated whenever the disk is inserted. The minifloppy drive head moves within the head window; the microfloppy moves the metal shutter aside to gain access to the disk inside. Then the head moves out to the edge of the disk, a process called **indexing,** which is essential to finding the data in its various locations. Then the head scans the sectors for data or program instructions.

The floppy disk is the primary means of delivering a personal computer software program from the publisher to the user. With the prominent use of hard disk drives on personal computers these days, programs are often copied to the hard disk and then used. The original program disks are stored for safekeeping. Conversely, hard disk drives are most commonly backed up on floppy disks. Therefore, floppy disks are direct access storage devices and backup storage devices as well.

THE HARD DISK DRIVE.   Hard disk drives operate in a similar fashion to floppy disk drives. While a floppy disk is made of mylar plastic, a hard disk is made of aluminum or other rigid material, such as glass, and coated with a magnetic material. Hard disks are sealed in a metal case to prevent smoke, dirt, or other contaminants from entering. Figure 9.24 shows an early hard disk drive, which is about 36 inches in diameter. Today's personal computer uses either 5¼-inch or 3½-inch hard disk drives, and the 2½-inch drive is becoming more common on laptops. Mainframes and minis commonly use 14-inch disk drives. Most hard disk drives are made up of several disks, or platters. Each has its own head, but all move together to read and write to the disk. Figure 9.25 shows a typical multiple-disk platter.

For many years, the hard disk was referred to as a *fixed disk* because it was fixed in place. That is no longer always true. Today we have the convenience of *removable hard disk drives* for personal computers, such as the one in Figure 9.26. Removable drives offer several advantages. First, your data is secure because you can take it home with you. Second, removable drives make it easy to copy data from one drive to another. Third, storage capacity is expanded because you can remove a drive that is full and replace it with a fresh one.

FIGURE 9.24

Barely recognizable these days, this is an early hard disk drive.

FIGURE 9.25

A typical multiple-disk platter, commonly called a disk pack.

A common hard disk drive for a personal computer holds 30MB, or 30 million bytes. A common hard disk drive for a mainframe holds 10 times that, or 300MB; some range up to the billions of bytes. However, personal computers are increasingly utilizing larger hard disk drives. It is not uncommon to see personal computers using the 386 microprocessor with hard disk drives from 40MB up to 650MB! Large system disk drives utilize **disk packs.** The average disk pack contains 11 disks, each 14 inches in diameter, and fits into the top of the disk drive.

Besides its higher storage capacity, the hard disk drive provides much faster access to data than a floppy disk drive. One reason for this is that the disk spins

FIGURE 9.26

A removable hard disk drive gives you security and the portability of moving applications and data from one computer to another.

much faster. This is extremely important in large businesses, where there may be dozens, even hundreds of disk drives, each holding nearly half a billion bytes of data.

OPTICAL DISK STORAGE.   Even though magnetic disks have great storage capacity, it's still never enough. Sidney Diamond, the vice president of information systems at Black & Decker, says, "You can't just add [new disk drives], or you'd be building new data centers all the time." This means the search for new and better storage technology goes on continuously.

Optical disc, or laser disc, storage holds great promise. Optical discs come in several sizes and formats. One is the 12-inch **laser videodisc,** which is also used in home videodisc players and holds a billion bytes, or one gigabyte. Another is the **optical disc,** which can be written to and read from and holds 256MB. A **compact disc-read only memory** (CD-ROM) disc holds 600MB, the equivalent of 1,600 minifloppies. A CD-ROM, just like its musical counterpart, the compact disc, is only written to once. Thus, a CD-ROM containing information, or the CD containing music, is manufactured, or "published," as a way to distribute its contents, much as book publishers distribute information in printed and bound books. (See Figure 9.27.)

The **write once, read many** (WORM) CD-ROM disc can be written to by the user, but cannot be erased. A WORM disc holds 200MB. Even better is the *erasable optical disc,* which can be used just like a magnetic disc to store and then dispose of data at will. WORM discs and drives are becoming inexpensive enough for the average personal computer user, but it will be a few more years before erasable CD-ROM discs are affordable.

Although optical discs hold a great deal more data, they are slower than

magnetic disks. This is the major reason they are not in wider use today. However, there is no reason to think problems with speed and erasability won't be overcome in time. By the mid-1990s, optical discs will be standard equipment on most personal computers.

SEQUENTIAL ACCESS STORAGE DEVICES

Today sequential access storage devices are most commonly used for backup purposes. No one wants to wait for data stored sequentially on tape these days!

REEL-TO-REEL TAPE.   **Reel-to-reel tape** was once a primary means of storage for mainframes, but now is commonly used as a backup storage medium. It probably won't be used much longer. There are several reasons for this. First, tape cartridges are falling in price and becoming much easier to work with. Second, loading and unloading reel-to-reel tapes requires a person, often called a "tape hanger," and personnel are growing scarce.

TAPE CARTRIDGES.   Early tape cartridges were nothing more than the Philips compact cassette most people use to listen to music. Over time listeners began using a higher-quality tape, but slow speed was a problem. This led to specially designed tape cassettes, or **cartridges,** and special **streaming tape** drives.

Tape cartridges offer several other distinct advantages. They have greater capacity than reel-to-reel tape (200MB compared to 180MB), and they are considerably more compact. Cartridges come in a library system, as shown in

Figure 9.28, with a robot arm that loads and unloads them. The robot has an eye that searches for a cartridge by reading the bar code serial number of the tape cartridge. It is able to find and load a cartridge in 10 seconds. No more tape hangers.

At the Harvard-Smithsonian Astrophysics Laboratory, CD-ROM is used to back up reel-to-reel tape. Satellites collected celestial images and data, transmitting it for many years back to earth where it was stored on reels of magnetic tape. Now that tape is growing old and subject to deterioration, data could be lost. Thus, the tapes are being copied onto CD-ROMs and sent to scientists at observatories all around the world. What once could only be used by an institution with a large computer system with the proper software capable of handling the tape reels is now available to any researcher with a CD-ROM drive.

There are many other types of peripherals for computers. Some are internal peripherals. They are designed as printed circuit boards and are inserted into an **expansion slot,** a type of interface connection, in the personal computer. These printed circuit boards serve as controllers for disk drives or as interfaces for external peripherals for a scanner, a joystick, or a mouse.

KNOWLEDGE CHECK

1. What are the two types of storage?   p. 298
2. What is the difference between direct access and sequential access?   p. 298
3. Name several types of direct access storage devices (DASDs).   p. 300
4. What is a major disadvantage of optical storage?   pp. 304–5
5. What is a major advantage of tape cartridges?   pp. 305–6

TOMORROW

VIRTUAL REALITY: THE ULTIMATE I/O?

Imagine one of these computer-created graphics: a protein molecule, the surface of Mars, a depiction of life on Earth 2 million years ago. Now imagine yourself within — actually part of — that graphic! This is **virtual reality** or cyberspace, a three-dimensional graphic system that creates the optical effect of walking through a 3-D image. NASA's Ames Research Center, Autodesk International, and other companies are developing computer-aided design tools that create a virtual reality. Virtual reality travelers wear a stereoscopic headset and "smart gloves" that enable them to control their journey. The traveler sees images displayed on a pair of miniature color CRTs or LCDs, while the gloves make it possible to move through or grasp objects anywhere in the field of view. There is a virtual reality scenario that allows two persons to play games in a phantom playground.

Early travelers report that the experience is disorienting and unlike anything they've previously experienced. For this reason, excursions are limited to 45 minutes or less. In 1992, the first movie to feature virtual reality, *Lawnmower Man,* was released. Later that year, the Computer Museum in Boston opened the first public virtual reality demonstration. It shouldn't be long until it arrives at a nearby video arcade.

WHAT LIES AHEAD?

The human-computer interface is central to understanding the evolution of input, output, and storage devices. Think of your brain as a CPU, and your nervous system as the interface to your peripherals — eyes, ears, voice, limbs. It's a great interface; we can control our senses and our bodies effortlessly. There is little doubt that computer engineers would like to develop a human-computer interface that makes communicating with the computer just as easy for us.

But where are these advances leading us? Toward a computer that we can touch or talk to; one that has unimaginably vast amounts of data storage; one that provides any type of output we feel in the mood for. This is just on the horizon and it's called *multimedia,* where text, images, and sound merge with

Careers for Knowledge Workers

Michele Harris, Systems Consultant, Xerox Corporation

Michele Harris is a beta test manager for laser printing systems products at Xerox Corporation. Her job is to manage the delivery of new printing systems, including printer, software, and peripherals, prior to their introduction to the market. "My ultimate responsibility is to monitor the processes that ensure Xerox launches quality products to our customers," says Michele. "This includes reviewing the technical specifications, writing the process plan, and testing the company's ability to market, sell, process orders, deliver, and support new printing system products."

Michele has a bachelor's degree in sociology and an interesting background. After college, she spent some time working as bookkeeper, secretary, and mechanic's helper for an aircraft maintenance company. Changing the oil and working on small aircraft enhanced her mechanical know-how. After that, she took a job as a customer service representative, where she coordinated orders and shipping and handled customer complaints. These jobs were good preparation for joining Xerox as a customer service engineer for its copiers and laser printers. "People are really unhappy when an office machine breaks down," says Michele, "and there will always be a requirement for service on a copier or printer. But almost as important as fixing the machine is repairing the relationship with the people. It's really important to leave with them happy with Xerox."

Michele has been with Xerox over 10 years, moving from her customer service position to printing systems customer support to her present position in preintroduction testing. There are two types of such testing: alpha and beta. Alpha testing is internal; beta testing is done with a select group of customers or potential buyers. At Xerox, beta testers are commonly se-

---

computer data to open a whole new world to us. You might walk down a Paris street with a guide that points things out, speaking a word in French as you see it displayed on the screen. You repeat the word to the computer, and your guide helps you with the correct pronunciation. In another multimedia scenario, an annual report is displayed to a company's board of directors in a wall-size digital display. A voice explains the company's performance while highlighting sales figures. Board members ask questions while touching points on the graph, and the voice answers them.

Multimedia is possible because of advanced input, output, and storage devices. Scanning devices allow us to enter text, photographs, and more. We can enter moving video images and even connect an electronic piano keyboard to record our own compositions. Optical storage will hold video, sound, text, and computer graphics in any combination. Advanced video displays will

lected by the sales representatives. Michele then interviews the key individual, establishes interest, explains the purpose of the beta test, and then asks them to respond to a questionnaire. All this information must be organized into the process plan, a written report she submits to the development, manufacturing, marketing, and service organizations for approval. She continues working very closely with other internal organizations to ensure that Xerox is ready to launch the product.

That accomplished, Michele launches the beta test, which commonly lasts for 30 to 90 days. She often travels during the early phase, working with the Xerox sales and marketing people and visiting customer sites. "I have to maintain constant interaction with customers and internal Xerox functional and field support groups to make sure the beta test is run-

ning smoothly and to learn how the product is doing," she says.

Michele enjoys combining her interest in working at an innovative company with her skills in sales and marketing. "People who want to succeed in their career have to have good sales and marketing skills," she says. "It's not enough to be technically competent. You have to have a positive attitude and enjoy interacting with people. That's most of what sales and marketing is anyway." Michele also enjoys making business presentations, such as presenting the new product to salespeople on her road trips. "It's an informal speech, with color slides showing the product and the beta test process, and presentation graphics portraying the market. It's fun, and I always get a lot of questions that end up helping me understand the product and the market better."

Michele's four years in the

beta test organization have led to a promotion to the Xerox executive communications center as a systems consultant. She will conduct major account customer exchange events and seminars, explaining the company's strategies and technological solutions for companies working with document management. It's a position that will take advantage of the best of her technical and public speaking and presentation skills.

Michele loves to sing and has attained semiprofessional status in her community. In addition to being a soloist at her church and the chaplain service for the local VA hospital, she is often hired to sing at banquets and formal affairs. "I'm mostly asked to sing classical," she says, "but my favorite music is country!"

provide more colors and clarity than the best high-definition television (HDTV). Audio output will be digital stereo — music, voice, and computer-generated sound effects. Clearly, peripheral devices are vital to making computers more and more useful.

HARDWARE ETHICS: THE PROPER USE OF PERIPHERALS

What promises to provide us with the most dramatic steps forward in making computers more useful also holds an inherent danger: altering facts and reality. A scanner could be used to enter the letterhead of the president of the United States, adding text that declares war on China. Anything from a business card to a birth certificate could conceivably be falsified.

Similarly, a photograph can be entered and then doctored to either remove images or insert images that were previously not there. We have seen this occur at computer trade shows as people demonstrate the powers and features of their products. In one instance, a photograph showed a building and an American flag. The image was scanned into the computer. Then, using a graphics program, the flag was literally erased from the photo.

There is nothing particularly new about falsifying documents, but the computer makes it easier; there is less need for expensive, specialized equipment.

What's more, the computer makes it seem like fun or entertainment. The demonstrator at the trade show did not exhibit feelings of guilt or remorse over falsifying or altering the photograph; on the contrary, she seemed to feel that it was a technological achievement to be able to do so. It is this attitude that knowledge workers must recognize and avoid. There is a sense of accomplishment associated with performing computer tasks. That is all the more reason we must be careful to constantly ask ourselves if we are acting prudently, ethically, and legally with our computers.

SUMMARY

1. *Define the peripheral device and explain the purposes of the different kinds of interfaces.* Peripherals allow us to communicate with the CPU. Input, output, and storage devices are connected to the CPU with a physical interface, a mechanical connection most commonly made by plugging a cable into connections. Sometimes a peripheral needs a software, or logical, interface as well. The connection between a human and a peripheral is called the *human-computer interface.*

2. *Identify the methods of data entry and the different types of input devices used.* The most common input peripheral is the keyboard. Its most common purpose is data entry. Other input peripherals include pointing devices, writing and drawing devices, video, OCR, and voice. Source data, or machine-to-machine input, is another way to enter data into the computer.

3. *Describe the different types of output devices and the uses for various output technologies.* Output devices for human use fall into two main categories: video displays and printers. Video displays may be monochrome or color, high-resolution or low-resolution. High-resolution color monitors are best suited to graphics. Liquid crystal displays (LCD) are used on laptops. Minis and mainframes use both dumb and smart terminals, which combine a keyboard and display. Printers may be dot-matrix, impact, laser, or inkjet; a special type of inkjet printer, called a *plotter,* is used for large drawings and graphics. As with input, computers can be used for machine-to-machine output; for example, to control processes or to produce computer-output microfilm output.

4. *Explain the uses and purposes for direct access and sequential access storage methods.* In addition to main memory, there is auxiliary storage. There are two types of storage peripherals: direct access and sequential access. Direct access, or random access, stores data in a particular location for quick retrieval. Sequential access stores data sequentially and is slower than direct access; it is mostly used for backup. Today's primary storage medium is magnetic disk, both hard and soft. Primary sequential access devices use tape cartridges, which are replacing reel-to-reel tape for backup purposes. Optical discs may supersede both magnetic disks and tape as the storage medium of the future. They also make it possible to move toward multimedia.

ISSUES

1. Auxiliary storage, whether it is a hard disk, floppy disk, or optical disc, is expensive. A concern in business, government, or your own personal work is having enough storage — in other words, enough room to store all the data you want to keep. As mentioned in the text, there never seems to be enough disk space; but how much of the data people store really must be retained? For example, is every memo announcing an office meeting kept? Do you keep letters

and notes you wrote to friends that you won't ever read again? Does it make more sense to simply keep paper copies of only some of your documents? How do you decide what should be deleted? How would a company or a government agency formulate such a policy?

2. Over the past few years, a debate has grown up over fact versus fiction on television news and documentaries. Reenactments of actual events have been filmed using actors, often with hypothetical scenarios of what really happened. Many people feel it is neither ethical nor proper to present re-creations as actual events; however, television executives seem to feel that this technique is a valid method of depicting events as close to the way they actually occurred as possible. Computers can be used — and misused — in the same way. A computer simulation could show a warplane attacking an American ship. A journalist's video image could be altered so that she appeared to be reporting on what was really a fictitious event. If these and similar events occurred, where — and how — could we draw the line between appearance and reality? What should we do about this?

CHAPTER REVIEW QUESTIONS

REVIEW QUESTIONS

1. What are the purposes of input, output, and storage devices?
2. What are the two types of interfaces called, and what is the purpose of each?
3. When is computer-to-machine output used?
4. What is the difference between a musical CD and a CD-ROM?
5. What media are most commonly used for backing up data and instructions stored on a DASD?
6. What input devices are commonly used for handwriting and drawing?
7. Why is it important to continually improve the quality of the video monitor display?

DISCUSSION QUESTIONS

1. Discuss the reasons for, and purposes of, the different kinds of physical interfaces.
2. Discuss the aspects of the human-computer interface you personally find important.
3. Describe three types of input devices and what tasks each is best suited to perform.
4. Classify the different types of printers according to print quality.
5. Discuss the purpose behind laying out disk access into track, sectors, and cylinders.
6. Discuss the pros and cons of voice input/output computers.

MULTIPLE-CHOICE

1. Source data input is used (check all that apply):
   a. When there is machine-to-machine input.
   b. When only a scanner is available.
   c. When scanning bar codes.
   d. For processing bank checks.
   e. By potato chip salespeople in grocery stores.
2. The two auxiliary storage methods are:
   a. Main memory.
   b. Reel-to-reel tape.
   c. Direct access.
   d. Microfloppy.
   e. Sequential access.
3. The major differences between personal computer hard disk drives and mainframe or mini hard disk drives are (check all that apply):
   a. Multiple disks.
   b. Disk platter size.
   c. Data capacity.
   d. PCs utilize disk packs.
   e. All of the above.

4. The reasons for the laser printer's popularity are (check all that apply):
   a. Speed.
   b. Low cost.
   c. Type fonts.
   d. Graphics.
   e. All of the above.

5. The first broad application of virtual reality will probably be in:
   a. Space exploration.
   b. Psychiatry.
   c. Entertainment.
   d. Television commercials.

FILL-IN-THE BLANK

1. The _____ task is performed with an input device.
2. The two types of video monitor displays are _____ and _____.
3. An example of computer-to-machine output is _____.

4. Sequential access auxiliary storage is best suited for _____.
5. A floppy disk that can store 1.2MB to 1.44MB is called a _____ disk.
6. The most widely used input device is the _____.

TRUE/FALSE

1. The light pen input device has been used longer than any other.
2. The punched card is still the most widely used input medium.
3. A bit-mapped computer display shows more detail than a character-mapped display.
4. It is quicker to find data using a direct access storage device than a sequential storage device.

5. The major advantage of optical discs is storage capacity.
6. FAX machines are capable of transmitting data files to a computer.
7. The trackball is a good alternative to the mouse.

KEY TERMS

bit-mapped, 290
cartridge, 305
character-mapped, 290
compact disc-read only memory (CD-ROM), 304
computer-output microfilm (COM), 296
computer-to-machine output, 296
cylinder, 300
daisy wheel, 294
data collection device, 286
data entry, 280
digital camera, 283
digitizer, 283
direct access, 298

direct access storage device (DASD), 300
disk pack, 303
dot-matrix, 292
double-sided disk, 300
dumb terminal, 292
expansion slot, 306
facsimile, 287
gas plasma display, 291
hard copy, 287
high-density disk, 300
impact printer, 292
indexing, 302
inkjet printing, 295
intelligent terminal, 292

interface, 277
I/O, 277
joystick, 281
laser printer, 294
laser videodisc, 304
letter-quality printer, 294
light pen, 283
liquid crystal display (LCD), 291
magnetic ink character recognition (MICR), 286
magnetic strip, 286
microfloppy, 300
minifloppy, 300
near-letter-quality (NLQ), 293

Software Concepts

"The computer is the most flexible machine invented, capable of a staggering diversity of applications," wrote noted futurist and consultant James Martin in his book *An Information Systems Manifesto.* "It is rapidly dropping in cost and its power needs to be used as fully as possible for improving the efficiency of organizations. The problem lies not in the machine itself, but in the methods we use for creating applications."*

To a certain extent, this has always been the case. One reason was that only a limited number of data processing professionals knew how to create applications. Another was that these professionals worked with a limited, and increasingly slow, awkward, and unwieldy set of tools and techniques. Yet another was that they had to create applications not only for use within the information systems organization, but for various departments and groups of knowledge workers.

While this is still a problem in many companies today, it is diminishing. The personal computer now has many of the software development tools that were once the prov-

ince of its larger predecessors, so that many more people can create the applications needed. In many cases, applications are localized by group, department, or division and require only a mini or a PC for hardware. In addition, we now have many more powerful and easy-to-use programming languages as well as simpler yet more sophisticated application development techniques than in the past. Last but not least, a lot of application development has been turned over to knowledge workers, just like you.

In this module, we'll study the three primary areas of software. Chapter 10 covers programming languages and concepts; Chapter 11 explains systems analysis and design; and Chapter 12 reveals the concepts underlying database technology. In each we'll first learn about the classical, more traditional methods, in most cases seeing how information systems professionals applied them. Then we'll explore their contemporary implementations and how they are used for knowledge work. In studying both aspects, it should become clear that the computer's versatility is wholly dependent on the quality and characteristics of its applications — quality and characteristics inspired by the people who create them.

---

*James Martin, *An Information Systems Manifesto* (Englewood Cliffs, N.J.: Prentice Hall, 1984), p. 3.

CHAPTER

10

Programming Languages and Concepts

CHAPTER OUTLINE

Programming and the Knowledge Worker

Programmers and Programming

The Evolution of Programming Languages

Machine Language
Assembly Language

YESTERDAY: HERMAN HOLLERITH AND THE FIRST I/O DEVICE

High-Level Programming Languages

FORTRAN: A Scientific Language
COBOL: A Business Language

TODAY: IN MEMORIAM: GRACE MURRAY HOPPER, A COMPUTER SCIENCE PIONEER

BASIC: A PC Language
C: A High-Level Language

Object-Oriented Programming

The Nature of Objects
Basic Principles of Object-Oriented Programming
OOP Languages
Advantages and Disadvantages

CASE: Computer-Aided Software Engineering

Program Design
Re-engineering
I-Case
Advantages and Disadvantages

TOMORROW: DECLINE AND FALL OF THE AMERICAN PROGRAMMER

CAREERS FOR KNOWLEDGE WORKERS: DAVE BALL, SOFTWARE TEST ENGINEER, MICROSOFT

What Lies Ahead?

Ethics in Programming: What Is "Intellectual Property"?

Summary

Issues in Programming

Chapter Review Questions

Key Terms

LEARNING OBJECTIVES

After reading and studying this chapter, you should be able to:

1. Explain the origins and development of machine programming.

2. Describe the evolution of computer programming languages.

3. Explain the characteristics of several popular high-level languages.

4. Identify the characteristics and benefits of object-oriented programming.

5. Identify the characteristics and benefits of computer-aided software engineering.

PROGRAMMING AND THE KNOWLEDGE WORKER

By this point in your studies, you know that programming is an activity of not only information systems professionals but knowledge workers as well. Preparing instructions for the computer is an everyday activity for people who use computers. However, programming did not begin with computers; it traces its roots to the textile industry in the year 1801. This business required the talents of skillful weavers with keen minds and nimble fingers. Creating fabrics with complex patterns was time consuming and expensive. A Frenchman named Joseph-Marie Charles Jacquard was probably the first to program a machine. He was a weaver who dreamed of a machine that would help do his weaving more quickly, inexpensively, and with fewer mistakes.

Jacquard studied the weaving process and the machine that did it, the loom. In doing so, he displayed the analytic qualities of a good programmer. The result was a loom that could be programmed to create patterns and designs, using a **punched card.** Jacquard's punched card was a wooden slat with holes cut in it, as shown in Figure 10.1. It was an invention that would continue to be used for over 180 years.

Jacquard's loom was complex, yet straightforward in design. Inside the loom, threaded needles pressed upward against the punched cards. If a needle passed through a hole in the card, it pushed up a thread to be woven into the fabric. If there was no hole, the thread remained unwoven below the card. Thus different patterns were generated by different hole patterns in the cards. Cards were fed into the loom in sequence, allowing many operations to take place automatically.

Jacquard's loom demonstrated two important ideas. First, we can translate complex designs into codes, or programs, that machines readily understand. Second, in so doing, machines can be instructed to perform repetitive tasks. Punched card technology was transferred to a machine devised by Herman Hollerith in the 1880s to count the U.S. Census, and proliferated with the advent of IBM computing machines (see the Yesterday feature). IBM punched cards were used for programming computers (and storing data) until the late 1980s, and still are used with some computers. Compare the cards on the Jacquard loom in Figure 10.1 to the IBM punched card in Figure 10.2.

Lady Augusta Ada Lovelace (1816–52) was another programmer who bears mention. The daughter of poet Lord Byron, she worked with English inventor Charles Babbage, who was attempting to build the first computational machine, called the *difference engine,* a great, complex set of meshing cogs and gears. It was followed by the *analytical engine,* neither of which Babbage ever made to work. "We may say most aptly that the Analytical Engine weavers algebraical patterns just as the Jacquard loom weaves flowers and leaves," she wrote. Lady Lovelace wrote a famous paper on the analytical engine in which she developed several types of instructions that would have to

FIGURE 10.1

The Jacquard loom. Note how the punched cards are fed through a primitive processing device to program the loom.

FIGURE 10.2

Although rarely used today, punched cards used to be a primary method for inputting large quantities of data into a computer.

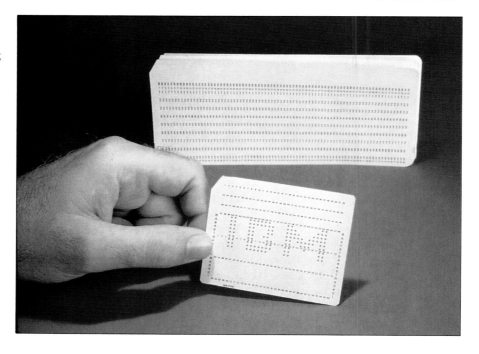

wait over a hundred years before they were put to use. And in 1991, a group of engineers and scientists were able to build an actual, working analytical engine.

PROGRAMMERS AND PROGRAMMING

For most of its life, the computer has been programmed by programmers — those knowledge workers we call *information systems professionals.* Programmers used specific languages for specific programs that would be used in science, business, general-purpose, and even military applications. However, the programming profession has undergone significant changes. The programming workload of information systems professionals has increased dramatically as more and more knowledge workers required more and more applications to perform their work. As a result, new languages and tools emerged to help the information systems professional. But in addition, it became possible for nonprofessional knowledge workers to do some of their own programming. This chapter discusses these tools and tasks.

John Xenakis, in an article entitled "The Automation of the Computer Programmer," writes:

> They did it to cobblers, they did it to telephone operators, they're doing it to bank tellers. Can they do it to programmers? We're beginning to see the outlines of how the programmer's job will be automated. . . . Although automation of the computer programmer will not occur entirely for several decades, enough partial automation will occur during the next few years so that the job of the computer programmer in the year 2000 will be dramatically different than it is today. . . . As coding jobs are eliminated, a systems analyst will do all the work, and leave the rest to automation.
>
> . . . People needed too many shoes, too many phone calls, too many bank deposits and withdrawals, for human cobblers, operators and bank tellers to handle, and so we started using shoe-making machines, dial telephones, and automated teller machines (ATMs). Likewise, there are now too many computer programs to be written for existing programmers to handle.[1]

How is the nature of programming, and the people who do it, changing? That is the subject of this chapter. We shall study the evolution of programming languages, from the first computer to the latest in automated programming. You will see how the knowledge worker is in many instances taking the place of the traditional programmer.

THE EVOLUTION OF PROGRAMMING LANGUAGES

Computer programming has been with us for over 50 years. Machines — computers included — are programmed with ordered, organized instructions. These instructions are written in a **programming language,** which is a formally designed set of symbols (often referred to as notation). Programming languages have evolved greatly over the years. Each evolutionary stage is

---

[1] John Xenakis, "The Automation of the Computer Programmer," *BCS Update,* March 1991, p. 8.

FIGURE 10.3   The five programming generations.

First: 1951–58	Second: 1958–64	Third: 1964–71	Fourth: 1977–88	Fifth: 1988–
Low-level	Low/high-level	High-level	Very high level	Object-oriented
Machine, assembly	Assembly, COBOL, FORTRAN	BASIC, Pascal	C++, Turbo Pascal, 4GLs	OOP, CASE

commonly referred to as a generation. Figure 10.3 shows the five generations of computer languages: Appendix B explains all aspects of the computer generations — hardware and software — in greater detail.

The Jacquard loom's programming language took the form of a series of punched holes. ENIAC was initially programmed by flipping toggle switches and changing cables. Needless to say, this was a slow, awkward process. Information systems professionals quickly began searching for a better, faster way to issue instructions to the computer. This was especially true when repetitive instructions needed to be issued, the same every time, without errors. Think of a payroll program; no one wanted a program that could not produce consistent, reliable results. One solution, the punched card, was mentioned earlier.

Punched cards evolved into other methods, such as punched metal and paper tape and then magnetic tape, but the most effective solution was what we now call programming languages. The first language closely resembled the toggle-switch method, issuing 0s and 1s to the computer by simply substituting software for hardware. As programming languages evolved and improved, they became more English-like. Here is how programming languages have developed.

MACHINE LANGUAGE

Electronic digital computers understand only **machine language** — the language of 0s and 1s that make up bits and bytes. Machine language requires no translation. From ENIAC to today's most sophisticated digital computers, machine language is the same. Machine language is directly understood, or executed, by hardware. Electronic circuitry turns these 0s and 1s into the operations the computer performs. The problem was that it was extremely tedious for a programmer to sit at a keyboard and type the instructions in endless sequences of 0s and 1s.

ASSEMBLY LANGUAGE

The first way this programming problem was addressed was by the assembly language. An **assembly language** uses letters, numbers, and symbols to represent individual 0s and 1s. For example, where in machine language multiply is set as 001011, in an assembly language you just write M, which is translated by an assembler into the 001011 of machine language. This greatly simplified programming.

Assembly languages are powerful programming tools because they allow programmers a large amount of direct control over the hardware. They pro-

Yesterday

Herman Hollerith and the First I/O Device

Herman Hollerith had a problem to solve: trying to count the 1890 census in less than the seven years it took to do the 1880 census. Aware of Jacquard's work, Hollerith applied punched card technology to mechanical tabulating machines. His card, called the Hollerith card, was the same size as a dollar bill. By 1884, Hollerith had developed an electromechanical tabulating machine. It used some of the same technology as an electric telegraph key and the same mechanical counters in an adding machine.

To read the cards, electrical contact was made by a pin passing through holes in the card, touching a bath of mercury below. The machine could read between 50 and 80 cards a minute. Counting the census involved tabulating data on 62,622,250 citizens. That amounted to 2 billion holes in punched cards. Hollerith's machine did it in just over two years. An article in a magazine of the time said, "This apparatus works as unerringly as the mills of the gods, and beats them hollow as to speed."

Hollerith was a good businessman; he leased his equipment to the U.S. government and to other governments as well. In 1896, he formed the Tabulating Machine Company. That company became International Business Machines, and the punched card became known as the IBM card. Billions and billions of punched cards have been used for storing both programs and data over the years. But now, other forms of output have replaced the punched card. The last IBM punched card plant closed its doors in 1986.

vide greater ease in writing instructions, but preserve the programmer's ability to declare exactly what operations the hardware performs.

Assembly languages are machine-specific or machine-dependent. **Machine-dependent** means the instructions are specific to one type of computer hardware, so they come packaged with the computer system. Assembly code for a Prime mini won't work on a Digital mini. Assembly code often can't even be transferred between different models built by the same manufacturer.

For the most part, assembly languages are used by systems programmers to develop operating systems and their components. Thus one early programming problem was solved, but another one remained: how to make programming languages portable, or transferable from one computer to another. The answer was, in theory at least, high-level programming languages.

Knowledge Check

1. How were the first computers programmed?   p. 320
2. What fundamental language do digital electronic computers understand?   p. 320
3. What is an example of assembly language?   p. 320
4. What does the term *machine-dependent* mean?   p. 321
5. What is an assembly language primarily used for?   p. 321

HIGH-LEVEL PROGRAMMING LANGUAGES

Assembly languages were the first bridge between our native tongue and the computer's binary language. However, it wasn't long before programmers realized they could take programming one step closer to a spoken language. The creation of high-level programming languages followed. **High-level languages** are a method of writing programs using English-like words as instructions.

High-level programming languages combine several machine language instructions into one high-level instruction. So, as we move up the ladder from machine language to high-level languages, less is more; fewer program instructions have a greater effect on programming the computer. Where a programmer had to correctly write a string of 0s and 1s in machine language, assembly language required only a single letter or a short **mnemonic,** a term or word that is easy to identify, such as ADD for addition. And where several instructions are required to program an operation in assembly code, a high-level language requires just a single statement.

STATEMENTS AND SYNTAX

A **statement** is an expression of instructions in a programming language. A statement usually translates into one or more instructions at the machine language level. For example, PRINT "Welcome to MetaSoftware version 6.0" is a statement that tells the program to display the words in quotation marks on the screen. Each programming language includes a set of statements and a syntax. **Syntax** is the set of rules governing the language's structure and statements. To write a program in any programming language, the programmer must use its statements and strictly abide by its syntax rules. These syntax rules may include how statements are written, the order in which statements occur, and how sections of programs are organized.

STRUCTURED AND UNSTRUCTURED LANGUAGES

We divide high-level programming languages into two categories: structured and unstructured. Here we encounter yet another use for the term structure that is distinct from either structured design or structured programming. A **structured** high-level programming language requires the programmer to write programs in well-defined sections, which are compiled in sequence. An **unstructured** language allows the programmer to create programs in a more random fashion.

TRANSLATING HIGH-LEVEL LANGUAGES INTO PROGRAMS

High-level programming must be translated before it is an executable program that can be read by the CPU. Thus each language must be converted from its English-like expressions into machine language, using one of the following types of programs.

ASSEMBLERS. The simplest translator is an **assembler.** It translates assembly language into machine language, the 0's and 1's the CPU understands.

COMPILERS. A **compiler** translates entire files of source code into **object code,** which in turn becomes an executable file. An **executable** file is one that can be read by and run by the CPU, such as the ones that start a word processing or graphics application program.

On personal computers, source code is translated directly into executable code. These files are easily recognizable in a personal computer's disk directory because their filenames end in .EXE. On minis and mainframes, source code is usually translated into object files, which must be linked together to create executable files.

Some advanced compilers also produce other kinds of files, like analysis and program error files. These can be very useful to programmers, because they contain important information about how clearly the computer understands the source code as written.

INTERPRETERS. An **interpreter** translates source code one line at a time for immediate execution by the CPU. Like the compiler, an interpreter translates from the language the programmer used to write the program. However, an executable file is not created in the process, resulting in a program that runs slower. And unlike the compiler, there is no analysis and program error correction; serious errors cause the program to simply stop running. Interpreters were widely used on early personal computers, which lacked the memory capacity to run larger compiler programs.

ADVANTAGES AND DISADVANTAGES

High-level languages provide benefits by utilizing the statements created, but they give up something in the process. Programmers no longer have the direct control over the hardware that they have with assembly languages. When high-level languages are compiled, statements are translated into specific machine instructions determined by the compiler. Programmers can't alter these translations without rewriting the compiler — a large task.

An additional problem high-level languages were meant to address was portability. You'll recall from Chapter 7 that *portable* refers to using one form of software, such as an operating system or an application, on several different kinds of hardware. Programmers hoped they could use the same version of a language, no matter what manufacturer's hardware they were working with. This didn't come to pass. In attempting to ensure customer fidelity, most computer manufacturers developed their own versions of the major high-level languages specifically for their own hardware. This means code often must be modified before a program written for a Sun computer will run on a Hewlett-Packard computer, for example. Nevertheless, code written in a high-level language is much more portable than assembly code. High-level source code can usually be easily modified to work on different hardware than it was written for, unlike assembly code.

High-level languages are used for all kinds of programming, but are especially valuable to applications programmers, who create specialized software. There are over two hundred general and special-purpose high-level languages in use today. Here are four widely used high-level programming languages and the features that make them powerful and effective tools for programming computers.

FIGURE 10.4

A FORTRAN program that
produces the average of 10
numbers.

```
C COMPUTE THE SUM AND AVERAGE OF 10 NUMBERS
C
        REAL NUM, SUM, AVG
        INTEGER TOTNUM, COUNTR
C
        SUM = 0.0
C INITIALIZE LOOP CONTROL VARIABLE
        COUNTR = 0
        TOTNUM = 10
C
C LOOP TO READ DATA AND ACCUMULATE SUM
  20 IF (COUNTR .GE. TOTNUM) GO TO 30
        READ, NUM
        SUM = SUM + NUM
C       UPDATE LOOP CONTROL VARIABLE
        COUNTR = COUNTR +1
        GO TO 20
C END OF LOOP - COMPUTE AVERAGE
  30 AVG = SUM / TOTNUM
C PRINT RESULTS
        PRINT, SUM
        PRINT, AVG
        STOP
        END
```

FORTRAN: A SCIENTIFIC LANGUAGE

One of the first high-level languages was **FORTRAN,** for FORmula TRANs-lator. It was created in 1954 by John Backus, one of IBM's most respected scientists, for developing scientific and engineering applications. FORTRAN allows programmers to calculate complex formulas with a few source code instructions. Like a wise mathematician, it readily understands and executes the language of numbers.

FORTRAN is an unstructured language. FORTRAN was patterned after the CPU: It reads and executes instructions, one after another, without much regard to categories and classes. If you want to define a data item, you can do so at any point in the program. Other languages, such as COBOL and Pascal, require that each major program element reside in one place, all together. FORTRAN doesn't have that requirement.

As with most high-level programming languages, FORTRAN has been revised and refined over the years. Even John Backus has been trying to write a "better" FORTRAN. Standardized versions, approved by the American National Standards Institute (ANSI), were released in 1957, 1958, 1962, and 1978. Computer manufacturers who adopt these standards make it possible to use the same version of FORTRAN on nearly any computer hardware. Figure 10.4 shows a sample FORTRAN program. For the sake of comparison, each of the programming language examples performs the same task (averaging 10 numbers) so note how differently each approaches the problem.

COBOL: A BUSINESS LANGUAGE

About the time FORTRAN was invented, COBOL was developed by the COnference on DAta SYstems Languages (CODASYL). It was issued by the U.S. Government Printing Office in 1960. **COBOL** stands for COmmon

TODAY

IN MEMORIAM: GRACE MURRAY HOPPER, A COMPUTER SCIENCE PIONEER

Few individuals can be said to have changed the world, yet one for whom this might be considered an understatement is Admiral Grace Murray Hopper. This colorful and brilliant woman truly gained a measure of immortality through her many accomplishments.

It would be hard to imagine a more distinguished career than hers. Consider these achievements:

- Graduated from Vassar, Phi Beta Kappa.
- Earned M.A. and Ph.D. degrees from Yale.
- Anchored Harvard's Mark I programming team.
- Joined the Eckert-Mauchly Computer Corporation as senior mathematician in 1948.

- Served as senior programmer on UNIVAC I project.
- Developed one of the first program translators at the University of Pennsylvania in 1952.
- Created the programming language Flow-Matic, which was the basis for COBOL.
- Wrote the compiler that made it possible for COBOL to run on almost any computer.
- Won the first Computer Sciences Man-of-the-Year award in 1969.
- Served 43 years in the Naval Reserve, retiring as a Rear Admiral at age 79.

In September 1991, President George Bush awarded the National Medal of Technology to Admiral Hopper "for her pio-

neering accomplishments in the development of computer programming languages that simplified computer technology and opened the door to a significantly larger universe of users." She was the first woman to receive the award as an individual. After careers in academia, the government, and the military, Hopper began a new career in 1988 as a senior consultant and industry spokesperson with Digital Equipment Corporation. On January 1, 1992, having recently celebrated her 85th birthday, Grace Murray Hopper died in her sleep at her home in Arlington, Virginia.

Business-Oriented Language. Its developers represented a cross-section of computer users in business, industry, government, and education. Among the COBOL developers was Grace Hopper, a pioneer in computer programming. Working for the U.S. Navy, Hopper was a driving force behind COBOL, working to ensure it would become a standard across the industry. (See the Today feature.)

COBOL is a structured programming language. This means that COBOL "has a place for everything" and requires programmers to "put everything in its place." COBOL programs are separated into four sections called *divisions:*

1. The Identification Division documents the program name, the programmer's name(s), dates, and any other important identification information.
2. The Environment Division names the computer hardware, including the CPU and I/O devices.
3. The Data Division identifies all associated files and working storage sections of the program.
4. The Procedure Division contains all the instructions in the COBOL program.

FIGURE 10.5

A COBOL program that produces the average of 10 numbers.

```
IDENTIFICATION DIVISION.
PROGRAM-ID.        AVERAGES.
AUTHOR.            DEB KNUDSEN.
DATE-COMPILED.
ENVIRONMENT DIVISION.
CONFIGURATION SECTION.
    SOURCE-COMPUTER. HP-3000.
    OBJECT-COMPUTER. HP-3000.
INPUT-OUTPUT SECTION.
FILE-CONTROL.
    SELECT NUMBER-FILE ASSIGN TO ''NUMFILE''.
    SELECT REPORT-FILE ASSIGN TO ''PRINT,UR,A,LP(CCTL)''.
DATA DIVISION.
FILE   SECTION.
FD  NUMBER-FILE
    LABEL RECORDS ARE STANDARD
    DATA RECORD IS NUMBER-REC.
01  NUMBER-REC                    PIC S9(7)V99.
FD  REPORT-FILE
    LABEL RECORDS ARE STANDARD
    DATA RECORD IS REPORT-REC.
01  REPORT-REC                    PIC X(100).

WORKING-STORAGE SECTION.
01  END-OF-NUMBER-FILE-FLAG       PIC X(3) VALUE SPACES.
    88  END-OF-NUMBER-FILE                 VALUE ''YES''.
01  SUM-OF-NUMBERS                PIC S9(7)V99.
01  AVERAGE-OF-NUMBERS            PIC S9(7)V99.
01  NUMBER-OF-NUMBERS             PIC 9(5).

01  WS-REPORT-REC.
    05  FILLER                    PIC X(2)    VALUE SPACES.
    05  FILLER                    PIC X(17)   VALUE
                                  ''SUM OF NUMBERS = ''.
    05  WS-SUM-OF-NUMBERS         PIC Z,ZZZ,ZZZ.99-.
    05  FILLER                    PIC X(3)    VALUE SPACES.
    05  FILLER                    PIC X(15)   VALUE
                                  ''# OF NUMBERS = ''.
    05  WS-NUMBER-OF-NUMBERS      PIC ZZZZ9.
    05  FILLER                    PIC X(3)    VALUE SPACES.
    05  FILLER                    PIC X(21)   VALUE
                                  ''AVERAGE OF NUMBERS = ''.
    05  WS-AVERAGE-OF-NUMBERS     PIC Z, ZZZ, ZZZ.99-.
    05  FILLER                    PIC X(8)    VALUE SPACES.
```

COBOL divisions are further divided into paragraphs and sections. This structure helps programmers write code efficiently and with a minimum of repetition and confusion. COBOL programs are self-documenting; the simplicity of structure and expressions make them almost self-explanatory.

COBOL is the nearest thing to a standard in business programming in the United States. Over the years, one programming language after another has threatened to displace COBOL, but so many COBOL programs have been written for large computer systems, it would be very costly to change at this point in time. The American National Standards Institute standardized COBOL in 1968 and issued a revised form in 1974 called ANSI – COBOL. After long years of industry debate, COBOL 85 was approved. Today, COBOL is among the most standardized high-level programming languages. Figure 10.5 shows a sample COBOL program.

```
PROCEDURE DIVISION.
100-MAIN-PROGRAM.
    OPEN INPUT   NUMBER-FILE
         OUTPUT REPORT-FILE.
    MOVE SPACES TO REPORT-REC.
    MOVE ZEROS TO SUM-OF-NUMBERS.
    MOVE ZEROS TO AVERAGE-OF-NUMBERS.
    MOVE ZEROS TO NUMBER-OF-NUMBERS.

    READ NUMBER-FILE
      AT END MOVE ''YES'' TO END-OF-NUMBER-FILE-FLAG.

    IF END-OF-NUMBER-FILE
      NEXT SENTENCE
    ELSE
      PERFORM 200-PROCESS-NUMBER-FILE
        UNTIL END-OF-NUMBER-FILE.

    PERFORM 300-COMPUTE-AVERAGE.

    PERFORM 400-PRINT-RESULTS.

    CLOSE NUMBER-FILE
          REPORT-FILE.

    STOP RUN.
200-PROCESS-NUMBER-FILE.
    ADD 1 TO NUMBER-OF-NUMBERS.
    ADD NUMBER-REC TO SUM-OF-NUMBERS.

    READ NUMBER-FILE
      AT END MOVE ''YES'' TO END-OF-NUMBER-FILE-FLAG.
300-COMPUTE-AVERAGE.
    DIVIDE SUM-OF-NUMBERS BY NUMBER-OF-NUMBERS
      GIVING AVERAGE-OF-NUMBERS.
400-PRINT-RESULTS.
    MOVE SUM-OF-NUMBERS TO WS-SUM-OF-NUMBERS.
    MOVE NUMBER-OF-NUMBERS TO WS-NUMBER-OF-NUMBERS.
    MOVE AVERAGE-OF-NUMBERS TO WS-AVERAGE-OF-NUMBERS.
WRITE REPORT-REC FROM WS-REPORT-REC.
```

BASIC: A PERSONAL COMPUTER LANGUAGE

BASIC, or the Beginners All-purpose Symbolic Instruction Code, was developed over a period of years by professors John Kemeny and Thomas Kurtz and students in the computer science program at Dartmouth College. It was released in 1965. Although originally developed on a mainframe computer, BASIC is the most popular programming language used by personal computer owners. In most versions, BASIC is an unstructured language. Its creators intended that it teach programming concepts as students wrote programs. It is sometimes called *conversational* because it uses terms such as START, READ, INPUT, and STOP.

The original BASIC was easy to learn, allowing novice computer users to write simple programs within a few minutes. Today many manufacturers have

FIGURE 10.6

A BASIC program that produces the average of 10 numbers.

```
10  REM COMPUTE SUM AND AVERAGE OF 10 NUMBERS
20  LET SUM = 0
30  FOR I = 1 TO 10
40    INPUT N(I)
50    LET SUM = SUM + N(I)
60  NEXT I
70  LET AVG = SUM / 10
80  PRINT ''SUM = '',SUM
90  PRINT ''AVERAGE = '',AVG
999 END
```

developed varieties of BASIC that are as complex as other high-level programming languages.

BASIC uses five major categories of statements:

- Arithmetic statements allow users to use BASIC like a calculator. Typing "print 2 + 2" programs your computer to display the result, "4."
- Input/output statements, including READ, DATA, INPUT, and PRINT, program fundamental data-flow functions.
- Control statements, including GOTO, IF-THEN, FOR, NEXT, and END, control the sequence of instructions executed by the computer.
- Other statements, including REM and DIM, help document BASIC programs and set up data dimensions, respectively.
- System commands tell the operating system how to work with BASIC programs. For example, RUN means execute a program; LIST directs the computer to display a BASIC program.

BASIC fundamentals are standardized and available as Standard Minimal BASIC, released in 1978. Today, there are many popular implementations of BASIC. One is Microsoft BASIC, which is commonly packaged with MS-DOS. Another is TrueBASIC, a structured version developed by Kemeny and Kurtz. It was developed in response to criticism of unstructured BASIC and is available for many computers. In addition, ANSI issued a standard for structured BASIC in 1987. Figure 10.6 shows a sample BASIC program. The most recent version of BASIC is Microsoft Visual BASIC for use in developing applications to run under Microsoft Windows.

C: A High-Level Language

C is a relatively new programming language developed by Bell Laboratories. It gives programmers a larger measure of control over the hardware, like an assembly language, but incorporates many of the statement features of high-level languages. Although it was originally designed to work with the UNIX operating system, C is a structured language that can be used effectively for almost any kind of programming. This is due to the fact that it was standardized by the American National Standards Institute (ANSI), making it almost universal for personal computer and workstation programming tasks.

C is a compiled language that uses a number of libraries of functions; a programmer wishing to use a specific function, such as PRINT, looks it up in the appropriate library and inserts it into the program. The newest version of C is called C++, and is an object-oriented language; it is discussed in detail in the next section. Figure 10.7 is an example of a C program.

FIGURE 10.7

A C program that produces
the average of 10 numbers.

```
#include <stdio.h>
main ()
    {
        int i, num;
        float sum;
        printf(''Enter numbers \n'');
        sum = 0;
        for (i = 0; i < 10; i++)
          {
            scanf(''%d'',&num);
            sum = sum + num;
          }
        printf(''Sum = %3.1f\n'',sum);
        printf(''Average = %3.1f\n'',sum / 10.0);
    }
```

This chart summarizes the characteristics of several high-level programming
languages.

FIGURE 10.8

Language \\ Feature	Ada	APL	BASIC	COBOL	FORTRAN	Pascal	PL/1	RPG
Scientific		✓	✓		✓	✓	✓	
Business			✓	✓		✓	✓	✓
Problem Oriented								✓
Procedure Oriented	✓	✓	✓	✓	✓	✓	✓	
Standardized	✓		✓	✓	✓	✓	✓	
English-like			✓	✓		✓	✓	
Highly Used			✓	✓	✓			✓
Interactive		✓	✓			✓		

OTHER HIGH-LEVEL LANGUAGES

There are many other commonly used high-level programming languages that
we haven't discussed here. Figure 10.8 shows several high-level languages and
some of their characteristics. The following list gives some additional facts
about these specialized programming languages:

- Ada was named for Augusta Ada Lovelace, the first female programmer mentioned earlier. Ada was developed by the U.S. Department of Defense for military programming.
- APL, standing for A Programming Language, is best suited for writing mathematical programs.

- PL/1 was developed by a committee especially for the IBM System/360. Originally it was to be called NPL, for New Programming Language, but the acronym was already being used by the National Physics Laboratory in England.

- Pascal, designed by one of the world's foremost programmers, Niklaus Wirth of the Netherlands, is a teaching language that helps students learn structured programming and good programming habits. It was popularized by Borland International upon introduction of Turbo Pascal in 1984.

- RPG (Report Program Generator) is an easy-to-learn programming language used mostly with mainframe computers and their DBMS applications. It is especially useful for creating reports.

Another type of high-level language, referred to in Figure 10.3, is called 4GL. 4GL stands for *fourth-generation language*. It is a programming language used in conjunction with database management systems. As such, it is more appropriately discussed in Chapter 12.

It's important to understand that great wealth and diversity of programming languages have evolved over the years. Some were designed for specific purposes, while others were intended to set broad standards or encompass a number of computer platforms. Each has served useful purposes; some, such as Jovial (1960) have faded into obscurity, while others, such as COBOL, may live forever. In all likelihood, you will rarely if ever have occasion to learn or use these programming languages. Next, let's look at even higher-level languages that you just might work with someday.

■ KNOWLEDGE CHECK

1. What is a statement? p. 322
2. What is syntax? p. 322
3. Explain what is meant by an unstructured language and identify one. p. 322
4. Explain what is meant by a structured language and identify one. p. 322
5. Describe three of the most popular programming languages. Give each one's specific purposes. pp. 327–28

OBJECT-ORIENTED PROGRAMMING

Object-oriented programming (OOP) is a tool both programmers and knowledge workers can use. Bits of code are put together to form an **object,** a set of instructions and data, that together form a unique programming entity that perfectly executes a specific routine. For example, an object might perform the task of placing an application's icons on the screen. The application might come with six screen icons, but a provision allows you to delete any or all and add others. If you make changes, they are stored in the object and, after your customization, they appear each and every time you start the application. A major feature of objects is their *reusability,* meaning an object can be used in more than one application — whenever that icon is needed again.

THE NATURE OF OBJECTS

Objects have both *attributes* and *behaviors*. For example, if the icons are buttons, when you press one with the mouse button it launches an action; that is its attribute. Its behavior might be the way it does so; for example, it might *zoom* the action onto the screen, or the colors might change. To make them function better, objects are organized into a hierarchy of *classes*. The class defines the kind of instructions and data found in an object; for example, some perform a specific action (such as calculating a column of spreadsheet numbers), while others make sure instructions, or messages, are properly carried out (such as closing a file).

The objects are fitted together to form a program. OOP is similar to building a modular house, where parts are prefabricated and fitted together according to the buyer's desires. In that respect, it differs greatly from the way programming in high-level languages is performed. A COBOL programmer, for example, may write portions of the program in no particular order; that may be followed by some outlining and then going back later to "flesh it out." The programmer may find the need to write little bridge programs to link larger portions, after the fact. The result is often termed **spaghetti code** because the program is convoluted and disorderly. It may be easy for that particular programmer to make corrections or modifications later, but no one else may ever be able to understand the program. This has been a common occurrence since the early 1950s and often makes maintenance difficult.

BASIC PRINCIPLES OF OBJECT-ORIENTED PROGRAMMING

OOP avoids this kind of problem by using very practical engineering techniques, much as an architect or engineer designs a building or an aircraft. OOP utilizes three basic principles in doing so: encapsulation, inheritance, and polymorphism.

ENCAPSULATION. **Encapsulation** means that a high degree of functionality is integrated or bundled into each object. Encapsulation makes an object *reusable* because it is totally self-sufficient. Thus when creating new programs or modifying old ones, it is much easier to link different objects together.

INHERITANCE. **Inheritance** means that objects within a specific class have the ability to share attributes with each other. Since the important traits have already been built in, using encapsulation, it is much easier for the programmer to create a new program that is similar to an existing one. For example, if the programmer had a highly sophisticated word processing program, he or she could view objects and, after examining their encapsulation and inheritance characteristics, then select specific objects, and build a desktop publishing program with them. Encapsulation assures the functionality; inheritance permits defining or redefining objects to suit them to the new application. A retrofit task such as this would be nearly unimaginable using a high-level language.

POLYMORPHISM. **Polymorphism** lets the programmer describe a set of actions or routines that will perform exactly as they are described regardless of the class of objects they are applied to. For example, in a conventionally written application program, the exact type of printer must be defined in order to print a file — even though a dozen or more printer driver files exist. If you connect another printer and do not tell the program to change printer drivers, when you issue the PRINT FILE command, it will not execute. Polymorphism would correct that by directing the print command to address any object in the class — in other words, any printer driver — and to always print the file.

OOP LANGUAGES

Smalltalk is probably the best-known example of an object-oriented programming language. It was developed by Alan Kay at the Xerox Palo Alto Research Center in 1972 and has undergone many changes and improvements on its long path to acceptance. Smalltalk pioneered the concept of programming with icons, rather than statements and syntax. Instead of the programmer typing character strings, programs are constructed by linking icons that take over the task of creating character strings — in other words, writing the code. Figure 10.9 shows what a typical Smalltalk development screen looks like.

There are many object-oriented languages available now; some, such as Borland's Turbo Pascal, are "new and improved" with OOP. Others, such as Borland's ObjectVision, are designed specifically to create applications that work under Microsoft Windows.

ADVANTAGES AND DISADVANTAGES

OOP acknowledges that changes in programs will occur, and allows *planning* for those changes. It is software that, like a well-built bridge or building, is

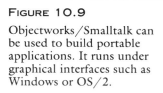

FIGURE 10.9

Objectworks/Smalltalk can be used to build portable applications. It runs under graphical interfaces such as Windows or OS/2.

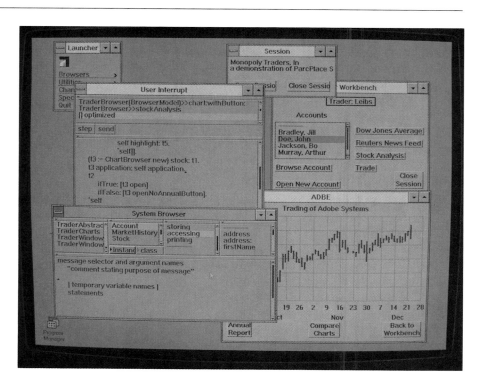

capable of withstanding stress. OOP speeds application development and requires less actual programming than a conventional high-level language.

OOP makes programming much easier for information systems professionals, but it also opens the door for knowledge workers to create software they need without having to learn a formal language or get a programmer involved. Another advantage with OOP is *reusability*. Modules created with OOP can be reused in other programs. In addition, software created with OOP can be modified and revised by adding or subtracting modules. An application can be created by simply selecting objects or, as shown in Figure 10.10, icons from a menu.

The greatest disadvantage with object-oriented programming is that it requires programmers to learn new languages. The most popular ones are C++ and Smalltalk, both quite powerful, flexible, and easy to use; yet inertia and the difficulties of starting all over with an entirely new programming methodology stand in the way. In addition, OOP applications are incompatible with older, spaghetti-code applications, making for problems in large information systems organizations.

CASE: COMPUTER-AIDED SOFTWARE ENGINEERING

An interesting new kind of software tool emerged in the 1980s: **computer-aided software engineering** (CASE). It is a methodology especially designed for programmers in large information systems organizations who need to quickly create new applications or re-engineer the older spaghetti-code applications previously discussed.

CASE automates the design and implementation of applications, as well as the procedures linking various applications, so they may be created more rapidly and efficiently. In this respect, CASE is similar to object-oriented programming; it differs primarily in that it is designed for applications of the

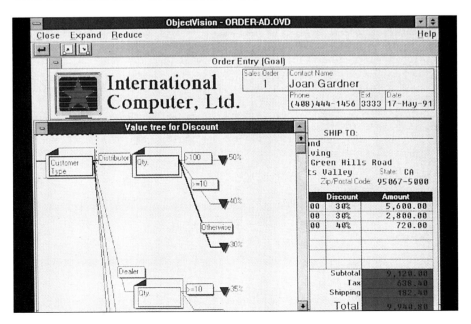

FIGURE 10.10

Object Vision, an object-oriented application, allows the nontechnical user to create specific Windows-based applications using objects or icons instead of complicated computer codes.

high-level programming environment. CASE tools are used in three ways: for program design, for re-engineering, and as an integrated set of application development tools.

PROGRAM DESIGN

Program design is, simply, creating a new application. It includes analysis, design, and documentation. CASE dramatically lowers these so-called "front-end" development costs by automating many manual operations and tasks. The computer itself replaces paper, pencil, and the flowchart template.

Excelerator is a CASE tool developed for the personal computer which designs, validates, and prepares specifications for applications and information systems. The systems analyst can create a system design, show it to knowledge workers, work with them to tailor it to their needs, and then create the program specifications. Figure 10.11 shows Excelerator.

RE-ENGINEERING

The second way CASE tools are used involves using programming, correcting programming errors, and maintaining software applications—the "back-end" of development. These tools streamline and automate many programming tasks, and include text editors with built-in language templates, source code management libraries, and program performance and efficiency analyzers. Many companies have at least one enormous database that has become increasingly expensive or difficult to maintain and update. One CASE activity called *re-engineering* adapts these older applications to current business requirements.

For example, if a company started using a database 30 years ago, many of its early departments may no longer exist. Accidentally entering a portion of the

---

FIGURE 10.11

CASE program design using Excelerator. Each of these graphic screen symbols represents a module of programming code that performs the functions described on the screen. By linking them together, a new application can quickly and simply be created.

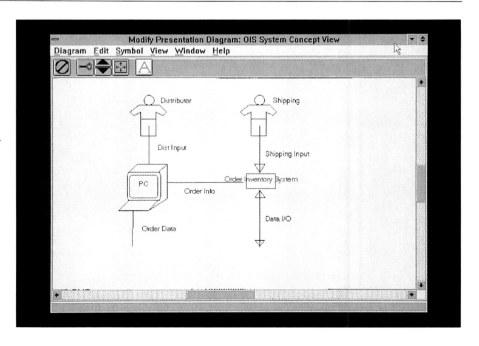

database designed for these departments can cause a malfunction or even a failure. A re-engineering CASE tool, such as the Bachman Data Analyst, will clean up existing files and redesign the database to bring it more in line with the company's current and future needs. It also paves the way for migrating from the old database to a new one. Figure 10.12 shows a Bachman Data Analyst screen. CASE and re-engineering tools have extended the life and usefulness of existing software applications that otherwise would cost millions to replace or re-create. "CASE is the fifth-generation programming language," says Charles Bachman, who with his son Jonathan started Bachman Information Systems and created the Bachman CASE tools.

I-CASE

The third type of CASE tool is called Integrated CASE (I-CASE). A tool for complete system development, it is being used in many large corporations to create more flexible systems and to create systems more quickly. I-CASE permits designing systems from block diagrams, as shown in Figure 10.13. This allows people to focus more concretely on who should get what information. TWA used I-CASE to design a system that monitors its frequent flier program. In the past, it took three working days to program changes in the program; now it takes half an hour.

Once the system is designed using I-CASE, it is often possible to use a **code generator,** a special software program, to create a large portion of the source code. The code generator writes code faster and more accurately than programmers, and once written, it maintains itself. Blue Cross/Blue Shield of North Carolina used a generator for a large health care system. Only 16,000 lines of code were written by programmers; the code generator wrote the remaining 194,000. A system that could have taken several years to complete was ready and working within six months.

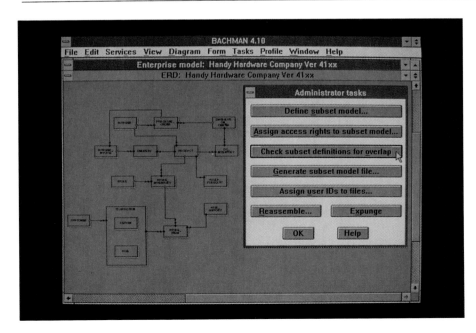

FIGURE 10.12

CASE re-engineering. As a company's needs grow and change, a re-engineering tool like the Bachman Data Analyst enables redesigning and updating a company's database. This product, termed a shared work manager, allows the administrator to manage task assignments and groups of analysts to share application models.

FIGURE 10.13

Integrated CASE. Texas Instruments' Information Engineering Facility (IEF) is shown here, with design work on an Entity Relationship diagram in the full screen, Diagram Testing in the lower window, and actual application execution in the upper window. Complete mainframe applications can be designed, generated, and tested on a single OS/2 workstation.

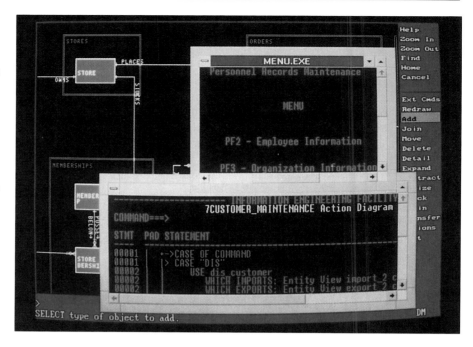

ADVANTAGES AND DISADVANTAGES

Computer-aided software engineering has rewritten many of the rules for how applications are designed and programmed. CASE makes it easier to understand the nature and intent of the application before it is designed, because objects are defined by real data or examples. When new applications are written in a conventional programming language, almost everything is custom-written; with CASE, objects can be reused again and again. Handwritten programs must be tested and retested to assure their reliability, which is often a complex and time-consuming task. CASE objects can be analyzed independently; changing or even removing one doesn't necessarily mean other functions in the application will change or be disrupted.

CASE is great, but it's no panacea. There are many instances where there are established applications that require ongoing programming work in COBOL. And, from the knowledge worker perspective, learning CASE is like starting over, when the programmer already has a great depth and breadth of skills already. For this reason, programmers are often teamed up with kindred knowledge workers — one team to work with COBOL or the prevalent language, and another to learn and practice with CASE. Thus CASE tools are more often used for new application development.

From a business perspective, CASE tools are expensive to purchase. Then there is the big expense of training knowledge workers in their use. One way CASE software vendors are trying to help customers reduce expense is by making the technology available on desktop personal computers instead of mainframes. The jury is still out on CASE. According to a Forrester Research survey of 50 senior information systems executives in 1992, about 38 percent are currently using CASE tools, while almost 80 percent say they plan to use them by 1996. Like most innovative new technologies, CASE acceptance and use is slow.

TOMORROW

THE DECLINE AND FALL OF THE AMERICAN PROGRAMMER

A major figure in the software industry, Edward Yourdon is a programming expert, newsletter editor, and author. In his book, *The Decline and Fall of the American Programmer,* he issues a warning: What happened to the U.S. consumer electronics and auto industries can happen to the software industry too.

The American programmer is about to share the fate of the dodo bird. By the end of this decade, I foresee massive unemployment among the ranks of American programmers, systems analysts, and software engineers. Not because fifth-generation computers will eliminate the need for programming, or because users will begin writing their own programs. No, the reason will be far simpler: *international competition will put American programmers out of work, just as Japanese competition put American automobile workers out of work in the 1970s.* And just as the American automobile industry was shocked and unprepared for its loss of dominance, so the

American software industry will find its fall from preeminence difficult and unexpected.

From my visits to data processing organizations in the United States and around the world, I am firmly convinced that most American programmers (and their managers) do not yet fully understand, deep in their psyches, that every product and every service provided by today's society depends on productive, high-quality information systems. An increasing number of manufactured products contains one or more embedded computer systems, systems that are software intensive, with 100,000 or more lines of code. And though the term "service economy" conjures up images of low-paid workers dishing out hamburgers at Burger King, today's service economy is information intensive and would collapse almost instantly without smoothly functioning information systems.

The average company spends a minuscule 1 to 3 percent of its revenues on data processing. But this paltry figure fails to empha-

size the point that a company's information technology is its Achilles' heel. As a project manager at the Jet Propulsion Laboratories remarked to me a few years ago, "Software represents only 10 to 15 percent of the money we spend around here, but it's 'in series' with 90 percent of what we do: if the software fails, the mission fails." And thus the people who build information systems—the programmers, systems analysts, database designers, telecommunications specialists, and others—play an increasingly crucial role in the fiscal health, and the very survival, of their employers. In the 1990s, a company whose programmers and systems analysts are an order of magnitude better than its competitors will have a dramatic advantage—and the company whose software folks are an order of magnitude worse than its competitors will go out of business.*

———————
*Edward Yourdon, *The Decline and Fall of the American Programmer* (Englewood Cliffs, N.J.: Prentice Hall, 1992), pp. 1–3.

KNOWLEDGE CHECK

1. What is an object in object-oriented programming?   p. 330
2. What is the term used to describe disorganized programs?   p. 331
3. How does OOP offer an advantage in addressing changes in programs?   pp. 332–33
4. What does the term *reusable* mean in OOP?   p. 333
5. What is the main difference between OOP and CASE programming tools?   p. 333
6. What is re-engineering? When and how should it be used?   p. 334
7. Who uses OOP tools, and who uses CASE tools?   pp. 333–36

CAREERS FOR KNOWLEDGE WORKERS
DAVE BALL, SOFTWARE TEST ENGINEER, MICROSOFT

Whenever you press the Help button in Microsoft Windows, think of Dave Ball. He's a software test engineer at Microsoft Corporation, the world's largest and most influential personal computer software publisher. Dave's work group ensures the quality of the Windows Help display system. Help is an important feature in any software application, as Dave will tell you. He's worked on the quality of Help for a number of Microsoft applications, including

word processing, the spreadsheet, integrated software, programming languages, and a CD-ROM package.

Dave graduated from Seattle Pacific University with a degree in business computing, which he says helped orient him to using computers to solve business problems. His first job was at Boeing Aircraft, working as a programmer/analyst on mainframe systems. He learned about software testing while working with the computer systems for

the Boeing 747-400, the world's largest passenger aircraft.

Dave liked software testing, and when he saw a HELP WANTED ad for Microsoft in the newspaper, he applied for the job and got it. "I had enormous respect for Microsoft and the integrity of their software, and I was fascinated with personal computers. But when I got the job offer, I was stunned.

"Most people have heard of debugging," says Dave, "which is different than testing. Debugging ensures that software does what you expect. Testing ensures that software won't do what you don't expect." For example, a spreadsheet expects to calculate numbers; what happens if you insert words where the spreadsheet expects numbers? Will it produce an error message or simply crash?

Microsoft takes testing so seriously that it has published an application called Microsoft Test for Windows, which Dave worked on. It is designed for companies that create applications for Windows, called *third-party developers,* so they can find bugs and problems in their soft-

WHAT LIES AHEAD?

As Figure 10.14 shows, programming computers has changed dramatically over the past two decades. Today there are far more computers and more people using them for a wider variety of tasks than before — creating a greater demand for applications. As John Xenakis says, there has been a drive for ways to automate programming. Even advanced programming tools require programmers at the keyboard. Are we moving toward a day when computers write their own programs, without human intervention?

ware. Test for Windows creates routines that simulate how a knowledge worker will actually use the application, and then performs the tasks, often repeating them over and over. "Sometimes a problem doesn't show up the first time you execute a task," says Dave. "Sometimes it doesn't show up for quite a while, so Test for Windows can repeat it hundreds, even thousands of times. If there's a problem, Test for Windows can set up a routine to find it."

Dave is a member of a small workgroup or team made up of a program manager, several test engineers, and a number of software development engineers. Microsoft is composed of many such workgroups, allowing people to develop strong, close working relationships. "The culture is outgoing and friendly here, and it's a very international community where women and men from all kinds of backgrounds and countries work together," he says. In fact, the Microsoft culture has even developed its own vocabulary: "bandwidth" is a term used to describe intellectual powers, and

when someone is "hardcore" it means they're serious about their work.

Microsoft is sometimes called "the velvet sweatshop," Dave says, "because we work hard but enjoy what we do. People have a very professional attitude toward their work. We're competitive, but it's focused on getting out an excellent product. This is a great place to be creative and solve problems; it's encouraged. You don't give up; you just keep hammering until you find an answer, or you ask others to help if you can't do it yourself."

One test of creative problem-solving ability is the "manhole question" asked of potential new hires: Why are manholes round? Dave, who has done some campus recruiting (Microsoft scours 137 U.S. campuses every year), says it's surprising how many people have never puzzled out the answer. Yet the way people respond can make the difference between getting an offer from Microsoft or not. Hiring smart people is a top priority.

Dave believes that opportunities for programmers are increas-

ing. "You're going to see more and more computers in more and more products. The quality of many household appliances can be improved by adding a hardware controller, even to a vacuum cleaner. Those controllers need instructions, or programming.

"Here at Microsoft, we're also developing more specialty software products for personal computers. For example, we've created a simple desktop publishing program called Microsoft Publisher from our Microsoft Word for Windows word processing program. And we used the core technology of our Microsoft Excel spreadsheet to create a budgeting program called Microsoft Money for Windows. College graduates with a major in, say, journalism, accounting, or marketing, combined with a minor in programming, will become tomorrow's vertical market software developers. There are all kinds of opportunities out there."

Dave ought to know. He's been promoted to lead engineer, testing, for the new version of Microsoft Money.

Those who say that the programmer's job is too sophisticated to be completely automated are actually correct. After all, we still have bank tellers and telephone operators filling niches that automation hasn't yet been able to handle. And I'll bet that somewhere there's still a cobbler who manufactures shoes entirely by hand.

But each year, another chunk of the programmer's job will be bitten off and assigned to automation. Those people and the companies whose livelihood depends on those chunks will have to change direction soon, or be out of business when the new century begins.[2]

---

[2] Xenakis, "Automation of the Computer Programmer."

FIGURE 10.14   Developments in programming.

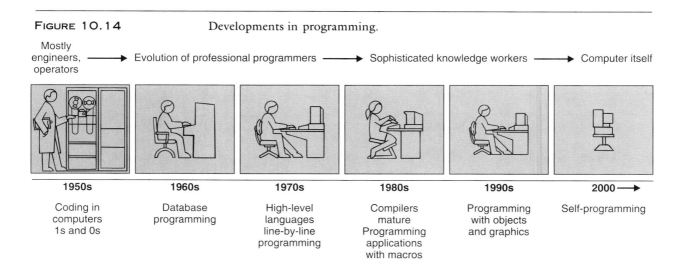

Mostly engineers, operators ⟶ Evolution of professional programmers ⟶ Sophisticated knowledge workers ⟶ Computer itself

1950s	1960s	1970s	1980s	1990s	2000 ⟶
Coding in computers 1s and 0s	Database programming	High-level languages line-by-line programming	Compilers mature Programming applications with macros	Programming with objects and graphics	Self-programming

ETHICS IN PROGRAMMING: WHAT IS "INTELLECTUAL PROPERTY"?

As we've seen, programming involves a degree of creativity. As a means of solving problems, we can accurately state that programs are creations or inventions. To underscore this fact, consider that in recent years, many companies and individuals have sought U.S. government patents on programs. Of course, whenever an individual originates a creation or invention, ownership can become an ethical issue.

Many computer corporations feel that they own the programming ideas of their employees. They insist that any and all programming output, while an employee is on the payroll, is actually the property of the corporation. This includes the programs themselves and even "intellectual property" (ideas). If we examine firms' perspective, we can see why they take this stance. Employees work together, attend meetings and seminars, and generally discuss programs under development. Their problem solving is valuable and has the potential to create profitable products. If an employee turns this information into a product he or she sells outside the corporation, we might consider this a form of theft. In this instance, the ideas of the individual are usurped for the group's advantage.

The line between ethical and unethical behavior in this type of situation is often drawn on the basis of monetary gain or loss. Has the programmer used company resources, such as computer time or corporate data? Does the company authorize using the computer to work on individual projects on personal time? Did the employee agree that all work he or she does belongs to the company? Was the project originally intended for company use? These and many more issues must be clarified.

Many companies now have a set of ethical guidelines for employees to follow; failure to do so often results in immediate dismissal. When systems people are found breaking the rules, it is not uncommon to see them escorted out of the building by the security guards. This ignominy is prompted by fear that they will take programs or software with them, or even possibly cripple the system with bugs.

Clearly, ethical behavioral means not breaking company rules. However, the rules must be clear: if the programmer is hired on a freelance basis, he or she may be entitled to retain ownership. If the company wishes to keep its system development private, it must inform employees of this fact. You can see that when it comes to programing, discretion plays a big part in determining what's right and what's wrong. Most important, it means developing and adhering to a strict set of personal ethical guidelines.

SUMMARY

1. *Explain the origins and development of machine programming.* The first programmed machine was the Jacquard loom; it used punched cards to create weaving patterns. The concept was used in a machine that counted the 1890 census and later was used at IBM for programming computers.

2. *Describe the evolution of computer programming languages.* The first computer programming language was machine language, requiring the programmer to write programs in the 1s and 0s the computer understands. Assembly language, although machine-dependent, used words to represent code.

3. *Explain the characteristics of several popular high-level languages.* All high-level languages use statements and syntax to create instructions. Some are structured languages, while others are unstructured. Compilers and interpreters turn code into executable programs. FORTRAN is an unstructured language for scientists. COBOL is a structured language for business. BASIC is commonly an unstructured general-purpose language for novices. C is a structured, all-purpose language.

4. *Identify the characteristics and benefits of object-oriented programming.* OOP combines bits of code into objects, which include instructions and data and act like modular building blocks. OOP objects are reusable, meaning they can be put to work in many different programs. OOP overcomes the problem of spaghetti code in high-level language programming, makes programming easier, and creates programs with less code.

5. *Identify the characteristics and benefits of computer-aided software engineering.* CASE is for large information systems organizations that need to quickly create new applications or re-engineer old applications that are based in high-level languages. CASE makes old systems more useful quickly, and I-CASE can produce entirely new applications and information systems in very short order.

ISSUES IN PROGRAMMING AND PROGRAMS

1. Gerald Weinberg, an expert on programmers and programming, says that programming is a complex human activity. Programmers would agree; most feel that their work is a form of artistic expression and don't want to be disturbed when they are "creating." Business managers want programmers held accountable for their work productivity, just like other employees, to avoid project delays and the application backlog. Is it possible to strike a happy medium between the two? Is it possible that tools such as CASE will eventually replace the programmer?

2. Despite the advances in computer hardware, many industry observers feel there have been relatively few innovations in software. They cite the spreadsheet as the only application developed during the 1980s. In addition, critics often contend that programmers design systems that are easy to create, but quite often difficult or awkward to use. An example is an order entry system that asks for the customer's zip code, phone number, catalog number, credit card number, and item number, rather than following the more natural way people convey personal information: name, address, phone number, catalog and item number, and credit card number. In your experience, have computers made any real progress in meeting people's needs or work styles, rather than making us conform to the way they work?

3. "Intellectual property," or the right of ownership, is a serious ethical and legal concern in the software industry. Employers asked programmers to sign away all rights to their work while on the company payroll, while some programmers feel any code they write is an original creative expression, no different than a novel or a painting. What's more, software publishers have sued each other for copying what is termed the *look and feel* of a program. Most notable has been the

lawsuit Lotus Development Corp. brought against Paperback Software and Mirror Technologies, two competitors against its Lotus 1-2-3 spreadsheet. Research the outcome of this and other software copyright court decisions. How will litigation affect creativity and innovation in software development?

CHAPTER REVIEW QUESTIONS

REVIEW QUESTIONS

1. Why is assembly language better for writing operating systems than it is for writing application programs?

2. Why are there both structured and unstructured languages?

3. Identify the two elements common to both human and computer languages.

4. What kind of applications is FORTRAN suited for?

5. What kind of applications is COBOL suited for?

6. What are the differences between BASIC and C?

7. Explain the main difference between OOP and CASE.

DISCUSSION QUESTIONS

1. Discuss the advantages of a machine that can be programmed to perform many different tasks over one that performs a single task. How many can you think of in the former group?

2. Discuss the evolution of programming languages, and the relative advantages and disadvantages as they get more English-like (as in high-level and object-oriented).

3. Discuss the major differences between how a compiler and an interpreter translate code.

4. How are the work and role of the programmer changing?

5. Edward Yourdon (Tomorrow feature) believes the programmer job is disappearing, while Dave Ball (Careers feature) sees new tasks and roles for the programmer. Discuss the merits of both points of view.

MULTIPLE-CHOICE

1. High-level languages (choose all that apply):
   a. Are closer to English.
   b. Are easier to use than machine or assembly language.
   c. Use statements to tell knowledge workers how to use them.
   d. Must be compiled before they can be used.
   e. Are more portable than lower-level languages.
   f. Can be used equally to write all different types of applications.

2. The advantage in using objects in object-oriented programming is (choose all that apply):
   a. An object forms a complete, unique programming entity.
   b. An object may be reused in different programs.
   c. Objects are customizable.
   d. Objects require less programming, or developmental time.
   e. All of the above.

3. The major strength of I-CASE is to:
   a. Correct the problems created in front-end CASE development.
   b. Create more flexible systems more quickly.
   c. Make knowledge workers do all the programming.
   d. Get rid of spaghetti code.

4. The first device used for programming a machine was:

a. The knitting needle.
b. The punched card.
c. Switches and cables.
d. The compiler.

5. A programming language shares in common with human languages the following (choose all that apply):

a. Statements.
b. Syllogisms.
c. Syntax.
d. Verisimilitude.
e. All of the above.

FILL-IN-THE-BLANK

1. A language that requires no translation for program execution is _____.

2. The _____ language doubles for high-level and object-oriented programming.

3. The _____ programming language was named after the first woman programmer.

4. _____ _____ is a language version designed to create applications for Windows.

5. Objects are modular, while high-level languages often produce _____ code.

6. CASE re-engineering is intended to improve the efficiency of _____.

TRUE/FALSE

1. The output file produced by a compiler is called an *executable file.*

2. OOP objects contain instructions, data, and icons.

3. A key advantage of OOP is reusability.

4. Turbo Pascal made it possible to more quickly program mainframes.

5. The cotton gin was the first machine to be programmed.

6. ENIAC was programmed with switches and cables.

7. A compiler creates code that becomes an executable file, but an interpreter only translates one executable line at a time.

KEY TERMS

assembler, 322

assembly language, 320

BASIC language, 327

C language, 328

COBOL language, 324

code generator, 335

compiler, 323

computer-aided software engineering (CASE), 333

encapsulation, 331

executable, 323

FORTRAN language, 324

high-level language, 322

inheritance, 331

interpreter, 323

machine-dependent, 321

machine language, 320

mnemonic, 322

object, 330

object code, 323

object-oriented programming (OOP), 330

polymorphism, 331

programming language, 319

punched card, 317

spaghetti code, 331

statement, 322

structured programming language, 322

syntax, 322

unstructured programming language, 322

CHAPTER

11

Software Engineering

LEARNING OBJECTIVES

After reading and studying this
chapter, you should be able to:

1. Identify the steps in the traditional system development life
cycle.

2. Describe software engineering
and how it is used.

3. Explain the structured techniques used in software development.

4. Explain the information engineering development process.

5. Describe some information
engineering approaches.

6. Describe the rapid application
development life cycle.

SOFTWARE ENGINEERING

As you know, *people* working with *software* and *hardware* create *computer systems.* This chapter explains that the majority of the work entails creating software—either systems software or application software. The application(s) used with the system largely determines how knowledge workers use it, and what type of productivity it provides for the business. This aspect of computer system development has become so important it has evolved its own name: **software engineering,** which involves the design, development, and implementation of production software systems on large-scale business computers. Software engineering, as defined by the Study Group on Computer Science of the NATO Science Committee in 1967, embraces all the human aspects, from programming to management, as well as all the project details, from concept to execution to documentation.

Programmers, systems analysts, application programmers, and other software and information systems professionals take part in software engineering. The degree of complexity and the number of steps in software engineering vary, depending on the size of the company, its business objectives, the number of information systems professionals on the development staff, the size and complexity of the problem that must be solved, and the number of knowledge workers who will be using the system.

The field of software development has evolved rapidly since the early 1980s. For that reason, we first study the traditional method of creating a system or an application, often called *system development life cycle.* This method, although tried and true, emphasizes the role of the information systems organization. The second, more modern method is called *information engineering,* where the system is designed and created by both the information systems professionals and knowledge workers. Each method is illustrated with a case study that shows how software development projects actually happen. The first, at *The New York Times,* involved only a programming team. The second, at Imperial Oil of Canada, shows the importance of the two groups —information systems professionals and knowledge workers—working together to design and create a new application.

TRADITIONAL SYSTEM DEVELOPMENT

In the past, developing systems was the responsibility of the information systems organization. The process was called the **system development life cycle** and it is comprised of these steps:

- *Analysis:* Identifying and defining the problem.
- *Design:* Planning the solution to the problem.

- *Coding:* Writing the program.
- *Debugging:* Correcting program errors.
- *Testing and acceptance:* Making sure the system works properly and turning it over to the users.
- *Maintenance:* Keeping systems working properly and improving them when necessary.
- *Documentation:* Writing software, user, and reference documentation.

ANALYSIS AND DESIGN

Let's begin our discussion by looking at the first steps in the system development process: systems analysis and design. **Systems analysis** is the study of an activity, a procedure, or even an entire business to determine what kind of computer system would make it more efficient. **Systems design** is the activity of planning the technical aspects for the new system. This activity is usually triggered when a knowledge worker requests a new system; for example, your company's telemarketing department might ask for an application that keeps track of customer ordering information. Analysis and design are essential steps in the early stages of defining a software project. Large software development companies have found that effective early planning can cut overall program development time and costs by as much as 60 percent.

Systems analysts gather and analyze the data necessary to develop the new application. Depending on the organization and its size, they might also be called *systems consultants, systems engineers, information analysts,* or *business analysts.* Whatever their title, the systems analyst's tasks are to:

- Analyze the problem to be solved, the data to be input, the expected output, and so on.
- Determine what people, software, and hardware resources are necessary to solve the problem.
- Design and specify the computer system and the methods for the information system to solve the problem.
- Guide or manage the project to a successful conclusion.

CODING

Analyzing and defining programs involves manual tasks, easily performed without computers, and comprise the first step. Coding and debugging, which follow, are the opposite — now the pencil is put away and replaced by the keyboard. **Coding** is programming in a specific programming language, or languages — writing the source code for the program. The code is compiled into the language the CPU understands.

Source code is the program, written in a specific programming language, that will be sent to the computer for processing. Coding is the same as programming, but specifically refers to writing source code. By the time we begin coding, the program planning stage should be finished. If we have defined the problem well and created a good design, coding can often take less time than the other steps in the system development process.

TEXT EDITORS. A **text editor** is an essential tool for the coding step in the system development process. It is a program with which to write, erase, and

YESTERDAY
THE EVOLUTION OF BUSINESS SYSTEM ANALYSIS TECHNIQUES

Professor J. Daniel Couger detailed the history of business system analysis in an ACM Computing Surveys article in 1973. There he explained that "Systems analysis consists of collecting, organizing, and evaluating facts about a system and the environment in which it operates. The objective of systems analysis is to examine all aspects of the system—equipment, personnel, operating conditions, and its internal and external demands—to establish a basis for designing and implementing a better system."

In the early 1900s, the *process flowchart,* pioneered by Frederick W. Taylor and the Gilbreths, was used to show the flow of materials. The flowchart has lived on in many iterations, being particularly useful in the early stages of designing a computer system on paper.

From 1920 to 1950, as paperwork burdens grew, the process flowchart was modified into a *forms flow.* It was found lacking, however, because it failed to identify data elements and volumes.

From 1951 to 1960, techniques especially for computer systems emerged. One was the *Information Process Chart* (IPC), a combination of flowcharts and block diagrams. IPC brought attention to the need for formal annotation, necessary for computerized analysis.

During the 1961–70 period, *Accurately Defined System* (ADS), a technique developed within NCR, was introduced. It was a well-organized approach to defining and specifying systems. ADS used five forms to define the application or system. Although paper-based, the technique led the way to other computerized system definition approaches.

The 1970s saw the emergence of IBM's *Business Strategy Planning* (BSP). It was a thoroughgoing paper- and computer-based planning methodology that took into consideration business goals, targets, trends, strategies, and critical success factors.

The 1980s saw BSP become *Information Strategy Planning* (ISP), which links information technology planning to business strategy planning. It is perhaps the most comprehensive way to view a business and its goals, and to examine how the computer technology can serve the business and achieve those goals. It helps identify strategic systems opportunities, provides a means for analyzing goals and problems, assesses technology impact, analyzes critical success factors, and helps create a model and an architectural framework for the information system.

manipulate words on the monitor screen. A text editor is very much like a word processor, but without many of the formatting features; in fact, word processing was the progeny of text editors.

Programming languages require certain formalities, and advanced text editors help programmers stick to the proper forms. For example, if a programming language asks that each line of source code be indented a certain number of spaces and end with a period, the text editor can be set to automatically begin each line with a tab and close each line with a period. Other functions like search, cut and paste, automatic word wrap, and automatic line spacing also make coding a little easier. And to make writing programs more orderly and disciplined, a technique called structured coding evolved.

STRUCTURED CODING.   **Structured coding** was the first structured technique, borne of the need for a more organized way to write programs. Structured coding states that all programs can be written using three basic

FIGURE 11.1

The three primary control structures used in structured programming.

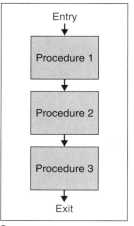

Sequence

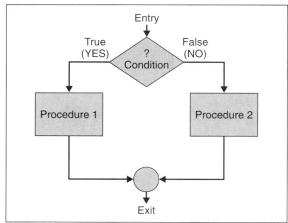

Selection (IF-THEN-ELSE)

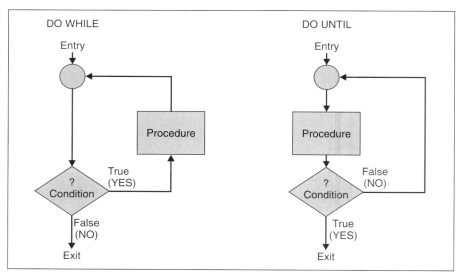

Looping (iteration)

constructs: sequence, selection, and repetition, as shown in Figure 11.1. Programs written using structured coding techniques are easier to read, understand, and maintain. Note, however, that structured coding is distinct from other structured techniques explained later in this chapter. You can use structured coding whether or not you use structured design techniques.

DEBUGGING

In the early 1940s, a programming team found a moth in a computer that had caused a program to fail. Ever since that incident, the term **bug** has been used to describe a program or hardware problem. Figure 11.2 shows the naval record of that first bug.

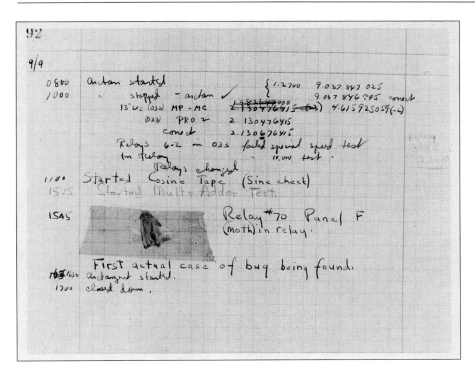

FIGURE 11.2

First computer bug. This moth was found caught in an early computer's relay, causing a program to fail. The term *debugging* is commonly used in identifying software program errors.

Detail and precision are required, almost to the point of perfection, to make a program run successfully; therefore bugs are quite common. A **debugger** is a system software program that identifies program errors. For example, the debugger may be used when a program runs but fails to produce the correct output. A debugger reports problems as error messages. The compiler also identifies program errors so the programmer can debug (correct) the program. Programmers use error message listings, as shown in Figure 11.3, to track down bugs. Debugging can be a costly process, consuming as much as 50 percent of program development time. Modern debugging tools, such as those found in the information engineering development environments discussed later in this chapter, help programmers spot troubles more quickly.

TESTING AND ACCEPTANCE

No system is truly worthwhile unless it meets the needs of the knowledge workers it was designed for. Therefore, once a system is debugged, it goes into **testing** so people can see how it works. There are two types of testing: system tests and user tests. **System testing** involves entering various kinds of data to see how the program reacts under different conditions.

User testing, as its name implies, means letting the knowledge workers test the system under actual working conditions. They look not only for system malfunctions, but also for such things as ease of use, the system's speed in performing tasks, and a number of design characteristics. Often knowledge workers are asked to try to cause the system to fail by performing unantici-

Figure 11.3   Error messages produced when compiling a BASIC program.

```
Diagnostic on source line 16, listing line 16
source file: CHECKBOOK.BAS;1

              IF answer = ''Y''
%BASIC-E-INSERTB,          assuming THEN before end of statement

Diagnostic on source line 17, listing line 17
source file: CHECKBOOK.BAS;1

              WHILE
%BASIC-E-FOUND,          found end of statement when expecting an expression

Diagnostic on source line 21, listing line 21
source file: CHECKBOOK.BAS;1

              THEN
................1
%BASIC-E-FOUND, 1:          found keyword THEN when expecting one of:
                                 an operator
                                 end of statement
                                 ''(''

Diagnostic on source line 30, listing line 30
source file: CHECKBOOK.BAS;1

              THEN
................1
%BASIC-E-FOUND, 1:          found keyword THEN when expecting one of:
                                 an operator
                                 end of statement

Diagnostic on source line 35, listing line 35
source file: CHECKBOOK.BAS;1

              END IF
%BASIC-E-MISMATFOR,          missing NEXT for UNTIL at listing line 25

%BASIC-E-ENDNOOBJ, CHECKBOOK.BAS;1 completed with 5
diagnostics - object deleted
```

pated functions — for example, opening the same file repeatedly without closing the previous one. Remember, a system should not only work as it is supposed to; it also should not fail even when used improperly. When this occurs, the system should give the knowledge worker an error or help message suggesting a course of corrective action.

Maintenance

Once accepted by the knowledge workers, the system goes into **production,** which means it is in daily use. That does not, however, mean it is perfect. Most systems are constantly corrected, updated, and improved; this ongoing phase of the system life cycle is called **maintenance.** The knowledge workers might ask that the system run faster or perform more tasks; or changing business procedures or conditions might necessitate updating or modifying the system. Also, since the system is not perfect, subtle bugs may reveal themselves after the system is in use, such as during periods of high-volume usage or when

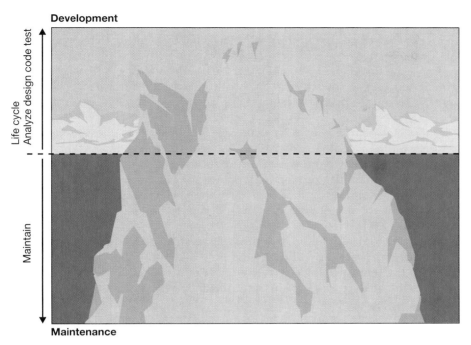

Development

Life cycle

Analyze design code test

Maintain

Maintenance

FIGURE 11.4

The relationship between the work involved in systems design and systems mainte- nance can be likened to how much of an iceberg floats above the water's surface.

unanticipated types of use occur. Regardless of the reasons, as Figure 11.4 shows, far more time and effort are put into systems maintenance than systems design.

DOCUMENTATION

Documentation is the set of instructions that accompany a system or an application. There are three kinds of documentation: software, user, and ref- erence documentation. They are differentiated by the people who use them. **Software documentation** is chiefly for programmers who will maintain the program. **User documentation** and **reference documentation** are for the knowledge workers who will use the program. Software documentation ex- plains how a program works. User and reference documentation explains what a program does and how to use it.

Writing the documentation is the final step in the system development life cycle, but ideally it is a *process* that continues throughout development. Even though the final details cannot be written until the programming is finished, waiting until the end of the project to begin writing often results in poor documentation. Good documentation is no accident; it is the result of careful planning and development, just like the software itself. Documentation can take many forms, including conventional paper-based manuals or memos, on-line electronic versions, or even context-sensitive help screens or messages that appear when summoned by pressing the Help key. In fact, the knowledge worker often contributes to producing the system's documentation, both during and after development.

STRUCTURED TECHNIQUES

By the mid-1960s, government institutions and corporations were floundering in a sea of programming problems. Programs written in many individualistic styles led to chaos in software development and maintenance. In response, people such as Edsger Dijkstra, Corrado Bohm, and Guiseppe Jacopini developed and advocated a variety of **structured techniques.** Structured means a technique that is orderly and that can be understood by others besides the program creator.

There are a number of structured techniques, including structured programming or coding, structured analysis, structured design, and so on. Structured techniques often result in reduced program development time, increased programmer productivity, less testing and debugging, and programs that are simpler and easier to maintain. Here are a few of the more commonly used structured analysis and design techniques.

STRUCTURED ANALYSIS. **Structured analysis** uses data flow diagrams to chart a system's progress. By showing how data moves from one point to another, the resulting concept is that of a logical system. Structured analysis requires the analyst to logically think through what the system should do, before determining how it should be done. The emphasis is on the end result —what knowledge workers need from the system to perform their work. Interestingly, the logic inherent in structured analysis often allows the analyst to come up with more creative solutions to problems.

STRUCTURED DESIGN. **Structured design** commonly utilizes a method called the *top-down approach,* which breaks the problem into parts and arranges these parts in a **hierarchy,** a series of steps arranged according to their size and level of detail, beginning with the overall problem to be solved and continuing down in a series of increasingly more detailed parts of the problem.

Computers work by performing tasks in step-by-step fashion. For this reason, they are good at working with algorithms. An **algorithm** is a limited set of step-by-step instructions that solve a problem. Once the steps are well defined, programmers can easily go on to write code in **modules** — distinct, logical parts of a program.

Structured techniques help programmers understand what they're doing before they begin writing code. They provide several kinds of road maps, in various levels of detail, to serve as guides in coding. Although you may never write code, it is probable you will participate in developing a system or application. Understanding the process will help you make a more meaningful contribution.

STRUCTURED TECHNIQUES CASE STUDY: *THE NEW YORK TIMES*

The first software engineering project to employ structured techniques was begun in 1969 at *The New York Times.* IBM was brought in to develop an information system that would replace the manual clipping file, or morgue as it was known. The system would make it possible to research articles by date of publication, section of the paper, key words, and so forth. The system was developed using what was termed a *chief programmer team* comprised of spe-

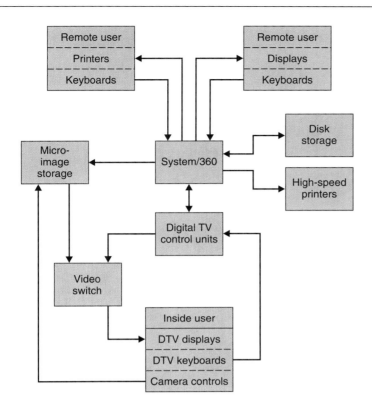

FIGURE 11.5

Data flow diagrams chart the course of data in an information system.

cialists, each of whom was responsible for specific tasks or modules of the programming code.

The work began with structured design, which involved creating data flow diagrams explaining how data would move between various hardware components, as shown in Figure 11.5. The team identified *descriptors,* bibliographic data that would be needed — for example, date or date range, whether the writer was a staff reporter or freelancer, the type of article (news, editorial, feature), accompanying illustrations or artwork, the section and page numbers, and the relative importance of the article.

The project used the top-down approach for its structured analysis. In their work, the control code, or most primary programming, was done first, followed by the functional code that was to work with the already-functioning computer system. This approach made it easier to integrate the new application and also resulted in fewer program errors and less need for debugging. Since debugging occurred in modules, or stages, overall system reliability was improved.

Remarkably, the project was finished in just six months. Using traditional development techniques, it would have taken an estimated 132 months. The experienced team members were highly motivated to finish the project on time, yet its small size was considered a benefit to its manageability and responsiveness to change. As a result, debugging, testing, and acceptance proceeded quickly and smoothly — especially since there were only 20 errors

TODAY

HOW (NOT) TO WORK WITH A SYSTEM DESIGNER

The following is a humorous essay by Dave Platt, a system designer.

The "spell-it-out-up-front," detailed-specification approach attempts to spell out THE SOLUTION in great detail. For example, the contract might call for a microprocessor-based implementation using a distributed network of FooBaz 413 MPUs, running a real-time operating system capable of responding to interrupts in no more than 0.8263 nanofidgets, and capable of processing 1763 meta-shift-cokebottle commands per cup of coffee.

These sort of solution-specifications are often very comforting to the contract-writer . . . they provide a detailed, measurable, and testable description of the solution which must be delivered. When the project ends, it's relatively easy to compare the solution-as-specified with the solution-as-delivered, and see whether there are any shortfalls.

This is all fine . . . as long as the person writing the specification really understands what the problem is, and is actually capable of specifying a package which will solve the problem. If so, everybody's happy.

However . . . as others have pointed out, the solution is often specified well before the problem is really understood, or by people who aren't as aware of the problem as they should be. The net result is a situation we've seen all too often . . . a solution is delivered, it meets all of the project specifications, and yet proves to be inadequate when actually tested in the field, or to be incompatible with other packages it really should work with, or . . .

Things can get much worse . . . if, for example, the specification is changed part-way through the project. Adding a new requirement or two to the specification can throw the whole implementation effort entirely out of joint . . . leading to schedule slippage, cost overruns, or a patchwork solution that proves to be unmaintainable. All too often, the solution must be thrown away, and a new one developed at great expense . . . often by the same process, alas.

To paraphrase a guy I work with: "Don't hire me as a designer, and then tell me what to implement. If you do, you've just done my job, and you don't need me. Instead, tell me about your problem."

discovered! But in large part, the project's success was attributed to structured programming techniques, as well as to the organization and tools used to achieve it.

KNOWLEDGE CHECK

1. What is software engineering?   p. 345
2. Which two program development steps work hand in hand to define the software project?   p. 346
3. Who is in charge during the early development stages?   p. 346
4. What makes coding different from programming?   p. 348
5. What tasks does a text editor perform?   pp. 346–47
6. What term is used to refer to the problems the debugger reports?   p. 348
7. What are the two types of testing?   p. 349
8. Why is more effort expended on maintenance than on system design?   pp. 350–51
9. What are the two categories of documentation?   p. 351

Traditional Development	Information Engineering
• Emphasis on coding and testing	• Emphasis on analysis and design
• Paper-based specifications	• Computer-based specifications
• Manual coding	• Automatic code generation
• Manual documentation	• Automatic documentation generation
• Often fails to meet user specs	• Joint application development
• Requires debugging	• Automated design verification generates bug-free code
• Constant code maintenance needed	• Code regenerated according to updated design specifications

FIGURE 11.6

Traditional development versus information engineering.

INFORMATION ENGINEERING

Information engineering is a software development methodology developed by Clive Finkelstein, an Australian information systems professional. In 1981, Finkelstein wrote:

> Software engineering is intended primarily for use by analysts and programmers. It was not designed to be applied directly by users (knowledge workers). Communication with knowledge workers comes primarily through the data flow diagram. Information engineering, on the other hand, brings user department personnel, management and data processing (the information systems organization) together in a partnership. Its techniques draw on the experience of all three groups.[1]

Finkelstein, working with James Martin, has refined and perfected this methodology over many years. Information engineering goes beyond the boundaries of a specific methodology. It creates a framework for developing companywide computer systems, automating the entire business and all its processes. In fact, its concentration is on creating systems that serve the business needs and company goals.

Knowledge workers play an integral role in information engineering; indeed, systems cannot be designed or created without their participation. And information engineering uses the latest software tools and techniques to design and create systems; the idea is to do quality work, but to do it quickly, so that the system can be put to work.

In almost all respects, information engineering is superior to traditional development techniques. By way of comparison, refer to the chart in Figure 11.6.

INFORMATION ENGINEERING DEVELOPMENT

There are four components or steps in an information engineering project. Everyone, from senior management to knowledge workers to information systems professionals, participates. The four steps are quite simple:

- *Information strategy planning,* in which top management reviews the enterprise goals and establishes information needs to support those goals.

---

[1] Clive Finkelstein, "Information Engineering," *Computerworld,* June 15, 1981.

- *Business area analysis,* which models the enterprise's activities and data with respect to the prior planning.

- *System design,* the actual specifications and attributes of the application, which are presented in a manner that is understandable to both senior management and knowledge workers. This design is periodically reviewed and updated.

- *Implementation,* where data and activities are integrated with the enterprise-wide plan, to accomplish business goals. The business now can react more quickly and effectively to changing conditions. Management understands the enterprise and the strategic uses of technology better. Knowledge workers work more productively, resolve problems faster, and produce both short-term and long-term returns.

INFORMATION ENGINEERING APPROACHES

There is no single way to use information engineering; rather, as mentioned, it is a new way of thinking about system development. Some of the techniques or methodologies and the development tools used may be "home grown," developed within a business as its own approach or for a single project. Others are developed by a consultant, a software company, or a software developer. Here are a few examples:

- *Application development without programmers:* Knowledge workers use languages or development tools that do not require extensive training to create their own application.

- *Joint application development (JAD):* A team of information systems professionals and knowledge workers is assembled on a one-time basis to work intensively on a single project.

- *Prototyping:* A partially working model of the system is quickly put together to show the knowledge worker how it will perform. If it seems appropriate, the working system is built with the knowledge worker's participation.

- *CASE projects:* A team of information systems professionals who have demonstrated an interest in using computer-aided software engineering (CASE) tools work together to complete a system project.

PROTOTYPING

Prototyping warrants more attention, since it can be used in just about any application development environment, regardless of the methodology used —whether structured design or information engineering. This is due to the fact that prototyping is done early in the process. Prototyping involves both knowledge workers who will use the system and the application programmers or developers. Its main functions are:

- It simulates the important interfaces between the system and knowledge worker.

- It performs all the major functions.

- It can be built quickly.

However, a prototype has limitations. It may not perform on a par with the actual system or be able to access all the databases. It may not respond

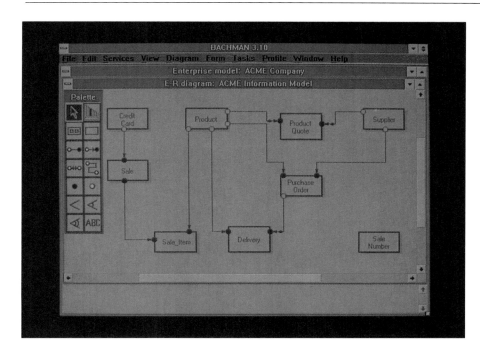

FIGURE 11.7

Prototyping. An entity-relationship diagram provides a graphic representation of a whole data model for a particular company, and shows the relationships between each of the entities. This prototyping tool enables data and business analysts to model their information systems quickly and effectively.

correctly to all the situations encountered when the actual application is in use. It is like a designer's model of an auto; it has form and some function, but it can't be driven. Early prototyping tools created a prototype and nothing more; once the knowledge workers liked it, the developers had to begin again from scratch using development tools. However, that is no longer the case. The prototype is the model upon which the real system is built, and almost always evolves into the final system. In doing so, prototyping speeds the development process.

Prototyping is usually accomplished with a prototyping software development tool. This program may be a stand-alone software product or part of an integrated CASE product. Figure 11.7 shows a working screen of a prototyping tool.

Yet another methodology is rapid application development, our next topic.

RAPID APPLICATION DEVELOPMENT

Rapid application development (RAD) is an information engineering technique promoted by James Martin. He defines RAD as a development life cycle designed to take maximum advantage of the integrated CASE (I-CASE) tools you learned about in Chapter 10. The goal is to produce systems of high quality, at high speed, at low cost. While better/faster/cheaper has certainly always been the ultimate goal of computing, Martin appends this goal by saying, "A top criteria for IS must be that it never interferes with business's ability to seize a competitive opportunity. Speed is essential."

In the traditional development approach, the knowledge worker is commonly involved in the process at the outset, prior to design, but then not again until the application reaches testing. In the RAD life cycle, the knowledge worker is involved during the entire process; only during actual construction does that involvement diminish at all.

The RAD life cycle is based on four foundations: the information engineering methodology; high-quality software engineering tools; using the most highly skilled people; and strong management support and involvement. RAD also presumes a departure from what James Martin calls the "classical development life cycle," in which applications are built "by hand" using paper schematics and line-by-line coding.

RAD CASE STUDY: IMPERIAL OIL

Imperial Oil, Ltd., of Canada is a $5 billion petroleum refiner and marketer with headquarters in Toronto. In 1986, at a time when the oil business was recovering from its worldwide slump, Imperial's information systems organization decided it must deliver better services in a shorter period of time to the various business divisions. It had tentatively settled on a methodology, but upon closer examination realized it could never manually implement a rigid methodology in a company the size of Imperial and be sure knowledge workers would conform to its design criteria. In addition, it had begun developing an architecture that utilized PC-based tools, but soon realized it really needed a mainframe-based, shared-data environment.

Imperial's Esso Petroleum Canada division employed the services of James Martin Associates to develop a mission-critical system for retail sales reporting and cash management for its retail outlets. The system also was to include a management reporting system for these two functions. The firm used the information engineering methodology with the rapid application development techniques, employing the Texas Instruments Integrated Engineering Facility (IEF) I-CASE development environment.

The system was designed to accomplish four goals. The first was to develop an application that processed transactions at the retail outlet, and then gathered that data from the outlet's point-of-sale (POS) terminal and stored it. Second was a management and control system that balanced the books, provided a quality assurance component, and then returned data results to the retail outlets for review. Third was a management and control system that put this data into a shared database. Fourth was a series of applications to extract and report on the data in the database. Since the firm was building a new system within a suite of systems, it used JMA's information engineering techniques to design the bridges between old and new.

There was a great deal of planning, communicating, and decision making before the project began. Moreover, Imperial felt it was essential that everyone on the development team — both the information systems professionals and the knowledge workers who would be using and managing the system — thoroughly grasp the business aspects of the system they were building. Everyone had to understand what they were working on and why they were working on it: delivering the system would mean giving the company a strong competitive advantage.

For example, since certain areas identified in the business area analysis for automating were considered a business priority, they were discussed with analysts who understood the current systems, as well as with employees in the

TOMORROW
THE SECRET LIFE OF SOFTWARE

The New York Times (February 28, 1990) published a story by John Markoff entitled "A Darwinian Creation of Software." It concerned *artificial life,* programs that are felt to be alive and "that can actually evolve into more powerful programs through their own interaction and merging to create a new generation—a Darwinian process similar to that of biological organisms." Artificial life techniques do indeed rival the process of living organisms. Basic rules are created, which then produce interactive software modules, which in turn build into more complex programs.

In its first attempt, Thinking Machines, Inc., used artificial life techniques to create a program that sorts a list of numbers that rivals the best programming of humans. The program creates thousands of parallel chains, each with an assigned list of numbers, that constantly com-bine and recombine instructions. The program sorts them; according to the instructions, the lists of numbers are sorted and the "best" numbers pulled out and passed to the next chain. There is a constant process of sorting and weeding out the undesirable numbers—much as an organism attempts to divest itself of germs or undesirable influences. When combined with a powerful parallel processing computer, like the Connection Machine with its 64,000 processors, a sorting program of this sort has enormous potential to solve problems that can be represented mathematically.

> Through the computerized equivalent of the survival of the fittest, a computer runs thousands of programs simultaneously and a specially tailored master program selects those that most efficiently accomplish a given task. The programs that do well are then com-bined to produce a next generation that is even better in accomplishing the task. Such evolution could produce software more reliable than that designed by human programmers, who cannot anticipate all the potential ways in which their software can fail.

Biologist Charles Taylor and computer scientist David Jefferson have teamed up at UCLA to create an artificial life technique simulation program for mosquito abatement. It determines the most effective places to apply insecticides, and has reduced the number of treatment sites from 20,000 to 3,000. In addition, Borland International is using the technique in its Reflex and Paradox DBMS software as well as in Quattro (its spreadsheet) to "teach" the software how to run faster within the memory limitations of the personal computer with which it is being used.

retail operations who used the data. In this way they were able to see how the new system would work with existing systems and what obstacles might stand in their way.

The system was deployed in three stages. In phase I, the business area analysis was done and a working prototype was developed in under 120 days. In phase II, business system design and technical design occurred simultaneously and took 150 days. Phase III was completion, testing, and moving to production and took 70 days. When finished, the system consisted of 500,000 lines of COBOL II, 45 user procedures, and 19 screens.

Development team issues were very important at Imperial. The project team consisted of three subteams, each with a group leader reporting to the project manager. Team members were information systems professionals and

01001011011
00101110010
100101011010
01010001001
10001101011
01010001001
10011000101
1000100101

CAREERS FOR KNOWLEDGE WORKERS
GEORGE BORHEGYI, PROJECT MANAGER,
CAMBRIDGE TECHNOLOGY PARTNERS

George Borhegyi considers himself a professional—and every aspect of his demeanor, from his impeccable dress to his telephone manners, exhibits his professionalism. George is rightly proud of his position as associate director and project manager at Cambridge Technology Partners, an information integration firm. CT Partners uses state-of-the-art system development techniques to design and quickly build strategic applications for its clients, and George is often in charge of such projects.

George began his career with CT Partners in 1987, shortly after graduating from the Massachusetts Institute of Technology with a degree in electrical engineering. "I wasn't what you'd say a 'technical' person," George says. "I've always been attracted to technology, but I never had a home computer. But in my studies, I always liked business, psychology, *and* technology. My work involves all three."

And he had to use all three right from the start. His first assignment was as a teaching assistant, helping business executives and salespeople learn how to use computer systems. He also took part in demonstrations of the company's strengths in quickly developing systems. He worked with knowledge workers and systems people, writing code and creating the user interfaces, to make the prototype work.

The first systems development project George was placed in charge of was for Royal Carib-

knowledge workers from the comptroller's office and retail departments. No one had any prior IEF experience; some, in fact, had never worked on a project before. One team worked on changes to the point-of-sale units, another on constructing the on-line transaction processing system and databases, and the third on connections to and from those databases to the corporate database. Imperial learned that not all people come to a project such as this with all the right skills. Some needed training in tools other than CASE, and training was delivered along with the project.

This project taught the people at Imperial several important things. First, they found they did not have to analyze the business excessively for the system to produce results. Second, they found that CASE tools are a means to an end, not an end themselves, and must be used under proper project management to

bean Cruises. The system was designed to provide a direct communication link between Royal Caribbean and the worldwide travel agents who booked tours for their customers. The agents wanted the ability to quickly book and confirm cruise reservations, and Royal Caribbean wanted to provide the best service possible to maintain the strong relationship they enjoyed with their agents. So George and his CT Partners staff built a system called CruiseFax. After entering the reservation on a computer terminal, Royal Caribbean's computer system prepared a confirmation that was immediately FAXed to the travel agent and handed to the customer. This immediate reply made customers happy — because their fare and stateroom reservations were confirmed — and helped the travel agent close the sale.

CT Partners put in the CruiseFax system in just 14 weeks. The project could have taken 6 to 8 months using traditional system development techniques. One travel agent was so happy with it that his agency is doing 33 percent more business with Royal Caribbean. Today over 4,000 travel agencies have access to CruiseFax.

George is proud of the system. "It's simple, and it gives the customer the kind of information they need when they need it. That should be a primary characteristic of any computer system. I find that more and more of our work is developing systems for customer service applications." Indeed, CT Partners sees project development as synonymous with customer support, and divides its work into seven practice areas: consulting, on-site demonstrations, rapid prototyping, design, development (systems integration), and customer support and empowerment. This means that the CT Partners team works with the client in each of these practice areas during a project.

George has worked in all these areas, and as his knowledge and skills have grown, he has been given different roles and more responsibilities. Currently he is working primarily in consulting. "I'm often called in to help explain our work when the salespeople are talking to potential customers. I can discuss our work in the business terms that executives understand. That's customer service too, because it's 'empowering the users,' to use a CT Partners phrase. When users or knowledge workers are empowered, they are then able to use, maintain, and enhance the computer system by themselves. Our ongoing goal is to help them become self-sufficient and more productive. That's what I like to see."

produce results. Third, a project's success is based in large part on having responsive, enthusiastic, hungry knowledge workers who want the system.

WHERE ARE WE GOING?

There is little doubt that software development tools and techniques are in a high state of evolution and change. Since the early 1980s, traditional programming languages such as COBOL, which has been in existence since the 1950s, have been challenged by newer, more powerful languages such as C++, Turbo Pascal, and Smalltalk. The "old tried-and-true" system development methodology, which was for many years known simply and generically as "system analysis and design," has given way to many new development techniques. And knowledge workers play a much more active and important role in development today.

Most human beings are somewhat resistant to change. This becomes more prevalent as we grow older or more accustomed to using the knowledge, skills, and tools we are familiar with. Information systems professionals are no different; their reluctance to embrace new software development tools and techniques, while quite understandable, has led to a riot in the hallways. Many have come forward with new, powerful, fast, inexpensive solutions to lingering problems, such as the applications backlog. Martin says the average information systems organization has at least five years' worth of development projects waiting to be completed.

Knowledge workers simply can't wait that long for their applications. They must take a more active role in design and, indeed, development. The result is getting applications that are more appropriate to their needs, and getting them sooner. As business sees the dramatically improved, easier-to-use, and more quickly developed systems and applications that these new tools and techniques produce, the end result will be higher productivity and a more competitive role in the marketplace.

SOFTWARE ENGINEERING ETHICS: WORKING IN DEVELOPMENT TEAMS

William James, the great 19th-century philosopher and psychologist, wrote that "an act has no ethical quality whatever unless it is chosen out of several equally possible." Choosing the proper ethical course to take when working in a development team or group is complex, because there are many people with often differing goals, priorities, needs, and agendas. That is why there is often a senior management *sponsor* for a team who does not actually work within the group, but who is available to make team decisions and resolve issues and disputes.

J. Daniel Couger of the University of Colorado at Colorado Springs has long been considered an authority on programmer motivation and training. He has identified the following mix of factors that enhance programmer motivation and productivity:

- *Skill variety:* The different activities necessary.
- *Task identity:* Completion from beginning to end.
- *Task significance:* The job's final outcome or effect.
- *Autonomy:* Freedom, independence, and discretion.

- *Feedback:* Clear communication about performance.

All five, in the correct amounts, will produce meaningfulness, responsibility, and knowledge of results, says Dr. Couger. The result is more satisfied programmers, lower turnover, and higher-quality programming.

These same factors can apply to development teams, where programmers work with knowledge workers. And when working in a mixed group such as this, conflicts occur less frequently when the atmosphere is open and free of the usual corporate bureaucracy. According to Gerald M. Weinberg, an internationally recognized software consultant, many development projects get into trouble, not because of technological issues, but due to people problems such as "status walls" and "boundary problems."

In all development projects, individuals must be called upon to set aside their individual agendas and focus on the good of the company. This is ethical behavior of the highest order, because as William James points out, it is *chosen* behavior.

SUMMARY

1. *Identify the steps in the traditional system development life cycle.* The steps include analysis, design, coding, debugging, testing and acceptance, maintenance, and documentation.

2. *Describe software engineering and how it is used.* Software engineering is the design, development, and implementation of production software systems on large-scale business computers. It covers all aspects of system development, including people, programming, management, and project details.

3. *Explain the structured techniques used in software development.* Structured techniques include structured analysis to chart the system and structured design, or the top-down approach.

4. *Explain the information engineering development process.* Information engineering stresses the need for knowledge workers to work in partnership with management and the information systems professionals. There are four steps: information strategy planning, business area analysis, system design, and implementation.

5. *Describe some information engineering approaches.* Approaches include application development without programmers, joint application development, prototyping, and CASE projects.

6. *Describe the rapid application development life cycle.* The RAD life cycle includes the information engineering methodology, high-quality software engineering tools, highly skilled people, and strong management support and involvement.

ISSUES IN SOFTWARE ENGINEERING

1. Richard Stallman, a programmer at MIT's Artificial Intelligence Laboratory, fights for free software. He doesn't believe software should be copyrighted, licensed, owned, or sold. As head of the Free Software Foundation, Stallman believes that software publishers' competition and greed are bad for consumers.

   He explains it this way. The publisher's programmers write the source code, but it is protected so that the user—or person who buys the program—can't tap into it. Therefore, only the publisher can revise, improve, or modify a program, and users cannot adapt it to their own particular needs or purposes—nor can they fix bugs. They have to wait until a revision is offered—for sale.

   Stallman embodies the thinking and ethos of the early hackers: free software that is shared, with each programmer adding value as the program is passed along. Stallman, a brilliant programmer, creates very similar duplicates of existing software and then distributes from his computer with what he calls a "copyleft" (the opposite of copyright), so that each user must distribute it to someone else for the cost of duplicating it.

   Do you agree or disagree with Stallman's position? Form two opposing groups and debate the issue of "free software."

2. Programmers and systems analysts often complain that they "don't get no respect," as Rodney Dangerfield says. Should they be considered "professionals"? One group says yes, because it's long past time for software development to be considered an engineering discipline, and for software developers to consider themselves engineers. Nurses, physicians, pilots, civil engineers, and even hair stylists are all licensed. Wouldn't you want the electronic instrument that monitors your heart or checks blood for AIDS or tells the pilot whether the landing gear is down to be built by licensed or certified professionals?

   The opposing group says no, that not everyone who graduates with a B.S. in engineering and who is employed at a company to work on engineering projects needs to become a Licensed Professional Engineer. The same should be true with software engineering. Whose side are you on?

3. You are working with an information engineering development team, and you're all taking a

coffee break. You overhear one of the programmers say he sold the module he recently created for the project to a third-party developer the night before. The programmer he's speaking to asks what the developer plans to do with it; the first programmer replies that he does not know, but he sure got paid well for it.

Has something illegal or unethical occurred here? Is the module the programmer created his own possession? Or, since it was created on company time for company purposes, does your employer own it? What should you do?

CHAPTER REVIEW QUESTIONS

REVIEW QUESTIONS

1. Toward what type of systems is software engineering oriented?
2. List the steps in the system development life cycle.
3. What parallels can you draw between designing and creating a software system and other endeavors?
4. How do debuggers assist programmers?

5. What is the difference between software documentation and user documentation?
6. What is the difference between user and reference documentation?
7. Describe the four steps in information engineering.

DISCUSSION QUESTIONS

1. Discuss the difference between software engineering and information engineering.
2. Why is it so important to have knowledge workers involved in the software engineering process?
3. Discuss some of the reasons for business's desire to develop systems more quickly and efficiently, and the results that accrue.

4. Discuss the role of prototyping and why it is important today.
5. Compare and contrast the traditional life cycle and the RAD life cycle.
6. How would you prioritize development team trust and mutual concern over ethical issues?

MULTIPLE-CHOICE

1. Software engineering includes the following types of people (choose all that apply):
   a. Programmers.
   b. Knowledge workers.
   c. Management.
   d. Systems analysts.
   e. All of the above.
2. More time and money is spent on which of the following than any other development activity?
   a. Debugging.
   b. Production.
   c. Maintenance.
   d. Meetings.

3. Some key differences in information engineering over traditional development are (choose all that apply):
   a. Less paper-based work is involved.
   b. There are fewer bugs.
   c. Knowledge workers don't need to participate.
   d. State-of-the-art tools and techniques are used.
   e. Programmers must work harder to accomplish the same objectives.
4. The following software tool is an essential component in RAD and information engineering:
   a. CASE.

b. OOP.

c. Spreadsheet.

d. Text editor.

e. Structured programming.

5. Debugging tools (check all that apply):

   a. Find insects in the hardware.

   b. Identify program errors.

   c. Locate problems as error messages.

   d. Produce error message listings.

   e. All of the above.

6. Information engineering (choose all that apply):

   a. Takes the corporate business strategy into consideration.

   b. Requires the involvement of knowledge workers.

   c. Permits using a wide variety of development techniques.

   d. Requires the use of rapid application development.

   e. All of the above.

Fill-in-the-Blank

1. Another name for system development life cycle is ——————.

2. The system development tool that paved the way for word processing is the ——————.

3. The first structured technique was ——————.

4. Another term for programming is ——————.

5. Improving a completed system for knowledge workers is called ——————.

6. An —————— is a set of step-by-step instructions to solve a problem.

True/False

1. There is no difference whatsoever between coding and programming.

2. If you know structured coding, you know structured design techniques.

3. A system in production means it is just about finished and ready to use.

4. RAD helps companies perform more competitively in the market because it makes their computers run faster.

5. A major difference between RAD and traditional development is that the knowledge worker participates in the entire RAD process.

Key Terms

algorithm, 352

bug, 348

coding, 346

debugger, 349

documentation, 351

hierarchy, 352

information engineering, 355

maintenance, 350

modules, 352

production, 350

rapid application development (RAD), 357

reference documentation, 351

software documentation, 351

software engineering, 345

source code, 346

structured analysis, 352

structured coding, 347

structured design, 352

structured techniques, 352

systems analysis, 346

systems analyst, 346

systems design, 346

system development life cycle, 345

system testing, 349

testing, 349

text editor, 346

user documentation, 351

user testing, 349

CHAPTER 12

Corporate Database Concepts

LEARNING OBJECTIVES

After reading and studying this chapter, you should be able to:

1. Describe the difference between the personal computer database concept and corporate database concepts.

2. Describe the role of the database administrator and the duties performed.

3. Discuss advantages and disadvantages of database management.

4. Describe database tools and how they are used.

5. Describe the different types of corporate databases.

6. Explain how different organizational database systems are used.

What Is a Corporate Database?

It has been predicted that the volume of existing data will double *19 times* in the decade of the 1990s. The sheer enormity of data that large corporations have amassed in the decades previous to this has pushed the data storage capacities from kilobytes to megabytes to terabytes. For quite a while, it was assumed that all this data should be stored in the "corporate database," which was at once a concept expressing intellectual and proprietary ownership, but also a physical location: the mainframe computer. Indeed, IBM developed and refined a database idea for doing this which they called the repository, but new hardware architectures, software concepts, and organizational changes have overshadowed this monolithic database.

In Chapter 6, you learned that a database is a group of related records and files. You also learned that a computerized DBMS is a software application for managing one or more databases. The discussion in that chapter focused on the DBMS as it is used with personal computers; nothing has changed here except that we will be discussing much, much larger database systems. In this chapter you'll learn about databases and DBMSs for all types of computer systems: mainframe, minicomputer, personal computer, and interconnected, or *networked,* computers.

Before proceeding, you might want to review the concept of the file from Chapter 2, and the different types of data representation — character, field, record, file, and database — in Chapter 6. All these concepts apply in this chapter as well. In Chapter 6, you learned about the different types of DBMSs as well: flat file, hierarchical, network, and relational. (The Yesterday feature explains the development of database technology.) In this chapter, the focus is specifically on the relational DBMS, which is most widely used for large, organizational applications in the business world.

The relational database management system was conceived by Dr. Edgar F. "Ted" Codd at IBM in 1969. For many years it was thought to be too theoretical and complex for use in business, but it gradually gained acceptance as computer hardware became powerful enough to process and sort relational data — particularly as the DBMS for personal computers. Recall that in a relational database, all data is viewed as essentially alike; data is interchanged and cross-referenced between different records.

As you know, every application has its commands and instructions; the DBMS is no exception, but the commands and instructions we need to work effectively with it are often more sophisticated and complex. There are two major reasons for this. First, there are so many ways of organizing, evaluating, combining, and viewing the data. Second, we must be able to **navigate,** or move among vantage points, in the DBMS. In business, we commonly navigate among such vantage points as the manufacturing or inventory database,

YESTERDAY

ORIGINS OF THE DATABASE MANAGEMENT SYSTEM

The DBMS was first used in manufacturing operations, to keep track of parts, but one of the earliest commercial database applications was American Airlines' SABRE reservation system, in 1962. While working at General Electric's computer division in the 1960s, Charles Bachman developed a DBMS called IDS (for Integrated Data Store). IDS was a network model DBMS, which in the mainframe world is sometimes referred to as a CODASYL model (named after

the committee that approved its approach). GE left the business by the end of the decade. Then, in 1969, IBM began selling software separately from hardware, which was termed *unbundling*. The same year John Cullinane formed Cullinane Corporation and introduced the first unbundled software program for IBM mainframe computers—IDS, which Cullinane had bought from GE. Cullinane Corp. soon became the most successful unbundled software company in

the industry. Bachman went to work for Cullinane, and in 1973 an improved version, Integrated Database Management System (IDMS), was introduced. It set the standard for database management software around the world. Today over 4,000 organizations worldwide use Cullinet software, which is now a division of Computer Associates, the largest computer software company in the world.

the human resources database, the marketing database, from division to division, and so forth. We also need to dissect, organize, and view data in many different ways. Navigation requires a more advanced set of commands, which are in fact grouped into a database manipulation language. The most common language for this is called *structured query language* (SQL), which you first learned about in Chapter 6 and will learn more about later in this chapter.

KNOWLEDGE CHECK

1. Define the term *corporate database*.   p. 367
2. Name some of the computer systems that use a DBMS.   p. 367
3. Who developed the relational DBMS?   p. 367
4. What is meant by the term *navigate* the databases?   p. 367
5. Name an example of a database manipulation language.   p. 368

THE CORPORATE DATABASE

You know that a computer system is comprised of people, software, and hardware; this is certainly true with respect to database technology. It is a highly advanced area, where information systems professionals — or sometimes knowledge workers — are trained and educated for specific duties; some universities have degrees for specific database information systems jobs. This section explores the people, software, and hardware DBMS concepts; it is followed by the steps or tasks involved in developing and managing a DBMS; then the advantages in using database technology are explained.

MANAGING A CORPORATE DATABASE

It is often best if databases are centrally managed, even if they are primarily used by individual departments. Each department has access to the files it needs, while common data can be shared between various departments. In a corporate system, there is often a *centralized database* with accounting, employee records, and other corporate data. Then there are a number of *decentralized databases,* specific to a department or function; for example, marketing may have its own customer database. All these databases are running under a single DBMS application program, on a single mainframe or minicomputer. Any data that is centralized can be shared with the decentralized databases, so that now everyone in the company sees the single most current file. With a DBMS, sharing data makes it easier for everyone to use the data, and it is more accurate and current. A well-managed database environment can make a major contribution to the company's success and productivity.

But all this doesn't just happen magically when a DBMS is installed. People who understand the company's line of business, its management structure, and its computer systems must install and maintain a complex database environment such as this. For these reasons, two things are key to success: a knowledge worker called a *database administrator* and a special type of software called a *data dictionary.*

THE DATABASE ADMINISTRATOR.

Banks, insurance companies, automobile manufacturers, and most other large companies have corporate databases so large they require the full-time attention of a **database administrator** (DBA). The DBA is responsible for maintaining the DBMS and for ensuring the accuracy and the integrity of its data. The DBA works with department and corporate managers to decide these key aspects of database usage:

- What data should go into the database.
- What relationships should exist between various data items.
- Who has permission to read database information.
- Who has authority to update the database.

For example, if inventory records are kept in the database, the DBA must find out if the manufacturing manager uses these records to make manufacturing plans. The DBA must find out what the inventory manager needs to know to maintain the records, such as part numbers, quantities, and stock levels. The DBA also must determine what the purchasing people need to know, such as the part number, description, company of manufacture, and price. The DBA will use all this information to set up a single inventory database that works for all who need to use it.

THE DATA DICTIONARY.

Managing a corporate database can be a complex job, with many relationships to consider and many people to serve. The work

FIGURE 12.1

A partial list of some common data dictionary terminology. Terms are also defined for the database administrator or others working with the database (as shown by *).

1-to-1_relation	integrated_tool	object-oriented_programming
1-to-n_relation	list	relation
argument_list	logical_object	repository
class	merge	root_partition
data_element	navigator	source_object*
error_stack	null_function	version

* source_object: A system object you can create and from which you can make derived objects.

would be almost impossible without the aid of a data dictionary. The **data dictionary** is a list of all the fields, files, and commands utilized in manipulating the database; it is often referred to as "data about the data." The data dictionary contains such things as file specifications (field size, etc.), different database specifications, or which users receive specific reports. The data dictionary also establishes the rules that govern using the database: data definition rules, database access rules, data usage rules. It is like an instruction list or a repair diagram for the system. The information it contains is essential to the DBA. A portion of a large corporate data dictionary is shown in Figure 12.1.

DATABASE DEVELOPMENT AND MANAGEMENT

The database administrator and the information systems professionals she or he works with are responsible for managing the DBMS and administering to the databases. This is often referred to as **database development.** Management involves planning, organizing, directing, and controlling, and these activities certainly apply in database development. Let's take a closer look at these activities.

DATA PLANNING.   The first management — and database — step is planning. Data planning involves two types of modeling. The first is modeling the business organization to determine what data needs exist. This can become very complex as the DBA and staff determine the **entity,** which is data that has a particular meaning — such as a job title or position. It is also necessary to establish the relationships between entities, or how different kinds of data interact with each other. For example, an employee is an entity; many facts or attributes about that employee exist in databases. Payroll needs to know how many income tax deductions a worker takes, which is usually the number of family dependents. Human resources needs the same information, but in more detail, for the employee's health insurance plan. That data forms an entity, and a relationship exists between the two databases concerning it.

The second type of data planning is modeling the data within the DBMS, where the different entities or data elements are defined. Some examples include the manner in which names are entered (last name first, then first name and initial), whether a customer can have only one account, or whether several members of a family each have separate accounts. All this information is used in the physical design of the database, which you learned about in Chapter 6.

DATA ORGANIZATION. Organizing data is similar to most other management organizing tasks. Databases are in a constant state of change, as data is added, deleted, modified, and shifted around. Therefore, it is important that the database design must be organized to reflect this constant change. Since the DBMS takes over managing disk space, access must be simple, easy, and fast. There are two commonly used methods of organizing data in databases:

- *Sequential organization,* where changes must be sorted and organized into proper sequence for updating the database. It is used primarily when accumulated data is processed periodically, such as once a week; it is slow.
- *Direct organization,* or random organization, where the DBMS keeps track of where data is supposed to go without sorting. *Key transformation* uses an arithmetic computation to conduct the transaction. *Indexed sequential access method* (ISAM) uses a key for each file that makes it easier to find; it is similar to the thumb index in a dictionary. It is fast and even though sequential, ISAM only processes transactions that need to be processed.

DATA PROCESSING. Data processing is the third management activity, directing. As you may have guessed, once the planning is accomplished, the processing takes place in accordance with the plan. Database processing on larger computer systems is somewhat different than what you may be accustomed to with a personal computer. A PC application transaction is processed almost immediately; in most cases, we issue the data processing order by pressing the Enter key. On older, larger systems, the CPU may be busy with hundreds of applications and may not be able to perform a task right away. So with these systems, the databases might only be updated once a day or several times a week, which is termed *batch processing.* Batch processing is best suited to tasks where there are hundreds, thousands, even hundreds of thousands of transactions to perform. It used to be the only type of processing; today there are others, but batch processing is still used for repetitive or non-time critical applications such as payroll.

More common is **on-line processing,** which processes transactions as they occur and updates the database in a steady stream. When you withdraw money from an automated teller machine (ATM), in most cases on-line processing subtracts the amount from your account balance as the transaction is completed.

When the application is time critical, **on-line transaction processing** (OLTP) is used; the entire transaction is completed as soon as it is entered. A common example is airline flight reservations and seat assignments. OLTP is more expensive, since it consumes more system resources. But wherever time is money, OLTP is becoming more commonplace.

DATA SECURITY. Data security is the equivalent of the fourth management task, control. The DBA is responsible for all access to the databases and for ensuring data integrity at all times. That means each knowledge worker must be given an unique password to use when he or she enters the database, along with a security-level clearance relative to the person's needs and skills. For example, some knowledge workers may only *view* data; others may copy data from the database, manipulate and change it, and then pass it back to the database to update files. Still others may enter any and all portions of the database and change data, or even database organization, at will. If we accept the fact that the corporate database contains invaluable information, we must acknowledge the need for security measures.

DATABASE ADVANTAGES AND DISADVANTAGES

There are many ways in which the DBMS is a superior way to store and organize data. These include:

- Data from many different sources can be stored and accessed from a common format. Different application programs are not needed for payroll, human resources, marketing, manufacturing, and so on. A single DBMS works for all.
- Data need be stored only once, not in a number of different applications. All data is accessible using the single DBMS.
- Program and data are independent of one another, so the DBMS application can be replaced with a more modern, useful version that can still access the data. DBMS programs are used for long periods, but business and organizational changes often demand their being upgraded. In the past, a database **conversion** project—changing from one DBMS program to another—was grueling work. Today the data can be left intact while the application is changed.
- Data integrity is assured by software design and security measures. The accuracy and integrity of the data are extremely important. In addition, unauthorized access, modification, and even destruction of data must be guarded against. Most larger companies have a **disaster recovery** plan or program that goes into effect in case of fire, flood, or loss of electrical or telecommunications services.

However, there can be disadvantages, such as:

- Hardware costs, specifically for intensive CPU processing activity and high-capacity auxiliary storage devices. Mainframe computers continue to be used for DBMS applications because of their vast processing power. Storage devices are expensive, and often more of these multiple disk drives are added rather than go through the tedious process of removing outdated or unnecessary data.
- Training in complicated, sophisticated DBMSs is costly and time-consuming. Information systems professionals often must attend training courses on a regular basis to keep up with database technology advances.
- Portability across hardware platforms, both in terms of the DBMS running on various mainframes, minis, and PCs, and in terms of accessing the DBMS from another computer. Today's knowledge workers don't care where the data physically resides. It may be on the mainframe or their own desktop computer; all they should have to know is the commands to work with it, rather than the commands to move from one hardware platform to another in search of it.

Most businesses realize they could not function without a corporate DBMS, and appreciate the advantages while taking the disadvantages in stride. And, in recent years, several DBMS software companies have made their DBMSs available on a wide range of computers, making portability less of an issue. Indeed, the relationship between hardware platforms is changing, as we shall see in the next section.

KNOWLEDGE CHECK

1. Describe the difference between a centralized and decentralized database. p. 369
2. What are several of the DBA's most important responsibilities? p. 369
3. Why do we need a data dictionary? p. 370
4. What is the management aspect of data planning? p. 370
5. What is the management aspect of data organization? p. 371
6. What is the management aspect of data processing? p. 371
7. What is the management aspect of data security? pp. 371–72

CORPORATE DBMS TOOLS

In the past, the computer staff was responsible for creating all new knowledge worker applications. However, as more and more employees began using computers, the demand for applications outstripped the information systems organization's ability to supply them. Today there are tools that allow knowledge workers to work flexibly with a database. This type of software tool is called a **front end,** and it performs a variety of tasks ranging from simple access to data to analysis to creating custom databases and database applications. A **database application** is a program designed to extract and organize specific data and then present it on the computer screen and in printed reports. It could be something as simple as a list of employees and the number of days they were absent due to illness, or as complex as an analysis of the fat, carbohydrates, and protein in a food product.

Front end tools are versatile; many are designed to be used as a mainframe or minicomputer application, accessible by the knowledge worker from a terminal. Others were designed to be used as a personal computer application and are often more versatile and powerful. They are more versatile because they can access many different types of databases and more powerful because they take advantage of the PC's processing power and storage capabilities. Here are some representative front end tools.

THE SPREADSHEET TOOL

Interestingly, a regular spreadsheet program, running on a PC, can act as a front end. For example, Lotus 1-2-3 can be used to perform a basic database **query,** which extracts data from the database and presents it in a usable format (the spreadsheet grid). The spreadsheet can be used to create or delete tables, or to add, update, or delete data in a database.

The Analysis Tool

Sometimes it can be difficult to review vast quantities of the data from a database, attempting to find precisely what you want. Here is where an analysis tool, such as Forest & Trees, is used. It is a good example of a more powerful PC-based tool, because it can combine data from not only a number of databases, but from spreadsheets as well. It lets the knowledge worker define what is important, and then it builds the tools to find and organize that data for you. Data results can be presented in text or graphical form. Figure 12.2 shows a typical screen created with an analysis tool.

The Fourth-Generation Language Tool

Another tool that allows knowledge workers to create their own applications is the fourth-generation language. A **fourth-generation language** (4GL) is a database front end tool that uses English-like phrases and sentences to issue instructions. Since it is built into the DBMS program and designed specifically to work with that particular DBMS, it is often called a 4GL/DBMS. The 4GL runs on either a terminal or a PC, and lets users express what they want the system to accomplish, rather than having to issue detailed instructions as to how to do it. They make programming easier by bringing the language syntax even closer to our own English. They also make programming easier by using menus and question-and-answer sequences to create instructions instead of strings of programming language procedures. The 4GL's features include:

- *The emphasis is on end results.* You specify the problem you want to solve rather than the means of arriving at a solution. Sophisticated underlying software does the rest.

FIGURE 12.2

Forest & Trees enables the knowledge worker to use a report format to define and create a custom analysis. This one shows sales revenue using both spreadsheet and database information.

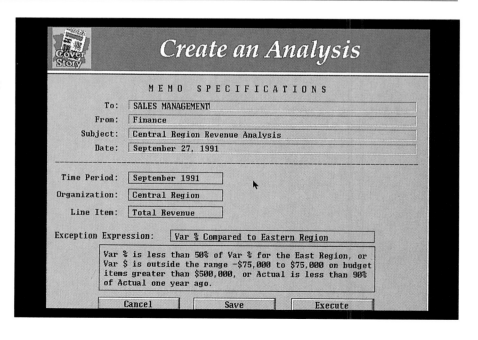

- *Limited training is required.* 4GLs don't require that you learn a traditional high-level programming language. Sometimes you have to know what certain terms or symbols mean, but you won't spend weeks learning a language and its syntax, as with COBOL or even BASIC.

- *Interactive dialogue replaces writing source code files.* With 4GLs, you simply type your request, such as "SHOW RESULTS OF MARKETING PROMOTION." Instead of writing programs, you interact directly with the computer by typing English-like phrases or by selecting symbols or menu choices.

- *Knowledge worker productivity increases.* 4GLs provide an even greater ability to perform instructions than high-level languages. Shorter statements and fewer total hours spent programming produce more results.

- *Memory requirements increase.* It's not all rosy. 4GLs do cost something — they require about 75 percent more memory than high-level languages.

Figure 12.3 shows a typical screen created with a 4GL.

Users often create their own applications using a 4GL/DBMS. One interesting instance took place at a company that produces frozen dinners. Government regulations and the company's own requirements for nutrition and calorie counts led to a need for monthly quality control reports. The company's chief chemist wanted to take sample dinners, analyze them, and determine if they were meeting quality standards. If the dinner didn't pass inspection, she wanted to know what was wrong, what plant produced the dinner, and on what day.

The chemist went to the MIS department and asked if it could create this application, which was basically analyzing data from the corporate database. She was told MIS had an enormous application development backlog and

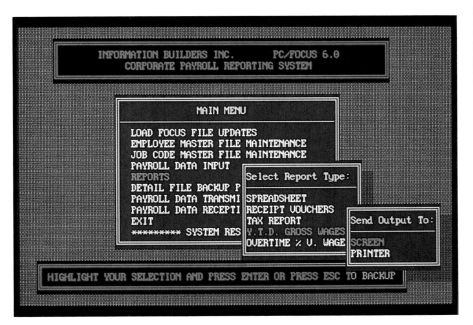

FIGURE 12.3

It's easier to define and create reports with a 4GL tool like PC/Focus because you don't have to write complex codes or detailed instructions.

could not get to the task for several years. She began exploring alternatives and learned about a 4GL/DBMS called NOMAD2. Although she was not a computer expert, she decided to give it a try. Within two weeks she had her application up and running, without any help from the MIS department. All the chemists in the department learned NOMAD2 and it is used constantly. It is a time saver too; the caloric content of a glazed chicken used to take over an hour to analyze manually. Now it only takes one or two minutes.

THE APPLICATION GENERATOR TOOL

Another type of 4GL is called an *application generator*. It is most commonly used by the information systems professionals in companies where large mainframe computers are used to manage a huge corporate database. Application generators often run on desktop PCs or workstations. They are standalone software programs that create applications which, in turn, interact with the DBMS. Some are created for use specifically with a particular vendor's DBMS, such as Ingres, Oracle, or Sybase. Others are designed to create specific types of applications, such as the client/server computing we shall study shortly. Figure 12.4 shows a typical screen created with an application generator.

THE QUERY LANGUAGE TOOL

Query languages simplify searching computer memory for information. Query languages are good examples of business-oriented 4GLs. They let knowledge workers program computers without having to learn a conventional programming language. They give access to computer data without having to execute COBOL or FORTRAN source code. Query languages run

FIGURE 12.4

Knowledge workers are able to better understand data when it is presented in its true context. This sophisticated database interface, developed with several application generation tools, displays textual information about autos with the corresponding graphic image.

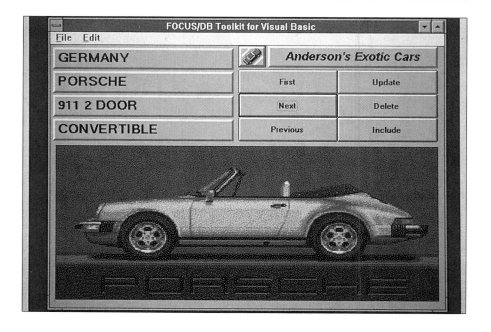

on both large systems and PCs, and produce excellent information. For example, if everyone in the company got a 6 percent raise, the query language could update all payroll files at once.

SQL, which stands for *structured query language,* is the standard query language for relational database management systems, for everything from the IBM mainframe to the Digital VAX to the PC to the Macintosh. SQL originated at IBM in the early 1970s, in a project called Structured English Query Language. And although IS professionals use it too, knowledge workers can use SQL to:

- Formulate interactive (immediate response) queries for the database in English-like phrases.
- Issue commands or instructions to the DBMS that would have required programming or assistance from the information systems staff.
- Manipulate and extract data from databases.
- Control user access or secure the data in the DBMS.

SQL may be a separate, standalone software product, or it may be built into a DBMS program. Its versatility has made it an extremely useful and popular front end. Figure 12.5 shows a typical SQL query. We'll see how SQL was used in an interesting case study in the next section.

It is important to remember that there are many definitions and interpretations of database front end tools, and there is bound to be some overlap among them. One tool may perform several of the tasks described here. In fact, SQL is gradually taking over most, if not all, the tasks each of these different tools has performed in the past. One day, perhaps one front end tool will do everything. That's good; it's a dynamic, growing field, and it is the knowledge worker who reaps the benefits.

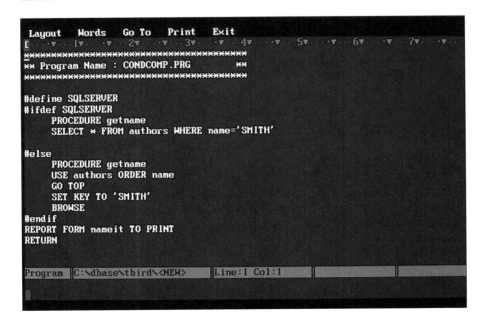

FIGURE 12.5

SQL is built into this DBMS program. Here it is being used to query the database for a report on authors named Smith.

KNOWLEDGE CHECK

1. Name some of the software tools used to work with corporate databases.   p. 373
2. Describe a database application.   p. 373
3. What is the simplest query tool that is also an application itself?   p. 373
4. For what tasks is the analysis tool useful?   p. 374
5. Explain several features of the 4GL/DBMS tool.   pp. 374–75
6. When is an application generator commonly used?   p. 376
7. What does SQL stand for?   p. 377
8. Describe several features of the SQL tool.   p. 377

TYPES OF CORPORATE DATABASES

DBMS programs and data are stored on auxiliary storage devices, most commonly magnetic media, and preferably on hard disk drives. However, the CD-ROM disc and its drive are in common use today. The CD-ROM is a convenient medium for many types of databases where the data doesn't change — literature, encyclopedias, books, magazines, newspapers, and other formerly published works, and many forms of statistical or informational research, as in engineering, law, and medicine.

For a long time, the only kind of information stored in databases was data: facts about people, places, and things. Today it's far more common to find all kinds of information in databases: data, text, images, and even sound. Let's take a closer look.

THE DATA DATABASE

Database data is just that: data. If it concerns an employee, a record is made up of the following data:

```
Last Name: Lawton
First Name: Shayne
Date of Birth: 10/12/69
Social Security No: 602-44-6962
Occupation: Sales Manager
Marital Status: Married
```

and so forth. The data is factual, and can be organized and tabulated in various ways. This is the oldest and most common type of database.

THE TEXT DATABASE

The text database contains documents, which you learned about in Chapter 1. Documents (text) provide richness and detail that are not found in the just-the-facts data database. For example, data about the employee might read:

```
Shayne Lawton was born in Park City, Utah, on October 12,
1969. He graduated Dartmouth College with a Bachelor's
```

FIGURE 12.6
Once they are logged in with
an ID number, residents of
Ocean Park, California, can
access the Public Electronic
Network Computer System, a
vast text database, through
their local public library.

```
degree in business administration, and a minor in applied
information systems. He joined the Onyx Corporation that
same year as a sales representative, but was promoted to
sales manager for the Northeast region six months later.
```

Text databases can hold many different types of corporate documents, from a personal resume like the preceding to memos, letters, reports, and other important text-based information. Text databases are emerging as an equally useful and valuable information resource in business and government. Figure 12.6 shows a text database in use in a college library.

THE IMAGE DATABASE

Early personal computer image databases were collections of noncopyrighted drawings and graphics, called *clip art*. Today, database-stored images include drawings, art, and photographs and have much wider application. Now we can add Shayne Lawton's photo to his personnel file. The insurance industry was quick to recognize the value of adding images to data in its claims adjustment. A field claims adjuster, investigating an auto accident, could write a report and include photographs, which would be scanned into the computer and stored in the database, along with the file report.

Today image databases abound. One growth area is the **geographic information system** (GIS), which combines computer graphics-generated maps and cartography with relevant data in a database. Geographic information systems are widely used in urban planning and by government agencies for

FIGURE 12.7

Where do you want to go?
This image database program
for your PC contains a database of over 350,000 miles of
roads and 52,000 cities and
towns. On-screen maps help
you plan your route and provide pertinent information on
cities and towns; then the
program prints the directions
and a detailed itinerary.

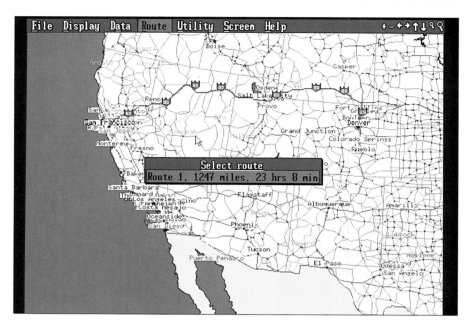

land use management. One of the most widely used is the U.S. Census Bureau's TIGER geographic database. More recently, GISs have made their way
to personal computers and even automobiles, for trip planning. Figure 12.7
shows a personal computer GIS.

The Multimedia Database

The multimedia database brings together all these databases — data, text, and
image — and combines them with sound and even full-motion video. Now we
can see Shayne Lawton walk and hear him talk. Each different type of information is commonly presented in its own window on the screen, which can be
moved or resized. Multimedia makes it possible to view and work with different types of information in their natural state, or *native mode*, in exactly the
way people are used to. At some point soon in your career as a knowledge
worker, you will be able to work with a multimedia computer system.

Organizational Database Systems

Database management systems of all types are used in business organizations
every day; that's nothing new. What is new is the growing need to obtain data
or information from diverse databases throughout the company. It often isn't
enough just to see data on your product's market share; it's much more
meaningful when compared to the norm of competing products, regional
markets, other products from the company, and so forth.

Some database systems are centralized and serve the entire company, while
others are either decentralized or distributed to individual divisions or departments. You'll recall that decentralized means the DBMS and databases are

TODAY

MULTIMEDIA: INFORMATION AT YOUR FINGERTIPS

Bill Gates, chairman and chief executive officer of Microsoft, gave the keynote speech at the Fall 1990 Comdex trade show. Gates presented his vision of the 1990s, which he calls the "PC decade." PCs should enable people to use them in the broadest ways possible; Gates calls this "information at your fingertips." To bring the demonstration to life, it was integrated with a film that portrayed a problem at a coffee bean importer, a small company in a highly competitive market.

A product manager arrives at work in the morning, goes to her multimedia PC, and points and clicks on the electronic mail icon. A window displays a list of messages; she clicks on the newest one, which happens to be a voice mail message embedded in a compound document. A manager informs her that a fire has destroyed one of their produc-

tion facilities; she clicks an icon for a news story and sees he has included a newspaper clipping with a photo of the fire.

Her concern is replacing the lost production, so she pulls up spreadsheet figures from an old report. She's not sure which report contains the figures she wants, but she is able to narrow the search, first by date, then by topic, until she has reduced 2,000 possibilities to just six. She finds the one she wants, then points and clicks on the ones that need to be revised in light of the lost plant.

Now she creates a new, blank memo form (a template) in another window and fills in the blanks for TO:, FROM:, and so forth. Then she types an introductory sentence, followed by cutting and pasting the chart from the old report. Now she clicks on the chart data, and the actual spreadsheet cells appear

in a window on top of the memo. She changes the data to today's, and the chart is automatically (and audibly) updated with the most current capacity information from the database server.

Next, she takes the forecasted sales projections from a recent E-mail message and updates the spreadsheet/graphic chart on capacity. It turns out that the company will be able to fulfill all its orders, even though the fire has put the plant out of commission. She copies (cc:) the memo and adds a voice message expressing relief that everything will be all right and prepares to send it to the managers who need to know. A window appears with color photographs of the managers; she selects three, clicks on them, moves the memo to the outbox, and sends it to them.

Now *that's* multimedia.

used by various groups, but still reside on a centralized system. **Distributed** means the hardware and software are physically located with the group and are connected to the centralized DBMS. These connections are usually made through a computer network, which we shall study in more detail in Chapter 13. There are two other types of organizational database concepts: client/server and enterprisewide systems. In the following case studies, we'll learn how some businesses and organizations have taken advantage of these different types of database concepts.

MAINFRAME DATABASE SYSTEMS

A mainframe database system is most useful when a homogenous group works with the same data on a regular basis. Facundo Rojo was data center manager for one of the most ambitious and short-lived mainframe computer installations in history: Los Juegos de la XXV Olympiada (The Games of the 25th

FIGURE 12.8

Where's the problem? Candle Corporation's Omegamon utility software works in conjunction with the mainframe DBMS. Its color-coded status indicators alerted knowledge workers at the 1992 Summer Olympics of impending or existing problems.

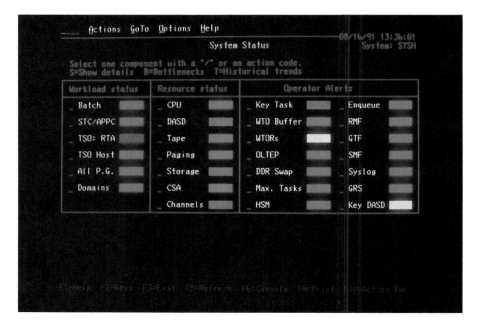

Olympiad) held in Spain in the summer of 1992. IBM donated several of its largest mainframe computers, as well as its DB2 database management software, which was used in conjunction with supporting DBMS software from Candle Corp, a leader in this field. The system posed a formidable challenge; there were nearly 4,000 workstations that knowledge workers would begin using only 15 days before the Olympic games began. "You could compare it to managing a bank. There are 3,000 cashiers all asking for money on the very first day of business . . . and they must have it!" said Rojo.

The DBMS software was used for two major application tasks. One was to take care of authorizations, inscriptions, volunteer selection, logistics, transportation, sanitary services, accommodations, reception and dispatch, press bookings, and a number of support services. The other was to manage historical data on the Olympic games of the past and of the 500 teams participating that summer, including biographical data on the individuals.

Once the summer games concluded, the system was shut down. The hardware and some software was returned to IBM, while COOB '92, the holding company for which Rojo worked, was dismantled. The data, however, remains intact, awaiting use for the summer games in 1996. Figure 12.8 shows a typical data screen.

DISTRIBUTED DATABASE SYSTEMS

Many organizations have multiple locations: offices, factories, distribution warehouses, retail outlets, etc. For such companies, distributed database systems are more a necessity than a choice. Domino's Pizza has over 5,000 retail stores in the United States and wants to keep its customers happy. It used to do so by asking pizza-eaters to fill out the "Mystery Customer Survey," a ques-

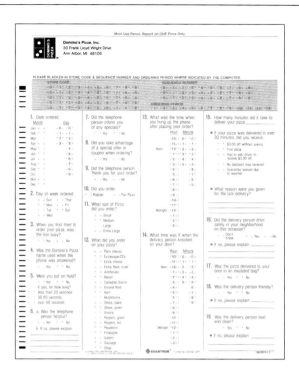

FIGURE 12.9

Domino's questionnaire is used to gather data for its DBMS system for improving quality and customer service.

tionnaire on a sheet of paper. The questionnaires were sent in; it then took weeks to input, process, and analyze the results.

But in 1992, Domino's shifted to a distributed DBMS to collect and analyze this data. A staff of telephone pollers calls customers and, using personal computers and Foxbase DBMS software, enters their responses into a form on the computer screen. They ask about the quality of both the pizza and the service from individual stores across the nation. The PCs send the data to Domino's mainframe computer in Ann Arbor, Michigan, where it is stored in a huge database. In addition to gathering information on crust thickness, staff friendliness, and timely delivery, the Foxbase system generates a thank-you letter and a rebate coupon for the next order. As a matter of fact, you may have received one yourself! Figure 12.9 shows the Domino's screen questionnaire.

CLIENT/SERVER DATABASE SYSTEMS

Client/server refers to a database system used by a group of knowledge workers in a specific work group, division, or department. Each *client,* a personal computer or workstation in use by a knowledge worker, has its own application software; they are all connected to a single computer, called a *server,* on which certain programs and data reside. The server may be as simple as a hard disk drive; it might be a powerful personal computer or workstation designed especially as a server; or it can even be an entire mainframe system and DBMS. Working together, the client and server stations each utilize their own — and each other's — processing and data storage capabilities to best advantage. Client/server takes good advantage of different hardware platforms and networking concepts and makes it much more efficient for knowledge workers to use corporate databases.

The Church of Jesus Christ of Latter-Day Saints in Salt Lake City, Utah, has the most extensive database of genealogical records in the world. In addition to its records on 7.5 million Mormons, it has information on another 6 million family names. The Church accepts requests for information from people around the world, and its information system has recently been upgraded with special client/server technology so that even more people can access their family records more conveniently.

The system employs over 70 Digital Equipment Corp. VAX minicomputers, and until recently access was provided by Digital terminals. Now, using a Digital tool called DECtp (for transaction processing) Desktop for ACMS (Application Control and Management), the databases running on VAX servers can be accessed using either Macintosh or MS-DOS personal computers. The client/server technology is being extended so that other types of computers connected in the church network can also be accessed, using Desktop for ACMS. But at the heart of the effort is using these new DBMS techniques to make it easier to track DBMS genealogical data and automate access to it. In addition, the church's *Family History Library Catalog* and *International Genealogical Index* are now available to its 1,100 Family History Centers on CD-ROM. Figure 12.10 shows a client-server screen.

ENTERPRISEWIDE DATABASE SYSTEMS

"Islands of automation" used to be the way most corporations described their various computer systems. There was one for finance, another for manufac-

---

FIGURE 12.10

Desktop ACMS provides the framework for integrating multivendor desktop clients so different types of personal computer and workstation users anywhere on the network can access transaction processing applications.

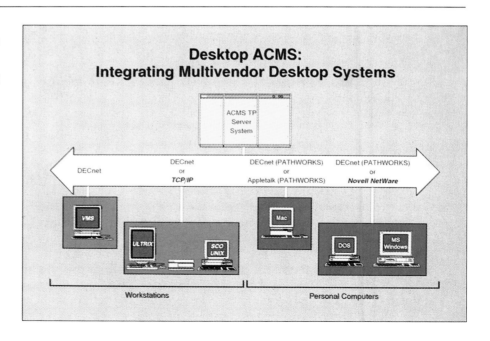

turing, and still others for office automation, order fulfillment, distribution, marketing, and engineering and manufacturing. Today those islands are becoming a continent in enterprisewide systems, where computers are not only physically connected but also able to share data and pass transactions. A true **enterprisewide database system** means that any data can be found anywhere it resides, immediately accessed, and put to use. While we'll go into this topic in more depth in the next chapter, here we'll see how its database aspect works.

For many years, manufacturing was hindered because of incompatibility between computer-aided design systems and computer-aided manufacturing. What's more, there was cost accounting data, marketing data, and so forth that could also be used in preparing to manufacture. Siemens Gammasonics, part of Siemens Medical Corp., manufactures nuclear medicine diagnostic imaging cameras and related products for hospitals around the world. It uses software from CIMLINC, running on Digital minis, and special terminals and workstations, to integrate data from different enterprisewide databases that automatically generates camera assembly instructions, machine setup, and tooling, and provides shop floor electronic instructions on terminal screens. Figure 12.11 shows a CIMLINC screen.

In addition, the CIMLINC system also provides a link to other relational databases in the enterprise. Some of the databases are local, in Hoffman Estates, Illinois, but others are at company headquarters in Iselin, New Jersey; however, all are equally accessible. Obtaining this data is important, since information concerning the manufacturing standards that differ from country to country must be available. Although most such systems must be customized to a great extent for the client, the move toward enterprisewide open systems is underway in full force.

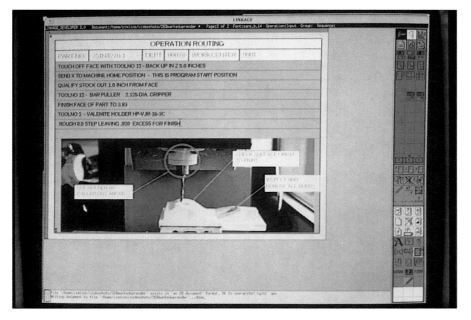

FIGURE 12.11

CIMLINC's multimedia information integration software, LINKAGE. This Operation Routing screen is being used to manage the process of engineering and manufacturing a specific tool. Critical areas can be called out for review and verification.

Tomorrow

The Object-Oriented DBMS

Combine the principles of object-oriented programming (which you studied in Chapter 11) with DBMS technology, and what do you have? The **object-oriented database management system** (OODBMS). Many industry analysts regard it as being the next generation in DBMS, but not necessarily replacing its predecessor. Ted Rybeck (an industry analyst at Advanced Manufacturing Research, Inc., a Cambridge, Massachusetts–based market research firm) says, "Object orientation does not have to be a replacement for relational DBMS. As its name implies, it is an orientation rather than a full-blown DBMS model. As such, it can blend with and build on the relational schema. There are no strict rules preventing a relational database management systems vendor from enhancing its product to become an object-oriented DBMS; in fact, many of them are now doing just that."

OODBMS uses the idea, or model, of the *object* to combine procedures, or instructions, with data and incorporate them together into a software entity. Thus, like OOP, creating a data-base involves selecting and linking objects to get what you want. This database design approach is termed *modular,* and messages are sent to the objects to define the actions to be taken. For the knowledge worker, the process is quite simple: objects are selected from menus, they appear as boxes on the screen, and the mouse and keyboard are used to create linking messages. And of course, objects can be reused so that rewriting code is unnecessary.

OODBMS is considered best for complex applications—such as the enterprisewide database discussed earlier. In addition, OODBMS makes it possible to use the multimedia database, incorporating data, text, graphics, voice, imaging, manufacturing, modeling, and group-oriented database applications—all with a single, relational OODBMS.

So far, CAD, CASE, and computer-aided publishing have found the greatest value from OODBMS. Eastman Kodak's Advanced Development Division has used an OODBMS from Object Design for its computer-aided printing and publishing. Bob Gordon, project director, says, "If you're trying to put out a newspaper, you have to manage pages that are made up of different-size articles, pictures, graphics, ads, and so on. You want an object-oriented database that can manage all of them and let you pass some of the attributes of one down to another. Relational databases don't handle very large and very small objects of the same data type efficiently."

But perhaps the greatest benefit from OODBMS is that it holds forth the possibility of working directly with the information, without having to issue commands and manipulate the database. Instead of moving through a file structure to identify a data element that is part of an employee's personnel record, OODBMS allows the knowledge worker to move through *classes of people*—for example, stockholder, employee, or customer—to find the individual in question. The data is subservient to the information—not the other way around.

Knowledge Check

1. Why is it important to have access to multiple databases? pp. 380–81
2. When is the mainframe database concept most useful? p. 381
3. When is the distributed database concept most useful? p. 382
4. When is the client/server database concept most useful? p. 383
5. When is the enterprisewide database concept most useful? pp. 384–85

WHAT LIES AHEAD?

Object-oriented programming (OOP) and the graphic user interface (GUI) are quickly making the world of DBMS friendlier and easier for the knowledge worker to use. Instead of issuing commands to the database, we will be able to work with objects and actions. Objects are pieces or sets of information that knowledge workers need to perform their work. For example, an insurance underwriter commonly works with a file name or number; in the new paradigm, she or he works with customers and policies, which are objects. Once the file is located, the database commands are commonly CREATE, VIEW, EDIT, or PRINT. Using actions, the tasks are work-oriented: add, cancel, delete, issue, or surrender. This makes for increased productivity and greater enjoyment in performing one's work.

The other significant change that lies ahead is the movement from Dr. Lucky's data-information-knowledge hierarchy, as it applies to database technology. This is another object-oriented direction, to be sure, and is designed to capture and store the business's *knowledge assets*. Although each company defines knowledge assets differently, it is generally considered to be the various forms of expert knowledge employees possess—from engineer and scientists to managers, salespeople, and, yes, knowledge workers.

DATABASE ETHICS: INSURING DATABASE INTEGRITY

There are several top priorities for both the database administrator and the knowledge worker when working with corporate databases. Safety and security must be meticulously maintained so that sensitive personal and corporate data are not exposed to any kind of risk. But first and foremost, the data stored in the database must be accurate—what is termed *database integrity*.

The Massachusetts Institute of Technology surveyed the heads of MIS in 50 large businesses in 1992 and learned that over half of them believed their corporate information was less than 95 percent accurate. This, they felt, limited its usefulness. In many cases they believed the data was so bad that it should not be used for making business decisions.

We know we live in the Information Age and that accurate information is essential. A small example of this can be found in our everyday lives: direct mail for advertising and marketing purposes. Direct mail is becoming a highly targeted process, with the recipient's name printed in the literature. What if it is the name of a household pet? What if the person is deceased? What if the mailing list data is old, and the people have long since moved away? For business, such errors are costly in terms of time, printing, and postage.

Another commonly used database is often filled with errors and erroneous information: credit reporting agencies. People have found their identities confused by inaccurate data entry of social security numbers, and have often found bad accounts listed on their report when they had no such account at all. Every citizen deserves the right to accurate credit data. From a business standpoint, the reporting agency has an equal desire for accuracy—if for no other reason than to avoid bad publicity and liability lawsuits.

Often the problem is that knowledge workers do not enter data completely or accurately, say customer complaints. Sometimes the computer system does not permit them to do so. For example, they may be required to use codes for complaints and no single code accurately describes the problem. Or they may have to type the complaint into a data field that is too short; or it simply may take too long to do so. Another problem is when data is transferred from one computer system to another; what was a back-ordered item in the former becomes a fulfilled item in the second, but there may be no way of tracking how long it took to fulfill the back orders—critical management decision-making information.

0100101101
0010110010
1001010110
0101000100
1000110101
0101000100
1001100010
1000100101

CAREERS FOR KNOWLEDGE WORKERS
PERRY MIZOTA, MARKETING MANAGER, SYBASE, INC.

Perry Mizota tells the story of his career evolution, from programming to marketing communications for a major software company, this way. He graduated from the University of Southern California as a computer science major and took his first job as a programmer at Hughes Aircraft. After two years

of work experience he enrolled in the Master's of Business Administration program at UCLA. That degree led to a position at Hewlett Packard, a major computer systems company. "I was a product manager for database management software products at HP, and one of my duties was to track our competitors. One up-and-coming company was Sybase, and I watched it closely because I was interested in going to a smaller company and growing with it. When a position in marketing communications opened up, I jumped at the opportunity."

Sybase is a software company that began developing a client/server-based relational database management system in 1984. In fact, the well-respected *Software* magazine credited Sybase with introducing the term *client/server*. The RDBMS was introduced in 1987, and since then

has been purchased by hundreds of businesses worldwide, including Salomon Brothers, American Airlines, Chevron, and Sun Microsystems. Because the Sybase RDBMS runs on personal computers, workstations, minis, and mainframes, it is called an enterprisewide application.

Perry characterizes the difference between being a product manager and being a marketing communications manager this way: "A product manager is a more technical person who works with engineers who are developing a software or hardware product. It's fairly detailed, technical work. A marketing communications manager must understand the company and its products, and communicate the benefits of both to the public at several different levels."

At Sybase, marketing communications involves the preparation of print advertising, sales

---

There is no single source of corporate database integrity problems. However, there is a single source of correcting them: each knowledge worker must assume complete responsibility for the data they work with. Any errors must be corrected or reported to the database administrator. No detail is too small nor too insignificant. The success of today's business depends on accurate data that knowledge workers can use for reliable information.

SUMMARY

1. *Describe the difference between the personal computer database concept and corporate database concepts.* The principles are the same; what differs is that corporate DBMS systems are much larger. Corporate DBMSs are most often relational, and megabytes of data become terabytes. There are many more ways of organizing, evaluating, combining, and viewing the data, and we must be able to navigate or move among vantage points in the DBMS. Corporate database management

materials, and public relations. Perry has one staff member who works with him and coordinates with two outside agencies — an ad agency and a public relations firm. Thus Perry acts as the creative director, or coordinator of creative services, to communicate about the company and its products to what he terms "three different constituencies."

The first constituency is the customers — businesses that buy Sybase software products. These are what he terms "business-to-business" sales since Sybase has its own direct sales staff calling on the Fortune 500 companies. The sales representatives need materials that explain products and their benefits to give to potential customers. In addition, Sybase advertises its products in the leading computer industry publications. The second constituency is journalists from technical, computer industry,

and business publications, who receive literature and press releases. The third is industry analysts and observers, technically inclined consultants whose advice is solicited by potential customers. Working to communicate effectively with these three constituents, Perry says, is the most challenging and creative part of his job.

Perry has made the successful transition from a computer, or technical, job to that of a knowledge worker with skills in both computer technology and business practices. He believes working with computers is unavoidable for tomorrow's knowledge workers. "Computers are tools for making organizations and companies more competitive, and your computer skills and knowledge are invaluable. You don't need a technical background for the kind of work I do, but the ability to understand

computer technology and how it affects business is essential.

"The world of client/server computing allows knowledge workers, using computers, to be more productive. It creates *power users*, the term we used to use to define people who were highly skilled with Lotus 1-2-3. Power users created macros that made their spreadsheet work more productive. It was a form of programming, and a very sophisticated use of the computer. Client/server will expand knowledge worker skills beyond the spreadsheet as they become power users of the RDBMS, developing and implementing their own applications. They will be able to affect and change their own personal work environment, and that's a nontrivial improvement over the old mainframe computing environment!"

encompasses mainframes, minis, personal, and interconnected (networked) computers.

2. *Describe the role of the database administrator and the duties performed.* The DBA is responsible for maintaining the DBMS and ensuring the accuracy and the integrity of its data. The DBA works with department and corporate managers to decide what data goes into the database, the relationships between various data items, who has permission to access the database, and who has authority to update it. The DBA is also responsible for the data dictionary (a list of all the fields, files, and commands utilized in manipulating

the database) and all aspects of data management (planning, organization, processing, and security).

3. *Discuss advantages and disadvantages of database management.* Advantages include working with data from many sources, storing data only once, maintaining program and data independence, and data integrity. Disadvantages include hardware costs, training time and costs, and portability across platforms.

4. *Describe database tools and how they are used.* The simplest front end tool is the spreadsheet for query and database design. The analysis tool

helps sift the data. The 4GL allows using English-like phrases to manipulate the database. The application generator allows building database applications, often on a personal computer. The most popular tool is the query language, SQL, which can perform many, if not most, of the front end tasks.

5. *Describe the different types of corporate databases.* The earliest and simplest type of DBMS is the data database. The text database contains documents; the image database contains graphics, photos, and images. The multimedia database contains data, text, image, sound, and video.

6. *Explain how different organizational database systems are used.* There are mainframe, distributed, client/server, and enterprisewide database systems. A mainframe system is best suited to a centralized company. A distributed system is best suited to companies with multiple locations. Client/server is the newest type of system, which maximizes processing and data storage capabilities. Enterprisewide joins many different systems, and is a point of evolution that many companies are evolving toward.

DATABASE ISSUES

1. *The Wall Street Journal* (August 21, 1991, p. B1) reported that Citicorp proposed giving marketers access to files on its 21 million customers. The marketers could use the records of purchases in creating targeted mailing lists. Privacy advocates "are aghast that outsiders could have access to data as revealing as credit-card records." Georgetown University professor Mary Culnan cited Citicorp's plans in testimony to Congress, saying, "These transaction records reflect the most intimate details of our personal lives, yet they do not receive any legal protection."

   Citicorp says it intends to disclose data only in broad categories — for example, it might release a list of cardholders who buy goods for children. It does not intend to disclose store-by-store details. How do you feel about your buying habits and patterns being made public and used for competitive marketing purposes?

2. In Austin, Texas, Malcolm Graham received a water bill for $22,000, for using almost 10 million gallons of water in one month. The meter reading for the month was slightly *less* than that for the previous month, which the computer interpreted as wrap-around. (A new meter had been installed between readings and was not set properly.) A manual review of unusually large bills failed to spot that one. A utility company spokesman said, "We have about 275,000 accounts each month. We just missed this one. If we only miss one a month, that's a pretty good percentage." Do you agree? How would you feel if this happened to your utility bill? Your bank statement? How would you address the prob-

lem? What would you consider a reasonable amount of your time and effort to resolve the problem?

3. *The New York Times* News Service reported in 1991 that law enforcement officials in Ohio searched the records of every telephone user in southwestern Ohio to determine who, if anyone, called a *Wall Street Journal* reporter to provide information that Proctor & Gamble said was confidential and protected by state law. The investigation went far beyond examining the telephone records of current and former employees of the giant consumer products company, an inquiry the Hamilton County prosecutor's office confirmed.

   Prosecutor Arthur Ney, Jr., responding to a complaint by Proctor & Gamble, ordered Cincinnati Bell to produce all the telephone numbers of calls to the home or office of reporter Alecia Swasy between March 1 and June 15, 1991. Proctor & Gamble, which makes many family and household products, asked the Cincinnati police to determine whether current or former employees were leaking confidential corporate information to *The Wall Street Journal.* Ms. Swasy, a reporter based in Pittsburgh sent to cover Proctor & Gamble, had written several articles citing unidentified sources who said a senior executive was being pressured to resign and that some unprofitable divisions might be sold.

   Alan F. Westin, a professor at Columbia University and an authority on technology and privacy, said, "When technology allows you to run millions of calls involving 650,000 telephone subscribers through a computer in order to identify who called a person, potentially to find out whether a crime was committed, you raise the question of whether technological capacity has gone over the line in terms of what is a reasonable search and seizure."

Was Proctor & Gamble within its legal rights to ask for this search? Do you feel a violation of Ms. Swasy's privacy occurred? What of the moral and ethical aspects? How would you feel if this happened to you?

CHAPTER REVIEW QUESTIONS

REVIEW QUESTIONS

1. Explain the difference between a centralized and a decentralized database.
2. Why is it necessary to establish entity relationships?
3. Explain the difference between on-line processing and on-line transaction processing, and where each is best suited.
4. Name some key features and advantages of the 4GL.
5. How do text databases differ from data databases?
6. What is meant by the term *islands of automation?*
7. What is the most useful DBMS tool?

DISCUSSION QUESTIONS

1. Discuss some of the reasons for the incredible growth in the volume of data.
2. Describe several of the database administrator's responsibilities.
3. Why do you suppose there is so much interest in geographic information systems?
4. Describe some ways you would put a multimedia database system to use.
5. Discuss the uses for the different front end tools.
6. Discuss some possible problems and issues relating to database security.

MULTIPLE-CHOICE

1. The major difference between the large organizational DBMS and the personal computer DBMS is:
   a. It's larger.
   b. It's relational.
   c. It may run on many different computers.
   d. All of the above.
2. A data dictionary:
   a. Contains the codes for unlocking the database.
   b. Is used by knowledge workers on a daily basis.
   c. Lists how much storage space the database occupies.
   d. Contains essential "data about the data."
3. The major advantages for client/server are (choose all that apply):
   a. All knowledge workers have their own computer processing and storage.
   b. All the data is stored on a single server.
   c. The mainframe can be powered down.
   d. The clients all rely on the server for processing.
   e. Many databases can be accessed from a client computer.
4. What technologies are making DBMSs friendlier and easier to use (pick all that apply):
   a. Color monitors.
   b. The graphic user interface.
   c. Object-oriented technology.
   d. CD-ROM.
5. The "data about the data" is stored in the
   a. DBMS.
   b. Database.
   c. Data dictionary.
   d. Data repository.
   e. Database administrator's head.

6. The organizational database designed for work-groups is:
   a. Distributed.
   b. Client/server.
   c. CODASYL.
   d. Relational.
   e. All of the above.

7. Some of the tools commonly used on PCs to access corporate databases are (choose all that apply):
   a. SQL.
   b. 4GL.
   c. Client/server.
   d. Spreadsheet.
   e. Application generator.

FILL-IN-THE-BLANK

1. The oldest form of data processing still in use today is _____ _____.

2. SQL stands for _____ _____ _____.

3. The knowledge worker who maintains the corporate database is called the _____ _____.

4. Another name for the network mainframe database is _____.

5. The next-generation type of database is _____.

TRUE/FALSE

1. Large DBMSs provide many ways of working with data and moving around the DBMS.

2. Database front end tools came into existence to help knowledge workers create their own applications.

3. SQL is used only by information systems professionals.

4. A mainframe database system is best suited to older, manufacturing businesses.

5. The distributed database is the most technologically advanced.

KEY TERMS

client/server, 383
conversion, 372
data dictionary, 370
database administrator, 369
database application, 373
database development, 370
disaster recovery, 372
distributed, 381

enterprisewide database system, 385
entity, 370
fourth-generation language, 374
front end, 373
geographic information system (GIS), 379

navigate, 367
object-oriented database management system (OODBMS), 386
on-line processing, 371
on-line transaction processing, 371
query, 373

Understanding and knowledge are not useful until they can be applied. Throughout this text, you have learned the basic concepts and seen examples of business computing as it is practiced in the modern world.

These chapters demonstrate how knowledge workers use computers to help the companies they work for achieve their business goals. We shall see if the computer is living up to the promise of performing its tasks *better, faster,* and *cheaper,* aiding knowledge workers as a productivity tool, and aiding businesses by providing competitive advantages. You will see personal computers, minis, and mainframes working together; you will learn about application development projects and their outcome; you'll understand why different software tools are suited to specific tasks. And you'll observe many types of knowledge workers at work.

Chapter 13, Management Information Systems, opens the door to the information systems organization, its knowledge workers, and its objectives. You'll learn what MIS stands for organizationally, technologically, and managerially. MIS knowledge workers are very much like knowledge workers in other business roles, and you'll learn

more about their important work responsibilities.

Chapter 14, Voice and Data Communications Systems, introduces you to the most dynamic and growing aspect of business computing. No modern knowledge worker or business can thrive without communications systems; computers are part of the phone systems, and with every passing day it becomes more imperative to transmit data from computer to computer. You'll learn about the wide diversity of information services available via computer for both the individual knowledge worker and the business organization.

Chapter 15, Office Automation and Departmental Computing, brings the knowledge worker and the business environment together. For over a hundred years there were few significant changes in office work or the office environment. However within the past decade the office has been utterly transformed. Not only are there many new technologies, from PCs to facsimile machines, but there is a new, more professional and respectful attitude about the importance of knowledge work. This chapter explores both aspects as they are practiced today, and it points out some work and career directions for the future.

CHAPTER 13

Management Information Systems

LEARNING OBJECTIVES

After reading and studying this chapter, you should be able to:

1. Define the term *MIS* and explain how it is used.
2. Describe three roles MIS plays in a company.
3. Name ways MIS is used, by whom, and for what purposes.
4. Discuss the impact of personal computers and new computer architectures on MIS.
5. Explain how centralized MIS is evolving and changing.

MANAGEMENT INFORMATION SYSTEMS AND THE KNOWLEDGE WORKER

There are many types of knowledge workers in business. By and large, these knowledge workers are white-collar professionals — people who use computers in a wide variety of tasks that help the company achieve its objectives. These tasks include managing, administration, order processing, accounting, purchasing, manufacturing support, sales, marketing, and many, many others you are probably familiar with.

However, there is a smaller yet no less significant group of knowledge workers whose job it is to create and support the computer systems in operation throughout the company. They are responsible in some way for nearly all the computers, from the largest mainframe to the personal and portable PCs. As you learned in the preceding chapters, these knowledge workers are often called *information systems professionals* for they have been educated and trained to work with the corporate computer systems.

There are three ways in which businesses are commonly supported by computer systems. First, in most large companies, there is a central computer facility, which provides services companywide. But the business environment is grouped into logical, functional systems, each with its own tasks to perform. Second, additional computer systems, usually designed and installed by the information systems professionals, support each of these individual functional groups or departments. And third, often a group or system must interact with other groups, so the information systems organization provides the linkages between them. Figure 13.1 demonstrates the interactions in an MIS between different departments, all contributing toward a common business goal.

Like the various hardware components in a computer system (such as the CPU, main memory, and peripherals), various business processes (such as order processing, accounting, manufacturing, and shipping) form a system for managing a business. Working together, these processes assure that the work gets accomplished properly and that the business achieves its goals, such as producing a service or product, satisfying customer needs, creating a profit, and distributing dividends to shareholders. It is the mandate of the company's information systems to ensure that the company remains viable and competitive in its market; that its knowledge workers have all the information they need to do their work in a timely manner; and that each and every business process achieve the highest levels of performance.

Generally speaking, when we talk about the computer in business and the various tasks it performs, we use the term *management information systems* (MIS). The term gained wide acceptance in 1968, when the Society for Management Information Systems (now the Society for Information Manage-

FIGURE 13.1   The computer provides essential links throughout the company. A sales order triggers a series of interrelated processes that utilize many aspects of an information system to produce the finished product or service.

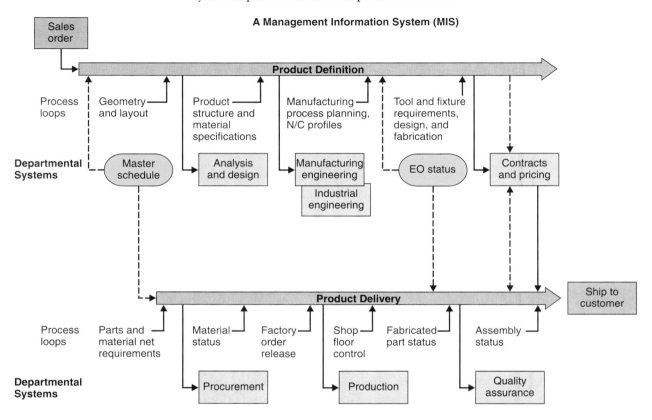

ment) was founded. The Society is made up of executives, information systems professionals, and academicians who meet to explore the latest trends and ideas in MIS. The goal of MIS is to deliver information systems to corporate knowledge workers.

MIS: A Definition

The term **management information system** refers to the computer system, working together with the business organization, to achieve the business goals. Figure 13.2 shows a typical business system with its human input, processing resources, and products or services output — you can see the similarity with a computer system. And like the business system, the computer system must be managed.

The computer system provides data that various knowledge workers in the business use, in the form of information, to solve problems, plan strategies, and make decisions affecting the health and livelihood of the business. In most cases, these knowledge workers are managers who are charged with decision-

The MIS department uses computer systems to create products and services in the same way as the business system.

FIGURE 13.2

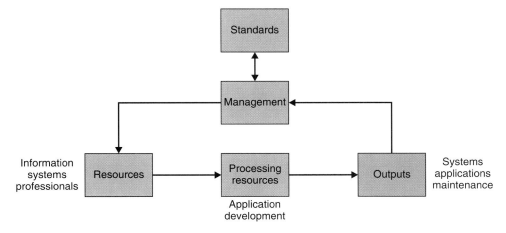

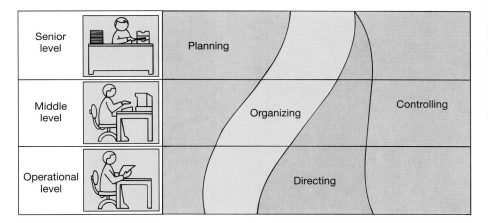

FIGURE 13.3

Management activities in business and MIS. Top management spends most of its time organizing and planning, middle management motivating and developing, and operational management directing and controlling.

making responsibilities. Generally, as you can see in Figure 13.3, managers are categorized into three levels:

- Top-level or senior management.
- Middle or line management.
- Operational or supervisory management.

These categories apply whether we are discussing corporate management or management in a specific department—including MIS. However, the MIS organization's role is changing considerably. There is a greater need for MIS to be able to respond quickly and effectively to the company's changing priorities. This chapter explains how it is doing so, and Figure 13.4 shows how a typical MIS organization is making the appropriate changes. But first, let's learn the purposes and uses for MIS.

FIGURE 13.4   An organization chart for an MIS organization in transition. Today's systems chart reflects a primary focus on technology issues. Tomorrow's systems chart shows a shift to an organization focused on people and business needs.

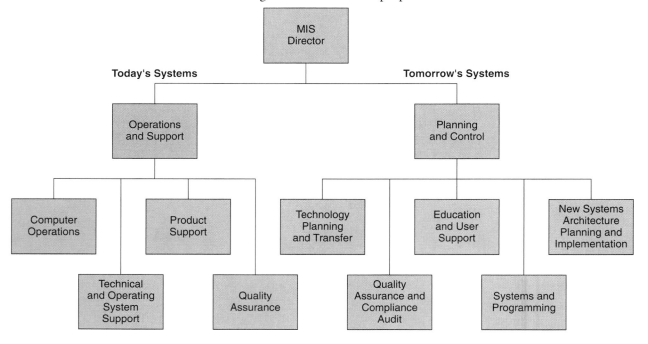

WHY USE A MANAGEMENT INFORMATION SYSTEM?

Let's study the acronym for management information systems — MIS — to answer this question.

THE M.   Regardless of the business function, it is essential there be some form of *management* to plan, organize, direct, control, and staff. Management accomplishes objectives through the efforts of many people. Lack of management is responsible for more failures than any other single aspect of business.

THE I.   To provide *information* for management decisions, for planning strategic directions for the future, for improving business performance, and for developing or sustaining a competitive advantage in the marketplace.

THE S.   To develop and maintain *systems* and applications that help make workers more productive and contribute to achieving the business's goals.

WHO USES MIS?

Who uses MIS? There are two answers to this question. First, MIS is primarily used in business, in government, and in the information industry. Even though an individual using a personal computer in home business could be considered an MIS user, in this chapter we are primarily interested in large MIS

YESTERDAY

RICHARD NOLAN: CREATING A VISION OF MIS

In the 1970s Richard L. Nolan, then an associate professor at the Harvard Business School, was studying data processing (DP) departments in a number of large companies. He developed what he termed the *stages theory* about why some DP departments were doing better with information systems than others. In 1974, he and a colleague published an article in the *Harvard Business Review* entitled "Managing the Four Stages of EDP Growth." (EDP stands for electronic data processing.) Five years later, Dr. Nolan published a second *Harvard Business Review* article, "Managing the Crises in Data Processing," which added two stages to his earlier model. Nolan identified these stages:

1. *Initiation.* Beginning to use computer technology and experiencing early successes, which in turn leads to increased interest and more experimentation.

2. *Contagion.* The factors in stage 1 lead to widespread interest and new applications and services for users. Information systems usage rapidly proliferates.

3. *Control.* Management begins to feel uneasy with this rapid growth and associated costs, and begins to curtail proliferation. Some DP projects are deemed impractical; attempts at integrating various applications and systems prove difficult since each was independently developed without planning for how it would work harmoniously with others at a later date. Users "give up on data processing."

4. *Integration.* DP has reorganized itself and started activating new applications and providing high-quality service to users.

5. *Data administration.* Applications are beginning to be integrated, and DP begins to exercise tighter control over data and systems.

6. *Maturity.* Full applications

integration occurs, and the structure and organization of DP are complete. Information flows duplicate the organizational structure of the company, which results in high-quality utilization of information systems.

Nolan's idea that there were life stages struck a powerful chord in DP managers, and has had a profound influence on many information systems departments. Once they recognized a stage they were stuck in, these managers were able to guide the operation into the next, more productive, stage.

As Nolan also pointed out, "It is important to realize how greatly DP technology spurs the development and codification of an external, or professional, body of knowledge." This fact has been largely responsible for the growth, development, and importance DP has assumed in the modern corporation and government organizations.

environments. *Information Week,* a magazine for information systems professionals, ranks the top 100 MIS organizations in business each year. The smallest of these MIS organizations has an annual budget of $100 million; the largest is in excess of a quarter of a billion dollars!

Second, management information systems are used by managers at the three levels we discussed earlier — senior management, middle management, and operational management — to plan, organize, direct, control, and staff MIS operations and projects for users. A **project** is an assignment for MIS to create an application for users in a business function. The project might be a way for a fast food chain to gather the daily receipts from its many restaurants or to set up a new customer database for a division introducing a new product.

How MIS Is Used

Management information systems are most widely used in business, where they are often considered a "strategic weapon" in "corporate combat." Management collects business data and, with the help of MIS, it is stored, processed, and retrieved as strategic information. This data collected in MIS comes from three sources:

- *Outside sources* such as feedback from customers, sales rep surveys, magazines or trade publications, on-line database information, and the informal human networks or "grapevines."
- *Inside sources* about the company, provided by operational management concerning its productivity, resources, and such, or by middle management regarding opinions or analysis of short-term goals, opportunities, and accomplishments.
- *The information system itself,* by feeding specific data into the computer in order to produce analyses or scenarios for senior management to set future goals, plan strategic directions, or create new competitive advantages. These are often customized information systems called *decision support systems* or *executive information systems,* designed especially for top-level managers without extensive computer skills. We will study these systems in greater detail in Chapter 15.

A typical large company has many types of information systems in use. While some are designed to assist customers, such as an automated teller network of ATMs at a bank, most are for internal use. In most large companies, each of the divisions requires its own information systems, some of which are centralized and shared by others, while others are unique to that organization. For example, central MIS provides sales figures that are used by finance to determine the firm's profitability, by marketing to set quotas and measure the sales staff's performance, and by human resources (in this case, payroll) to pay salaries and sales commissions. An organizational MIS for distribution might keep track of local inventories at half a dozen regional warehouses.

From a management perspective, the sales information helps the operational manager know how much product to manufacture and how many workers to hire. It also helps the middle manager set goals for new products or market share, and it helps senior management plan for expansion. So in a sense, anyone who is involved in managerial decisions is often using management information systems.

The MIS Concept

There are many ways to manage a business. In the study of management, there are various schools of thought: classical management, scientific management, behavioral management, and so forth. Most management experts agree that managers usually make decisions based on acquired experience and personal judgment, sometimes backed up or verified with empirical evidence.

The idea or concept behind MIS is that *it is a system that works in conjunction with the business system, like an overlay that helps conceptually chart, support, and verify the business plans, directions, and strategies.* It does this at three levels of information management:

- *Record keeping,* the simplest (and earliest) use for information systems.

TODAY
A CHARTER FOR MIS

Charles P. Lecht (see the Epilogue) wrote in a column about MIS for *Computerworld* newspaper. "I wrote the following charter at a friend's behest (over) 20 years ago. It may be even more relevant today than when it was written," he says.

The primary mission of the information systems department is to create the proper procedural environment for the orderly regeneration of the corporation's operational environment as it pertains to (1) the acquisition, purification, storage, processing, retrieval, presentation and dissemination of information for management at all levels and (2) the creation of organic harmony in the integration of man/machine information technology systems into the day-to-day affairs of the corporation.

The IS department's primary mission is supportive of, subservient to and embedded in the overall corporate plans, procedures and objectives as established by the corporate planning committee.

Its role in the corporate environment is unique in that it cannot create a product to be delivered to the corporation without the dynamic and day-to-day participation of the various corporate organizations that the product is to serve.

Its measure of success is in its ability to proliferate its capabilities throughout the corporation and to ultimately lose its identity as a corporate organization.

In concert with the broad objectives outlined above are those involving the IS department's role in providing guidance in the allocation of funds to be invested in data processing resources. In doing this, the IS department is required to achieve a proper, timely and in-context capability to ascertain the technical, politi-

cal, psychological and financial impact of the use of information technology in support of the corporation.

The IS department will prepare and maintain a plan to include long-range objectives, each defined as the outgrowth of a set of short-range accomplishments. The IS department must prepare and maintain its own operational procedures and standards to serve as an in-flight guidance system to ease the corporation's transition from systems of the past to those of the future in an atmosphere of realism dedicated to fulfilling the urgent needs of the present.

"Never before has the job of managing an IS department been so difficult."

Source: Charles P. Lecht, "Now More Than Ever, a Plan," *Computerworld,* April 27, 1992, p. 88.

- *Operations control,* improving such things as order entry and processing or inventory control.
- *Strategic planning,* for such things as increasing market share, outperforming the competition, and in general gaining a competitive advantage.

These three levels roughly correspond to the three levels of business functions and management, as you will recall from Figure 13.3. Consider a company that owns a chain of retail outlets. The store manager uses the computer information system for record keeping and other light management tasks. The operations manager uses the system to keep track of retail stores, make operational changes, and assemble data for management reports. The chief executive officer uses the system for planning the company's business directions.

In this context, MIS provides a management information system that acts as a model for conducting and managing the business. The magazine advertisement in Figure 13.5 is a parable that characterizes many a modern busi-

FIGURE 13.5

Computerworld newspaper has been the most trusted source of information for IS professionals since it was launched in 1964.

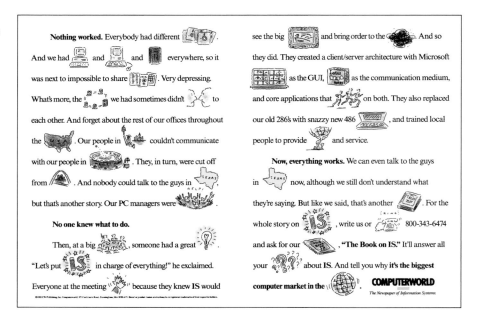

ness's problems with computers and how MIS helps solve those problems. Let's take a look at how MIS is used in real companies and government organizations.

THE BUSINESS PERSPECTIVE

TransCanada PipeLines (TCPL), with headquarters in Calgary, Alberta, Canada, transports natural gas via 11,000 km of pipeline in Canada as well as the United States. Several years ago, a number of changes in business dynamics — such as deregulation, pipeline expansion, the need to increase markets, and the demand for new services — led to TCPL's reevaluation of its information systems directions.

The MIS organization was faced with the task of rebuilding all its business and operational information systems in a very short time. The first conclusion was that its existing, mainframe-based approach to systems development would deliver the needed business solutions neither within an acceptable time frame nor at an affordable cost. As a result, the first step was reorganizing the MIS into 17 distributed partnership teams designed to facilitate a closer bond with business groups.

The partnership teams are supported by shared technology groups as well as by a distributed technology architecture based on 17 networked Digital VAX midsize departmental computers that have, over time, replaced the mainframe. In addition, over 1,300 Macintoshes have been deployed, acting as workstations in the distributed network. Implementing these technologies demanded a new kind of *infrastructure,* or underlying support structure, that encompasses the interpersonal, software, and hardware aspects of MIS for both the information systems professionals and the knowledge workers. Dr. Doron Cohen, vice president of information systems, says this new infrastructure has helped MIS strengthen its understanding of how computer technology can be used to facilitate the business's goals and objectives.

"We had to change this paradigm and create a new model for our company's information systems," says Dr. Cohen. "Until we did so, it was not possible to truly take advantage of the new and emerging technologies, such as the GUI." The GUI (graphical user interface) they developed runs on the Macintosh workstations and is consistent with the Mac's GUI. The new infrastructure was completed in just three and a half years, less than half the time it might normally take a company to convert from one technology infrastructure to another. Once it was in place, the MIS organization was able to create an important application that has helped transform the way senior management uses information systems at TCPL.

Up until a few years ago, the CEO, COO, senior vice presidents, and vice presidents still received mostly paper-based reports. They felt the Macs on their desktops were being underutilized and wondered if they could be used to provide better access to the information they needed. The project became known as GIS, for Graphical Information for Senior executives. A team of three or four people worked on two aspects of the project. One was interpreting and translating the paper-based reports to the user interface. The second was working with other information systems staff and knowledge workers to understand what information was needed.

The team conducted short interviews with the knowledge workers — senior managers — and then quickly created modules for them to use and work with for a few weeks. A module contains specific information, presented graphically either as pie, line, and bar graphs or as custom layouts, such as maps or diagrams. After the team had solicited feedback, the module was adjusted and returned to the knowledge worker. This was usually done for two to three iterations, until it was complete. Each module was created by a member of the project team and took between two and four weeks to complete, depending on the person's experience.

The various report categories helped determine the visual metaphor on the opening screen: a rotating hexagonal nut which reflects the engineering nature of the company with each side representing a control panel. The hexagon revolves, presenting different views of the company. Each control panel corresponds to a report category, with a title and accompanying icon for identification. Reports provide information in the categories of pipeline, construction, planning, external information, human resources, and financials. Clicking and holding the mouse button on an icon produces a pop-up menu list of the modules available in the category.

Pipeline is the largest category, containing extensive information about the pipeline, its operation, and the gas flows. Figure 13.6 presents the screen display seen after selecting "Estimated Volumes" from the Mainline side of the hexagon. This is a map of the TCPL pipeline with gas flow information displayed at key points along the pipeline. Volume can be displayed in either metric or imperial units. The date in the upper-right corner is the current date; the arrows permit moving ahead or back in time. Clicking on any value on the

FIGURE 13.6

FIGURE 13.6

Making data easy to understand: The TransCanada PipeLines GUI screen. The MIS organization worked extensively with senior management to develop an information system that met with their needs.

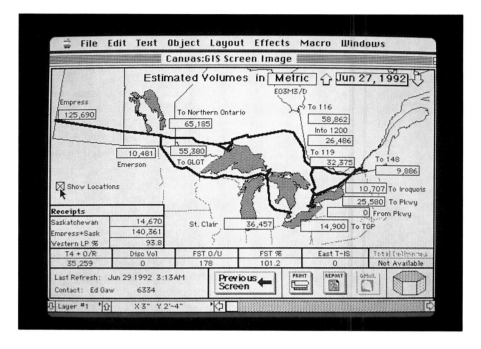

map results in the display of a line chart showing the trends over the current month, as well as the previous month, at that location. When the screen is loaded, all the past, present, and forecast data is retrieved at once so it is instantaneously accessible.

At the bottom-left corner of the screen is a status box, displaying the date and time the data was last refreshed plus the name and telephone extension of the *information custodian,* who is responsible for the information presented in the modules. Generally these custodians were previously responsible for providing senior management with paper reports; now they do the same work electronically. Either the information is automatically updated from the source system and transferred to GIS from a Microsoft Excel spreadsheet, or GIS reads the source files directly.

Senior management enjoys using GIS; they are receiving more information than was previously available, in a more useful and understandable format, and more quickly, than they had earlier gotten on paper. What's more, it has triggered a constant stream of ideas and requests for ways to make the system even more useful.

"No amount of technical expertise alone can create a system such as this," says Dr. Cohen. "It is important to understand that first you must have a technical infrastructure. By that I mean you must understand the hardware, software, and communications architecture that is the basis for information systems. Second, you must have a cultural infrastructure; that is to say there must be a sound relationship within MIS as well as between MIS and the business people we serve. We strongly believe in teamwork, and we have a clearly defined set of values that guide the way we work and interact with people. We believe in forming partnerships with the users, and that providing continuing support for them is extremely important. Yes, the GUI is a beautiful screen, and we are very proud of our GIS. But it was only possible because we looked at the changing business world of TransCanada Pipelines, and changed our MIS infrastructure along with it."

THE GOVERNMENT PERSPECTIVE

Management information systems are used in almost every aspect of city, county, state, and federal government. At the federal level, they are used to provide census data, research and reports for the legislative bodies, as well as files on taxpayers, Medicare recipients, and many other groups. Most of these systems are used by the government's employees, but here is one that is used by its citizens.

Tulare County, California, is a largely agricultural area with many farm workers of Hispanic and Southeast Asian descent. These people are unemployed at different times of the year and are then eligible for various forms of public assistance: unemployment, welfare, food assistance, dependent children aid, and so forth. To help these people, knowledge workers at the Department of Public Social Service must work with state and federal regulations that form a stack of paper nearly seven feet tall. An information system helps them, but Tulare County's information systems organization created a system that the public could use themselves.

It's called "the Tulare Touch" because it uses a computer terminal with a touch screen monitor; there is no keyboard. It is also a multimedia information system that uses videotape, audio, graphics, and electronic forms which the person applying for assistance fills in. At the beginning, a host or hostess from the client's native country appears on the screen and introduces the system in their native language — English, Spanish, or one of four Southeast Asian languages. Then highly graphic screens and forms appear, with the voice guiding the client's activities in the background. The applicant's eligibility and benefits are calculated by the system, and at the end of the interview a completed eligibility form is printed out.

The Tulare Touch runs on an IBM mainframe system. Eligibility workers and information systems professionals worked together to design and create the system, preparing it with all the conceivable questions an applicant might be asked. It was designed so that the applicant would not have to answer all the questions — there are over 1,000 — but only those that are pertinent. The other important aspect of the system was the GUI, for it had to be fun and friendly. A videodisc is used to present the host or hostess and to give instructions; a hard disk drive stores and replays the audio portion.

The system has been very successful. Now county eligibility workers can spend their time helping their clients rather than sifting through regulations and filling out forms. They are able to help more people on a daily basis than they could before. The system makes fewer errors and is often able to detect fraud when it occurs. Management likes it because applicants say they are more comfortable disclosing information to the computer. And the Tulare Touch is

FIGURE 13.7

The Dow Jones News/Retrieval service offers users a range of information services. This submenu shows the diversity of published information available at the touch of a key.

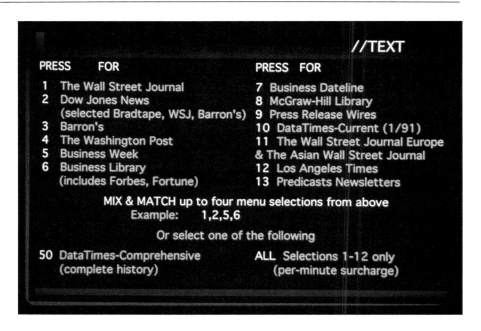

saving the county a great deal of money. It cost $3 million to create and is saving over $20 million annually.

INFORMATION PROVIDERS

The Information Age has created a new type of business: information providers. In the past, we obtained information from libraries and published materials. Now we can obtain it from computers, which have the ability to store and retrieve many more kinds of information, from film reviews to corporate performance reports to competitive intelligence. Dow Jones & Company sees itself as an information provider, using computers to do so and also using computers — and MIS — to maintain its product.

Dow Jones is no stranger to selling information; it has done so for over 150 years, starting with credit reports. *The Wall Street Journal* has been published for over 100 years. All Dow Jones services make extensive use of MIS, but it is Dow Jones News/Retrieval (DJN/R), the on-line, electronic source of information, that is on the leading edge (Figure 13.7).

A few years ago, DJN/R's director of MIS bought two Connection Machines from Thinking Machines, Inc., of Cambridge, Massachusetts. It was the first business (rather than scientific) use for the powerful computer. The Connection Machine is a state-of-the-art parallel processor, with over 65,000 microprocessors all working at once.

In the past, as more subscribers logged on DJN/R, the more it slowed down the conventional, single-processor mainframes and minis. And as more data was added to the database, it became more difficult — and slower — to find things. Now, using the Connection Machine, a DJN/R user can quickly obtain any tidbit of information she needs. But that's all the subscriber needs to care about; from her perspective, who cares what kind of computer does it?

What Dow Jones News/Retrieval seems to understand quite well is that management must provide the linkages between strategy and technology, and that channels of communication must be wide open and available for its customers.

KNOWLEDGE CHECK

1. What is the name given to computer systems used in business to achieve business goals?   p. 398
2. What are the three levels of management?   p. 399
3. Describe what the three letters in the acronym MIS stand for.   p. 400
4. What are the three sources of data used for strategic or competitive information?   p. 402
5. Explain the purpose behind the MIS concept.   p. 402
6. What term describes a MIS department that sells information?   p. 408

MIS: THREE COMPONENTS

In the early days, a business had a computer that kept track of accounting data and records. It was considered an office machine or just a large calculator that could speed up manual processing. Today, computer information systems are essential in every aspect of a well-run business. A company would literally grind to a halt without MIS. Even when the computer function is lost ("goes down") for just a short period of time, the losses quickly add up. To give you an idea of how important MIS is to a business, look at the pie chart in Figure 13.8 explaining what a typical *Computerworld* subscriber spends annually on information technology.

Throughout this book, it's been stressed that the computer is a system made up of people, software, and hardware. The same is true of MIS. There are many people to consider in MIS: managers, staff, and end-users. MIS software takes many forms; MIS hardware is often complex and ubiquitous. Let's take a closer look.

THE PEOPLE COMPONENT

MIS is unique in that it touches just about everyone in the company. MIS is a department or organization itself with all its own internal computing needs. Yet it is also an organization providing services to other departments. Within those departments are many people who use computers.

THE MIS ORGANIZATION

Just as business has its organizational chart, so do individual departments throughout the company. Refer again to Figure 13.4; as you can see, MIS is no exception. It takes many different people to run a large MIS organization.

FIGURE 13.8

Buying power of the *Computerworld* reader. With 86
percent of our readers in IS
or corporate management,
we reach the most important
buyers in the market, each
of whom spends an average
of $3.2 million a year on
information technology.

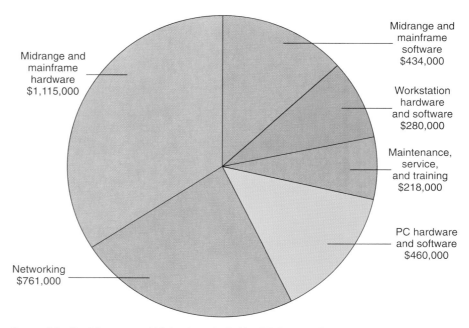

Midrange and
mainframe
hardware
$1,115,000

Midrange and
mainframe
software
$434,000

Workstation
hardware
and software
$280,000

Maintenance,
service,
and training
$218,000

PC hardware
and software
$460,000

Networking
$761,000

Source: A Profile of *Computerworld* Subscribers, April 1991. IDG Research Services Buying Power Survey,
October 1991.

In years past, data processing functions were loosely managed; the atmosphere was fraternal. Projects often ran over budget and past the scheduled
completion date because programmers tend to write and rewrite code or
"tweak" it to make it better. Often the improvements were barely noticeable
to the user and were a waste of time and money. In other cases, the application
was a programming marvel but was difficult to use or did not provide the
information managers needed.

Without firm management controls, MIS often ran afoul of other business
departments and gained a reputation for being difficult to work or communicate with. On the other hand, more and more functions and departments
wanted information systems, creating a work overload in MIS. As a result, an
application backlog grew; in large companies, some estimated there would be
a lag time of five to six years before a project could be completed! An improved
management structure has helped get MIS better organized and able to accomplish its tasks in a more businesslike fashion.

MIS MANAGEMENT.   At the head of the MIS organization is the senior executive, sometimes known as the vice president, general manager, or director of
MIS. In most cases, these individuals have worked their way up through the
ranks over a period of 10 to 20 years. Many have an undergraduate degree in
computer science or MIS and often an MBA to go with it. They are highly paid
individuals with a great deal of authority and responsibility. They often report
to the executive vice president or even the president of the company. They
spend a great deal of their time in planning meetings, helping chart directions

for the company and determining the role of MIS in corporate strategies. It is not uncommon to find them in a corner office, sitting at a large walnut desk.

Reporting directly to the MIS executive is the middle manager, commonly known as the manager of MIS. This is a senior person as well, but one with day-to-day responsibilities. His or her job is to make sure the director's wishes are carried out and implemented by the operational managers. For example, if the company decides to begin its fiscal year with a new reporting system, the director must orchestrate the operational managers and their staff to make sure the necessary hardware is purchased, the programming is completed, the debugging is finished, terminals or PCs are installed on desks, and so forth.

The operational managers oversee such things as software maintenance, new application development, and user training. These managers are often appointed to head a team of programmers working on a specific application or project. They are given detailed instructions and schedules for completing portions of the projects, some of which take years to finish.

MIS STAFF. The MIS staff is made up of people with many different skills, in much the same organizational tasks as the business itself. Most staff members have completed college programs in computer science. There are systems analysts who are responsible for analyzing and designing new applications as well as complete systems. For example, the head of manufacturing might ask a systems analyst to create a system, from hardware to software, to control the entire manufacturing process of a new product.

Programmers write software with programming languages. They can be found working at terminals or personal computers in conventional office environments, just like any other knowledge worker. In a Fortune 500 firm, there might be several hundred programmers working on various projects. Some are systems programmers, meaning their work involves expanding, improving, or maintaining the systems software or the existing software applications, such as the accounting system or the manufacturing resource planning (MRP) system.

Others are application programmers, who are assigned to work with various departments in the company, such as customer service, or to help users develop new applications. For example, a company planning to implement electronic data interchange (EDI) might have several systems programmers working in the MIS department, while assigning application programmers to order processing, inventory, and shipping to set up and install the EDI applications.

Still others are operations technicians, responsible for maintaining the hardware. Some are responsible for installing terminals and setting up personal computers, while others troubleshoot malfunctioning equipment. Some are in charge of backup systems, such as changing disk packs, tapes, and tape cartridges.

END-USER COMPUTING

The IBM PC, introduced to corporate America in 1981, truly changed the way the world computes. Its proliferation was spurred by users' growing frustration with MIS and its inability to provide them with computing services. The result became known as **end-user computing,** giving knowledge workers their own computers so they could be more productive in their work. Since MIS could not or would not provide them, the end-user departments funded such purchases from their own budgets. In time, some large companies actually opened their own computer stores, where knowledge workers could select their own PCs.

The reluctance on the part of MIS to support end-user computing was due to several factors: the application backlog noted earlier in this chapter, a purported lack of CPU power to add an infinite number of new terminals, and a general reluctance to let the unsophisticated novice have access to the corporate mainframe and its data. However, the widespread need on the part of knowledge workers to use more information in their work, combined with the need to be ever more productive, made end-user computing inevitable. Thus many knowledge workers began using mainframes or minis, working at terminals, but far more turned to PCs.

But PCs are no panacea. Naomi Karten, editor of *Managing End-User Computing,* has identified a number of erroneous assumptions about what PCs can or cannot do. For example it is wrong to assume that:

- *PCs reduce work load.* They often increase the work load because they can do so many things that simply weren't possible before.
- *Training results in immediate expertise.* Training is the beginning of the expertise-building process, not the end.
- *All we need to know is how to make the software work.* Clients who ask only for features or functions and don't want to be bothered with understanding how to analyze a business problem from a computer perspective, or how to evaluate alternative systems solutions, need more training.[1]

At first, knowledge workers with personal computers were not interested in using central MIS services, but were content with spreadsheets and word processing. But it soon became clear that for staff to be truly productive, access to mainframe data was essential. This spawned a number of significant changes in the way MIS functions and the way companies use information, as will be seen in the software and hardware sections.

THE PC MANAGER

Educating and training knowledge workers has become a primary objective for business. Where once acquiring new computer technology had been many firms' top priority, today it is employee training and motivation. Quality people are needed to use information systems effectively in the future. Concerns businesses have voiced include:

- How have job descriptions changed?
- What types of people or skills do we need now?
- Are we finding these people?

---

[1] "Expectations and Assumptions," *Managing End-User Computing* 5, no. 9 (April 1992), p. 11. © Auerbach Publishers.

FIGURE 13.9
The department's PC manager helps knowledge workers with hardware and software installation and configuration so that systems meet individual needs and further business goals.

- Where will we find these people in the future?
- Do we need to retrain people who have lost their jobs due to departmental computing, attrition, or downsizing?

Due to these increased training needs, a new occupation has emerged in many large companies: the **PC manager.** These people are commonly from an end-user group or department, and they not only understand the business process but have grasped computer technology and intuitively understand application software programs. Their job is to help other knowledge workers in their department learn to be more productive with their PCs, and often to troubleshoot and correct hardware and software problems. In addition, PC managers may counsel senior management on how to solve the preceding questions (Figure 13.9).

At first, it was an ad hoc position; that is, the PC manager unofficially helped fellow employees learn to use personal computers and software. In time, the position became more or less official; while most PC managers continue to do their regular work, their training role is sanctioned by management. In some cases, training is their only job. In Chicago, PC managers are such a powerful force that Julian Horwich formed the Chicago Area Microcomputer Professionals, which is now over 10,000 strong.

PC managers are a diverse, self-reliant group. Few use the technical support help telephone lines provided by software companies, preferring to learn application programs on their own time or at independent training seminars. Most say staying ahead of users' needs is a full-time job.

1. What is the senior MIS manager called, and who does he or she report to?   p. 410
2. What is the manager second in command called?   p. 410
3. Name several staff positions that report to the second in command.   p. 411
4. What has been responsible for the growth in end-user computing?   p. 412
5. What are the primary responsibilities of the PC manager?   p. 412

THE SOFTWARE COMPONENT

MIS is responsible for keeping many, many applications running on a daily basis, and making them available to knowledge workers. These include order processing, accounting, inventory control, computer-aided drawing, manufacturing, and database management. Remember, large computer systems are multiuser, multitasking machines; there could be a hundred or more applications running at once. The manner in which these many systems and applications are organized and monitored has been given various names and appellations over the years. The distinctions often blend into one another, but what follows describes the general evolution of the MIS software component.

DISTRIBUTED COMPUTING

For many years, all MIS functions were called **centralized computing,** kept in the central MIS facility. Eventually, there was more to do than MIS could handle. For that and other reasons, many computers and applications are dispersed, which is called **distributed computing,** and placed where they can be most effective (Figure 13.10).

George P. DiNardo, chief of information management and research at Mellon Bank in New York, after spending 30 years in two highly centralized MIS operations, reorganized his MIS department to reflect a decentralized or distributed computing environment. Over half of the applications are now developed by people in the end-user departments. Mr. DiNardo says, "The totally centralized systems shop can — if it is a quality shop — build systems better, but the business unit (knowledge workers) can build better systems. Application programming really belongs under the control of the business units that use that application. How do I feel about this transformation? I feel very good, thank you!"

COOPERATIVE PROCESSING

For most of the half-century computers have been in use, computer systems have been intentionally incompatible with each other. Vendors, wishing to develop a loyal market and customer base, made their hardware and software proprietary, as you learned with PCs in Chapter 2. However, in recent years businesses have found that no single computer is really appropriate for all the company's needs: the mainframe is good for corporate data, but engineers often want workstations, some knowledge workers prefer Macintoshes, banks want transaction processing for their ATMs, and so forth.

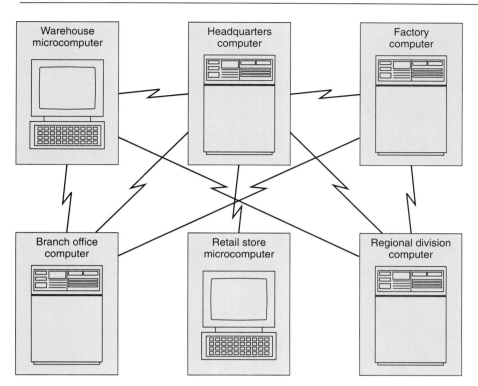

FIGURE 13.10

Distributed computing makes computer resources available throughout the organization.

The result is the drive toward **cooperative processing,** which means different computer systems are able to exchange data between their diverse operating platforms. The **operating platform** includes the computer itself, its operating system, its networking system (which is presented in the following chapter), its applications (e.g., databases) and services (e.g., transaction processing), and its development languages and tools, which you learned about in Chapters 10 and 11. The ultimate goal is to make it possible for any application to share data with any other.

This is often referred to as **interoperability,** which is simply another way of saying it is possible to perform any work task, regardless of its original resident operating platform, from whatever computer you are using. This is depicted in Figure 13.11. The reality today is that knowledge workers who have to use applications that reside on different platforms either have to know complex log-in and log-out procedures to change from one to another, or alternately may have two or three different terminals on their desk. Thus it is easy to see why interoperability, where it is possible to have mainframe, mini, workstation, and PC application work sessions all available or even running simultaneously, is highly desirable.

John R. Rymer, editor of *Network Monitor: Guide to Distributed Computing,* writes

> Interoperability is the defining user requirement for the 1990s. All large corporations and public institutions are trying to use distributed computing technology to get more value from their older standalone applications . . . [and are] seeking to integrate existing applications with new applications [with]

FIGURE 13.11   Interoperability: having your work session your way, regardless of the platform.

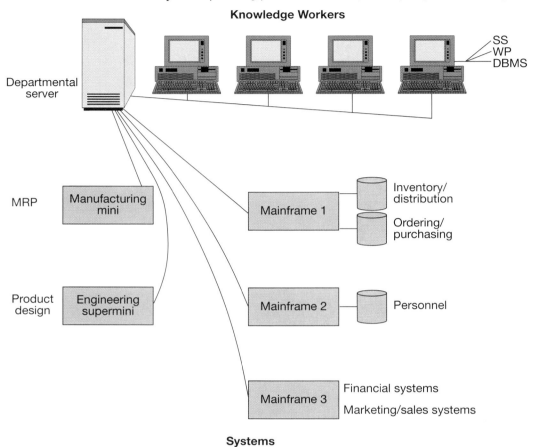

a set of distributed computing structures known as cooperative processing. In cooperative processing, two or more systems collaborate to perform a task. . . . We are moving slowly but inexorably toward distributed, object-oriented computing as the most important applications platform for the '90s and beyond.[2]

MIS AS A CORPORATE RESOURCE

As information systems have evolved, the manner of collecting data and transforming it into information has itself become a strategic tool. Just as a manager becomes more valuable as he or she gains experience, so have information systems. Companies are often reluctant to discuss certain aspects of their information systems, for fear that competitors may gain a competitive advantage by employing the same strategies.

For that reason, many corporate information systems use a security system that restricts access to certain types of information. For example, access to the

----

[2] John R. Rymer, *Network Monitor* 7, no. 4 (April 1992), pp. 2–3, © Patricia Seybold's Office Computing Group.

data center is restricted to key personnel by use of passwords and special locks. Security systems create passwords and security levels, so a clerk cannot read memos between senior executives that discuss a new product introduction. Programmers are often asked to sign employment agreements stating they will not divulge details about the projects they are at work on or the contents of programs they write. For example, an expert system might contain proprietary details about a product's ingredients or custom manufacturing techniques that would cause great loss if it fell into a competitor's hands.

Often computer-generated information, and in some cases proprietary programs, have demonstrated a usefulness that does not conflict with the company's strategic goals. Smart companies realize this material can be sold to others, providing a return on the investment made in developing it and perhaps even a profit. Mailing lists are a profitable information resource. Banks and insurance companies often sell specialized programs they have developed in-house. Clearly MIS is a valuable corporate resource in many different ways.

KNOWLEDGE CHECK

1. What kinds of applications is MIS responsible for running?   p. 414
2. Describe the two different ways in which MIS can be organized. pp. 414–15
3. What are the advantages in distributed computing?   p. 414
4. Why is cooperative processing desirable?   p. 415
5. What do we mean when we say MIS is a corporate resource?   pp. 416–17

THE HARDWARE COMPONENT

In the early days of business computing, the computer was kept in a separate room. By the late 1950s most businesses had IBM computers so they called the computer site the "IBM Room." Over the years, the names data processing and electronic data processing became fashionable. By the mid-1970s, the term MIS was commonplace; in the 1980s it was shortened to simply *information systems* (IS). In the 1990s it is not uncommon to refer to it as *information technology* (IT).

These changes reflect the information systems professional's desire to provide the kinds of computer services the enterprise seeks. There is still a computer room today, but more often it is an area, perhaps an entire floor in the building, designed to house the computer equipment. There is usually a shift supervisor and several operations people on duty, monitoring the system, backing up hard disk drives on tape cartridges, and performing other maintenance tasks. But MIS extends throughout the business. There are minicomputers in manufacturing, workstations in engineering, and personal computers in offices everywhere. This is why there is so much interest in the high-level, managerial organization of the software and hardware components. It is the reason for software, or information, engineering at the development level and cooperative processing at the application level. And as we shall see, there is also managerial organization at the hardware level.

FIGURE 13.12   New computer architectures are designed to take maximum advantage of all types of computer systems.

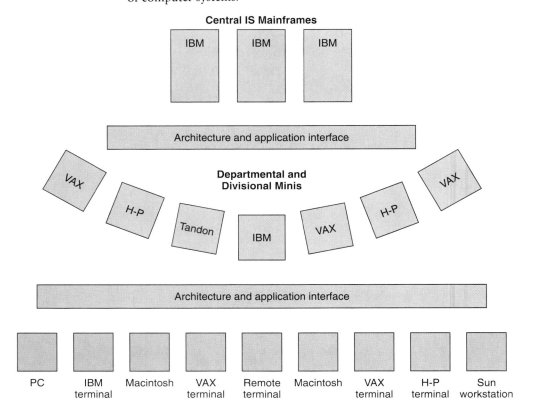

Central IS Mainframes

Departmental and Divisional Minis

Architecture and application interface

Architecture and application interface

PC | IBM terminal | Macintosh | VAX terminal | Remote terminal | Macintosh | VAX terminal | H-P terminal | Sun workstation

NEW COMPUTER ARCHITECTURES

Like nature and its systems, the evolution of computers and management information systems hasn't always been logical or carefully planned. A **computer architecture** is the design and implementation of computer systems in an organization. With the wide variety of peripherals and separate systems that must connect to the centralized computer, new computer architectures have emerged. A computer architecture is quite similar to a building architecture in that it determines how best to use physical facilities to help people work efficiently. Many businesses have devised their own, while others are promoted by computer vendors.

Figure 13.12 shows an architecture design used by an aerospace division of TRW, Inc., that maximizes the distributed computing concept. Centralized MIS services are retained as they are, with smaller mainframes and minicomputers connected; departmental processing is done in the appropriate departments. Personal computers and workstation computers are connected to departmental computers. The strategy behind TRW's architecture is to disperse computer power to reach as many users as possible; their belief is that the

NAS currently supports a growing number of desktops, systems, and servers with a variety of operating systems. This scenario shows how data is exchanged across NAS.

FIGURE 13.13

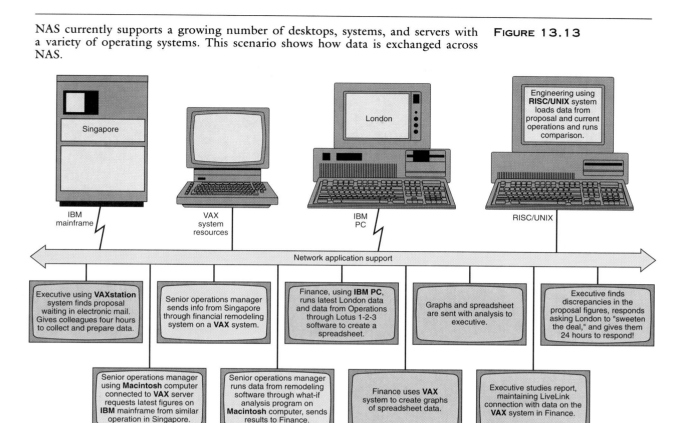

newest uses and innovations with the information system come from those users. This is the basic design architecture for modern information systems. The two major trends today are open systems and client/server computing.

OPEN SYSTEMS. **Open systems** means just what it implies: computer systems from various vendors can be easily connected to one another. This is true at the hardware level, the systems software level, and the application level. Open systems is the concept of interconnecting hardware, system software, and applications from many manufacturers into one *heterogeneous* system. In a truly open system, the knowledge worker is able to work with any application or any data, regardless of its platform, in exactly the same way, using the same or similar keystrokes and seeing the same screen displays. Trade groups, such as the Open Software Foundation (OSF), were formed to develop solutions to open systems problems, and great strides have been made. OSF's Motif graphic user interface is one result. Digital Equipment Corporation's Network Application Support (NAS), shown in Figure 13.13, is probably the most comprehensive open systems solution from a single vendor.

Tomorrow

X Windows: The Emerging Client/Server Standard?

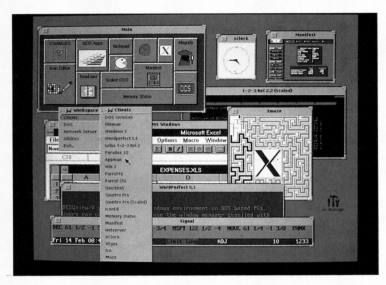

In real estate, the three criteria for property are "location, location, and location." In computer technology, it might be said that the three criteria are "standards, standards, and standards." Cooperative processing, open systems, and client/server computing are emerging with the UNIX operating system in common, and it could evolve into a standard for the simple reason that it is available on so many different computing platforms.

That's fine, but knowledge workers have no desire to work at the operating system level—thus the question is, what is the user interface? X Windows is the answer. "X Windows is the only means of distributing a windowed environment across a company's computing resources," says analyst Steve Auditore of the X Business Group market research company.

X Windows is both a GUI and an operating environment that runs under UNIX and competes with Microsoft Windows, OS/2, and a variety of other window-oriented GUIs, both commercial and proprietary. Developed at MIT in the early 1980s, it is licensed to develop-

ers by the X Consortium, which is comprised of 35 vendors. Simply put, X Windows allows developers to create applications that span a variety of platforms while allowing the user interface to present the same windowed environment to the knowledge worker.

X Windows runs on terminals of all kinds, which are less expensive than PCs. What's more, it runs on PCs as well. Some computer systems vendors have made the X Windows interface available to customers on UNIX workstations, terminals, and PCs. Quarterdeck Office Systems offers its DesQview menu-driven operating environment in an X Windows version, making it a direct competitor with Microsoft Windows. DesQview/X is powerful; it runs X Window terminal sessions, it manages any kind of PC application, and it runs Windows as if it too were an application, as well as the applications running under Windows.

X Windows grew popular in the manufacturing environment, where graphic terminals are used for design, engineering, and other tasks. Yet the growth into the business market in the past few years has been phenomenal, nearly doubling in 1991 from 66,970 units in 1990. Growth is expected to increase by at least 40 percent for the next few years.

A great deal of open systems work involves personal computers, and it is estimated that about 15 million personal computers will need to be integrated in the first part of the 1990s. This is because some users need access to the corporate mainframe's database (for example, to perform analyses and projections using current figures). MIS grew concerned that the data passed back from the personal computer may have been "corrupted," and for several years there ensued the battles and problems of micro-mainframe connections, or trying to connect personal computers to the central computer. Much of the problem was solved by appointing a database administrator in MIS to maintain database integrity.

CLIENT/SERVER COMPUTING. **Client/server computing** is a hardware architecture that takes advantage of the processing power of two computers working together to perform a task. One is called the **client**, usually a PC used by a knowledge worker, which is the "front end" of the system. The other, called the **server,** is the "back end" computer that holds data the client needs to process. It might be a mainframe, mini, workstation, or even another PC; often servers are the most powerful PCs available, and they serve many PCs. While this architecture resembles the traditional distributed model with its mainframe and terminals, it differs significantly in that *both computers are involved in the data processing.* Each processes its data in the best way it knows how to do. For example, if the knowledge worker is working with a large DBMS stored on the server, the PC only works with the data it needs; the rest stays at the server. If the server database is updated, that processing is done at the server. In addition, servers often serve more than one client PC, thus the need for more processing power.

FACILITIES MANAGEMENT

In the 1960s, many companies wanted to install data processing equipment but lacked the staff or the expertise to do it themselves. So they brought in **facilities management** companies, which contract for and run the entire information systems operation. Electronic Data Systems (EDS) was formed by H. Ross Perot, a Texan with firm convictions about himself, his employees, and his company. Facilities management takes many forms today. It is used to get a new MIS operation up and running quickly; it is used to breathe new life into one that is performing below par; and it is used by companies that simply no longer wish to operate the computers, often termed **outsourcing.**

Today, industry leader EDS is a $5 billion company, with employees in 26 foreign countries. Figure 13.14 shows the EDS MIS facility in Dallas, Texas. EDS buys more computers than any other corporation on earth, installing and operating them at customer sites. It has created management information systems for insurance companies, banks, the federal government, and agencies of the armed forces. In the 1980s, it had contracts with the U.S. Army, First City Bancorp of Houston, and Blue Cross/Blue Shield, each representing well over half a billion dollars. In 1984, Perot sold EDS to General Motors, which wanted to enhance its computer operations and develop sophisticated factory automation systems. Perot became a significant investor in Steve Jobs' NeXT computer and went on to form Perot Systems, a more specialized counterpart to EDS, in 1988.

FIGURE 13.14

FIGURE 13.14

Electronic Data Systems (EDS) MIS facility in Dallas, Texas.

KNOWLEDGE CHECK

1. Why do we say there is a computer "room" even though MIS extends throughout the business?   p. 417
2. What is another acronym commonly used in place of MIS?   p. 417
3. Explain the concept of a computer architecture and why it is important to management.   p. 418
4. What is the goal of open systems?   p. 419
5. What is the advantage of client/server computing?   p. 421
6. Name some of the reasons for facilities management.   p. 421

WHAT LIES AHEAD?

The nature of MIS continues to change rapidly. *I/S Analyzer,* a newsletter for information systems management, reported five personnel and organizational issues facing MIS in the 1990s:

- The "new individualists" are a new type of information systems professional — more complex in their needs and interests, and motivated by different things than their predecessors — now entering the work force and taking positions of leadership.

- Organizational dynamics are changing. Influence is no longer measured by the number of employees one manages; "influence without authority" is a new management skill; and people-relationships are based on exchange, reciprocity, and forming alliances.

- Corporate and organizational cultures are changing as a result of mergers and acquisitions as well as more frequent changes in management. Behavioral science is playing a growing role in helping MIS people assess culture, for they must work with it every day.

- The business environment is changing. There is a shift away from industrial and material capital to a knowledge-value base, which is accelerating the rate of change worldwide.

- MIS managers must be ever more active in assessing their own personality and behavior as they affect personnel and organizational matters. Understanding the various personality types one encounters is a way to better understand oneself.[3]

In addition to the push for cooperative and open systems, hardware technology is driving many changes as well. The large mainframe computer has been surpassed in speed and flexibility by desktop computers, which have microprocessors even more powerful than mainframes. Even so, mainframes will not leave us soon; they represent a significant investment and will act as database machines and file servers for many years to come.

Furthermore, as computing power and information systems are distributed throughout the business more and more, MIS people are moving out of the information systems organization and being assigned to end-user organizations. They are working side by side with knowledge workers to build and maintain departmental information systems. As the mainframe becomes a database storage bank, the centralized operation will require fewer staff; however knowledge workers, as they assume more technical responsibilities, will need more help maintaining their systems and building new applications.

MIS ETHICS: CORPORATE DATA SECURITY

Corporate data security is every employee's business. Corporate computer crimes demoralize employees and make the company look bad. According to the experts, most computer crimes are committed by insiders. Here are three true stories:

- A secretary created phony vendors in a computer database and then authorized $80,000 in payments to them.

- A chemical company salesman programmed the computer to pay him double commissions.

- A commodities broker skimmed $1.5 million off his trading pool.

The best defense is an offense — a corporate policy and set of guidelines — experts advise. Here are five ways to create a sense of computer ethics and to prevent computer crime:

1. Top management must be educated about computer crime and its consequences. Studies have shown that when the president or chief executive understands use and abuse, and takes a public stand against computer crime, employees are less likely to commit it.

2. Managers should warn employees that the company takes a hard line on computer crime,

---

[3] *I/S Analyzer* 29, no. 11 (November 1991) © United Communications Group.

CAREERS FOR KNOWLEDGE WORKERS

TIM YANCY, MANAGER, CUSTOMER SERVICE MANAGEMENT SYSTEMS, SOUTHERN CALIFORNIA EDISON

"My job is really interesting," says Tim Yancy. "I work on the business side, and it's different from the technical world. I find it more important and exciting. Tasks that five years ago were done by programmers can be done today by knowledge workers, using the new PC tools,

in just a few months. The real key is understanding the business your company is in; that's what it boils down to."

Tim Yancy represents the modern information systems professional. He earned his undergraduate degree in business administration, with a minor in computer science, from Oral Roberts University in Tulsa, Oklahoma. "It seemed like a good combination," he says. Upon graduation he was hired by Southern California Edison, an electric utility that provides service to a 50,000–square-mile area of central and southern California. The computer systems at Southern California Edison are complex and vast; there are over 650 employees in the information systems organization.

Tim's first job was as a programmer trainee, which he did for three years, "but it just wasn't my strongest suit." He transferred to a staff planning

group, charged with evaluation and planning issues such as whether to lease or buy computer hardware and software. "We also used the mainframe computer to do our work—for example, analysis software and some 4GLs to prepare our reports." While in this position, Tim returned to college and earned an MBA degree from California State University at Los Angeles.

He then moved on to a senior information systems analyst position, where he helped knowledge workers learn how to use PCs to be more productive in their work. "End-user support is what we called it, and it was here I began learning about the business of the company. I learned there were a lot of people who didn't care about computers, and some who even felt they were in the way. When you work with personal computers, it can be easy to lose sight of the

---

whether it's theft of a floppy disk or stealing information from a database. They should spell out that offenders will be prosecuted.

3. There should be a company code of ethics, and every employee should receive a copy. It should state explicitly what the company considers a computer crime, as well as what is ethical and unethical. It should also tell employees what actions are grounds for dismissal and/or prosecution.

4. Employees should have a contact person to notify if they suspect there has been a computer crime.

5. Data security systems must be instituted that re-

quire employees to use passwords or other security systems. Passwords should be changed every 30 days. There should be a corporate director of security to investigate possible crimes and to make sure employees are protecting their passwords.

It may seem odd, but people will often do things with the computer without thinking they are unethical or illegal. Therefore most experts agree that educating employees is the first step in computer security. This weeds out the true criminal from the accidental rule-breaker by ensuring that those who violate the rules are doing so with full knowledge of what the company deems ethical and unethical.

fact that you need to get something done with it. You need to be *productive* with it. This was an important learning experience for me."

Tim took what he learned into his next assignment, Macintosh product manager for the company. He evaluated knowledge workers' needs and recommended the appropriate Macintosh for the job. He also became actively involved with MacIS, a computer user group dedicated to helping information systems organizations maximize the productivity potential of the Macintosh. "It was really one of my favorite jobs," says Tim, but again he was promoted, this time to his current position as manager of customer service management systems.

"My group develops computer systems for the managers of customer service at Southern California Edison," he says. There are 500 managers and

about 6,500 employees in customer service, spread across the entire 50,000-mile area. Working with a core group of managers, Tim and his staff are delivering information to help them better understand customer service operations. "This is new information they've never had before, and we're trying to deliver it in a very timely manner.

"It's a Macintosh system, and the managers use the mouse to click on icons or make choices from menus. They need to see operational reporting data, such as monthly reports on key indicators of business performance. They also need financial reports. The graphical user interface is important, and so is being able to view financial data in graphical form."

There is a significant shift in the way information systems are developed and used at Southern California Edison. Here is one example: "We've always been a

centralized data processing shop built around mainframes in the corporate office," says Tim. "That worked well, and we did everything we could centrally. But now we realize the usefulness of the PC tools, the limitations of the old systems, and the fact that knowledge workers can often develop their own applications faster.

"IS also spends a disproportionate amount of time maintaining the old systems, such as updating electricity rate structures. A modern, flexible system can be updated quicker and easier. We have good, solid operational mainframe systems in place; now my mission is to build managerial systems on top of them. To do that well means understanding the business, and in the future I believe we will need more people who understand both computers and the business world. It's worth going out of your way to know both."

SUMMARY

1. *Define the term MIS and explain how it is used.* A company's management information system works together with the business to help it achieve its goals. The same business systems and management structure that work in the company are used in MIS as well. People, software systems, and hardware make up MIS.

2. *Describe three roles MIS plays in a company.* The people component includes MIS staff, end-users, and company management. The software component provides systems that make various services available on a wide variety of computers

across the company. These are often referred to as distributed computing, enterprise-wide computing, and information systems that are offered outside the company as a product. The hardware component includes the physical location of the computers; some are centralized, while others are in various departments. Most companies want their hardware integrated, so data can be used everywhere. Often new hardware architectures must be designed to accomplish this.

3. *Name ways MIS is used, by whom, and for what purposes.* MIS provides information for the com-

pany with computer systems. It is used for record keeping, operations control, and strategic planning. MIS is primarily used in business, government, and the information industry.

4. *Discuss the impact of personal computers and new computer architectures on MIS.* MIS has grown from a centralized to a distributed computing environment. Personal computers have contributed to dispersing processing power in the company. The current trends are in cooperative processing, open systems, and client/server computing.

5. *Explain how centralized MIS is evolving and changing.* People issues are growing in importance. Mainframe computers are not going away, but information systems are spreading throughout the business. As this occurs, the MIS people are moving from their organization out into user organizations, to work side by side with knowledge workers. MIS executives are increasingly being called upon to help solve business problems and assist in making strategic business decisions.

INFORMATION AGE ISSUES

1. In the past, we had corporate MIS departments run by computer professionals. When the company needed a new application or system, the professionals designed it. But over the years, computers have grown easier to program and use. Now many users can create their own applications or systems. In the process, the need for MIS professionals is declining. In many companies, cutbacks in the corporate MIS department and decentralization are resulting in layoffs and firings. Do you feel this is a fair way to treat the people who have maintained computer systems over the years? Can you think of better ways to handle MIS personnel, whose job descriptions are becoming obsolete?

2. It is not uncommon to hear about companies using computer technology to gain a competitive advantage in their industry. These firms utilize the computer in some innovative way that the competitors haven't yet thought of, and thus are able to sell more products or services. Yet sooner or later, the competitors figure out the technique; eventually the entire industry uses it. Can you foresee a day when there are no competitive advantages to be gained through computers? What happens to competitive business practices if that happens?

3. In the movie *Jumpin' Jack Flash,* an employee discovers she has a talent for stealing small amounts of money from the computer system. Before long, she has enough to buy a fancy sports car. The idea that she is stealing does not seem to bother her; rather, she is quite proud of her ability to manipulate the computer so effectively. Would this same employee reach into a co-worker's pocketbook, or even the company safe, and steal money? Why, then, does she steal without compunction using the computer?

CHAPTER REVIEW QUESTIONS

REVIEW QUESTIONS

1. What are the two types of knowledge workers in large businesses?
2. Name the three levels of management in business operations.
3. Why is it important that MIS act as an "overlay" to chart and support the business and its functions?
4. Describe some of the jobs of MIS staff.
5. What are the objectives and benefits of cooperative processing and open systems?
6. What are the objectives and benefits of client/server computing?
7. When does facilities management or outsourcing make sense?

DISCUSSION QUESTIONS

1. Discuss the definition of MIS and what it means. How do the newer names affect its corporate goals and objectives?
2. Discuss some practical applications of the M in MIS.
3. Discuss some practical applications of the I in MIS.
4. Discuss some practical applications of the S in MIS.
5. Discuss Nolan's model of the stages of growth in MIS. Does it apply in other areas of business or life as well?
6. Name some examples of each of the three sources from which management collects data to be stored, processed, and retrieved by MIS.
7. Describe MIS's key advantages in the TransCanada PipeLines case.
8. Describe MIS's key advantages in the Tulare Touch case.

MULTIPLE-CHOICE

1. The different levels of computer support are:
   a. Centralized.
   b. Executive.
   c. Departmental.
   d. Groups.
   e. White collar workers.
2. MIS supports the following levels of management:
   a. Supervising.
   b. Record keeping.
   c. Plant supervisor.
   d. Operations control.
   e. Strategic planning.
   f. Layoffs.
   g. All of the above.
3. An operating platform includes:
   a. The operating system.
   b. The networking system.
   c. The knowledge worker group.
   d. Common data.
   e. Applications and services.
   f. Development languages and tools.
   g. All of the above.

FILL-IN-THE-BLANK

1. A _____ _____ _____ is the creation of a business application by MIS.
2. An MIS organization that packages and sells information is called a _____.
3. The three components of MIS are _____, _____, and _____.
4. The name given for knowledge workers taking responsibility for their own computing needs is _____.
5. The first way in which MIS software functions were organized was called _____.
6. Interoperability is the same as _____.

TRUE/FALSE

1. The computer systems in a company should be consistent in operations with the business processes.
2. MIS personnel rarely need a college education.
3. The PC manager works in the MIS organization.
4. In the broad sense, all computer systems are distributed.
5. All companies should insist that MIS have a computer architecture.

KEY TERMS

Voice and Data Communications Systems

LEARNING OBJECTIVES

After reading and studying this chapter, you should be able to:

1. Identify the hardware, software, and network components necessary for communications.

2. Describe the difference between analog and digital signals.

3. Identify two kinds of networks.

4. Name three network topologies.

5. Identify the different types of network applications.

6. List several methods of maintaining network security.

Voice and Data Communications and the Knowledge Worker

In 1844, Samuel F. B. Morse tapped in dots and dashes with a metal key, sending the first telegraph message from Washington, D.C., to Baltimore, Maryland. Using Morse code, as it became known, was inconvenient and restricted both speed and content by today's standards, but back then it greatly sped the transmission of information; it is still in use today. Data communications was born. By 1871, the Western Union telegraph company eclipsed the Pony Express as the means of moving messages quickly.

Five years later, patent number 174,465 was issued to Alexander Graham Bell for the harmonic telegraph — today known as the telephone — and the world was never the same again. Now people could hear each other's voices over wires, surely a miracle. The telephone network grew rapidly; in just 25 years there were 6 million phones in the United States.

This chapter explores the two types of communications used in business today to convey information: voice and data communications. Both involve the use of computers, but our primary concentration throughout will be on data communications. As with MIS, the terms in use have changed over the years. The first was **telecommunications,** which James Martin, a noted industry expert, defines in his seminars as

> Any process that permits the passage from a sender to one or more receivers of information of any nature, delivered in any usable form (printed copy, fixed or moving pictures, visible or audible signals, etc.) by means of any electromagnetic system (electrical transmission by wire, radio, optical transmission, guided waves, etc.). [Telecommunications] includes telegraphy, telephony, videotelephony, data transmission, etc.

Today it is common to simply hear the term *communications* used in its place. Another term you might hear is *data communications,* which involves sending data from one computer-like device to another.

When communications is applied in a business setting, it is often termed *networking.* **Networking** means to connect two or more computers to exchange programs and data through a communications channel. A **communications channel** is a physical means of connecting the communicating computers so they can exchange the programs or data. This means of connection or transmission is commonly wires of one sort or another, but may also take just about any form, from satellite and radio signals to infrared beams. The simplest network is two people using tin cans connected by a string to transmit primitive voice communications. But it points up the fact that networking takes place when *people* use computer systems and communications.

Today our networking options are numerous. Sophisticated phone systems link knowledge workers and companies wishing to do business with one another. We use facsimile machines to, in effect, copy whole sheets of paper long distance. But by far the most diverse of our communications options is linking computers into networks that span the globe. Large computer systems are connected in networks with other computers around the world, performing a vast number of transactions—often without any human intervention—at speeds that boggle the mind. Personal computers are linked with each other, as well as with larger office systems and corporate mainframes, to conduct daily commerce. PCs are also used in both business and personal lives to send and receive electronic mail, read the news, shop for merchandise, manage investments, converse with friends, meet new people, conduct international teleconferences, and browse in vast electronic information libraries. Figure 14.1 shows the diversity of communications services used by today's knowledge worker.

FIGURE 14.1   Today's knowledge worker is in electronic contact with an array of both voice and data communications systems.

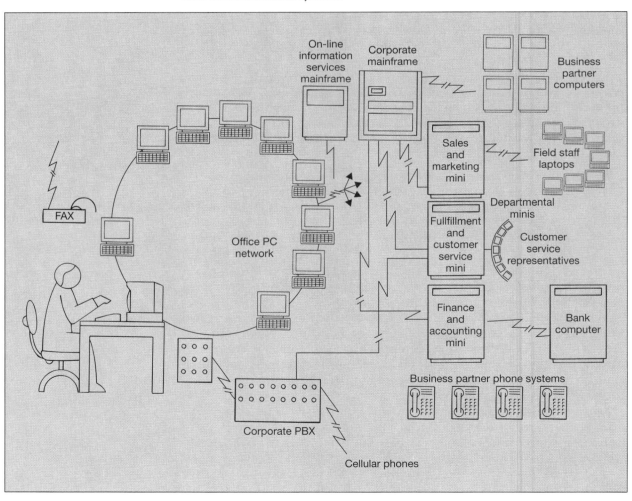

In this chapter we'll explore how knowledge workers use voice and data communications and networking to do their work and help the business achieve its goals. You'll learn about the hardware and software necessary for voice and data communications as well as the role of the PC in today's networking. You'll become familiar with the various types of networks and transmission technologies. Case studies will demonstrate how business and government use networking, and you'll find out about the many on-line information services now available. We'll also explore the serious problem of network security and how certain people use networks to invade and damage computer systems.

COMMUNICATIONS HARDWARE

A computer communications system has the same components as any other type of computer system: input devices, a processor, routing devices, and output devices. Like other computer systems, it also has certain standards or rules that must be followed precisely, and it has some sort of operating system as well. And knowledge workers use specific procedures and application software to work with the communications system. There are always computers —at least two. The main difference is in the peripherals used to connect the computers to networks.

Not that many years ago, voice communications and data communications were completely separate technologies in a company. Rarely did the two organizations even interact. But in the late 1980s, that began changing dramatically. Today voice and data communications technologies and organizations are often merged, working together to meet the rapidly expanding needs of the business. Let's take a closer look at the two technologies.

VOICE COMMUNICATIONS HARDWARE

Knowledge workers use the telephone every day, but the phone used in the office is often very different from the one at home. Its many calling and messaging features are attributable to the computer circuitry that lies within its case. In voice communications, your desk phone is a terminal, attached to a powerful computer-powered device called a *PBX*.

PBX. Aside from the telephone, probably the most common voice communications hardware device is the **private branch exchange (PBX),** also known as the *switchboard*. The PBX was modeled after the public branch exchange switchboard used at the telephone company to route calls. In the past, the switchboard was controlled by an operator who connected outside callers with the destination phone by plugging cables into a panel. In time, it became possible to dial the extension number; today many PBXs allow for direct dialing. Most modern PBXs have computer power built in, so that many of the functions performed by the operator are done automatically. The "intelligent PBX," often called a *computerized branch exchange* (CBX) or *private automated branch exchange* (PABX), has many other features, some of which we'll discuss in the software section.

YESTERDAY
THE DARTMOUTH TIME-SHARING EXPERIMENT

The BASIC programming language was developed as a teaching tool at Dartmouth College in Hanover, New Hampshire, by Dr. John Kemeny and Dr. Thomas Kurtz. Coincident with developing BASIC, Kemeny and Kurtz sought a way to "provide interactive computing, to give the students the capability of actually talking with the machine while the program was running, to give immediate feedback," Kemeny explained. At the time this was known as time-sharing, as explained in Chapter 7.

I wanted to hear how BASIC was implemented, and Kemeny smiled as he told me the story. John McGeachie and Michael Busch, two graduate students, were working with Kemeny late into the night. Indeed, much of the work had to go on at night, for everyone had their regular daytime duties as well. "I've always been a late-night worker, always have been," says Kemeny. "But these two were carrying a full-time load, and what they did

was remarkable. The solution to time-sharing was two machines talking to one another. The big problem was how to get them communicating, which one was the master, and which the slave. It was a problem that had never been solved before, and McGeachie and Busch solved it."

The team had gotten BASIC working a few days prior and had turned their attention to trying to get the two machines communicating. One was a General Electric 225 mainframe and the other a GE "front end," a programmable telephone switching device. They'd had a few responses work, but nothing conclusive. Teletype terminals (TTYs) were connected to the front end, and two people would try simultaneously to send a computation in BASIC to the mainframe and get an answer back. As it turned out, the front end became the master, telling the mainframe what to do (the reverse of what some had expected).

Time after time, they'd send their programs and nothing would happen. Each time the mainframe dumped the program (refused to store it in memory) and the experiment failed.

Time after time, the team tinkered with the equipment and then returned to their keyboards, typing in any BASIC program that came to mind and sending it to the mainframe once again. Then, at 4:00 A.M., May 1, 1964, it worked. Just like that, it worked; the mainframe responded and returned correct answers to both terminals! Kemeny was elated. And Kurtz? Ecstatic, of course, when he heard about it in the morning. "Tom Kurtz knows he was not there," grins Kemeny, "for he's an early bird."

Source: Jack B. Rochester, "The Most Popular Language on Earth: A Pop History of BASIC," Boston Computer Society Computer Update, January–February 1985, pp. 30–35.

There are also a number of voice communications peripheral devices used in voice communications and integrated voice/data communications. Needless to say, each requires software to activate its functions. Here are a few.

T-1 SWITCH.   The **T-1 switch** makes it possible to turn one incoming phone line into many lines. T-1 switches are electronic devices that split the incoming calls using binary logic (2, 4, 8, 16, 32, 64, and so on) and route them to another computer or controller that disperses them to their destination. For example, a company may have one incoming line that splits to eight lines, routing them to the PBX; or it might route them to the order processing or customer service department, where the calls are answered by the first available representative.

AUTOMATIC CALL DIALING.   **Automatic call dialing (ACD)** is a computer-managed electronic dialing function for outgoing calls, often used by telephone marketing companies. It picks an exchange, such as 745, and then begins dialing all the suffix numbers in that exchange. Each time a call is answered, it is routed to the salesperson or customer service representative to pick up.

AUTOMATIC NUMBER IDENTIFICATION.   **Automatic number identification (ANI)** is used to determine the number of the caller dialing in. ANI uses its computer circuitry to identify the number from the telephone network, displaying it on a computer screen or an LCD (liquid crystal display) readout. It too is used in telephone marketing as a tool for determining customer demographics. For example, customers calling an 800 toll-free number to order a product or magazine subscription can be identified regionally (city, state, etc.) by their area code and phone number prefix. In this way, companies can perform targeted test marketing and then learn customer responses.

BRIDGE.   The **bridge** is computer circuitry that links phones and computers together. Some bridges are very simple; all they do is enable the computer to perform dialing tasks such as speed dialing or predictive dialing, which combines the features of automatic call dialing with a screening function. Unanswered calls or those picked up by an answering machine are rejected, so that the knowledge worker's time is not wasted.

There are two other devices in the bridge family: the *router* and the *gateway.* They perform similar functions: making connections between communications systems whether voice or data. The goal of all bridge devices is to create enterprisewide open systems, which you learned about in the previous chapter.

More sophisticated bridges answer an incoming call and use ANI to identify the caller as a new or existing customer. If the latter, the computer finds the customer's file and routes *both* the voice call *and* the on-screen data file to the customer service representative automatically. This is termed **voice/data integration,** and it not only saves time but helps customers feel they are being treated courteously, efficiently, and professionally.

DATA COMMUNICATIONS HARDWARE

In order to connect a computer to any kind of communications network, there must be some kind of device that links the two. The most common device, a *modem,* is used extensively with personal computers and along with other devices in large systems.

THE MODEM.   A **modem** is a hardware device that allows computers to communicate via telephone lines. Modem is an acronym of the terms **modu**lator and **dem**odulator. You connect a terminal or personal computer to a modem, and the modem to the telephone line, as shown in Figure 14.2. At the sending end, the modem *modulates* (converts) the computer's signals so they can be transmitted over the phone line. At the receiving end, the modem

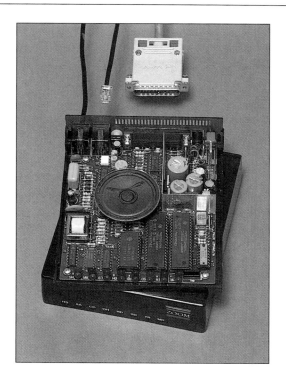

demodulates (reconverts) telephone signals back into signals the computer understands.

ANALOG AND DIGITAL COMMUNICATIONS.   Why are modulation and demodulation necessary? Because telephone systems were designed to carry analog, not digital, signals. An **analog signal** is continuous and changes in tone, pitch, and volume, like our voices. A **digital signal** is a single discrete signal, a steady stream of pulses that does not change in tone, pitch, or volume. Figure 14.3 shows the differences between digital and analog signals.

A series of digital signals makes up a data transmission, like a series of letters makes up a word. You can hear a digital signal when you use a modem or a FAX machine. When a connection is made, you'll hear a high-pitched squeal. This is a **carrier signal,** a tone that indicates the computer is available. After connection, the carrier signal is modulated to convey the binary information of the computer over the telephone line.

Most of the communications channels in the United States and Canada today are analog, although that is changing. However once the signals — whether voice or data — reach the first switch in a business, they are converted from analog to digital; that is the only way computers and computer-controlled devices can work with them. Without digital processing, it would not be possible to provide voice/data integration. We'll return to the subject of digital signals when we discuss communications channels in more detail.

TYPES OF MODEMS.   Modems come in many shapes and designs. The earliest modem, called an **acoustic coupler,** has two cups the telephone receiver

Modulated, digital computer signals and demodulated, analog signals.

FIGURE 14.3

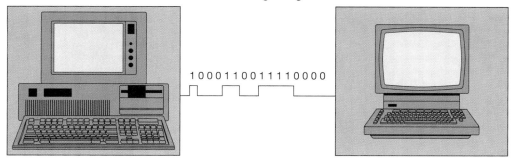

FIGURE 14.4

Acoustic couplers make it possible to use the nearest phone to establish a data communications link.

An internal modem is a printed circuit board that is inserted into an expansion slot inside the computer. Most modern internal modems are also smart modems (see Figure 14.5).

fits into. The acoustic coupler allows us to use almost any phone anywhere, including pay phones, to network computers. However acoustic couplers can be unreliable, in part because noise entering the cups can disrupt transmission.

An **internal modem** is mounted on a printed circuit board that fits into an expansion slot inside your computer. It usually requires no adjustments and is the least expensive modem. Figure 14.4 shows an acoustic coupler and an internal modem. Still somewhat more common is the **external modem.** It is enclosed in a case and connects to the computer with a cable; it has a receptacle for a modular phone plug.

FIGURE 14.5

External smart modems can be easily shifted from one PC to another. Many of today's smart modems also offer FAXing capabilities, such as the one shown here.

THE "SMART" MODEM. The **smart modem** has advanced circuitry that performs many functions for the knowledge worker. It can automatically dial a number or answer the phone. It can also redial a busy number over and over, and is able to adjust to the characteristics of the modem it is connecting to. External smart modems have lights that provide a visual signal as to what the modem is doing: the data transmission speed, when it has made the connection, when it's sending or receiving data, in addition to a speaker for audible monitoring, and more. By contrast, consider the first modems of the 1960s that had to be taken apart and rewired to dial a different telephone number. Figure 14.5 shows an external smart modem.

MODEM SPEED. Modems are also classified by data transmission speed, measured as *baud rate*. The **baud** is a unit for measuring signal speed, and is roughly equivalent to one *bit per second (bps)*. Early personal computer modems could only transmit at 300 bps, but 2,400-bps and 9,600-bps modems are common today. Larger mainframe computer modems can transmit at speeds of 19,200 to 1.25 million bps.

CONTROLLER. Communications controllers perform the same functions as regular computer controllers. A **controller** routes data between the CPU and the terminal, making it possible for many knowledge workers to work more efficiently. The controller is a kind of middleman, handing work off to the terminal and then, when it's ready, passing it to the CPU for processing. Every step is performed more efficiently. Controllers are used primarily with mini-computers and mainframes, and act as an intermediate computer between the terminal and the CPU. A controller is useful when sales representatives are

TODAY

NETWORKING TIPS

Standalone Personal Computers

1. Buy a smart modem. They are often pre-set to work on specific personal computers. Buy either a 2,400-bps or 9,600-bps modem, the standard operating speeds for most telecommunications.

2. Buy an easy-to-use software program. Evaluate them carefully for ease of setup, entering phone numbers and communications protocols, and redial features. Make sure you can program the software to dial and log into on-line services with ease.

3. When selecting on-line services, ask if there is an additional surcharge for using a faster modem. Depending on the work you're doing and your financial resources, you may want to set your software to dial at the less-expensive 1,200 or 2,400 bps. Check the hourly rates for on-line services; some are less expensive at night or on weekends. Watch the clock while you're on-line; it's easy to rack up big charges fast.

4. Plan on-line database searches before you dial. Use the manual to plan the keystrokes to find the information you want; otherwise you could spend expensive time searching in vain.

5. Do not use a modem on a telephone line with the call waiting feature. If someone calls while you are on-line, call waiting will disconnect you. It is possible to program most modems to begin a dialing sequence with *70, the code that temporarily disables the call waiting feature; call your phone company business office if you need help.

Reasons to Consider a Local Area Network

1. If knowledge workers share files and are passing disks back and forth with fre-quency. A problem frequently encountered is: who has the latest version of the file?

2. If there is a central peripheral, such as a laser printer or modem, connected to just one computer. Do people have to interrupt the knowledge worker or wait in line to use it?

3. If backups are a problem and there is no regularly scheduled plan for backing up.

4. If hard disk storage is a problem — perhaps some PCs have no hard disk, or an older, small hard disk, and a file server with a large hard disk would alleviate storage problems.

5. If knowledge workers need to communicate regularly without physically interrupting one another; E-mail on the LAN is a solution. This provides an opportunity to establish a gateway to external on-line resources as well.

submitting their daily sales reports. A file arrives and is routed by the controller to an operator at a terminal, where it is checked and prepared for processing. Then it is sent to the CPU for processing and storage.

MULTIPLEXER. The T-1 switch is a voice multiplexer; the term **multiplexer** is used to describe the peripheral device that splits one incoming *data line* into many, so that more than one terminal can be used to service incoming data transmissions. Multiplexers also speed up the data transmission, often raising it from 2,400 baud to 56,000 baud (often shown as 56Kbps, for kilobits per second). For example, a multiplexer is useful when multiple credit card authorizations are being handled at a processing center.

CONCENTRATOR. A **concentrator** is a controller and multiplexer combined into one peripheral to manage, amplify, and ensure the integrity of data signals. It is usually a computer- or microprocessor-controlled device, and like its two counterparts is connected between the primary computer and the terminals and other peripherals (such as a printer or modem). A concentrator is useful in situations where terminals or peripherals perform operations slowly, but task processing must be completed promptly. For example, customers at a bank ATM may take all the time they want to check account balances and decide how much to withdraw from their accounts, but the debiting should be quickly accomplished. The concentrator is also used when the data must be passed through wires or cables over long distances and needs to be boosted, or amplified. This ensures that the processing tasks are performed promptly and accurately. As you can see, there is similarity between controllers, multiplexers, and concentrators, but the trend is toward circuitry that combines and even adds functions, while at the same time reducing the size, cost, and unnecessary complexity of yet another peripheral device.

KNOWLEDGE CHECK

1. Name the voice and data device that turns a single incoming line into multiple lines. p. 434
2. What is an advanced use of a bridge? p. 435
3. What is the most commonly used communications peripheral for personal computers? p. 435
4. What is the difference between analog and digital signals? p. 436
5. What is the unit of measurement for communications speed? p. 438
6. What is the difference between a controller and a concentrator? p. 440

COMMUNICATIONS SOFTWARE

The hardware devices just discussed commonly provide the physical link between the computer and the communications network, but without software issuing commands to the computer, nothing will happen. Voice communications software automates certain PBX functions and is the key ingredient in voice/data integration. Data communications software routes signals to and from the devices, dials telephone numbers, and transmits data between remote computers.

VOICE COMMUNICATIONS SOFTWARE

Computers have made it much easier to work with PBXs. For example, if the marketing department was launching a new promotion that asked customers to call to place orders, they might need additional incoming lines. In the past this meant physical rewiring, but today it simply means a little reprogramming. The same is true of the messages and manner in which incoming calls are placed on hold until answered.

VOICE MAIL.   Perhaps the most familiar voice communications software is **voice mail,** which uses the computer to capture (input), digitize (process), store (on disk), and forward (output) spoken-word messages. Voice mail usually permits each employee to record a personal outgoing message. It is the corporate answering machine at every extension so that no one ever misses a call.

CALL CENTER MANAGEMENT.   The most sophisticated voice (often voice/data integration) communications application is in customer service. The *call center* is the department or function that works with customers; it often handles the largest volume of calls. Customer service is one of the most important services any company delivers, for satisfied customers are a top priority; therefore, the way they are handled on the phone is critical. Customer service is much more than simply handling incoming orders or complaint calls, as Figure 14.6 shows. Using computer systems that integrate voice and data is often referred to as *computer-telephone integration* (CTI). CTI systems make it possible for business not only to help customers, but also to add value to services and to increase business as well.

Call center management software runs on larger systems, such as minis and mainframes. In addition to voice/data integration, it's possible to completely customize the application to conform to the specific business, individual product lines, and even differing skill levels of the customer service representatives. A case in point is Blue Cross/Blue Shield of Rhode Island (BC/BS RI), whose customer service representatives handle over half a million calls per year. They must explain benefits and answer a wide variety of coverage questions for their insured.

BC/BS RI realized it must simplify the customer service process, so it decided to design and install a new call center management system. Among its

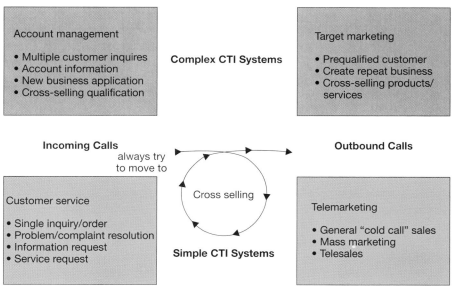

FIGURE 14.6

Computer-telephone integration uses voice and data communications to create new business opportunities from simple customer service calls.

goals were reducing the number of incoming customer calls for information (in the belief that a better-informed customer needs to make fewer inquiries) and improving the level of service for customer calls — ideally, to satisfy the inquiry on the first call. The new system was created by the Blue Cross/Blue Shield information systems organization and Cambridge Technology Partners, a systems development company.

BC/BS RI's IT infrastructure is made up of IBM mainframes storing all the insurance and customer data; they call these the *back end systems*. CT Partners installed an IBM RS/6000 UNIX midrange computer as an intermediary processor between the back end systems and the customer service reps' terminals. The reps participated in selecting the hardware: IBM PS/2 personal computers with large color monitors and easy-to-use trackballs for pointing and clicking operations.

CT Partners terms this a *three-tier client/server architecture,* where back end data is sent to the middle processing tier for formatting and routing transactions, then delivered as information to the representative at the workstation. CT Partners was responsible for writing the gateways from the back end systems to the UNIX processor, and for creating the graphic user interface for the PCs.

Customer service management and representatives are pleased with the Blue Ribbon system, as they call it. They have experienced marked improvements in ease of use, the quality of their interaction with customers, and higher productivity in expediting requests. From an information systems perspective, the Blue Ribbon system employs today's most modern technologies — powerful workstations with a GUI and a client/server architecture — that still make it possible to use the data from existing mainframe applications.

DATA COMMUNICATIONS SOFTWARE

There are two types of data communications software. One, generically known as *communications software,* is used to make connections from the individual computer making the inquiry to the **host** computer, the computer in charge of the work session and that stores the data the knowledge worker seeks. The other, communications management software, is used to establish connections from host computers to individual computers to provide services and data.

COMMUNICATIONS SOFTWARE. Communications software programs

work just like any other application, such as word processing. Some communications software uses a simple command structure; some use a menu; others are graphical and designed to work with Windows. Communications software can usually be programmed with telephone numbers that dial the modem and connect to another computer. Once connected, or on-line, you can send or receive communications. **On-line** means, literally, in direct communications with another computer. In a few cases, there are proprietary communications software programs that are designed to provide access to a single vendor's computer. This approach is used to restrict and control access to these information sources and thus ensure security and fiscal accountability. Whether an off-the-shelf or proprietary package, all communications software provides the following capabilities.

Anatomy of PC-to-host communications. Database services permit downloading files from the host, but not uploading files from the PC.

FIGURE 14.7

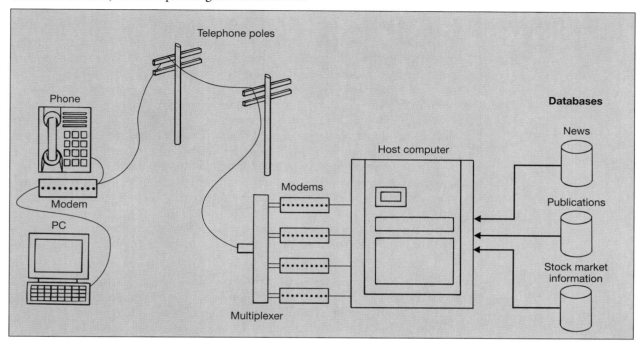

FILE TRANSFER. The most common communications activity is transferring files that contain useful information. This is called **uploading** when files are sent from a remote computer, such as a laptop or personal computer, to a larger, central computer (a mini or mainframe), as depicted in Figure 14.7. The opposite is **downloading** or receiving files. File transfer lets you send or receive data very efficiently, since you don't have to type it in while you are on-line. For example, a report can be prepared using word processing and then uploaded to the destination computer. This saves time and money. However, the file must be in the proper format for transmission.

THE ASCII FORMAT. Applications such as word processing and spreadsheets format data, making it appear correctly in the documents you create. Communications software has the ability to transmit just about any kind of data, but not always in the format of the originating application. **ASCII** (pronounced *askey*) stands for the American Standard Code for Information Interchange and applies to all aspects of communications and networking. It is the most commonly used format for file transfer. ASCII data interchange requires that all the special codes and formats from the application program be stripped from a file. This is the only aspect of the ASCII standards that you control, and it is very simple to do. Most applications offer the option of storing your work as an ASCII file (sometimes referred to as **text file**) as well as, say, a standard word processing file. Although it is often possible to exchange files created by a particular word processing or spreadsheet program, the ASCII format makes it possible to share a file between incompatible programs as well.

COMMUNICATIONS PROTOCOLS. Computers and communications programs differ, therefore it can be difficult to get two to "talk" to each other. But we can adjust these differences by setting **communications protocols,** the rules and standards, baud rate, and other important settings that make it possible for two computers to communicate with each other.

Many communications software products have a feature called a **script file** that allows you to create and store the protocol settings for each individual system you communicate with, as well as each computer's telephone number and the information you need to connect on-line. In most cases where one computer is directly connected to another, such as two personal computers, their communications protocols must be set to match. Synchronizing two communicating computers is called **handshaking.** Some communications applications are designed to work on many different brands of computers, to overcome hardware incompatibility and expand communications capabilities.

COMMUNICATIONS MANAGEMENT SOFTWARE. Our software discussion thus far has centered on the standalone computer calling a host computer. Now let's look at **communications management software,** sometimes called **dialup** software, which controls most computers that receive calls from a number of single knowledge workers. Like an airport traffic controller, this software determines which computers can participate in a network and the proper paths for communications to take.

Communications management software manages the use of the network, ensuring that only properly authorized knowledge workers get connected, keeping records of their on-line time, and charging their accounts when services are used. It also manages all the various services and makes them available to knowledge workers. When a network becomes overloaded, communications management software decides which computers have priority and which have to wait.

Commonly, all communications software performs error checking and security procedures. **Error checking** is an important process by which networked computers assure the accuracy and integrity of data transmissions. There are many factors that introduce errors, among them mis-keying, electrical power surges, and telephone line noise. Often when errors are found, the software tells the transmitting computer to re-send the data. Security procedures are used to prevent someone from intruding in a network without proper authorization. The software requests that potential knowledge workers identify themselves and prove they are authorized to use the computer before they actually get into the network's computers.

Communications management software runs on mainframes, minis, and personal computers; its characteristics and capabilities are determined by the number of people using it and the extent of the services it offers. Figure 14.8 shows the main menu for a popular on-line information service's communications management software. We'll learn more about on-line information services later in this chapter.

FIGURE 14.8

A Prodigy service menu from one of the many different on-line information services offered by Prodigy. Note the window in the lower portion of the screen that announces other Prodigy services.

KNOWLEDGE CHECK

1. What is the most common voice communications application?   p. 441
2. What does the term *on-line* mean?   p. 442
3. What are the two terms used for file transfer?   p. 443
4. What is the most common format for file transfer?   p. 443
5. What are the two types of data communications software?   pp. 442, 444
6. Why is error checking important?   p. 444

COMMUNICATIONS NETWORKS

In general, a **network** is any computer system that connects two or more points in a communication channel. Practically speaking, a network is made up of three components: computers and peripheral devices, one or more communications channels, and a set of standards, or protocols, that assure proper understanding and communication. There are many kinds of networks, and we shall learn about them — how they differ and how they often interconnect with one another. You are already familiar with computers and peripheral devices, so let's begin by discussing communications channels.

COMMUNICATIONS CHANNELS

As you know, a communication channel can be something as simple as a string between two tin cans. In computer communications, each point in the chan-

FIGURE 14.9

Several factors influence the choice in communication channels. Twisted-pair and coaxial are widely installed, but fiber optic cable is essential for our expanding communications needs.

Twisted-pair wiring.

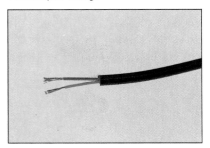

Coaxial cable.

Fiber optic cable.

nel is called a **node.** Thus the tin cans are nodes in a network, and telephones are nodes of a voice communications network. The oldest communication channel for telephones is two copper wires, termed **twisted-pair** wiring. These two wires and a little electricity are all phones need. Yet those same twisted-pairs are quite adaptable to data communications as well. There are many networks built with twisted pair wiring. Refer to Figure 14.9 as you study these other common methods:

- *Coaxial cable* — used by cable television companies.
- *Fiber optic cable* — thin wires of glass fiber.
- *Infrared transmission* — sending signals via a beam of infrared light.
- *Microwave transmission* — high-frequency radio signals beamed between earth stations.
- *Satellite transmission* — high-frequency radio signals beamed between satellites and earth stations.

Two additional factors that determine the use of communications channels are bandwidth and speed — the topics we shall study next.

CHANNEL BANDWIDTH.   "Why so many methods?" you may ask. The issue is **bandwidth,** the capacity of a communications channel to carry data or information. Voice bandwidth is not much of an issue; the frequency range of the human voice is quite narrow. But what happens when a friend plays music for you over the phone? Chances are you notice it doesn't sound quite as good as on your stereo. Obviously twisted-pair has a limited bandwidth.

This becomes problematic in two ways. The first is the number of messages the channel can carry, in both voice and data. The more, the better. The second is the nature and quality of the signal. Data must have a very clear channel; what you hear as noise on the phone line can completely corrupt a data transmission. Coaxial cable is affected by inclement weather, and falling autumn leaves can downgrade microwave transmissions. Imagine the significance of this to a bank that is electronically transferring several billion dollars. In addition, full-motion video used in multimedia applications requires very high bandwidth channel capabilities. The channel must be as wide as possible to accommodate a large number of complex signals.

SPEED. You already know that communications speed is measured in baud or Kbps. When considered in terms of bandwidth and speed, the channels are classified into three categories:

- *Narrow band transmission,* the slowest at 45–150 baud; used by telegraph and teletype machines; commonly twisted-pair wires.
- *Voice-grade transmission,* the middle speed at 300–9600 baud; the human voice is in this range, thus so are telephones as well as inexpensive or home-use modems; commonly twisted-pair wires.
- *Wideband transmission,* for highest speed at 19,200 baud to 500Kbps or more; this is for commercial grade channels used in business, finance, the government, and so on. Commonly coaxial, fiber optic, or microwave transmission.

The last issue concerning communications channels is the media mode. **Media mode** refers to message-routing technique. There are three media modes:

- *Simplex,* meaning one direction only (for example, from host to recipient).
- *Half-duplex,* meaning one direction at a time although both directions are possible.
- *Full-duplex,* meaning both directions at the same time.

Today, most voice and data communications channels are full-duplex; the need for information and instantaneous feedback requires it. However the computer-to-printer channel is simplex, and most large host-to-terminal computer systems still use half-duplex.

NETWORK STANDARDS

Communications network **standards** are the rules and guidelines for achieving satisfactory performance and communication between different networks and computer systems. These standards are analogous to those you learned about with different proprietary hardware platforms in Chapters 2, 3, and 13—except in communications they often become more complicated. Each new communications technology or application seems to require its own standards. Here is a sampling:

- ASCII, for data file transfer.
- FDDI, for high-speed fiber optic transmissions.
- T1 (and T3), for wideband circuits.
- CCITT X.400, for electronic mail message handling.
- SNA, for IBM mainframe communications.
- DECNET, for Digital mini communications.

These are just a few, and there is no practical reason for you to understand them all. However, for the purpose of understanding the importance and usefulness of standards, we will study two that attempt to bring uniformity to data communications. One, OSI, has been in existence for some time; the other, SMP, is emerging as the new business computing standard.

FIGURE 14.10   The seven layers of OSI. When properly implemented, the only layer the knowledge
worker must interact with is the application.

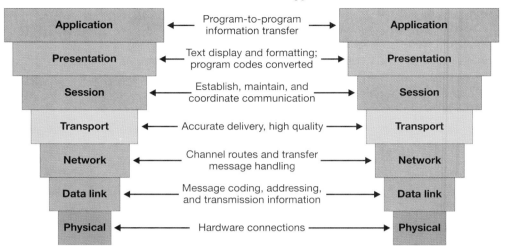

OSI.

Open systems interconnect (OSI) is a standard that separates computer-to-computer communications into seven layers or levels, each building one atop the next. The OSI model was created by the European International Systems Organization in the 1970s, and in the 1980s came to be regarded as a solution, not just for communications, but for the enterprise-wide open systems issue. As its name implies, its stated goal is to make differing systems "open" from the hardware through the application, as shown in Figure 14.10. Dr. Peter G. W. Keen (author, professor, and consultant on communications) says of OSI, "The OSI model has generated several of the most important and useful standards in the telecommunications field. The architecture, not OSI, is the strategy, although OSI may be a key element of the architecture."

SMP.

Simple management protocol (SMP) is another set of standards that emerged in the late 1980s. Originally called *Simple Network Management Protocol,* it was used for the Internet, an academic and research network widely employed in North America. Many hardware, software, and communications vendors were quick to see the versatility of this new standard, and in lending their support have given it wide credibility. One of SMP's strengths is that it manages a wider variety of networks used in business today, and is considered a more "generic management technology," says Marshall Rose, a consultant and one of the original architects of SMP.

TYPES OF NETWORKS

There are many different types and sizes of networks, each designed for a different purpose. Basically they fall into two groups: public networks, that individuals and businesses can use for a fee, and private networks, whose use is limited by its owners. Let's take a look at both.

Public Networks

A **public network** is an *open* communications network available for use by anyone, usually on a fee basis. The U.S. Sprint, MCI, and AT&T telephone networks are examples of public networks. They span the world. Even though initially designed for voice messages, these telephone networks carry a large volume of computer communications today.

In France, the telephone network was intentionally turned into a computer network by a project called Teletel. Teletel was launched in 1981, when the French telephone and post office department put a terminal called Le Minitel in every home in France. Over 4 million have been installed.

Initially Teletel was to replace printed phone books by giving people on-line directory assistance. However, enterprising companies soon realized they could provide other on-line services to the public. The program was a success — the number of on-line services in France has jumped from 200 to over 9,000. One popular service, Dialog, allows people to form groups and have typed on-line conversations.

Data Communications Networks.   In the United States, some networks are used exclusively for computer communications. These are called **packet-switching networks.** A *packet* is a block of data prepared for data transmission. Packets are routed to their destination very quickly — in just a few milliseconds. For example, on a packet-switching network, you could send the entire text of the novel *Moby Dick* — 220,000 words — in less than 30 seconds. There are two advantages to packet-switching: (1) It is more economical to send data in packets; and (2) packets are less prone to errors and corruption. The most prominent packet-switching networks are Tymnet and Telenet in the United States and Datapac in Canada. The first packet-switching network was ARPANET, created in 1968 by the U.S. Department of Defense Advanced Research Projects Agency. It links various government agencies, research labs, and universities. Today it is called Internet, and it links hundreds of locations and thousands of computers in North America. Figure 14.11 shows the scope of services provided by Internet.

Private Networks

In addition to public networks, many private networks exist in the United States. A **private network** is a *closed* communication system, usually confined to a particular company, government entity, or other group. An example of a private network is American Airlines' SABRE reservation service. SABRE stands for Semi-Automated Business Research Environment. Developed by IBM in the mid-1960s, SABRE now has more than 68,000 terminals that connect 8,000 reservation operators and 14,000 travel agents around the world. Over 470,000 reservations are made on SABRE every day.

Several types of private networks exist in business today, serving a variety of needs for knowledge workers. The networks are categorized in two ways: one is by topology, the physical layout of network devices and nodes, and the other is by the proximity of the devices and nodes to each other. Let's look at these types of networks and examples of how they are used.

FIGURE 14.11   Internet is the world's largest computer network, develped from the U.S.
                      Department of Defense's ARPANET. It has grown from being a network for
                      government and military researchers to providing information and services for
                      businesses, college professors and students, and a variety of individual knowledge
                      workers and citizens.

Internet Resources
Note: In most cases, there are a number of special interest topics or groups under each of these main resource headings.

Internet Networks

The Internet communicates via gateways with other networks such as CompuServe, MCI Mail, BITNET, FIDONet, UUNET, and USENET. The Internet has several component networks (which themselves include other networks):

- CREN/CSNET
- DDN (Defense Data Net)
- ESNET (Energy Sciences Network)
- NASA Science Internet
- NSFNET (National Science Foundation Network)

Aeronautics and Astronautics
Agriculture
Astronomy
Aviation
Biotechnology
Chemistry
Computer Science
Computing
Cooking
Education
Electrical Engineering
Engineering
Environment
Environmental Studies
Freenet
Geography
Geology and Geophysics
Government, U.S.
Health
History
Hobbies and Crafts
Horticulture
Humanities
Internet
Law
Libraries

Library and Information Science
Literature
Mathematics
Meteorology and Climatology
Music
Network Information
Network Organizations
News, Network
Nutrition
Oceanography
Political Activism
Popular Culture
Recreation, Games
Recreation, Sports
Reference Books
Religion
Resource Directories
Science
Security
Society and Culture
Standards
Travel
Weather
White Pages
Zymurgy

Source: *The Whole Internet Catalog and User's Guide* by Ed Krol. © 1992. Sebastopol, California: O'Reilly & Associates, Inc.

NETWORK TOPOLOGY.   **Topology** defines the layout of computers and other devices and how they are connected. Figure 14.12 illustrates the three most common topologies: star, bus, and ring networks.

- A **star network** gives many knowledge workers access to central files and system resources through a host CPU.

- A **bus network** has no central computer, but shares other network resources, such as printers, in the same way as the star network.

- In a **ring network,** individual computers are connected serially to one another. This arrangement is somewhat more expensive but has the advantage of providing many routing possibilities.

LOCAL AREA NETWORKS

The most widely used type of private network is the **local area network** (LAN). As the name suggests, LANs are set up to allow a small group of knowledge workers in the same geographic location, such as an office or a

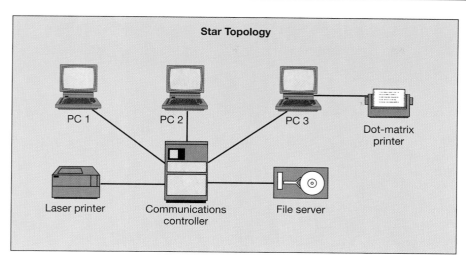

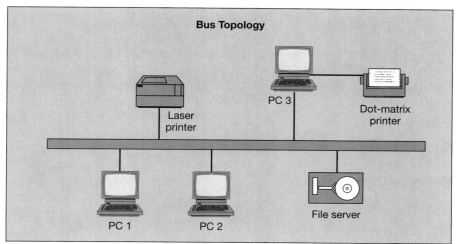

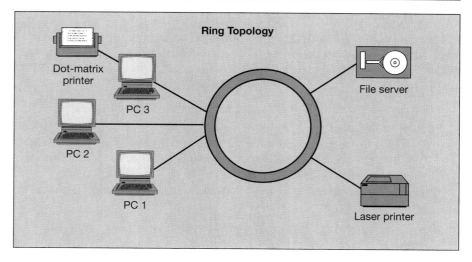

FIGURE 14.12

The three most common network topologies: star, bus, and ring.

small company, to share data, programs, and hardware resources. A LAN may use any of the three networks — star, bus, or ring — mentioned previously.

CLIENT/SERVER LANS.   For the most part, LANs are made up of PCs and file servers. The file server is the most powerful PC in the network and has the largest-capacity hard disk drive. In most network architectures, there is a *client/server hierarchy;* that is, the server or host assumes primary duties, since it must deliver files and manage resources for the clients.

PEER-TO-PEER LANS.   However, a new network architecture called *peer-to-peer networking* is emerging. **Peer-to-peer** means that every computer on the network is an equal, so that it can act as a server, a workstation, or both. All programs, data, and peripherals on the network are available to all knowledge workers. Exchanging files and programs between workstations becomes very easy to do with peer-to-peer networking. By comparison, in a client/server architecture, all resources must be shared from the server, and each client workstation is subservient to the server. Figure 14.13 shows a typical peer-to-peer networking architecture.

The PCs and server(s) in most LANs are usually hard-wired, meaning they are physically connected with cables. An exception is infrared LANs, which transmit data via light beam rather than cabling. Each PC has a network adapter card installed in an expansion slot that is connected to the cable. Hard-wired LANs don't require modems. The cabling may be twisted pair, but coaxial cable is often used and fiber optic use is growing in popularity since it can handle more data and transmit it much faster.

LAN SOFTWARE.   All networks require software, and the LAN is no exception. Refer to Figure 14.10 showing the OSI layers. The LAN utilizes four of these layers:

Application: Network applications.
Transport: Network operating system.
Network: Network BIOS.
Physical: Network adapter card.

The network BIOS (Basic Input/Output System) functions in the same way as the DOS operating system BIOS. The network operating system (NOS) performs functions similarly to a computer operating system such as DOS. Its tasks include:

- *File service,* sending files from the server to the workstations.
- *Print service,* routing print jobs from workstations to printers.
- *Security,* ensuring that file integrity is maintained. For example, two knowledge workers cannot be allowed to edit and change the same file at once.
- *Utilities* that manage and direct certain tasks and help configure the network.

By far the most popular NOS is Novell Netware, which is compatible with most topologies and is capable of supporting up to a few hundred knowledge workers, depending on the specific Netware version in use. Some NOSs are even designed to work with Windows.

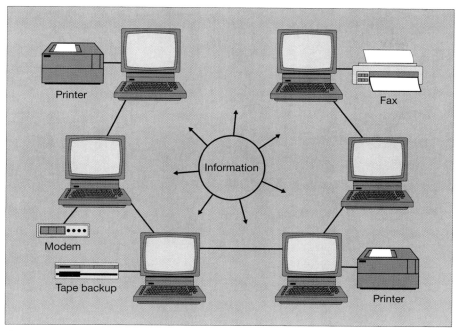

FIGURE 14.13

Peer-to-peer networking is the latest trend in LANs.

Source: Courtesy Artisoft.

Knowledge workers use many of the same application software programs they would use on a standalone PC when they work in a networked environment. There are LAN versions of most major applications, such as WordPerfect, Lotus 1-2-3, and Paradox. In addition, there are special applications designed for knowledge workers working in teams or groups. One of the best-known is Lotus Notes, which we will study in the following chapter. A very common application on networks of all kinds is **electronic mail** (E-mail), which is creating, sending, storing, and forwarding written messages (files) to other knowledge workers.

WIDE AREA NETWORKS.   The **wide area network** (WAN) is another type of private network. WANs use phone lines, microwave relaying stations, and satellites to connect computers located miles apart. WANs allow knowledge workers to do the same things as LANs. Even over great distances, WANs allow users to send electronic mail, share data and programs, and use the printers and memory devices linked to the network. Figure 14.14 is an example of a WAN.

1. What is the term used to refer to points on a network?   p. 446
2. Name several methods for creating communications channels.   p. 446
3. Why is bandwidth important in networks?   p. 446
4. What is the purpose behind a standard such as OSI?   p. 447–48
5. Name a type of public network.   p. 449

KNOWLEDGE CHECK

FIGURE 14.14

This corporate WAN allows the company to send voice and data transmissions between its computer centers at greatly reduced cost (see legend).

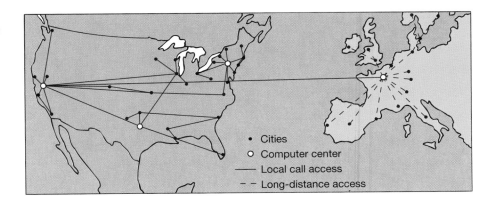

- • Cities
- ○ Computer center
- —— Local call access
- – – Long-distance access

6. What is the most widely used type of private network?   p. 449
7. What is the difference between a LAN and a WAN?   p. 453

NETWORK APPLICATIONS

Networks provide a wide range of personal, business, and government services. In general, these network services fall into two categories: information services, which allow us to read local and remote databases; and interactive services, which allow us to exchange information via networks. Here are some examples of these two kinds of network services.

INFORMATION SERVICES

Information services maintain and provide access to data repositories. They offer a wide variety of information. Subscribing to an information service is similar to subscribing to a magazine. Once you are registered, you're given a telephone dial-up number that allows you to connect to the service. Many information services require an initial fee and then bill you for usage on a monthly basis.

Information services are one-way services; you can read their data but cannot add to their databases. There are two general categories into which information services fall: news services and database services.

NEWS SERVICES. As the name implies, **news services** provide the latest news, including general interest, business, and financial news. You can read *The New York Times, Forbes, USA Today,* and many newsletters on news services.

The Dow Jones News/Retrieval (DJN/R) service is an example of a news service. DJN/R provides financial information, stock quotations for over 6,000 companies, and other investment information. Since it is owned by Dow Jones, it also offers the full text of articles from *Barron's* and *The Wall Street Journal.* But DJN/R doesn't confine itself to financial information. It

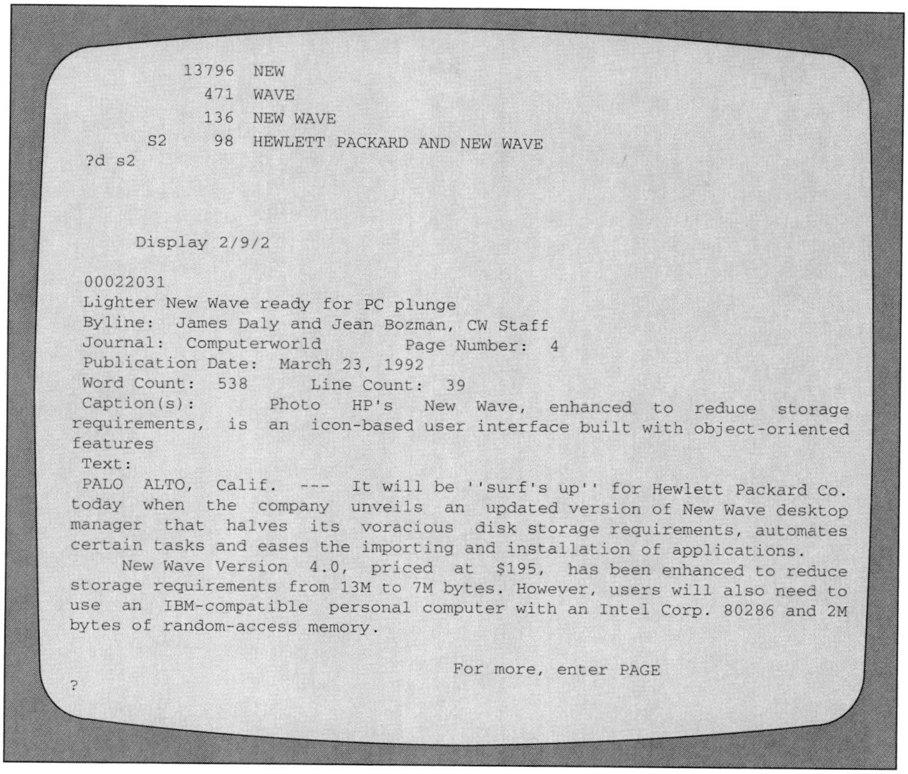

FIGURE 14.15

Downloaded data. A search
was conducted for the terms
"Hewlett Packard" and
"New Wave" resulting in 98
matches. The first file is
partially displayed.

```
           13796  NEW
             471  WAVE
             136  NEW WAVE
       S2     98  HEWLETT PACKARD AND NEW WAVE
    ?d s2



       Display 2/9/2

    00022031
    Lighter New Wave ready for PC plunge
    Byline:  James Daly and Jean Bozman, CW Staff
    Journal:  Computerworld     Page Number:  4
    Publication Date:  March 23, 1992
    Word Count:  538    Line Count:  39
    Caption(s):      Photo  HP's  New Wave, enhanced  to  reduce  storage
    requirements,  is  an  icon-based user interface built with object-oriented
    features
    Text:
    PALO  ALTO,  Calif.  ---  It will be ''surf's up'' for Hewlett Packard Co.
    today  when  the  company  unveils  an  updated version of New Wave desktop
    manager  that  halves  its  voracious  disk storage requirements, automates
    certain tasks and eases the importing and installation of applications.
        New Wave Version  4.0,  priced  at  $195,  has  been enhanced to reduce
    storage requirements from 13M to 7M bytes. However, users will also need to
    use  an  IBM-compatible  personal computer with an Intel Corp. 80286 and 2M
    bytes of random-access memory.

                               For more, enter PAGE
    ?
```

FIGURE 14.15

Downloaded data. A search
was conducted for the terms
"Hewlett Packard" and
"New Wave" resulting in 98
matches. The first file is
partially displayed.

also provides film reviews, a college selection service, an encyclopedia, and a medical and drug reference.

DATABASE SERVICES. A **database service** is an information service whose primary purpose is to provide comprehensive information. These services store very large amounts of data on large-capacity hard disk drives. Database services allow you to connect your personal computer to a host computer, read data, and download it to your computer. Writers, students, lawyers, medical practitioners, and other knowledge workers use database services to research topics of interest. Figure 14.15 shows a topic researched on a database service.

The U.S. government has hundreds of specialized databases for such topics as agriculture, population, jobs, health, and science. In some ways, subscribing to a database service is like having the Library of Congress on your desktop.

There are many commercial databases available to business and individuals as well. One of the largest and most widely used is Dialog, which contains hundreds of industry-specific databases (chemistry, petroleum, etc.) as well as news, magazines, and special-interest databases. Dialog is used by businesses, but offers a limited number of its databases to individuals as Knowledge Index. Other commercial databases include Nexis for news and articles, Lexis for legal, Bibliographic Retrieval Services (BRS) for news and articles, Investext for financial information, and Prodigy for shopping and consumer information.

FIGURE 14.16

The main menu of a small CBBS. Note the several special-interest topics.

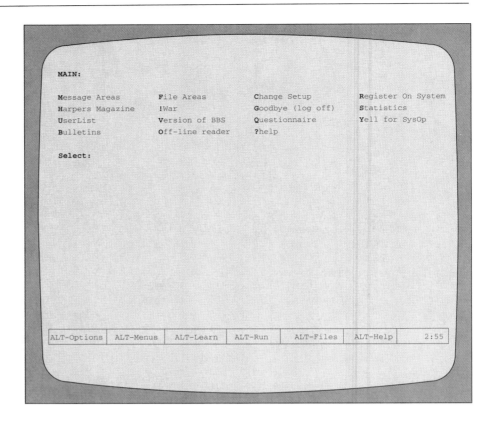

```
MAIN:

Message Areas     File Areas        Change Setup        Register On System
Harpers Magazine  !War              Goodbye (log off)   Statistics
UserList          Version of BBS    Questionnaire       Yell for SysOp
Bulletins         Off-line reader   ?help

Select:
```

```
ALT-Options | ALT-Menus | ALT-Learn | ALT-Run | ALT-Files | ALT-Help |  2:55
```

INTERACTIVE SERVICES

Where information services are one-way streets, interactive services can be two-, four-, six-, and more-way streets. Interactive services allow you to connect your personal computer to a community of computer users to both obtain and exchange information. You can interact with other users in the same way you would over the telephone, but with added dimensions. In effect, you and your information become part of the service to whatever extent you choose.

ELECTRONIC BULLETIN BOARDS. One of the most popular interactive services for personal computer users is the electronic bulletin board, sometimes called a CBBS, for *computerized bulletin board system*. An **electronic bulletin board** lets people read and post messages on an information service. Bulletin board messages are topic-specific or personal, depending on the type of bulletin board. Figure 14.16 shows a menu on a typical small BBS.

For example, a bulletin board might specialize in bringing buyers and sellers of personal computers together, like classified ads. However you may also read and post personal messages on any of thousands of topics, from business to politics to personal hobbies or outdoor activities. For example, during the Tour de France bicycle race, observers posted daily race results. There are bulletin boards for just about any and every interest.

FIGURE 14.17

Levi Strauss developed LeviLink, an EDI system designed to manage inventory and order requirements. It is administered across a private network to retail stores that carry Levi Strauss clothing.

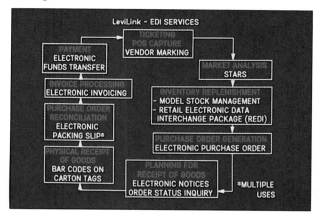

A shipping clerk verifies order fulfillment by checking the barcodes on the shipping carton.

EFT AND CONSUMER SERVICES.   Probably the most common example of an interactive service is **electronic funds transfer** (EFT). EFT means making any type of financial transaction using a network. EFT often involves using a bank card to make withdrawals and deposits via an ATM. Consumer shopping networks are also growing in popularity. These services allow shopping worldwide for virtually every kind of product or service, from dry cleaners that pick up and deliver to large-volume auto dealers.

INFORMATION UTILITIES.   A third type of on-line service called **information utilities** combines elements of information and interactive services. Utilities such as CompuServe, Delphi, and The Source give subscribers access to news, extensive databases, bulletin boards, and shopping services, all for a very reasonable fee. Typical start-up subscription packages cost $25 to $30.

BUSINESS AND GOVERNMENT NETWORKS

Business and government regard communications and networking as serious tools, even as they experiment with this technology to create new services. Let's look at a few ways business and government use networks.

EDI.   **Electronic data interchange** (EDI) is using networks to transfer forms, such as invoices, purchase orders, shipping, shipping notices, and even payments with computers. The data is loaded into EDI software with the appropriate forms, similar to on-screen templates. The completed forms are most commonly transmitted computer-to-computer using compatible hardware and software, or via a private network. Figure 14.17 shows an EDI transaction.

TOMORROW

THE NEW PROMISE OF INFORMATION UTILITIES

In their formative years, information utilities such as Delphi and CompuServe were oriented toward the home user and individual knowledge worker. Today CompuServe is the most-used service of its kind, providing hundreds of thousands of knowledge workers of all types with data from over 40 mainframe computers at its headquarters in Columbus, Ohio. Knowledge workers, from the self-employed to the Fortune 100, use CompuServe on a daily basis, downloading information about 8 million businesses from Dun's Electronic Yellow Pages, reading newsletters, regional business and trade publications, searching for trademark information, checking the stock market, reading and gathering government-collected information, and, yes, learning about computers and application programs.

Forums, as they are called, have sprung up for nearly every interest, from current events to computers. The application forums look like a Who's Who in Software; they are organized by platform (IBM PC, Macintosh, etc.), type of software (graphics), and so forth. You can participate in conferences (where topics are currently being discussed on-line), research previous conferences, or take a look around the library to see if there are any files or programs you wish to download.

Software vendors quickly came to appreciate the value of the forum, for it provides direct feedback from knowledge workers using the application. Knowledge workers also benefit, for the vendor staffs the forum with skilled technical support people who can answer questions. The topics are so diverse and of such wide interest that

many computer publication journalists and columnists regularly "cruise" the forums in search of topics for their next article.

James Glieck, who has written several books about technology such as *Chaos: Making a New Science,* joined a CompuServe forum to obtain help with a new word processing program with which he was having difficulty. Writing about his experiences in *The New York Times Magazine,* Glieck says he found several bugs and that he would encounter a message on his screen reading "unrecoverable application error — terminating current application." He writes of his personal experience:

Searching for help, I stumbled into an odd corner of the electronic village, a "forum" on the CompuServe Information Service devoted entirely to a permanent

---

Many accountants and individuals are now using EDI technology to submit federal income tax returns. The Internal Revenue Service now makes it possible for many people to use their personal computers to file tax returns. To do so, you use an income tax preparation software program. The electronic forms that comprise your tax return are electronically transmitted to IRS computers.

CALS. Some years ago, the U.S. Department of Defense instituted **computer aided acquisition and logistics support** (CALS), a program conceived for image processing and paperless document management associated with the design, manufacture, acquisition, and maintenance of weapons systems. Under the CALS requirement, defense contractors involved in large weapons systems for the Air Force, Army, and Navy must now submit engineering drawings and text information in digital form — usually computer tapes or

floating conversation about the ins and outs of (my software) . . . . CompuServe fosters a strange form of communication, more casual than letters, more formal than telephone conversation, and extremely public. An electronic culture has developed with its own evolving rules of decorum, its own politesse and its own methods of conveying rage, not to mention its indispensable acronyms: IMHO (in my humble opinion), FWIW (for what it's worth), PMJI (pardon my jumping in), ROFL (rolling on the floor laughing), IANAL (I am not a lawyer). The characters ;) are supposed to mean "just kidding"—on the theory that they suggest, sideways, a face that is smiling and winking.*

Bill Dunn, formerly the head of the Information Services Division at Dow Jones & Co., commented on the future of interactive, on-line information from the business point of view:

To peer into the future, I found I needed a new view of the information world; Dow Jones & Co. began to develop a model based more on biological evolution than technical revolution. The model recognizes increasing competition but also greater cooperation—the need for foes to work together to develop competitive standards. It also recognizes greater interdependence—the need for complex multivendor solutions to work seamlessly in the customer's eye. The fittest will continue to survive but in a more interdependent, cooperative landscape.

Companies and their customers are developing more links and becoming more interdependent to create competitive advantage; a biologist might liken the process to specialized organs connecting to serve a larger need. Also, clusters of people are working in a more independent and more cooperative fashion, just like cells evolve into multicell

bodies to serve a specific purpose. Competitive technology providers band together to promulgate a standard for their mutual benefit, just as competition in nature operates within bounds, alongside a surprising measure of cooperation.†

This model became the basis of DowVision, an on-line service from Dow Jones.

---

* James Glieck, "Chasing Bugs in the Electronic Village," *NYT Sunday Magazine,* June 14, 1992, pp. 38–42.
† *Computerworld,* June 4, 1990, p. SR19.

CD-ROM—instead of paper. In time, mainframe databases at defense and industry sites will be connected to share CALS data electronically.

A new aspect of the CALS network, made operational in 1992, links NATO offices and contractors in France, Germany, Italy, and the United Kingdom for the access and exchange of weapons systems data stored on mainframes at the Huntsville, Alabama, Missile Command (MICOM) in CALS format. The new network will use fiber optic channels to link over 10,000 workstations and Macintoshes to the MICOM mainframe.

---

1. What is the difference between an information service and an interactive service?   p. 456
2. Identify two types of information services.   pp. 454–55

KNOWLEDGE
CHECK

3. Identify two types of interactive services.　pp. 456–57
4. What is an information utility?　p. 457
5. What does EDI stand for?　p. 457
6. What does CALS stand for?　p. 458

NETWORK SECURITY

Computer security and the need to physically protect data was discussed in Chapter 2. This need for protection exists in networking as well, for whenever a computer is connected to a phone line, it is extremely vulnerable to unauthorized people gaining access to the data stored there. We'll explore some of the problems and their remedies, and then discuss the ethics of networking.

PROTECTING NETWORKS

Because networks can make computer systems vulnerable to intrusion, security systems exist to protect computers and networks. One such system employs usernames, or account numbers, and a **password,** a special character string unique to the individual, to differentiate between authorized users and intruders. To make this system work, knowledge workers must keep their passwords both unique and confidential.

Another method of ensuring network security is the callback system. In this system, you begin by connecting to the computer with telephone and modem. Next, the computer prompts you for your username and password, which you enter. At this point the computer terminates the connection. The computer verifies your username and password, and then calls you back to establish your work session.

Despite these security systems, unauthorized parties still find ways to intrude on computer systems. One term used for these computer abusers is *intruders.* Let's take a look at who these people are and the crimes they commit.

INTRUDERS

People who intrude, or break in to computer systems, are sometimes inappropriately called hackers. A **hacker** is someone who demonstrates great skill in programming and working with computers. A computer abuser is an **intruder,** who is behaving either unethically or illegally in the use of computer systems. Intruders interfere with computer systems owned or operated by others. They usually gain access by circumventing username/password security. They use an automatic telephone dialer to find the numbers of computer systems. When they locate a number, their computer attempts to guess usernames and passwords by trying every possible combination of letters and numbers. Intruders have been known to attack voice communications systems as well. A few years ago, two teenaged intruders were able to gain unauthorized access to a publisher's phone mail system. Angered that they had not received a free poster for subscribing to one of its magazines, they left lewd outgoing voice mail messages and erased valuable incoming advertising queries. The voice mail system had to undergo extensive reprogramming, rendering it out of service for almost three weeks.

To thwart intruders, some systems use **lockouts,** software that only lets you have three tries at entering a username or password. After several incorrect attempts to enter a correct username and password, the phone connection is broken. This can certainly slow down an intruder's efforts. Another security measure requires that authorized users change passwords at assigned intervals.

The latest technology uses keycards, fingerprints, voiceprints, and retinal eye scans to secure multiple-user systems. Although these require additional sophisticated hardware and software, many military, government, corporate, and private institutions feel their information security is worth the extra cost and effort.

There are numerous other ways to break into computers and networks. To try figuring out the loopholes before intruders do, some computer owners try breaking into their own systems. For example, the U.S. Air Force employs experts from Mitre Corporation to look for weaknesses in its computer security. Here are two other methods of thwarting unauthorized access to computer systems.

ENCRYPTION.   **Encryption** involves putting coding devices at each end of the communication line. Before transmitting a message, one computer encodes the text by substituting gibberish characters for real letters. At the other end, it is decoded by the receiving computer. This makes it very hard for transmissions to be intercepted and read by unauthorized people.

FILE PROTECTION.   File protection is now common on personal computers, whether they are used by one person or connected in a network. Programs have been created to protect personal files so that others may not read them. For example, Word Perfect 5.1 permits closing a file with password protection. In addition, programs "lock" a floppy disk or hard disk drive against prying eyes. Figure 14.18 shows how a program of this type works. It prompts the user for a password, and it reveals if unauthorized attempts to log on have been attempted.

THE COMPUTER VIRUS

In recent years, computer systems have been plagued with an insidious program called a **computer virus,** which corrupts or "infects" computer files by inserting a copy of the virus itself. Most computer viruses are very small, short programs that enter computer systems via other programs or through communications networks, and then hide. A virus can go unnoticed for long periods as it insidiously infects the computer and then, at a predetermined time and date, or often when the computer is powered up, causes it to crash.

Viruses are often created by an employee who has been fired and wants to strike back at the company in anger; by talented young intruders who want to demonstrate their computer skill; or by programmers with antisocial tendencies or a perverted sense of humor. We have had many virus attacks over the past few years, and although they can be stopped there does not seem to be a way to prevent them. One recurring virus that has gained a certain notoriety is the Michelangelo virus, so named because it launches itself on the great inven-

FIGURE 14.18

Disk protection program.

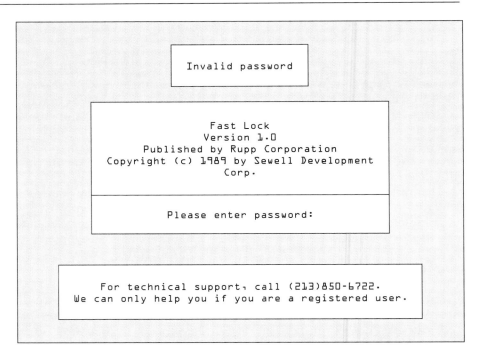

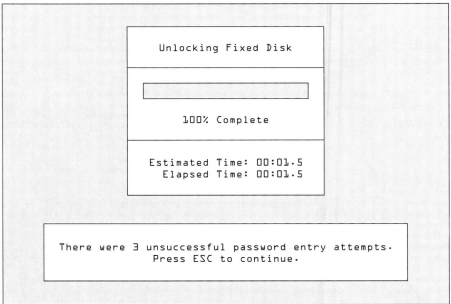

tor and Renaissance man's birthday, March 6. The Michelangelo virus is
contracted from a floppy disk which is not bootable itself. Thus it is passed
from one knowledge worker to the next on a data disk, and commonly infects a
computer when the infected disk is left in the drive. Knowledge workers and
businesses are becoming more conscious of the danger, and many use anti-

virus programs on a regular basis. One, the Norton Anti-Virus, runs a check for most known viruses when the computer is first powered up.

THE COMPUTER WORM.   A relative of the computer virus is the **computer worm,** which duplicates itself from one computer's memory to the next. Once in memory, it continues to propagate itself, over and over, consuming ever more space until the computer crashes. The most widely publicized worm attack occurred in 1988. Robert Morris, a graduate computer science student at Cornell University, placed a computer worm on ARPANET. It brought 6,000 computers to a halt. Morris was brought to trial and convicted.

Aaron Haber, who teaches at Harvard University, has written:

> As a society, we must link computer files with the realization that this material often represents the life work and innermost thoughts of a person and is highly confidential. It is more than property and must be treated accordingly.
>
> [The intruder] is an example of how we have failed, and his example is one that will be followed until we change society. Intruders will continue breaking into systems and implanting viruses as a game. They know they would not physically ever harm someone, yet do not comprehend the violence of their seemingly benign actions. They rarely see, in person, the results of their activities and this distance promotes their insensitivity.
>
> Unless and until new standards are set and accepted in this country, we will continue to suffer from people such as [intruders] and their computer viruses.[1]

KNOWLEDGE CHECK

1. Identify some of the problems that have led to the creation of computer security systems.   p. 460
2. In computing, what is an intruder?   p. 460
3. What is a lockout?   p. 461
4. Describe how encryption provides computer security.   p. 461
5. What is a computer virus?   p. 461

WHAT LIES AHEAD?

For large companies, the network is becoming the computer and, in the process, is changing the definition of MIS and its management. John J. Donovan, an MIT professor and head of an educational and consulting company, sees the MIS executive becoming a network manager in the increasingly decentralized computing and business environment. In such an environment, the computer is literally the network. He says:

> I believe the 1990s will witness the emergence of a new breed of senior information executive — the network manager — whose priorities and challenges

---

[1] *Boston Globe* editorial, December 13, 1988.

CAREERS FOR KNOWLEDGE WORKERS
PAUL WILCZYNSKI, KRISLYN COMPUTER SERVICES

One of the notable side effects of the computer is that it has created entire new businesses, even industries, to support computer systems, knowledge workers, and customers. One of the more interesting businesses that has grown up around public electronic mail is the service agency, which acts as a liaison between customers and the E-mail utility.

Paul Wilczynski is owner of

Krislyn Computer Services, one of the first service agencies for MCI Mail. "I encountered MCI Mail in its infancy," says Paul. "Registration was free, and while I wasn't quite sure what to do with it, I thought it was pretty neat and began using it." Paul graduated from Oberlin with a degree in sociology, but followed a fascination with technology into radio broadcasting and, ultimately, computers. He

learned FORTRAN and COBOL, worked as a programmer, and taught college programming courses. When the personal computer burst upon the scene, he started his own programming and systems development company.

By the mid-1980s, Paul had mastered not only the personal computer but the modem as well, managing the Business Forum on Delphi. This experience and understanding of how to help on-line knowledge workers undoubtedly contributed to his enthusiasm for becoming an MCI Mail service agency. "When I received the letter describing the MCI Mail agency program, I was ecstatic. I was going to be paid for doing something I loved doing anyway. Instead of writing back, I responded with an MCI Mail message. I think they were a little surprised!"

Krislyn Computer Services' mission is to provide services relating to the electronic transmission of information. Krislyn pro-

will differ in many important respects from the CIOs. [Chief information officer is another term for MIS executive.] Unless CIOs successfully transform themselves into network managers, they will be ill-equipped to confront user dissatisfaction, organizational squabbles, and technological roadblocks invariably triggered by the advance of decentralized computing. . . . Network managers understand that in a world of accelerating decentralization, the most effective way to oversee a company's computer resources is to relinquish control of them and instead focus on the networks that connect them. Network managers won't merely accept the inevitability of decentralized computing. They will encourage it by surrendering authority over hardware purchases and

vides not only MCI Mail but also fax broadcasting (one message to many recipients) and a "fax on demand" service. You call an 800 number, press a five-digit code corresponding to a document, and enter the recipient's fax number; the document is then transmitted to the fax machine within one minute or so.

"As an agency, we do two things," says Paul. "One, we offer MCI Mail to new customers, often through referrals. Two, we work with existing customers, helping them use MCI Mail effectively throughout their organizations. With some companies, one-to-two–person shops, for example, MCI Mail is used in a very specific way and there isn't much room to add new applications.

In larger companies, though, there are lots of potential uses that usually haven't been considered. MCI Mail can be used for electronic data interchange, for example, to send and receive standard documents such as purchase orders and invoices. There are also lots of custom applications possible, which are currently called "mail-enabled applications." These are applications where knowledge workers work with their electronic documents on the screen as they normally would, but the completed work is forwarded using electronic mail instead of paper. There are lots of things that fall into this category."

Paul spends a lot of time on MCI Mail and on the phone, helping customers. "I'm very service-oriented," he says, "even if the customer only spends $5 to $10 a month. It's just my personality. But if you don't provide superior service in business these days, you don't stand a prayer of succeeding." Paul also suggests to customers ways to get more value from MCI Mail. For example, one of his customers is Irwin, publisher of this textbook. Each campus representative has their own laptop computer and MCI Mail account for communicating with others in the company. But Paul has also explained to them how to access the communications gateway to Internet so they can exchange mail with professors on campus.

He is also helping champion ease of use in computer communications. "The technology is often retarding growth in this industry," he says. "It's too technically difficult to do things that are very simple. The computer and modem are not yet as easy to use as the phone or fax, but they need to be." To this end, one of Paul's sales associates is currently offering "one-button mail" to MCI Mail customers. Paul is very active in tracking the growth and direction of the electronic communications services industry over the next few years. "We saw phenomenal growth in the latter half of the 80s, and the growth will continue. But it will be more in the direction of transmitting data such as spreadsheets, word processing documents, and business transactions than in individual messaging."

software development while seizing control of communications systems and policies.[2]

On the technology side, as more and more people and companies use networking, the importance of being able to connect networks to one another grows. This is true both in the United States and internationally. And as

[2] John J. Donovan, "Beyond Chief Information Officer to Network Manager," *Harvard Business Review,* September–October 1988, pp. 134–40.

twisted pair wire and coaxial cable are replaced by fiber optics cables, more and more networks are becoming digital.

Digital networks have three advantages. First, voice transmissions work just fine on digital networks, which make it possible to leave stored messages, as if an answering machine were built into the network. Second, in an all-digital network, modems are unnecessary. And third, many more services can be added. Regional Bell Operating Companies are experimenting with on-line telephone directories and special circuits that do call screening, identify incoming calls before you pick up the phone, and offer a variety of push-button audio services.

The culmination of this drive for new, improved networking is called the **integrated services digital network** (ISDN). An ISDN is an all-digital network that connects computers directly to one another; a modem is unnecessary. The goal for ISDNs is to make every network digital, whether voice or data, and compatible with every other network in the world. An ISDN would make it possible to send video images from point to point; for example, a hospital could send a patient's X-rays to the doctor's office. Not only does ISDN have higher bandwidth, but it speeds up the delivery of information as much as six times. A single communications line — most likely a fiber optic cable — can be used for telephone, computer, facsimile, and television and even teleconferencing when it's used for business.

COMMUNICATIONS ETHICS

It is unethical to gain access to someone else's computer system without their express permission (in other words, without a legitimate username and password). It is unethical to read the files of a welfare recipient, a doctor's patient, or an employee unless it is your job to do so. And it is unethical to damage or destroy programs or data — considered proprietary — on someone else's computer.

Stewart Brand, a leading thinker, computer user, and author of *The Whole Earth Catalog* and *The Whole Earth Software Catalog,* says this of people who are challenged to crack into computers: "When you are linked into such computer power, you are no longer a mensch. You are an *ubermensch* [superman]. . . . What they know is that they are outside the law. The information technology that they are moving with is going so fast that they're

ahead of the law. It's like we've come upon a vast new continent, we've just spent a couple of years on the shore — and the closest thing to native dwellers are the intruders."

Others do not take such a poetic view of intruders. Our government has responded to our computer security problems and begun to get tough. The Computer Fraud and Abuse Act of 1986 makes it a felony to cause more than $1,000 in damages by breaking into computers across state lines or by maliciously trespassing into banking or security dealers' computers. The FBI investigates these cases. In addition, most states have similar laws either on the books or pending. To some people, intruders used to be heroes. Now they may also be felons and convicts.

SUMMARY

1. *Identify the hardware, software, and network components necessary for communications.* Communications systems fall into two categories: voice and data. Voice communications hardware includes the PBX and T-1 switch. Data communi-

cations hardware includes the modem. Voice communications software applications include voice mail and call center management. Data communications software includes communications software for the individual and communications management software for the host. Both voice and data communications can share the same communications channels, which include twisted pair and fiber optic cables. Network standards make it easier to integrate voice and data, and to have distributed computing.

2. *Describe the difference between analog and digital signals.* An analog signal is continuous and changes in tone, pitch, and volume, like our voices. A digital signal is a single discrete signal, a steady stream of pulses that does not change in tone, pitch, or volume. Most telephone networks are still designed to carry analog signals.

3. *Identify two kinds of networks.* The public network is open to use by anyone willing to pay for the service. The AT&T and packet switching networks are examples. A private network is a closed communications system, usually managed by a company or private group, such as the SABRE

airlines reservation network between American Airlines and its travel agents.

4. *Name three network topologies.* A star network gives many knowledge workers access to central files and system resources through a host CPU. A bus network has no central computer, but shares other network resources, such as printers, in the same way as the star network. A ring network has individual computers connected serially to one another.

5. *Identify the different types of network applications.* There are information services, such as news and database services. There are interactive services, such as electronic bulletin boards and information utilities.

6. *List several methods of maintaining network security.* Lockout, callback, encryption, and file protection are some network security methods.

COMMUNICATIONS ISSUES

1. One of the great principles of democracy, applied to modern communications, maintains that access to information is a public right. Yet recent intrusions on networks have seriously disrupted their operations and threaten even more extensive, permanent damage to software and data. Each intrusion makes information providers fear damage to their computer systems, so tighter security measures — which end up restricting access to information — are discussed. In light of these issues, do you think there should be more security and more restrictions on access to public networks?

2. Do you believe that intruders should be punished as criminals and sentenced to prison? Do you think a distinction should be made between curious intruders and malicious intruders? What alternatives to lawful punishment do you propose?

3. A proposed U.S. law reads, "It is the sense of

Congress that providers of electronic communications services and manufacturers of electronic communications service equipment shall ensure that communications systems permit the government to obtain the plain text contents of voice, data, and other communications when appropriately authorized by law." How do you feel about the fact that anything you say over the phone or send in an electronic mail message could be made available to any government agency? Business consultant William Hugh Murray says, "It should not be illegal for the people to have access to communications that the government cannot read. We should be free from unreasonable search and seizure; we should be free from self-incrimination. The government already has powerful tools of investigation at its disposal; it has demonstrated previous little restraint in their use." Discuss the Constitutional aspects of this issue.

CHAPTER REVIEW QUESTIONS

REVIEW QUESTIONS

1. What three components are necessary for voice or data communications?

2. Name some differences between a regular modem and a smart modem.

3. What is a communications channel?
4. When and why is channel bandwidth important?
5. What advantage does EDI provide?

6. What is a computer virus or worm, and what can be done about them?

DISCUSSION QUESTIONS

1. Why would businesses want a private network?
2. Discuss the advantages and disadvantages of electronic news services.
3. Discuss the seven layers of OSI as they might apply in a computing situation familiar to you, your fellow knowledge workers, or your classmates.
4. When would a client/server LAN be advantageous?

5. When would a peer-to-peer LAN be advantageous?
6. Name some of the technologies used for communications channels.
7. Discuss the difference between analog and digital signals. What do you think is holding back the all-digital, or ISDN, networks?
8. Discuss the guidelines for the selection and care of passwords.

MULTIPLE-CHOICE

1. The T-1 switch (check all that apply):
   a. Makes many communications channels from one.
   b. Is a digital switch.
   c. Can be used for voice or data communications.
   d. All of the above.
2. The ASCII file format (check all that apply):
   a. Is a recognized standard.
   b. Permits data interchange between applications.
   c. Works with just about any communications software.
   d. Is also called a *text file*.
   e. Is handy for uploading.
3. The most common voice communications hardware today is (check all that apply):
   a. The PBX.
   b. The telephone.
   c. The cellular phone.
   d. The T-1 switch.
   e. The concentrator.
4. When your fax machine or modem makes a high-pitched squeal, it is (check all that apply):
   a. Not operating properly.
   b. The carrier signal.

   c. Signaling for human intervention.
   d. Making connection with another device.
5. The most common uses for computers in voice communications are (check all that apply):
   a. Voice mail.
   b. Automating switchboard functions.
   c. Callbacks.
   d. Call center management.
   e. All of the above.
6. A network (check all that apply):
   a. Uses standards, protocols, and software.
   b. Connects to points in the communications channel.
   c. Has the same components as a computer system.
   d. May be interconnected with another network.
   e. May have its own operating system.
   f. All of the above.
7. Someone who uses computer systems without the owner's permission or without proper authorization is called:
   a. A hacker.
   b. A systems programmer.
   c. Abusive.
   d. An intruder.

FILL-IN-THE-BLANK

1. The primary data communications device is the _____.
2. Another term used for *baud* is _____.

3. The individual knowledge worker established an on-line work session using _____ software, and the host computer provides data

services with _____ _____ software.

4. The different types of network topologies are _____, _____, and _____.

5. Making connection with another computer is termed _____.

6. Each point in a communications channel is called a _____.

TRUE/FALSE

1. A script file makes it possible to send the same electronic mail message to many different computers.

2. Today's typical modem speed is 2,400 megahertz per minute.

3. Some information and interactive services charge for downloading.

KEY TERMS

acoustic coupler,   436

analog signal,   436

ASCII,   443

automatic call dialing (ACD),   435

automatic number identification (ANI),   435

bandwidth,   446

baud (bps),   438

bridge,   435

bus network,   450

carrier signal,   436

communications channel,   431

communications management software,   444

communications protocol,   444

communications software,   442

computer aided acquisition and logistics support (CALS),   458

computer virus,   461

computer worm,   463

concentrator,   440

controller,   438

database services,   455

dialup,   444

digital signal,   436

downloading,   443

electronic bulletin board,   456

electronic data interchange (EDI),   457

electronic funds transfer (EFT),   457

electronic mail,   453

encryption,   461

error checking,   444

external modem,   437

hacker,   460

handshaking,   444

host,   442

information services,   454

information utility,   457

integrated services digital network (ISDN),   466

internal modem,   437

intruder,   460

local area network (LAN),   450

lockout,   461

media mode,   447

modem (modulator-demodulator),   435

multiplexer,   439

network,   445

networking,   431

news services,   454

node,   446

on-line,   442

open systems interconnect (OSI),   448

packet-switching network,   449

password,   460

peer-to-peer,   452

private branch exchange (PBX),   433

private network,   449

public network,   449

ring network,   450

script file,   444

simple management protocol (SMP),   448

smart modem,   438

standards,   447

star network,   450

T-1 switch,   434

telecommunications,   431

text file,   443

topology,   450

twisted pair,   446

uploading   443

voice/data integration,   435

voice mail,   441

wide area network (WAN),   453

CHAPTER

15

Office Automation and Departmental Computing

LEARNING OBJECTIVES

After reading and studying this chapter, you should be able to:

1. Define office automation and explain its relationship to the information systems in business.

2. Name the four fundamental office automation technologies.

3. Describe the importance of the knowledge worker in the modern office environment.

4. Describe trends in distributed computing and integrated computing environments.

Office Automation and the Knowledge Worker

From the late 1800s, when the typewriter was introduced, to the late 1900s, the way work was accomplished in business offices changed very little. Manual typewriters gave way to electric typewriters, but typists still worked in "typing pools." Paper documents accumulated everywhere and were stored in filing cabinets. Perhaps most important, the *procedures* that office workers used to work with information and with each other changed very little.

Computer technology in the 1980s dramatically changed the office environment. The personal computer began replacing typewriters. Secretarial jobs began to disappear as more knowledge workers used PCs to create, edit, and print their own documents. Although most still worked with documents, first overnight delivery services and then the desktop facsimile machine changed forever the *speed* with which knowledge workers processed transactions. And once MIS began networking PCs, the way knowledge workers work together, as well as the procedures they used, changed forever.

But all was not rosy. A hard lesson business had to learn was that computers alone do not improve productivity. In fact early, less-sophisticated computer hardware and software sometimes retarded productivity. The equipment was often difficult to learn; many hours were spent trying to master it, resulting in lost productive hours when the knowledge workers should have been performing their regular work. Over time, hardware and software was designed to more closely resemble actual work processes — in other words, the way people do their work, rather than a convenient way for the computer to do the work. Then real productivity improvements began to occur.

For example, in the past a single knowledge worker might be responsible for collecting, organizing, analyzing, and formatting a printed monthly report of his department's activities. Now, several people contribute information based on their individual areas of expertise — the supervisor, the analyst, and the sales manager. Data is collected from several application programs, either on disks or transmitted across the local area network. Significant tables or charts are electronically turned into overhead transparencies or color slides. Indeed, the report may be distributed electronically rather than on paper. The subsequent "meeting" to discuss its contents may occur on-line, using electronic mail, without all parties being physically present in a conference room. In fact, the sales manager, who could be on the road with her salespeople, may participate from a remote site using a notebook computer.

This chapter explores what it means to be a knowledge worker in today's office environment. You'll learn about the new roles people play in knowledge work, as well as the rapid evolution of new procedures they use as they work with some of the most exciting and versatile computer technology on the market today. And you'll see how the idea of the document, which we first studied in Chapter 1, has come full circle with office automation.

FIGURE 15.1   Office automation in the 1990s. All these technologies are in use in modern businesses.

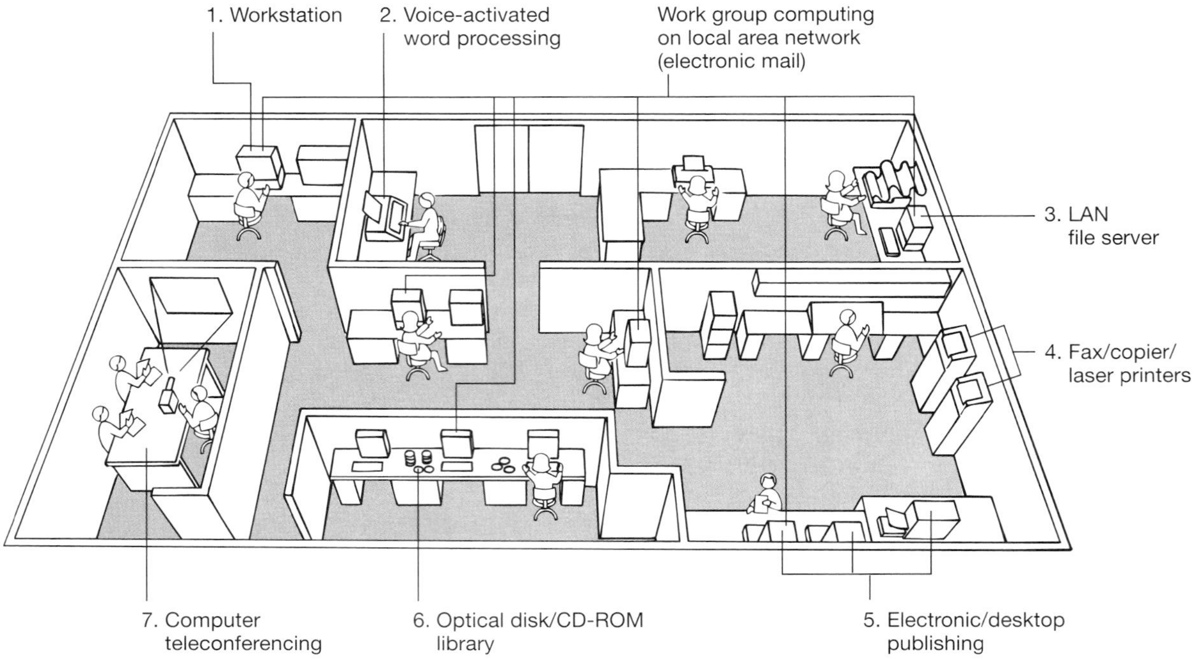

1. Workstation   2. Voice-activated word processing   Work group computing on local area network (electronic mail)   3. LAN file server   4. Fax/copier/ laser printers   7. Computer teleconferencing   6. Optical disk/CD-ROM library   5. Electronic/desktop publishing

OFFICE AUTOMATION: A DEFINITION

Office automation is using computer and communications technology to help people better use and manage information. Office automation technology includes all types of computers, telephones, electronic mail, and office machines that use microprocessors, or other high technology components. Figure 15.1 shows a state-of-the art office.

Knowledge workers using office automation (OA) include senior executives, managers, supervisors, analysts, engineers, and other white-collar office workers. In most offices, information is the end product, often in paper form. It is essential for managing, organizing, analyzing, and conducting the company's business. OA systems keep track of the information originating in various other processing operations throughout the company, such as order processing, accounting, inventory, and manufacturing. Office automation provides knowledge workers with information-producing systems to collect, analyze, plan, and control information about the many facets of the business, using text, voice, graphics, and video display technologies.

The term *office automation* was first used in 1955 to describe computer-automated bookkeeping, an adjunct of data processing. The term—and to some extent the entire notion of automating the office—fell into disuse as the emphasis turned to management information systems. There was renewed interest toward the end of the 1970s, when futurists such as Alvin Toffler envisioned the "office of the future." By the mid-1980s, office automation was a popular concept again. The road to OA has been a bumpy one, from

YESTERDAY

THE EVOLUTION OF THE TYPEWRITER

1714: An anonymous British inventor claims to be working on "an artificial machine or method of impressing or transcribing of letters singly or progressively one after another, as in writing, whereby writing whatever may be engrossed in paper or parchment so neat and exact as not to be distinguished from print." No such machine is forthcoming.

1857: W. A. Burt, an American, builds the first working typewriter and types this message to his wife: "Dear Companion, I have but jest got my second machine into operation and this is the first specimen I send you except a few lines to regulate the machine."

1867: Another American, Christopher Sholes, develops the first commercial typewriter. In 1873, he sells the rights to Remington. IT COULD ONLY TYPE IN UPPER CASE.

1872: Thomas Edison creates an electric typewriter. However, it is so crude that it is converted into a ticker-tape printer.

1874: Mark Twain becomes the first author to buy and use a Remington typewriter.

1935: The first commercially successful electric typewriter is introduced by IBM.

1961: The first IBM Selectric typewriter using interchangeable "golfball" typing elements is introduced. The golfball was developed by happenstance by Kenneth Iverson of IBM, who was looking for a way to suitably type the characters for his new programming language, APL.

1964: The first IBM stand-alone word processing system, called the MT/ST, is a combination of two technologies: magnetic tape (MT) to record and store keystrokes, and the Selectric typewriter (ST) for playback.

1969: The IBM MC/ST is introduced. This system uses a plastic magnetic IBM card to store data, rather than the more cumbersome reels of magnetic tape.

1972: The first electronic memory typewriters appear. They can store up to a full page in their tiny memory.

1976: The Wang multiuser Word Processing System (WPS) is introduced. Within two years, it becomes the most popular word processor in the world.

1979: "Intelligent" electronic typewriters are introduced. They can store documents on floppy disk and are capable of acting as printers in computer systems.

1981: Typewriters with dedicated word processing built in are introduced.

1986: Portable dedicated word processing typewriters are introduced.

being a poor cousin to data processing to finding its own identity in text and information processing.

KNOWLEDGE WORKERS: THE MOST IMPORTANT ELEMENT

As this text has stressed throughout, people are the most important component in any computer system. Knowledge workers are found in many different occupations in modern business, turning data into useful information. A hundred years ago, office workers were treated in much the same way as factory workers, performing rote tasks under strict supervision. Today's knowledge workers, and the work they perform, have redefined office work. In many instances, knowledge work has significantly altered the established organizational chart hierarchy, turning managers into their own secretaries and turning administrative assistants into decision makers. There are two ways to characterize knowledge workers, and in both cases it is by the work they do: collaboration and power users.

COLLABORATION. Knowledge workers used to be defined by their department or function. Today people are selected to work together for their knowledge and skills to accomplish a task or project, and then regroup to work with others on the next project. This is termed **collaboration,** and it simply means working together with the aid of computer systems. Collaboration is sometimes referred to as *computer-supported collaborative work,* and the knowledge workers working together are often referred to as a **work group.** Collaboration makes use of PCs and workstations in local area networks, often connected to the corporate computers for downloading data, using everyday applications, electronic mail, and sometimes special work group software.

THE POWER USER. Certain knowledge workers are able to assimilate and learn to use computer technology more quickly than others. The **power user** is a knowledge worker who understands the business and work group objectives, as well as the computer systems in use (specifically personal computers), and is able to help formulate strategies for getting the most productivity from computers for the work group. For example, Sarah, the graphic designer in the advertising department who uses a Macintosh, is a power user. So is Mike, the sales representative who has configured his notebook computer for maximum productivity. Indeed, almost any knowledge worker can become a power user. Both of these power users will be active in sharing their computer skills and knowledge with other knowledge workers to help them solve business problems and become more productive.

ERGONOMICS. Office tasks involve a great deal of thinking and decision making. As a result, hardware and software engineers understand that office systems must be flexible and versatile. Moreover, they must be designed so that any knowledge worker, regardless of background, can easily use them. This is called **ergonomics,** the study of how to create safety, comfort, and ease of use for people who use machines. It is not a new field of study; in fact, it has existed for over a hundred years. With the advent of computers, ergonomics engineers became particularly interested in OA systems, furniture, and environments for the knowledge worker.

Computer ergonomics developed most rapidly in Europe, where standards committees insisted upon common electrical connections and ease-of-use criteria. Intensive studies determined the best designs for keyboards, set eye fatigue levels for monitors, and specified desk and seating designs that alleviate physical stress. These standards were adopted by the U.S. computer industry, which in many cases enhanced and improved them. Office furniture companies soon introduced ergonomically designed chairs and equipment. Refer to Figure 15.2 as you review the following concerns that ergonomics addresses:

- Desktop height (for the keyboard) and distance to the chair seat.
- The chair seat and back; both must be adjustable for proper seat angle and back lumbar support.
- Keyboard angle and hand rest, key sound feedback, and key pressure.

The ergonomically designed office.   **FIGURE 15.2**

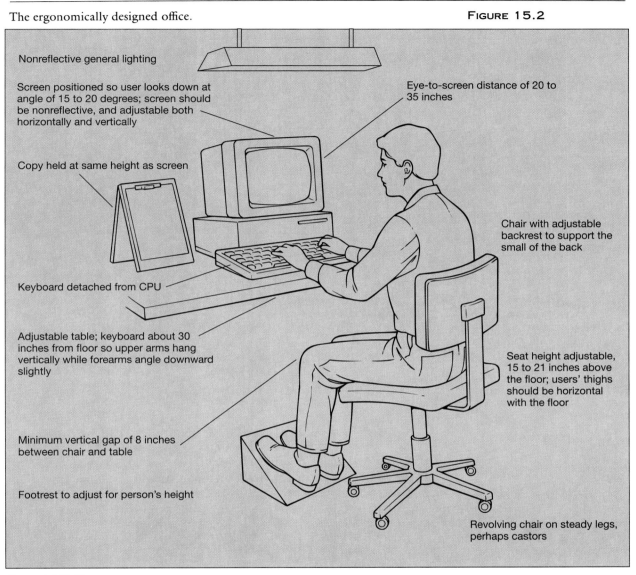

Nonreflective general lighting

Screen positioned so user looks down at
angle of 15 to 20 degrees; screen should
be nonreflective, and adjustable both
horizontally and vertically

Eye-to-screen distance of 20 to
35 inches

Copy held at same height as screen

Keyboard detached from CPU

Chair with adjustable
backrest to support the
small of the back

Adjustable table; keyboard about 30
inches from floor so upper arms hang
vertically while forearms angle downward
slightly

Seat height adjustable,
15 to 21 inches above
the floor; users' thighs
should be horizontal
with the floor

Minimum vertical gap of 8 inches
between chair and table

Footrest to adjust for person's height

Revolving chair on steady legs,
perhaps castors

Source: *InfoWorld* newspaper.

- Video monitor angle, screen brightness, radiation factor, and ambient
  room light.
- Sound from the computer itself—its fan and disk drives.

Many studies have been conducted to determine the optimum ergonomic
configuration, but often it depends on individual workers and any ailments,
such as back problems, they may have. Knowledge workers are prone to a
unique form of stress from looking at monitors for extended periods, so
frequent breaks are recommended. According to the U.S. government's National Institute of Occupational Safety and Health, there is no conclusive

TODAY

TELECOMMUTING FROM THE VIRTUAL OFFICE

For some knowledge workers, the next best thing to office automation is no office. While there are many jobs that require working in the company offices, and the vast majority of knowledge workers prefer working and socializing with fellow employees, there are many who enjoy telecommuting. Telecommuting, for most of these people, means working from a home office. For others, the office is wherever they are: in the car, at a customer site, in a hotel room. This anytime, anywhere office has been dubbed *the virtual office.*

Los Angeles, that paradise for commuters, is a testing ground for telecommuting. The Los Angeles County Telecommuting Project has about 1,700 employees working from home offices on a part-time basis. For many, it involves learning some new skills: self-management and self-discipline, and how to overcome the feeling that they are cut off from the office. In the office, managers are learning to trust that the telecommuters are doing their work without supervision. The county expects to continue expanding the pro-

gram, from office workers to public service employees, reaching 10,000 people by the mid-1990s. As more companies and organizations realize the savings in allowing employees to work at home, along with the additional benefits of reducing traffic congestion, pollution, and stress, we can expect to see telecommuting make futurist Alvin Toffler's prediction of the "electronic cottage" a reality.

evidence, however, that radiation from monitors affects unborn infants. Another ailment that some knowledge workers contract, *carpal tunnel syndrome,* affects the wrists. But medical practitioners and ergonomists alike agree that one way to avoid the stress, strain, and backache of working with computers is to change positions often — at least every 15 minutes — and to take a short break every two hours.

OFFICE SYSTEMS: SOFTWARE AND HARDWARE

Office automation utilizes computer-based systems to provide information to help knowledge workers make decisions that benefit the business. You have already studied software and hardware separately. In this chapter, we see them functioning together in office automation systems. Several distinct technologies, or systems, comprise OA:

- *Text management systems,* including electronic typewriters, word processing systems, and electronic publishing.
- *Business analysis systems,* including spreadsheet analysis, decision support systems, and executive information systems.
- *Document management systems,* including database management and document storage and management.

■ *Network and communication management systems,* including the telephone, electronic mail, voice messaging systems, teleconferencing, and facsimile (FAX).

In the following sections of this chapter, we'll see how knowledge workers put these four types of office systems to use.

KNOWLEDGE CHECK

1. What is the end product of office automation?   p. 472
2. Describe how office automation is essential to the business as a whole.   p. 472
3. What are people who use office automation often called?   p. 473
4. What is the purpose behind ergonomics?   p. 474
5. Describe the four systems or technologies that comprise office automation, and identify the goals they serve.   pp. 476–77

OFFICE AUTOMATION SYSTEMS

As mentioned earlier, office automation systems are used to collect, analyze, plan, and control information in order for the business to thrive. Order processing, inventory management, manufacturing resource planning, and distribution are distinct systems unto themselves and are not considered part of office automation.

As also mentioned earlier, there are four primary technologies used to manage information in office automation: text management systems, business analysis systems, document management systems, and network and communication systems. They are used to manage these various types of information:

■ *Text,* as in written text form.
■ *Data,* as in numbers and other nontext forms.
■ *Graphics,* including drawings, charts, and photographs.
■ *Video,* such as captured images, videotapes, and teleconferencing.
■ *Audio,* such as phone conversations and dictation.

In the past, each of these forms of information was created using different technologies. Text was created using conventional typewriters or, more recently, word processing. Data, such as sales reports, was provided by the central computer. Charts and graphs were either hand-drawn or created using 35mm slide photography, and videotapes were used for training. The telephone was the primary audio medium. It wasn't possible to combine them in any effective manner.

Today the computer combines or integrates these different media and others as well. Data, sound, and images can all be input into a computer, stored, then translated into the kind of output we need. At the center of this integration are networking and communications systems. Let's look at the four office technologies of information management and some of their applications.

TEXT MANAGEMENT SYSTEMS

A **text management system** includes all kinds of typewriters, word processing systems, PCs with word processing, desktop publishing and text editing systems, and even computerized typesetting equipment. Text management systems are used for:

- Writing memos, notes, letters, and other short documents requiring little if any revision.
- Printing envelopes and labels.
- Preparing preprinted forms, such as invoices or purchase orders.
- Composing longer documents, such as proposals and reports, that involve several reviews and revisions.
- Retrieving and editing documents that are often reused, such as form letters and contracts, that contain standard replaceable (boilerplate) text.
- Creating display documents, ranging from advertising brochures to in-house or client newsletters or other documentation.

AT&T Federal Systems Advanced Technologies has a Proposal Development Engineering facility in Greensboro, North Carolina. Its work involves preparing high-quality documents, or proposals, for U.S. government bids. Technical writers from all over the country write and edit the text, and send it on disk or electronically to Greensboro. There it is published, incorporating different typefaces, drawings and graphics, and formats. These proposals must be published without delay, and they often must meet strict federal guidelines for size, length, and other matters. Therefore, it is a critical publishing operation.

In addition to its ongoing proposal preparation, the Proposal Development Engineering facility is developing a proposal database. Most proposals contain over 50 percent new information, but there is a great deal of repetitive information that can be reused, such as facility plans, business plans, personnel resumes, and product descriptions. The facility is creating a text library of this boilerplate information. The key is in indexing it so it can be easily found. To do this, the facility is using the Workgroup Technologies text management software (shown in Figure 15.3) because of its organizing, categorizing, and search-and-retrieval capabilities. Using this text management system has eliminated a great deal of paper as well as an elaborate system for organizing and storing old paper proposals.

BUSINESS ANALYSIS SYSTEMS

A manager or executive needs solid data from which to extract the information necessary to make good decisions for the business. In the past, these knowledge workers had to rely on their experience and other personal factors to make decisions. A **business analysis system** provides data that, when used with the proper software, aids in business analysis and decision making. The

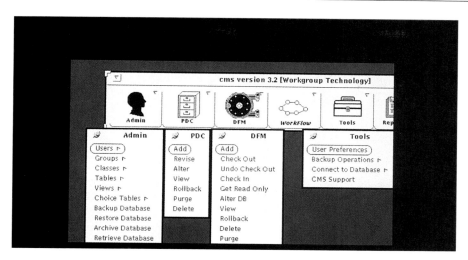

FIGURE 15.3

A portion of Workgroup Technologies document management pulldown menu showing how the information is organized for use by the work group.

spreadsheet is routinely used by corporate power users for such things as honing cost-benefit analyses and creating budgets. Yet there are other computer-based software tools for performing business analyses. Two that are commonly used are decision support systems and executive information systems.

DECISION SUPPORT SYSTEMS.   Since its origins in the late 1970s, the **decision support system** (DSS) has evolved in its usefulness and the tasks it performs. A decision support system, as its name implies, helps a manager extract information from various MIS databases and reporting systems, analyze it, and then formulate a decision or a strategy for business planning. The DSS does this by collecting data and analyzing it with special modeling software.

For example, the manager can create a scenario to see what would happen if a product's sales skyrocketed or if a division were closed down. The software creates charts and graphs from the data, showing how expenses, profits, and other financial factors would be affected. Some DSSs have an artificial intelligence component to help formulate decisions and analyze outcomes.

EXECUTIVE INFORMATION SYSTEMS.   The **executive information system** (EIS) is designed for top management who often want nothing to do with a computer. Typically the EIS is a PC with brilliant color graphics and extremely easy-to-use software that can present data with just a keystroke or two, as shown in Figure 15.4. The idea is to create an executive tool that isn't intimidating. The EIS replaces conventional reports, such as a thick stack of computer printouts that contain only a few things of interest to the executive. The EIS has access to the corporate mainframe and is able to project most of the information in graphical form. Using the EIS, the executive can evaluate the company's performance, track product lines, create scenarios for future product introductions, plot emerging trends in the industry, or plan new directions in which to take the company.

FIGURE 15.4

Managers shouldn't need to
concern themselves with
where data is stored or what
application produced it. This
executive information system
displays information in its
business context, as shown in
each of the four windows.

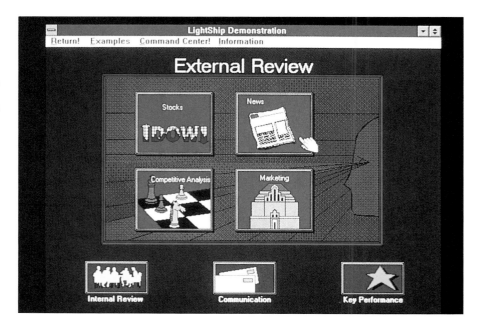

Robert Kidder, chief executive officer of Duracell, once used his EIS to
compare U.S. and European sales staff productivity. The EIS captured the data
from the corporate mainframe and displayed it on his screen as multicolored
graphics. It showed the U.S. salaried sales staff producing more sales than the
Europeans. He tapped the mouse button a few more times and finally learned
that in Germany, too many salespeople were calling on small shops that did
not generate sufficient revenues. Kidder corrected the problem by licensing
distributors to service the small shops instead of having expensive salespeople
call on them.

EXPERT SYSTEMS.   There is a software technology called artificial intelligence (AI). **Artificial intelligence** attempts to replicate many human
thought processes, such as reasoning, learning, self-improvement, and associative learning, in a computer. The goal many AI researchers have strived for
is a machine that can think. On the immediate horizon is to simply have
smarter programs. Raymond Kurzweil, a leading proponent of artificial intelligence, says, "I believe that by the end of this century, AI will be as ubiquitous
as personal computers are today. The majority of software will be intelligent,
at least by today's standards."

Computers systems are able to store and randomly retrieve information, in
close approximation with how a human would, and it is here that AI has
achieved the most success. These are called expert systems. An **expert system**
offers solutions for problems in a specialized area of work or study, based on
the stored knowledge of human experts. Expert systems have been developed

for medicine, oil exploration, civil engineering, food preparation, monitoring plant operations, and hundreds of other applications. For example, MYCIN is an expert system that can diagnose blood and bacterial infections, based on the knowledge of many doctors stored in its knowledge base; it then recommends antibiotics for treatment. In another example, when the chief cook at Campbell Soup Company decided to retire, the firm stored his soup preparation knowledge in an expert system.

Another AI technology is the **neural network,** which uses many various connections between input, processing, and output. A neural network may be either a software or hardware technology; the first neural network integrated circuit chip was introduced in 1992. Neural networks in software have been in use in business for several years, where their great strength is in recognizing patterns in data. For example, Chase Manhattan Bank, the second largest credit card issuer, uses neural network software to detect credit card abuse patterns in transactions. If a card is used repeatedly in a short time, or just after being reissued, it could mean the card has been stolen. The neural network was exposed to the patterns of legitimate and illegitimate credit card use until it "learned" how to detect fraud. It also was able to learn to detect new and emerging types of fraud. In this way, Chase was able to reduce the time between detecting possible misuse or fraud from three days to just one, saving the bank untold millions of dollars.

DOCUMENT MANAGEMENT SYSTEMS

OA demands that data be immediately accessible and instantaneously retrievable. For that reason we are slowly moving away from paper, toward document forms that can be stored on the computer. What you learned about the document in Chapter 1 comes full circle in this chapter. In order for computer systems to be truly useful, they must be information managers. Managing data is not enough. Information is often stored in documents.

Document management systems aid in filing, tracking, and managing documents, whether they are paper or computer-based. The document may be a file from word processing, spreadsheet, database, or other applications, such as image files. There are document management systems for many different types of applications, such as on-line information organization and insurance agency file organization. These systems can organize a document for entire divisions of a company on a mainframe or mini, or on personal computers for smaller applications.

One common PC application is document management for documents created by collaborative work groups with word processing. It does not take the place of word processing, but acts like a database manager for word processing files. This type of software permits gathering and organizing files stored on various computers or servers in a network, then indexing them like a DBMS would. It permits viewing and previewing files for their content, and archiving them for long-term storage. Perhaps most important, document management software maintains version control, so that knowledge workers only use the most current revision of a document. Thus the AT&T proposal case mentioned before integrates both text management and document management. Figure 15.5 shows a document management screen.

FIGURE 15.5

Keyfile is an integrated document manager for both paper and electronic documents that provides for easy sharing and quick access of information in a work group environment.

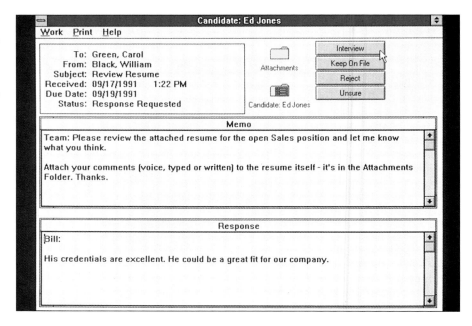

NETWORK AND COMMUNICATION MANAGEMENT SYSTEMS

In the previous chapter, you learned there are many ways for knowledge workers to communicate with one another. It's possible for them to communicate right now, in real time, via phone or computer. And they can also communicate at some point in the future, using the computer-controlled PBX voice mail system or the computer network to leave an electronic mail message. In both instances, today's modern corporations make extensive use of **network and communication management systems** to manage both voice and data communications.

The Associated Press (AP) has combined document management with its network connecting news offices across the United States. The document management system, called SelectNews, runs on a 386-based PS/2. The software scans news stories arriving from AP news offices on average about every six seconds and then routes them to a predefined news category. Editors in charge of the news categories, or "beats," check their PS/2, connected via local area network to the server PC, for incoming stories. They are in turn assigned or routed to AP's wire services. Similarly, computer-based telephone systems can help track phone usage and costs with printed reports. Often they can also switch service between long-distance carriers to take advantage of lower rates.

WORK GROUP COMPUTING

As mentioned earlier, many knowledge workers enjoy their work more, and are more productive, when they can work together in small, collaborative

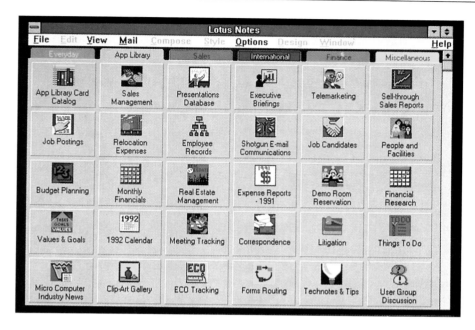

FIGURE 15.6

Lotus Notes is an open work group computing environment that helps knowledge workers perform collaborative tasks more effectively. It is used to build applications that provide an easy means for work groups to communicate and share information across geographic, technical, and organizational boundaries. This screen shows an application library used to generate new applications.

groups. A work group is comprised of knowledge workers, each of whom has a different task, but all of whom are working toward a common goal. Work group computing is spreading throughout business organizations, and encompasses all four of the different systems we've just discussed.

Groupware is a software product designed for sharing information, both text and graphics, from both corporate and on-line sources, among networked PCs and workstations. Lotus Notes is groupware that helps people track ideas, analyze data, create continuing dialogues with one another, and present results. Groupware, such as Notes (Figure 15.6), helps knowledge workers present ideas better, organize information, create brainstorming sessions, obtain feedback, and solve problems within work groups.

Groupware reduces the time a work group spends in live meetings by providing them with a 24-hour-a-day forum. People can log on or off the system from their office, from a PC at home, or from a laptop on the road. They read the meeting dialogue and add their comments; the group works on the project until everyone agrees upon a decision or course of action. People say they feel freer to say what's really on their minds in an on-line forum.

Groupware is used by executives for planning and strategy, by groups such as traders in a mutual funds financial brokerage, and by information systems developers creating software requirements for new applications. Once again we see how the Information Age has changed the way we communicate. In the 1990s, we can expect to see our most important information exchange relayed via computer, using electronic mail or electronic data interchange. Routine correspondence containing a signature or graphics will be FAXed. However, long documents, reports, and highly confidential material may continue to be sent via overnight express services.

KNOWLEDGE
CHECK

1. What five types of information do OA systems manage?   p. 477
2. What has changed with respect to the people using text management systems?   p. 478
3. What is the primary purpose behind an executive information system?   p. 479
4. Why do we need sophisticated document management systems?   p. 481
5. What technology is essential to exchanging information in office automation systems?   p. 482

OFFICE AUTOMATION TECHNOLOGIES AT WORK

Three technology trends have created today's office automation environment. One is the rise of the PC, which is perfectly suited for many routine office tasks. Knowledge workers who did not have access to the corporate computer now are able to do their own computing. The second trend is the local area network, which makes sharing information possible. Once it was possible to do either standalone computing or workgroup computing, the corporate mainframe assumed a new usefulness in distributed computing, the third trend.

In a truly distributed computing office, you can have access to the data on any computer, whether it is another PC, a mini, or a mainframe. All systems are *integrated;* that is, we can enter data with any device, store data anywhere in the system, and produce output in a variety of ways, as shown in the integrated image/data management systems in Figure 15.7.

In this environment, we can say "everything is everywhere," or "the network is the computer." This is the ideal OA environment. An outstanding example of distributed computing is Project Athena at the Massachusetts Institute of Technology. Begun in 1983 and completed in 1990, Project Athena is a network of over 1,100 personal computers, minicomputers, and workstations, all linked together, for the use of faculty and students alike. Athena is based on the client/server model and uses computers from Cray, Digital, IBM, and Sun, among others, the UNIX operating system, and the Motif graphic user interface. There are over 80 network servers and about 100 laser printers. On an average day, over 2,500 campus knowledge workers log on the system. Figure 15.8 diagrams Athena. Other examples of distributed office environments include the integrated desktop and large system integration.

THE INTEGRATED DESKTOP

Software makes it possible for today's knowledge worker, using a PC or workstation, to have an integrated electronic desktop. In such an environment, all the various office management functions are available on the PC at the touch of a key. An example is Norick's Paperless Office (Figure 15.9), which creates an integrated work environment with your existing productivity applications on the PC. It will run under Windows or can be used as its own operating

An image/data management system. Note the variety of image sources available across the network.

FIGURE 15.7

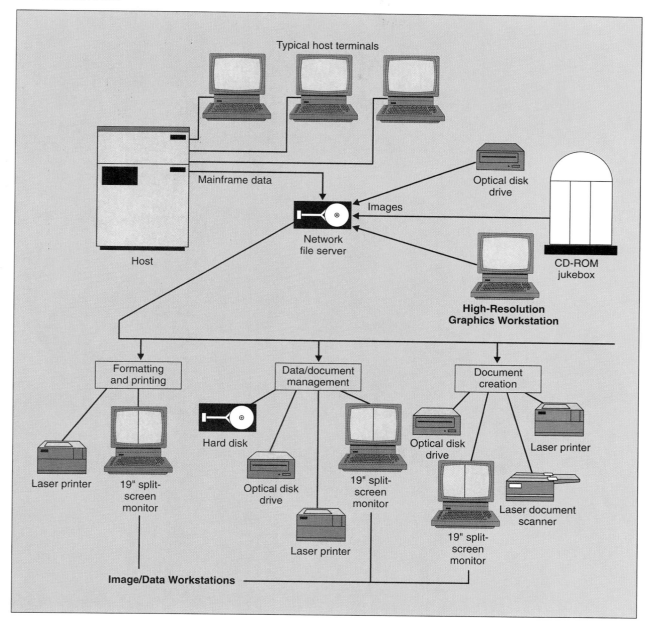

environment. This software manages all documents, including storage and retrieval and routing them to different applications. Documents are stored according to the way the knowledge worker organizes information — not by the application that created it. In addition, Norick's Paperless Office permits storing different types of documents with established relationships together in

FIGURE 15.8   Athena: distributed computing at MIT.

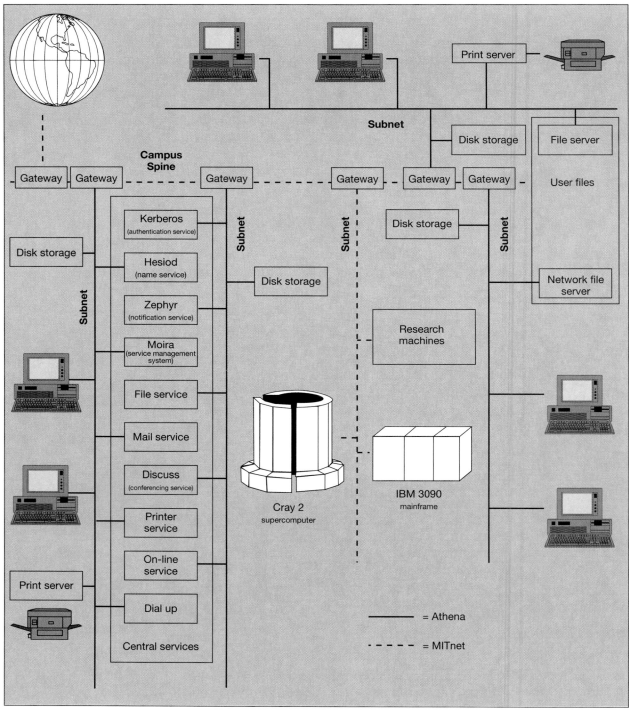

Source: *Information Technology Quarterly,* Fall 1990.

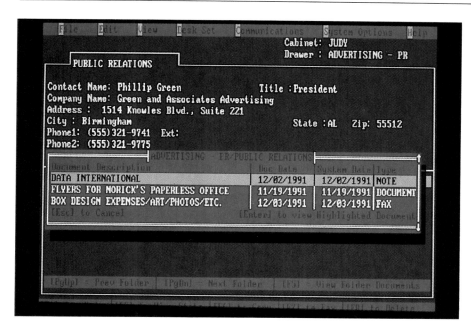

FIGURE 15.9

Paper becomes electronic: Using Norick's Paperless Office, this Rolodex-style card need never be printed. In addition, pertinent files from other applications are referenced at the bottom of the card.

a single electronic file folder. It also permits sending electronic documents by FAX, right from the PC.

LARGE SYSTEM INTEGRATION

Office automation in large systems expands on the multi-tasking, multi-user concept. In large systems, it is not always necessary that every knowledge worker use the same brand of application, such as WordPerfect; sophisticated software interfaces make it possible to exchange data between PC, mini, and mainframe applications. This additional functionality makes it possible to create standards for applications that apply across the company, so the emphasis is on the business benefits, not on trying to make the technology work properly. The ideal situation is to make the entire computer system transparent to the knowledge workers; their sole concentration is on obtaining and properly utilizing information to make decisions.

Digital Equipment Corporation's All-in-1 integrated OA software offers word processing and text management, electronic mail, facsimile, database management, a calendar, appointment scheduler, computer teleconferencing, and many other features. When one worker sends another an E-mail message, the recipient's terminal or PC beeps to signal an incoming message. With All-in-1, if a meeting time or date is changed, each attendee automatically receives an electronic message.

Digital is continuing to expand the frontiers of office automation in a collaborative project with the MAYA Design Group of Pittsburgh, Pennsylvania. The design integrates image-based documents, electronic communications, FAX, and office work flow management, all working with an innovative graphical user interface (Figure 15.10). The GUI permits manipulating

FIGURE 15.10

Work in progress: This screen shows the various elements of a GUI from Maya, an independent software developer —graphic images, commands, icons, buttons, text fonts, and information windows—as they are being created and refined.

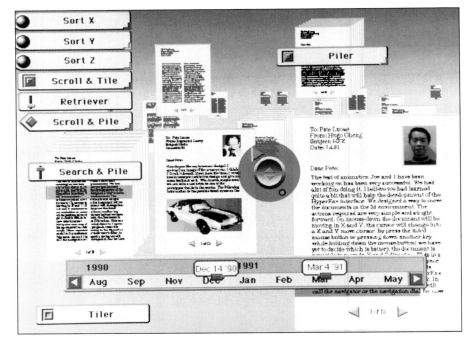

hundreds of documents at a time in a simulated three-dimensional space. While many sophisticated distributed OA systems require extensive training, MAYA's design assures ease of use.

KNOWLEDGE CHECK

1. What is distributed computing, and why is it desirable?   p. 484
2. What is holding back distributed computing?   p. 484
3. Describe two characteristics of the integrated desktop environment. pp. 484, 487
4. What additional function makes large systems integration desirable? p. 487
5. What is the ultimate goal of office automation?   p. 487

WHAT LIES AHEAD?

The document is truly the center of OA, as witnessed by the many supporting technologies. It is common to see photocopy machines, facsimile machines, micrographics recorders, and optical scanners, as well as various incoming information sources, such as stock market tickers or business news wire services. Each has emerged as a separate technology; however, the computer is emerging as the center of integrated office systems.

TOMORROW

DISTRIBUTED NETWORK COMPUTING: MORE OF THE SAME, ONLY BETTER

Distributed computing is far from a new idea. It had its origins in the 1970s and had made several reappearances, often with slightly different names. Why won't it go away? To paraphrase the words of an anonymous pundit, because you have to keep doing it until you get it right.

Distributed computing in the 1990s is driven by knowledge worker need: there is no way any single-vendor solution can provide the diversity of services today's business needs. In addition, technology has matured; it's increasingly possible, especially given the advances in communications and networking, to make distributed computing a reality today.

The ideal state is termed *distributed network computing,* which means that any number of network nodes can be processing data in parallel with one another, and even sharing processing if necessary. It also means

that any and all computers can be interconnected for data- and processing-sharing; the knowledge worker doesn't know if the IBM mainframe or the Hewlett-Packard mini or the Macintosh is doing the work—nor does he or she even care.

What the knowledge worker does care about is the character and quality of the work being accomplished in this distributed network environment. Since it is an all-digital network of high bandwidth, it is capable of voice, data, and image processing. The insurance underwriter is able to view a videotape of the ship she has been asked to insure, stem to stern, port to bow, inside and out. Digital color still photographs of employees and work-in-progress are visible in pertinent files.

Perhaps best of all, a wide diversity of applications run in a full multitasking environment, seamlessly with one another. It's

hard to tell when one is left and another begun because all the knowledge worker has done is start typing in different information. The software senses the need for word processing as opposed to a spreadsheet and shifts automatically. What's more, when an analysis or opinion is needed, all he need do is click the mouse on the ? icon and the expert system renders its views.

Most of this technology is available separately today. What's been lacking in the past is the desire on the part of technology vendors to collaborate on such a system. As distributed network computing takes firm hold over the next few years, we'll see such a system quickly come into focus because everything will interface with everything else. Why? Because the knowledge workers demand it and, as anyone in business knows, the customer is *always* right.

What office could survive without a photocopy machine? The basic technology, xerography, originated in the mid-1940s. Today the line between a copy machine and a laser printer is blurring. Many feel there is an unneeded step in printing a document and passing it through a copier for multiple copies. The answer is the intelligent laser printer/copier, which combines the two operations.

Scanning text and images to be combined in documents is becoming commonplace in offices. Furthermore, the tasks a FAX machine performs are not so different from copying or printing. Why not have one machine that combines the laser printer, copier, scanner, and FAX? In 1992, Okidata introduced Doc-It, just such a multifunction machine, that connects to a PC.

Here is an example of multifunctionality. Let's say we create and store a magazine advertisement, with text, graphics, a photograph, and the company

Careers for Knowledge Workers
Sue Stokes, Senior Workers' Compensation Underwriter, Transamerica Insurance

When Sue Stokes first began using a computer at age 13, she never thought she'd become a highly skilled knowledge worker in the insurance profession. No, at the time Sue thought the computer was mostly fun, and it also helped her get her homework done. "I found out computers weren't so bad. In fact, I even took programming courses — BASIC as a sophomore, FORTRAN as an independent study when I was a junior, and COBOL my senior year."

In college, Sue combined her interests in computers and medicine. She studied biology, statistics, mathematics, and computer science to earn a B.S. in bio-metry, a field of medical research, from the University of Minnesota. Her ambition took her to the University of San Diego for an MBA. She then "sort of fell into insurance."

With her educational background, Sue was well qualified for a position in insurance underwriting. "I went into workers' compensation, which took advantage of my medical background. I quickly understood the medical reports for injury claims and could visualize medical problems when assessing risks." That "fall" had a nice landing, as Sue was soon promoted to senior workers' compensation underwriter.

And she was already computer-literate as well. "Workers' compensation underwriting involves the ability to make decisions based on pieces of an information puzzle. Each risk — that's what we call a company applying for coverage — is different. Cleri-

logo. Now, using mail merge, we address it to each of the people on the distribution list and the printer produces an original for each party. There are three managers on the premises who are to get a copy, so the copier produces three. Two other managers are in different cities, so we FAX copies to them. All this can be accomplished in just a few keystrokes, saving a great deal of time.

And what of color? The color inkjet printer is affordable for most knowledge workers now, and it won't be long until the color laser printer becomes affordable as well. Soon we will be printing out documents just the way they appear on the screen and think nothing of it. Will wonders never cease? Indeed, as Arthur C. Clarke once said, "Any sufficiently advanced technology is indistinguishable from magic."

cal workers have less severe exposure in accidents, or claims, than carpenters. Interestingly, the highest premium rates are among circus and carnival workers. I like making those decisions, and I use the computer to help me."

Sue primarily uses a terminal attached to an IBM mainframe. "I have access to our insureds' policy information, electronic mail, our insurance rate information, and Transamerica company data, such as profits and losses." She uses electronic mail to correspond and send risk information to others in the company: home office underwriters, claims adjusters, and loss control representatives.

Sue also uses a personal computer, although not as much as her terminal. "I prepare monthly reports that are about six pages long," she says. She uses word processing and a spreadsheet for this work. In addition to the text

writing, she must prepare a great deal of numerical and statistical information, such as the amount of new policies her department has written (in premium dollars), policies that have been renewed, a comparison of new business with historical activity, and staff and customer service information.

To help her compile the numerical and statistical information, an artificial intelligence system called Intellect is used to extract the pertinent data from about a dozen databases on the mainframe. Intellect responds to English-like commands and collects policy, profit and loss, and other data Sue requests for her report. For example, Intellect gathers the amount of premium business written and the losses incurred; then the spreadsheet is used to compare the figures against the monthly goals. Monthly and year-to-date figures are automatically updated at the

same time. Once the report is finished, it is sent via electronic mail to the appropriate managers to review. No paper.

Sue believes the paperless office is just around the corner, "although we're not there yet," she says. "Almost all the documents we work with are on the computer. When we become paperless, about the only time we'll need paper is for a legal signature. An underwriting file can quickly grow to over half an inch thick. But reviewing just what you want to see on the computer screen is much easier and faster. I can look up the policy information, the risk information, and the endorsements on the screen. That's often all I need to see, but still sometimes it's quicker to look through the file. But I think most insurance companies will be paperless in another five years."

The computer plays an increasingly important role in office systems integration, as more and more office machines are linked. Today computers large and small, file servers, mass storage, and peripherals such as modems, microfilm copiers, and laser printer/copiers are linked in networks. When a laser printer/copier is linked into the computer system so that a letter can be electronically sent to it and then copied, it is called an *intelligent copier*. When a number of complementary machines are linked together in an office, we call that an *intelligent network*. As this happens, the computer and the network become the same; the network is the computer. We have true office automation; we have put it all together.

For many years, people feared that computers would put them out of work. For you, tomorrow's knowledge worker, it seems safe to say the computer is still busily creating many new jobs and opportunities. A U.S. government study states that three out of five jobs people will need to be trained and educated for in the year 2000 do not exist today. These new jobs will be a result of new technologies that are emerging as industries. Furthermore, there is increasing need for people to enter the computer industry in a wide variety of occupations.

Regardless of whether your career takes you into a business-oriented occupation or the information systems organization, welcome, knowledge worker, to the second great renaissance: the Information Age.

WORK GROUP ETHICS: RESPECTING EACH OTHER

Human beings are, by nature, competitive. It's part of the survival instinct to want to get ahead in life. For many years, people have used war terminology and metaphors to describe business practices. It's no secret that certain people will do unethical — even illegal — things to make money or boost their careers. But can we say, "All's fair in love and war"? This is an issue of particular concern in the office, where so many people can easily gain access to your computer and the data stored on it.

Work group computing is founded on the premise that people work *together* to achieve common goals. There should be respect for others' rights, privacy, and data in such an environment. However, it is likely that in the real world unethical people will read other knowledge workers' private files; in fact, some might even sabotage a colleague's work to make him or her look bad. To some extent, security systems should take care of this, but as the old saying goes, locks only keep honest people honest.

In order to respect fellow knowledge workers, it's important to respect the new office automation technologies and accompanying procedures. For example, proper text management means being careful to avoid plagiarizing, just as rigorous business analysis demands honest interpretation and communication of the facts. It is essential that all employees know and understand the company's policies and guidelines on ethical behavior. Most important, to quote Shakespeare, "To thine own self be true."

SUMMARY

1. *Define office automation and explain its relationship to the information systems in business.* Office automation is the marriage of computer and communications technologies that bring a variety of office machines together to serve the knowledge worker. The goal is to more efficiently manage information so that the company can steer other systems — accounting, manufacturing, and so on — toward specific business goals.

2. *Name the four fundamental office automation technologies.* OA is comprised of four systems: text management, business analysis, document management, and network and communications management. The four systems are used to manage text, data, graphics, video, and audio.

Text management includes typing, word processing, and electronic publishing. Business analysis includes decision support systems, executive information systems, and expert systems. Document management means working with information in paper and electronic form on the computer, from either corporate or on-line sources. Network and communications management means adding the ability to share information between computers, facilitating work group computing.

3. *Describe the importance of the knowledge worker in the modern office environment.* The knowledge worker is the person using office automation technology either to make decisions or to support the business. For over 100 years, there were

few improvements in the way we accomplished office work; today we realize that to increase productivity we must do more than simply replace the typewriters with computers. We must change procedures, and knowledge workers are doing that themselves with systems like work group computing.

4. *Describe trends in distributed computing and integrated computing environments.* Distributed computing brings various computer systems together so they may share data and programs. When it is complete, we call it an integrated environment, from an integrated desktop to a large integrated system. An integrated desktop may reside on a single computer or on many workstations across a local area network. A relatively sophisticated large integrated system is the image/data management system.

OFFICE AUTOMATION ISSUES

1. Women have, for many years, been discriminated against in the workplace. Can you think of some examples, either from your own experience or from books, movies, or TV? How do you feel about this form of discrimination? Do you think office automation technology can reduce this discrimination?

2. A recent concern has been what is termed the "dumbing down" of the work force. Often people without extensive education, training, or computer skills operate computers (or computerized devices such as cash registers or data entry point-of-sale terminals) and insist that the data is correct — even when it's obvious that it is not. You are familiar with the term *garbage in, garbage out.* How well are we preparing people to understand the issue of computer accuracy? For instance, is the accuracy of the data a life and death matter? For medical diagnostic equipment, the answer is yes, but for certain simple transactions, it's not. If the computer in a bookstore says there are two copies of a particular title on the shelf though there are none, that does not necessarily signify a computer error. It might only mean that both copies were sold since the computer was last updated. How can we help people to work with common sense as well as with computers?

3. There are many reported instances of employees being monitored or tracked at work. According to the U.S. government's Office of Technology Assessment, over 26 million employees have their work tracked electronically, and over 10 million have their pay based on computer evaluations. The work habits of knowledge workers can be monitored either by viewing their screen to see what they are doing or even by using electronic mail messages. Some say we're living in a surveillant society and that we have to make daily choices about what we are willing to give up about ourselves. Ostensibly, the purpose behind tracking is to ensure high productivity, but people being people, it often turns into something more. Some recent studies have shown that tracking is counterproductive because, among other reasons, it increases stress. A focus on quality, not quantity of output, makes workers happier and more productive. What do you think about tracking? Is there ever a time when it is a good idea?

CHAPTER REVIEW QUESTIONS

REVIEW QUESTIONS

1. How does office automation help knowledge workers make better decisions?

2. Name some of the machines used in office automation.

3. How have text management systems changed the way knowledge workers work with text?

4. Explain the concept of distributed computing.

5. Explain the purposes of the four OA technologies.

6. Why is ergonomics important?

7. Explain the differences between text manage-

ment and document management systems, and how they complement one another.

DISCUSSION QUESTIONS

1. Discuss the differences between computer systems that concentrate on producing data versus those in OA that must produce information.
2. Discuss the importance of ergonomics in OA.
3. Describe some ways in which it would be important to integrate text, data, graphics, video, and audio in an office environment.
4. Discuss how collaborative, or work group, computing is changing the way knowledge workers work, how they are evaluated, and their productivity.
5. Discuss the new paradigms in office organization and the way work gets accomplished.
6. Discuss the role of networking—especially the LAN—in OA.
7. Form a work group and define a mission, then discuss how you would use groupware to collaborate.
8. Explain the reasons for the different types of business analysis systems.

MULTIPLE-CHOICE

1. A document can take the following forms (check all that apply):
   a. Paper.
   b. Electronic.
   c. Numbers.
   d. Text.
   e. Image.
   f. All of the above.
2. Groupware (check all that apply):
   a. Is collaborative.
   b. Incorporates electronic mail.
   c. Lets people work whenever, wherever they want.
   d. Checks to make sure people work eight hours a day.
3. The power user (check all that apply):
   a. Is from the information systems organization.
   b. Understands the business.
   c. Teaches other knowledge workers.
   d. Often helps formulate technology strategies.
   e. All of the above.
4. Expert systems (check all that apply):
   a. Are based on artificial intelligence.
   b. Are the same as neural networks.
   c. Can reason out decisions like humans.
   d. Are useful in decision making.

   e. All of the above.

FILL-IN-THE-BLANK

1. The main characteristic of a decision support system is _____ _____.
2. The main characteristic of an executive support system is _____.
3. The main characteristic of an expert system is

   _____.

4. _____ is the study of the human safety factors in working with machines.
5. Making various hardware and software work compatibly together is called _____

   _____.
6. _____ software requires the stored knowledge of experts to perform its tasks.

TRUE/FALSE

1. Document management systems help us re-use portions of text.
2. The integrated desktop takes the place of Windows.

3. Collaborative work groups are generally more productive than conventionally organized office workers.

4. Large system integration benefits distributed computing.

5. Neural networks excel at pattern recognition.

KEY TERMS

artificial intelligence (AI), 480

business analysis systems, 478

collaboration, 474

decision support systems (DSS), 479

document management systems, 481

ergonomics, 474

executive information systems (EIS), 479

expert systems, 480

groupware, 483

network and communications management systems, 482

neural network, 481

office automation (OA), 472

power user, 474

text management systems, 478

work group, 474

EPILOGUE

A Futurist Looks Back

By Charles P. Lecht

Since computer and communications technologies are rapidly synthesizing to be mutually dependent, if not one and the same, I'll start with the big picture — today's emerging global networks of computers — and end with the solitary device we now call the computer system. I'll then offer my humble opinion as to why our technology is so important to our survival.

Today's versatility in computer and communications technologies is a marvelous phenomenon. The discrete computer upon which I write this essay will, upon its completion, be connected via Japan's Venus-P network to an AT&T network so that I can ship these words to my publisher's computer to be processed into the first chapter of a book. Thus, my computer is at once a discrete desktop computer and a terminal to a larger system whenever I want it to be. It automatically shares local and international facilities with a keystroke.

I mention this to set the scene for what is to follow. For I see little essential difference between the computer that may be spread over a continent (whose circuits are the veins and arteries of a massive communications system) and the microchip that resides on a sliver of silicon. If you were a microbe suspended above a silicon chip and looking down upon it, you would see essentially the same scene as a human astronaut might see suspended above the landscape of a national communications network.

If you accept this model, that is, that the computer on a chip and that which girdles our globe are essentially the same, then unfolding before us is a 21st-century computer usage scenario which involves an ad hoc synthesis of the following three computer power repositories: foremost use will be through the sharing of massive computer systems power invested in our public and private communications utilities; next will be through the use of discrete and disconnected computing devices; and last, but not least, will be through the use of unseen embedded computer systems (computers which are within other technologies such as cars, video sets, and even such mundane devices as vacuum cleaners).

I'll start with the shared communications-cum-computer Goliaths. Not only will we share their massive computer power, but we will also share the entire spectrum of what we do with computers, including the

gathering of inputs, the use of processing facilities, and the creation of outputs. These are the three most fundamental principles upon which all computing is based. Disparate groups of people will prepare data for the same
applications, massive systems will process it in an ever-changing kaleidoscope
of network syntheses, and the results will be retrievable by whoever wants
these wherever they may be.

Of course, communications will have to improve to create the optimum
environment for this sharing. High-speed broadband wire, cable, fiber optic,
and broadcast facilities will have to become commonplace. But we needn't
wonder whether this will ever happen; the only question is when. Rewiring the
in-place networks will take decades, longer than creating new networks piggy-
backed on old facilities such as telephone poles, railroad sidings, and television and microwave towers. So, we can expect the latter to happen. In-place
facilities will, of course, continue to be used, but only while economic considerations prevent their replacement.

And there are other considerations impeding the kind of ad hoc synthesis I
envision. The current mostly national networks are too expensive to make
their utility commonplace for users.

Crossing national boundaries that are tariffed locally ensures that users
essentially pay a duty on importing or exporting information much as they do

on material goods. In addition, the need to negotiate separate service arrangements with each national service provider is a barrier impeding the development of truly global multinational networks.

But the situation is changing with the establishment of cooperatives that cross state and national boundaries. Examples of such cooperatives in their embryonic forms exist today. For example, Electronic Data Systems Corp. operates an extensive data network for itself and for General Motors Corp.'s domestic and international operations. SITA, an airline cooperative based in Paris, operates a specialized data network reaching 187 countries. Cable & Wireless, a British firm, has begun the construction of what it describes as "the global information highway" linking all continents with optical fibers. And Syncordia, a joint venture of British Telecom PLC, France Telecom, Deutsche Bundespost, and Nippon Telegraph & Telephone Corp., has announced its intention to assemble a global broadband multilateral communications utility.

To work in parallel with communications carried by wire, wireless communications — including satellites — will also have to be upgraded. Vast improvement is needed in this area; today's wire-connected systems are burdensome on offices, are expensive to maintain, and impede technological advancement.

Before the end of this decade, wired LAN facilities may well be augmented by the wireless broadcast of data between disparate computer systems/devices and in the first decade of the 21st century, be replaced by it. This should clean up the wired mess that characterizes many office communications to this very day, reduce maintenance costs, and prepare the way for a nonmaterial upgrading (one that doesn't involve the ripping out of walls and floors and the laying of cables) of LAN facilities as new innovations appear.

Through the use of broadcast, wireless data/voice communications will become ever-more encompassing so that, even for one specific company, this phenomenon, which began in a LAN environment in a single office, will be spread to service several offices. In the distant future, such communications will be possible between the company's buildings and compounds too. Later it will spread to the communities, cities, and continents where the company has its operations.

Of course, wireless satellite communications systems already exist, but these are unavailable for everyday use, say between a printer and a PC in an office in today's techno-economic environment. And even if they were available, such use is so mired in a web of national and international bickering and so expensive that no one would use them. However, as these problems are overcome, we can expect our data processing world to take off and such broadcasted connections to become commonplace. This will take at least 25 years.

With communications barriers eliminated, we will once again focus our efforts on improving our local processing facility — namely, the discrete device we all call a computer system — which occupies a room, at most, these days, and even comes small enough to sit on a desk or a lap, or be held in the palm of our hand. I'll not talk about supercomputers and their esoteric technologies such as massively parallel systolic megaflops (millions of floating point instructions per second) or megalips (millions of logical inferences per second) systems; these are beyond the know-how or, for that matter, the economic reach of the overwhelming majority of our computing community. Most of us do commercial data processing with discrete, much lower performance devices and it is these to which I make reference below.

We'd be hard-pressed not to notice that there have been vast improvements in computer technology in the past 40 years. But the future is even brighter. Current RISC systems offer up to 50 MIPS at a personal workstation. By using CPUs in a parallel, by the end of this decade we will be able to acquire small systems technologies featuring CPU clusters, each producing 200 MIPS or more. These MIPS will be packaged on a board or in a housing that today holds only one CPU. Such configurations will break today's processor speed barriers and make possible those applications we've only dreamed of in a personal computer — like articulate language translation, perfected database engines which feature instantaneous data storage/retrieval, the mathematical modeling of a corporation's economy, and easy-to-use multimedia.

For example, we will perfect voice inputs so that users needn't remain slaves to the keyboard. We will never be entirely free of the keyboard, nor will we want to be, for that matter. Workplace noise considerations, the need to speak and enter data virtually simultaneously as an airline agent does, password recognition in a public place, and the boredom of speaking a long list of numbers to a computer will ensure that the keyboard is around indefinitely. Besides, who wants a hundred people in an office shouting "Copy!" to their computer or a hundred computers audibly begging for more data? There is a place for both input modes; which a user chooses will depend upon his data creation/entry/receiving requirements. Nevertheless, the capability to speak to a computer and have it respond with voice will offer a quantum leap in the quality of our use of it.

With sound, we will have at our disposal all the human faculties to help us communicate with computers as naturally as possible — our five senses will have been augmented. Just as computers can now help us "see" into a suitcase at an airport, "smell" and "taste" substances, or help a robot "touch" an automobile part, they will now be able to "hear" sound and respond with sound as we wish them to.

Special-purpose personal computers (in which I include expert systems) will appear everywhere. These are systems that are dedicated to performing one task only like word processing, communicating, graphics creation, desktop publishing, financial reporting, and virtually all the other things we do in our day-to-day lives. There is just too much hassle in dealing with today's general-purpose computer. For one thing, they do not come as neatly packaged as even a modern hi-fi system. Electronic boards and chips have to be inserted into them and software has to be configured to make them usable. Cables and wires whose connecting ends are as fragile as they are invisible come in separate packages to be connected only by the neighbor's young and budding Leonardo da Vinci. Some have instructions that are unreadable and getting it all together can frustrate the patience of otherwise intelligent people just wanting to get on with using them.

This problem can only be overcome by the development of intelligent computing devices that require no preparation save opening the package and clearing space on a desk for their use. Some special-purpose computers are available today, but it is just the beginning. They are typically word processors, word translation, calendar, telephone and memo devices, alarm systems, cash dispensing/register machines, and those fuzzy-logic home appliances like washing machines, vacuum cleaners, and rice cookers. But these barely scratch the surface of what could be. I see an endless marketplace for embedded computer-driven devices that touches almost all that we do intelligently as well as physically. It may be the most fertile marketplace for computer manufacturers for the remaining part of this century and into the first half of the next century.

Then there is the software issue in the general-personal computer area. While new operating system software, such as Windows, OS/2, UNIX, and NT, among others, offers users greater and greater capabilities, it has also become commensurately harder to use. Even installing this software can require help from the kid next door who is taking a computer course. Wouldn't it make things easier to preinstall operating system software in computers? And to make their use self-prompting if not transparent to users? It is my forecast that preinstallation will occur within the next year or two. For example, IBM will preinstall OS/2 and the other manufacturers will follow their lead. The self-prompting feature will take another 10 years and transparency another 25.

But the operating system software isn't the only problem. For example, my word processor comes with a manual of almost 600 pages. Others are even longer. You have to take the equivalent of a university course to be able to use the software. How can software creators reasonably expect anyone to simply load and operate their products if they require so much effort to understand them? The first company that comes out with any reasonable desktop publishing/word processing software that brings a user up to par quickly, without reading a boring, voluminous treatise, and that anticipates his skill (or lack thereof) is in for big bucks in my view. A word processor/desktop publishing computer with enough MIPS could conceivably do this, and it's my bet that such a machine will arrive by the end of this decade.

That computers continue to arrive with ever-increasing amounts of RAM and disk memories is a boon to users weary from managing flocks of floppies. My IBM PC has a 2-gigabyte hard disk capacity and 24MB of RAM. To me, who has been in the computer field for more years than I care to remember, this amount of memory is truly astonishing. It hardly seemed possible just a few, maybe five, years ago.

If nothing else, large memory eliminates the need to write applications employing "paging" much the same as monks had to do reading an ancient manuscript. But of far greater consequence is the capability this offers to manage very large databases (including backing them up) in a highly unified environment and to access these in ever-shorter time frames from just about any location. But the future holds much more. How would you like to have a memory so large that it could never be filled up in a lifetime and accessed so fast that data location could be freed from the tyrant of hardware geography? A terabyte (trillion bytes), solid-state, nonvolatile memory could once and for all do this. Plug-in memory modules containing high density chips whose circuits are etched in the fermi (trillionths of a meter) world are required.

Such capacity would enable a user to hold more information than he is ever likely to produce, more than 400 million pages at 300 words per page. Users would never again have to face the issue of where to store data to free the computer for more.

I foresee such memories available by the turn of the century or shortly thereafter. Think about it. Valuable data, impossible to keep in the past simply because of a lack of available storage space, could be retained. Imagine the impact this could have on our lives, particularly in the fields of science and philosophy. Had such memories been available from time immemorial we would have long ago learned to model the phylogenetic process to study how life evolved and maybe even how it originated. We'd have learned how to reproduce the programs running in cells and how to create these synthetically so we could replace those gone defective. Disease would have been eradicated.

Massive memories could provide us with the means to create holographic replicas of things past and things to come and to experience these without suffering their effects. The virtual could become real until we flipped the switch to turn the images off. Our intelligence, artificial and real, could be augmented with artificial experience to enrich and refresh our memories.

We'd be hard-pressed not to notice that we need to artificially augment our natural faculties so that we can process and communicate life's messages and data in ever-more effective ways. Our computer technology may offer the only means to do this. That's not to say that augmentation is impossible to achieve naturally; however, there may not be time enough for this to occur. Even though people are becoming smarter and stronger, and living longer as time passes, we cannot help but notice that we still haven't figured out how to live in peace or how to forecast and become free of those disasters that Mother Nature is sure to bring.

Just as the lever is an amplifier of our physical strength, so is the computer an amplifier of our intellectual power. We improve technology in a quest to improve our lives, where we are going, and what we'll find when we get there. Surely, if the past 40 years of computer technology development offer any indication of what's possible in the next 40 years, we may look forward to the discovery of at least some of the solutions to our earth-bound problems and a much brighter future for the generations to come.

APPENDIX

A

Number Systems

LEARNING OBJECTIVES

After reading and studying this appendix, you should be able to:

1. Define a number.

2. Explain the purpose of a number system.

3. Understand how number systems are used for different purposes.

4. Understand the number systems unique to computers.

5. Describe the two common types of computer codes and their relationship to number systems.

WHAT IS A NUMBER?

The *Oxford English Dictionary* defines a **number** as a "particular mark or symbol, having arithmetical value, by which anything has a place assigned to it in a series." Strictly speaking, a number is a *concept* associated with a numeral. For example, we look in our hand and see a number of pennies, three to be exact; the numeral 3 appears in our mind. A **numeral** is a symbol that represents a value in a specific number system. In common, everyday language, we use the term *number* to refer to a *numeral,* as we shall do in this appendix.

WHAT IS A NUMBER SYSTEM?

We use numbers to keep track of things, to place a value on things, to measure and compare things, and for many other purposes. No one can accurately say when the human race began using numbers, but it's assumed the first number systems derived from counting on our fingers. A **number system** is a set of symbols or numbers combined with *rules* for how those numbers are used.

THE EGYPTIAN NUMBER SYSTEM

The ancient Egyptians created a number system around 2850 B.C. based on *hieroglyphics* (representational characters). They were no different than our 1 or 2 or 3, but perhaps more interesting to look at:

Our Numeral (decimal)	Egyptian Numeral	Descriptive Name
1	I	Stroke
10	∩	Heel bone
100	⌒	Scroll
1,000	⌇	Lotus flower
10,000	⌐	Pointing finger
100,000	⌒	Polliwog
1,000,000	⚊	Astonished man

Try writing the year you were born in the Egyptian number system.

THE DECIMAL NUMBER SYSTEM

The number system we use most commonly today is the Hindu-Arabic or **decimal number system,** which is also referred to as a **base 10** number

Numbers	1	9	9	2
	(Thousands)	(Hundreds)	(Tens)	(Ones)
Base 10	1,000	100	10	1
Powers	10^3	10^2	10^1	10^0

system. That means it is based on 10 numbers. The number symbols 1 through 9 appear to have originated in India around 300 B.C. The decimal system did not use the 0 (zero) at the time, although the 0 is believed to have predated the Hindu-Arabic numbers.

The decimal or base 10 number system places values on numbers according to their position. The lowest values are to the right, the values increasing as they move to the left, each position raising the value by 10. We refer to these increments of 10 as **powers,** or exponents, which means the number is multiplied by itself. For example:

$10^1 = 10$
$10^2 = 10 \times 10 = 100$
$10^3 = 10 \times 10 \times 10 = 1,000$
$10^4 = 10 \times 10 \times 10 \times 10 = 10,000$

Another very famous example is the mathematical equation demonstrating Einstein's theory of relativity, which looks like this:

$E = mc^2$

The ^{2} means the number is taken to the second power. Figure A.1 shows how the base 10 system of powers works, using the calendar year 1992 as an example.

COMPARING NUMBER SYSTEMS

By way of comparison, there is another base 10 number system we still see in use today. It's the Roman system, which uses letters of the alphabet as numbers. Figure A.2 compares it with the Hindu-Arabic number system.

Do you see the structure in the Roman number system? It changes symbols at 5 and 10, but the numbers preceding each combine the previous number. Once you grasp the logic, when you watch old movies you can tell what year they were made. For example:

Hindu-Arabic	**Roman**
1992	MCMXCII

Try writing the year you were born in Roman numbers.

Interestingly, there was a battle in Europe over which number system to use that went on for hundreds of years. The "algorists" favored the decimal system and the "abacists" favored the Roman (and performed their math on the abacus, hence their name). The decimal number system has only been in wide use since about the year 1500. Figure A.3 shows the development of the decimal number system; notice when the zero appears.

Hindu-Arabic and Roman
number systems.

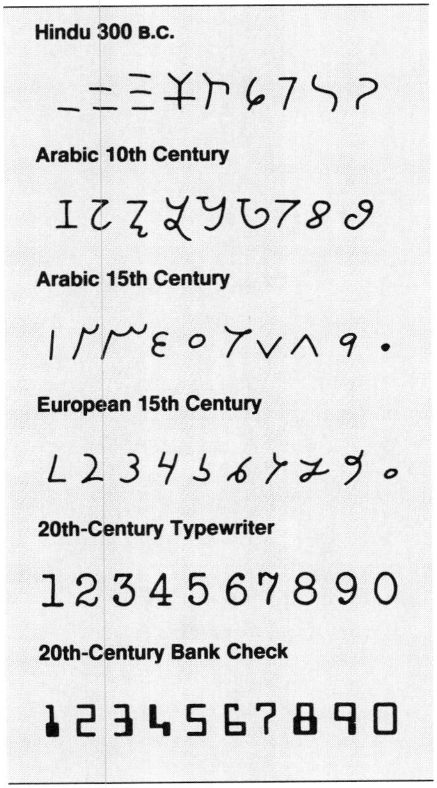

Arabic	Roman	Arabic	Roman	Arabic	Roman
1	I	16	XVI	90	XC
2	II	17	XVII	100	C
3	III	18	XVIII	200	CC
4	IV	19	XIX	300	CCC
5	V	20	XX	400	CD
6	VI	21	XXI	500	D
7	VII	22	XXII	600	DC
8	VIII	23	XXIII	700	DCC
9	IX	24	XXIV	800	DCCC
10	X	30	XXX	900	CM
11	XI	40	XL	1,000	M
12	XII	50	L	2,000	MM
13	XIII	60	LX	3,000	MMM
14	XIV	70	LXX	4,000	$\overline{MV}$
15	XV	80	LXXX	5,000	$\overline{V}$ (or 8)

FIGURE A.3

Development of the decimal
number system.

Hindu 300 B.C.

Arabic 10th Century

Arabic 15th Century

European 15th Century

20th-Century Typewriter

1234567890

20th-Century Bank Check

NUMBER SYSTEMS FOR COMPUTERS

There have been many calculating and computational machines designed to use the decimal or base 10 number system. Yet none have proven to work as fast as the modern electronic digital computer that we have studied in this book. The computers we are familiar with use the binary number system. The story of how the binary number system came to be used for computers is the story of pioneering research in mathematics by two men who lived a century apart from one another.

GEORGE BOOLE + CLAUDE SHANNON = THE BINARY COMPUTER

George Boole (1815–1864) proved that logic could be expressed in simple algebraic equations. Over time, this became known as Boolean algebra. His concepts provided the foundation for a number of experiments in building mechanical counting devices. In the 20th century, those same concepts were applied to the study of electronics.

In 1937, Claude Shannon was a student at the Massachusetts Institute of Technology, studying for his master's degree. The title of his master's thesis was "A Symbolic Analysis of Relay and Switching Circuits," and in it he applied Boolean logic (binary arithmetic) to the circuits that comprise a computer.

Shannon's ideas were first put into use by AT&T's Bell Laboratories to speed telephone call connections, and later to reduce noise. However, his contribution to electronic digital computer technology is equally if not more significant. For his work in switching circuits and information theory, he was awarded the Nobel prize.

THE BINARY NUMBER SYSTEM

The binary number system, as you already know from Chapter 2, uses just two numbers: the 1 and the 0 (zero). Therefore, we call it a **base 2** number system. Modern electronic digital computers use the binary number system for internal processing. This is because the two numbers, 1 and 0, easily represent the two electrical states, *on* and *off*. This simplicity enables computers to perform mathematical operations with incredible speed.

Numbers, letters, and symbols are represented as a series of 1s and 0s. For example, people enter decimal numbers into the computer; a special translation program in the computer converts decimal into binary. This same translation program converts binary into decimal output. Figure A.4 shows the binary equivalents for decimal numbers.

In the decimal system, we count by powers of 10: 1, 10, 100, and so on. In the binary system, we count by powers of 2:

$2^1 = 2$
$2^2 = 4$
$2^3 = 8$
$2^4 = 16$

If you recall, computer memory is incremented by powers of 2. Early personal computers had 64K of RAM, which then grew to 128K, doubling 256K, doubling 512K, then 640K (512 + 128), and so forth.

Decimal Place		
100	10	1
		0
		1
		2
		3
		4
		5
		6
		7
		8
		9
	1	0
	1	1
	1	2
	1	3
	1	4
	1	5
	1	6

Binary Place					
32	16	8	4	2	1
					0
					1
				1	0
				1	1
			1	0	0
			1	0	1
			1	1	0
			1	1	1
		1	0	0	0
		1	0	0	1
		1	0	1	0
		1	0	1	1
		1	1	0	0
		1	1	0	1
		1	1	1	0
		1	1	1	1
	1	0	0	0	0

FIGURE A.4

Binary equivalents for decimal numbers.

WHY COMPUTERS USE NUMBER SYSTEMS

Machine language, which you learned about in Chapter 10, uses the binary number system to provide instructions for the CPU. It is the most basic language for the computer; it requires no translation to be understood. Therefore, the people most interested in number systems and how they translate one into another are programmers. As you can imagine, it would be extremely tedious to write every character and instruction in binary or machine language; that's why programming languages evolved.

However, it is sometimes necessary for programmers to work with the computer at or near the machine language level. Even so, there are two number systems that have helped make their work easier: the octal and hexadecimal number systems. These number systems have been used as a kind of shorthand so that the programmer does not have to write programs in 0s and 1s. As you read about these systems, refer to Figure A.5, which compares decimal and binary number systems to octal and hexadecimal.

THE OCTAL NUMBER SYSTEM

The **octal** number system is a **base 8** system that uses eight symbols, the numbers 0 through 7. Like the decimal system, the octal system places values on numbers according to their position. In this case, numbers are raised by the power of 8. When converting octal numbers to binary, the equation is $8 = 2^3$. This means that a set of three binary digits equals one octal digit. Octal was the first programming language (as opposed to binary or machine language) that programmers actually used to write instructions for the earliest computers.

FIGURE A.5   Comparison of decimal and binary to octal and hexadecimal number systems.

Decimal Place

100	10	1
		0
		1
		2
		3
		4
		5
		6
		7
		8
		9
	1	0
	1	1
	1	2
	1	3
	1	4
	1	5
	1	6

Binary Place

32	16	8	4	2	1
					0
					1
				1	0
				1	1
			1	0	0
			1	0	1
			1	1	0
			1	1	1
		1	0	0	0
		1	0	0	1
		1	0	1	0
		1	0	1	1
		1	1	0	0
		1	1	0	1
		1	1	1	0
		1	1	1	1
	1	0	0	0	0

Octal Place

64	8	1
		0
		1
		2
		3
		4
		5
		6
		7
	1	0
	1	1
	1	2
	1	3
	1	4
	1	5
	1	6
	1	7
	2	0

Hexadecimal Place

256	16	1
		0
		1
		2
		3
		4
		5
		6
		7
		8
		9
		A
		B
		C
		D
		E
		F
	1	0

THE HEXADECIMAL NUMBER SYSTEM

The **hexadecimal** number system is a **base 16** number system that uses 16 symbols. This means using additional, distinct symbols after we reach 9. Thus, hexadecimal uses letters of the alphabet: A for 10, B for 11, through F for 15, and 10 for 16. Again, symbols have value according to their position. When converting hexadecimal symbols to binary, the equation is $16 = 2^4$. Today, hexadecimal is more commonly used in computers than the octal system.

In the past, it was useful for programmers to know how to convert from binary to octal or hexadecimal. In fact, expert programmers could perform conversions in their heads while they wrote programs. Yet in time it became possible to use special software programs to perform these tasks automatically so that few today use these number systems extensively. However, systems programmers still find occasions when it is necessary to rewrite or revise portions of the computer system code using these basic tools.

NUMBER SYSTEMS AND COMPUTER CODES

In the same way that number systems are used to represent instructions sent to the CPU, computer codes are used to represent data sent for processing. **Computer codes** are a set of symbols and rules that assure that the characters we send to the computer system are consistently and accurately represented. There are two computer codes in common use today: EBCDIC and ASCII.

Character	EBCDIC	ASCII
0	11110000	00110000
1	11110001	00110001
2	11110010	00110010
3	11110011	00110011
4	11110100	00110100
5	11110101	00110101
6	11110110	00110110
7	11110111	00110111
8	11111000	00111000
9	11111001	00111001
A	11000001	01000001
B	11000010	01000010
C	11000011	01000011
D	11000100	01000100
E	11000101	01000101
F	11000110	01000110
G	11000111	01000111
H	11001000	01001000
I	11001001	01001001
J	11010001	01001010
K	11010010	01001011
L	11010011	01001100
M	11010100	01001101
N	11010101	01001110
O	11010110	01001111
P	11010111	01010000
Q	11011000	01010001
R	11011001	01010010
S	11100010	01010011
T	11100011	01010100
U	11100100	01010101
V	11100101	01010110
W	11100110	01010111
X	11100111	01011000
Y	11101000	01011001
Z	11101001	01011010
Special Characters		
!	01011010	01000001
"	01111111	01000010
#	01111011	01000011
$	01011011	01000100
%	01101100	01000101
&	01010000	01000110
(	01001101	01001000
)	01011101	01001001
*	01011100	01001010
+	01001110	01001011

FIGURE A.6

Comparison of EBCDIC and ASCII.

Figure A.6 compares these two computer codes and the binary number system.

EBCDIC

EBCDIC stands for Extended Binary Coded Decimal Interchange Code. Developed by IBM for its mainframe computers, it is now used by most IBM computers. EBCDIC can represent 256 different letters, numbers, and characters.

ASCII

ASCII stands for the American Standard Code for Information Interchange. It was developed so that computer systems made by a wide variety of different companies could exchange data with ease, especially with respect to computer networking and communications. Like EBCDIC, ASCII can represent 256 characters.

USING NUMBER SYSTEMS AND COMPUTER CODES

Needless to say, there are times when non-IBM computers must communicate with IBM computers; then it is necessary to convert from ASCII to EBCDIC and vice versa. Again, this is similar to converting between the number systems we studied previously, and is primarily accomplished by special software programs.

It would be difficult to use computers without numbers and number systems. If you compare what you've learned in this appendix with what you learned about bits and bytes in Chapter 2, you can now understand how the concepts of the bit and byte are based on the binary number system. You can also understand the translation process between the characters — both as programs and as data — we type into the computer and the way they are represented to the CPU.

SUMMARY

1. *Define a number.* A numeral is a symbol that represents a value in a specific number system, such as the V in the Roman system or the 5 in the Hindu-Arabic system. We commonly refer to a numeral as a number.

2. *Explain the purpose of a number system.* A number system is a set of symbols or numbers used according to specific rules. We use number systems to keep track of things or to place a value on things.

3. *Understand how number systems are used for different purposes.* Both Roman and Hindu-Arabic number systems are decimal, or base 10, systems which we are most familiar with.

4. *Understand the number systems unique to computers.* Computer number systems are used to represent instructions sent to the CPU. The

computer uses the binary, or base 2, system which evolved out of research by Claude Shannon, based on George Boole's algebra. It is tedious for programmers to work with the instructions sent to the CPU in binary, so two shorthand methods have evolved to make their work easier. One is the octal number system, which is called base 8; the other is hexadecimal, or base 16, the more popular of the two.

5. *Describe the two common types of computer codes and their relationship to number systems.* Computer codes are used to represent data being sent to the CPU. The one common to IBM computers is EBCDIC. The one common to almost all other computers is ASCII, which can be used to communicate between IBM and non-IBM computers.

REVIEW AND DISCUSSION QUESTIONS

1. Explain the difference between a number and a numeral.

2. Discuss the reasons why there are different number systems.

3. What are the advantages to using the binary number system for computers?

4. Try taking a number that has a relationship to distance, such as the miles from your home to school, out to as many powers as you can. Discuss the significance to the powers of 10.

5. Create an exercise in working with the binary number system, such as spelling your name or creating your date of birth. Discuss the patterns that the 1s and 0s form.

6. Learn more about George Boole and his special algebra. What kind of man was he? Do you think he realized the importance of his algebra at the time he created it?

7. Learn more about Claude Shannon. What is the special relationship between Boolean algebra and electronic theory?

8. Discuss why it might be easier to use another rather complex number system, such as octal or hexadecimal, as a shorthand for the binary system.

9. Identify the most common number system used for sending data to a wide variety of computer systems.

10. During what computer activity are you most likely to encounter a number system used for representing instructions? For representing data?

KEY TERMS

base 2,   506

base 8,   507

base 10,   503

base 16,   508

computer codes,   508

decimal number system,   503

EBCDIC,   509

hexadecimal,   508

number,   503

number system,   503

numeral,   503

octal,   507

powers,   504

The Computer Generations

LEARNING OBJECTIVES

After reading and studying this appendix, you should be able to:

1. Understand how computer technology has evolved throughout the five generations.

2. Describe the various electronic devices that have driven computer technology from one generation to the next.

3. Understand the most significant advances in circuit technology, CPU speed, memory, programming languages, and software for each generation.

INTRODUCTION

The best way to understand where we are going is to understand the events that have led us to where we are. In the same way we want to understand how human society has evolved, it is important that we understand computer evolution. Indeed, computer evolution has had a dramatic impact on human society and will surely continue to do so in the future.

The **computer generations** are the stages in the evolution of electronic circuitry, hardware, software, programming languages, and other technological developments. These generations help us measure the progress of computer technology. They are an artificial schema people have superimposed on computer history in order to understand events and advancements. You won't find the generations beginning or ending exactly on schedule; some developments overlap from one generation to the next, while others just don't fit neatly into one generation or another. Yet what the computer generations help us do is find a frame of reference with which to measure progress and evaluate advances in computer technology.

This appendix explores the five generations of progress we have made in detail. This should be of particular interest to students who are interested in studying the evolution of the computer industry, who plan to pursue a career in computer science or information systems, or who are seeking background material for a term paper or class project.

This appendix begins with a brief survey of the field of electronics, which paved the way for the computer. Then each of the five generations is discussed. The following topics are covered:

- Circuit technology.
- CPU speed.
- I/O devices.
- Memory and storage.
- Programming languages.
- Software (operating systems and applications).

A BRIEF HISTORY OF ELECTRONICS

Perhaps the best way to begin our discussion is to give credit to Benjamin Franklin for flying a kite in a rainstorm, demonstrating how to harness and use electricity. Franklin was truly a Renaissance man; he was interested in statesmanship, writing, printing, and science. In the 1750s, he tied a key to a kite string and sent it up in a rainstorm. Lightning struck the key and magnetized it.

Around the same time, a French physicist named Francois du Fay determined that there are two types of electricity. He termed them vitreous and resinous; they later became known as positive and negative. Electricity flows from the negative to the positive. By controlling this flow, in much the same way a water faucet controls water flow, scientists eventually learned to manipulate electricity's two states: on and off. As we shall see, this is essential to how computers operate.

THE VACUUM TUBE

In the latter part of the 19th century, American Thomas Edison invented the incandescent light bulb and Italian Guglielmo Marconi developed the wireless telegraph. But it wasn't until John Fleming, an Englishman, invented the first vacuum tube in 1904 that people were able to control electricity. A **vacuum tube** is a device for controlling the flow of electrical current. It is composed of metal plates and wires sealed in a glass enclosure. It performs special tasks such as receiving radio signals, amplifying sound, and switching electrical signals on and off. In the early days, the vacuum tube, like its water-controlling counterpart, was called a valve.

The first vacuum tube was a **diode,** which permits electricity to flow in only one direction. Then in 1907, an American named Lee DeForest invented a better vaccum tube, the **triode.** Instead of just controlling the flow of electricity, the triode can amplify it, like raising or lowering the volume on your stereo, or completely switch it on or off. The triode and the more advanced tubes that followed it led to the invention of the radio, radar, television, and ultimately the computer. DeForest was truly the father of modern electronic communications.

Necessity is the mother of invention. This was certainly the case with vacuum tubes, for they drew vast amounts of electrical power and generated a great deal of heat. It was said that when ENIAC was first switched on, the lights of Philadelphia dimmed. The tremendous heat ENIAC's vacuum tubes generated made them burn out at the rate of one an hour. Computer scientists had to overcome these obstacles to make computing less expensive and more efficient.

THE TRANSISTOR

The **transistor** is a device that performs the functions of a triode vacuum tube but with a great deal less heat and much higher reliability. It is also much, much smaller. The transistor is made from **semiconductor** materials, usually germanium or silicon, that can achieve electrical potential.

The first transistor was invented at AT&T's Bell Laboratories in 1947 by William Shockley, Walter Brattain, and John Bardeen. They were awarded the Nobel prize for their discovery, which changed the course of electronics. Over time, transistors grew more versatile and powerful, while growing smaller as well.

THE INTEGRATED CIRCUIT

Complex computer circuitry that once filled entire rooms now rests in a sliver of silicon you can hold on the tip of your finger. ENIAC was composed of 18,000 vacuum tubes that made up 100,000 circuits. Now, a single chip, a mere quarter of an inch square, contains over 1 million circuits.

Type	Generation	Circuits	Used for
Small scale or SSIC	3	10s	Switching
Medium scale or MSIC	3	100s	Memory
Large scale or LSIC	4	1,000s	Digital watch
Very large scale or VLSIC	4	10,000–100,000s	Early CPU
Very high speed or VHSIC	5	1,000,000s	Microprocessor
Ultra high speed or UHSIC	5	500,000,000+	Smart machine

FIGURE B.1

The evolution of integrated circuits and their uses.

The integrated circuit (IC) is comprised of many transistors, diodes, and other electronic circuit devices. The more devices in an IC, the more complex it is. **Integration** is the term used to refer to this complexity. Integration, and thus integrated circuits, have evolved over the years, as shown in Figure B.1. As a point of reference, we compare each stage of integration according to the number of on/off switches or circuits it could place on one chip.

As you learned in Chapter 8, Jack Kilby of Texas Instruments is credited with creating the first integrated circuit or IC. Gary Boone, another engineer at Texas Instruments, was granted the first patent for a microprocessor, or, to quote from the U.S. Patent, for "a computing system including a central processing unit integrated on a single chip." A microprocessor is one particular type of integrated circuit; ICs can be used for many different purposes. Today, the most widely used microprocessor chips for personal computers are manufactured by Intel and Motorola.

Let's look at electronic circuitry in terms of the computer generations. The vacuum tube was first generation; the transistor was second generation. Refer again to Figure B.1. The SSIC and MSIC chips were third generation; the LSIC and VLSIC were fourth generation. We are now beginning to see the first VHSIC and UHSIC chips that could be called fifth generation. With this understanding of electronics, let's take a closer look at the computer generations.

THE FIRST GENERATION

Computers that used vacuum tubes are considered part of the first generation. Yet the ENIAC, developed at the University of Pennsylvania, and the Mark I, developed about the same time at Harvard University, were early noncommercial computers. They were developed by research teams in an academic setting, mostly to see if the machine could be built, not necessarily to sell it on the open market. Therefore, it is more practical to refer to first-generation computers as the commercial machines made from approximately 1951 to 1958.

The term *commercial* means computers that were sold to businesses or research institutions. The UNIVAC I was the first commercial computer sold. In 1951, the U.S. Bureau of the Census bought two, and the Prudential Insurance Company of Boston bought one. IBM was not long in offering its first commercial computer, the 701, in 1953. In 1955, IBM introduced the 704, the most powerful computer of its time. Both were scientific computers but complementary models, the 702 and 705, were developed for business data processing. By this time, computers were somewhat smaller than ENIAC, only filling a room the size of a gymnasium instead of an entire building.

CIRCUIT TECHNOLOGY

Vacuum tubes were the electrical switching devices of the first generation. Early tubes were quite large, some as big as a soft drink can. Due to the heat they generated, their life span was rather short. Over time, they became more reliable, faster, cooler — and smaller. Yet as we have seen, the search for better reliability and better switching components was on from the start.

CPU SPEED

First-generation computers were quite slow by today's standards, performing an average of 39,000 operations per second. Just to refresh your memory, operations refers to arithmetic operations such as adding and subtracting. ENIAC could perform only 5,000 calculations or operations per second. Yet it was able to analyze in just two hours a problem that would have taken 100 mathematicians a year to figure out. What an incredible savings in time! Within 10 years, computers were almost eight times faster than ENIAC.

I/O DEVICES

Early first-generation computers didn't have keyboards for input operations. Instructions and data were usually fed in using paper tape or punched cards. Punched cards were fine for recording and storing data, but people also needed a convenient way to read computer output. For that purpose, electric typewriters programmed to type on paper tape or punched card readers were used for printing reports.

The punched card was an extremely significant tool throughout the history of computers. Originally devised and patented by Herman Hollerith, it has been in use for over 100 years. During the first generation, it was used for both program and data input and output. IBM perfected the punched card machines, also called *unit record equipment,* because each punched card was a unit with a complete set of data recorded on it. The punched card became known as the "IBM card."

MEMORY AND STORAGE

In Chapter 2, you learned about computer memory and that it is measured in bytes. One kilobyte (1K) is 1,024 bytes. First-generation computers had between 1K and 4K of RAM. On the early computers, programs and data were stored first on punched paper tape and punched cards, and then electronically on devices such as mercury delay lines and special tubes. First-generation computers used magnetic drums or cores.

The **magnetic drum** was used as random access memory or RAM, and it was just that: a slowly rotating drum. That was a major problem, since promptly storing and retrieving data is central to a computer's usefulness. Dr. An Wang, an engineer at the Harvard Computation Laboratory in 1948, was a pioneer in developing **magnetic core** for memory. He figured out a way to make the magnetic core memory from little magnetic donuts electrically charged to store data. This was used for auxiliary storage. Wang worked with Howard Aiken on the Mark IV, a successor to the Mark I computer mentioned earlier. The idea was picked up by Jay Forrester at MIT and further developed, creating grids with the cores that made it easier to locate data. IBM, which provided support to MIT, was the first to introduce magnetic core memory on its 704, one of its most popular and profitable systems.

Wang's magnetic core memory was used in computers for many years. It was much faster and more reliable than anything else available at the time. An Wang went on to start his own computer company, Wang Laboratories.

PROGRAMMING LANGUAGES

There were no programming languages as we know them today for first-generation computers. The computer received its instructions in machine language or as electrical on/off signals. On the early computers, these signals were "programmed" into the computer by flipping switches. On first-generation computers, these instructions were typically fed into the machine on punched cards or punched paper tape.

SOFTWARE

A typical application during this time was **tabulating,** which means totaling figures or organizing data into tables (that we now term a *spreadsheet*). Insurance companies performed accounting and statistics, and the Bureau of the Census maintained statistics, files, and records. Because the data and instructions were loaded all at once, and since computers could only perform one task at a time, computer work was done in batches, like baking a batch of cookies. As you learned in Chapter 2, this is called *batch processing.*

For example, the computer might be given the job of totaling all the claims processed at an insurance company. Once the job was loaded into the computer, it would run until the job was finished (or until it hit an error, which stopped the computer). Once finished, the computer was available for another job. For that reason, the operating systems of the 1950s were simply called *batch processing systems.*

THE SECOND GENERATION

Resting in the Computer Museum in Boston is the TX-0, the first all-transistorized computer. It was an MIT Lincoln Labs project that was finished in 1958, heralding the second generation (1958–64). TX-0 was a test to see how well transistor circuitry worked, and the test proved that it worked very well indeed. It was also one of the first computers with a video display, a 12-inch round CRT. Once completed, the TX-0 was installed at MIT's main campus and remained in use until 1975.

Meanwhile, work was underway at IBM on a new, all-transistorized computer. Its purpose was to perform relatively simple business tasks. When it was introduced, the IBM 1401 was an instant success: it set the standard for business computing and outsold every other computer on the market.

Second-generation computers were much more reliable than first-generation machines. The industry coined a term, **mean time between failures** (MTBF), to describe reliability. Second-generation machines would go days instead of just minutes or hours between failures, in large part due to replacing many of the less reliable vacuum tubes with transistors. As a result, they were smaller as well, occupying just a large room instead of a gym.

Circuit Technology

Transistors replaced vacuum tubes in the second generation. The transistor performed the same function as a tube but was much smaller, cooler, and more reliable because it was made of a crystalline substance.

The transistor was about the size of a pea, with wires that attached it to an electronic circuit. It generated very little heat, did not require a glass enclosure, and was far less expensive to manufacture. Equally or more important, on an electrical level it was far more efficient and reliable than a tube.

Bell Labs introduced the junction transistor, an improvement on the original, in 1951. Then in 1952, Bell gave the transistor to the world, gratis. This was a rare occurrence, since inventors or companies usually require royalty payments when others use their technology. Bell had spent millions of R&D dollars on the device, but apparently thought there was more to be gained by letting others find new uses for the transistor — which they did.

CPU Speed

The 1401 wasn't the fastest business computer available. Honeywell offered a machine that was faster, but the IBM was more popular — over 14,000 were put into use. However, processing speeds had improved by this time, by a factor of five; on average, computers could process 200,000 instructions per second.

I/O Devices

The second-generation computers utilized keyboards and video display monitors. It was during this period that the first light pen was used as an input device for drawing on the face of the monitor. High-speed printers came into use, and the first computer that could produce output for a typesetting machine was developed.

Memory and Storage

During this period, RAM grew from 4K to 32K, making it possible for the computer to hold more data and instructions. Magnetic tape was developed in the early 1950s for audio recording, and was adapted to computers as a storage medium for programs and data. "Mag tape" was wider than audio tape and came on large metal spools. You have probably seen a computer's tape drives spinning away in a movie at some time or other. That's because it's often the only way to show that a computer is doing anything.

There were also great advances in auxiliary storage, led by the hard disk drive. One of the first was about four feet in diameter and stood upright, looking very much like a blacksmith's grinding stone. But most significant was IBM's RAMAC (Random Access Method of Accounting and Control) in 1957. The IBM disk drive was refined and improved; within a few years it resembled a jukebox, with six 14-inch disks stacked one atop the other. This disk drive was first used on IBM's 1400 series computers. All together, the disks held 3 million bytes or 3 megabytes (MB). Compare this with today's personal computer hard disk drive, 3½-inch which commonly holds 80 to 105 MB.

PROGRAMMING LANGUAGES

The IBM 1401 didn't have an operating system; instead, it used a special language called the Symbolic Programming System (SPS) to create programs. SPS was an assembly language, the second-generation form of computer programming language. As you already know, earlier computers were programmed with switches and cables, then punched cards, that sent either positive or negative electrical signals—machine language—directly to the machine's circuits. Assembly language permitted using *mnemonics* or special symbols that were in turn translated into machine language—1s and 0s.

Although there were two high-level languages available (FORTRAN, developed in 1954, and COBOL, developed in 1959), the 1401 had its own language called Autocoder. FORTRAN was created as a scientific language, and COBOL as a business language, in hopes that many programmers would use them and create standards.

SOFTWARE

At this time, programmers were writing complete application programs in assembly language, or in FORTRAN or COBOL, for a specific computer. The most significant application software developed during this time was records management, which held many of the most important files and records for a business. These might be an employee's personnel files or inventory records for a product. Another was manufacturing control systems.

Almost every computer had its own unique operating system, programming language, and application software. Standards were slowly adopted over the years, but most large system manufacturers still prefer to make their computer systems proprietary to retain their customers. For example, the original IBM PC was developed as an open system, so any software developer can write applications for it, but Apple Computer systems are proprietary. In the past few years, standards foundations and consortiums have helped make this less of a problem than it was 30 years ago.

THE THIRD GENERATION

Fortune magazine's cover story in September 1966 was entitled, "IBM's $5,000,000,000 Gamble." Its topic was the IBM System/360, introduced in 1964, which heralded the third-generation computers (1964–71). The article quoted Bob Evans, the project manager, as saying, "We called this project 'you bet your company.' " The $5 billion cost of developing the 360 was far more than IBM's annual revenues at the time. The gamble paid off, for the 360 was an enormous success. It was the first IBM computer to use the integrated circuit, which, as you know, is a number of electrical components on a single slice of silicon.

The 360 was so named because there are 360 degrees in a perfect circle (see Figure 3.12 on p. 85), and IBM wanted its customers to think of it as the perfect computer for all their needs. It apparently worked, because IBM took orders for over $1 billion worth of 360s in the first month. The first one was installed at Globe Exploration Company, Midland, Texas, in May 1965.

The 360 series and its successor, the 370 series, set real standards for the first time. Other companies introduced computers that worked like the 360, such as RCA with its Spectra computers. In fact, most of the mainframe computers in use today are molded after the 360/370 machines. Even IBM's top-line 3090 series of computers is based on the 370 system.

As you might expect, third-generation computers were even more reliable than their predecessors. A study of electronic computer failure once showed that circuits such as the ones used in the 360 had an MTBF of 33 million hours — that's over 545 years! The computer would have problems from time to time, of course, but at last it could be depended on to run for weeks and months at a time without component failures. And the shrinking computer continued to shrink; now it was the size of a refrigerator, filling a large cabinet or set of cabinets in a room. The IBM 360 wasn't the only family of computers. By 1968, Digital's PDP-8 had spawned several models and was by far the most popular minicomputer.

CIRCUIT TECHNOLOGY

The IBM 360 utilized what was termed *hybrid integrated technology,* where separate transistors and diodes were inserted into circuits. Thought was given to using fully integrated circuits, but IBM felt the new technology was too risky. Thus, IBM established a technology policy of using solid, proven methods rather than pushing the state of the art. Just a year later, in 1965, General Electric introduced a computer using all integrated circuits. Within the next few years, many computers began employing ICs in various circuits. In 1971, Intel introduced the first commercial microprocessor chip, the 4004.

CPU SPEED

Even though the IBM 360 wasn't the fastest computer introduced in 1964 — the CDC 6600 supercomputer wears that crown — processing speed increased from the second to the third generation by a factor of five. By 1971, computers were able to process nearly 1 million instructions per second and thus gave us another acronym: MIPS.

I/O DEVICES

The third generation marked the full shift from punched cards to magnetic storage media. Now it was possible to type data on the keyboard and have it stored on tapes or disks. This was called *interactive data processing,* what today we term *on-line transaction processing*. This meant that tasks were performed while you actually worked with the computer. Another new way to enter data was called *optical character recognition* (OCR). An OCR scanner would "read" a document typed in the special OCR characters. Networking equipment allowed sending and receiving data between a remote terminal and the computer, and between computers as well. The IBM Selectric typewriter was used for printing word processing letters and reports.

MEMORY AND STORAGE

Hard disks and magnetic tape made an interesting flip-flop in the third generation. RAM took giant strides as it became possible to use hard disks for main memory. Some computers had up to 3 megabytes of main memory. On the other hand, computers began using magnetic tape for auxiliary storage, primarily as backup, to make an additional copy of data stored on auxiliary storage hard disk drives for safety.

PROGRAMMING LANGUAGES

During the third generation, software really flourished for the first time. One reason was because FORTRAN and COBOL were more widely established as standards for writing application programs. This made writing programs much easier. Many high-level programming languages were developed during the third generation, among them BASIC and Pascal.

SOFTWARE

Another reason software flourished was that operating systems had matured. Multiprogramming, discussed in Chapter 7, was in use. In order to make all the 360 series computers compatible (and to make its earlier 1401 compatible as well), IBM created the OS/360 operating system. And since other computer companies were making computer systems that worked just like an IBM—termed **plug-compatible machines** (PCM)—they had to emulate the 360's operating system as well as its hardware.

Yet another reason for software's growth was due to something called **unbundling,** or selling the software separate from the hardware. In the past, if you purchased a computer from, say, Sperry Univac, you also purchased your software from them. If you didn't like that software or if it didn't meet your needs, you had to hire a custom programmer to modify it. But in the early 1960s, Charles Lecht started an independent software company called Advanced Computer Techniques and stimulated the industry into unbundled software; in other words, he made it possible to buy software from someone other than the computer manufacturer.

ACT, followed by other software companies, sold what is called *third-party software*. If a program was written for one machine and was popular, it could be modified and rewritten for another machine. Personal computer software has always been unbundled, except for IBM's proprietary PC–DOS and OS/2 operating systems (although Microsoft offers versions for non-IBM machines).

Two of the most significant applications of the third generation were networking communications and word processing. The advent of computer-to-computer communications made it possible for a number of people, using terminals, to use a single computer, even different programs, at the same time. This was called *time-sharing* and it led to multiprocessing. IBM introduced word processing to the world in 1964, in a machine called the Magnetic Tape/Selectric Typewriter, or MT/ST.

The Fourth Generation

The fourth generation (1971–88) brought us many different innovations, several as a result of advances in chip technology. The integrated circuit of the third generation, considered a marvel in its time, now seems rather simple when compared to microprocessor chips. Large-scale integration, a technique for packing more and more circuitry on a single chip, has given us microprocessors as powerful as an entire mainframe computer. The fourth generation brought major advances in second-generation mainframes and in third-generation minicomputers, and added a brand new category of machine: the microcomputer or personal computer.

Mainframes

Mainframes continued to grow more powerful, but there was another interesting development. IBM introduced the 370, its successor to the 360, which was *compatible* with the older series. That meant that, for the first time, operating systems and applications software from 360s would work on 370s. The PCM industry continued to expand. Although RCA failed in its attempt (to the tune of almost half a billion dollars) to successfully market its 360 PCMs, Gene Amdahl, a former IBM engineer and architect who designed the 704 and was on the 360 team, started several successful PCM companies.

Minicomputers

Edson de Castro, a computer designer at Digital Equipment Corporation, left DEC to form Data General and began building minis that competed with Digital's. Other notable mini companies are Hewlett-Packard, Prime Computer, Tandem Computer, and others. Hewlett-Packard and Prime have concentrated more on scientific and engineering machines. Tandem came up with an innovative idea: two complete CPUs within one computer, so that if one failed, the other would immediately take its place. Tandem called this "nonstop computing" and has been very successful selling its computers to banks and other businesses that can't afford to have the computer "go down."

But Digital's VAX is probably the biggest success story in minicomputer history. Begun in 1975, the VAX (which stands for Virtual Address Extension) was an improvement over the PDP-11 mini. The design team was led by Gordon Bell, one of Digital Equipment Corporation's most brilliant engineers. The goal was to create a new, faster 32-bit machine that was compatible with the older, and very popular, 16-bit PDP-11. This was counter to IBM's strategy, which was to introduce a new and improved computer about every five years, one that was incompatible with older models. This, of course, meant that companies would have to replace their old computers, buy the new ones, and then (the suppliers hoped) convert the old software. Often this was neither practical nor necessary, since the MTBF for fourth-generation computers had grown to months, if not years.

PERSONAL COMPUTERS

The personal computer's growth and development is nearly identical to that of the mainframe computer. It started out as a hobbyist's kit, an experimental machine, but people quickly found many uses for it. What is dramatically different is that the personal computer has evolved about four times faster than the mainframe. Today we have personal computers and workstations with as much processing power as a mainframe or a VAX. Larger computers often have more RAM and are designed to work with dozens, even hundreds, of disk and tape drives. They also permit hundreds of users, working at terminals, to use the computer at the same time. But personal computer memory is growing larger, and now small work groups can use personal computers that are connected together in networks. The picture is rapidly changing in favor of the smaller, easier-to-use personal computer and the more powerful workstations.

CIRCUIT TECHNOLOGY

Curiously, the company that initiated commercial development of the microprocessor—which heralded the fourth computer generation—went out of business. Busicom was a Japanese electronic calculator company that asked Intel, a California electronics firm, to create an advanced integrated circuit for a programmable calculator. Marcian E. "Ted" Hoff was the engineer in charge. He pioneered the 4004, a four-chip microprocessor, in 1969, although it was never used for its intended purpose. The advanced process of packing more circuits on a chip is termed *large-scale integration* (LSI). The fourth generation brought us very large scale integration (VLSI).

The 4004 was a breakthrough. Even before it was finished, Intel engineers were working on the next chip, the 8008. It was introduced in 1971; Texas Instruments, Fairchild Semiconductor, RCA, and other electronics firms were introducing competing chips soon after. In 1974, Intel introduced the 8080, which was 10 times faster than the 8008 and had four times the memory capacity. This microprocessor literally launched the personal computer industry. It has been superseded by the 8086, 8088, 80286, the 80386, and the 80486.

Meanwhile, companies specializing in manufacturing memory chips were working to pack more circuits—and thus more memory capacity—on an individual IC. In 1969, memory chip capacity was 256 bits; by 1976, it had risen to 64,000 bits (64K bits). By 1983, it had quadrupled to 256K bits.

CPU SPEED

The fourth generation gave us a dramatic increase in processor speed. In the early 1970s, processing speed was 1 million instructions per second (MIPS). By the late 1980s, that had increased to 4.77 MIPS in the standard personal

FIGURE B.2

Advances in microprocessor and memory chips in the 1990s.

| Intel Microprocessors | | | |
Year	Model	Speed	Number of Transistors
1989	80486	25–50 MHz	1 million
1992	80586	75–100 MHz	4 million
1995	80686	150 MHz	22 million
1999	80786	250 MHz	100 million

| American DRAM Chips | | |
Year	Memory Size	Number of Chip Components
1989	1 megabit	More than 1 million
1991	4 megabits	More than 10 million
1994	16 megabits	More than 10 million
1996	64 megabits	More than 100 million

computer and up to 12 MIPS in the PC/AT models. In 1988, some 80386-based personal computers and workstations ran at 25 MIPS; today, speeds commonly reach 50 MIPS.

Grosch's Law, put forth by Herbert R. J. Grosch in the late 1940s, says that computing power increases by the square of its cost. According to Grosch, every time you buy a new system, you obtain four times the computing power for just twice the cost. Grosch's Law has never produced less, but it has produced more.

Grosch's Law was broken in the fourth generation; doubling the speed no longer costs twice as much. Often it doesn't cost any more at all. Throughout the late fourth generation and into the fifth generation, it's almost impossible to keep up with microprocessor and memory chip advances. Chip manufacturers announce improved performance every few weeks, and, as Figure B.2 shows, we can expect to see this continue well into the late 1990s.

I/O DEVICES

The keyboard and video monitor have become standard I/O devices, but in the fourth generation, the mouse began playing a major role. The mouse is especially useful for issuing commands to the operating system or the software, which formerly required pressing several keys. Some knowledge workers still find keys or control commands quicker and easier, while others wouldn't trade their mouse for anything.

There were three major fourth-generation printer advances. The first was the Diablo daisy wheel letter-quality printer, the first automatic printer for computers. The second was the incredibly fast inkjet printer, often used for printing bulk mail promotions. Dot-matrix printers have also improved, offering high speed and print quality almost as good as a letter-quality printer. Most in demand is the laser printer, with its variety of professional, printer-quality typefaces, superb graphics, and multiple printing formats.

MEMORY AND STORAGE

VLSI has also allowed us to progress from computers with only a few kilobytes of memory to personal computers with 2, 4, and often 16 *megabytes* of memory. This additional memory makes it possible to use multitasking operating systems and more complex or graphically oriented applications.

In the early 1970s, an IBM engineer named Alan Shugart invented the floppy disk. The first one was 8 inches in diameter, but floppy disks have now shrunk from 5¼ inches to the popular 3½-inch disk used in Macintoshes, 386-based personal computers, and PS/2s. Floppy disk storage capacity has increased dramatically as well.

Hard disk drives have also grown in capacity; mainframes and minis now have disk drives that hold data in quantities known as *gigabytes*. Alan Shugart also invented the Winchester hard disk for personal computers. Early models held only 5MB, but that quickly increased to 20MB. Personal computers now have hard disks capable of holding over 600MB.

PROGRAMMING LANGUAGES

The fourth generation introduced fourth-generation languages, more English-like languages that nonprogrammers could use to design their own applications. Fourth-generation languages are commonly used with a database management system program, on all classes of computers. The fourth generation also saw the development of new languages for artificial intelligence, including Prolog, which was developed in England.

SOFTWARE

Operating systems made it easier for users to work with computers by creating a more friendly user interface. The most notable example is the Macintosh graphical interface, which allows the user to point at images on the screen with a mouse, rather than memorize keyboard commands. Microsoft Windows for DOS and IBM's Presentation Manager for OS/2 were responses to creating a more friendly user interface. Today, most personal computers offer an improved user interface or a DOS shell program that makes it possible to issue commands from a graphical screen.

Application software likewise became easier to use, with many programs offering "pull-down" or "pop-up" menus that display a list of commands or actions on the screen. Many programs that were only available on mainframes or minis migrated to the personal computer environment (for example, database management systems and accounting programs). The spreadsheet was a new and original application for the personal computer, as was desktop publishing.

THE FIFTH GENERATION

In the past, applications often required designing both computer hardware and software from scratch. Today we are approaching a time when computer systems will automatically create new applications without any human help or intervention. We have entered the fifth generation of computing (1983–?), where we will have personal computers as powerful as mainframes and software that performs certain thinking functions only our brains can now do. One sign of fifth-generation activity was the recognition of legitimate expert systems research around 1983. Another was the fifth-generation government-funded research project that Japan formally launched in the early 1980s. The goal was to develop computer systems that combine advances in speech recognition, vision systems, database technology, and the telephone booth so that the average citizen would have extraordinarily easy access to computer power and information. The Japanese project ended and has been replaced by a new endeavor, but today, fifth-generation projects are in development around the world — especially in the United States.

CIRCUIT TECHNOLOGY

One fifth-generation goal is to develop VHSIC and UHSIC chips (see Figure B.1), more commonly called superchips. Early superchips are two to three times faster than the fastest personal computer microprocessor chip. The first uses for these superchips are in military applications, but scientists say they'll be widely used in consumer products such as digital television sets. Not only will superchips be fast, they'll be self-repairing, too. They'll be able to diagnose their own malfunctions and substitute spare transistors on the same chip.

Chip development is truly at the center of the fifth generation. Other research is underway in the following areas:

- New materials such as gallium arsenide to replace silicon.
- New techniques such as superconductivity or operating in extremely low temperatures that speeds the flow of electricity.
- New applications such as the neurocomputer or neural computing chip.

First developed by Drs. Carver Mead and Federico Faggin, the neural chip works very similarly to the neurons in our own brains. The chips can be linked into massive, complex circuits that scientists hope will eventually lead to "thinking" computers.

CPU SPEED

The fifth generation has seen an accleration in the introduction of Intel CISC microprocessors. The 80586 has been introduced, and the 80686 is scheduled for 1995. As Figure B.2 shows, its speed will be six times the 80486. No matter how powerful today's computer, there are still times when we must sit and wait for an operation to be completed. This is because the CPU can only process one instruction at a time, and even though it may be processing at 25, 33, or even 50 million instructions per second, we often may end up staring at the screen for what seems like hours.

Fifth-generation computers will overcome the problem of speed in several ways. One is the new generation of reduced-instruction-set computers, or RISC machines. They take advantage of the traditional von Neumann CPU architecture by utilizing, as the name implies, fewer instructions. The Alpha RISC microprocessor chip, developed by Digital Equipment Corp., shows great promise in this regard. Another is the parallel processing architecture that allows many CPUs to share the processing work. Perhaps the most promising is the optical computer chip, which uses light instead of electricity. Such a computer would be able to process instructions at *nearly the speed of light.*

I/O DEVICES

Touch screens will be in common use for simple tasks in the fifth generation. Instead of typing, we'll be able to give these computers voice instructions. In time, they will reply vocally or by more conventional means if we prefer. As the computer input and output devices change, so will the user interface — to a point where it will be entirely transparent, as it should be.

MEMORY AND STORAGE

Memory chips have acquired vast storage capabilities (see Figure B.2); economies of scale in manufacturing will drop so dramatically that they will be able to hold tremendous amounts of mass storage. Optical storage devices, based on today's CD-ROM and videodisc technologies, will largely replace magnetic disks. Gradually we will be able to store data on networks as well, so we won't have to pay for our own storage devices at all.

PROGRAMMING

Object-oriented programming (OOP) and computer-aided software engineering (CASE) tools are in more common use for developing applications in business. Indeed, many knowledge workers will be able to utilize OOP for creating personalized applications. This is a dramatic advance; applications can be designed to one's own personal needs and tastes. No longer will it be necessary to learn how to use a program; the computer will "learn" how to perform a particular task exactly as you want it done. In time, the "programming language" will be our own spoken language, which the computer interprets into its own machine language. The instructions themselves will be programmable, so that computer "crashes" will be a thing of the past: programs will be self-repairing.

SOFTWARE

The fifth generation will bring us intelligent GUIs that learn to respond to our personal workstyle or lifestyle. For example, the computer knows that you like to wake up in the morning to the morning news headlines, then you like to read your electronic mail. It will alert you when you need to attend a meeting or write a report. As you change between types of data, it will automatically switch to the appropriate application. Image processing and voice recognition will be an important part of fifth-generation systems. We will be on-line continuously as the computer searches for and retrieves data we have previously programmed it to find for us.

WHAT LIES AHEAD?

The computer has made advances that are unparalleled by any other invention or achievement of the human race. Yet many believe its greatest contributions are yet to come. The fifth generation is leading us into an age where the computer will be our sidekick, companion, and an extension of our brain. We will not have to spend so much time learning how to use it or manipulating its hardware and software to get what we need from it. In this exciting new generation, the computer is becoming a genuine productivity tool. As it does so, we will find that the fifth generation is bringing us computer systems capabilities we can scarcely imagine.

Yet are people's attitudes changing and advancing along with improvements in machines such as the computer? We have seen great resistance on the part of people to change, especially with respect to learning how to understand and use a computer. However, whether we are ready or not, the computer will begin making dramatic changes in our lives over the next 30 years.

We will see much of our daily activities automated by computers. Those who hold jobs will be those who make business decisions or those who work in entertainment and the creative arts: business and government leaders, salespeople, artists, composers, sports players. There will be a vast explosion in creativity, but also a huge leisure class. The quality of life will improve for everyone — but at the same time, the world's population will continue to grow at a rapid pace.

Meanwhile, we will enter the sixth, and perhaps the seventh, computer generations. Computers will be ubiquitous and possibly invisible. We will issue instructions to walls, sidewalks, autos, appliances. Robots will tend to our personal needs, and all information and entertainment will be delivered to us, automatically via a multimedia home entertainment center with a computer at its center, across fiber optic networks.

Can we effectively deal with all this change? Author-adventurer Laurens Van der Post said, "Life is its own journey, presupposes its own change and movement, and one tries to arrest them at one's eternal peril." We must begin learning how to develop our capacity to change, and expanding our mental and human potential now, in order to prepare for this new world. It is ours and we must be its master, not its slave.

SUMMARY

1. *Understand how computer technology has evolved throughout the five generations.* Advances in electronics in the early part of the 20th century made it possible to develop electronic digital computers. We call the stages in the evolution of computer electronic circuitry, hardware, software, and programming languages the computer generations.

2. *Describe the various electronic devices that have driven computer technology from one generation to the next.* Early computers used vacuum tubes, but they proved unreliable for computing purposes. Real progress in reliability began with transistors and was fulfilled by integrated circuits. ICs evolved into microprocessors and are also used for computer memory and other pur-

poses. The amount of electronic circuitry that can be packed on an IC is called *integration* — for example, very large scale integrated circuit (VLSIC).

3. *Understand the most significant advances in circuit technology, CPU speed, memory, programming languages, and software for each generation.* The first generation (1951–58) mainframe computers used vacuum tubes; CPU speed was measured in thousands of instructions per second. I/O was primarily punched cards and paper tape. Magnetic drum and magnetic core were used for memory and storage. There were no languages and typical applications were tabulating or maintaining files.

The second generation (1958–64) saw the

introduction of the minicomputer. Transistors began to be used; speed was about 200,000 instructions per second. I/O devices were keyboards and video displays; memory and storage devices were magnetic tape and large disk drives. Programming languages were mostly machine-specific, but FORTRAN and COBOL were introduced. Records management was the primary software application.

The third generation (1964–71) used integrated circuits; speed increased to nearly 1 million instructions per second. I/O included improved keyboard techniques and optical character recognition. Hard disks and magnetic tape drives made memory and storage advances. High-level programming languages flourished, and through unbundling, many new applications were introduced.

The fourth generation (1971–88) heralded the personal computer. Speed increased to 20 million instructions per second. The mouse was a preeminent I/O device. Memory and storage capacity increased dramatically, especially with personal computers. Programming languages became more English-like, and thousands of new applications were developed in business, education, entertainment, and personal improvement.

4. The fifth generation (1983–?) promises the ubiquitous computer, everywhere but rarely seen. Current chip technology will make dramatic improvements and new chip technologies will be introduced. Speed will approach that of light. Touch screens and the human voice will be common I/O devices. Users will write their own tailor-made applications in object-oriented programming modules—or software will write itself. Applications will continually adapt to user needs.

REVIEW AND DISCUSSION QUESTIONS

1. What were the major problems with using vacuum tubes in computers?
2. What is the basic material used in transistors and integrated circuits?
3. What electronic components are found in ICs?
4. Why weren't the computers of the 1940s considered first-generation machines?
5. Explain how Grosch's Law works, and how it has changed over the years.
6. Why do you think the punched card was used for almost 100 years?
7. Describe the advantages of third-generation over second-generation computers.
8. What generation has produced the most significant advances for users?
9. What should our greatest concerns be for the future computer generations?
10. Discuss the historical significance of the Information Age and the computer generations. How do they complement one another? Where are they leading us?

KEY TERMS

computer generations,   513
diode,   514
integration,   515
magnetic core,   517
magnetic drum,   516

mean time between failures (MTBF),   518
plug-compatible machine (PCM),   521
semiconductor,   514

tabulating,   517
transistor,   514
triode,   514
unbundling,   521
vacuum tube,   514

DOS Command Chart

APPEND: Used to specify a search path for data files; functionally equivalent to the PATH command.

ASSIGN: Reroutes requests from one drive to another.

ATTRIB: Makes a file read-only (cannot be revised).

AUTOEXEC.BAT: Starts a series, or batch, of commands. One of the most useful DOS commands, it combines and simplifies many instructions into one file to execute.

BACKUP: Makes a copy of one or more files on a new disk.

BREAK: Enables or disables the CTRL-BREAK function that ends a DOS operation.

CHDIR: Changes or displays the default directory.

CHKDSK: Checks a disk's status, such as amount of space used.

CLS: The command to clear all text from the screen display.

COPY: Copies one or more files to a new destination directory or disk.

DATE: Displays the current date.

DEL (DELETE): Deletes a file from a disk (same as ERASE).

DIR: Displays a directory listing of all files on a disk.

DISKCOMP: Allows you to compare the contents of two disks.

DISKCOPY: Copies the entire contents of one disk to another, including hidden files and COMMAND.COM. It will FORMAT the disk at the same time.

ECHO: Displays or suppresses (ECHO OFF) batch command messages; that is, does not show text on screen while AUTOEXEC.BAT file is running.

ERA (ERASE): Deletes a file from a disk (same as DELETE).

FDISK: Used to create and set the DOS partition(s) on a hard disk.

FIND: Used to search for a filename or other character strings.

FORMAT: Command to prepare a new disk for use by DOS.

LABEL: Used to create a label, or name, for a disk or hard disk drive. See VOL.

MKDIR: Creates a new subdirectory on a disk (floppy or hard). See RMDIR.

MODE: Sets computer characteristics, such as display width (40 or 80 characters).

PATH: Specifies that DOS should execute commands or programs found in specific subdirectories.

PRINT: Prints a DOS file.

PROMPT: Lets you customize or individualize a DOS prompt (C:). For example, PROMPT PG displays the prompt: C:\>

REM (REMARK): Displays nonexecutable comments during the execution of a BATCH file.

REN (RENAME): Allows you to rename a file.

REPLACE: Replaces all the files on the disk you are copying from to the disk you are copying to; in other words, only new files are copied.

RESTORE: Allows you to restore files saved by BACKUP.

RMDIR: Removes a subdirectory. See MKDIR.

SELECT: Lets you specify international languages for use with the keyboard.

SYS (SYSTEM): The command for transferring the hidden files and DOS command interpreter (COMMAND.COM) from the DOS disk to a new disk during formatting; creates a ''bootable'' disk.

TIME: Displays the current time.

TREE: Displays the subdirectory structure.

TYPE: Displays a file's contents on the screen.

VER (VERSION): Displays the version of DOS you are using.

VERIFY: Confirms that disk sectors are correctly recording data during format or copying.

VOL (VOLUME): Displays a disk volume label. See LABEL.

XCOPY: Copies subdirectories and files together.

Accumulator
A register that temporarily stores the results of continuing arithmetic and logical operations.

Acoustic coupler
A modem with two cups that the telephone receiver fits into.

Address register
A register that holds instructions or pieces of data in a specific memory location.

Algorithm
A limited set of step-by-step instructions that solve a problem.

Alternate (Alt)
A computer keyboard key used in conjunction with standard keyboard keys to issue commands or instructions to the application software.

Analog
A computer that does not count in two digits, but rather continuously measures and compares changing values.

Analog signal
A signal that is continuous, but changing in tone, pitch, and volume.

Application development environment
Using the DBMS's built-in programming language to create applications.

Application generator
A DBMS programming language that permits programming either by using English-like commands or by making selections from menus.

Application software
Computer programs used by knowledge workers to produce useful work.

Arithmetic-logic unit (ALU)
The electronic circuitry in the CPU that performs the arithmetic and logical operations; one of three components of the central processing unit.

Arithmetic operations
Functions of the arithmetic-logic unit that perform addition, subtraction, multiplication, and division.

Artificial intelligence
A software technology that attempts to replicate many human thought processes (such as reasoning, learning, self-improvement, and associative learning) in a computer. See **expert system.**

ASCII
Acronym for American Standards Code for Information Interchange. A standard for telecommunications and application file transfer requiring that all the special codes and formats from the application program be stripped from a file. Also called a text file.

Assembler
Software that translates assembly language into machine language.

Assembly language
A programming language that uses letters, numbers, and symbols to represent individual 0s and 1s.

Attribute
A characteristic of an entity.

Automatic call dialing (ACD)
A computer-managed electronic dialing function for outgoing calls.

Automatic number identification (ANI)
A computer-assisted operation used to identify from the telephone network the number of the caller dialing in, displaying it on a computer screen or an LCD readout.

Auxiliary storage
Used to keep instructions and data more permanently. Also known as storage device.

Backspace
A computer keyboard key that deletes the previously typed character.

Backup
The process of making duplicate copies of programs and files for safekeeping.

Bandwidth
The capacity of a communications channel to carry data or information.

BASIC
The most popular programming language used by personal computer owners; most commonly an unstructured language.

Batch processing
Taking data that is collected in a batch over a period of time and then usually input, processed, and output all at once.

Baud (bps)
The unit for measuring signal speed, roughly equivalent to one bit per second (bps).

Binary number system
A number system based on just two numbers or digits, 1 and 0.

Bit
The basic unit of data recognized by a computer.

Bit-mapped
A high-resolution display. See character-mapped.

Boldface
Accentuating type characters by making them darker.

Boot
Loading the operating system in computer memory.

Bridge
Computer circuitry that links phones and computers together.

Bug
A program or hardware problem.

Bus network
A network with no central computer that shares other network resources in common.

Business analysis systems
A system that provides data that, when used with the proper software, aids in business analysis and decision making.

Byte
A group of bits that can be operated on as a unit by the computer.

C language
A programming language similar to assembly language, but incorporating many of the statement features of high-level languages.

Cache memory
A small memory accumulation area, part of either the CPU integrated circuit chip or a software program, that creates an additional memory staging area just before the CPU where instructions can be gathered for more efficient processing.

CALCULATE
An automatic calculation command built into the spreadsheet's operation.

Caps Lock
A keyboard key used to lock the keyboard for typing capital letters.

Carrier signal
A tone that indicates the computer is available.

Cartridge
A specially designed tape cassette used for backup.

Cell
A square on the spreadsheet screen indicating where to type in data.

Cell pointer
Illuminates the particular cell it is located in, taking the place of the cursor to indicate where data may be entered.

Center
To place text equidistant from each side of the page.

Centralized computing
The concept of keeping all MIS functions in one location or facility.

Central processing unit (CPU)
The computer component that executes instructions and processes data.

Character
A single symbol, letter, number, or punctuation mark defined in the database.

Character-based
An application program capable of displaying only ASCII text, not graphics.

Character-mapped
A lower-resolution display than bit-mapped displays.

Click and drag
A technique used with pointing devices, such as the mouse, to issue commands and accomplish tasks.

Client
A PC used by a knowledge worker; the "front end" of a client/server system.

Client/server
A database system used by a group of knowledge workers in a specific work group, division, or department.

Client/server computing
A hardware architecture that takes advantage of the processing power of two computers working together to perform a task.

Clip art
Universally recognized images available in books or stored on computer disks.

Closed architecture
A computer designed so that a competitor would need permission to obtain its specifications and duplicate them.

Clusters
Individual storage compartments on a disk, defined by their track and sector designation.

COBOL
A structured programming language most widely used in business; a structured language.

Code generator
A software program used to create a large portion of the source code.

Coding
Programming in a specific programming language or languages; creating source code for the program.

Collaboration
Knowledge workers working together with the aid of computer systems.

Column
The cells running vertically down the spreadsheet screen.

Command
An instruction given to the computer.

Command language
A common vocabulary of codes, words, and phrases used to communicate quickly and efficiently with the CPU.

Command line
The portion of the screen where DOS commands or instructions are issued.

Command line interface
A human-computer interface that requires typing a command in the proper syntax.

Communications channel
A physical means of connecting the communicating computers so they can exchange the programs or data.

Communications management software
An application that controls computers that receive calls from a number of knowledge workers. Also called dialup or host software.

Communications protocol
A rule and standard that make it possible for two computers to communicate with each other.

Communications software
An application programmed with telephone numbers to dial a modem and connect to another computer, to send or receive data communications.

Compact disc-read only memory (CD-ROM)
Auxiliary storage medium that uses laser technology instead of magnetics to read and write to a CD-sized disk. See **write once, read many.**

Compiler
Software that translates entire files of source code into object code, which in turn becomes an executable file.

Complex-instruction-set computing (CISC)
A microprocessor or CPU architecture and operating system design that recognizes 100 or more instructions. See **reduced-instruction-set computing.**

Computer
A device that accepts data, then performs arithmetic or logical operations that manipulate or change the data, and finally produces new results from that data.

Computer-aided acquisition and logistics support (CALS)
A U.S. Department of Defense program for image processing and paperless document management associated with the design, manufacture, acquisition, and maintenance of weapons systems.

Computer-aided software engineering (CASE)
A methodology especially designed for programmers in large information systems organizations who need to quickly create new applications, or re-engineer older applications.

Computer architecture
The design and implementation of computer systems in an organization.

Computer literacy
Being knowledgeable or educated about the computer and how it works in our daily lives.

Computer-output microfilm (COM)
Miniature photography used to condense, store, and retrieve data on film.

Computer system
People, using data and procedures, to work with software and hardware components.

Computer-to-machine output
Using the input/output process to control machine operations.

Computer virus
A program that corrupts or "infects" computer files by inserting a copy of the virus itself into those files.

Computer worm
A program that damages computers by duplicating itself from one computer's memory to the next.

Concentrator
A controller and multiplexer combined into one peripheral to manage, amplify, and ensure the integrity of data signals.

Configuration
The various hardware components that make up a computer system.

Constant
The raw number or data entered for spreadsheet processing.

Control (Ctrl)
A computer keyboard key used in conjunction with standard keyboard keys to issue commands or instructions to the application software.

Controller
A peripheral device that routes data between the CPU and the terminal.

Control unit
One of three components of the central processing unit; directs the step-by-step operation of the computer.

Conversion
Changing from one DBMS program (or other application) to another.

Cooperative processing
The ability to use different computer systems which are able to exchange data between their diverse operating platforms.

Co-processor
An additional CPU microprocessor chip, often utilized for improving the speed of mathematical operations.

Corporate electronic publishing
A type of electronic publishing used for documents intended for both external and internal use.

Cursor
Usually a blinking rectangle or a blinking underline that indicates where the next typed keyboard character will appear on the screen.

Cursor control
The four computer keyboard arrow keys.

Cut and paste
Moving portions of files, often created by different applications, from one file to another.

Cycle
The length of time it takes the CPU to process one machine instruction.

Cylinder
A vertical stack of tracks on a disk.

Daisy wheel
A printer with a print hammer that strikes each "petal" of a plastic print

wheel against a ribbon to form an impression.

Data
Facts and numbers suitable for communication or interpretation. A single unit of data may be termed a datum; technically data is the plural term.

Database
A group of related records and files.

Database administrator
The information systems professional responsible for maintaining the DBMS as well as for ensuring the accuracy and integrity of its data.

Database application
A program designed to extract and organize specific data, and then present it on the computer screen and in printed reports.

Database design
Planning the nature and purpose of the database using paper and pencil.

Database development
Managing the DBMS and administering to the databases.

Database management system (DBMS)
Application software that lets you organize, store, and retrieve data from a single database or several databases.

Database service
An on-line information service whose primary purpose is to provide comprehensive information.

Data collection device
A source-data input computerlike device used for such tasks as scanning UPC codes for inventory purposes.

Data definition
Creating a detailed description of the data.

Data dictionary
A list of all the fields, files, and commands utilized in manipulating a database.

Data disk
The disk on which work is stored.

Data elements
Individual pieces of data that are joined to produce information; also called data items.

Data entry
The process of entering data into computer memory.

Data processing
The activity of a computer system using specific procedures that turn data into useful information for people.

Data refinement
The interaction or relationships between various data elements.

Data representation
The characters used to present data to the computer for processing in a language it understands.

Debugger
A system software program that identifies program errors.

Decision support systems (DSS)
A system that helps a manager extract information from various MIS databases and reporting systems, analyze it, and then formulate a decision or a strategy for business planning.

Default mode
The editing mode in which the application software begins automatically.

Delete (Del)
A computer keyboard key that deletes the current character.

DELETE
A DBMS command used to remove a record from the database.

Desk accessories
Utility software that replaces common objects on the knowledge worker's desk.

Desktop personal computer
A computer that fits on a desktop, is designed for a single user, and is affordable for an individual to buy for personal use.

Desktop publishing
Combined word processing and graphics applications with advanced formatting capabilities.

Dialup
See **communications management software.**

Digital camera
A still-photograph camera that connects to a computer and transfers the image digitally to disk.

Digital computer
A computer that uses the binary arithmetic system as the basis for its operation.

Digital signal
A single discrete signal; a steady stream of pulses that does not change in tone, pitch, or volume.

Digitizer
An electronic drawing tablet used as an input device.

Direct access
A method to quickly retrieve data stored in a particular memory location with a specific address. Also called random access. See **sequential access.**

Direct-access storage device (DASD)
The electromechanical device used with direct-access media, such as a hard disk.

Directory
A list of the files stored on a disk or a portion of a disk.

Disaster recovery
A plan or program that goes into effect in case of fire, flood, or loss of electrical or telecommunications services.

Disk operating system (DOS)
The operating system for a personal computer.

Disk pack
The device that holds a number of disks and is fitted onto a large-system DASD.

Distributed computing
Placing MIS functions where they are the most effective.

Distributed system
A system in which the hardware and software are physically located with the group and are connected to the centralized DBMS.

Document
A self-contained work, created by a knowledge worker using a computer and an application program, that can be saved and later retrieved as a file.

Document and image processing
The process of turning computer-aided designs into working specifications in both graphics and text.

Documentation
The instructions that accompany a system or an application.

Document management systems
A system that aids in filing, tracking, and managing documents, whether they are paper or computer-based.

Dot-matrix
Output produced by printers that utilize moving wires in the print head.

Double-sided disk
A disk that can be written to on both sides.

Downloading
The data communications activity of receiving files. See **uploading.**

Draft
One of successive versions of a document.

Dumb terminal
A video monitor and keyboard connected to a large system that performs the simplest input and output operations, but no processing. See **intelligent terminal.**

Ease of use
The term used to characterize aspects of computer system design; the way in which a person, regardless of their computer knowledge, skills, or background, can quickly become productive with the computer.

Electronic
A machine that uses components such as vacuum tubes, transistors, or silicon chips.

Electronic bulletin board
An interactive telecommunications service that permits posting and receiving electronic mail messages; sometimes called a bulletin board system (BBS) or computerized bulletin board system (CBBS).

Electronic data interchange (EDI)
The use of communications networks to transfer forms (such as invoices, purchase orders, shipping notices, and even payments) with computers.

Electronic funds transfer (EFT)
The use of communications networks to perform financial and banking transactions.

Electronic mail
Creating, sending, storing, and forwarding written messages (files) to other knowledge workers.

Electronic publishing
The process of converting text materials, commonly produced with word processing software, into a professionally published format.

Encapsulation
In object-oriented programming, adding a high degree of functionality to each object, making it reusable.

Encryption
The use of coding devices at each end of the communication line to prevent transmissions from being intercepted and read by unauthorized people.

End
A computer keyboard key that may be used in conjunction with the cursor control keys for moving through text.

End-user computing
Giving knowledge workers their own computers so they can be more productive in their work.

Enter
A computer keyboard key used to complete and issue a command or instruction to the computer.

Enterprisewide database system
One in which computers are physically connected and able to share data and pass transactions. Data can be found anywhere it resides, immediately accessed, and put to use.

Entity
Data that has a particular meaning. Something about which data is to be collected in a database.

Ergonomics
The study of how to create safety, comfort, and ease of use for people who use machines such as computers.

Error checking
The process whereby networked computers ensure the accuracy and integrity of data transmissions.

Escape (Esc)
A computer keyboard key that removes control of the computer system from the program in use, either stopping a task in progress or exiting from the program altogether.

Executable
Describing a file that can be read by and run by the CPU; with PCs, a file with the .EXE extension.

Execution cycle
The portion of the machine cycle in which the data is located and the instruction is executed.

Executive information system (EIS)
A system for top management that utilizes a PC with brilliant color graphics and extremely user-friendly software that can present data easily.

Expansion slot
A type of interface connection for printed circuit board peripherals in the personal computer.

Expert system
A type of software application that offers solutions for problems in a specialized area of work or study, based on the stored knowledge of human experts. See **artificial intelligence.**

External modem
A modem enclosed in a case and connected to the computer with a cable.

Facilities management
A vendor company that contracts for and runs a corporation's entire information systems operation.

Facsimile
A type of source data input; either a standalone machine or a printed circuit board peripheral in the personal computer.

Field
A group of characters that represent an attribute.

File
A group of related records and the primary unit of data storage.

Filename
A unique designation for a file created with an application. In DOS, it is up to eight characters long, followed by an optional period or dot and three-character filename extension.

Financial model
A mathematical representation of a real-world financial or economic situation, used to test different hypotheses in order to find a solution.

Flat file database
A file management system in which each file is stacked on top of the previous one.

Floating point operations per second (FLOPS)
The measurement of supercomputer performance.

Floppy disk
A magnetic disk used for auxiliary storage.

Floppy disk drive
The auxiliary storage device used with floppy disks.

Footer
Information about the document that appears at the bottom of the page, in most cases repetitively throughout a document, such as the page number. See **header.**

Formatting
The process of emphasizing and arranging text on the screen or the printed page.

Formula
A mathematical statement that sets up a calculation with values.

FORTRAN
A programming language.

Fourth-generation language
A database front end tool that uses English-like phrases and sentences to issue instructions.

Frame
A box in desktop publishing that contains text or graphics.

Front end
A tool that allows knowledge workers to work flexibly with a database. It may assist in access to data, analysis, and creating custom databases and database applications.

Function
A formula or set of formulas that have already been created and programmed into the spreadsheet for use.

Function key (F-key)
A computer keyboard key used in conjunction with standard keyboard keys to issue commands or instructions to the application software.

Gas plasma display
A deep orange, flat-panel display composed of three sheets of glass with plasma, an illuminant gas, between them.

General-purpose computer
One that is used for a variety of tasks without the need to modify or change it as the tasks change. See **special-purpose computer.**

Geographic information system (GIS)
An image database that combines computer graphics–generated maps and cartography with relevant data in a database.

Gigabyte
One billion bytes, or 1 GB.

Graphics
Pictorial representations of numeric data produced by the spreadsheet; also a standalone application.

Groupware
A software application designed for sharing information, both text and graphics, from both corporate and on-line sources, among networked PCs and workstations.

Hacker
Someone with great skill in programming and working with computers.

Handshaking
Synchronizing two communicating computers for data exchange.

Hard copy
Output on paper, from a printer or plotter. See **soft copy.**

Hard disk drive
An auxiliary storage device with a rigid magnetic disk enclosed in a permanently sealed housing.

Hard return
The act of pressing the Enter key to end a line manually.

Hardware
The components or physical devices that make up a computer system.

Header
Information about the document that appears at the top of the page. See **footer.**

Help
A function built into the application that contains instructions, tips, pointers, explanations, and guidance.

Hertz (Hz)
A unit of measure for machine cycle frequency. One Hertz equals one cycle. Also used to gauge the speed of personal computers, measured in millions.

Hidden file
A file that contains software information that is the copyrighted property of the computer company.

Hierarchical database
A DBMS that creates relationships between logical data elements by establishing an inverted or upside-down tree structure from the central root to the branches.

Hierarchy
A series of steps in structured design, beginning with the overall problem to be solved and continuing down in a series of increasingly more detailed parts of the problem.

High-density disk
One that has the number of tracks doubled or quadrupled.

High-level language
A method of writing programs using English-like words as instructions.

High-resolution graphics
Output of a monitor capable of displaying sharp, crisp video with curving lines, shading, detail, color, and so on.

Home
A computer keyboard key that is used (often in conjunction with the cursor control keys) for moving through text.

Host
The computer in charge of a data communications work session.

Human-computer interface
The point of meeting between the person using the computer and the computer itself.

Hypertext
Software that dynamically associates words and concepts so that searching for a specific word also produces other related words or text.

Hyphenation
The process of correctly splitting a word at the end of a line.

I/O
The process of input and output. Also, the devices, or peripherals, used for input and output.

Icon
A pictorial figure or representation that is designed to be easily recognizable by most people.

Icon bar
A menu of icons running across the top or bottom of the screen.

Impact printer
A printer that strikes characters on the paper. See **nonimpact printer.**

Import
To bring a file created by another type or brand of application into the one currently in use.

INDEX
A DBMS command that puts data in either alphabetical or numerical order.

Indexing
The process by which the read-write head moves to the outer edge of the disk to find data in its various locations.

Information Age
An era in which information has become a commodity, has value, and is bought and sold.

Information engineering
A software development methodology that brings knowledge workers, management, and information systems personnel together into a working partnership.

Information services
On-line services that maintain and provide access to data repositories.

Information utility
An on-line service that combines information and interactive services to provide access to news, extensive databases, bulletin boards, shopping services, and so on.

Inheritance
In object-oriented programming, giving objects within a specific class the ability to share attributes with each other.

Inkjet printing
A printing technique where characters and images are transferred to paper by spraying a fine jet of ink.

Input devices
Components used for entering data or instructions into the computer.

Insert (Ins)
A computer key that toggles between the two modes for entering text. See **typeover mode.**

Insert mode
The default mode for the Insert key.

Instruction
A group of characters, usually in the form of a program, that the computer understands.

Instruction cycle
The portion of the machine cycle in which the CPU fetches (retrieves) an instruction from RAM and gets ready to perform processing.

Instruction register
A register that holds an instruction (for example, add, multiply, or a logical comparison operation).

Integrated circuit
An electronic component with hundreds or thousands of electronic circuits on a single piece of silicon.

Integrated services digital network (ISDN)
An all-digital network that connects computers directly to one another; no modem is necessary.

Integrated software
The combination of several stand-alone applications, capable of freely exchanging data with each other, into a single program.

Intelligent terminal
A terminal with its own CPU or processing capabilities built in. See **dumb terminal.**

Interface
The point where a peripheral device, software, or a human meets the computer.

Internal modem
A modem mounted on a printed circuit board that fits into an expansion slot inside a personal computer.

Interoperability
The ability to perform any work task, regardless of its original resident operating platform, from any computer.

Interpreter
Software that translates source code one line at a time for immediate execution by the CPU.

Intruder
Someone behaving either unethically or illegally in the use of computer systems.

Italics
Tilting text for emphasis.

Joystick
A pointing device most commonly used for playing computer games.

Justification
Aligning text against the left, right, or both margins.

Kerning
Proportionally separating individual characters within a word to make text easier to read.

Keyboard
An input device used to enter data or instructions.

Keyword
A searchable term common to several topics.

Kilobyte
One thousand bytes, or 1 KB.

Knowledge worker
Someone who routinely uses a computer to enhance work productivity.

Label
Text in a spreadsheet.

Landscape
Laying the sheet of paper on its side so it measures 11 × 8½ inches. See **portrait.**

Laptop
A portable computer weighing between 8 and 15 pounds with a desktop-quality keyboard.

Laser printer
A printer that creates output by directing a laser beam onto a drum, creating an electrical charge that forms a pattern of letters or images, and transferring them to paper.

Laser videodisc
A type of media used for optical storage.

Leading
Proportionally altering the space between lines.

Ledger sheet
A sheet of columnar paper with columns and rows, used for accounting and calculating.

Letter-quality printer
A printer similar to a typewriter that creates high-quality impact printing.

Light pen
An input device used to draw, write, or issue commands when it touches the specially designed video monitor screen.

Line spacing
The amount of space between lines of text; for example, single space, double space, etc.

Link
A common data item.

Liquid crystal display (LCD)
A type of flat-screen display commonly used with laptops.

LIST
A DBMS command to display information, such as fields or records.

Load
To read software into the computer.

Local area network (LAN)
A network that allows a small group of knowledge workers in the same geographic location to share data, programs, and hardware resources. See **star network, bus network,** and **ring network.**

Lockout
Security software that permits only three tries at entering a username or password.

Logical data representation
An organized method for storing data about an entity in a database.

Logical operations
Functions of the ALU that compare two pieces of data to determine if one is greater than, less than, or equal to the other.

Machine cycle
The steps involved in processing a single instruction. See **instruction cycle and execution cycle.**

Machine-dependent
Describes instructions that are specific to one type of computer hardware.

Machine language
A programming language.

Macro
A sequence of keystrokes or instructions, recorded and saved in a file, used while working in an application.

Magnetic ink character recognition (MICR)
A type of source-data input that allows the computer to recognize characters printed using magnetic ink.

Magnetic strip
A type of source-data input that allows the computer to recognize data encoded in a magnetic strip, most commonly on the back of bank or credit cards.

Mail merge
Combining information from separate files (such as a name and address) to create special documents.

Mainframe
A large, general-purpose computer capable of performing many tasks simultaneously for hundreds or thousands of people.

Main memory
The storage area directly controlled by the computer's CPU. Also called **random access memory (RAM).**

Maintenance
The ongoing corrections, updatings, and improvements made to applications; part of the system development life cycle.

Management information systems (MIS)
The computer system, working together with the business organization, to achieve the business goals. It includes human input, processing resources, and products or services output.

Margin
The blank space on the sides or top and bottom of the text.

Massively parallel processing
A parallel processing computer that utilizes hundreds to thousands of microprocessors.

Math co-processor
A separate microprocessor designed to improve the speed of ALU functions.

Media
The physical material used to store data and instructions.

Media mode
Message-routing techniques: simplex, half-duplex, full-duplex.

Megabyte
One million bytes, or 1 MB.

Memory management
The process of controlling the quantity of data and instructions that can be held in RAM at any given time.

Menu-driven interface
A human-computer interface that presents a list of the commands, tasks, or projects most often worked with.

Menu line
The area on the screen that displays the various options you have for working with a document.

Microfloppy
A 3½-inch magnetic disk.

Millions of instructions per second (MIPS)
The measure of CPU speed in mainframes and minicomputers.

Minicomputer
A versatile, medium-sized computer that can be used by more than one person at the same time.

Minifloppy
A 5¼-inch magnetic disk.

Mnemonic
A term or word that is easy to identify, such as ADD for addition.

Modem (modulator-demodulator)
A peripheral device that allows computers to communicate via telephone lines.

MODIFY
A DBMS command to adjust the width of a field, to redefine it, or to add additional fields.

Modules
Distinct, logical parts of a program.

Monitor
A video display that presents computer work.

Motherboard
The component where a computer's primary electronic circuitry resides.

Mouse
A hand-held device moved across the desktop surface to electronically move the **pointer** correspondingly across the screen.

Multimedia
An interactive application that lets the knowledge worker and the computer engage in an ongoing exchange or presentation of information.

Multiplexer
A data communications peripheral device that splits one incoming data line into many so that more than one terminal can be used to service incoming data transmissions.

Multiprogramming
Term commonly used to refer to multitasking on mainframes and minicomputers.

Multitasking
An operating system function that permits using more than one application at the same time. See **task-switching.**

Multiuser
An operating system able to process the work of two or more users, working at different terminals or personal computers, at the same time.

MVS
An IBM mainframe operating system.

Native format
The format in which a file was formatted by its originating application.

Navigation
The ability to move from one point in the database to another.

Near-letter-quality (NLQ) printer
A dot-matrix printer with additional print wires, usually 24, designed to produce higher-quality output.

Network
Any computer system that connects two points or more in a communication channel.

Network and communications management system
System that allows knowledge workers to communicate with each other in real time or in the future using voice and data communications.

Network database
A DBMS that utilizes many-to-many relationships.

Networking
Connecting two or more computers to exchange programs and data through a communications channel.

Neural network
Either a hardware or software technology that uses many input, processing, and output connections to recognize patterns in data.

News service
An on-line telecommunications service that provides the latest news, including general interest, business, and financial news.

Node
A point in a communications channel.

Nonimpact printer
A printer that forms a character by means other than striking the paper, most commonly by using laser or inkjet technology. See **impact printer.**

Nonvolatile
A type of memory in which instructions and data are retained regardless of whether the computer is turned on or off.

Notebook
A portable computer weighing between four and seven pounds, with a limited keyboard.

Number Lock (Num Lock)
The computer keyboard key that locks the numeric keypad into its numbers mode.

Numeric keypad
The set of number and mathematical operations keys to the right of the QWERTY keypad.

Object
In object-oriented programming, a set of prewritten instructions and data that form a program module.

Object code
Programming code turned from source code into an executable file by a compiler.

Object-oriented DBMS (OODBMS)
A DBMS that uses objects to combine procedures or instructions with data and incorporate them together into a software entity.

Object-oriented programming (OOP)
A programming technique that puts prewritten modules of programming code and data together to form a unique programming entity that perfectly executes a specific routine. See **encapsulation, inheritance, object,** and **polymorphism.**

Office automation
Use of computer and communications technology to help people better use and manage information.

On-line
Two computers in direct telecommunications with each other.

On-line processing
A type of computer processing in which data is processed immediately, as soon as it is input.

On-line transaction processing (OLTP)
A type of computer processing in which the computer system completes the entire sequence of processing transactions as soon as it is entered.

Open architecture
Making computer specifications available to outside organizations so they may develop compatible software and hardware products.

Open system
A computer environment where all types and sizes of computers, regardless of their operating systems, can work together.

Open Systems Interconnect (OSI)
A standard that separates computer-to-computer communications into seven layers or levels.

Operating environment
A form of software that works between the operating system and the application software that makes the computer system easier for knowledge workers to use.

Operating platform
The computer, operating system, networking system, applications and services, and development languages and tools.

Operation
A set of instructions or a programming statement; with a supercomputer, termed a **floating point operation.**

Optical character recognition (OCR)
A specific typeface developed specifically to be read by early scanners.

Optical disc
Storage media that is read or written to using a laser beam.

Optical disc storage
The storage device used with optical disc media.

OS/2
The IBM PS/2 operating system.

Outliner
A word processing feature that creates an outline and paragraph numbering for a document.

Output
The product or result of the computer's data processing.

Output devices
Devices used to see the results of data processing.

Outsourcing
Another term for **facilities management.**

Overstrike mode
The Insert key toggle that deletes each old character as you type a new character. (See **Insert.**) Also called **typeover mode.**

Packet-switching network
A data communications network that transmits data in blocks, or packets.

Page break
The last line of text at the bottom of a particular page.

Page Down
A computer keyboard key that may be used in conjunction with the cursor control keys for moving through text.

Page Up
A computer keyboard key that may be used in conjunction with the cursor control keys for moving through text.

Palmtop
A handheld portable computer weighing less than a pound, with a low-quality keyboard.

Parallel interface
An interface designed so that data passes through the interface simultaneously. See **serial interface.**

Parallel processing
A computer architecture utilizing many microprocessors working together so that many programs, operations, or transactions can be processed simultaneously.

Password
A special character string unique to the individual that allows the computer to differentiate between authorized users and intruders.

PC manager
A knowledge worker (commonly from an end-user group or department) who understands the business processes, computer

technology, and software programs, and helps other knowledge workers become more productive using them.

Peer-to-peer
A network architecture where every computer on the network is an equal and can act as a server, a workstation, or both.

Pen-based computing
A computer that employs an electronic stylus to draw simple characters and to issue instructions.

Peripheral device
A device connected to the computer; may be input, output, or storage.

Personal computer (PC)
A computer designed for use by a single individual and priced so that the average person can afford it. Usually small enough to fit on a desktop. Sometimes called a microcomputer.

Personal information manager (PIM)
A DBMS that combines other desktop tools (such as the appointment calendar, calculator, and "to do"list) and word processing.

Physical data representation
How data is stored and retrieved on the computer system's auxiliary storage devices.

Pixel
The dots of light that create the monitor screen display and determine its resolution. See **resolution.**

Plotter
A type of printer that uses inkjet technology to create scientific and engineering drawings as well as other graphics, often in color.

Pointer
The arrow or character moved across the screen by the mouse.

Pointing devices
Peripherals used to move the cursor, usually working in conjunction with a keyboard.

Point-of-sale (POS) terminal
A source-data input device that scans the bar codes of the UPC to register the price (which is programmed into the host computer) as well as to deduct the item from inventory.

Polymorphism
In object-oriented programming, describing a set of actions or routines that will perform exactly as they are described regardless of the class of objects they are applied to.

Port
Connections at the rear of the motherboard for peripherals such as the keyboard, monitor, and printer.

Portability
An operating system characteristic meaning it can be used on several different computers regardless of their manufacturer.

Portable
A personal computer used by a single individual that can be used in many different places.

Portrait
A piece of paper oriented 8½ by 11 inches. See **landscape.**

Power user
A knowledge worker who understands the business and work group objectives as well as the computer systems in use (specifically personal computers), and who is able to help formulate strategies for getting the most productivity from computers for the work group.

Presentation graphics
Computer graphics or visuals for business that present numerical, statistical, financial, or other quantitative data in a pie chart, a bar chart, a line graph, or a scatter graph.

Printer
A device that displays the results of computer work.

Printing
The final step in working with an application and document that creates hard copy.

Private branch exchange (PBX)
The voice communications device used for routing telephone calls; also called a switchboard, computerized branch exchange (CBX), or private automated branch exchange (PABX).

Private network
A closed communication system, usually confined to a particular company, governmental entity, or other group.

Processing
See **data processing.**

Production
Putting an application into daily use.

Program
A series or set of instructions that give us a more complex result from the computer.

Program disk
The disk on which the application instructions are stored.

Programmer
A person who understands the problem or task the computer is supposed to work on and can translate it into the language the computer understands.

Programming
The activity of programmers.

Project
An assignment for MIS to create an application for users in a business function.

Prompt
A character or message that indicates the computer system is ready to accept a command or input.

Proprietary
An operating system for which the exact workings are private, protected information.

Public network
An open communications network available for use by anyone, usually on a fee basis.

Pulldown menu
A menu hidden behind the individual menu options that provides more command options.

Punched card
The earliest input media. A stiff cardboard card with holes punched into it, used to feed instructions or data into a computer.

Query
A software tool or a function that extracts data from the database and presents it in a usable format.

Query language
A type of programming language that allows knowledge workers to make DBMS inquiries without using programming "codes"or keywords.

Random access
See **direct access.**

Random access memory (RAM)
One of the three components of the central processing unit. It provides temporary storage for the programs being executed and for data as it passes through processing. Also called **main memory.**

Rapid application development (RAD)
An information engineering technique designed to take maximum advantage of the integrated CASE (I-CASE) tools.

Read
To copy data from disk to memory.

Read-only memory (ROM)
Memory chips that store permanent instructions and perform many routine tasks for the CPU; these instructions cannot be changed.

Read/write head
The element in the data storage device that scans the magnetic surface of the disk. Reading the disk is searching for data or instructions; writing to disk is storing data or instructions.

Recalculate
A built-in spreadsheet function that refigures the calculations whenever a change is made.

Record
A collection of related data items or fields that a DBMS treats as a unit.

Reduced-instruction-set computing (RISC)
A microprocessor or CPU architecture that uses a condensed set of instructions for its operating system. See **complex-instruction-set computing.**

Reel-to-reel tape
A data storage medium used with sequential storage devices; often used for backup.

Reference documentation
Instructions for the knowledge workers who will use the program that organizes information in a nonprocedural way, such as listing commands alphabetically.

Register
A temporary storage area designed to hold instructions and data during processing.

Relational database (RDBMS)
A DBMS in which all data is viewed as essentially alike; therefore it creates any-to-any relationships.

Report writer
A DBMS tool that organizes and formats data into an attractive format for printing.

Resolution
The degree of detail in a graphics display. See **pixel.**

Results
Presenting data into a form that a person can use; the final step in data processing.

Revising
The process of re-reading, changing, and replacing text written in word processing.

Ring network
A network in which individual computers are connected serially to one another.

Root directory
The primary directory. Subdirectories are stored under the root directory.

Row
The cells running horizontally across a spreadsheet screen.

Ruler
A tool for measuring the size of frames and columns in desktop publishing.

Saving
Storing a document or file on disk.

Scanner
An input device that uses a light-sensitive device to enter text (and, depending on the software, graphics) into the computer.

Scheduling
The operating system's ability to make maximum use of the CPU by performing tasks in a precise sequence.

Script file
A communications software feature that creates and stores the settings for individual systems, computer telephone numbers, and protocols.

Scrolling
A word processing function that continuously feeds an electronic sheet of paper for entering work.

Scrolling bars
Bars on the side and bottom of the screen that permit using the mouse pointer to move through text.

Sector
Wedges on a floppy or hard disk that compartmentalize the data into addresses for the read/write head to locate.

Sequential access
The method of storing data in a particular order, such as alphabetically or by date and time. See **direct access.**

Serial interface
An interface where the data passes through the interface sequentially. See **parallel interface.**

Server
The "back end"computer in a client/server system that holds data the client needs to process. Also called a file server.

Simple Management Protocol (SMP)
A set of network standards that make it possible to interconnect many types of computer systems.

Sizing
In electronic desktop publishing, trimming a graphic image to fit into a predefined frame.

Smart modem
A modem that can automatically dial a number or answer a call, redial a busy number, and adjust to the characteristics of the modem to which it is connecting.

Soft copy
The output produced by the video monitor. See **hard copy.**

Software documentation
Instructions for the programmers who will maintain the program.

Software engineering
The aspect of computer system development that involves the design, development, and implementation of production software systems on large-scale business computers.

SORT
A DBMS command to order or separate one or more records in a database.

Sort keys
The fields used by the SORT command to separate records.

Source code
The program, written in a specific programming language, that will be sent to the computer for processing.

Source data input
Feeding data directly into the computer without human intervention. See **magnetic ink character recognition, magnetic strip,** and **data collection device.**

Spaghetti code
A program or code that was not written sequentially or was written with little regard to rules or good organization.

Special-purpose computer
A computer designed and used solely for one application. See **general-purpose computer.**

Spreadsheet
An application that uses mathematical formulas to perform calculations on data arranged in a matrix or grid. Often used in accounting.

Stand-alone program
An individual application that works alone.

Standards
The rules and guidelines for achieving satisfactory performance and communication between different networks and computer systems.

Star network
A network that provides access to central files and system resources through a host CPU.

Statement
An expression or instruction in a programming language.

Status line
An area at the top or bottom of the screen that provides information about a word processing session.

Storage
Holding data in computer memory.

Storage register
A register that holds data retrieved from RAM temporarily, prior to processing.

Streaming tape
A specially designed tape cassette for backup.

Structured coding
Guidelines for programming in system development.

Structured design
A design method that uses the top-down approach to break a problem into parts and arrange them into a hierarchy, according to their size and level of detail.

Structured programming
A way of programming that requires the programmer to write programs in well-defined sections that are compiled in sequence.

Structured query language (SQL)
A popular query language for DBMSs. See **query language.**

Structured techniques
An orderly way of programming that can be understood by others as well as the original programmer.

Style sheet
A template that makes document design progress more quickly and smoothly.

Supercomputer
A special type of computer that is commonly used to perform a single, very complex task that requires massive processing power.

Syntax
The set of rules governing the language's structure and statements.

System analysis
The study of an activity, procedure, or an entire business to determine what kind of computer system would make it more efficient.

System analyst
An information systems professional who gathers and analyzes the data necessary to develop a new application.

System design
The activity of planning the technical aspects for a new system.

System development life cycle
The traditional method of creating a system or an application. Consists of analysis, design, coding, debugging, testing, and acceptance.

System 7
The Macintosh operating system.

System software
Software that controls the computer's primary operations, such as the operating system.

System testing
Entering various kinds of data to see how a program reacts under different conditions.

System unit
The cabinet in which the computer's electronic and mechanical components are stored.

T-1
A peripheral device that takes multiple calls from a single incoming line and routes them to another computer or controller that disperses them to their destinations.

Tab
In word processing, an automatic

indentation from the margin, usually to begin paragraphs.

Task switching
The process of keeping several applications or tasks active at the same time. See **multitasking.**

Technological innovation
The pace of new advances in technology and the propagation of those advances throughout the culture or society, toward the goal of performing work better, faster, and/or at lower cost.

Telecommunications
Sending data, including voice, from one computerlike device to another. Also called communications or data communications.

Template
A worksheet with labels, commands, and formulas already created and saved in a file.

Terabyte
One trillion bytes; 1 TB.

Terminal
A keyboard and monitor connected to a mainframe or minicomputer.

Terminate and stay resident (TSR)
A program that boots up and then waits in the background during use of an application program until it is needed.

Testing
The process of determining how an application or system works.

Text editor
A program with which to write, erase, and manipulate words on the monitor screen; similar to a word processor, but without many of the formatting features.

Text file
See **ASCII.**

Text management systems
A system that utilizes typewriters, word processing systems, PCs with word processing, desktop publishing and text editing systems, and even computerized typesetting equipment to work with text.

Thermal printer
A printer that uses heat to form a nonimpact image on chemically treated paper.

Thimble
The print element on an impact printer that resembles the IBM Selectric "golfball."

Time-sharing
A computer system that can be used by many people simultaneously for different purposes or applications.

Title line
An area of the screen that presents the program name and often the document name.

Toggle
A function of a specific computer keyboard key that alternates between two related tasks.

Topology
The layout of computers and other devices as well as their connections.

Touch-sensitive screen
An input device that permits using the finger as the input device.

Trackball
A pointing device that acts like an upside-down mouse to move the cursor on the screen.

Tracks
The concentric storage rings upon which data is recorded on a floppy or hard disk.

Twisted pair
Two copper wires that create a communications channel. Commonly used as phone lines.

Typeface
The type character design. Also called the font.

Typeover mode
The Insert key toggle that deletes each old character as you type a new character; see **Insert.** Also called overstrike mode.

Underline
Highlighting text by drawing a line under words.

UNIX
A popular operating system.

Unstructured programming
A way of programming that allows the programmer to create programs in a more random fashion.

Uploading
In telecommunications, the process of sending files from a remote computer to a large central computer. See **downloading.**

User documentation
Instructions for the knowledge workers who will use the program, explaining procedures step by step.

User testing
Allowing knowledge workers to test the system under actual working conditions.

Utility software
A type of software that performs a variety of helpful tasks with the ease and efficiency of an application program.

Value
A quantity assigned to a variable, or simply a number.

Vector graphics
Early graphics program that connected lines between points on the screen.

Virtual memory
A portion of hard disk space that the CPU regards in the same way it does RAM, so that RAM appears in essence to have more capacity than it actually does.

Virtual reality
A three-dimensional graphics system that creates the optical effect of walking through a 3D image. Also called cyberspace.

VMS
The Digital Equipment Corporation's VAX operating system.

Voice/data integration
The computer-assisted ability to route a data call and a voice call to a knowledge worker so that both transmissions occur simultaneously.

Voice mail
The use of the computer to capture (input), digitize (process), store on

disk, and forward (output) spoken-word messages.

Voice output
Spoken output produced by a computer. Also called speech synthesis.

Voice recognition
Entering data into a computer by speaking into a microphone. Also called voice input.

Volatile
A type of memory in which the contents are removed when replaced by new instructions and data, or lost when electrical power to the computer is turned off.

Volatile memory
Short-term memory. Everything stored is lost when the computer's power is shut off.

What-if analysis
Substituting one number for another to see what difference it will make.

Wide area network (WAN)
A type of private network that uses phone lines, microwave relaying stations, and satellites to connect computers located miles apart.

Widow
A single word on a line, left dangling at the end of a paragraph.

Windows
Individual boxes in which separate applications are displayed on the monitor screen.

Word
A logical unit of information. Word length is the term used to describe their size, counted in numbers of bits.

Word processing
An application that permits creating and revising written work.

Word wrap
A word processing feature that automatically moves a word from the end of one line to the beginning of the next.

Work area
The blank area of the screen that accepts text.

Work group
A number of knowledge workers, each of whom has different job duties or tasks, but all of whom are working toward a common goal.

Working copy
A duplicate copy of a program disk used for everyday work. The original is stored for safekeeping.

Work session
The period of time during which a knowledge worker is computing.

Worksheet
The data document created by the spreadsheet program, containing the words, values, formulas, and so on.

Workstation
A powerful desktop computer most commonly used by a single individual, but which may be shared by others.

Write
To copy data from memory to disk.

Write once, read many (WORM)
An optical disc storage media that allows the knowledge worker to store data once on the disc and then re-use it many times.

Writing
The process of conveying information with words.

WYSIWYG
The ability to display text exactly as it will appear on the printed page; the acronym stands for What You See Is What You Get.

CHAPTER 1

REVIEW QUESTIONS

1. Being knowledgeable or educated about the computer and how it works, and being able to use a computer properly and ethically. Each of us is responsible.
3. The system unit, keyboard, and monitor; the fourth is the printer.
5. Input, processing, output, storage, and results.
7. A document contains data in the form of text and graphics; it is also the record of a transaction.

DISCUSSION QUESTIONS

1. It is routinely used for banking and financial transactions, and we trust it to work correctly.
3. Computers may be incorrectly programmed; they may not be up-to-date; they may be used by unethical people.
5. Q.E.D.

MULTIPLE-CHOICE

1. *d.* All of the above.

3. *b.* It is mostly used as a storehouse for corporate data.
   c. It is used in conjunction with minis and personal computers.
   d. It is not used for all computing tasks.
5. *d.* Input, processing, output, storage, and results.

FILL-IN-THE-BLANK

1. Digital and electronic.
3. People, data, procedures, hardware, and software.
5. System unit, keyboard, and monitor.

TRUE/FALSE

1. False.
3. False.
5. False; they are the same.

CHAPTER 2

REVIEW QUESTIONS

1. Humans control or interact with input and output. They do not with processing.
3. The command is an instruction the knowledge worker issues to the computer system.

DISCUSSION QUESTIONS

1. The result is fewer mistakes.
3. They both have input, processing, and output components. The main difference is that the computer can perform many tasks, whereas the stereo can only play music.

5. Q.E.D.

7. Directories provide a way to store files in an orderly manner. The root directory is the place for primary files used for starting up the system. Separate subdirectories for individual applications and their data files make it easier to locate and manage both applications and data.

9. On a two-floppy system the application program is on one disk and the data files are on the other. On a hard disk the application is in one subdirectory and its data files are in an adjacent sub-subdirectory.

MULTIPLE-CHOICE

1. *a.* The control unit.
   b. The arithmetic-logic unit.
   c. Random access memory.

3. *a.* The PS/2 uses Micro Channel Architecture.
   c. The PS/2 has a newer operating system.

FILL-IN-THE-BLANK

1. Read only.
3. Q.E.D.
5. 1 kilobyte, or 1KB.

TRUE/FALSE

1. False.
3. True.
5. True.
7. False.

CHAPTER 3

REVIEW QUESTIONS

1. General-purpose means the computer may be used for many tasks. Special-purpose means the computer is used for a single task.

3. Science and engineering, office automation, and education.

5. Because it uses state-of-the-art circuit technology, such as parallel processing.

7. Q.E.D.

DISCUSSION QUESTIONS

1. The application software grows more complex, as do the needs of knowledge workers, placing ever greater demands for speed on the computer.

3. A notebook is lighter and has sufficient battery power for short trips. A palmtop is good for note taking and desktop management, but its keyboard is often inadequate for, say, word processing.

5. Advantages: More than one application is active and available at all times; data can be transferred between applications.
   Disadvantages: The computer usually performs more slowly; it requires another layer of software which must be learned and mastered.

7. Its size and cost have delimited its options. The concept of OEM computers reached maturity with minicomputers, which are smaller, less expensive, and more easily moved.

MULTIPLE-CHOICE

1. *a.* Is usually more expensive than a desktop PC.
   b. Does not always have a floppy disk drive.
   c. Performs all the same tasks as a desktop PC.
   d. Can transfer data to other computers.
   e. Sometimes comes with built-in software.

3. *a.* They are too expensive.
   c. Knowledge workers want processing power on their desktops.
   d. The mainframes were too busy for all the tasks required of them.

FILL-IN-THE-BLANK

1. Better, faster, and less expensive.
3. Reduced-instruction-set computing.
5. Integrated circuit chip.

TRUE/FALSE

1. True.
3. True.
5. True.

CHAPTER 4

REVIEW QUESTIONS

1. It is the primary way that information is formally shared in business; it has been shown to improve employee motivation; it helps knowledge workers' productivity.
3. Word wrap means you don't have to press the typewriter carriage return at the end of a line. Scrolling makes it possible to continuously view pages in a document of any length.
5. It not only corrects spelling but also helps find related words.
7. Creating forms, designing different types of pages in a single document, and standardizing documents such as memos, reports, and letters.

DISCUSSION QUESTIONS

1. Written information is the most common form of business communication. Well-presented documents make information more accessible.
3. It makes it possible to observe progress, recheck portions of a document, and ensure that there is a copy of the last draft for safekeeping.
5. To organize your thoughts before you begin writing. Prewriting helps keep documents focused on the most important topics, omitting needless words. Prewriting with word processing makes it possible to expand the topics into sentences and paragraphs, whereas prewriting with pen and paper must be keyed in, adding an additional step.
7. Q.E.D.

MULTIPLE-CHOICE

1. *e.* All of the above.
3. *a.* Makes commands graphical.
   c. Makes good use of a color monitor.
   d. Doesn't require the use of toggle on/off keys.
   e. Is more fun to use.
5. *a.* Is only for training and education.
   b. Is a very sophisticated form of electronic publishing.
   c. Allows mixing movies and sound with text and graphics.
   e. Takes good advantage of hypertext.

FILL-IN-THE-BLANK

1. Document.
3. QWERTY; Dvorak.
5. Information.

TRUE/FALSE

1. True.
3. True.

CHAPTER 5

REVIEW QUESTIONS

1. It is a replica or copy that can be tested or changed without disturbing the original.
3. A formula is the mathematical equation; the constants are the numbers the formula works with. The constant appears in the spreadsheet cell, while the formula appears on the status line.
5. Character-based spreadsheets require use of plotting procedures to transform the numeric data into a chart or graph, whereas graphically based programs do so with the click of the mouse button.
7. The dot of light used as a measure of computer monitor resolution. The more pixels, the clearer and more colorful the high-resolution graphics.

DISCUSSION QUESTIONS

1. Macros are shortcuts for commonly repeated tasks and functions. Q.E.D.
3. Incorrect formulas and values produce incorrect results. GIGO.
5. Advantages: Functions are chosen from a menu bar; instant graphics; cut and paste.
   Disadvantages: Often is slower; sometimes is more complex to learn; often requires a more powerful computer.

MULTIPLE-CHOICE

1. *a.* Several applications can work together.
   b. It's easy to exchange data between applications.
   c. All applications work similarly.
3. *e.* All of the above.
5. *a.* Illustrating documents.
   b. Animation.
   c. Graphic novels.
   d. Mapping.

FILL-IN-THE-BLANK

1. Calculator, pencil, and ledger sheet.
3. Template.
5. Command; status.
7. Presentation graphics.

TRUE/FALSE

1. False.
3. False.
5. True.

CHAPTER 6

REVIEW QUESTIONS

1. A database is a group of related records and files; a DBMS is a software application program.
3. Data definition and data refinement.
5. Hierarchical: An inverted or upside-down tree structure from the central root to the branches. Network: Many-to-many relationships. Relational: Any-to-any relationships.
7. To automate commands or create easier procedures for working with data.
9. It is awkward and expensive to store all data in a single database. In many companies, specific data often resides in departmental databases.

DISCUSSION QUESTIONS

1. Flexibility, discrimination, and extensibility.
3. The field is part of a record, and the unique aspects of each make it possible to use the information they contain in organizing and using a database.
5. The RDBMS is the most modern, easiest to understand, and most flexible of the three types of DBMSs.

MULTIPLE-CHOICE

1. *b.* Character.
   e. Field.
   f. Database.
   g. File.
3. *b.* Helps manage daily work activities.
   c. Can store data in more than one format.
   d. Works the way the knowledge worker works.
   e. Uses keywords to form associative links.

FILL-IN-THE-BLANK

1. Flat file, hierarchical, network, and relational.
3. Pencil and paper.
5. Attributes.

TRUE/FALSE

1. True.
3. True.
5. False.

CHAPTER 7

REVIEW QUESTIONS

1. It runs the computer system, performing a variety of fundamental operations, and includes the operating system.
3. Input and output control; CPU task scheduling; data management and storage; and command languages and utilities.

5. Multitasking commonly refers to personal computers, while multiprogramming is a term used more often for larger computer systems.

7. Accounting, project management, investment management, mailing list management, and vertical market applications.

DISCUSSION QUESTIONS

1. Multitasking is used when there is a need to keep several applications active or to perform tasks that don't involve the knowledge worker in the background, such as printing.

3. Advantages: Shares data easily between applications; switching is easy between applications; commands are commonly the same. Disadvantages: Not all applications are equally powerful or useful; takes up a large amount of disk space.

5. Q.E.D.

7. The need for keeping data private with regard to other knowledge workers; the need to protect one's personal computer, and also the office computers, from viruses, etc.

MULTIPLE-CHOICE

1. *a.* Only available on IBM mainframes.
   b. Capable of driving several CPUs.
   d. Designed for all types of processing.
   e. Able to run hundreds of simultaneous applications.

3. *c.* Operating environment.

FILL-IN-THE-BLANK

1. Virtual memory.
3. Lotus 1-2-3.
5. Hardware, operating system, operating environment, application software, and human.

TRUE/FALSE

1. False.
3. True.
5. True.

CHAPTER 8

REVIEW QUESTIONS

1. Its ability to perform many different types of tasks.

3. Control unit, arithmetic-logic unit, and main memory.

5. Main memory.

7. Instruction cycle and execution cycle.

DISCUSSION QUESTIONS

1. Q.E.D.

3. Q.E.D.

5. Von Neumann architecture uses a single processor to process one instruction at a time; parallel processing uses many processors to process multiple instructions.

7. Batch processing is good for work that isn't time-critical; on-line processing is suited to financial transactions and fast throughput, such as merchandise orders.

MULTIPLE-CHOICE

1. *a.* Was invented by Jack Kilby.
   b. Was invented at Texas Instruments.
   c. Integrates many electronic circuit components into a single chip.

3. *b.* A cycle.

FILL-IN-THE-BLANK

1. Beach sand.
3. Read-only memory.
5. Bits; bytes; words.
7. Batch processing.

TRUE/FALSE

1. True.
3. False.
5. True.

CHAPTER 9

REVIEW QUESTIONS

1. They make the computer processor useful to people.
3. When it is necessary to control other machines or their processes.
5. Floppy disks.
7. The higher the resolution, the crisper and sharper the video images.

DISCUSSION QUESTIONS

1. Physical interfaces make it possible to connect peripheral devices. The three most common types are serial, parallel, and monitor.
3. Keyboard, text entry; mouse, issuing commands; light pen, drawing.
5. To form an orderly way of storing and then retrieving data.

MULTIPLE-CHOICE

1. *a.* When there is machine-to-machine input.
   c. When scanning bar codes.
   d. For processing bank checks.
   e. By potato chip salespeople in grocery stores.
3. *b.* Disk platter size.
   c. Data capacity.
5. *c.* Entertainment.

FILL-IN-THE-BLANK

1. Data entry.
3. Microfilm.
5. High density.

TRUE/FALSE

1. False.
3. True.
5. False.

CHAPTER 10

REVIEW QUESTIONS

1. It allows programmers more direct control over the hardware and greater ease in writing instructions.
3. A set of words and a set of language usage rules.
5. Business.
7. CASE is designed for applications in a high-level programming environment.

DISCUSSION QUESTIONS

1. Q.E.D.
3. A compiler creates executable code, while an interpreter does not.
5. Q.E.D.

MULTIPLE-CHOICE

1. *a.* Are closer to English.
   b. Are easier to use than machine or assembly language.
   c. Use statements to tell knowledge workers how to use them.
   d. Must be compiled before they can be used.
3. *b.* Create more flexible systems more quickly.
   d. Get rid of spaghetti code.
5. *a.* Statements.
   c. Syntax.

FILL-IN-THE-BLANK

1. Machine language.
3. Ada.
5. Spaghetti.

TRUE/FALSE

1. True.
3. True.
5. False.
7. True.

CHAPTER 11

REVIEW QUESTIONS

1. Large-scale business computers.
3. Q.E.D.
5. Software documentation is for programmers; user documentation is for knowledge workers.
7. Information strategy planning, business area analysis, system design, and implementation.

DISCUSSION QUESTIONS

1. Software engineering is primarily used by programmers and analysts. Information engineering involves knowledge workers.
3. The goal is to make knowledge workers more productive and to make the business more efficient and competitive.
5. Traditional life cycle: Analysis, design, coding, debugging, testing and acceptance, maintenance and documentation. RAD life cycle: Information engineering methodology, high-quality software engineering tools, highly skilled people, strong management support and involvement.

MULTIPLE-CHOICE

1. *e.* All of the above.
3. *a.* Less paper-based work.
   b. There are fewer bugs.
   d. State-of-the-art tools and techniques are used.
5. *b.* Identify program errors.
   c. Locate problems as error messages.
   d. Produce error message listings.

FILL-IN-THE-BLANK

1. Traditional.
3. Structured coding.
5. Maintenance.

TRUE-FALSE

1. False.
3. False.
5. True.

CHAPTER 12

REVIEW QUESTIONS

1. Centralized holds corporate data; decentralized is usually specific to a department or business function.
3. On-line processing processes transactions as they occur and updates the database in a steady stream. OLTP completes the entire transaction as soon as it is entered. OLTP is more expensive.
5. Text databases contain documents and have more informative richness than data databases.
7. The query language.

DISCUSSION QUESTIONS

1. Q.E.D. The Information Age.
3. Urban planning and government agencies for land use management.
5. Query, database design, analysis, manipulative data.

MULTIPLE-CHOICE

1. *a.* It's larger.
   c. It may run on many different computers.
3. *a.* All knowledge workers have their own computer processing and storage.
   b. All the data is stored on a single server.
   c. The mainframe can be powered down.
   d. The clients all rely on the server for processing.
   e. Many databases can be accessed from a client computer.
5. *c.* Data dictionary.
7. *a.* SQL.
   d. Spreadsheet.
   e. Application generator.

FILL-IN-THE-BLANK

1. Batch processing.
3. Database administrator.
5. Image.

TRUE/FALSE

1. True.
3. False.
5. True.

CHAPTER 13

REVIEW QUESTIONS

1. White-collar professionals and information systems professionals.
3. To help conceptually chart, support, and verify the business plans, directions, and strategies.
5. It shifts the emphasis away from the hardware component to making any and all information available to knowledge workers.
7. Helps get a new MIS operational quickly, improves performance, and removes responsibility for operating an internal MIS organization.

DISCUSSION QUESTIONS

1. Q.E.D.
3. Q.E.D.
5. The stages are based in psychological theory and apply to people, groups, organizations, business, societies, etc.
7. The system was developed simply and inexpensi-

vely, using existing technology, and provided great value and benefit to the managers.

MULTIPLE-CHOICE

1. *a.* Centralized.
   c. Departmental.
3. *g.* All of the above.

FILL-IN-THE-BLANK

1. Management information system.
3. People, software, and hardware.
5. Centralized.

TRUE/FALSE

1. True.
3. False.
5. True.

CHAPTER 14

REVIEW QUESTIONS

1. Hardware, software, and a network.
3. A physical means of connecting computers for communications.
5. Forms can be transmitted electronically, computer-to-computer.

DISCUSSION QUESTIONS

1. To save on costs and to control usage.
3. Campus network, office LAN, telephone network, packet switching network.
5. When there is no server or need for a central storage device.

7. Analog is modulated; digital involves 1s and 0s. Primarily cost and the vast amount of installed wiring are restraining ISDN.

MULTIPLE-CHOICE

1. *d.* All of the above.
3. *a.* The PBX.
   b. The telephone.
   c. The T-1 switch.
5. *e.* All of the above.
7. *d.* An intruder.

Fill-in-the-Blank

1. Modem.
3. Communications; communications management.
5. Handshaking.

True/False

1. False.
3. True.

Chapter 15

Review Questions

1. By redefining the way people in offices work together, and by using the computer as a productivity tool to get more done.
3. By making it possible to create more types of documents, and by producing them without the use of typesetting and printing services.
5. To manage text, data, graphics, and video and audio information.
7. Text management focuses on creation and dissemination, while document management is concerned more with storage and retrieval. Thus once a document is created with the former, it is managed with the latter.

Discussion Questions

1. The former are traditional data management; the latter are concerned with not only data but also text, graphics, video, audio, and formatted documents that produce more than data — information. The latter are more complex to work with, to store, and to retrieve.
3. Q.E.D.

5. Collaborative work groups; work procedures have changed dramatically; the document, the network, and the personal computer all created new paradigms.
7. Q.E.D.

Multiple-Choice

1. *f.* All of the above.
3. *e.* All of the above.

Fill-in-the-Blank

1. Business analysis.
3. Stored expertise or knowledge.
5. Distributed computing.

True/False

1. True.
3. True.
5. True.

Chapter 1

Figure 1.1, p. 6: Poulides/Thatcher/ Tony Stone Worldwide. **Figure 1.2,** p. 8: Courtesy of National Center for Atmospheric Research. **Figure 1.3,** p. 9: Mark Mangold/Courtesy of U.S. Census Bureau. **Figure 1.4,** p. 13: Fredrik D. Bodin. **Figure 1.6,** p. 15: John Greenleigh/Courtesy of Apple Computer, Inc. **Figure 1.7,** p. 16: Stuart McCall/Tony Stone Worldwide. **Figure 1.8,** p. 17: Diana Kassir. **Figure 1.10,** p. 19: Courtesy of Cray Research, Inc. **Yesterday,** p. 21: left—Bettman Newsphotos; right—The Computer Museum, Inc. **Today,** p. 24: Courtesy of Cornell University Library. **Careers for Knowledge Workers,** p. 28: Courtesy of Garry Fairbairn.

Chapter 2

Yesterday, p. 35: top—Jack Rochester; right—Courtesy of Apple Computer, Inc.; bottom—Courtesy of Tandy Corporation. **Figure 2.2,** p. 36: Courtesy of Motorola, Inc. **Figure 2.3,** p. 41: Fredrik D. Bodin. **Figure 2.14,** p. 53: Fredrik D. Bodin. **Figure 2.16,** p. 55: top—Courtesy of IBM Corporation; left—Courtesy of Compaq Computer Corporation; right—Courtesy of Zeos International, Ltd. **Figure 2.17,** p. 56: Courtesy of Bestinfo, Inc. **Figure 2.18,** p. 58: Fredrik D. Bodin/ Courtesy of Project Services International, Inc. **Careers for Knowledge Workers,** p. 60: Courtesy of Susan Wells.

Chapter 3

Figure 3.1, p. 69: Jack Rochester. **Figure 3.2,** p. 70: top left—Lou Jones; top right—Lou Jones; bottom left—Lou Jones; bottom right—Courtesy of Cimlinc Inc. **Figure 3.3,** p. 71: The Computer Museum, Inc. **Figure 3.4,** p. 72: Courtesy of Mission Cyrus Corporation. **Figure 3.5,** p. 73: Fredrik D. Bodin. **Figure 3.6,** p. 74: Courtesy of Poqet Computer Corporation. **Figure 3.7,** p. 74: Courtesy of Hewlett Packard. **Figure 3.8,** p. 77: Courtesy of NeXT Computer Corporation. **Figure 3.9,** p. 79: Charles Thatcher/Tony Stone Worldwide. **Figure 3.10,** p. 81: Courtesy of Digital Equipment Corporation. **Figure 3.11,** p. 84: Courtesy of IBM Corporation. **Figure 3.12,** p. 85: Courtesy of IBM Corporation. **Figure 3.13,** p. 87: Courtesy of Thinking Machines Corporation. **Figure 3.14,** p. 89: Hank Morgan/Rainbow. **Figure 3.15,** p. 91: Courtesy of Momenta Corporation. **Careers for Knowledge Workers,** p. 92: Courtesy of Michael Dell.

Chapter 4

Figure 4.1, p. 103: Fredrik D. Bodin. **Figure 4.3,** p. 107: Fredrik D. Bodin. **Figure 4.5,** p. 110: left—Courtesy of IBM Corporation; right—Fredrik D. Bodin/Courtesy of Dvorak International. **Figure 4.7,** p. 113: Fredrik D. Bodin. **Figure 4.8,** p. 114: Fredrik D. Bodin. **Figure 4.11,** p. 117: Fredrik D. Bodin. **Figure 4.12,** p. 120: Courtesy of Microsoft Corporation. **Figure 4.13,** p. 121: left —Fredrik D. Bodin; right—Courtesy of Reference Software, Inc. **Figure 4.14,** p. 122: Fredrik D. Bodin. **Tomorrow,** p. 125: left—Courtesy of Microsoft Corporation; center—Courtesy of Lotus Development Corporation; right—Courtesy of Word Perfect Corporation. **Figure 4.16,** p. 126: left —Courtesy of Interleaf Corporation;

right—Fredrik D. Bodin. **Figure 4.20,** p. 132: Fredrik D. Bodin. **Figure 4.21,** p. 134: Courtesy of Business Research Institute. **Careers for Knowledge Workers,** p. 136: Betsy H. Harbinson/Atlanta Stock Associates.

Chapter 5

Figure 5.4, p. 151: Fredrik D. Bodin. **Figure 5.5,** p. 152: Fredrik D. Bodin. **Figure 5.7,** p. 158: Courtesy of StatSoft. **Figure 5.10,** p. 162: A— Fredrik D. Bodin/Courtesy of Symantec Corporation; B—Fredrik D. Bodin/Courtesy of Personics; C— Courtesy of Business Forecast Systems, Inc. **Figure 5.11,** p. 164: left— Courtesy of IBM Corporation; right— Mosgrove Photo/Courtesy of Apple Computer, Inc. **Figure 5.12,** p. 165: Courtesy of Digital Equipment Corporation. **Figure 5.13,** p. 166: Courtesy of Corel Draw Corporation. **Figure 5.14,** p. 167: A—Courtesy of Joni Carter; B—Dan McCoy/Rainbow; C—Courtesy of Wang Laboratories, Inc. **Figure 5.15,** p. 168: Custom Medical Stock Photo. **Figure 5.17,** p. 171: A—O.S.U./Cranston Graphics (Rainbow); B—Peter Yates; C— Courtesy of Precision Visuals, Inc. **Careers for Knowledge Workers,** p. 172: Courtesy of Tim Tran.

Chapter 6

Figure 6.7, p. 192: left—Courtesy of Borland International, Inc.; center— Courtesy of Borland International, Inc.; right—Courtesy of Fox Software, Inc. **Figure 6.8,** p. 195: Courtesy of IBM Corporation. **Figure 6.9,** p. 196: Courtesy of Cortex Corporation. **Tomorrow,** p. 198: Courtesy of Lotus Development Corporation. **Careers for**

Knowledge Workers, p. 199: Courtesy of Philippe Kahn.

Chapter 7

Figure 7.4, p. 211: John Greenleigh/ Courtesy of Apple Computer, Inc. **Figure 7.6,** p. 213: Fredrik D. Bodin. **Figure 7.10,** p. 219: A—Fredrik D. Bodin; B—Fredrik D. Bodin; C— Courtesy of Quarterdeck Office Systems, Inc. **Figure 7.11,** p. 221: A— Fredrik D. Bodin; B—Courtesy of IBM Corporation; C—Courtesy of Borland International, Inc.; D—Courtesy of Digital Equipment Corporation. **Figure 7.13,** p. 227: Courtesy of Geo-Works International. **Figure 7.14,** p. 228: Courtesy of Lotus Development Corporation. **Figure 7.15,** p. 230: Fredrik D. Bodin. **Figure 7.16,** p. 232: Courtesy of Intuit, Inc. **Figure 7.17,** p. 233: Courtesy of Symantec Corporation. **Figure 7.18,** p. 236: A— Courtesy of Borland International, Inc.; B—Fredrik D. Bodin; C—Courtesy of XTree Company; D—Fredrik D. Bodin. **Figure 7.19,** p. 237: A— Courtesy of Berkley Systems, Inc.; B— Courtesy of Hewlett Packard Company; C—Fredrik D. Bodin. **Tomorrow,** p. 238: Courtesy of Xerox Palo Alto Research Center. **Careers for Knowledge Workers,** p. 240: Steve Knoll.

Chapter 8

Figure 8.1, p. 251: Courtesy of Texas Instruments. **Figure 8.2,** p. 252: Courtesy of NovaSensor Corporation. **Figure 8.3,** p. 255: Courtesy of Apple Computer, Inc. **Careers for Knowledge Workers,** p. 270: Courtesy of Laszlo Belady.

Chapter 9

Figure 9.3, p. 281: Fredrik D. Bodin. **Figure 9.4,** p. 282: Fredrik D. Bodin. **Figure 9.5,** p. 282: Courtesy of Gravis Corporation. **Figure 9.6,** p. 284: Courtesy of Skip Morrow. **Figure 9.7,** p. 284: Courtesy of Logitech, Inc. **Figure 9.8,** p. 285: left—Courtesy of Hewlett Packard Company; right— Courtesy of Logitech, Inc. **Figure 9.9,** p. 286: Monte H. Gerlack/Courtesy of Schneider Associates. **Figure 9.10,** p. 287: Fredrik D. Bodin. **Figure 9.11,** p. 288: top left—Charles Gupton/ Stock Boston; top right—John Co-

letti/Stock Boston; bottom—Courtesy of Poqet Corporation. **Figure 9.12,** p. 289: James Wilson/Woodfin Camp and Associates. **Figure 9.13,** p. 290: Fredrik D. Bodin. **Figure 9.15,** p. 292: Courtesy of Grid Systems Corporation. **Figure 9.18,** p. 295: left —Courtesy of Hewlett Packard Company; right—Courtesy of Kodak Corporation. **Figure 9.19,** p. 296: Courtesy of Hewlett Packard Company. **Figure 9.20,** p. 297: Courtesy of Monologue Systems. **Figure 9.21,** p. 300: left—Courtesy of IBM Corporation; right—Courtesy of Hewlett Packard Company. **Figure 9.24,** p. 303: Jack Rochester. **Figure 9.25,** p. 303: Courtesy of IBM Corporation. **Figure 9.26,** p. 304: Courtesy of Tandon Inc. **Figure 9.27,** p. 305: Courtesy of Gravis Corporation. **Figure 9.28,** p. 306: Courtesy of National Center for Atmospheric Research. **Tomorrow,** p. 307: Courtesy of Auto-Desk, Inc. **Careers for Knowledge Workers,** p. 308: Dave Smith/Courtesy of Michele Harris.

Chapter 10

Figure 10.1, p. 318: Courtesy of IBM Corporation. **Figure 10.2,** p. 318: Courtesy of IBM Corporation. **Figure 10.9,** p. 332: ParcPlace Systems. **Figure 10.10,** p. 333: Courtesy of Borland International, Inc. **Figure 10.11,** p. 334: Courtesy of Index Technology Corporation. **Figure 10.12,** p. 335: Courtesy of Bachman Information Systems. **Figure 10.13,** p. 336: Courtesy of Texas Instruments. **Careers for Knowledge Workers,** p. 338: Courtesy of Dave Ball.

Chapter 11

Figure 11.2, p. 349: Courtesy of U.S. Naval Archives. **Figure 11.7,** p. 357: Courtesy of Bachman Information Systems, Inc. **Careers for Knowledge Workers,** p. 360: Fredrik D. Bodin.

Chapter 12

Figure 12.2, p. 374: Courtesy of Information Resources, Inc. **Figure 12.3,** p. 375: Courtesy of Information Builders, Inc. **Figure 12.4,** p. 376: Courtesy of Borland International, Inc. **Figure 12.5,** p. 377: Courtesy of Information Builders, Inc. **Figure 12.6,** p. 379: Mi-

chael Grecco/Picture Group. **Figure 12.7,** p. 380: Courtesy of AutoMap, Inc. **Figure 12.8,** p. 382: Courtesy of Candle Corporation. **Figure 12.9,** p. 383: Courtesy of Domino's Pizza, Inc. **Figure 12.10,** p. 384: Courtesy of Digital Equipment Corporation. **Figure 12.11,** p. 385: Courtesy of CimLinc Inc. **Careers for Knowledge Workers,** p. 388: Courtesy of Perry Mizota.

Chapter 13

Figure 13.5, p. 404: Courtesy of *Computerworld.* **Figure 13.6,** p. 406: Fredrik D. Bodin/Courtesy of Trans-Canada Pipeline. **Figure 13.7,** p. 408: Courtesy of Dow Jones News Retrieval. **Figure 13.9,** p. 413: Courtesy of Pilot Software, Inc. **Tomorrow,** p. 420: Courtesy of DesQView, Inc. **Figure 13.14,** p. 422: Courtesy of Electronic Data Systems, Inc. **Careers for Knowledge Workers,** p. 424: Courtesy of Tim Yancy.

Chapter 14

Figure 14.2, p. 436: Fredrik D. Bodin. **Figure 14.4,** p. 437: left— Fredrik D. Bodin/Offshoot; right— Courtesy of Hayes Microcomputer Products, Inc. **Figure 14.5,** p. 438: Courtesy of Supra Corporation. **Figure 14.8,** p. 445: Courtesy of Prodigy Information Service. **Figure 14.9,** p. 446: left—Fredrik D. Bodin; center— Fredrik D. Bodin; right—Michael A. Keller/The Stock Market. **Figure 14.17,** p. 457: Courtesy of Levi Strauss Inc. **Careers for Knowledge Workers,** p. 464: Fredrik D. Bodin.

Chapter 15

Figure 15.3, p. 479: Courtesy of Workgroup Technologies, Inc. **Figure 15.4,** p. 480: Courtesy of Pilot Software, Inc. **Figure 15.5,** p. 482: Courtesy of Keyfile Corporation. **Figure 15.6,** p. 483: Courtesy of Lotus Development Corporation. **Figure 15.9,** p. 487: Courtesy of Norick Software, Inc. **Figure 15.10,** p. 488: Courtesy of Digital Equipment Corporation/Maya Design Group. **Careers for Knowledge Workers,** p. 490: Kate E. Schermerhorn.

Epilogue

p. 497: Jack Rochester.

INDEX

Index